CIMA Official
Learning System

CIMA PUBLISHING

Operational Level

P1 – Performance Operations

Bob Scarlett

ELSEVIER

AMSTERDAM   BOSTON   HEIDELBERG   LONDON   NEW YORK   OXFORD
PARIS   SAN DIEGO   SAN FRANCISCO   SINGAPORE   SYDNEY   TOKYO

CIMA Publishing is an imprint of Elsevier
Linacre House, Jordan Hill, Oxford OX2 8DP, UK
30 Corporate Drive, Suite 400, Burlington, MA 01803, USA

British Library Cataloguing in Publication Data
A catalogue record for this book is available from the British Library

Library of Congress Cataloguing in Publication Data
A catalogue record for this book is available from the library of congress

978-1-85617-722-1

For information on all CIMA publications
visit our website at www.elsevierdirect.com

Typeset by Macmillan Publishing Solutions
(www.macmillansolutions.com)

Printed and bound in Hungary

09 10 11   11 10 9 8 7 6 5 4 3 2 1

Contents

5 Developments in Management Accounting

The CIMA Learning System

Acknowledgements

Every effort has been made to contact the holders of copyright material, but if any here have been inadvertently overlooked the publishers will be pleased to make the necessary arrangements at the first opportunity.

How to use your CIMA *Learning System*

This *Performance Operations Learning System* has been devised as a resource for students attempting to pass their CIMA exams and provides:

- a detailed explanation of all syllabus areas;
- extensive 'practical' materials, including readings from relevant journals;
- generous question practice, together with full solutions;
- an exam preparation section, complete with exam standard questions and solutions.

This Learning System has been designed with the needs of home-study and distance-learning candidates in mind. Such students require very full coverage of the syllabus topics, and also the facility to undertake extensive question practice. However, the Learning System is also ideal for fully taught courses.

The main body of the text is divided into a number of chapters, each of which is organised on the following pattern:

- *Detailed learning outcomes.* This is expected after your studies of the chapter are complete. You should assimilate these before beginning detailed work on the chapter, so that you can appreciate where your studies are leading.
- *Step-by-step topic coverage.* This is the heart of each chapter, containing detailed explanatory text supported where appropriate by worked examples and exercises. You should work carefully through this section, ensuring that you understand the material being explained and can tackle the examples and exercises successfully. Remember that in many cases knowledge is cumulative: if you fail to digest earlier material thoroughly, you may struggle to understand later chapters.
- *Readings and activities.* Most chapters are illustrated by more practical elements, such as relevant journal articles or other readings, together with comments and questions designed to stimulate discussion.

THE CIMA LEARNING SYSTEM

- *Question practice.* The test of how well you have learned the material is your ability to tackle exam-standard questions. Make a serious attempt at producing your own answers, but at this stage do not be too concerned about attempting the questions in exam conditions. In particular, it is more important to absorb the material thoroughly by completing a full solution than to observe the time limits that would apply in the actual exam.
- *Solutions.* Avoid the temptation merely to 'audit' the solutions provided. It is an illusion to think that this provides the same benefits as you would gain from a serious attempt of your own. However, if you are struggling to get started on a question you should read the introductory guidance provided at the beginning of the solution, and then make your own attempt before referring back to the full solution.

Having worked through the chapters you are ready to begin your final preparations for the examination. The final section of this CIMA *Learning System* provides you with the guidance you need. It includes the following features:

- A brief guide to revision technique.
- A note on the format of the examination. You should know what to expect when you tackle the real exam, and in particular the number of questions to attempt, which questions are compulsory and which optional and so on.
- Guidance on how to tackle the examination itself.
- A table mapping revision questions to the syllabus learning outcomes allowing you to quickly identify questions by subject area.
- Revision questions. These are of exam standard and should be tackled in exam conditions, especially as regards the time allocation.
- Solutions to the revision questions. As before, these indicate the length and the quality of solution that would be expected of a well-prepared candidate.

If you work conscientiously through this CIMA *Learning System* according to the guidelines above you will be giving yourself an excellent chance of exam success. Good luck with your studies!

Guide to the Icons used within this Text

 Key term or definition

π Equation to learn

 Exam tip to topic likely to appear in the exam

 Exercise

? Question

 Solution

! Comment or Note

Study technique

Passing exams is partly a matter of intellectual ability, but however accomplished you are in that respect you can improve your chances significantly by the use of appropriate study and revision techniques. In this section we briefly outline some tips for effective study during the earlier stages of your approach to the exam. Later in the text we mention some techniques that you will find useful at the revision stage.

Planning

To begin with, formal planning is essential to get the best return from the time you spend studying.

Estimate how much time in total you are going to need for each subject that you face. Remember that you need to allow time for revision as well as for initial study of the material. The amount of notional study time for any subject is the minimum estimated time that students will need to achieve the specified learning outcomes set out earlier in this chapter. This time includes all appropriate learning activities, for example, face-to-face tuition, private study, directed home study, learning in the workplace, revision time and so on. You may find it helpful to read *Better Exam Results* by Sam Malone, CIMA Publishing, ISBN: 05066357X. This book will provide you with proven study techniques. Chapter by chapter it covers the building blocks of successful learning and examination techniques.

The notional study time for *Performance Operations* is 200 hours. Note that the standard amount of notional learning hours attributed to one full-time academic year of approximately 30 weeks is 1,200 hours.

By way of example, the notional study time might be made up as follows:

	Hours
Face-to-face study: up to	60
Personal study: up to	100
'Other' study – e.g. learning in the workplace, revision, etc.: up to	40
	200

Note that all study and learning-time recommendations should be used only as a guideline and are intended as minimum amounts. The amount of time recommended for face-to-face tuition, personal study and/or additional learning will vary according to the type of course undertaken, prior learning of the student, and the pace at which different students learn.

Now split your total time requirement over the weeks between now and the examination. This will give you an idea of how much time you need to devote to study each week. Remember to allow for holidays or other periods during which you will not be able to study (e.g. because of seasonal workloads).

With your study material before you, decide which chapters you are going to study in each week, and which weeks you will devote to revision and final question practice.

Prepare a written schedule summarising the above – and stick to it!

The amount of space allocated to a topic in the study material is not a very good guide as to how long it will take you. For example, 'Summarising and Analysing Data' has a weight of 25 per cent in the syllabus and this is the best guide as to how long you should spend on it. It occupies 45 per cent of the main body of the text because it includes many tables and charts.

It is essential to know your syllabus. As your course progresses you will become more familiar with how long it takes to cover topics in sufficient depth. Your timetable may need to be adapted to allocate enough time for the whole syllabus.

Tips for effective studying

(1) Aim to find a quiet and undisturbed location for your study, and plan as far as possible to use the same period of time each day. Getting into a routine helps to avoid wasting time. Make sure that you have all the materials you need before you begin so as to minimise interruptions.

(2) Store all your materials in one place, so that you do not waste time searching for items around the house. If you have to pack everything away after each study period, keep them in a box, or even a suitcase, which will not be disturbed until the next time.

(3) Limit distractions. To make the most effective use of your study periods you should be able to apply total concentration, so turn off the TV, set your phones to message mode and put up your 'do not disturb' sign.

(4) Your timetable will tell you which topic to study. However, before diving in and becoming engrossed in the finer points, make sure you have an overall picture of all the areas that need to be covered by the end of that session. After an hour, allow yourself a short break and move away from your books. With experience, you will learn to assess the pace you need to work at. You should also allow enough time to read relevant articles from newspapers and journals, which will supplement your knowledge and demonstrate a wider perspective.

(5) Work carefully through a chapter, making notes as you go. When you have covered a suitable amount of material, vary the pattern by attempting a practice question. Preparing an answer plan is a good habit to get into, while you are both studying and revising, and also in the examination room. It helps to impose a structure on your solutions, and avoids rambling. When you have finished your attempt, make notes of any mistakes you made or any areas that you failed to cover or covered only skimpily.

(6) Make notes as you study, and discover the techniques that work best for you. Your notes may be in the form of lists, bullet points, diagrams, summaries, 'mind maps' or the written word, but remember that you will need to refer back to them at a later date, so they must be intelligible. If you are on a taught course, make sure you highlight any issues you would like to follow up with your lecturer.

(7) Organise your paperwork. There are now numerous paper storage systems available to ensure that all your notes, calculations and articles can be effectively filed and easily retrieved later.

Paper P1
Performance Operations

Syllabus Overview

This paper primarily deals with the tools and techniques that generate information needed to evaluate and control present and projected performance. Thus, forecasting key variables, recognising uncertainties attached to future events, is a basis for budget construction; the budget is then used with costing systems to evaluate actual performance. Project appraisal relies similarly on future financial projections to provide the information on which managers can evaluate expected performance and actual outcomes. Both budgeting and project appraisal emphasise the critical importance of optimising cash flow and the final section of the paper continues this theme from the perspective of managing working capital.

Syllabus Structure

The syllabus comprises the following topics and study weightings:

A	Cost Accounting Systems	30%
B	Forecasting and Budgeting Techniques	10%
C	Project Appraisal	25%
D	Dealing with Uncertainty in Analysis	15%
E	Managing Short-Term Finance	20%

Assessment Strategy

There will be a written examination paper of 3 hours, plus 20 minutes of pre-examination question paper reading time. The examination paper will have the following sections:

Section A – 20 marks
A variety of compulsory objective test questions, each worth between 2 and 4 marks. Mini scenarios may be given, to which a group of questions relate.

Section B – 30 marks
Six compulsory short answer questions, each worth 5 marks. A short scenario may be given, to which some or all questions relate.

Section C – 50 marks
One or two compulsory questions. Short scenarios may be given, to which questions relate.

Learning Outcomes and Indicative Syllabus Content
P1 – A. Cost Accounting Systems (30%)

Learning Outcomes		Indicative Syllabus Content
Lead	**Component**	
1. Apply and discuss costing methods and interpret their results. (4)	(a) Compare and contrast marginal (or variable), throughput and absorption accounting methods in respect of profit reporting and stock valuation.	• Marginal (or variable), throughput and absorption accounting systems of profit reporting and stock valuation. (A, B)
	(b) Prepare and discuss a report which reconciles budget and actual profit using absorption and/or marginal costing principles.	• Activity-based costing as a system of profit reporting and stock valuation. (C)
	(c) Compare and discuss activity-based costing as compared with traditional marginal and absorption costing methods, and discuss including its relative advantages and disadvantages as a system of cost accounting.	• Criticisms of standard costing in general and in advanced manufacturing environments in particular. (C)
		• Integration of standard costing with marginal cost accounting, absorption cost accounting and throughput accounting. (A, B, D)
	(d) Apply standard costing methods within costing systems, including and demonstrate the reconciliation of budgeted and actual profit margins.	• Manufacturing standards for material, labour, variable overhead and fixed overhead. (D, E)
		• Price/rate and usage/efficiency variances for materials, labour and variable overhead. (D, F)
	(e) Explain why and how standards are set in manufacturing and in service industries with particular reference to the maximisation of efficiency and minimisation of waste.	• Further subdivision of total usage/efficiency variances into mix and yield components. (Note: The calculation of mix variances on both individual and average valuation bases is required.) (D, F)
	(f) Calculate and interpret material, labour, variable overhead, fixed overhead and sales variances, distinguishing between planning and operational variances.	• Fixed overhead expenditure and volume variances. (Note: the subdivision of fixed overhead volume variance into capacity and efficiency elements will not be examined.) (D, F)
		• Planning and operational variances. (D, F)
	(g) Prepare reports using a range of internal and external benchmarks and interpret the results.	• Standards and variances in service industries (including the phenomenon of 'McDonaldisation'), public services (e.g. Health), (including the use of 'diagnostic related' or 'reference' groups), and the professions (e.g. labour mix variances in audit work). (D, E, F)

(h) Explain the impact of just-in-time manufacturing methods on cost accounting and the use of 'backflush accounting' when work-in-progress stock is minimal.

- Sales price and sales revenue/margin volume variances (calculation of the latter on a unit basis related to revenue, gross margin and contribution margin). Application of these variances to all sectors, including professional services and retail analysis. (D, E, F)
- Interpretation of variances: interrelationship, significance. (D, E, F)
- Benchmarking. (G)
- Backflush accounting in just-in-time production environments. The benefits of just-in-time production, total quality management and theory of constraints and the possible impacts of these methods on cost accounting and performance measurement. (H)

2. Explain the role of MRP and ERP systems in supporting standard costing systems, calculating variances and facilitating the posting of ledger entries. (2)

(a) Explain the role of MRP and ERP systems in supporting standard costing systems, calculating variances and facilitating the posting of ledger entries.

- MRP and ERP systems for resource planning and the integration of accounting functions with other systems, such as purchase ordering and production planning.

3. Apply principles of environmental costing in identifying relevant internalised costs and externalised environmental impacts of the organisation's activities. (3)

(a) Apply principles of environmental costing in identifying relevant internalised costs and externalised environmental impacts of the organisation's activities.

- Types of internalised costs relating to the environment (e.g. emissions permits, taxes, waste disposal costs) and key externalised environmental impacts, especially carbon, energy and water usage. Principles for associating such costs and impacts with activities and output.

P1 – B. Forecasting and Budgeting Techniques (10%)

Learning Outcomes

Lead (Level)	Component	Indicative Syllabus Content
1. Explain the purposes of forecasts, plans and budgets. (2)	(a) Explain why organisations prepare forecasts and plans. (b) Describe and explain the purposes of budgets, including planning, communication, co-ordination, motivation, authorisation, control and evaluation, and how these may conflict.	● The role of forecasts and plans in resource allocation, performance evaluation and control. (A) ● The purposes of budgets and the budgeting process, and conflicts that can arise (e.g. between budgets for realistic planning and budgets based on 'hard to achieve' targets for motivation). (B)
2. Prepare forecasts of financial results. (3)	(a) Calculate projected product/service volumes employing appropriate forecasting techniques. (b) Calculate projected revenues and costs based on product/service volumes, pricing strategies and cost structures.	● Time series analysis including moving totals and averages, treatment of seasonality, trend analysis using regression analysis and the application of these techniques in forecasting product and service volumes. (A, B) ● Fixed, variable, semi-variable and activity-based categorisations of cost and their application in projecting financial results. (B)
3. Prepare budgets based on forecasts. (3)	(a) Prepare a budget for any account(s) in the master budget, based on projections/forecasts and managerial targets. (b) Apply alternative approaches to budgeting, and identify differences between them.	● Mechanics of budget construction: limiting factors, component budgets and the master budget, and their interaction. (A) ● Alternative approaches to budget creation, including incremental approaches, zero-based budgeting and activity-based budgets. (B)

P1 – C. Project Appraisal (25%)

Learning Outcomes

Lead	Component	Indicative Syllabus Content
1. Prepare information to support project appraisal. (3)	(a) Explain the processes involved in making long-term decisions.	• The process of investment decision-making, including origination of proposals, creation of capital budgets, go/no-go decisions on individual projects (where judgements on qualitative issues interact with financial analysis), and post-audit of completed projects. (A)
	(b) Apply the principles of relevant cash flow analysis to long-run projects that continue for several years.	• Identification and calculation of relevant project cash flows taking account of inflation, tax, and 'final' project value where appropriate. (B, C)
	(c) Calculate project cash flows, accounting for tax and inflation, and apply perpetuities to derive 'end of project' value where appropriate.	• Activity-based costing to derive approximate 'long-run' costs appropriate for use in strategic decision-making. (D)
	(d) Apply activity-based costing techniques to derive approximate 'long-run' product or service costs appropriate for use in strategic decision-making.	• Need for and method of discounting. (E) • Sensitivity analysis to identify the input variables that most affect the chosen measure of project worth (payback, ARR, NPV or IRR). (F)
	(e) Explain the financial consequences of dealing with long-run projects, in particular the importance of accounting for the 'time value of money'.	• Identifying and integrating non-financial factors in long-term decisions. (G) • Methods of dealing with particular problems: the use of annuities in comparing projects with unequal lives and the profitability index in capital rationing situations. (G)
	(f) Apply sensitivity analysis to cash flow parameters to identify those to which net present value is particularly sensitive.	
	(g) Prepare decision support information for management, integrating financial and non-financial considerations.	
2. Evaluate project proposals. (5)	(a) Evaluate project proposals using the techniques of investment appraisal.	• The techniques of investment appraisal: payback, discounted payback, accounting rate of return, net present value and internal rate of return. (A, B, C)
	(b) Compare and contrast and discuss the alternative techniques of investment appraisal.	• Application of the techniques of investment appraisal to project cash flows and evaluation of the strengths and weaknesses of the techniques. (B, C)
	(c) Compare and rank prioritise projects that are mutually exclusive, involve unequal lives and/ or are subject to capital rationing.	

P1 – D. Dealing with Uncertainty in Analysis (15%)

Learning Outcomes

Lead	Component	Indicative Syllabus Content
1. Analyse information to assess the impact on decisions of variables with uncertain values. (4)	(a) Identify and analyse the impact of uncertainty and risk on decision models that may be based on relevant cash flows, learning curves, discounting techniques, etc. (b) Apply sensitivity analysis to both short-and long-run decision models to identify variables that might have significant impacts on project outcomes. (c) Analyse risk and uncertainty by calculating expected values and standard deviations together with probability tables and histograms. (d) Prepare expected value tables. (e) Calculate the value of information. (f) Prepare and apply decision trees.	• The nature of risk and uncertainty. (A) • Sensitivity analysis in decision modelling and the use of computer software for 'what if' analysis. (B) • Assignment of probabilities to key variables in decision models. (B) • Analysis of probabilistic models and interpretation of distributions of project outcomes. (C) • Expected value tables and the value of information. (D, E) • Decision trees for multi-stage decision problems. (F)

P1 – E. Managing Short Term Finance (20%)

Learning Outcomes

Lead	Component	Indicative Syllabus Content
1. Analyse the working capital position and identify areas for improvement. (4)	(a) Explain the importance of cash flow and working capital management.	• The link between cash, profit and the balance sheet. (A)
	(b) Calculate and interpret working capital ratios for business sectors.	• The credit cycle from receipt of customer order to cash receipt and the payment cycle from agreeing the order to making payment. (A)
	(c) Prepare and analyse cash flow forecasts over a twelve-month period.	• Working capital ratios (e.g. debtor days, stock days, creditor days, current ratio, quick ratio) and the working capital cycle. (B)
	(d) Identify and discuss measures to improve a cash forecast situation.	• Working capital characteristics of different businesses (e.g. supermarkets being heavily funded by creditors) and the importance of industry comparisons. (B)
	(e) Analyse trade debtor and creditor information.	• Cash flow forecasts, use of spreadsheets to assist in this in terms of changing variables (e.g. interest rates, inflation) and in consolidating forecasts. (C)
	(f) Analyse the impacts of alternative debtor and creditor policies.	• Variables that are most easily changed, delayed or brought forward in a forecast. (D)
	(g) Analyse the impacts of alternative policies for stock management.	• Methods for evaluating payment terms and settlement discounts. (E, F)
		• Preparation and interpretation of age analyses of debtors and creditors. (E, F)
		• Establishing collection targets on an appropriate basis (e.g. motivational issues in managing credit control). (F)
		• Centralised versus decentralised purchasing. (F)
		• The relationship between purchasing and stock control. (G)
		• Principles of the economic order quantity (EOQ) model and criticisms thereof. (G)

(Continued)

Learning Outcomes

Lead	Component	Indicative Syllabus Content
2. Identify short-term funding and investment opportunities. (2)	(a) Identify sources of short-term funding. (b) Identify alternatives for investment of short-term cash surpluses. (c) Identify appropriate methods of finance for trading internationally. (d) Illustrate numerically the financial impact of short-term funding and investment methods.	• Use and abuse of trade creditors as a source of finance. (A) • Types and features of short-term finance: trade creditors, overdrafts, short-term loans and debt factoring. (A) • The principles of investing short term (i.e. maturity, return, security, liquidity and diversification). (B) • Types of investments (e.g. interest-bearing bank accounts, negotiable instruments including certificates of deposit, short-term treasury bills, and securities). (B) • The difference between the coupon on debt and the yield to maturity. (B) • Export finance (e.g. documentary credits, bills of exchange, export factoring, forfaiting). (C)

1

Basic Aspects of
Management Accounting

Basic Aspects of Management Accounting

1

LEARNING OUTCOMES

The contents of this chapter provide underpinning material for the content of later chapters and contribute to the stated learning outcomes of those chapters. However, none of the learning outcomes for Performance Operations draw wholly or directly from the content of this chapter.

1.1 Introduction

You should have encountered the basic principles of cost and revenue behaviour in your certificate or equivalent studies. The major part of this chapter amounts to a revision of those basic principles.

Much of the content of this chapter is 'assumed prior knowledge' for Performance Operations studies and for material covered in subsequent chapters of this text. If you are entirely familiar with the basic aspects of management accounting, then you may prefer just to skim-read this chapter. However, you are advised not to ignore it completely – particularly the sections on relevant costs and limiting factor analysis.

1.2 Cost behaviour

Many factors affect the level of costs incurred; for instance, inflation will cause costs to increase over a period of time. In management accounting, when we talk about cost behaviour we are referring to the way in which costs are affected by fluctuations in the level of activity.

The level of activity can be measured in many different ways. For example, we can record the number of units produced, miles travelled, hours worked, percentage of capacity utilised and so on.

An understanding of cost behaviour patterns is essential for many management tasks, particularly in the areas of planning, decision-making and control. It would be impossible for managers to forecast and control costs without at least a basic knowledge of the way in which costs behave in relation to the level of activity.

In this section, we will look at the most common cost behaviour patterns and we will consider some examples of each.

1.2.1 Fixed cost

> The CIMA *Terminology* defines a fixed cost as 'a cost which is incurred for an accounting period, and which, within certain output or turnover limits, tends to be unaffected by fluctuations in the levels of activity (output or turnover)'.

Another term which can be used to refer to a fixed cost is 'period cost'. This highlights the fact that a fixed cost is incurred according to the time elapsed, rather than according to the level of activity.

A fixed cost can be depicted graphically as shown in Figure 1.1.

Examples of fixed costs are rent, rates, insurance and executive salaries.

The graph shows that the cost is constant (in this case at £5,000 for all levels of activity). However, it is important to note that this is only true for the relevant range of activity. Consider, for example, the behaviour of the rent cost. Within the relevant range it is possible to expand activity without needing extra premises and therefore the rent cost remains constant. However, if activity is expanded to the critical point where further premises are needed, then the rent cost will increase to a new, higher level.

This cost behaviour pattern can be described as a stepped fixed cost (Figure 1.2).

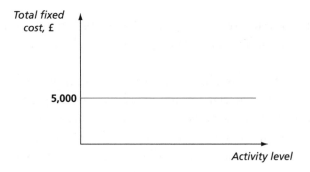

Figure 1.1 Fixed cost

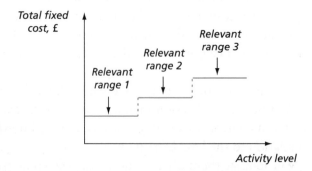

Figure 1.2 Stepped fixed cost

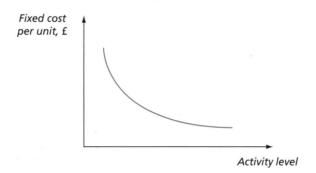

Figure 1.3 Fixed cost per unit

The cost is constant within the relevant range for each activity level but when a critical level of activity is reached, the total cost incurred increases to the next step.

The possibility of changes occurring in cost behaviour patterns means that it is unreliable to predict costs for activity levels which are outside the relevant range. For example, out records might show the cost incurred at various activity levels between 100 and 5,000 units. We should therefore try to avoid using this information as the basis for forecasting the level of cost which would be incurred at an activity of, say, 6,000 units, which is outside the relevant range.

> **!** This warning does not only apply to fixed costs: it is never wise to attempt to predict costs for activity levels outside the range for which cost behaviour patterns have been established.

When you are drawing or interpreting graphs of cost behaviour patterns, it is important that you pay great attention to the label on the vertical axis. In Figures 1.1 and 1.2 the graphs depicted the total cost incurred. If the vertical axis had been used to represent the fixed cost per unit, then it would look as shown Figure 1.3.

The fixed cost per unit reduces as the activity level is increased. This is because the same amount of fixed cost is being spread over an increasing number of units.

1.2.2 Variable cost

> The CIMA *Terminology* defines a variable cost as 'a cost which varies with a measure of activity'.

Examples of variable costs are direct material, direct labour and variable overheads.

 Exercise 1.1

Figure 1.4 depicts the total variable cost at each activity level. Can you draw a sketch graph of the variable cost per unit?

Figure 1.4 depicts a linear variable cost. It is a straight line through the origin which means that the cost is nil at zero activity level. When activity increases, the total variable cost increases in direct proportion, that is if activity goes up by 10%, then the total variable cost also increases by 10%, as long as the activity level is still within the relevant range.

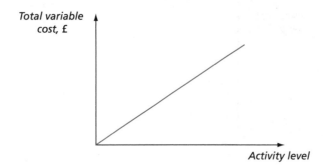

Figure 1.4 Linear variable cost

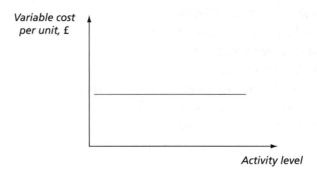

Figure 1.5 Variable cost per unit

The gradient of the line will depend on the amount of variable cost per unit.

If you attempted Exercise 1.4, then your graph of variable cost per unit should look like Figure 1.5.

The straight line parallel to the horizontal axis depicts a constant variable cost per unit, within the relevant range.

In most examination situations, and very often in practice, variable costs are assumed to be linear. Although many variable costs do approximate to a linear function, this assumption may not always be realistic. A variable cost may be non-linear as depicted in either of the diagrams in Figure 1.6.

These costs are sometimes called curvilinear variable costs.

The graph of cost A becomes steeper as the activity level increases. This indicates that each successive unit of activity is adding more to the total variable cost than the previous unit. An example of a variable cost which follows this pattern could be the cost of direct labour where employees are paid an accelerating bonus for achieving higher levels of output. The graph of cost B becomes less steep as the activity level increases. Each successive unit of activity adds less to total variable cost than the previous unit. An example of a variable cost which follows this pattern could be the cost of direct material where quantity discounts are available.

Exercise 1.2

Can you think of other variable costs which might follow the behaviour patterns depicted in Figure 1.6?

The important point is that managers should be aware of any assumptions that have been made in estimating cost behaviour patterns. They can then use the information which is based on these assumptions with a full awareness of its possible limitations.

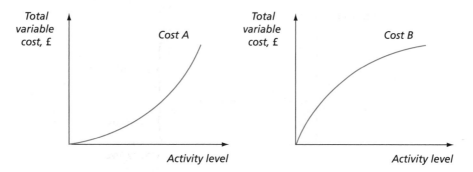

Figure 1.6 Non-linear variable costs

1.2.3 Semi-variable cost

> 🔑 A semi-variable cost is also referred to as a semi-fixed, hybrid, or mixed cost. The CIMA *Terminology* defines it as 'a cost containing both fixed and variable components and which is thus partly affected by a change in the level of activity'.

A graph of a semi-variable cost might look like Figure 1.7.

Examples of semi-variable costs are gas and electricity. Both of these expenditures consist of a fixed amount payable for the period, with a further variable amount which is related to the consumption of gas or electricity.

Alternatively a semi-variable cost behaviour pattern might look like Figure 1.8.

This cost remains constant up to a certain level of activity and then increases as the variable cost element is incurred. An example of such a cost might be the rental cost of a photocopier where a fixed rental is paid and no extra charge is made for copies up to a certain number. Once this number of copies is exceeded, a constant charge is levied for each copy taken.

✋ Exercise 1.3

Can you think of other examples of semi-variable costs with behaviour patterns like those indicated in Figures 1.7 and 1.8?

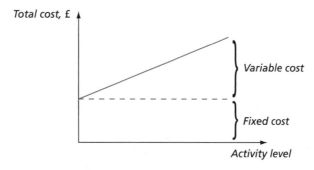

Figure 1.7 Semi-variable cost

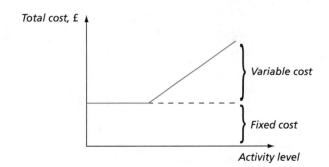

Figure 1.8 Semi-variable cost

1.2.4 Analysing semi-variable costs

The semi-variable cost behaviour pattern depicted in Figure 1.7 is most common in practice and in examination situations.

When managers have identified a semi-variable cost they will need to know how much of it is fixed and how much is variable. Only when they have determined this will they be able to estimate the cost to be incurred at relevant activity levels. Past records of costs and their associated activity levels are usually used to carry out the analysis. The three most common methods used to separate the fixed and variable elements are as follows:

(a) The high–low method.
(b) The scattergraph method.
(c) The least squares method of regression analysis.

You will be learning about the least squares method in your studies of *Business Mathematics.* In this text we will look at methods (a) and (b) in more depth.

The high–low method

This method picks out the highest and lowest activity levels from the available data and investigates the change in cost which has occurred between them. The highest and lowest points are selected to try to use the greatest possible range of data. This improves the accuracy of the result.

Example: the high-low method

A company has recorded the following data for a semi-variable cost:

Month	Activity level units	Cost incurred £
January	1,800	36,600
February	2,450	41,150
March	2,100	38,700
April	2,000	38,000
May	1,750	36,250
June	1,950	37,650

The highest activity level occurred in February and the lowest in May. Since the amount of fixed cost incurred in each month is constant, the extra cost resulting from the activity increase must be the variable cost.

	Activity level	£
	units	
February	2,450	41,150
May	1,750	36,250
Increase	700	4,900

The extra variable cost for 700 units is £4,900. We can now calculate the variable cost per unit:

$$\text{Variable cost} = \frac{4,900}{700} = \text{£7 per unit}$$

Substituting back in the data for February, we can determine the amount of fixed cost:

February	£
Total cost	41,150
Variable cost (2,450 units × £7)	17,150
Therefore, fixed cost per month	24,000

Now that the fixed and variable cost elements have been identified, it is possible to estimate the total cost for any activity level within the range 1,750 units to 2,450 units.

The scattergraph method

This method takes account of all available historical data and it is very simple to use. However, it is very prone to inaccuracies that arise due to subjectivity and the likelihood of human error.

1. First a scattergraph is drawn which plots all available pairs of data on a graph.
2. Then a line of best fit is drawn by eye. This is the line which, in the judgement of the user, appears to be the best representation of the gradient of the sets of points on the graph. This is demonstrated in Figure 1.9.

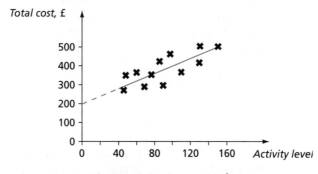

Figure 1.9 Scattergraph

 The inaccuracies involved in drawing the line of best fit should be obvious to you. If you had been presented with this set of data, your own line of best fit might have been slightly different from ours.

3. The point where the extrapolation of this line cuts the vertical axis (the intercept) is then read off as the total fixed cost element. The variable cost per unit is given by the gradient of the line.
   From Figure 1.9, the fixed cost contained within this set of data is adjudged to be £200.
   The variable cost is calculated as follows:

Cost for zero units = £200
Cost for 150 units = £500

$$\text{Gradient (i.e. variable cost)} = \frac{500 - 200}{150 - 0} = \text{£2 per unit.}$$

1.2.5 Using historical data

The main problem which arises in the determination of cost behaviour is that the estimates are usually based on data collected in the past. Events in the past may not be representative of the future and managers should be aware of this if they are using the information for planning and decision-making purposes.

1.3 Costs and activity-based techniques

Since the mid-1980s, activity-based techniques (ABTs) have been at the forefront of developments in management accounting. The use of ABTs will be explored in some depth later in this text.

The general background to ABTs is discussed in 'Activity-Based Techniques', in Chapter 2. This article should be accessible to you at this point and you may care to read forward to it if the topic interests you.

The key point to note for now is that costs can be collected and reported in various different ways. One way is to report them according to the activities that they contribute to. For example, the overhead costs associated with the stores operation of a manufacturing business for period X can be reported as follows:

(1) Chart of accounts view

	£
Indirect wages	50,000
Rent of premises	25,000
Maintenance of equipment	5,000
Total	80,000

And/or:

(2) Activity-based view

	£	Activities	£ per Activity
Placing orders	40,000	2,000 orders	20
Receipt of deliveries	30,000	3,000 receipts	10
Issues of supplies	10,000	10,000 issues	1
Total	80,000		

The traditional management accounting treatment of these costs would be to treat them as fixed overheads and absorb them into product costs using some arbitrary overhead absorption base such as direct labour hours. This logic follows the chart of accounts view shown above.

In fact, few costs are truly fixed if you take a long enough time horizon, consider a wide enough span of activity levels and study the costs carefully to determine what activities they vary with. If costs are reported according to the activities they relate to, then one obtains the activity-based view shown above. This provides a sensitive view of costs that can be used for a variety of management purposes. We will explore those purposes as we progress through this text and consider ABTs such as activity-based costing (ABC), activity-based budgeting (ABB) and activity-based management (ABM).

1.4 Breakeven or cost–volume–profit analysis

> *Cost–volume–profit* (CVP) analysis is defined in CIMA's *Official Terminology* as 'the study of the effects on future profit of changes in fixed cost, variable cost, sales price, quantity and mix'.

A more common term used for this type of analysis is 'breakeven analysis'. However, this is somewhat misleading, since it implies that the focus of the analysis is the *breakeven point,* that is the level of activity that produces neither profit nor loss. The scope of CVP analysis is much wider than this, as indicated in the definition. However, you should be aware that the terms 'breakeven analysis' and 'CVP analysis' tend to be used interchangeably.

1.4.1 Calculating the breakeven point

Contribution is so called because it literally does contribute towards fixed costs and profit. As sales revenues grow from zero, the contribution also grows until it just covers the fixed costs. This is the breakeven point where neither profits nor losses are made.

It follows that to break even the amount of contribution must exactly match the amount of fixed costs. If we know how much contribution is earned from each unit sold, then we can calculate the number of units required to break even as follows:

$$\text{Breakeven point in units} = \frac{\text{Fixed costs}}{\text{Contribution per unit}}$$

For example, suppose that an organisation manufactures a single product, incurring variable costs of £30 per unit and fixed costs of £20,000 per month. If the product sells for £50 per unit, then the breakeven point can be calculated as follows:

$$\text{Breakeven point in units} = \frac{£20,000}{£50 - £30} = 1,000 \text{ units per month.}$$

1.5 The margin of safety

The margin of safety is the difference between the expected level of sales and the breakeven point. The larger the margin of safety, the more likely it is that a profit will be made, that is if sales start to fall there is more leeway before the organisation begins to incur losses. (Obviously, this statement is made on the assumption that projected sales volumes are above the breakeven point.)

In the above example, if forecast sales are 1,700 units per month, the margin of safety can be easily calculated.

$$\begin{aligned}
\text{Margin of safety} &= \text{projected sales} - \text{breakeven point} \\
&= 1,700 \text{ units} - 1,000 \text{ units} \\
&= 700 \text{ units per month, or } 41\% \text{ of sales } (700/1,700 \times 100\%)
\end{aligned}$$

The margin of safety should be expressed as a percentage of projected sales to put it in perspective. To quote a margin of safety of 700 units without relating it to the projected sales figure is not giving the full picture.

The margin of safety might also be expressed as a percentage of the breakeven value, that is 70 per cent of the breakeven value in this case.

The margin of safety can also be used as one route to profit calculation. We have seen that the contribution goes towards fixed costs and profit. Once breakeven point is reached the fixed costs have been covered. After the breakeven point there are no more fixed costs to be covered and all of the contribution goes towards making profits grow.

In our example the monthly profit from sales of 1,700 units would be £14,000.

$$
\begin{aligned}
\text{Margin of safety} &= 700 \text{ units per month} \\
\text{Monthly profit} &= 700 \times \text{contribution per unit} \\
&= 700 \times £20 \\
&= £14,000.
\end{aligned}
$$

1.6 The contribution to sales (C/S) ratio

The contribution to sales ratio is usually expressed as a percentage. It can be calculated for the product in our example as follows:

$$
\begin{aligned}
\text{Contribution to sales ratio (C/S ratio)} &= £20 / £50 \times 100\% \\
&= 40\%
\end{aligned}
$$

A higher contribution to sales ratio means that contribution grows more quickly as sales levels increase. Once the breakeven point has been passed, profits will accumulate more quickly than for a product with a lower contribution to sales ratio.

You might sometimes see this ratio referred to as the profit–volume (P/V) ratio.

If we can assume that a unit's variable cost and selling price remain constant, then the C/S ratio will also remain constant. It can be used to calculate the breakeven point as follows (using the data from the earlier example):

$$
\text{Breakeven point in sales value} = \frac{\text{Fixed costs}}{\text{C/S ratio}} = \frac{£20,000}{0.40} = £50,000
$$

This can be converted to 1,000 units as before by dividing by the selling price of £50 per unit.

 Exercise

A company manufactures and sells a single product that has the following cost and selling price structure:

	£/unit	£/unit
Selling price		120
Direct material	22	
Direct labour	36	
Variable overhead	14	
Fixed overhead	12	
		84
Profit per unit		36

The fixed overhead absorption rate is based on the normal capacity of 2,000 units per month. Assume that the same amount is spent each month on fixed overheads.

Budgeted sales for next month are 2,200 units.
You are required to calculate

(i) the breakeven point, in sales units per month;
(ii) the margin of safety for next month;
(iii) the budgeted profit for next month;
(iv) the sales required to achieve a profit of £96,000 in a month.

✓ Solution

(i) The key to calculating the breakeven point is to determine the contribution per unit.

Contribution per unit = £120 − (£22 + £36 + £14) = £48

$$\text{Breakeven point} = \frac{\text{Fixed overhead}}{\text{Contribution per unit}}$$

$$= \frac{£12 \times 2,000}{£48} = 500 \text{ units}$$

(ii) Margin of safety = budgeted sales − breakeven point
= 2,200 − 500
= 1,700 units (or, 1,700/2,200 × 100% = 77% of budgeted sales)

(iii) Once breakeven point has been reached, all of the contribution goes towards profits because all of the fixed costs have been covered.

Budgeted profit = 1,700 units margin of safety × £48 contribution per unit
= £81,600

(iv) To achieve the desired level of profit, sufficient units must be sold to earn a contribution that covers the fixed costs and leaves the desired profit for the month.

$$\text{Number of sales units required} = \frac{\text{Fixed overhead + desired profit}}{\text{Contribution per unit}}$$

$$= \frac{(£12 \times 2,000) + £96,000}{£48} = 2,500 \text{ units}$$

1.7 Drawing a basic breakeven chart

A basic breakeven chart records costs and revenues on the vertical axis and the level of activity on the horizontal axis. Lines are drawn on the chart to represent costs and sales revenue. The breakeven point can be read off where the sales revenue line cuts the total cost line.

We shall use our basic example to demonstrate how to draw a breakeven chart. The data is

Selling price	£50 per unit
Variable cost	£30 per unit
Fixed costs	£20,000 per month
Forecast sales	1,700 units per month

> ✎ You must be able to prepare breakeven charts to scale using data provided. To give yourself some practice it would be a good idea to follow the step-by-step guide that follows to produce your own chart on a piece of graph paper.

- *Step 1. Select appropriate scales for the axes and draw and label them.* Your graph should fill as much of the page as possible. This will make it clearer and easier to read. You can make sure that you do this by putting the extremes of the axes right at the end of the available space.

  The furthest point on the vertical axis will be the monthly sales revenue, that is,

  1,700 units × £50 = £85,000

  The furthest point on the horizontal axis will be monthly sales volume of 1,700 units. Make sure that you do not need to read data for volumes higher than 1,700 units before you set these extremes for your scales.

- *Step 2. Draw the fixed cost line and label it.* This will be a straight line parallel to the horizontal axis at the £20,000 level.

  The £20,000 fixed costs are incurred in the short term even with zero activity.

- *Step 3. Draw the total cost line and label it.* The best way to do this is to calculate the total costs for the maximum sales level, which is 1,700 units in our example. Mark this point on the graph and join it to the cost incurred at zero activity, that is £20,000

	£
Variable costs of 1,700 units	
(1,700 × £30)	51,000
Fixed costs	20,000
Total cost for 1,700 units	71,000

- *Step 4. Draw the revenue line and label it.* Once again, the best way is to plot the extreme points. The revenue at maximum activity in our example is 1,700 × £50 = £85,000. This point can be joined to the origin, since at zero activity there will be no sales revenue.
- *Step 5. Mark any required information on the chart and read off solutions as required.* Check that your chart is accurate by reading off the measures that we have already calculated in this chapter: the breakeven point, the margin of safety, the profit for sales of 1,700 units.
- *Step 6. Check the accuracy of your readings using arithmetic.* We already have the solutions calculated arithmetically for our example. However, it is always good examination practice to check the accuracy of your answers and make adjustments for any errors in your chart (if you have time!).

The completed graph is shown in Figure 1.10.

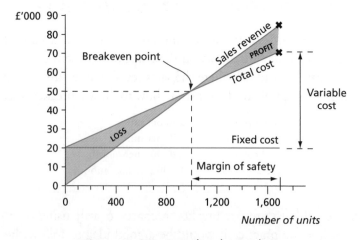

Figure 1.10 Basic breakeven chart

> ✎ Your own graph should be considerably larger than this: a full A4 graph-ruled sheet is recommended to facilitate ease of interpretation.

1.8 The contribution breakeven chart

One of the problems with the conventional or basic breakeven chart is that it is not possible to read contribution directly from the chart. A contribution breakeven chart is based on the same principles but it shows the variable cost line instead of the fixed cost line (Figure 1.11). The same lines for total cost and sales revenue are shown so the breakeven point and profit can be read off in the same way as with a conventional chart. However, it is also possible to read the contribution for any level of activity.

Using the same basic example as for the conventional chart, the total variable cost for an output of 1,700 units is 1,700 × £30 = £51,000. This point can be joined to the origin since the variable cost is nil at zero activity.

The contribution can be read as the difference between the sales revenue line and the variable cost line.

This form of presentation might be used when it is desirable to highlight the importance of contribution and to focus attention on the variable costs.

1.9 The PV chart

Another form of breakeven chart is the PV chart. This chart plots a single line depicting the profit or loss at each level of activity. The breakeven point is where this line cuts the horizontal axis. A PV graph for our example will look like Figure 1.12.

The vertical axis shows profits and losses and the horizontal axis is drawn at zero profit or loss.

At zero activity the loss is equal to £20,000, that is the amount of fixed costs. The second point used to draw the line could be the calculated breakeven point or the calculated profit for sales of 1,700 units.

The PV graph is also called a profit graph or a contribution–volume graph.

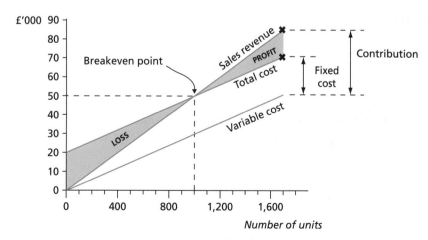

Figure 1.11 Contribution breakeven chart

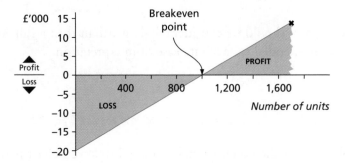

Figure 1.12 Profit–volume chart

 Exercise

Make sure that you are clear about the extremes of the chart axes. Practise drawing this chart to scale on a piece of graph paper.

1.9.1 The advantage of the PV chart

The main advantage of the PV chart is that it is capable of depicting clearly the effect on profit and breakeven point of any changes in the variables. An example will show how this can be done.

Example

A company manufactures a single product that incurs fixed costs of £30,000 per annum. Annual sales are budgeted to be 70,000 units at a sales price of £30 per unit. Variable costs are £28.50 per unit.

(a) Draw a PV graph, and use it to determine the breakeven point.

The company is now considering improving the quality of the product and increasing the selling price to £35 per unit. Sales volume will be unaffected, but fixed costs will increase to £45,000 per annum and variable costs to £33 per unit.

(b) Draw, on the same graph as for part (a), a second PV graph and comment on the results.

Solution

The PV chart is shown in Figure 1.13.
The two lines have been drawn as follows:

- *Situation (a).* The profit for sales of 70,000 units is £75,000.

	£'000
Contribution 70,000 × £(30 − 28.50)	105
Fixed costs	30
Profit	75

This point is joined to the loss at zero activity, £30,000, that is the fixed costs.

- *Situation (b).* The profit for sales of 70,000 units is £95,000.

	£'000
Contribution 70,000 × £(35 − 33)	140
Fixed costs	45
Profit	95

This point is joined to the loss at zero activity, £45,000, that is the fixed costs.

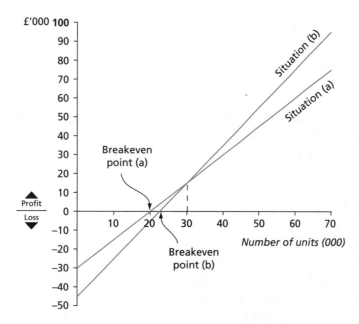

Figure 1.13 Showing changes with a PV chart

Comment on the results

The graph depicts clearly the larger profits available from option (b). It also shows that the breakeven point increases from 20,000 to 22,500 units but that this is not a large increase when viewed in the context of the projected sales volume. It is also possible to see that for sales volumes above 30,000 units the profit achieved will be higher with option (b). For sales volumes below 30,000 units option (a) will yield higher profits (or lower losses).

The PV graph is the clearest way of presenting information like this. If we attempted to draw two conventional breakeven charts on one set of axes, the result would be a jumble that would be very difficult to interpret.

1.10 The limitations of breakeven (or CVP) analysis

The limitations of the practical applicability of breakeven analysis and breakeven charts stem mostly from the assumptions that underline the analysis:

(a) Costs are assumed to behave in a linear fashion. Unit variable costs are assumed to remain constant and fixed costs are assumed to be unaffected by changes in activity levels. The charts can in fact be adjusted to cope with non-linear variable costs or steps in fixed costs, but too many changes in behaviour patterns can make the charts very cluttered and difficult to use.

(b) Sales revenues are assumed to be constant for each unit sold. This may be unrealistic because of the necessity to reduce the selling price to achieve higher sales volumes. Once again, the analysis can be adapted for some changes in selling price but too many changes can make the charts unwieldy.

(c) There is assumed to be no change in stocks. Reported profits can vary if absorption costing is used and there are changes in stock levels.

(d) It is assumed that activity is the only factor affecting costs, and factors such as inflation are ignored. This is one of the reasons why the analysis is limited to being essentially a short-term decision aid.

BASIC ASPECTS OF MANAGEMENT ACCOUNTING

(e) Apart from the unrealistic situation described above of a constant product mix, the charts can only be applied to a single product or service. Not many organisations have a single product or service, and if there is more than one then the apportionment of fixed costs between them becomes arbitrary.

(f) The analysis seems to suggest that as long as the activity level is above the breakeven point, then a profit will be achieved. In reality certain changes in the cost and revenue patterns may result in a second breakeven point after which losses are made. This situation will be depicted in the next section of this chapter.

1.11 The economist's breakeven chart

An economist would probably depict a breakeven chart as shown in Figure 1.14.

The total cost line is not a straight line that climbs at a constant rate as in the accountant's breakeven chart. Instead, its slope increases moving from left to right because marginal costs are likely to increase with output – given short-term capacity constraints.

The revenue line is not a straight line as in the accountant's chart. The line becomes less steep to depict the need to reduce unit selling prices in order to achieve higher sales volumes.

However, you will see that within the middle range the economist's chart does look very similar to the accountant's breakeven chart. This area is marked as the relevant range in Figure 1.14.

For this reason it is unreliable to assume that the CVP relationships depicted in breakeven analysis are relevant across a wide range of activity. In particular, Figure 1.14 shows that the constant cost and price assumptions are likely to be unreliable at very high or very low levels of activity. Managers should therefore ensure that they work within the relevant range for the available data, that is within the range over which the depicted cost and revenue relationships are more reliable.

1.12 Using costs for decision-making

Most management decisions involve a change in the level, method or mix of activities in order to maximise profits. The only costs that should be considered in decision-making are

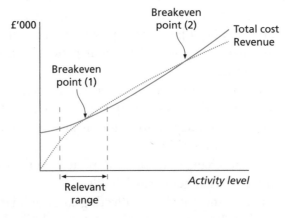

Figure 1.14 The economist's breakeven chart

those that will be altered as a result of the decision. Those costs that will be affected by the decision may be referred to as *relevant costs,* while others are non-relevant and should be ignored in the analysis.

It is often the case that variable costs are relevant whereas fixed costs are not, unless the decision affects the cost structure of the organisation. Thus, information for decision-making should always be based on marginal costing principles, since marginal costing focuses on the variable costs and is not concerned with arbitrary apportionment of fixed costs that will be incurred anyway.

1.12.1 Short-term decision-making

An important point that you should appreciate for all of the decision-making techniques that you learn about in this chapter is that they are usually most relevant to short-term, one-off decisions. Furthermore, as you will see with the example of the minimum-price quotation, the analysis provides only a starting point for management decisions. The financial figures are only part of the information needed for a fully informed decision. It is also important to consider the non-financial factors which might be relevant to the decision.

> You must get into the habit of considering non-financial and qualitative factors in any decision. Many exam questions will specifically ask you to do so.

1.13 Evaluating proposals

As an introduction to using cost information to evaluate proposals, use your understanding of breakeven analysis and cost behaviour patterns to evaluate the proposals in the following exercise.

Exercise

A summary of a manufacturing company's budgeted profit statement for its next financial year, when it expects to be operating at 75% of capacity, is given below.

	£	£
Sales 9,000 units at £32		288,000
Less		
Direct materials	54,000	
Direct wages	72,000	
Production overhead – fixed	42,000	
– variable	18,000	
		186,000
Gross profit		102,000
Less admin., selling and dist'n costs		
Fixed	36,000	
Varying with sales volume	27,000	
		63,000
Net profit		39,000

It has been estimated that

(i) if the selling price per unit were reduced to £28, the increased demand would utilise 90% of the company's capacity without any additional advertising expenditure;

(ii) to attract sufficient demand to utilise full capacity would require a 15% reduction in the current selling price and a £5,000 special advertising campaign.

You are required to

(a) calculate the breakeven point in units, based on the original budget;
(b) calculate the profits and breakeven points that would result from each of the two alternatives and compare them with the original budget.

☑ Solution

(a) First calculate the current contribution per unit.

	£'000	£'000
Sales revenue		288
Direct materials	54	
Direct wages	72	
Variable production overhead	18	
Variable administration, etc.	27	
		171
Contribution		117
Contribution per unit (49,000 units)		£13

Now you can use the formula to calculate the breakeven point.

$$\text{Breakeven point} = \frac{\text{Fixed costs}}{\text{Contribution per unit}} = \frac{£42{,}000 + £36{,}000}{£13} = 6{,}000 \text{ units}$$

(b) Alternative (i)

Budgeted contribution per unit	£13
Reduction in selling price (£32 − £28)	£4
Revised contribution per unit	£9

$$\text{Revised breakeven point} = \frac{£78{,}000}{£9} \qquad 8{,}667 \quad \text{units}$$

Revised sales volume = 9,000 × 90/75	10,800	units
Revised contribution = 10,800 × £9	£97,200	
Less fixed costs	£78,000	
Revised profit	£19,200	

Alternative (ii)

Budgeted contribution per unit	£13.00
Reduction in selling price (15% × £32)	£4.80
Revised contribution per unit	£8.20

$$\text{Revised breakeven point} = \frac{£78{,}000 + £5{,}000}{£8.20} \qquad 10{,}122 \quad \text{units}$$

Revised sales volume = 9,000 units × 100/75	12,000	units
Revised contribution = 12,000 × £8.20	£98,400	
Less fixed costs	£83,000	
Revised profit	£15,400	

Neither of the two alternative proposals is worthwhile. They both result in lower forecast profits. In addition, they will both increase the breakeven point and will therefore increase the risk associated with the company's operations. This exercise has shown you how an understanding of cost behaviour patterns and the manipulation of contribution can enable the rapid evaluation of the financial effects of a proposal. We can now expand it to demonstrate another aspect of the application of marginal costing techniques to short-term decision-making.

 Exercise

The manufacturing company decided to proceed with the original budget and has asked you to determine how many units must be sold to achieve a profit of £45,500.

 Solution

Once again, the key is the required contribution. This time the contribution must be sufficient to cover both the fixed costs and the required profit. If we then divide this amount by the contribution earned from each unit, we can determine the required sales volume.

$$\text{Required sales} = \frac{\text{Fixed costs} + \text{required profit}}{\text{Contribution per unit}}$$

$$= \frac{(\pounds 42,000 + \pounds 36,000) + \pounds 45,500}{\pounds 13} = 9,500 \text{ units.}$$

Now we shall move from this very basic analysis to consider specific types of cost that may assist management decision-making.

1.14 Relevant costs

Relevant costs are those which will be affected by the decision being taken. All relevant costs should be considered in management decision-making. If a cost will remain unaltered regardless of the decision being taken, then it is called a non-relevant cost.

1.14.1 Non-relevant costs

Costs that are not usually relevant in management decisions include the following:

(a) Sunk or past costs, that is money already spent that cannot now be recovered. An example of a sunk cost is expenditure that has been incurred in developing a new product. The money cannot be recovered even if a decision is taken to abandon further development of the new product. The cost is therefore not relevant to future decisions concerning the product.

(b) Absorbed fixed overheads that will not increase or decrease as a result of the decision being taken. The amount of overhead to be absorbed by a particular cost unit might alter because of the decision; however, this is a result of the company's cost accounting procedures for overheads. If the actual amount of overhead incurred by the company will not alter, then the overhead is not a relevant cost.

(c) Expenditure that will be incurred in the future, but as a result of decisions taken in the past that cannot now be changed. These are known as committed costs. They can sometimes cause confusion because they are future costs. However, a committed cost will be incurred regardless of the decision being taken and therefore it is not relevant. An example of this type of cost could be expenditure on special packaging for a new product, where the packaging has been ordered and delivered but not yet paid for. The company is obliged to pay for the packaging even if they decide not to proceed with the product; therefore it is not a relevant cost.

(d) Historical cost depreciation that has been calculated in the conventional manner. Such depreciation calculations do not result in any future cash flows. They are merely the book entries that are designed to spread the original cost of an asset over its useful life.

(e) Notional costs such as notional rent and notional interest. These are only relevant if they represent an identified lost opportunity to use the premises or the finance for some alternative purpose.

In these circumstances, the notional costs would be opportunity costs. This explanation will become clearer when you learn more about opportunity costs later in this chapter.

 ## Exercise

Test your understanding of relevant and non-relevant costs by seeing if you can identify which of the following costs are relevant:

(a) The salary to be paid to a market researcher who will oversee the development of a new product. This is a new post to be created specially for the new product but the £12,000 salary will be a fixed cost. Is this cost relevant to the decision to proceed with the development of the product?

(b) The £2,500 additional monthly running costs of a new machine to be purchased to manufacture an established product. Since the new machine will save on labour time, the fixed overhead to be absorbed by the product will reduce by £100 per month. Are these costs relevant to the decision to purchase the new machine?

(c) Office cleaning expenses of £125 for next month. The office is cleaned by contractors and the contract can be cancelled by giving 1 month's notice. Is this cost relevant to a decision to close the office?

(d) Expenses of £75 paid to the marketing manager. This was to reimburse the manager for the cost of travelling to meet a client with whom the company is currently negotiating a major contract. Is this cost relevant to the decision to continue negotiations?

Solution

(a) The salary is a relevant cost of £12,000. Do not be fooled by the fact that it is a fixed cost. The cost may be fixed in total but it is definitely a cost that is relevant to the decision to proceed with the future development of the new product. This is an example of a directly attributable fixed cost.

A directly attributable fixed cost may also be called product-specific fixed cost.

(b) The £2,500 additional running costs are relevant to the decision to purchase the new machine. The saving in overhead absorption is not relevant since we are not told that the *total* overhead expenditure will be altered. The saving in labour cost would be relevant but we shall assume that this has been accounted for in determining the additional monthly running costs.

(c) This is not a relevant cost for next month since it will be incurred even if the contract is cancelled today. If a decision is being made to close the office, this cost cannot be included as a saving to be made next month. However, it will be saved in the months after that so it will become a relevant cost saving from month 2 onwards.

(d) This is not a relevant cost of the decision to continue with the contract. The £75 is sunk and cannot be recovered even if the company does not proceed with the negotiations.

Conclusion

It is essential to look to the future when deciding which costs are relevant to a decision. Costs that have already been incurred or that will not be altered in the future as a result of the decision being taken are not relevant costs.

1.15 Opportunity costs

An opportunity cost is a special type of relevant cost. It is defined in the CIMA *Terminology* as 'the value of the benefit sacrificed when one course of action is chosen, in preference to an alternative. The opportunity cost is represented by the forgone potential benefit from the best rejected course of action.'

With opportunity costs we are concerned with identifying the value of any benefit forgone as the result of choosing one course of action in preference to another.

1.15.1 Examples of opportunity costs

The best way to demonstrate opportunity costs is to consider some examples.

(a) A company has some obsolete material in stock that it is considering to use for a special contract. If the material is not used on the contract it can either be sold back to the supplier for £2 per tonne or it can be used on another contract in place of a different material that would usually cost £2.20 per tonne.

The opportunity cost of using the material on the special contract is £2.20 per tonne. This is the value of the next best alternative use for the material, or the benefit forgone by not using it for the other contract.

(b) Chris is deciding whether or not to take a skiing holiday this year. The travel agent is quoting an all-inclusive holiday cost of £675 for a week. Chris will lose the chance to earn £200 for a part-time job during the week that the holiday would be taken.

The relevant cost of taking the holiday in £875. This is made up of the out-of-pocket cost of £675, plus the £200 opportunity cost, that is the part-time wages forgone.

1.15.2 Notional costs and opportunity costs

Notional costs and opportunity costs are in fact very similar. This is particularly noticeable in the case of notional rent. The notional rent could be the rental that the company is forgoing by occupying the premises itself, that is it could be an opportunity cost. However, it is only a true opportunity cost if the company can actually identify a forgone opportunity to rent the premises. If nobody is willing to pay the rent, then it is not an opportunity cost.

> If an examination question on relevant costs includes information about notional costs, read the question carefully and state your assumptions concerning the relevance of the notional cost.

BASIC ASPECTS OF MANAGEMENT ACCOUNTING

1.16 Avoidable, differential and incremental costs

There are two other types of relevant cost that you will need to know about: avoidable costs and differential/incremental costs.

1.16.1 Avoidable costs

CIMA defines avoidable costs as 'the specific costs of an activity or sector of a business which would be avoided if that activity or sector did not exist'.

For example, if a company is considering shutting down a department, then the avoidable costs are those that would be saved as a result of the shutdown. Such costs might include the labour costs of those employed in the department and the rental cost of the space occupied by the department. The latter is an example of an attributable or specific fixed cost. Costs such as apportioned head office costs that would not be saved as a result of the shutdown are unavoidable costs. They are not relevant to the decision.

1.16.2 Differential/incremental costs

CIMA defines a differential/incremental cost as 'the difference in total cost between alternatives; calculated to assist decision-making'.

For example, if the relevant cost of contract X is £5,700 and the relevant cost of contract Y is £6,200, we would say that the differential or incremental cost is £500, that is the extra cost of contract Y is £500.

1.16.3 Using incremental costs

Incremental costs can be useful if the cost accountant wishes to highlight the consequences of taking sequential steps in a decision. For example, the accountant might be providing cost information for a decision about whether to increase the number of employees in a department. Instead of quoting several different total-cost figures, it might be more useful to say 'the incremental cost per five employees will be £5,800 per month'.

Remember that only relevant costs should be used in the calculations.

1.16.4 Incremental revenues

Just as incremental costs are the differences in cost between alternatives, so incremental revenues are the differences in revenues between the alternatives. Matching the incremental costs against the incremental revenue will produce a figure for the incremental gain or loss between the alternatives.

 Exercise

To consolidate the material so far on relevant costs and opportunity costs, work through the following exercise to identify the relevant costs of the decision. Try to work out the relevant cost of each item before you look at the solution.

ABC Ltd is deciding whether or not to proceed with a special order. Use the details below to determine the relevant cost of the order.

(a) Materials P and Q will be used for the contract. 100 tonnes of material P will be needed and sufficient material is in stock because the material is in common use in the company. The original cost of the material in stock is £1 per tonne but it would cost £1.20 per tonne to replace if it is used for this contract. The material Q required is in stock as a result of previous over-purchasing. This material originally cost £500 but it has no other use. The material is toxic and if it is not used on this contract, then ABC must pay £280 to have it disposed of.

(b) The contract requires 200 hours of labour at £5 per hour. Employees possessing the necessary skills are currently employed by the company but they are idle at present due to a lull in the company's normal business.

(c) Overhead will be absorbed by the contract at a rate of £10 per labour hour, which consists of £7 for fixed overhead and £3 for variable.

(d) The contract will require the use of a storage unit for 3 months. ABC is committed to rent the unit for 1 year at a rental of £50 per month. The unit is not in use at present. A neighbouring business has recently approached ABC offering to rent the unit from them for £70 per month.

(e) Total fixed overheads are not expected to increase as a result of the contract.

 ## Solution

(a) The relevant cost of a material that is used regularly is its replacement cost. This will ensure that the business profits are unaffected by the use of the material for this contract. The relevant cost of material P is therefore £1.20 per tonne.

   Material Q has a 'negative' cost if used for the contract. This is the saving that will be made through not having to pay the disposal cost of £280.

(b) The relevant cost of labour is zero. The labour cost is being paid anyway and no extra cost will be incurred as a result of this contract.

(c) The fixed overhead is not relevant because we are told that fixed overheads are not expected to increase. The relevant variable overhead cost is £3 per hour × 200 hours = £600.

   Even if you are not specifically told that fixed overheads will remain unaltered, it is usual to assume that they will not increase, stating the assumption clearly.

(d) The rental cost £50 per month is not relevant because it will not be affected by the contract. The relevant cost of using the storage unit is the forgone rental income of £70 per month.

Summary of relevant costs

		£
(i)	Material P	120
	Material Q	(280)
(ii)	Labour	–
(iii)	Variable overhead	600
(iv)	Rent forgone	210
	Total relevant cost	650

1.17 Limiting factor decision-making

A limiting factor is any factor that is in scarce supply and that stops the organisation from expanding its activities further, that is it limits the organisation's activities.

The limiting factor for many trading organisations is sales volume because they cannot sell as much as they would like. However, other factors may also be limited, especially in the short term. For example, machine capacity or the supply of skilled labour may be limited for one or two periods until some action can be taken to alleviate the shortage.

1.17.1 Decisions involving a single limiting factor

If an organisation is faced with a single limiting factor, for example machine capacity, then it must ensure that a production plan is established that maximises the profit from the use of the available capacity. Assuming that fixed costs remain constant, this is same as saying that the contribution must be maximised from the use of the available capacity. The machine capacity must be allocated to those products that earn the most contribution per machine hour.

This decision rule can be stated as 'maximising the contribution per unit of limiting factor'.

Example

LMN Ltd manufactures three products, L, M and N. The company that supplies the two raw materials that are used in all three products has informed LMN that their employees are refusing to work overtime. This means that supply of the materials is limited to the following quantities for the next period:

Material A   1,030 kg
Material B   1,220 kg

No other source of supply can be found for the next period.
Information relating to the three products manufactured by LMN Ltd is as follows:

	L	M	N
Quantity of material used per unit manufactured			
Material A (kg)	2	1	4
Material B (kg)	5	3	7
Maximum sales demand (units)	120	160	110
Contribution per unit sold	£15	£12	£17.50

Owing to the perishable nature of the products, no finished goods stocks are held.

Requirements

(a) Recommend a production mix that will maximise the profits of LMN Ltd for the forthcoming period.
(b) LMN Ltd has a valued customer to whom they wish to guarantee the supply of 50 units of each product next period. Would this alter your recommended production plan?

Solution

(a) The first step is to check whether the supply of each material is adequate or whether either or both of them represent a limiting factor.

	L	M	N	Total
Maximum sales demand (units)	120	160	110	
Material A required per unit (kg)	2	1	4	
Total material A required (kg)	240	160	440	840
Material B required per unit (kg)	5	3	7	
Total material B required (kg)	600	480	770	1,850

There will be sufficient material A to satisfy the maximum demand for the products but material B will be a limiting factor.

The next step is to rank the products in order of their contribution per unit of limiting factor. The available material B can then be allocated according to this ranking.

	L	M	N
Contribution per unit sold	£15	£12	£17.50
Material B consumed (kg)	5	3	7
Contribution per kg of material B	£3	£4	£2.50
Ranking	2	1	3

The available material B will be allocated to the products according to this ranking, to give the optimum production plan for the next period.

Product	Recommended production (units)	Material B utilized (kg)
M	160 (maximum)	480
L	120 (maximum)	600
N	20	140 (balance)
		1,220

The available material B is allocated to satisfy the maximum market demand for products M and L. The balance of available material is allocated to the last product in the ranking, product N.

(b) The recommended production plan in part (a) does not include sufficient product N to satisfy the requirement of 50 units for the valued customer. Some of the material allocated to product L (second in the ranking) must be allocated to product N. The recommended production plan will now be as follows:

Product	Recommended production (units)	Material B utilised (kg)
N	50	350
M	160	480
L	78	390 (balance)
		1,220

This recommendation makes the best use of the available material B within the restriction of the market requirements for each product.

Exercise

Gill Ltd manufactures three products, E, F and G. The products are all finished on the same machine. This is the only mechanised part of the process. During the next period the production manager is planning an essential major maintenance overhaul of the machine. This will restrict the available machine hours to 1,400 hours for the next period. Data for the three products is

	Product E £ per unit	Product F £ per unit	Product G £ per unit
Selling price	30	17	21.00
Variable cost	13	6	9.00
Fixed production cost	10	8	6.00
Other fixed cost	2	1	3.50
Profit	5	2	2.50
Maximum demand (units/period)	250	140	130

No stocks are held.

Fixed production costs are absorbed using a machine hour rate of £2 per machine hour.

You are required to determine the production plan that will maximise profit for the forthcoming period.

Solution

The first step is to calculate how many machine hours are required for each product. We can then determine whether machine hours are really a limiting factor.

	Product E	Product F	Product G	Total
Fixed production costs per unit @ £2 per hour	£10	£8	£6	
Machine hours per unit	5	4	3	
Maximum demand (units)	250	140	130	
Maximum hours required	1,250	560	390	2,200

1.18 Product costing

The attribution of costs to products is a core element in much of cost and management accounting technique. A business will normally incur a wide range of costs in buying supplies and services and in undertaking various activities. Management seeks to attribute those costs to specific outputs – being the goods and services that the business generates. Knowing how much it costs the business to deliver a good or service to customers can act as a guide to various aspects of business management including product pricing, output and marketing decisions, management remuneration and inventory holding decisions. It also impacts on the inventory valuation decision in the context of external financial reporting.

For the purposes of product costing, costs are traditionally classified under two broad headings. These are direct costs and indirect costs.

1.18.1 Direct costs

 Direct cost – Expenditure that can be attributed to a specific cost unit, for example material that forms part of the product.

Direct costs include materials physically embodied in the finished product, wages for labour that is physically engaged in the production process and expenses that are related solely to the manufacture of a particular product. Direct costs (regardless of whether they are fixed or variable) are charged to the cost units (that is the accounts for the products) that they relate to.

1.18.2 Indirect costs

 Indirect cost – Expenditure on labour, materials or services that cannot be identified with a specific saleable cost unit.

The term 'indirect costs' is normally synonymous with 'overheads'. The attribution of such costs to individual products may be undertaken with varying possible levels of refinement. The traditional approach involves the use of cost centres and overhead absorption rates.

1.18.3 Attributing overhead costs to products and jobs
(a) Production overheads

The successful attribution of production overhead costs to cost units depends on the existence of well-defined cost centres and appropriate absorption bases for the overhead costs of each cost centre. It must be possible to record accurately the units of the absorption base which are applicable to each job. For example, if machine hours are to be used as the absorption base, then the number of machine hours spent on each job must be recorded on the job cost card. The relevant cost centre absorption rate can then be applied to produce a fair overhead charge for the job.

Indirect costs are first apportioned between cost centres (or production departments) on an appropriate basis.

Example

A factory incurs €600 security costs. It has three departments, details as follows:

A – 1,000 m² floor space and 80 staff
B – 2,000 m² floor space and 120 staff
C – 3,000 m² floor space and 100 staff

If the security costs relate to excluding intruders then floor space is the appropriate apportionment basis – giving a charge split of €100 to A, €200 to B and €300 to C. But if security costs relate to preventing theft by staff then staff numbers is the appropriate apportionment basis – giving a charge split of €160 to A, €240 to B and €200 to C. Each type of overhead should be apportioned between cost centres using the most appropriate basis.

Where an indirect cost relates to a specific cost centre (A, B or C in the above case), then it may be allocated direct to that centre, without any apportionment.

Once all indirect costs have been apportioned and allocated to cost centres, then the resultant cost centre overhead figures (the sum total of indirect costs allocated and apportioned to individual cost centres) may be absorbed into product costs (or 'cost units').

Example

If cost centre X incurs €1,000 overheads and spends 50 direct labour hours on product 1 and 150 direct labour hours on product 2 then the obvious overhead absorption base will be direct labour hours and the overhead absorption rate will be €5 per direct labour hour - with €250 absorbed into 1 and €750 into 2. But what constitutes an appropriate absorption rate depends on circumstances. If most cost centre overheads relate to the employment of labour then labour hours may be the appropriate overhead absorption basis. But, if overheads mainly relate to machine usage then machine hours might be the appropriate overhead absorption basis.

Note that the choice of overhead absorption base impacts on reported product costs. A reported product cost is only meaningful if the overhead absorption base is appropriate.

Overhead absorption rates are commonly calculated on budgeted costs and budgeted levels of activity, giving what are known as 'pre-determined' overhead absorption rates. Thus if a cost centre is budgeted to incur €10,000 overheads and work 1,000 direct labour hours then it will adopt an overhead absorption rate of €10 per hour. That cost centre will charge the products it works on in the accounting period at a rate of €10 per hour regardless of what overheads actually are how many hours it actually works.

The use of pre-determined overhead absorption rates means that an over- or under- absorption of overheads may occur. If the cost centre referred to previously actually incurs €10,500 overheads and works 980 hours then there will be an overhead under-absorption of €700. This €700 is not normally charged to products and is a straight charge to profit for the period.

The use of predetermined overhead absorption rates is often favoured by management since it avoids product costs being distorted by random movements in costs or activity during the period. It also allows product costs to be predicted in advance of production.

(b) Non-production overheads

The level of accuracy achieved in attributing costs such as selling, distribution and administration overheads to jobs will depend on the level of cost analysis which an organisation uses.

Many organisations use a predetermined percentage (see earlier discussion of absorption costing) to absorb such costs, based on estimated or budgeted levels of activity for the forthcoming period. The following example will demonstrate how this works.

Example

A company uses a predetermined percentage of production cost to absorb distribution costs into the total cost of its jobs. Based on historical records and an estimate of activity and expenditure levels in the forthcoming period, they have produced the following estimates:

Estimated distribution costs to be incurred £13,300
Estimated production costs to be incurred on all jobs £190,000

$$\text{Therefore, predetermined overhead absorption rate of distribution costs} = \frac{£13,300}{£190,000} \times 100\%$$

$$= 7\% \text{ of production costs}$$

The use of predetermined rates will lead to the problems of under- or over-absorbed overhead which we discussed in the previous section. The rates should therefore be carefully monitored throughout the period to check that they do not require adjusting to more accurately reflect recent trends in costs and activity.

It may not always be considered appropriate to attribute non-production overheads to individual products. Some categories of administration and management costs relate to a whole production facility and it is meaningless to try and split them between products. In such cases, the overhead costs concerned are simply charged to the profit account without any attempt to absorb them into individual products.

1.18.4 A worked example

The following example will help you to practise presenting a cost analysis for a specific job. The approach used can be applied equally to products, services or contracts.

Example

Jobbing Limited manufactures precision tools to its customers' own specifications. The manufacturing operations are divided into three cost centres: A, B and C.

An extract from the company's budget for the forthcoming period shows the following data:

Cost centre	Budgeted production overhead	Basis of production overhead absorption
A	£38,500	22,000 machine hours
B	£75,088	19,760 machine hours
C	£40,964	41,800 labour hours

Job number 427 was manufactured during the period and its job cost card reveals the following information relating to the job:

Direct material requisitioned	£6,780.10
Direct material returned to stores	£39.60
Direct labour recorded against job number 427	
Cost centre A	146 hours at £4.80 per hour
Cost centre B	39 hours at £5.70 per hour
Cost centre C	279 hours at £6.10 per hour
Special machine hired for this job: hire cost	£59.00
Machine hours recorded against job number 427	
Cost centre A	411 hours
Cost centre B	657 hours
Price quoted and charged to customer, including delivery	£17,200

Jobbing Limited absorbs non-production overhead using the following predetermined overhead absorption rates:

Administration and general overhead	10% of production cost
Selling and distribution overhead	12% of selling price

You are required to present an analysis of the total cost and profit or loss attributable to job number 427.

Solution

First, we need to calculate the predetermined overhead absorption rates for each of the cost centres, using the basis indicated.

$$Cost\ centre\ A = \frac{£38,500}{£22,000} = £1.75\ per\ machine\ hour$$

$$Cost\ centre\ B = \frac{£75,088}{£19,760} = £3.80\ per\ machine\ hour$$

$$Cost\ centre\ C = \frac{£40,964}{£41,800} = £0.98\ per\ labour\ hour$$

Now we can prepare the cost and profit analysis, presenting the data as clearly as possible.

Cost and profit analysis: job number 427

	£	£
Direct material*		6,740.50
Direct labour		
Cost centre A (146 hours × £4.80)	700.80	
Cost centre B (39 hours × £5.70)	222.30	
Cost centre C (279 hours × £6.10)	1,701.90	
		2,625.00
Direct expenses: hire of jig		59.00
Prime cost		9,424.50
Production overhead absorbed		
Cost centre A (411 hours × £1.75)	719.25	
Cost centre B (657 hours × £3.80)	2,496.60	
Cost centre C (279 hours × £0.98)	273.42	
		3,489.27
Total production cost		12,913.77

Administration and general overhead	1,291.38
(10% × £12,913.77)	
Selling and distribution overhead	2,064.00
(12% × £17,200)	
Total cost	16,269.15
Profit	930.85
Selling price	17,200.00

* The figure for material requisitioned has been reduced by the amount of returns to give the correct value of the materials actually used for the job.

1.19 Summary

In this chapter we have explored the basic ideas behind and cost and revenue behaviour that are used by management accountants in the design and operation of product costing, budgetary planning and financial control systems. These ideas are fundamental to much of what follows in this text, so you should have a clear understanding of them.

Self-test quiz

(1) Explain the term 'fixed cost' (Section 1.2.1).
(2) Explain the term 'variable cost' (Section 1.2.2).
(3) Explain the term 'semi-variable cost' (Section 1.2.3).
(4) Explain the 'high-low' method for analysing cost structures (Section 1.2.4).
(5) Distinguish between the 'chart of accounts' view and the 'activity view' of a set of costs (Section 1.3).
(6) State the possible uses of the 'margin of safety' measure (Section 1.5).
(7) Distinguish between the CVP chart and the PV chart (Sections 1.4 and 1.9).
(8) Explain the term 'limiting factor' in the context of decision making where there is a constraint (Section 1.17).

Revision Questions

1

? Question 1

GHI manufactures three products – X, Y and Z. GHI's factory is highly automated and labour can be quickly recruited to support any level of production. However, machine capacity is limited to 18,000 hours. GHI's goods dispatch department is equipped in a manner which makes it impossible to send out more than 1,000 units of any one product to customers in a single period.

Details concerning production in the coming period are as follows:

	X	Y	Z
Market demand, units	900	1,000	1,200
Variable cost per unit, £	21	28	9
Selling price per unit, £	38	52	29
Machine hours per unit	8.5	10.0	5.0

Fixed costs are £ 35,000 per period.

Requirements

(a) Calculate the mix of X, Y and Z production that will achieve the maximum possible profit in the current period. Prepare a statement showing how that maximum profit is made up. **(9 marks)**

(b) Advise GHI's management on whether or not it should hire new equipment (rental per period £ 1,100) for the dispatch department in order to allow its handling capacity to be increased from 1,000 units of any one product to 1,200 units. **(9 marks)**

(c) Explain the full range of things that can be limiting factors in a business situation. Explain why these things might be only 'short-term' problems. **(7 marks)**

(Total marks = 25)

? Question 2

A company provides three services that use the same machine, M1. The budgeted details per service are as follows:

	Service X £ per unit	Service Y £ per unit	Service Z £ per unit
Selling price	12	14	24
Variable costs	6	4	13

Fixed cost	2	5	8
Profit	4	5	3
Number of M1 machine hours	2	3	6

The fixed costs are general fixed costs that have been absorbed by the services by their direct labour content.

If M1 hours are scarce, the most and least profitable services are

	Most profitable	Least profitable
(A)	Y	Z
(B)	Z	X
(C)	Y	X
(D)	X	Z

? Question 3 Objective test questions

3.1 OT Ltd plans to produce and sell 4,000 units of product C each month, at a selling price of £18 per unit. The unit cost of product C is as follows:

	£per unit
Variable cost	8
Fixed cost	4
	12

Calculate (to the nearest whole number) the monthly margin of safety, as a percentage of planned sales.

3.2 Is the following statement *true* or *false*?
The P/V ratio is the ratio of profit generated to the volume of sales.

3.3 Product J generates a contribution to sales ratio of 30%. Fixed costs directly attributable to product J amount to £75,000 per month. Calculate the sales revenue required to achieve a monthly profit of £15,000.

3.4 Match the following terms with the labels **a** to **d** on the graph:

- Margin of safety
- Fixed cost
- Contribution
- Profit.

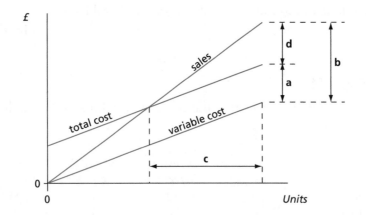

3.5 Which of the following statements about a PV chart are *true*?

(a) The profit line passes through the origin.
(b) Other things being equal, the angle of the profit line becomes steeper when the selling price increases.
(c) Contribution cannot be read directly from the chart.
(d) The point where the profit line crosses the vertical axis is the breakeven point.
(e) Fixed costs are shown as a line parallel to the horizontal axis.

3.6 Put the following tasks in the correct sequence for deciding on the optimum production plan when a limiting factor exists.

- Rank the products according to the contribution per unit of limiting factor used.
- Calculate each product's contribution per unit of limiting factor used.
- Identify the limiting factor.
- Allocate the limited resource according to the ranking.

3.7 The following details relate to three services provided by JHN plc.

	Service J £	Service H £	Service N £
Fee charged to customers	84	122	145
Unit service costs			
Direct materials	12	23	22
Direct labour	15	20	25
Variable overhead	12	16	20
Fixed overhead	20	42	40

All three services use the same type of direct labour which is paid £30 per hour.

The fixed overheads are general fixed overheads that have been absorbed on the basis of machine hours.

If direct labour is a scarce resource, the most and least profitable uses of it are

	Most profitable	Least profitable
A	H	J
B	H	N
C	N	J
D	N	H

(2 marks)

? Question 4 Profit statements and decision-making

BSE Veterinary Services is a specialist laboratory carrying out tests on cattle to ascertain whether the cattle have any infection. At present, the laboratory carries out 12,000 tests each period but, because of current difficulties with the beef herd, demand is expected to increase to 18,000 tests a period, which would require an additional shift to be worked.

The current cost of carrying out a full test is

	£ per test
Materials	115
Technicians' wages	30
Variable overhead	12
Fixed overhead	50

Working the additional shift would

(i) require a shift premium of 50% to be paid to the technicians on the additional shift;
(ii) enable a quantity discount of 20% to be obtained for all materials if an order was placed to cover 18,000 tests;
(iii) increase fixed costs by £700,000 per period.

The current fee per test is £300.

Requirements

(a) Prepare a profit statement for the current 12,000 capacity.
(b) Prepare a profit statement if the additional shift was worked and 18,000 tests were carried out.
(c) Comment on three other factors that should be considered before any decision is taken.

Question 5 PV graphs

(a) MC Ltd manufacturers one product only, and for the last accounting period has produced the simplified profit and loss statement below:

	£	£
Sales		300,000
Costs		
Direct materials	60,000	
Direct wages	40,000	
Prime cost	100,000	
Variable production overhead	10,000	
Fixed production overhead	40,000	
Fixed administration overhead	60,000	
Variable selling overhead	40,000	
Fixed selling overhead	20,000	
		270,000
Net profit		30,000

You are required to construct a PV graph from which you should state the breakeven point and the margin of safety.

(b) Based on the above, draw separate PV graph to indicate the effect on profit of each of the following:

(i) an increase in fixed cost;
(ii) a decrease in variable cost;
(iii) an increase in sales price;
(iv) a decrease in sales volume.

Question 6 Decision-making, limiting factor

ABC Limited makes three products, all of which use the same machine, which is available for 50,000 hours per period.

The standard costs of the product, per unit, are

	Product A £	Product B £	Product C £
Direct materials	70	40	80
Direct labour			
Machinists (£8/hour)	48	32	56
Assemblers (£6/hour)	36	40	42
Total variable cost	154	112	178
Selling price per unit	200	158	224
Maximum demand (units)	3,000	2,500	5,000

Fixed costs are £300,000 per period.

Requirements

(a) Calculate the deficiency in machine hours for the next period.
(b) Determine the production plan that will maximise ABC Ltd's profit for the next period.
(c) Calculate the profit that will result from your recommended production plan.

Solutions to Revision Questions

✓ Solution 1

(a) The products are ranked according to the contribution they offer in regard to the primary limiting factor (machine hours). This is so because maximum production allowed by both market demand and handing capacity cannot be achieved because of the machine hour constraint. Resources are then allocated according to this ranking and the secondary limiting factor (handling capability). The results are

	X	Y	Z	Total
Selling price p.u. (£)	38	52	29	
Variable cost p.u. (£)	21	28	9	
Contribution p.u. (£)	17	24	20	
Mac. Hrs. p.u.	8.5	10	5	
Cont. per mac. hr. (£)	2	2.4	4	
Rank	3	2	1	
Units	353	1,000	1,000	
Contribution (£)	6,001	24,000	20,000	50,001
Fixed costs (£)				−35,000
Profit (£)				15,001

(b) Increasing the handling capability from 1,000 units of any one product to 1,200 units of any one product has the following results:

Units	235	1,000	1,200	
Contribution (£)	3,995	24,000	24,000	51,995
Fixed costs (£)				−36,100
Profit (£)				15,895

Since the new arrangement increases profit, it should be adopted.

(c) Machine hours, skilled labour hours, material availability and transport capacity are all factors that are capable of being limiting factors. They are usually only short-term factors because in a dynamic economy some means can usually be found to evade them. A new source of materials may be opened up, new skilled labour may be trained and products may be redesigned to have a lower machine hour requirement.

For example, one of the key limiting factors in the Second World War for UK armaments industry was availability of aluminium. So, aircraft were designed that could be built with wood rather than aluminium. These did not have the same performance, service life or reliability as metal built aircraft – but they were available in numbers that a metal building programme would not have allowed.

However, it is often found that as soon as one limiting factor is eliminated or avoided, then another one tends to appear. For example, there is no point in producing more aircraft if there are no spare pilots to fly them.

✓ Solution 2

Service type	X	Y	Z
	£	£	£
Selling price	12	14	24
Variable costs	6	4	13
Contribution/unit	6	10	11
	Hours	*Hours*	*Hours*
Type M1 machine hours/unit	2	3	6
	£	£	£
Contribution/unit	3.00	3.30	1.83

Therefore the answer is (A), as the smallest additional cost.

✓ Solution 3

3.1   Monthly fixed costs = 4,000 units × £4 = £16,000.

$$\text{Breakeven point} = \frac{\text{Fixed costs}}{\text{Contribution per unit}} = \frac{£16,000}{£18 - £8} = 1,600 \text{ units}$$

$$\text{Margin of safety}\% = \frac{\text{Planned sales} - \text{breakeven sales}}{\text{Planned sales}} \times 100\%$$

$$= \frac{4,000 - 1,600}{4,000} \times 100\% = 60\%$$

3.2   *False.* The P/V ratio is another term for the C/S ratio. It measures the ratio of the contribution to sales.

3.3   Required sales value $= \dfrac{\text{Required contribution}}{\text{C/S ratio}} = \dfrac{£75,000 + £15,000}{0.30} = £300,000.$

3.4   (a) Fixed cost
     (b) Contribution
     (c) Margin of safety
     (d) Profit.

3.5   (a) *False.* The profit line passes through the breakeven point on the horizontal axis, and cuts the vertical axis at the point where the loss is equal to the fixed costs.
     (b) *True.* Profits increase at a faster rate if the selling price is higher.
     (c) *True.* A contribution breakeven chart is needed for this.
     (d) *False.* The breakeven point is where the profit line cuts the horizontal axis.
     (e) *False.* No fixed cost line is shown on a PV chart.

3.6   1. Identify the limiting factor.
     2. Calculate each product's contribution per unit of limiting factor used.

3. Rank the products according to the contribution per unit of limiting factor used.
4. Allocate the limited resource according to the ranking.

3.7

	J	H	N
Contribution/unit	£45	£63	£78
Direct labour/unit	£15	£20	£25
Contribution/ £1 of direct labour	£3.00	£3.15	£3.12

Therefore the answer is (A).

☑ Solution 4

- In part (b) do not be tempted to use unit rates to calculate the new level of fixed costs. The current level of fixed costs is £600,000 *per period*. This will increase by £700,000.
- Also in part (b), notice that the shift premium applies only to the technicians working on the additional shift. It does not apply to all technicians' wages.
- In part (c) you may have thought of other, equally valid, factors to be considered. In an examination, if you are asked for three factors do not waste valuable time by suggesting more than three.

(a) Profit statement for current 12,000 capacity:

		£'000
Sales	12,000 tests @ £300/test	3,600
Direct materials	12,000 tests @ £115/test	(1,380)
Direct labour	12,000 tests @ £30/test	(360)
Variable overhead	12,000 tests @ £12/test	(144)
Contribution		1,716
Fixed costs	12,000 tests @ £50/test	(600)
Profit		1,116

(b) Profit statement for 18,000 capacity, with additional shift:

		£'000	£'000
Sales	18,000 tests @ £300/test		5,400
Direct materials	18,000 tests @ £92/test		(1,656)
Direct labour	12,000 tests @ £30/test	(360)	
	6,000 tests @ £45/test	(270)	
			(630)
Variable overhead	18,000 tests @ £12/test		(216)
Contribution			2,898
Fixed costs			(1,300)
Profit			1,598

(c) Three other factors that should be considered are

1. Will the increase in demand continue in the long run, or is it short-lived? If it is thought that it will continue in the long run, management should consider expanding its permanent workforce so that shift premiums can be avoided.

2. Will the quality of the test decrease if more tests are carried out in the same time period? Also purchasing materials at a 20% discount may indicate a decrease in the quality of the materials.

3. The elasticity of demand for the test. If demand is relatively inelastic, it may be more economic to increase the price of the test.

✅ Solution 5

- Try to obtain a piece of graph paper and practise drawing your graphs to scale. Remember to use the whole of the paper – do not produce a tiny graph in the corner of the sheet.
- Remember that the graph in part (a) will cut the vertical axis at the point equal to the fixed costs, that is, the loss when no sales are made.
- Practise good exam technique: check your breakeven point arithmetically to verify that your graph is accurate.

(a)

Profit

£30,000

£0

Break-even point
£240,000

Margin of safety
£60,000

–£120,000

| 0 | 50 | 100 | 150 | 200 | 250 | 300 |

Sales revenue, £'000

(b) These graphs show increase or decrease in profit by $+x$ or $-x$.

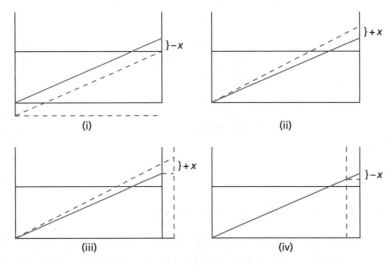

(i) $\}-x$

(ii) $\}+x$

(iii) $\}+x$

(iv) $\}-x$

(i) An increase in fixed cost
(ii) A decrease in variable cost
(iii) An increase in sales price
(iv) A decrease in sales volume.

Solution 6

- In part (b) remember to rank the products according to their contribution per machine hour. Then allocate the available machine hours according to this ranking.
- Do not attempt to apportion the fixed costs to the individual products. When you are calculating the profit in part (c), simply deduct the total fixed costs from your calculated contribution.

(a) Deficiency in machine hours for next period:

	Product A	Product B	Product C	Total
Machine hours required per unit	48/8 = 6	32/8 = 4	56/8 = 7	
Maximum demand (units)	3,000	2,500	5,000	
Total machine hours to meet maximum demand	18,000	10,000	35,000	63,000
Machine hours available				50,000
Deficiency of machine hours				13,000

(b)

	Product A £	Product B £	Product C £
Selling price per unit	200	158	224
Variable cost per unit	(154)	(112)	(178)
Contribution per unit	46	46	46
Machine hours required per unit	6	4	7
Contribution per machine hour	£7.67	£11.50	£6.57
Order of production	2	1	3

Therefore, make

	M/C hours
2,500 units of product B, using machine hours of (4 × 2,500)	10,000
3,000 units of product A, using machine hours of (6 × 3,000)	18,000
	28,000
Machine hours left to make product C	22,000
	50,000

Therefore, the company should make 3,142 i.e. (22,000/7) units of product C.

(b) Profit for the next period:

	Total £	Product A £	Product B £	Product C £
Contribution from recommended production:				
£46 × 3,000		138,000		
£46 × 2,500			115,000	
£46 × 3,142				144,532
	397,532	138,000	115,000	144,532
Fixed costs	(300,000)			
Profit for the period	97,532			

2

Cost Accounting
Systems

Cost Accounting Systems

2

LEARNING OUTCOMES

After completing study of this chapter you should be able to

► compare and contrast marginal (or variable), throughput and absorption costing methods in respect of profit reporting and stock valuation;

► discuss a report which reconciles budget and actual profit using absorption and/or marginal costing principles;

► discuss activity-based costing as compared with traditional marginal and absorption costing methods including its relative advantages and disadvantages as a system of cost accounting.

2.1 Introduction

In your certificate studies (or equivalent) you should have already encountered the basic principles and concepts involved in cost accounting. Specifically, you should be familiar with the manner in which the costs of objects and activities are determined through an exercise of cost allocation, apportionment and absorption. You should also be familiar with basic cost accounting practices such as stock valuation (LIFO, FIFO and average), profit determination, accounting in particular types of production environment (job, batch and process) and the principles of cost behaviour (fixed and variable). You should refer back to your earlier studies if you are unfamiliar with any of the topics referred to.

In this chapter we will revisit some of these basic principles and develop our understanding of their use into more advanced areas. The content of this chapter will lead into an exploration of modern innovations in management accounting systems in Chapter 5.

2.2 The difference between marginal costing and absorption costing

You should already be aware that the difference between marginal costing and absorption costing lies in their treatment of fixed production overhead.

You are reminded that direct costs are expenditures on materials, labour and expenses that relate strictly to individual products. Indirect or overhead costs are expenditures incurred in running a factory that do not relate specifically to individual products.

With absorption costing, the fixed production overhead cost is absorbed into the cost of units and all stock items are valued at their full production cost.

Example

ABC Ltd manufactures units. Relevant forecast details for the current period are:

Budget fixed production overheads	€10,000
Budget production	500 units
Variable production cost	€10 per unit

The predetermined overhead absorption rate is therefore €20 per unit (€10,000/500) giving a unit cost of €30 (€20 fixed plus €10 variable).

Predetermined OARs are commonly used in cost accounting systems in order to minimise the vulnerability of product costs to random movements in output levels and overhead costs. The production overhead cost of a unit is determined in advance of the current period and nothing that happens in the period will alter that.

Relevant actual details for the period are as follows:

Actual production	520 units
Actual sales	480 units (at €40 per unit)

The profit for the period, calculated on the absorption costing principle is:

		€
Sales		19,200 (480 × €40)
Production costs	15,600 (520 × €30)	
Closing stock	1,200 (40 × €30)	
Cost of sales		14,400
Gross profit		4,800
Overhead over absorption		400 (20 × €20)
Profit		5,200

By producing 520 units and charging €20 fixed overheads each, then we have charged €10,400 against profit. But only €10,000 fixed overheads have been incurred so we must credit €400 back to profit. This is the overhead over absorption figures referred to above.

Note that only production overheads are normally attributed to unit costs. Selling and administration overheads are not usually attributed to unit costs, although there may be circumstances when this is appropriate.

In contrast, marginal costing values all stock items at their variable or marginal cost only. Fixed costs are treated as period costs and are written off in full against the profit for the period.

Example

Given the details stated in the previous example, the profit calculated on the marginal costing principle is:

		€
Sales		19,200
Production costs	5,200 (520 × €10)	
Closing stock	400 (40 × €10)	
Cost of sales		4,800
Contribution		14,400
Fixed overheads		10,000
Profit		4,400

Since the two systems value stock differently, it follows that each will report a different profit figure for the period if stock levels alter.

The €800 (€5,200 − €4,400) difference between profits calculated above according to absorption and marginal costing principles is essentially a stock valuation thing. Absorption costing values stock at €1,200 while marginal costing values it at €400.

2.3 Preparing profit statements using each method

The best way to demonstrate how profit statements are prepared for each of the methods is to look at a worked example.

Example

Using the information below, prepare profit statements for June and July using (a) marginal costing and (b) absorption costing.

A company produces and sells one product only which sells for £50 per unit. There were no stocks at the end of May and other information is as follows:

	£
Standard cost per unit	
Direct material	18
Direct wages	4
Variable production overhead	3
Budgeted and actual fixed costs per month	
Fixed production overhead	99,000
Fixed selling expenses	14,000
Fixed administration expenses	26,000
Variable selling expenses	10% of sales value

Normal capacity is 11,000 units per month.
The number of units produced and sold was:

	June units	July units
Sales	12,800	11,000
Production	14,000	10,200

2.3.1 Profit statements using marginal costing

Marginal costing will value all units at the variable production cost of £25 per unit (£18 + £4 + £3).

Profit statements using marginal costing

	June		July	
	£'000	£'000	£'000	£'000
Sales revenue		640		550
Less: variable cost of sales				
Opening stock	–		30	
Variable production cost				
(14,000 × £25)	350			
(10,200 × £25)			255	
	350		285	
Closing stock				
(1,200 × £25)	(30)			
(400 × £25)			(10)	
Variable production of sales	320		275	
Variable selling expenses	64		55	
Variable cost of sales		(384)		(330)
Contribution		256		220
Less: fixed overhead				
Fixed production overhead	99		99	
Fixed selling expenses	14		14	
Fixed administration expenses	26		26	
		(139)		(139)
Profit		117		81

2.3.2 Profit statements using absorption costing

Fixed production overheads are absorbed on the basis of normal capacity which is often the same as budgeted capacity. You should recall that predetermined rates are used partly to avoid the fluctuations in unit cost rates which arise if production levels fluctuate.

$$\text{Fixed production overhead per unit} = \frac{£99,000}{11,000} = £9 \text{ per unit}$$

Full production cost per unit = £25 variable cost + £9 fixed cost = £34 per unit

This full production cost of £34 per unit will be used to value all units under absorption costing.

Since the production level is not equal to the normal capacity in either June or July there will be under- or over-absorbed fixed production overhead in both months. It is probably easier to calculate this before commencing on the profit statements.

	June	July
	£'000	£'000
Fixed production overhead absorbed		
(14,000 × £9)	126	
(10,200 × £9)		91.8
Fixed production overhead incurred	(99)	(99.0)
Over/(under) absorption	27	(7.2)

Profit statements using absorption costing

	June		July	
	£'000	£'000	£'000	£'000
Sales revenue		640.0		550.0
Less: full production cost of sales				
Opening stock	–		40.8	
Full production cost				
(14,000 × £34)	476.0			
(10,200 × £34)			346.8	
	476.0		387.6	
Closing stock				
(1,200 × £34)	(40.8)			
(400 × £34)			(13.6)	
	435.2		374.0	
(Over-)/under-absorbed fixed				
production overhead*	(27.0)		7.2	
Full production cost of sales		408.2		381.2
Gross profit		231.8		168.8
Less: selling/admin. expenses				
Variable selling expenses	64.0		55.0	
Fixed selling expenses	14.0		14.0	
Fixed administration expenses	26.0		26.0	
		(104.0)		(95.0)
Net profit		127.8		73.8

*If overheads have been over-absorbed then too much has been charged as a cost of production. This amount is, therefore, deducted to derive the full production cost of sales. If overheads are under-absorbed, the amount is added to increase the production cost of sales.

2.4 Reconciling the profit figures

In addition to preparing profit statements using absorption costing and marginal costing, you should also recall how to reconcile the profits given by each method for the same period and by the same method for different periods.

2.4.1 Reconciling the profits given by the different methods

The profit differences are caused by the different valuations given to the closing stocks in each period. With absorption costing, an amount of fixed production overhead is carried forward in stock to be charged against sales of later periods.

If stocks increase, then absorption costing profits will be higher than marginal costing profits. This is because some of the fixed overhead is carried forward in stock instead of being written off against sales for the period.

If stocks reduce, then marginal costing profits will be higher than absorption costing profits. This is because the fixed overhead which had been carried forward in stock with absorption costing is now being released to be charged against the sales for the period.

A profit reconciliation for the previous example might look like this:

	June £'000	July £'000
Marginal costing profit	117.0	81.0
Adjust for fixed overhead in stock		
Stock increase (1,200 × £9)	10.8	
Stock decrease (800 × £9)		(7.2)
Absorption costing profit	127.8	73.8

2.4.2 Reconciling the profits for different periods

You should also recall how to reconcile the profits for different periods using the same method.

(a) For marginal costing, the unit rates and the amount of fixed costs charged each period are constant. Therefore, the only thing which could have caused the profit difference was the change in sales volume. The lower sales volume in July resulted in a lower contribution and therefore a lower profit (since the amount of fixed cost remained constant).

The contribution per unit is £20 as follows:

	£per unit
Selling price	50
Variable production cost	(25)
Variable selling cost	(5)
Contribution	20

The marginal costing profit figures can be reconciled as follows:

	£'000
Marginal costing profit for June	117
Decrease in sales volume for July	
1,800 units × £20 contribution	(36)
Marginal costing profit for July	81

(b) For absorption costing the major part of the profit difference is caused by the change in sales volume. However, a further difference is caused by the adjustments for under- and over-absorbed fixed production overhead in each of the two periods.

The profit per unit with absorption costing is £11 as follows:

	£per unit
Selling price	50
Total production cost	(34)
Variable selling cost	(5)
Profit	11

The absorption costing profit figures can be reconciled as follows:

	£'000
Absorption costing profit for June	127.8
Decrease in sales volume for July	
1,800 units × £11 profit	(19.8)
Adjustments for under-/over-absorption	
June	(27.0)
July	(7.2)
Absorption costing profit for July	73.8

This may look confusing because both the under- and the over-absorption are deducted. This is because the over-absorption for June made profit for that month higher, therefore it must be deducted to arrive at July's profit. Similarly, the under-absorption in July made July's profit lower than June's, therefore it must also be deducted in the reconciliation.

2.4.3 Profit differences in the long term

The two different costing methods produce profit differences only in the short term when stocks fluctuate. If stocks remain constant then there will be no profit differences between the two methods.

In the long term the total reported profit will be the same whichever method is used. This is because all of the costs incurred will eventually be charged against sales; it is merely the timing of the sales that causes the profit differences from period to period.

2.4.4 Throughput accounting

In Chapter 5 we will consider 'throughput accounting' which offers an approach to performance evaluation which is adapted to the characteristics of the modern manufacturing environment. Essentially, it proceeds on the premise that in the very short term, all costs are fixed excepting for materials purchased and used. The impact of this on cost attribution leads tathroughput accounting sometimes being described as 'super-variable costing'.

If stock is valued and profit calculated on this basis it gives rise to an extreme form of marginal costing. Apart from materials in stock and the direct material cost component of inventory, all costs are charged to profit in the period in which they are incurred. Throughput accounting is most commonly used to provide a guide to performance evaluation in the context of modern just-in-time management systems wherein the focus is on organising production in a manner that makes the most effective use of bottleneck resources. It is less likely to be used as part of a conventional management reporting system. Throughput accounting is not used commonly as a system of product costing although it can be adapted for this purpose.

2.5 Marginal costing or absorption costing?

There is no absolutely correct answer to when marginal costing or absorption costing is preferable. However, it is generally accepted that marginal costing statements provide the best information for the purposes of management decision-making.

Supporters of absorption costing argue that fixed production overheads are a necessary cost of production and they should therefore be included in the unit cost used for stock valuation. SSAP 9 requires the use of absorption costing for external reporting purposes.

If stocks are built up for sale in a future period – for example in distilling – then absorption costing smoothes out profit by carrying forward the fixed production overheads to be matched against the sales as they are made.

Supporters of marginal costing argue that management attention is concentrated on the more controllable measure of contribution. They say that the apportionment of fixed production overhead to individual units is carried out on a purely arbitrary basis, is of little use for decision-making and can be misleading.

However, it is widely accepted that for general accounting purposes (as opposed to business decision-making purposes) both fixed and variable overhead costs should be attributed to cost units in some meaningful way. Absorption costing is therefore in wide use. The problem lies in adopting an appropriate method of attributing overhead costs to cost units.

Modern thinking in regard to product costing is that most costs are actually variable if you take a long enough view of them and understand what they vary with. The core issue is that a particular cost may not vary directly with units output but rather with the level of some activity required to achieve a given level of units output.

2.6 Activity-based costing

2.6.1 Traditional versus activity-based cost

Throughout this text we encounter the idea that the modern business environment is one which is much more dynamic than that in which traditional management accounting practices were developed. This applies also to the manner in which we determine the costs of individual products and services.

Traditional cost accounting involves attributing indirect costs to individual products on the basis of an overhead absorption base related to some proxy such as direct labour hours or machine hours ('volume-related measures'). One can apply this approach with varying degrees of sophistication but it is unlikely to give an unambiguous result in modern circumstances.

In the 'new manufacturing' environment a high proportion of costs are indirect and the only meaningful way to attribute such costs to individual products is through a study of the activities that give rise to them. One is seeking an approach to product costing that reflects the manner in which costs are actually incurred and the question is whether or not traditional absorption costing offers such an approach for both decision-making and performance evaluation purposes. This last question can be split into three strands:

1. Are production overheads significant relative to total full absorption cost?
2. Is there any causal link between the incurrence of these production overhead costs and the production volume, and hence products?
3. Are there causal links between the incurrence of production overhead and the particular product that are not volume-related?

Part (1) is important in the context of materiality. If production overhead costs represent only 1 per cent of total production costs, the argument as to how that 1 per cent should be spread among products would not have the same significance as one relating to the spreading of an amount representing, say 50 per cent of total production costs. In fact, overhead costs have become an increasing proportion of production costs during recent times, and in many industries now represent the single largest element of product costs. This change in the make-up of production costs has two main causes: the nature of the production process itself, and the nature of competition faced by firms.

In terms of production processes, it would be hard to think of a single industry in which there has not been a significant shift from the use of human labour to the use of machinery. The effect has been a reduction in the cost of direct labour and an increase in long-term variable production overhead (fixed costs) through increased depreciation charges. Furthermore, modern manufacturing machinery tends to be much more accurate than manual labour, so wastage of material has also declined over time, leading to a further fall in the proportion of direct costs in the total mix.

In the early part of the twentieth century, much competition was on the basis of price. While price remains an important competitive weapon in many industries, there are also other factors that determine a firm's success. As we saw in an earlier chapter, businesses now compete on time, quality, innovation and so on. This had led many producers to offer a great variety of products, and necessitated very complex production schedules. This complexity and diversity has also been responsible for some of the increase in production overheads in recent decades.

It will readily be appreciated that, as overheads have become an increasing proportion of total production cost, any arbitrariness in the method in which they are charged to products assumes increasing significance in a decision-making context.

Part (2) asked whether there was any causal link between the incurrence of production overhead costs and the production volume, and hence products. As noted above, some short-term variable overheads are observed to change in response to a volume-related measure, such as direct labour or machine hours worked – that is, there is a causal link between the production volume and the level of production overhead cost incurred. We gave the example of the volume-related activity of running a machine, which results in the variable overhead cost of power being incurred. However, other production overhead expenditure, such as the cost of material procurement, clearly has no direct relationship with the number of direct labour hours worked or the number of hours machines are operating. Nevertheless, the production volume-related basis that appears to drive some short-term variable overheads is usually used to absorb all overheads. It can be argued that this is the only sensible way to operate: by definition, the long-term variable production overheads are fixed in the short term; in the short term, therefore, there can be no causal link between any particular volume-related activity and the particular overheads incurred. Any absorption of cost must be arbitrary, but an absorption must be made nevertheless in order to meet financial accounting requirements. However, it follows that the information is unlikely to be useful for decision-making purposes.

Part (3) asked whether there were causal links between the incurrence of production overhead and the particular product that were not volume-related. In many companies, overhead continues to be absorbed by products on the same basis year after year, with little thought being given to the appropriateness for decision-making of this basis in a situation in which overhead is increasing relative to direct cost. However, the activity-based costing (ABC) approach is based on the premise that there may be a causal link between these overheads and individual activities, particularly when a perspective of more than one year is taken.

We must conclude that traditionally calculated product costs are not useful for decision-making, as they are unable to provide satisfactory explanations for the behaviour of costs. This does not mean, however, that ABC costs, without modification, are decision-relevant.

ABC and ABM have been very much at the leading edge of management accounting practices since the late 1980s.

Activity-Based Techniques

Bob Scarlett, *CIMA Insider,* **May 2002**

For the last 15 years, activity-based techniques (ABTs) have been at the forefront of developments in management accounting. The advent of ABTs has been associated with changes in production technology and organisational practices.

The origins of ABC

In the early 1980s, many organisations became aware that their traditional cost accounting systems were generating information that was either misleading or irrelevant. Organisations and manufacturing processes were becoming increasingly complex, products were becoming more highly customised and product life cycles were shortening. It was found that calculating product costs using traditional volume-based absorption methods (such as direct labour hours or machine hours) no longer produced meaningful results.

For example, let us say that a business manufactures many products including the X and the Y. Production of the two takes place at a rate of 10 units per hour and total production is 500 units of each in the period. Overheads in the period are £100,000 and a total of 20,000 direct labour hours are worked on all products. If the business uses a traditional overhead absorption rate of £5 per labour hour, then the overhead cost of both the X and the Y will be £0.50 per unit.

Enquiry reveals that X manufacture is organised in the form of 2 production runs per period and Y manufacture is organised in the form of 10 production runs per period. Enquiry also reveals that overhead costs mainly related to 'batch level activities' associated with machine set-ups and materials handling for production runs. If there are a total of 1,000 production runs in the period, then overheads may be attributed to products at a rate of £100 per run. On that basis the overheads cost of X will be £0.40 (2 runs X £100/500 units) and the overhead cost of the Y will be £2.00 (10 runs X £100/500 units).

The reported unit costs of £0.40 (X) and £2.00 (Y) are activity based, recognising that overhead costs are incurred through batch level activities. It is likely that this statements offers a more meaningful version of product costs than the traditional unit-volume-based version of £0.50 for both the X and the Y. ABC gives more meaningful results because it attributes costs to products in a more sensitive manner that recognises the way in which overhead costs are actually incurred.

In the case described, production of the Y is a more complex operation than production of the X. The need to organise Y production in frequent small batches (perhaps because it is perishable) means that it requires greater resource usage than production of the X -something that ABC recognises but traditional product costing does not.

This is particularly critical in the modern manufacturing environment. Continuous mass production of simple, homogenous products is becoming increasingly rare. Production now typically takes place in short, discontinuous runs and a high proportion of product costs are determined at the design phase. Hence, an increasing proportion of overhead costs are incurred at batch level or product level.

ABC is capable of providing a statement of product costs which may be used with confidence for both performance management and decision-making in the modern world.

Activity-based management (ABM)

The terms ABC and ABM are sometimes used interchangeably. This is inappropriate since ABC refers only to the actual technique used to determine the cost of activities and the cost of the outputs that those activities achieve. The aim of ABC is to provide improved cost data for use in managing the activities of a business.

ABM is a broader concept. It refers to the fundamental management philosophy that focuses on the planning, execution and measurement of activities as the key to competitive advantage. ABC and ABB are likely to be elements in the practice of ABM. A business that uses ABC and ABB is likely to have a good appreciation of

> its own cost structures and is therefore able to apply that appreciation for a variety of management purposes ranging from product design to departmental efficiency measurement.
>
> It is often found that the adoption of ABC and ABB yields only disappointing results in terms of profitability and performance. A recent American study by the Institute of Management Accountants disclosed that 80 per cent of ABC users reported that ABC had not yet resulted in any profit increase. Why should this be so?
>
> One problem identified by researchers is that the information generated by ABC and ABB systems has to be used effectively in order to achieve the expected results:
>
> An ABC implementation failure could be defined as the inability of a company to move from simply generating ABC information towards actually using the information.
>
> Roberts & Silvester, 'Why ABC failed and why it may yet succeed', JCM 1996

The writers quoted above suggest that organisations sometimes contain structural barriers to change that make it difficult to progress from ABC to ABM. The design and installation of sophisticated accounting systems is pointless if the information from those systems is not used.

2.6.2 Transaction analysis and cost drivers

As noted above, overhead in traditional systems is absorbed by products using volume-related measures. The activity-based approach, where appropriate, seeks explanations other than volume for the level of overhead. In this context, it is recognised that overhead costs are incurred in carrying out a number of different types of transactions. These have been summarised as follows:

 (i) logistical transactions, that is those activities that relate to the organisation of the flow of materials and other resources throughout the production process;
 (ii) balancing transactions, that is those that relate to ensuring that the supply of resources is matched with the demand for them;
(in) quality transactions, that is those concerned with ensuring output conforms to requirements;
(iv) change transactions, that is those concerned with meeting customers' requirements for altered specifications, product designs, delivery dates and so on.

The important point about the transactions identified by Miller and Vollman is that the primary driver behind them is usually not production volume. For example, logistical and balancing transactions are likely to be driven by the number of batches produced, rather than the total number of individual units. Similarly, change transactions might be related to the number of customers and number of different product types, rather than the volume of production. By identifying non-volume-related drivers, a better understanding of the behaviour of costs in the long term is provided. Such an analysis also facilitates the aggregation of cost-by-cost object, such as distribution channel, which again provides a better understanding for the management of the business than traditional approaches are able to produce.

The resources necessary to carry out the above transactions will tend to be variable in the short term only in an upward sense. As the number of customers increases, the potential for change transactions, for example, also increases. If the number or mix of customers were to change in the short term, in such a way that the overall workload is reduced, it is unlikely that any of the personnel employed to carry out the change transactions would be dismissed. Similarly, a short-term increase in the workload might be absorbed by existing staff, and overtime may be worked, which may or may not increase costs, depending on individual contracts. However, if the increased workload persists, more staff will eventually be hired. As the volume of these change transactions increases, the total overhead cost of the business will increase. In a traditional costing system (Figure 2.1), the increased cost of these transactions is automatically transferred to particular products by the use of a volume-related absorption rate. However, as noted above, such costs are not primarily volume-driven. It is conceivable that, for example, small batches of highly customised products could give rise to costs in terms of all four types of transactions listed above. Through the operation of a traditional costing system, the increased costs associated with carrying out these small-batch transactions will be spread among all the products on an inappropriate volume-related basis, such as direct labour hours or machine hours. It is this sort of anomaly that has led to the criticism of traditional costing as being arbitrary in its cost absorption, and thus providing information that is not useful for decision-making.

The ABC identifies the activities that cause cost to be incurred, and searches for the fundamental cost drivers of these activities. Once the activities and their drivers have been identified, this information can be used to attach overhead to those cost objects (e.g. products) that have actually caused the cost to be incurred. In comparing the ABC approach with the traditional approach, the obvious starting point is a comparison of the costs of individual products as determined under a traditional costing system with those same costs under an ABC system (Figure 2.2). However, this would be a pointless exercise if it simply stopped there: for a given sales revenue and a given level of total costs, the overall company

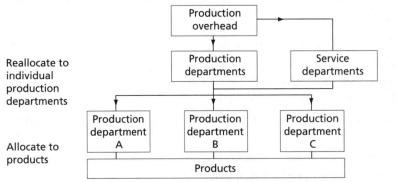

Sum of production departments' allocated costs = total production overhead

Figure 2.1 Traditional product costing system

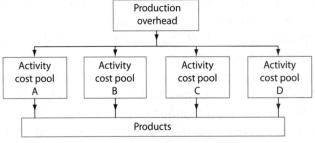

Sum of activity cost pools = total production overhead

Figure 2.2 Activity-based costing system

profit will be precisely the same whatever method of allocation is used to allocate the total cost between individual product lines.

2.7 Favourable conditions for ABC

The purpose of moving from a traditional costing system to an ABC system must therefore be based on the premise that the new information provided will lead to action that will increase the overall profitability of the business. This is most likely to occur when the analysis provided under the ABC system differs significantly from that which was provided under the traditional system, which is most likely to occur under the following conditions:

 (i) When production overheads are high relative to direct costs, particularly direct labour.
 (ii) Where there is great diversity in the product range.
(iii) Where there is considerable diversity of overhead resource input to products.
(iv) When consumption of overhead resources is not driven primarily by volume.

Information from an ABC analysis may indicate opportunities to increase profitability in a variety of ways, many of which are long term. For example, an activity-based analysis often reveals that small-batch items are relatively expensive to produce, and are therefore unprofitable at current prices. A number of responses to this information could be adopted. The first response might be to consider stopping production of such items, and concentrate on the apparently more profitable high-volume lines. Another approach would be to investigate how the production process could be organised in such a way as to bring the cost of producing small-batch items closer to that of producing high-volume goods. By identifying the cost of carrying out particular activities, the new approach provides opportunities for directing attention to matters of cost control. It can therefore be viewed as a much longer-term technique than the word 'costing' in the title suggests. The establishment of an ABC product cost may thus be considered to be merely the beginning of a process, rather than an end in itself. The recent use of the term activity-based management suggests this forward-looking orientation, which is assuming increasing importance. Activity-based management is discussed briefly in a later section.

2.8 Establishing an activity-based product cost

2.8.1 Comparison with traditional costing

Figures 2.2 and 2.3 illustrate the differences between a traditional product costing system and an ABC system.

A simplified description of the various steps associated with the operation of the basic ABC approach, and a comparison with the traditional costing approach, is given below. An example is set out in Section 2.8.4.

- *Step 1 – Identify the main production-related activities of the organisation.* In a traditional cost system, these will often be related to the department, for example machining, assembly, ordering, receiving, packing and despatching. Note that, for ABC, 'activities' can apply to services as well as to products.
- *Step 2 – Identify the cost of each of the activities identified in Step 1.* This analysis would include the direct costs of the activities, and might include some apportioned costs, such

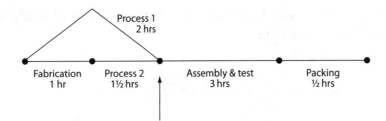

Figure 2.3 Network chart of a manufacturing process

as rent and rates, but it would exclude costs that would have been allocated to departments under a traditional system. For example, under the latter, a production department would be charged an allocation to cover the cost of the receiving department, but in an activity-based system, the receiving department either becomes an activity cost pool in itself, or is part of a greater activity cost pool and is not reallocated to production departments.

- *Step 3 – Determine the cost driver for each activity identified in Step 1.* The cost driver is the thing that best explains why resources are consumed by a particular activity, and therefore why the activity incurs cost, that is, it provides an explanation of the size of the cost pool. For example, although the resources consumed by the order processing activity can be explained by the number of orders processed, a more precise explanation might be the number of items processed therein, that is an order for one item will usually take less processing than an order for ten items, but ten single-item orders will require more processing than an order for ten items. A decision must be made as to what constitutes the most appropriate driver.
- *Step 3a – Select the activity cost pools and cost drivers that will be used within the system.* This step reflects the need for some compromise within an ABC system. As we have just seen, in order processing, the driver could be the number of orders processed, or the number of items per order. The outcome of the process will clearly be dependent on the particular decision made. The diagram above does not show Step 3a separately, but makes the implicit assumption that a driver can be identified.
- *Step 4 –* Calculate a cost driver rate for each activity cost pool in the same way as an overhead rate is calculated in a traditional system.

$$\text{Cost driver rare} = \frac{\text{Activity cost pool}}{\text{Activity driver}}$$

- *Step 5 –* Apply the activity cost driver rates to products (cost units) to arrive at an activity-based product cost.

2.8.2 Analysis of activities

The original impetus for the adoption of ABC is often the desire to provide a more accurate unit product cost. Indeed, the first reference to ABC, which appeared in the *Official Terminology* as late as 1991, is consistent with this objective: ABC was defined as: 'Cost attribution to cost units on the basis of benefit received from indirect activities, e.g. ordering, setting up, and assuring quality.' However, any unit cost, no matter how it is derived, can be misinterpreted. There is temptation to adopt a simplistic approach, which would say, for example, that if it cost £1,000 to produce ten units, it will cost £10,000 to produce 100 units. As we know, this in incorrect in the short term, owing to the existence of short-term fixed costs. The ABC approach does not eliminate this problem any more than the traditional approach. The alternative to presenting full absorption costing information in a traditional costing system has been to provide the user with a statement which distinguishes clearly between the variable cost of production and the fixed cost of production. This carries an implication for the decision-maker that if the variable cost of production is £50 for 10 units, the additional cost of producing a further 40 units will be $40 \times £5 =$ £200. Activity-based costing, on the other hand, can provide the user with a more sophisticated breakdown of cost. This breakdown relates cost to the level of activities undertaken. The structure of reporting will vary from company to company, but Cooper (1992) has suggested that four levels of activity, which he terms a hierarchy of cost, will commonly be found in practice. These are shown below:

(i) *Unit-level activities.* These are activities where the consumption of resources is very strongly correlated with the number of units produced. Costs traditionally defined as direct costs would fall into this category, for example direct material and direct labour.

(ii) *Batch-level activities.* Some activities – for example, machine set-up, materials handling and batch inspection – consume resources in proportion to the number of batches produced, rather than in proportion to the number of units produced. By identifying the consumption of resources at a batch rather than a unit level, it is easier than in a traditional costing system for a user to visualise the changing cost that will come about in the long term by changing a product mix or production schedule.

(iii) *Product-level activities.* Consumption of resources by, for example, administration, product specification or purchasing may be related to the existence of particular products. If the activity is performed to sustain the existence of a particular product line, it is a product-level activity.

(iv) *Facility-level activities.* Even within an ABC system, it is accepted that there are some costs that relate simply to being in business and that therefore cannot be related in any way to the production of any particular product line. Grounds maintenance, plant security and property taxes would be examples of this type of cost.

Consideration of (i)–(iv) shows that the difference between traditional costing and ABC costing will be dependent on the proportion of overhead cost that falls into each of the four categories. If this overhead is made up primarily of (i) and (iv), it is obvious that the traditional approach and the ABC approach will lead to very similar product costs. However, if the bulk of overhead cost falls into category (ii) and/or category (iii), there will be a very significant difference between the two.

Exercise

A company produced three products, the standard costs of which are shown below:

	£	£	£
Direct material	50	40	30
Direct labour (@ £10/hour)	30	40	50
Production overhead*	30	40	50
	110	120	130
*Absorbed on basis of direct labour hours			
Quantity produced/sold (units)	10,000	20,000	30,000

Total production overheads are £2,600,000 giving rise to an overhead absorption rate of £10 per hour (being £2.6 m overheads / 260,000 total direct labour hours worked).

The company wishes to introduce ABC, and has identified two major cost pools for production overhead and their associated cost drivers.

Information on these activity cost pools and their drivers is given below:

Activity cost pool	Cost driver	Cost associated with activity cost pool
Receiving/inspecting quality assurance	Purchase requisitions	£1,400,000
Production scheduling/machine set-ups	Number of batches	£1,200,000

Further relevant information on the three products is also given below:

	P	R	S
Number of purchase requisitions	1,200	1,800	2,000
Number of set-ups	240	260	300

From the information given, calculate the activity-based production cost of products, P, R and S. Also, comment on the differences between the original standard costs and the activity-based costs you calculate.

 ## Solution

We are in a position to move straight to Step 4, that is the calculation of the cost-driver rates.

$$\text{Cost-driver rate for receiving/inspecting quality assurance} = \frac{£1,400,000}{5,000} = £280$$
per purchase requisition

$$\text{Cost-driver rate for production scheduling/machine set-ups} = \frac{£1,200,000}{800} = £1,500$$
per set-up

Therefore ABC production costs of these products are as follows.

	P £	R £	S £
Direct material	50.00	40.00	30.00
Direct labour	30.00	40.00	50.00
Production overhead:			
Receiving/inspecting/quality assurance			
£280 × 1,200/10,000	33.60		
£280 × 1,800/20,000		25.20	
£280 × 2,000/30,000			18.66
Production scheduling/machine set-ups			
£1,500 × 240/10,000	36.00		
£1,500 × 260/20,000		19.50	
£1,500 × 300/10,000			15.00
	149.60	124.70	113.66

Comparison of the ABC cost with the original traditionally calculated cost reveals that product S was significantly overcosted by the traditional system relative to the ABC system, while product P was seriously undercosted. Product S is high-volume product with a high direct labour content, while product P is a low-volume product with a low direct labour content; this result is therefore to be expected. Both the activities in this simple example are batch-related, not unit-related. ABC reflects this reality in its allocation of production overhead costs to the product. The traditional approach allocated all production overhead costs to products as if the overheads were driven by unit-level activities, that is the number of direct labour hours worked – with the inevitable costing consequence seen above.

You should note that this example, with only two activity cost pools, will almost certainly have necessitated some arbitrary cost allocations. All that is being claimed is that the resulting ABC costings give a better insight into the cost of producing the products than traditional costs.

The debate as to whether ABC is actually a new technique, or whether it simply encourages a more accurate tracing of costs to products in a manner that is perfectly consistent with the traditional approach, is interesting but sterile – and misses the point of ABC, as is demonstrated in the rest of this chapter. Nevertheless, it is worth pointing out that ABC product costs are full absorption costs and, as such, suffer from the same type of deficiencies in a decision-making context as do traditional full absorption costs – they are historical, based on current methods of organisation and operation and, at the level of the product, contain allocations of joint/common costs, a point which is illustrated in the comprehensive example of ABC appearing later in this chapter. However, it can be strongly argued that ABC has an important 'attention-directing' role to play in both cost management and decision-making Indeed, the cost management, or monitoring, role of ABC is explicitly acknowledged in the definition which appears in the latest CIMA *Official Terminology:*

> *ABC:* An approach to the costing and monitoring of activities which involves tracing resource consumption and costing final outputs. Resources are assigned to activities and activities to cost objects based on consumption estimates. The latter utilise cost drivers to attach activity costs to outputs.

This particular role is discussed below.

In decision-making, it is arguable that activity-based costs are much more helpful than traditional costs in determining the costs relevant for decision-making and, more particularly, in drawing attention to the likely impact on long-run variable costs of short-term decisions. This point is discussed further later in the chapter.

Exercise – activity-based costing

(a) Distinguish between,
   (i) short-run variable costs and long-run variable costs, and give an example of each;
   (ii) the marginal cost and the average cost of production, and describe the conditions likely to cause such costs to vary.
(b) Explain how long-run variable production costs are allocated to cost units in traditional costing methods. In what ways are modern manufacturing methods making this approach less relevant?

2.8.3 Cost management and ABC

The ABTs have a wide range of applications in the areas of business planning and decision-making The application of an awareness of operational activities in the management of a business is known as Activity-Based Management'. ABM is a topic that is relevant to all three papers in CIMA's Performance pillar.

2.8.4 A comprehensive example of ABC

Exercise section I: traditional analysis

A company manufactures three products – X, Y and Z, whose direct costs are given below:

	X	Y	Z
	£	£	£
Direct material	67.92	63.27	56.79
Direct labour (@ £3/hour):			
Machining	13.08	14.73	17.01
Assembly	24.00	27.00	31.20
	105.00	105.00	105.00

The data below was used in calculating the direct labour costs above, and will be used to determine the production overhead charged to each product under the 'traditional' costing method.

	X	Y	Z	Total
Machine time (hours)	11.00	9.00	8.00	
Direct labour (hours)				
Machining	4.36	4.91	5.67	
Assembly	8.00	9.00	10.40	
Production (units)	50,000	30,000	16,250	
Total machine hours	500,000	270,000	130,000	900,000
Total labour hours				
Machining	218,000	147,300	92,137	457,437
Assembly	400,000	270,000	169,000	839,000
				1,296,437

Information on the company's overheads is as follows:

Production overhead	£'000	£'000
Indirect labour		
Machinery	900	
Assembly	600	
Purchasing/order processing	600	
Factory management	100	
		2,200
Power		
Machining	400	
Assembly	100	
		500
Indirect materials		
Machining	200	
Assembly	200	
Purchasing	100	
Factory management	100	
		600

Depreciation		
Machining	600	
Assembly	300	
Purchasing	200	
Building	400	
		1,500
Security		100
Grounds maintenance		100
Total production overhead		5,000

Prepare a traditional overhead analysis and calculate product costs for the three products. Assume that the machining department uses a machine hour absorption rate and the assembly department a labour hour rate.

 ## Solution

Step 1 – Assign production overhead to cost centres

	£'000	£'000
Machining		
Indirect labour	900	
Power	400	
Indirect materials	200	
Depreciation	600	
		2,100
Assembly		
Indirect labour	600	
Power	100	
Indirect materials	200	
Depreciation	300	
		1,200
Purchasing/order processing		
Indirect labour	600	
Indirect materials	100	
Depreciation	200	
		900
Factory management		
Indirect labour	100	
Indirect materials	100	
Depreciation	400	
Security	100	
Ground maintenance	100	
		800
Total production overhead		5,000

Step 2 – Reallocate services department costs to production departments on a suitable basis

	£'000	£'000
Machining		
Indirect costs (from step 1)	2,100	
Reallocation of service centre costs	600	
		2,700
Assembly		
Indirect costs (from step 1)	1,200	
Reallocation of service centre costs	1,100	

		2,300
Purchasing/order processing		
Indirect costs (from step 1)	900	
Reallocate on basis of direct labour cost	(900)	
		–
Factory management		
Indirect costs (from step 1)	800	
Reallocate on basis of direct labour cost	(800)	
		–
Total production overhead		5,000

Step 3 – Calculate absorption rate
   Machining: based on total machine hours

$$\frac{\text{Total overhead costs}}{\text{Total machine hours}} = \frac{£2,700,000}{900,000} = £3 \text{ per machine hour}$$

Assembly: based on total assembly labour hours

$$\frac{\text{Total overhead costs}}{\text{Total labour hours}} = \frac{£2,300,000}{839,000} = £2.74 \text{ per machine hour}$$

Step 4 – Calculate full product cost

	X	Y	Z
	£	£	£
Direct cost (as before)	105.00	105.00	105.00
Production overhead:			
Machining	30.00	27.00	24.00
Assembly	21.92	24.66	28.50
	156.92	156.66	157.50

Exercise section II: ABC analysis – allocating all costs to products

The information and data in the following tables will be used to determine cost drivers and calculate overheads.

Product X	*Product Y*	*Product Z*
High volume	Medium volume	Low volume
Large batches	Medium batches	Small batches
Few purchase orders placed	Medium purchase orders placed	Many purchase orders placed
	Medium components	Many components
Few customer orders placed	Medium customer orders placed	Many customer orders placed

	Product X	Product Y	Product Z	Total
Typical batch size	2,000	600	325	
No. of production runs	25	50	50	125
No. of inspections	25	50	50	125
Purchase orders placed	25	100	200	325
Customer orders received	10	100	200	310

Prepare an ABC analysis and calculate product costs.

 **Solution**

- Step 1 – Identify production-related activities

	£'000	£'000
Analysis of indirect labour		
Machining		
Supervision	100	
Set-up	400	
Quality control	<u>400</u>	
		900
Assembly		
Supervision	200	
Quality control	<u>400</u>	
		600
Purchasing/order processing		
Resource procurement	300	
Customer liaison/expediting	<u>300</u>	
		600
Factory management		
General administration		<u>100</u>
		<u>2,200</u>

Activities

1. Machining
2. Machine set-up
3. Machining quality control
4. Assembly
5. Assembly quality control
6. Resource procurement
7. Customer liaison/expediting
8. Factory management.

The table below shows the specific details of

- Step 2 – identify the cost of activities;
- Step 3 – identify cost driver;
- Step 4 – reallocate factory management costs pro rata to other costs.

STEP 2		Total	STEP 3	STEP 4	Total
	£'000	£'000		£'000	£'000
1. Machining					
Supervision	100				
Power	400				
Indirect materials	100				
Depreciation	600				
		1,200	Machine running time	230	1,430
2. Machine set-up					
Indirect labour	400				
Indirect materials	50				
		450	No. of set-ups (batch size)	85	535
3. Machining quality control					
Indirect labour	400				
Indirect materials	50				
		450	No. of inspections (batch size)	85	535
4. Assembly					
Supervision	200				
Power	100				
Indirect materials	100				
Depreciation	300				
		700	Direct labour hours worked	135	835
5. Assembly quality control					
Indirect labour	400				
Indirect materials	100				
		500	No. of inspections (batch size)	95	595
6. Resource procurement					
Indirect labour	300				
Indirect materials	50				
Depreciation	100				
		450	No. of orders placed (product batch size)	85	535
7. Customer liaison/expediting					
Indirect labour	300				
Indirect materials	50				
Depreciation	100				
		450	No. of orders rec'd (product)	85	535
8. Factory management (see note)					
Indirect labour	100				
Indirect materials	100				
Depreciation	400				
Security	100				
Grounds maintenance	100				
		800	No obvious (size of business?)	(800)	0
		5,000		0	5,000

There is no obvious driver for the common costs collected under the heading 'factory management', so they have been reallocated to other activity cost pools on the basis of their total costs.

- Step 5 – Calculate overhead from cost drivers.

  Rate per machine hour

$$\frac{\text{Total overhead costs}}{\text{Total machine hours}} = \frac{£1,430,000}{900,000} = £1.59 \text{ per machine hour}$$

Rate per set-up

$$\frac{\text{Total overhead costs}}{\text{Total set-ups}} = \frac{£535,000}{125} = £4,280 \text{ per batch}$$

Rate per machining inspection

$$\frac{\text{Total overhead costs}}{\text{Total inspections}} = \frac{£535,000}{125} = £4,280 \text{ per batch}$$

Assembly rate per direct labour hour

$$\frac{\text{Total overhead costs}}{\text{Total assembly hours}} = \frac{£835,000}{839,000} = £1.00 \text{ per labour hour}$$

Rate per assembly inspection

$$\frac{\text{Total overhead costs}}{\text{Total inspections}} = \frac{£595,000}{125} = £4,760 \text{ per batch}$$

Rate per order placed

$$\frac{\text{Total overhead costs}}{\text{Total orders placed}} = \frac{£535,000}{325} = £1,646 \text{ per order}$$

Rate per order received

$$\frac{\text{Total overhead costs}}{\text{Total orders received}} = \frac{£535,000}{310} = £1,726 \text{ per order}$$

- Step 6 – Calculate full product cost.

	X	Y	Z
	£	£	£
Direct costs (as before)	105.00	105.00	105.00
Overhead			
Per machine hour	15.90	14.31	12.72
Per set-up			
£4,280/2,000	2.14		
£4,280/600		7.13	
£4,280/325			13.17
Per machine inspection			
£4,280/2,000	2.14		
£4,280/600		7.13	
£4,280/325			13.17
Assembly rate @ £1 per DLH	8.00	9.00	10.40
Per assembly inspection			
£4,760/2,000	2.38		
£4,760/600		7.93	
£4,760/325			14.65
Per order placed			
£1,646 × 25/50,000	0.82		
£1,646 × 100/30,000		5.49	
£1,646 × 200/16,250			20.26

Per order received

£1,726 × 10/50,000	0.35		
£1,726 × 100/30,000		5.75	
£1,726 × 200/16,250			21.24
Overhead subtotal	31.73	56.74	105.61
Direct costs + overheads	136.73	161.74	210.61

Rationalisation of overhead charged

Product	Overhead (£)	Production	Total (rounded)
	£		£'000
X	31.73	50,000	1,580
Y	56.74	30,000	1,700
Z	105.61	16,250	1,720
			5,000

Comparison of product costs under each method

	X	Y	Z
'Traditional'	156.92	156.66	157.50
Activity-based costing	136.73	161.74	210.61

Product Z – with a low total production volume, many purchase and customer orders, and frequent small production runs – has a significantly higher cost under ABC than under the 'traditional' method. The opposite is the case with product X, which has a high total production volume, relatively few orders and large production runs.

 Exercise section III: ABC analysis – excluding facility-level costs

In the calculation in section II the ABC costs, like traditional costs, contain an allocation of the factory management costs within each cost driver – or absorption – rate. Factory management costs were attributed to other activities simply because of the lack of an identifiable driver with which to associate them with products.

However, it can be argued that this cost should not be identified arbitrarily with the other activities, but should be left within its own cost pool.

If this is done, Step 4 in the ABC analysis above would be omitted, and the calculation would proceed as follows

ABC analysis when factory management costs are not reallocated to other activities This shows the detail for

- Step 2 – Identify the cost of activities
- Step 3 – Identify cost drivers

STEP 2	£'000	STEP 3
1. Machining	1,200	Machine running time
2. Machine set-up	450	No. of set-ups (batch size)
3. Machining quality control	450	No. of inspections (batch size)
4. Assembly	700	Direct labour hours worked
5. Assembly quality control	500	No. of inspections (batch size)
6. Resource procurement	450	No. of orders placed (product/batch size)
7. Customer liaison/expediting	450	No. of orders received (product)
8. Factory management	800	No obvious driver (size of business)
	5,000	

- Step 4 – Omitted
- Step 5 – Calculate overhead from cost drivers.

Rate per machine hour

$$\frac{\text{Total overhead costs}}{\text{Total machine hours}} = \frac{£1,200,000}{900,000} = £1.33 \text{ per machine hour}$$

Rate per set-up

$$\frac{\text{Total overhead costs}}{\text{Total set-ups}} = \frac{£450,000}{125} = £3,600 \text{ per batch}$$

Rate per machining inspection

$$\frac{\text{Total overhead costs}}{\text{Total inspections}} = \frac{£450,000}{125} = £3,600 \text{ per batch}$$

Assembly rate per direct labour hour

$$\frac{\text{Total overhead costs}}{\text{Total assembly hours}} = \frac{£700,000}{839,000} = £0.83 \text{ per labour hour}$$

Rate per assembly inspection

$$\frac{\text{Total overhead costs}}{\text{Total inspections}} = \frac{£500,000}{125} = £4,000 \text{ per batch}$$

Rate per order Placed

$$\frac{\text{Total overhead costs}}{\text{Total orders placed}} = \frac{£450,000}{325} = £1,385 \text{ per order}$$

Rate per order received

$$\frac{\text{Total overhead costs}}{\text{Total orders received}} = \frac{£450,000}{310} = £1,452 \text{ per order}$$

Factory management costs of £800,000 have no obvious driver, and are not included in the costs above.

- Step 6 – Calculate full product cost

	X	Y	Z
	£	£	£
Direct costs (as before)	105.00	105.00	105.00
Overhead			
Per machine hour	13.33	12.00	10.67
Per set-up			
£3,600/2,000	1.80		
£3,600/600		6.00	
£3,600/325			11.08
Per machine inspection			
£3,600/2,000	1.80		
£3,600/600		6.00	
£3,600/325			11.08

Assembly rate @ £0.83 per DLH	6.67	7.51	8.67
Per assembly inspection			
£4,000/2,000	2.00		
£4,000/600		6.67	
£4,000/325			12.31
Per order placed			
£1,385 × 25/50,000	0.69		
£1,385 × 100/30,000		4.62	
£1,385 × 200/16,250			17.05
Per order received			
£1,452 × 10/50,000	0.29		
£1,452 × 100/30,000		4.84	
£1,452 × 200/16,250			17.87
Overhead subtotal	26.58	47.64	88.73
Direct costs + overheads	131.58	152.64	193.73

Rationalisation of overhead charged

Product	Overhead	Production	Total Tail
	£		£'000
X	26.58	50,000	1,329
Y	47.64	30,000	1,429
Z	88.73	16,250	1,442
			4,200

In this second approach, the £800,000 factory management costs have been left unallocated. Obviously, for stock valuation purposes, it would be necessary to allocate them to products, albeit on an arbitrary basis. They could be allocated to products in proportion to the allocation of other overhead costs, as shown below:

Product	Total Overhead	Factory management cost	Total production overhead allocated
	(1)	(2)	(1) + (2)
	£'000	£'000	£'000
X	1,329	253	1,582
Y	1,429	272	1,701
Z	1,442	275	1,717
	4,200	800	5,000

Apart from minor rounding differences, the total allocation as shown in the final column above is identical to that in the same column in section II, and thus the total overhead charged to the three products is identical under both approaches. However, the second approach may be much more helpful to management by directing attention to the resource implications of manufacturing particular products. For example, the table below shows product Y's comparative costs.

	Factory management costs allocated to other activities	Factory management treated as a separate activity
ABC COST OF PRODUCT Y	£	£
Direct costs (as before)	105.00	105.00
Overhead		
Unit-level activity cost		
Per machine hour	14.31	12.00
Assembly rate	9.00	7.51

Batch-level activity cost			
Per set-up	7.13	6.00	
Per machine inspection	7.13	6.00	
Per assembly inspection	7.93	6.67	
Per order placed	5.49	4.62	
Product-level activity cost			
Per order received	5.75	4.84	
Overhead subtotal	56.74	47.64	
Facility-level activity cost			
Factory management costs:		9.10	(£272,000/30,000)
Total production overhead	56.74	56.74	
Direct costs + overheads	161.74	161.74	

In the first analysis, the cost-driver rates do not give an accurate reflection of the resource consumption implications of performing particular activities, as they contain an arbitrary allocation of factory management costs. The second analysis provides cost-driver rates that do reflect truly the long-run costs of performing particular activities. This information may be useful to management in identifying cost-reduction opportunities, as well as for product costing purposes.

In addition to identifying 'factory management' as a separate cost pool, the table above has also grouped costs in accordance with the hierarchy outlined above. This provides management with a clear view of the resource consumption that will result in the long run, if production of Y is maintained at 30,000 units and the organisation of production remains the same. If the volume of production of Y were to change, both ABC analyses draw management's attention to the fact that the change in overhead resource consumption brought about by the change in volume would not be proportionate to the change in the number of units produced. In the first analysis, even the resource consumption of unit-level activities would not change proportionately to the change in production volume, as there is no reason to expect the facility-level costs of factory management, included therein via the allocation process, to change proportionately with change in volume. In the second analysis, where there are no arbitrary cost allocations, the resource consumption of unit-level activities would change proportionately with the change in volume. However, the change in consumption of the other overhead resources would depend on precisely how the change in volume was achieved – for example, were there more batcher? For example, volume could be expanded by increasing the size of each batch of Y, in which case the consumption of batch-level resources would remain constant, despite the rise in volume. ABC analyses thus provide a clearer insight into the way in which resource consumption, and ultimately cost, will change as a result of the specific changes in activities that accompany a particular change in volume.

It pays to know your abc

Sarah Perrin, *Management Today*, December 1997 Full Text: © Haymarket Publishing Ltd. 1997

It's difficult to calculate the true cost of a product when the same resources are used to generate different goods, says Sarah Perrin. Activity-based costing may be the answer.

Businessmen may think they already know how profitable their widgets are. They know the materials and labour costs which, hopefully, are covered by the price. But what about those extra indirect costs? For example, does the marketing department spend a major percentage of its time on one product line, devising promotions to shift stock? Does the finance department have to keep chasing one customer for payment? All these activities incur a cost whenever the same resources are being harder to calculate the true cost of a product.

Activity-based costing (ABC) is one answer. It takes every cost generated by the business and allocates it proportionately to the products or services that it has helped create. Customers too can be analysed to see whether some are more costly to serve than others. Only once all costs have been allocated do you have a complete picture of how profitable each of the different products or services really are.

That's the simple explanation, but the process is easier talked about than done. 'It's difficult to get a simple explanation of activity-based costing', says Colin Drury, professor of accounting at the University of Huddersfield. 'It's about trying to break an organisation down into many different activities rather than departments. It's about finding the causes of costs.'

The process itself does appear complex to the uninitiated. It requires the identification of all the activities performed within the company. 'For small or medium-sized companies, I would expect to divide the business into 300–400 activities', says John McKenzie, director of consulting for ABC software developer Armstrong Laing. Most departments could be broken down into 30–50 activities. Within accounts receivable, for example, one key activity would be chasing late payers. Having identified that activity, the next step is to customers. This can be done by getting staff to fill out time sheets or answer questionnaires. You can then estimate the cost of debt-chasing activity and allocate it proportionately over those late-paying accounts. Suddenly you have a better idea of how much each customer costs to service. By applying the technique to all the other departments, and all the activities within departments, the complete cost picture for each product or client appears.

So far so good. But it is what you do with the information that counts. Hence the term 'activity-based management' (ABM). One example of ABM would involve looking at all the activities in the company and breaking them down into four types: those that add value to a customer, those that add value to the business; non-value-added activities (such as correcting mistakes in invoices); and sustaining activities (such as the annual audit, which is required by law). Those non-value-added costs can then be compared with their value-added counterparts. If they make up a high proportion of the total, then there is scope for cost-cutting 'Sustaining and non-value-added costs often come out at around 50% of the total', says McKenzie. 'That's when you find you can eliminate some of them. That's when people get excited.'

Further analysis shows which products or customers are profitable. You can find yourself in the uncomfortable position of learning that, say, 10% of your company's products account for 100% of profits. In other words, 90% are loss-making or just breaking even.

2.9 Summary

In this chapter, we have considered basic principles involved in the design and use of management accounting systems. In particular we have considered alternative manners in which costs may be attributed to products and charged to profit. These range from the utilitarian approach of marginal costing (wherein costs considered to be 'fixed' are not attributed to products) through to the elaborate ABC approach wherein costs are attributed to products through an analysis of activities and cost drivers.

Self-test quiz

(1) State the factors that distinguish profit calculated according to (a) marginal costing and (b) absorption costing principles (Section 2.3).

(2) What are the respective uses for profit figures calculated using the two alternative principles? (Section 2.5)

(3) Explain the term 'overhead absorption rate' (Section 2.7.3).

(4) What is an 'over or under-absorption' of overheads? (Section 2.3.2)

(5) In the context of ABC, what is a cost pool? (Section 2.7)

(6) In the context of ABC, what is a cost driver? (Section 2.8.1)

(7) In the context of ABC, what is a batch-level activity? (Section 2.8.2)

(8) Explain the relationship between ABC and ABM (Section 2.6.1)

Revision Questions

2

? Question 1

1.1 The marginal costing convention of profit is more relevant to decision-making than the absorption costing convention because

   (A) So long as stock levels are rising, marginal costing gives a more conservative impression of profit than does absorption costing.

   (B) When stock levels are falling, the profit disclosed by marginal costing is less influenced by costs from the previous period than is the case with absorption costing.

   (C) Marginal costing provides a version of profit that relates only to those costs the level of which are influenced by the matters being decided upon.

   (D) Marginal costing provides a valuation of stock that conforms with current accounting standards relevant to the preparation of published accounts.

1.2 The use of predetermined overhead absorption rates is generally favoured by management accountants because

   (A) It allows product costs to be determined before the end of a given accounting period.

   (B) It avoids the over-or under-absorption of overheads.

   (C) It provides a more conservative version of product costs.

   (D) It relates more to the activities that give rise to overhead costs than do more traditional methods of overhead absorption.

1.3 The following details have been extracted from the budget papers of LK plc for June 2003:

Selling price per unit	£124
Variable production costs per unit	£54
Fixed production costs per unit	£36
Other variable costs per unit	£12
Sales volume	12,500 units
Production volume	13,250 units
Opening stock of finished items	980 units

If budgeted profit statements were prepared by using absorption costing and then by using marginal costing,

   (A) Marginal costing profits would be higher by £27,000.

   (B) Absorption costing profits would be higher £27,000.

(C) Absorption costing profits would be higher £35,000.

(D) Absorption costng profits would be higher £62,000.

1.4 In a period when finished stock levels increase, the profit and closing stock valuations shown under marginal costing and absorption costing would be

	Profit	*Closing stock valuations*
(A)	Marginal higher than absorption costing	Marginal lower than absorption costing
(B)	Marginal lower than absorption costing	Marginal higher than absorption costing
(C)	Marginal higher than absorption costing	Marginal higher than absorption costing
(D)	Marginal lower than absorption costing	Marginal lower than absorption costing

? Question 2

The following budgeted profit statement has been prepared using absorption costing principles:

	January–June		July–December	
	£'000	£'000	£'000	£'000
Sales		540		360
Opening stock	100		160	
Production costs				
Direct materials	108		36	
Direct labour	162		54	
Overhead	90		30	
	460		280	
Closing stock	160		80	
		300		200
GROSS PROFIT		240		160
Production overhead				
(Over-)/under-absorption	(12)		12	
Selling costs	50		50	
Distribution costs	45		40	
Administration costs	80		80	
		163		182
Net profit/(loss)		77		(22)
Sales units		15,000		10,000
Production units		18,000		6,000

The members of the management team are concerned by the significant change in profitability between the two 6-month periods. As management accountant, you have analysed the data upon which the above budget statement has been produced, with the following results:

1. The production overhead cost comprised both a fixed and a variable element, the latter appears to be dependent on the number of units produced. The fixed element of the cost is expected to be incurred at a constant rate throughout the year.
2. The selling costs are fixed.
3. The distribution cost comprises both fixed and variable elements, the latter appears to be dependent on the number of units sold. The fixed element of the cost is expected to be incurred at a constant rate throughout the year.
4. The administration costs are fixed.

Requirements

(a) Present the above budgeted profit statement in marginal costing format. **(10 marks)**

(b) Reconcile each of the 6-monthly profit/loss values reported respectively under marginal and absorption costing. **(4 marks)**

(c) Reconcile the 6-monthly profit for January to June from the absorption costing statement with the 6-monthly loss for July to December from the absorption costing statement. **(4 marks)**

(d) Calculate the annual number of units required to break even. **(3 marks)**

(e) Explain briefly the advantages of using marginal costing as the basis of providing managers with information for decision-making. **(4 marks)**

(Total marks = 25)

? Question 3

XYZ Inc has scheduled production of 20,000 Units (a new product) in the coming period and has budgeted for £200,000 of production costs (50% fixed). XYZ executives TW (Management Accountant), IS (Financial Accountant) and HF (Sales Manager) meet to consider the following market research data for the coming period:

Unit selling price (£)	Sales volume (Units)
15	20,000
20	16,000
25	11,500

TW advocates adopting a Unit selling price of £20 because this will maximise contribution. IS advocates a Unit selling price of £25 because this will maximise profit calculated according to normal accounting practice. HF advocates a Unit selling price of £15 because this will result in all output being sole and maximise market share.

Requirement

Explain each of these three points of view with supporting figures. Having regard to whatever facts you consider relevant, state which of the three points of view you consider to be correct. **(25 marks)**

? Question 4

ABC Ltd produces a large number of products including the A and the B. The A is a complex product of which 1,000 are made and sold in each period. The B is a simple product of which 25,000 are made and sold in each period. The A requires one direct labour hour to produce and the B requires 0.6 direct labour hours to produce.

ABC Ltd employs 12 salaried support staff and a direct labour force that works 400,000 direct labour hours per period. Overhead costs are £500,000 per period.

The support staff are engaged in three activities - six staff engaged in receiving 25,000 consignments of components per period, three staff engaged in receiving 10,000 consignments of raw materials per period and three staff engaged in disbursing kits of components and materials for 5,000 production runs per period.

Product A requires 200 component consignments, 50 raw material consignments and 10 production runs per period. Product B requires 100 component consignments, 8 raw material consignments and five production runs per period.

Requirements

(a) Calculate the overhead cost of the A and the B using a traditional system of overhead absorption based on direct labour hours. **(10 marks)**

(b) Identity appropriate cost drivers and calculate the overhead cost of the A and the B using an activity-based costing system. **(10 marks)**

(c) Compare your answers to (a) and (b) and explain which gives the most meaningful impression of product costs. **(5 marks)**

(Total marks = 25)

Scenario for questions 5 and 6

During the last 20 years, KL's manufacturing operation has become increasingly automated, with computer-controlled robots replacing operatives. KL currently manufactures over 100 products of varying levels of design complexity. A single, plant-wide overhead absorption rate (OAR), based on direct labour hours, is used to absorb overhead costs.

In the quarter ended March 20 3 9, KL's manufacturing overhead costs were

	£'000
Equipment operation expenses	125
Equipment maintenance expenses	25
Wages paid to technicians	85
Wages paid to storemen	35
Wages paid to dispatch staff	40
	310

During the quarter, Rapier Management Consultants were engaged to conduct a review of KL's cost accounting systems. Rapier's report includes the following statement:

In KL's circumstances, absorbing overhead costs in individual products on a labour-hour absorption basis is meaningless. Overhead costs should be attributed to products using an activity-based costing (ABC) system.

We have identified the folio wings as being the most significant activities:

1. receiving component consignments from suppliers;
2. setting up equipment for production runs;
3. quality inspections;
4. dispatching goods orders to customers.

Our research has indicated that, in the short term, KL's overheads are 40 per cent fixed and 60 per cent variable. Approximately half the variable overheads vary in relation to direct labour hours worked and half vary in relation to the number of quality inspections. This model applies only to relatively small changes in the level of output during a period of 2 years or less.

Equipment operation and maintenance expenses are apportionable as follows: component stores (15 per cent), manufacturing (70 per cent) and goods dispatch (15 per cent).

Technician wages are apportionable as follows: equipment maintenance (30 per cent), setting up equipment for production runs (40 per cent) and quality inspections (30 per cent).

During the quarter:

- a total of 2,000 direct labour hours were worked (paid at £12 per hour);
- 980 component consignments were received from suppliers;
- 1,020 production runs were set up; 640 quality inspections were carried out; and
- 640 quality inspections were carried out; and
- 420 goods orders were dispatched to customers.

? **Question 5** (see scenario)

KL's production during the quarter included components *r*, *s* and *t*. The following information is available:

	Component r	Component s	Component t
Direct labour hours worked	25	480	50
Direct material costs	£1,200	£2,900	£1,800
Component consignments received	42	24	28
Production runs	16	18	12
Quality inspections	10	8	18
Goods orders dispatched	22	85	46
Quantity produced	560	12,800	2,400

In April 20x9 a potential customer asked KL to quote for the supply of a new component *(z)* to a given specification. 1,000 units of *z* are to be supplied each quarter for a 2-year period. They will be paid for in equal instalments on the last day of each quarter. The job will involve an initial design cost of £40,000 and production will involve 80 direct labour hours £2,000 materials, 20 component consignments, 15 production runs, 30 quality inspections and 4 goods dispatches per quarter.

KL's sales director comments:

Now we have a modern ABC system, we can quote selling prices with confidence. The quarterly charge we quote should be the forecast ABC production cost of the units plus the design cost of the *z* depreciated on a straight-line basis over the 2 years of the job - to which we should add a 25 per cent mark-up for profit. We can base our forecast on costs experienced in the quarter ended March 20x9.

Requirements

(a) Calculate the unit cost of components *r*, *s* and *t*, using KL's existing cost accounting system (single-factory, labour-hour OAR). **(5 marks)**

(b) Explain how an ABC system would be developed using the information given. Calculate the unit cost of components *r*, *s* and *t*, using this ABC system. **(11 marks)**

(c) Calculate the charge per quarter that should be quoted for supply of component *z* in a manner consistent with the sales director's comments. Advise KL's management on the merits of this selling price, having regard to factors you consider relevant.

Note: KL's cost of capital is 3 per cent per quarter. **(9 marks)**

(Total marks = 25)

? **Question 6** (see scenario)

It is often claimed that ABC provides better information concerning product costs than traditional management accounting techniques. It is also sometimes claimed that ABC provides better information as a guide to decision-marking. However, one should treat these claims with caution. ABC may give a different impression of product costs but it is not necessarily a better impression. It may be wiser to try to improve the use of traditional techniques before moving to ABC.

Comment by KL's management accountant on the Rapier report

Requirements

(a) Explain the ideas concerning cost behaviour that underpin ABC. Explain why ABC may be better attuned to the modern manufacturing environment than traditional techniques. Explain why KL might or might not obtain a more meaningful impression of product costs through the use of ABC. **(10 marks)**

(b) Explain how the traditional cost accounting system being used by KL might be improved to provide more meaningful product costs. **(6 marks)**

(c) Critically appraise the reported claim that ABC gives better information as a guide to decision-making than do traditional product costing techniques. **(9 marks)**

(Total marks = 25)

Solutions to Revision Questions

 Solution 1

1.1 Answer: (C)

(A), (B) and (C) are all correct statements under most circumstances, but it is (C) that explains why the marginal costing convention is most applicable to decision-making (D) is a false statement since it is absorption costing that is consistent with current accounting standards.

1.2 Answer: (A)

(B), (C) and (D) are all false statements.

1.3 Finished goods stock increases during the period by 750 unit.
Fixed overhead absorbed per unit = £36
Difference in profits = 750 units × Fixed overhead absorbed per unit
Difference in profits = £27,000
When stock levels increase higher profits are reported under absorption costing. Therefore the answer is (B).

1.4 Answer: (D)

 Solution 2

- The emphasis in your PI syllabus is on the use of marginal costing information for performance evaluation. Ensure that you can produce a clear and complete answer to part (e).
- A common mistake is to include selling and distribution costs in stock valuations. Remember that stocks are valued at production cost only: variable production cost with marginal costing and total production cost with absorption costing, including absorbed fixed production overhead.

(a) The unit cost structure is the same in each 6-month period.

	£	£
Selling price		36
Direct materials	6	
Direct labour	9	
Variable overhead[2]	3	
Distribution cost[3]	1	
		19
Contribution		17

Notes:

1. Overhead January–June:
   £90,000 – £12,000 over-absorbed = £78,000
   Overhead July–December:
   £30,000 + £12,000 under-absorbed = £42,000

2. (£78,000 – £42,000)/12,000 = £3 variable
   £78,000 – (18,000 × £3) = £24,000 fixed

3. (£45,000 – £40,000)/5,000 = £1 variable
   £45,000 – (15,000 × £1) = £30,000 fixed

	January–June		July–December	
	£'000	£'000	£'000	£'000
Sales		540		360
Variable costs		285		190
Contribution		255		170
Fixed costs				
Production overhead	24		24	
Selling costs	50		50	
Distribution costs	30		30	
Administration	80		80	
		184		184
Profit		71		(14)

(b) Distribution costs are not included in stock valuation. Therefore, marginal cost unit stock valuation = £19 – £1 = £18 per unit.

	£
Marginal cost unit stock valuation	18
Absorption cost unit stock valuation	20

	January–June	July–December
	£'000	£'000
Absorption profit	77	(22)
c/fwd of fixed overhead in stock:		
(3,000 × £2)	6	
(4,000 × £2)		(8)
Marginal profit	71	(14)

(c) Absorption-based gross profit per unit is £400,000/25,000 = £16

	£'000
Profit from January–June	77
Reduction in sales volume (5,000 × £16)	(80)
Difference in overhead recovery (12,000 × £2)	(24)
Reduction in distribution cost	5
Profit/(loss) from July–December	(22)

(d) Fixed costs per annum £184,000 × 2 = £368,000

Contribution per unit £17
Annual breakeven sales in units £368,000/17 = 21,647 units

(e) Marginal costing is based on an understanding of cost behaviour, and attempts to model the real cash flows which will be the consequence of using resources and generating income. It can be represented graphically, giving simple, flexible and clear models of different scenarios. Marginal costing is closely associated with incremental costing and opportunity costing, which form a powerful grouping of financial modelling techniques which have common roots in the understanding of cost behaviour.

Solution 3

Profit can be calculated according to two alternative conventions. The first of these is the marginal costing convention being advocated by TW

XYZ profit – marginal costing convention

£			
Unit sp	15	20	25
Sales	300,000	320,000	287,500
Variable costs	100,000	100,000	100,000
Stock	0	20,000	42,500
Cost of Sales	100,000	80,000	57,500
Contribution	200,000	240,000	230,000
Fixed costs	100,000	100,000	100,000
Profit	100,000	140,000	130,000

The second is the absorption costing convention advocated by IS.

XYZ profit – absorption costing convention

£			
Unit sp	15	20	25
Sales	300,000	320,000	287,500
Costs	200,000	200,000	200,000
Stock	0	40,000	85,000
Cost of Sales	200,000	160,000	115,000
Profit	100,000	160,000	172,500

The two are distinguished by their treatment of fixed production costs in the stock valuation. The marginal costing convention adopts a stock valuation based on variable cost only – £5 per unit. The absorption costing convention adopts a stock variation based on full cost (including absorbed fixed costs) – £10 per unit. This latter method effectively allows a part of the fixed costs incurred in the current period to be carried forward into a subsequent period.

The absorption costing convention does give a maximum profit with a Unit selling price of £25. However, this involves carrying £42,500 of current period fixed costs forward into a subsequent period where they will have no impact on costs actually to be incurred. Those fixed costs are therefore 'decision relevant' to the current period and cannot be simply excluded from the decision before us.

The marginal costing convention charges all fixed costs to profit in the period in which they are incurred. Variable costs can be carried forward in the stock valuation – however, those variable costs will impact on the costs to be incurred in the subsequent period. Units produced in Period 1 and sold in Period 2 will allow production in Period 2 to be reduced and associated variable costs avoided.

Both sets of calculations given above assume that the stock will be marketable in the subsequent period. Were this not the case then the closing stock would have nil value and it would it would be appropriate to adopt a revenue maximising strategy. That would suggest a Unit selling price of £20. So, the Unit sales maximising strategy advocated by HF is unlikely to be appropriate – unless one wishes to maximising market share as part of some long term marketing concept.

The contribution maximising Unit selling price of £20 is therefore probably most appropriate in all the circumstances.

 # Solution 4

This is a basic product costing question that invites students to demonstrate their understanding of the principles of ABC.

(a) Overhead costs of £500,000 and direct labour hours of 400,000 give an overhead absorption rate of £1.25 per hour. Applied to the two products this OAR gives overhead costs as follows:

	Per unit £
A	1.25
B	0.75

(b) Three appropriate cost drivers are
   (i) receiving components;
   (ii) receiving raw materials;
   (iii) disbursing kits of components and raw materials.

Relating overhead costs to these drivers using the number of indirect staff engaged in each activity as the basis gives the following results:

- receiving components – £250,000; £10 per receipt;
- receiving raw materials – £125,000; £12.50 per receipt;
- disbursing kits – £125,000; £25 per issue

The products therefore attract overheads as follows:

	Total £	Per unit £
A	2,875	2.87
B	1,225	0.05

(c) Advocates of ABC would argue that the product costs shown in (b) are more meaningful than those shown in (a) because the former are based on a more sensitive analysis of the activities giving rise to overhead costs.

It is clear that the relative cost impact of the activities involved in producing the two products appears much more clearly when ABC is used.

 # Solution 5

The question covers much the same ground as Question 2 in this chapter. It invites students to demonstrate a grasp of the basic principles of ABC and how they compare to traditional product costing.

(a) Labour hour overhead absorption rate:

$$\frac{£310,000}{2,000} = £155 \text{ per labour hour}$$

Traditional unit costs:

	r	s	t
	£	£	£
Direct labour costs	300	5,760	600
Direct material costs	1,200	2,900	1,800
Overheads	3,875	74,400	7,750
Total costs	5,375	83,060	10,150
Cost per unit	£9.60	£6.49	£4.23

Workings for *r*

Direct labour costs	25 × £12	£300
Direct material costs	as stated	£1,200
Overheads	25 × £155	£3,875
Cost per unit	£5,375/560	£9.60

(b) An ABC system would be developed by analysing the cause of overhead costs as a function of the support activities carried out within the organisation. The 'cost drivers' are then used to apportion costs in a meaningful way to the different products produced in a multi-product company.

Rapier Consultants have already identified the cost drivers for KL, that is

- receiving components from suppliers;
- setting up production runs;
- quality inspections;
- dispatching goods to customers.

The apportionment of costs to *r, s* and *t* is carried out as follows:

Step 1 – Determine the total costs for each activity (£'000).

Activities	Operations	Maintenance	Costs Technicians	Stores	Dispach	Total
	£	£	£	£	£	£
Receiving supplies	18.75	3.75	3.83	35.00		61.33
			34.00			
Set-ups	87.50	17.50	17.85			156.85
Quality inspections			25.50			25.50
Dispatching goods	18.75	3.75	3.83		40.00	66.33
Total	125.00	25.00	85.00	35.00	40.00	310.00

Operations (equipment), maintenance and the portion of technicians' wages for maintenance are all apportioned on the book value of equipment.

Workings for set-up cost activities:

Operations and maintenance have 70% of their costs apportionable to manufacturing (i.e. set-ups):

$$125 \times 0.70 = 87.50$$

and

$$25 \times 0.70 = 17.50$$

Technicians have 40% of their cost apportionable to set-ups, that is

$$85 \times 0.40 \times 34$$

They also have 30% of their costs apportionable to maintenance, which in turn has 70% of its costs apportionable to set-ups, that is

$$85 \times 0.30 \times 0.70 = 17.85.$$

Step 2 – Calculate the cost for each activity.

		£
Receiving suppliers	£61,330/980	62.58
Set-ups	£156,850/1,020	153.77
Quality inspections	£25,500/640	39.84
Dispatching goods	£66,330/420	157.93

Step 3 – Apply these rates to calculate the unit costs.

	r	*s*	*t*
	£	£	£
Direct labour costs	300.00	5,760.00	600.00
Direct material costs	1,200.00	2,900.00	1,800.00
Receiving supplies	2,628.36	1,501.92	1,752.24
Set-ups	2,460.32	2,767.86	1,845.24
Quality inspections	398.40	318.72	717.12
Dispatching goods	3,474.46	13,424.05	7,264.78
Total	10,461.54	26,672.55	13,979.38
Cost per unit	£18.68	£2.08	£5.82

Example working for overhead costs: receiving supplies for *r*

$$£62.58 \times 42 = £2,628.36$$

(c) Quarterly charge (for 1,000 units):

		£
Design costs	£40,000/8	5,000
Direct labour	80 × £12	960
Direct materials		2,000
Overheads		
Receiving supplies	£62.58 × 20	1,252
Set-ups	£153.77 × 15	2,307
Quality inspections	£39.84 × 30	1,195
Dispatching goods	£157.93 × 4	632
Total		13,346
25% mark-up		3,337
Charge per quarter		16,683

The actual quarterly marginal cost is as follows:

	£
Design costs: £40,000/7.02	5,698
Direct labour	960
Direct materials	2,000

Variable overheads:
Labour-related:
80 × ((310,000 × 0.6 × 0.5)/2,000)   3,720
Inspection-related:
30 × ((310,000 × 0.6 × 0.5)/640)   4,359
16,737

The method suggested by the sales director does not cover the actual marginal costs.

In the short term, the use of Rapier's analysis of fixed and variable overheads allows the traditional method to give a more accurate costing. Work needs to be undertaken to discover the reasons for the discrepancies between the two methods, that is a more fundamental understanding of cost drivers and their unit costs is still required.

Workings for the actual quarterly marginal cost 7.02 represents the cumulative discount factor for the eight quarters at 3 per cent per quarter.

The labour-related overhead is found from the fact that 60 per cent of the overheads are variable of which 50 per cent vary with labour hours, that is

$$\frac{310,000 \times 0.6 \times 0.5}{2,000} = \text{ per labour hour.}$$

☑ Solution 6

- The question invites an evaluation of ABC practice relative to traditional product costing.
- It also invites discussion of how the traditional product costing system used by KL might be improved. This invites students to draw on knowledge gained in their Foundation level studies or equivalent.

(a) Activity-based costing (ABC) is based on the principle that all overhead costs can vary over the medium to long term and that each category varies with the level of support activity that is being provided. This is a more sophisticated argument than the simplistic division into fixed or variable costs with respect to one measure of activity, that is production output.

This more complicated approach was developed in response to a significant change in many modern manufacturing environments. Specifically, these change include

- constant and low levels of materials and products owing to the implementation of just-in-time (JIT) principles;
- constant and how direct labour costs owing to the high level of automation and a multi-skilling and teamworking approach;
- high capital investment cost, driving up overheads;
- many production set-ups to provide a wide range of customer-specific products while keeping low product inventory – this will influence the production overhead costs;
- more paperwork and progress expediting is required to ensure supply of materials and delivery of product – this also drives production overheads.

The ABC approach is to identify the relevant activities that drive up overhead costs, and to use the need for these activities for each product, as the basis for apportionment of these costs. Advocates claim that this is more attuned to the situation of high overhead and low direct costs than the traditional method, which catered for the opposite situation.

The company KL manufactures several products:

r complex, low-volume product;
s a simple, high-volume product;
t an intermediate product in terms of composition and volume.

The traditional system will tend to over-apportion costs to large volumes of production and under-apportion costs to complicated products.

Thus *r* will be undercharged and *s* overcharged by both inadequacies in the traditional system. This may make the product costs grossly inaccurate in some situations.

(b) The existing system uses a single overhead absorption rate (OAR), which produces the gross inaccuracies highlighted in part (a). This could be replaced with several OARs, one for each cost centre, and, rather than using direct labour hours, direct material costs, machine hours or power usage might be chosen as the basis for apportionment.

This might reflect more accurately the extra costs attributable to more complex products but would not reflect the extra costs attributable to small production batches.

Thus the system needs to be fully augmented with a complete analysis of overhead cost drivers to give meaningful results.

(c) The proponents of ABC claim that it gives more meaningful results in both AMT industries and service industries. Specifically, they state that it gives not only accurate and meaningful product costs, but that it also gives management a handle on controlling and reducing overhead costs.

This is based on the fuller understanding gained of how the overhead costs vary with the operating strategy and indirect support activities undertaken within the organisation.

Management decision-making for pricing, project appraisal, buy-or-make options, and so on depend on an accurate and meaningful cost analysis. The ABC system is the most sophisticated system developed for this purpose.

ABC produces an average cost per unit. However, when this changes with the level of activity (e.g. a stepped fixed cost, a discount on bulk purchases, etc.) this average cost per unit may not be the marginal cost per unit that should be taken into consideration.

Although the theory of ABC is simple, the process of analysis required to implement it is complex and costly. If the analysis is flawed, then the results obtained will also be flawed and may be less accurate and less meaningful than the 'arbitrary' traditional approach.

The Theory and Practice
of Standard Costing

The Theory and Practice of Standard Costing

3

3.1 Introduction

You should be familiar with the basic principles of standard costing and variance analysis from your certificate (or equivalent) studies. The initial content of this chapter amounts to a revision of these basic principles. You are advised to devote adequate time to this revision. The CIMA examination scheme is cumulative and Performance Operations examination questions in this particular area may draw heavily on material from certificate studies.

Standard costing and variance analysis represent a particular approach to performance evaluation. The concept that underpins them is that efficiency can be monitored by periodically comparing actual costs incurred with standard costs for output achieved. This concept is not valid under all circumstances. In subsequent chapters, the text goes on to explore both the practice and the limitations of standard costing.

3.2 The theory and practice of standard costing

CIMA's *Terminology* defines standard costing as follows:

 Standard costing: Control technique that reports variances by comparing actual costs to pre-set standards so facilitating action through management by exception.

You will see from this definition that there are very close relationships between standard costing and budgetary control (the practice of making continuous comparison between budget and actual results). They both compare the actual results with the expected performance to identify any variances. The difference is that with standard costing the comparison is usually made at a unit level, that is, the actual cost per unit is compared with the standard cost per unit. The resulting variances may be analysed to show their causes and we will see how this is done later in this chapter.

In order to be able to apply standard costing it must be possible to identify a measurable cost unit. This can be a unit of product or service but it must be capable of standardising: for example, standardised tasks must be involved in its creation. The cost units themselves do not necessarily have to be identical: for example, standard costing can be applied in some job costing situations where every cost unit is unique. However, the jobs must include standardised tasks for which a standard time and cost can be determined for monitoring purposes.

3.3 What is a standard cost?

A standard cost is a carefully predetermined unit cost which is prepared for each cost unit. It contains details of the standard amount and price of each resource that will be utilised in providing the service or manufacturing the product.

The standard cost may be stored on a standard cost card like the one shown below, but nowadays it is more likely to be stored on a computer, perhaps in a database. Alternatively, it may be stored as part of a spreadsheet so that it can be used in the calculation of variances.

The standard cost may be prepared using either absorption costing principles or marginal costing principles. The example which follows is based on absorption costing.

Example: Standard cost card: product 176

		£ per unit
Direct materials	40 kg @ £5.30	212.00
Direct wages		
Bonding	48 hours @ £2.50	120.00
Finishing	30 hours @ £1.90	57.00
Prime cost		389.00
Variable production overhead		
Bonding	48 hours @ £0.75	36.00
Finishing	30 hours @ £0.50	15.00
Variable production cost		440.00
Fixed production overhead		40.00
Total production cost		480.00
Selling and distribution overhead		20.00
Administration overhead		10.00
Total cost		510.00

For every variable cost the standard amount of resource to be used is stated, as well as the standard price of the resource. This standard data provides the information for a detailed variance analysis, as long as the actual data is collected in the same level of detail.

Standard costs and standard prices for direct cost items provide the basic unit information which is needed for valuing budgets and for determining total expenditures and revenues.

The principles of overhead absorption used to construct the standard cost shown in the above Example follow those explained earlier in the text. There are two cost centres (Bonding and Finishing) and it appears that variable overheads are being absorbed into the product on a direct labour hour basis. The basis on which the fixed overheads have been attributed to the product are less clear but that is not critical for present purposes.

3.4 Performance levels

3.4.1 A standard

CIMA's *Terminology* defines a standard:

 Standard: A benchmark measurement of resource usage, set in defined conditions.

The definition goes on to describe a number of bases which can be used to set the standard, including:

- a prior period level of performance by the same organisation;
- the level of performance achieved by comparable organisations;
- the level of performance required to meet organisational objectives.

Use of the first basis indicates that management feels that performance levels in a prior period have been acceptable. They will then use this performance level as a target and control level for the forthcoming period.

When using the second basis management is being more outward looking, perhaps attempting to monitor their organisation's performance against 'the best of the rest'.

The third basis sets a performance level which will be sufficient to achieve the objectives which the organisation has set for itself.

3.4.2 Ideal standard

Standards may be set at ideal levels based on any of the three alternative bases stated in Section 3.4.1 above, which make no allowance for normal losses, waste and machine downtime. This type of ideal standard can be used if managers wish to highlight and monitor the full cost of factors such as waste, and so on; however, this type of standard will almost always result in adverse variances since a certain amount of waste and so on is usually unavoidable. This can be very demotivating for individuals who feel that an adverse variance suggests that have performed badly.

3.4.3 Attainable standard

Standards may also be set at attainable levels which assume efficient levels of operation, but which include allowances for factors such as normal loss, waste and machine downtime. This type of standard does not have the negative motivational impact that can arise with an ideal standard because it makes some allowance for unavoidable inefficiencies. Adverse variances will reveal whether inefficiencies have exceeded this unavoidable amount.

3.4.4 Basic standard

A basic standard is one which is kept unchanged over a period of time. It is used as the basis for preparing more up-to-date standards for control purposes. A basic standard may be used to show the trend in costs over a period of time.

3.5 Setting standard costs

You have already seen that each element of a unit's standard cost has details of the price and quantity of the resources to be used. In this section we shall list some of the sources of information that may be used in setting the standard costs.

3.5.1 Standard material price

The sources of information include the following:

(a) Quotations and estimates received from potential suppliers.
(b) Trend information obtained from past data on material prices.
(c) Details of any bulk discounts which may be available.
(d) Information on any charges which will be made for packaging and carriage inwards.
(e) The quality of material to be used: this may affect the price to be paid.
(f) For internally manufactured components: the predetermined standard cost for the component will be used as the standard price.

3.5.2 Standard material usage

The sources of information include the following:

(a) The basis to be used for the level of performance.
(b) If an attainable standard is to be used, the allowance to be made for losses, wastage and so on. Work study techniques may be used to determine this.
(c) Technical specifications of the material to be used.

3.5.3 Standard labour rate

The sources of information include the following:

(a) The personnel department for the wage rates for employees of the required grades with the required skills.
(b) Forecasts of the likely outcome of any trades union negotiations currently in progress.
(c) Details of any bonus schemes in operation.

3.5.4 Standard labour times

The sources of information include the following:

(a) The basis to be used for the level of performance.
(b) If an attainable standard is to be used, the allowance to be made for downtime, and so on.

(c) Technical specifications of the tasks required to manufacture the product or provide the service.

(d) The results of work study exercises which are set up to determine the standard time to perform the required tasks and the grades of labour to be employed.

The determination of standard labour hour requirements has a significant history and theoretical basis.

Extract from 'What is a fair day's work?'

Gene Gagnon, *Transport & Distribution,* **29:12, November 1998**
Full Text © Penton Media Inc. 1998

In 1884, Frederick Winslow Taylor, a foreman with Bethlehem Steel, was in charge of a system that brought coal and coke to the furnace. He determined that there were three things needed to maximise warehouse productivity: a definite task, proper method, and a time for completion of the task. He made observations about the proper size shovel and wheelbarrows in order to develop the best method. He was primarily interested in the information so he could establish the right crew size and not have to send anyone home, but the whole area of 'working smarter, not harder' sparked his interest. He expanded the concept to include what we now call Work Simplification. In 1911, he wrote Scientific Management which discussed management's role in dealing with workers.

In the early 1900s, Frank Gilbreth was watching bricklayers and determined that their task was, in reality, a conglomeration of small motions. He installed a number of methods improvements and reduced the tasks of the bricklayer from 18 to 5. He called each of these small tasks a 'therblig' which became the first scientific classification of motions. In 1920, he used a movie camera to document the time that certain motions took. By counting the frames he could estimate a length of time for each motion.

The expansion of the ideas of these measurement pioneers resulted in what we know today as 'predetermined times', tables that have predetermined time values for a given body motion or combinations of motions. This is the basis of the standard costing techniques now widely used in manufacturing industries.

In the early 1940s, the Westinghouse Electric Corporation sponsored a series of studies into sensitive drill press work. These duties yielded a predetermined time value system known as MTM (Methods Time Measurement). This system was much too detailed for long-cycled or non-repetitive operations so it was simplified.

The simplification was named the Master Standard Data (MSD) and is applicable to any type of work. It can measure work that has never before been considered measurable from an economic standpoint. MSD clearly identifies the exact work content of each element of an activity. The engineers stated 'in literally thousands of instances, it was accurate well within the accepted work measurement consistency limits of plus or minus five per cent'.

3.5.5 Production overhead costs

Overhead absorption rates represent the standard hourly rates for overhead in each cost centre. They can be applied to the standard labour hours or machine hours for each cost unit.

The overheads will usually be analysed into their fixed and variable components so that a separate rate is available for fixed production overhead and for variable production overhead.

3.6 Updating standards

The main purpose of standard costs is to provide a yardstick against which actual performance can be monitored. If the comparison between actual and standard cost is to be meaningful, then the standard must be valid and relevant. It follows that the standard cost should be kept as up to date as possible. This may necessitate frequent updating of standards to ensure that they fairly represent the latest methods and operations, and the latest prices which must be paid for the resources being used.

3.7 Standard costing in the modern industrial environment

There has recently been some criticism of the appropriateness of standard costing in the modern industrial environment. The main criticisms include the following:

(a) Standard costing was developed when the business environment was more stable and operating conditions were less prone to change. In the present dynamic environment, such stable conditions cannot be assumed.
(b) Performance to standard used to be judged as satisfactory, but in today's climate constant improvement must be aimed for in order to remain competitive.
(c) The emphasis on labour variances is no longer appropriate with the increasing use of automated production methods.

These criticisms and the responses to them will be discussed fully later in this text. Standard costing is commonly identified with manufacturing and most of the examples used in this text are set in a traditional manufacturing context. However, the basic ideas involved can be easily adapted for use in the service sector. Examples of this adaption will be encountered later in this text in the discussion of McDonaldisation and diagnostic reference groups.

3.8 What is variance analysis?

A variance is the difference between the expected standard cost and the actual cost incurred. A unit standard cost contains detail concerning both the usage of resources and the price to be paid for the resources. Variance analysis involves breaking down the total variance to explain how much of it is caused by the usage of resources being different from the standard, and how much of it is caused by the price of resources being different from the standard.

These variances can be combined to reconcile the total cost difference revealed by the comparison of the actual and standard cost.

A variance is said to be favourable if it causes actual profit to be greater than budget; it is said to be adverse if it causes actual profit to be less than budget.

3.9   Variable production cost variances

We will use a simple example to demonstrate how the variances are calculated for direct material, direct labour and variable overhead.

 Exercise

A company manufactures a single product for which the standard variable cost is as follows.

		£ per unit
Direct material	81 kg × £7 per kg	567
Direct labour	97 hours × £4 per hour	388
Variable overhead	97 hours × £3 per hour	291
		1,246

During January, 530 units were produced and the costs incurred were as follows.

Direct material	42,845 kg purchased and used; cost £308,484
Direct labour	51,380 hours worked; cost £200,382
Variable overhead	cost £156,709

Calculate the variable cost variances for January.

3.9.1   Direct material cost variances

 Solution

(a) Direct material total variance

	£	
530 units should cost (× £567)	300,510	
But did cost	308,484	
Total direct material cost variance	7,974	Adverse

Note that this is an adverse variance because actual cost exceeds standard, hence causing actual profit to be less than budget.

This variance can now be analysed into its 'price' and 'quantity' elements.

(b) Direct material price variance

The direct material price variance reveals how much of the direct material total variance was caused by paying a different price for the materials used.

	£	
42,845 kg purchased should have cost (× £7)	299,915	
But did cost	308,484	
Direct material price variance	8,569	Adverse

The adverse price variance indicates that expenditure was £8,569 more than standard because a higher than standard price was paid for each kilogram of material.

π   *Material price variance:*   (Actual quantity of material purchased × standard price) − actual cost of material purchased.

(c) Direct material usage variance

The direct material usage variance reveals how much of the direct material total variance was caused by using a different quantity of material, compared with the standard allowance for the production achieved.

		kg	
530 units produced should have used (× 81 kg)		42,930	
But did use		42,845	
Variance		85	Favourable
× standard price per kg (£7)			
Direct material usage variance		£595	Favourable

The favourable usage variance indicates that expenditure was £595 less than standard. This was because a lower amount of material was used compared with the standard expected for this level of output.

CIMA's *Official Terminology* offers a slightly different statement of the materials usage variance to the one demonstrated above. However, the logic in both cases gives the same outcome.

π *Material usage variance:* (Actual production × standard material cost per unit) – (actual material used × standard cost per unit of materials).

Check: £8,569 adverse + £595 favourable = £7,974 adverse (the correct total variance).

3.9.2 The direct material price variance and stock valuation

One slight complication sometimes arises with the calculation of the direct material price variance. In this example the problem did not arise because the amount of material purchased was equal to the amount used.

However, when the two amounts are not equal then the direct material price variance could be based either on the material purchased or on the material used. In the example, we used the following formula (we will call it method A):

(A) Direct material price variance:

	£
Material *Purchased* should have cost	X
But did cost	X
Direct material price variance	X

Alternatively we could have calculated the variance as follows (we will call it method B):

(B) Direct material price variance:

	£
Material *used* should have cost	X
But did cost	X
Direct material price variance	X

Obviously if the purchase quantity is different from the usage quantity, then the two formulae will give different results. So how do you know which formula to use? The answer lies in the stock valuation method.

If stock is valued at standard cost, then method A is used. This will ensure that all of the variance is eliminated as soon as purchases are made and the stock will be held at standard cost.

If stock is valued at actual cost, then method B is used. This means that the variance is calculated and eliminated on each bit of stock as it is used up. The remainder of the stock will then be held at actual price, with its price variance still 'attached', until it is used and the price variance is calculated.

3.9.3 Direct labour cost variances

 Exercise

Using the data from the previous exercise, calculate the direct labour cost variances for January.

 Solution

(a) Direct labour total variance:

	£	
530 units should cost ($\times$ £388)	205,640	
But did cost	200,382	
Total direct labour cost variance	5,258	Favourable

Note that this is a favourable variance because actual cost is less than standard.

This variance can now be analysed into its 'price' and 'quantity' elements. The 'price' part is called the labour rate variance and the 'quantity' part is called the labour efficiency variance.

(b) Direct labour rate variance:

The direct labour rate variance reveals how much of the direct labour total variance was caused by paying a different rate for the labour hours worked.

	£	
51,380 hours should have cost ($\times$ £4)	205,520	
But did cost	200,382	
Direct labour rate variance	5,138	Favourable

The favourable rate variance indicates that expenditure was £5,138 less than standard because a lower than standard rate was paid for each hour of labour.

π *Labour rate variance:* (Actual hours paid $\times$ standard labour rate per hour) $-$ (actual hours paid $\times$ actual direct labour rate per hour).

(c) Direct labour efficiency variance:

The direct labour efficiency variance reveals how much of the direct labour total variance was caused by using a different number of hours of labour, compared with the standard allowance for the production achieved.

	Hours	
530 units produced should take ($\times$ 97 hours)	51,410	
But did take	51,380	
Variance	30	Favourable
$\times$ standard labour rate per hour (£4)		
Direct labour efficiency variance	£120	Favourable

The favourable efficiency variance of £120 is the saving in labour cost (at standard rates) resulting from using fewer labour hours than the standard expected for this level of output.

 Labour efficiency variance: (Actual production in standard hours × standard direct labour rate per hour) − (actual direct labour hours worked × standard direct labour rate per hour).

Check: £5,138 favourable + £120 favourable = £5,258 favourable (the correct total variance).

CIMA's *Official Terminology* offers a slightly different statement of the labour efficiency variance to the one demonstrated above. However, the logic in both cases gives the same outcome.

3.9.4 Variable overhead cost variances

Exercise

Using the data as before, calculate the variable overhead cost variances for January.

✓ Solution

(a) Variable overhead total variance:

	£
530 units should cost (× £291)	154,230
But did cost	156,709
Total variable overhead cost variance	2,479 Adverse

This variance can now be analysed into its 'price' and 'quantity' elements. The 'price' part is called the variable overhead expenditure variance and the 'quantity' part is called the variable overhead efficiency variance.

(b) Variable overhead expenditure variance:
The variable overhead expenditure variance reveals how much of the variable overhead total variance was caused by paying a different hourly rate of overhead for the hours worked.

	£
51,380 hours of variable overhead should cost (× £3)	154,140
But did cost	156,709
Variable overhead expenditure variance	2,569 Adverse

The adverse expenditure variance indicates that expenditure was £2,569 more than expected for the hours worked.

 Variable overhead expenditure variance: Actual overhead cost incurred − (actual hours worked × standard variable production overhead absorption rate per hour).

(c) Variable overhead efficiency variance:
The variable overhead efficiency variance reveals how much of the variable overhead total variance was caused by using a different number of hours of labour, compared with the standard allowance for the production achieved. Its calculation is very similar to the calculation of the labour efficiency variance.

Variance in hours (from labour efficiency variance)	<u>30</u>	Favourable
× standard variable overhead rate per hour (£3)		
Variable overhead efficiency variance	<u>£90</u>	Favourable

The favourable efficiency variance of £90 is the saving in variable overhead cost (at standard rates) resulting from using fewer labour hours than the standard expected for this level of output.

As with the earlier cases, CIMA's *Official Terminology* offers a slightly different statement of the variance to the one demonstrated above. However, the logic in both cases gives the same outcome.

π *Variable overhead efficiency variance:* (Actual hours worked × standard variable production overhead absorption rate per hour) − (actual production in standard hours × standard variable overhead absorption rate per hour).

Check: £2,569 adverse + £90 favourable = £2,479 adverse (the correct total variance).

All the above variable production cost variances are common to both absorption costing and marginal costing.

3.10 Fixed production overhead variances

In this section you will learn about the fixed production overhead variances in an absorption costing system. The variances in a marginal costing system will be covered in a later section.

The most important point to grasp about fixed production overhead variances is in an absorption costing system:

π *Total fixed production overhead variance:* This is equal to the under- or over-absorbed fixed production overhead for the period.

When you are analysing the total fixed production overhead variance you are therefore trying to explain the reasons for the over- or under-absorption. Factors which could lead to under-absorption will cause adverse fixed overhead variances. Factors which could lead to over-absorption will cause favourable fixed overhead variances.

The above points apply in a standard costing system. For example, say we are producing units and each unit requires 2 standard hours. If budget fixed overheads are £1,000 and budget hours are 200, then the overhead absorption rate will be £5 per hour. This translates into £10 per unit. So, if we actually produce 120 units (20 over budget) then we absorb £1,200 of overheads (120 units × 2 hours × £5). This is the same as the standard cost of the units produced. If we actually incur £1,050 of fixed overheads then the over-absorption is £150, which is a favourable cost variance under a standard costing system.

But matters may be different in a non-standard costing system where overheads are absorbed on the basis of actual rather than standard hours. In the above case, let us say we actually worked 230 hours (compared to the 240 standard hours). Then the overhead absorbed would be £1,150 giving an over-absorption of only £100. In this case the overhead cost variance (standard cost minus actual cost) is not the same as the over-absorption. This issue does not arise when absorption is simply on a per-unit basis.

The discussion that follows relates to standard costing systems.

3.10.1 The reasons for under- or over-absorption of overhead

There are basically two reasons why fixed overheads are under- or over-absorbed, and they are both linked to the calculation of the overhead absorption rate:

$$\text{Overhead absorption rate} = \frac{\text{Budget fixed overhead}}{\text{Budgeted output}}$$

The overhead will be under- or over-absorbed for either or both of the following reasons:

(a) The actual overhead expenditure was different from budget (this difference is expressed by the overhead expenditure variance).
(b) The actual output was different from budget (this difference is expressed by the overhead volume variance).

It is easiest to look at an example to see how the variances are calculated.

Example

A company manufactures a single product. Budget and actual data for the latest period are as follows:

- *Budget.* Fixed production overhead expenditure £103,000. Production output 10,300 units.
- *Actual.* Fixed production overhead expenditure £108,540. Production output 10,605 units.

3.10.2 The fixed production overhead total variance

$$\text{Predetermined overhead absorption rate} = \frac{£103,000}{\text{Budgeted output}} = £10 \text{ per unit}$$

	£
Overhead absorbed during period £10 × 10,605 Units	106,050
Actual overhead incurred	108,540
Fixed production overhead total variance	2,490 Adverse

This variance represents an under-absorption of fixed overheads.

3.10.3 The fixed production overhead expenditure variance

This is the amount of the total variance which is caused by the expenditure on overheads being different from the budgeted amount.

	£
Budgeted fixed production overhead expenditure	103,000
Actual fixed production overhead expenditure	108,540
Fixed production overhead expenditure variance	5,540 Adverse

π   *Fixed overhead expenditure variance.* Budgeted fixed overheads – actual fixed overheads.

Stop for a moment and look at the difference between the expenditure variances for fixed overhead and for variable overhead. With the variable overhead expenditure variance an allowance is made for the actual number of hours worked (i.e. the budget is flexed to the actual activity level). With the fixed overhead expenditure variance the allowance is not flexed because fixed overhead expenditure should not change if activity levels alter.

3.10.4 The fixed production overhead volume variance

This is the amount of the total variance which is caused by the volume of output being different from the budget.

	Units	
Actual output	10,605	
Budgeted output	10,300	
Difference	305	
$\times$ fixed production overhead absorption rate (£10)		
Fixed production overhead volume variance	£3,050	Favourable

π *Fixed overhead volume variance*:   (Actual production in standard hours $\times$ fixed overhead absorption rate) − budgeted fixed overhead.

The above formula is one taken from CIMA's *Official Terminology*. It expresses things in a different manner to the one demonstrated above. However, the logic in both cases gives the same outcome. The formula from the Terminology links calculation of the volume variance to an hourly absorption rate in order to facilitate the split of the volume variance into two subordinate components (capacity and efficiency variances). However, we will not consider this further analysis of the volume variance in this text.

In this case the volume variance is favourable because a higher output than budget was achieved, which would potentially lead to over-absorption.

Check: £5,540 adverse + £3,050 favourable = £2,490 adverse (the correct total variance).

3.11   Sales variances

In this section we shall be continuing with the study of variances from the viewpoint of reconciling budget and actual profits in an absorption costing system. There are two main variances for sales: the selling price variance and the sales volume variance. These variances can be demonstrated using the following data.

Example

A company manufactures a single product. Budget and actual data for the latest period is as follows:

Budget	
Sales and production volume	81,600 units
Standard selling price	£59 per unit
Standard variable cost	£24 per unit
Standard fixed cost	£4 per unit

	Actual results	
	Sales and production volume	82,400 units
	Actual selling price	£57 per unit
	Actual variable cost	£23 per unit
	Actual fixed cost	£6 per unit

This data will be used to calculate the sales variances below.

3.11.1 The selling price variance

This variance calculates the profit difference which is caused by charging a different selling price from the standard.

	£	
Selling price per unit should have been	59	
But was	57	
Selling price variance per unit sold	2	Adverse
× units sold (82,400)		
Selling price variance	164,800	Adverse

As with the earlier cases, CIMA's *Official Terminology* offers a slightly different statement of the variance to the one demonstrated above. However, the logic in both cases gives the same outcome.

π *Selling price variance:* (Actual sales volume × standard selling price per unit) − actual sales revenue.

The adverse variance indicates that the actual selling price was lower than the standard price leading to £164,800 less profit than budget.

3.11.2 The sales volume profit variance

This variance calculates the gross profit difference which is caused by selling a different quantity from that budgeted.

	Units	
Budgeted sales volume	81,600	
Actual sales volume	82,400	
Sales volume variance	800	Favourable
× standard profit per unit (£59 − £24 − £4 = £31)		
Sales volume profit variance	£24,800	Favourable

As with the earlier cases, CIMA's *Official Terminology* offers a slightly different statement of the variance to the one demonstrated above. However, the logic in both cases gives the same outcome.

π *Sales volume profit variance:* (Budgeted sales units × standard gross profit per unit) − (actual sales units × standard gross profit per unit). Be aware that some texts and practitioners refer to 'sales volume variance' when they actually mean sales volume profit variance.

The favourable variance indicates that the increased sales volume could have increased gross profit by £24,800 (if the selling price and the cost per unit had been equal to the standards).

An important point to note from this example is that the sales variances did not make use of the data on actual costs. All of the cost differences are analysed in the cost variances which you have already learned about in this chapter. The sales volume variance is expressed in terms of the *standard* gross profit lost or gained as a result of the change in sales volume.

3.12 Reconciling the actual and budget profit

Now that you have seen how to calculate all the main operating variances, you should be in a position to produce a statement which reconciles the actual and budget gross profit for the period.

First, to get some important practice, you should calculate all of the operating variances using the data given in the following exercise. Then you can learn to put all the variances together in a reconciliation statement like the one shown at the end of the solution.

Exercise

A company produces and sells one product only, the standard cost for which is as follows:

	£per unit
Direct material: 11 litres at £2	22
Direct wages: 5 hours at £6	30
Variable production overhead	10
Fixed production overhead	20
Total standard production cost	82
Standard gross profit	38
Standard selling price	120

The variable overhead is incurred in direct proportion to the direct labour hours worked.

The unit rate for fixed production overhead is based on an expected annual output of 24,000 units produced at an even rate throughout the year. Assume that each calendar month is equal and that the budgeted sales volume for May was 2,000 units.

The following were the actual results recorded during May.

Number of units produced and sold: 1,750 units

	£	£
Sales revenue		218,750
Directs materials: 19,540 litres purchased and used	41,034	
Direct labour: 8,722 hours	47,971	
Variable production overhead	26,166	
Fixed production overhead	37,410	
		152,581
Gross profit		66,169

Calculate the operating variances and present them in a statement which reconciles the budget and actual gross profit for May.

✓ Solution

Direct material price variance:

	£	
19,540 litres purchased should have costs (× £2)	39,080	
But did cost	41,034	
Direct material price variance	1,954	Adverse

Direct material usage variance:

	Litres	
1,750 units produced should have used (× 11 litres)	19,250	
But did use	19,540	
Variance	290	Adverse
× standard price per litre (£2)		
Direct material usage variance	£580	Adverse

Direct labour rate variance:

	£	
8,722 hours should have cost (× £6)	52,332	
But did cost	47,971	
Direct labour rate variance	4,361	Favourable

Direct labour efficiency variance:

	Hours	
1,750 units produced should take (× 5 hours)	8,750	
But did take	8,722	
Variance	28	Favourable
× standard labour rate per hour (£6)		
Direct labour efficiency variance	£168	Favourable

Variable production overhead expenditure variance:

	£	
8,722 hours of variable overhead should cost (× £2)	17,444	
But did cost	26,166	
Variable overhead expenditure variance	8,722	Adverse

Variable production overhead efficiency variance:

Variance in hours (from labour efficiency variance)	28	Favourable
× standard variable overhead rate per hour (£2)		
Variable overhead efficiency variance	£56	Favourable

Fixed production overhead expenditure variance:

	£	
Budgeted fixed overhead (2,000 units × £20)	40,000	
Actual fixed overhead	37,410	
Fixed overhead expenditure variance	2,590	Favourable

Fixed production overhead volume variance:

	Units	
Actual activity level	1,750	
Budgeted activity level	2,000	
Difference	250	
× fixed production overhead absorption rate (£20)		
Fixed overhead volume variance	£5,000	Adverse

Selling price variance:

	£	
Selling price per unit should have been	120	
But was (£218,750/1,750)	125	
Selling price variance per unit sold	5	Favourable
× units sold (1,750)		
Selling price variance	£8,750	Favourable

Sales volume profit variance:

	Units	
Budgeted sales volume	2,000	
Actual sales volume	1,750	
Sales volume variance in units	250	Adverse
× standard profit per unit (£38)		
Sales volume variance	£9,500	Adverse

A reconciliation statement begins with the original budgeted gross profit. It then adds favourable or subtracts adverse variances to arrive at the actual profit for the month.

Profit reconciliation statement for May

		£	£	£
Original budgeted gross profit:				
2,000 units × £38				76,000
Sales volume variance				(9,500)
Standard gross profit from actual sales				66,500
Selling price variance				8,750
				75,250
Cost variances				
Direct material:	price	(1,954)		
	usage	(580)		
			(2,534)	
Direct labour:	rate	4,361		
	efficiency	168		
			4,529	
Variable overhead:	expenditure	(8,722)		
	efficiency	56		
			(8,666)	
Fixed overhead:	expenditure	2,590		
	volume	(5,000)		
			(2,410)	
Actual gross profit				66,169

Note: variances in brackets are adverse.

3.13 Standard marginal costing

You should not be surprised to learn that the only variances in a marginal costing system which are different from those in an absorption costing system are those which involve fixed overheads. You are reminded that when a marginal costing system is in use, all fixed overheads are charged direct to profit without any attempt to attribute to units produced.

3.13.1 The fixed overhead volume variance

This variance does not arise in a marginal costing system. In an absorption costing system it represents the value of the under- or over-absorbed fixed overhead due to a change in production volume. When marginal costing is in use there is no overhead volume variance, because marginal costing does not absorb fixed overhead.

3.13.2 The fixed overhead expenditure variance

This is the only variance for fixed overhead in a marginal costing system. It is calculated in exactly the same way as in an absorption costing system.

3.13.3 The sales volume contribution variance

The sales volume contribution variance calculates the standard contribution gained or lost as a result of an increase or decrease in sales volume.

In the previous example the standard contribution per unit is £58.

	£ per unit
Standard selling price	120
Standard variable cost	62
Standard contribution	58

The sales volume contribution variance in a marginal costing system is calculated as follows:

	Units	
Budgeted sales volume	2,000	
Actual sales volume	1,750	
Sales volume variance	250	Adverse
× standard contribution per unit (£58)		
Sales volume contribution variance	£14,500	Adverse

3.13.4 Reconciling the actual and budget profit

The marginal costing variances can now be put together in a reconciliation statement. You should spend some time studying the statement which follows, noting the difference between this statement and the one prepared using absorption costing. Think carefully about the reasons for the differences and ensure that you understand each figure in the statement. The format of the statement is not prescriptive but it is a useful layout because it focuses the reader's attention on the contribution for the period.

Profit reconciliation statement for May: standard marginal costing

		£	£
Original budgeted contribution: 2,000 units × £58			116,000
Sales volume variance			(14,500)
Standard contribution from actual sales			101,500
Selling price variance			8,750
			110,250
Variable cost variances			
Direct material:	Price	(1,954)	
	Usage	(580)	
			(2,534)
Direct labour:	Rate	4,361	
	Efficiency	168	
			4,529
Variable overhead:	Expenditure	(8,772)	
	Efficiency	56	
			(8,666)
Acutal contribution			103,579
Fixed production overhead			
Budget		(40,000)	
Expenditure variance		2,590	
			(37,410)
Actual gross profit			66,169

Note: variances in brackets are adverse.

3.14 Idle time variances

You may come across a situation where idle time has occurred. Idle time is defined by CIMA as follows.

 Idle time: The period for which a workstation is available for production but is not used due to, e.g., shortage of tooling, material or operators.

During idle time, direct labour wages are being paid but no output is being produced. The cost of this can be highlighted separately in an idle time variance, so that it is not 'hidden' in an adverse labour efficiency variance. In this way, management attention can be directed towards the cost of idle time.

Variable production overhead variances can also be affected by idle time. It is usually assumed that variable production overhead expenditure is incurred in active hours only – for example, only when the machines are actually running, incurring power costs and so on – therefore variable overhead expenditure is not being incurred during idle hours. The variable production overhead efficiency variance is affected in the same way as the labour efficiency variance.

Example

To demonstrate this, suppose that in the previous exercise you were given the following additional information about the actual results recorded during May.

Of the 8,722 hours of direct labour paid for, 500 hours were idle because of a shortage of material supplies.

An idle time variance could be calculated as follows:

Idle hours × standard labour rate per hour
= 500 = £6
= £3,000 adverse

This is the standard cost of wages incurred during the idle time.

These idle hours must be eliminated from the calculation of the labour efficiency variance, so that the efficiency of labour is being measured only during the hours when they were actually working. This gives a much more meaningful measure of labour efficiency.

Direct labour efficiency variance

	Hours	
1,750 units produced should have taken (× 5 hours)	8,750	
But did take (active hours)	8,222	
Variance	528	Favourable
× standard labour rate per hour (£6)		
Direct labour efficiency variance	£3,168	Favourable

The total of these two variances is the same as the original labour efficiency variance (£168 favourable). The effect on the variable production overhead variances would be as follows:

Variable overhead expenditure variance

	£	
8,222 active hours of variable overhead should cost (× £2)	16,444	
But did cost	26,166	
Variable overhead expenditure variance	9,722	Adverse

Variable production overhead efficiency variance

	Hours	
1,750 units produced should have taken (× 5 hours)	8,750	
But did take (active hours)	8,222	
Variance	528	Favourable
× standard variable overhead rate per hour (£2)		
Variable overhead efficiency variance	£1,056	Favourable

The total of £8,666 adverse for the two variable production overhead variances is not affected by the idle time (you should check this for yourself). However, we have now measured efficiency during active hours only, and we have allowed expenditure only for active hours.

3.14.1 Expected idle time

Some organisations may experience idle time on a regular basis. For example, if demand is seasonal or irregular, but the organisation wishes to maintain and pay a constant number of workers, they will experience a certain level of 'expected' or 'normal' idle time during less busy periods.

In this situation the standard labour rate may include an allowance for the cost of the expected idle time. Only the impact of any unexpected or abnormal idle time would be included in the idle time variance.

Example

IT plc experiences seasonal demand for its product. During the next period the company expects that there will be an average level of idle time equivalent to 20% of hours paid. This is incorporated into the company's standard labour rate, which is £9 per hour before the adjustment for idle time payments.

The standard time to produce one unit of output is 3 active (productive) hours.

Actual results for the period were as follows:

Number of units produced	3,263
Actual hours paid for	14,000
Actual active (productive hours)	10,304

Requirement

Calculate the following variances for the period:

(i) the idle time variance;
(ii) the labour efficiency variance.

Solution

The basic standard rate per hour must be increased to allow for the impact of the idle time:

$$\text{Standard rate per hour worked} = \frac{£9.00}{0.8} = £11.25$$

The variances can now be evaluated at this increased hourly rate.

Idle time variance

		Hours
Expected idle time = 20% × 14,000 hours paid		= 2,800
Actual idle time = 14,000 − 10,304 hours		= 3,696
		896
× standard rate per hour worked (£11.25)		
Idle time variance	£10,080	Adverse

Labour efficiency variance

	Hours	
3,263 units should have taken (×3)	9,789	
But did take (productive hours)	10,304	
Variance	515	Adverse
× standard rate per hour worked (£11.25)		
Labour efficiency variance (to the nearest £)	£5,794	Adverse

3.15 Calculating actual data from standard cost details and variances

An excellent way of testing whether you really understand the reasons for and the calculation of operating variances is to 'work backwards' from standard cost data and variances to arrive at the actual results.

Try the following example for yourself before looking at the solution. If you have difficulty in solving it, then you should go back and reread this chapter to obtain a better understanding of variance analysis.

 Exercise

Q Limited operates a system of standard costing and in respect of one of its products, which is manufactured within a single cost centre, the following information is given.

For one unit of product the standard material input is 16 litres at a standard price of £2.50 per litre. The standard wage rate is £5 per hour and 6 hours are allowed to produce one unit. Fixed production overhead is absorbed at the rate of 120% of direct wages cost. During the last 4 weeks accounting period the following occurred.

- The material price variance was extracted on purchase and the actual price paid was £2.45 per litre.
- Total direct wages cost was £121,500.
- Fixed production overhead incurred was £150,000.
- Variances included:

	Favourable £	Adverse £
Direct material price	8,000	
Direct material usage		6,000
Direct labour rate		4,500
Direct labour efficiency	3,600	
Fixed production overhead expenditure		6,000

Calculate the following for the 4-week period:

(a) budgeted output in units;
(b) number of litres purchased;
(c) number of litres used above standard allowed;
(d) actual units produced;
(e) actual hours worked;
(f) average actual wage rate per hour.

Solution

The best thing to do as a first step is to pull together all of the standard cost information to calculate a standard cost per unit.

	£
Direct material: 16 litres × £2.50 per litre	40
Direct labour: 6 hours × £5 per hour	30
Fixed production overhead: £30 × 120%	36
Total	106

Calculating the required figures is now just a series of exercises in logic. These exercises can seem difficult to the novice – but the logic becomes simple and obvious with familiarity.

(a) If actual fixed production overhead was £150,000 and the fixed production overhead expenditure variance was £6,000 adverse, then it follows that the budget fixed overhead was £144,000. From this it follows that the budget must have been 4,000 units (that is, £144,000 budgeted overhead/£36 standard overhead per unit).

(b) If the standard material purchase price was £2.50 per litre and the actual purchase price was £2.45, then it follows that the material price variance is £0.05 per litre favourable. We are told that the material price variance was £8,000 favourable, so it follows that 160,000 litres must have been purchased (that is, £8,000 price variance/£0.05 price variance per litre).

(c) If the direct material usage variance was £6,000 adverse and the standard price of materials is £2.50 per litre, then it follows that the number of litres used above the standard allowance is 2,400 (£6000/£2.50/litre).

(d) If the actual direct wages paid was £121,500 and labour cost variances totalling £900 adverse (£4,500 adverse rate plus £3,600 favourable efficiency) were experienced, then the standard wages for the output achieved was £120,600. It follows that the units produced were 4,020 (that is, £120,600 standard labour cost/£30 standard labour cost per unit).

(e) The total hours actually worked is 24,120 standard hours worked (that is, 4,020 units produced × 6 standard hours per unit) minus the 720-hour favourable labour efficiency variance (that is, £3,600 efficiency variance/£5 standard rate per hour). This gives a total of 23,400 actual hours worked.

(f) If the actual wages paid was £121,500 and the actual hours worked was 23,400, then it follows that the actual wage rate per hour was £5.1923.

3.16 Example: Preparing a reconciliation statement

By way of illustration and revision, a report reconciling budgeted and actual profit via variance analysis will be prepared from the data below.

Kenden Limited is a small company producing a single product, the 'flixten'. Flixtens have the following production specifications:

Component	Standard quantity	Standard unit price £
FLIX	15	75
TEN	10	75

The standard direct labour hours to produce a flixten are 75; the standard wage rate is £10.50 per hour.

The fixed production overhead budget for the year is divided into calendar months, on the basis of equal production per month. The fixed overheads are £645,750 for the budgeted output of 2,460 flixtens for the year. The budgeted variable overhead, absorbed on the basis of labour hours, is £184,500 for the year.

The above data has been used to arrive at a standard cost for a flixten of £3,000, as shown below:

Flixten standard product cost

	£
Direct materials:	
FLIX (15 × £75)	1,125.0
TEN (10 × £75)	750.0
	1,875.0
Direct labour: (75 hours at £10.50 per hour)	787.5
Variable production overheads:	
75 hours per unit × £1 per direct labour hour*	75.0
Fixed production overheads: (£645,750/2,460 units)	262.5
Standard product cost	3,000.0

The budgeted sales of flixtens for March were 205 units at a standard selling price of £3,500 each, giving a £500 gross profit per unit and a budgeted profit for the month as follows:

*£184,500/(2,460 units × 75 hours per unit) = £1 per direct labour hour

	£	£
Sales		717,500
Cost of sales		
Direct materials	384,375.0	
Direct labour	161,437.5	
	545,812.5	
Variable production overheads	15,375.0	
Fixed production overheads	53,812.5	
		(615,000)
Gross profit (205 units × £500)		102,500
Administration expenses		(13,000)
Selling and distribution expenses		(21,000)
Net profit		68,500

Information relating to Kenden's actual costs and revenues for the month of March is shown below:

	£	£
Sales		612,000
Cost of sales		
Direct materials	342,864	
Direct labour	140,400	
	483,264	
Variable production overheads	14,000	
Fixed production overheads	53,250	
		(550,514)
Gross profit		61,486
Administration expenses		(13,938)
Selling and distribution expenses		(21,613)
Net profit		25,935

Despite the budgeted sales figure of 205 units, actual sales of flixtens in March were only 180 units, at a selling price of £3,400 each.

The company operates a JIT system (explored later in this text), so that there are no components or finished goods stocks. Works in progress is negligible.

The actual direct material cost represents the use of 2,850 FLIXs, which had been acquired at a cost of £199,500, and 1,838 TENs, which had been acquired at a cost of £143,364.

The actual number of direct labour hours worked in March was 14,625, considerably lower than the production manager had budgeted.

3.16.1 Reconciliation of budgeted and actual profit

From the standard cost information given above, you should have noted that the company employs absorption costing, and the variances appropriate to that particular system are used in the analysis. Adverse variances are shown in brackets, where appropriate.

	£	£
Budgeted gross profit		
205 units × £500 gross profit per unit		102,500
Sales variances		
Sales price variance 181 × (£3,400 – £3,500)	(18,100)	
Sales volume variance		
(205 − 180) × (£3,500 − £3,000)	(12,500)	
		(30,600)
Standard gross profit on actual sales		72,900

	Favourable £	Adverse £	
Cost variances			
Materials usage			
FLIX		11,250.0	
TEN		2,850.0	
Material price			
FLIX	14,250.0		
TEN		5,514.0	
Direct wage rate	13,162.5		
Labour efficiency		11,812.5	
Variable production overhead efficiency		1,125.0	
Variable production overhead expenditure	625.0		
Fixed production overhead expenditure	562.5		
Fixed production overhead volume		6,562.5	
	28,600.0	39,114.0	(10,514)
Actual gross profit			61,486
Budgeted administration and selling costs (total cost)			(34,000)
Administrative cost variance			(938)
Selling and distribution cost variance (marketing)			(613)
Actual net profit			25,935

As you are aware, cost variances involve a comparison of the standard cost of production with the actual cost of production. In this example, as the company does not hold stocks of finished goods or work in progress, the actual units *produced* are equal to the actual units *sold*. The total cost variance of £10,514(A) in the above reconciliation can be reconciled in turn as follows:

	£
Standard cost of production: 180 × £3,00	540,000
Actual cost of production	550,514
Total cost variance	(10,514)

It is assumed that users of this text will be familiar with the calculation of all the summary variances listed in the reconciliation above. However, for purposes of revision, details of these calculations are provided below. Confident readers may omit this section!

3.16.2 Calculation of cost variances shown in reconciliation above

Hitherto, we have explained the individual variances using a narrative logic. You may have noticed that the definitions of the variances taken from Chapter 6 of CIMA's *Official Terminology* use a rather more sparse algebraic logic. You may find it best to use either of these approaches or a mix of the two for your own working purposes – it all depends on how your mind works. The notes below tend to follow an algebraic reasoning but in appropriate cases a narrative explanation is also given.

Material variances:
Direct material usage variances: (standard quantity − actual quantity) × standard price
FLIX: ((180 × 15) − 2,850) × £75   £11,250(A)
TEN: ((180 × 10) − 1,838) × £75   £2,850(A)

Direct material price variances: (standard price – actual price) × actual quantity
FLIX: (£75 × 2,850) − £199,500   £14,250(F)
TEN: (£75 × 1,838) − £143,364   £5,514(A)

FLIXs used cost £199,500 (given). At standard price, FLIXs used should have cost £213,750 (that is, 2,850 FLIXs × £75). The FLIX material price variance is £14,250 favourable (i.e. £213,750 minus £199,500). Exactly the same reasoning can be applied to usage of TENs.

Labour variances:
Labour efficiency variance (standard hours – actual hours) × standard rate
(180 × 75 hours – 14,625 hours) × £10.50 £11,812.5(A)

Output of 180 units involves a standard labour requirement of 13,500 hours (180 units × 75 hours per unit), whereas 14,625 hours were used. The labour efficiency variance is therefore 1,125 hours, which has a cost of £11,812.50 adverse (that is 1,125 hours × £10.50).

Wage rate variance: (standard rate − actual rate) × actual hours
(£10.50 × 14,625) − £140,400 £13,162.5(F)

Production overhead variances:

From standard cost sheet, variable overhead absorption rate is £1 per direct labour hour

Variable production overhead efficiency variance: (standard – actual labour hours) × variable production overhead absorption rate

1,125 (see labour efficiency variance above) × £1   £1,125(A)

Variable production overhead expenditure variance: budgeted variable production overhead for actual hours worked – actual variable overhead incurred

14,625 × £1 – £14,000   £625(F)

Fixed production overhead expenditure: budgeted fixed production overhead – actual fixed production overhead £53,812.5 – £53,250   £562.5(F)

Fixed production overhead volume : (actual – budgeted units output) × absorption rate per unit – (180 – 205) × £262.5 = £6,562.5 (A)

3.17   Variance analysis and ABC

An ABC approach to the analysis of overhead costs is possible. This follows the ABC logic that all overheads are variable if one understands what they vary with. Let us illustrate the approach with a simple example.

Example

ABC Ltd produces the Unit and all overheads are associated with the delivery of Units to its customers. Budget details for the period include £8,000 overheads, 4,000 Units output and 40 customer deliveries. Actual results for the period are £7,800 overheads, 4,200 units output and 38 customer deliveries.

The overhead cost variance for the period is

Actual cost	£	7,800
Standard cost		8,400 (4,200 Units at £2 per Unit standard cost)
Cost variance		600 Fav

Applying the traditional fixed overhead cost variance analysis gives the following result:

Volume variance	£	400 Fav (£8,400 standard cost – £8,000 budget cost)
Expenditure variance		200 Fav (£8,000 budget cost – £7,800 actual)
Cost variance		600 Fav

Adopting an ABC approach gives the following result:

Activity variance	£	800 Fav ((42 standard – 38 actual deliveries) × £200)
Expenditure variance		200 Adv ((38 deliveries × £200) – £7,800)
Cost variance		600 Fav

The ABC approach is based on an assumption that the overheads are essentially variable (but variable with the delivery numbers and not the Units output). The ABC cost variances are based on a standard delivery size of 100 Units and a standard cost per delivery of £200. Both of these figures are derived from the budget. The activity variance reports the cost impact of undertaking more or less activities than standard, and the expenditure variance reports the cost impact of paying more or less than standard for the actual activities undertaken.

3.18 Variance analysis and throughput accounting

Throughput accounting has been introduced earlier in the context of accounting systems. It should be noted that throughput accounting is not a system of cost accounting or costing, since it is not directly concerned with the attribution of costs to products.

'TA is used to answer 3 basic questions: What is the impact of the decision on throughput? What is the impact of the decision on inventory? What is the impact of the decision on operating expenses? To answer these questions, no cost need be allocated to products.'

– Thomas Corbett, Journal of Cost Management, Jan/Feb 2000

However, it is possible to construct a profit statement with supporting variance figures using throughput accounting principles. The following example is adapted from a 1999 article appearing in Management Accounting titled 'Theory of constraints: it doesn't mean goodbye to variances' by Coate and Frey.

Example

A business produces two products, the A and the B, details as follows:

Per unit £	Selling price	Materials	Throughput
A	925	250	675
B	1,600	400	1,200

Other costs (all assumed fixed under throughput accounting) are:

Overheads £	
Machine	10,500
Labour	9,000
Expenses	7,000

The production of 30 units of A and 10 of B is budgeted with labour hours as the main constraint. One A requires 5 machine hours and 10 labour hours. One B requires 20 machine hours and 15 labour hours. A throughput accounting budget profit statement would be:

	£
Throughput:	
A	20,250
B	12,000
Total	32,250
Operating costs	
Machine	10,500
Labour	9,000
Expenses	7,000
Total	26,500
Profit	5,750

It is possible to attribute the machine and labour operating costs to products A and B using labour and machine hours respectively. This gives the following product standard costs and profits:

Products £	A	B
Materials	250	400
Machine	150	600
Labour	200	300
Total	600	1300
Selling price	925	1600
Profit	325	300

(specimen calculation: the budget labour hour rate is £9,000/450 hours = £20; it follows that the standard labour cost of A is 10 hours @ £20 = £200)

Let us say that, during the period budgeted for, an extra £1,500 labour cost was incurred in order to expand labour capacity so as to increase the output of A by 5 units. In the absence of any other departure from budget this event would give an actual profit of £7,625. That is the £5,750 budget profit plus £3,375 extra throughput contribution (5A × £675) less £1,500 extra labour costs. Using throughput accounting treatments (assuming all costs other than materials are fixed), a variance analysis report for the period appears as follows:

	£		Workings
Budget profit	5,750		
Sales volume var	1,625	fav	5A × £325
	–		
Labour expenditure var	1,500	adv	
Labour volume var	1,000	fav	5A × £200
Machine volume var	750	fav	5A × £150
Actual profit	7,625		

It might be argued that this statement offers particular insights into what has happened during the period. Labour costs have increased above those budgeted for but these extra costs were incurred in order to expand capacity in the bottleneck resource. The net labour cost impact (£500 adverse) has been more than offset by other effects.

3.19 Summary

In this chapter we have explored the means by which performance can be measured by comparison of actual results with the standards used to compile the budget. The technique known as variance analysis involves systematic reconciliation of the budget and actual profit for a given period through calculation of specific cost and sales variances. The concept is that a study of variances allows the manager to identify problems or opportunities on the 'principle of exception' basis.

At the core of this concept is the idea that where there is no exception, there is no problem or opportunity. Some observers consider that this idea may lack substance in the modern economic environment – a proposition that we will consider further as we progress through this text.

Self-test quiz

(1) Distinguish between an 'ideal standard', an 'attainable standard' and a 'basic standard' (Section 3.4).

(2) Explain the term 'cost variance' (Section 3.8).

(3) Explain the manner in which a labour cost variance is split into rate and efficiency component variances (Section 3.9.3).

(4) Explain the term 'variable overhead efficiency variance' (Section 3.9.4).

(5) Explain the manner in which a fixed overhead cost variance is split into expenditure and volume component variances (Section 3.10).

(6) Explain the term 'sales volume variance' (Section 3.11.2).

(7) What are the main differences between variance analyses carried out using (a) absorption costing and (b) marginal costing principles (Section 3.13).

(8) Explain the terms 'idle time' and 'idle time variance' (Section 3.14).

(9) What are the main criticisms of standard costing (Section 3.7).

(10) What factors help to make a standard cost 'meaningful' (Sections 3.6 and 3.10).

Revision Questions

3

? Question 1

The following data is to be used to answer questions 1.1 and 1.2 below.　　　　**(2 marks)**

SD plc is a new company. The following information relates to its first period:

	Budget	*Actual*
Production (units)	8,000	9,400
Sales (units)	8,000	7,100
Break-even point (units)	2,000	
Selling price per unit	£125	£125
Fixed costs	£100,000	£105,000

The actual unit variable cost was £12 less than budgeted because of efficient purchasing.

1.1 If SD plc had used standard absorption costing, the fixed overhead volume variance would have been

(A) £15,638(F)
(B) £17,500(F)
(C) £25,691(F)
(D) £28,750(F)

1.2 If SD plc had used marginal costing, valuing finished goods stock at actual cost, the profit for the period would have been nearest to

(A) £335,200
(B) £337,600
(C) £340,200
(D) £450,400

(3 marks)

The following data is to be used to answer questions 1.3 and 1.4 below.

W plc uses a standard absorption costing system. The absorption rate is based on labour hours. The following data relates to April 2003:

	Budget	*Actual*
Labour hours worked	10,000	11,135
Units produced	10,000	10,960
Variable overhead cost	£45,000	£46,200

1.3 The variable overhead expenditure variance to be reported for April 2003 is nearest to

(A) £40 (adv)
(B) £40 (fav)
(C) £3,907 (adv)
(D) £3,907 (fav)

1.4 The variable overhead efficiency variance to be reported for April 2003 is nearest to

(A) £710 (A)
(B) £730 (A)
(C) £740 (A)
(D) £790 (A)

1.5 A passenger transport company has developed the following formula to forecast the fuel cost to be included in its monthly budget:

$$Y = 10M - 0.4P + 5,000$$

where Y is the total fuel cost ($) per month,
         M is the number of miles travelled per month,
         P is the number of passengers carried per month.

The budgeted and actual miles travelled and passengers carried for April were as follows:

	Budget	Actual
Miles traveled	10,000	9,450
Passengers	6,000	6,050

The actual total cost of the fuel for April was $99,035.
The total fuel cost variance to be reported for April is

(A) $3,565 (F)
(B) $1,955 (F)
(C) $1,955 (A)
(D) $3,565 (A)

❓ Question 2

Details of the manufacturing operation of Drudge Ltd for the current period are:

	Budget total	Standard per unit	Actual total
Units	500		520
Labour hours	1,000	2.0	1,200
Material (kg)	750	1.5	740
£			
Wages	5,000	10.00	5,100
Purchases	1,500	3.00	1,550
Variable o/h	250	0.50	300
Fixed o/h	4,000	8.00	3,800
Total	10,750	21.50	10,750

Requirement

(a) Reconcile standard and actual cost for the output achieved by calculating cost variances.

You are now told that the unit selling price was £25 (budget) and £24 (actual).

(10 marks)

Requirement

(b) Reconcile budget and actual profit by calculating sales variances. **(10 marks)**

 Question 3

A local restaurant has been examining the profitability of its set menu. At the beginning of the year the selling price was based on the following predicted costs:

		£
Starter	*Soup of the day*	
	100 g of mushrooms @ £3.00 per kg	0.30
	Cream and other ingredients	0.20
Main course	*Roast beef*	
	Beef 0.10 kg @ £15.00 per kg	1.50
	Potatoes 0.2 kg @ £0.25 per kg	0.05
	Vegetables 0.3 kg @ £0.90 per kg	0.27
	Other ingredients and accompaniments	0.23
Dessert	*Fresh tropical fruit salad*	
	Fresh fruit 0.15 kg @ £3.00 per kg	0.45

The selling price was set at £7.50, which produced an overall gross profit of 60%.

During October 20X8 the number of set menus sold was 860 instead of the 750 budgeted: this increase was achieved by reducing the selling price to £7.00. During the same period an analysis of the direct costs incurred showed:

	£
90 kg of mushrooms	300
Cream and other ingredients	160
70 kg of beef	1,148
180 kg of potatoes	40
270 kg of vegetables	250
other ingredients and accompaniments	200
140 kg of fresh fruit	450

There was no stock of ingredients at the beginning or end of the month.

Requirements

(a) Calculate the budgeted profit for the month of October 20X8. **(2 marks)**
(b) Calculate the actual profit for the month of October 20X8. **(3 marks)**
(c) Prepare a statement that reconciles your answers to (a) and (b) above, showing the variances in as much detail as possible. **(14 marks)**
(d) Prepare a report, addressed to the restaurant manager, that identifies and discusses the two most significant variances. **(6 marks)**

(Total marks = 25)

Question 4

The following profit reconciliation statement summarises the performance of one of SEW's products for March 20X7.

			£	
Budgeted profit			4,250	
Sales volume profit variance			850	(A)
Standard profit on actual sales			3,400	
Selling price variance			4,000	(A)
			(600)	
Cost variances	*Adverse*	*Favourable*		
	£	£		
Direct material price		1,000		
Direct material usage	150			
Direct labour rate	200			
Direct labour efficiency	150			
Variable overhead expenditure	600			
Variable overhead efficiency	75			
Fixed overhead expenditure		2,500		
Fixed overhead volume		150		
	1,175	3,650	2,475	(F)
Actual profit			1,875	

The budget for the same period contained the following data:

Sales volume	1,500	units
Sales revenue	£20,000	
Production volume	1,500	units
Direct materials purchased	750	kg
Direct material used	750	kg
Direct material cost	£4,500	
Direct labour hours	1,125	
Direct labour cost	£4,500	
Variable overhead cost	£2,250	
Fixed overhead cost	£4,500	

Additional information
- Stocks of raw materials and finished goods are valued at standard cost.
- During the month the actual number of units produced was 1,550.
- The actual sales revenue was £12,000.
- The direct materials purchased were 1,000 kg.

Requirements
(a) Calculate
 (i) the actual sales volume;
 (ii) the actual quantity of materials used;
 (iii) the actual direct material cost;
 (iv) the actual direct labour hours;
 (v) the actual direct labour cost;
 (vi) the actual variable overhead cost;
 (vii) the actual fixed overhead cost. **(19 marks)**

(b) Discuss the nature of the direct materials usage variance, direct labour rate variance and sales volume variance.

(6 marks)

(Total marks = 25)

? **Question 5**

The following details have been extracted from the standard cost card for product X:

	£/unit
Variable overhead	
4 machine hours @ £8.00/hour	32.00
2 labour hours @ £4.00/hour	8.00
Fixed overhead	20.00

During October 20X7, 5,450 units of the product were made compared with a budgeted production target of 5,500 units. The actual overhead costs incurred were:

	£
Machine-related variable overhead	176,000
Labour-related variable overhead	42,000
Fixed overhead	109,000

The actual number of machine hours was 22,000 and the actual number of labour hours was 10,800.

Requirements

(a) Calculate the overhead cost variances in as much detail as possible from the data provided.

(12 marks)

(b) Explain the meaning of, and discuss the variable overhead variances that you have calculated.

(8 marks)

(c) Explain the benefits of using multiple activity bases for variable overhead absorption.

(5 marks)

(Total marks = 25)

? **Question 6**

QBD plc produces souvenirs for international airline operators. The company uses a standard absorption costing system. The standard cost card for one of QBD plc's souvenirs is as follows:

		$
Materials	1.5 kg	6.00
Labour	1.6 hours	8.00
Overheads		
Variable	1.6 hours	4.00
Fixed	1.6 hours	12.00
Total cost		30.00
Selling price		40.00

Production and sales information for April:

	Budget	Actual
Production	5,000 units	6,000 units
Sales	5,000 units	4,300 units
Sales revenue	$200,000	$164,800

The resources used and actual costs for April were as follows:

		$
Materials	10,300 kg	38,720
Labour	11,420 hours	71,200
Overhead		
Variable		29,650
Fixed		83,300

The 11,420 labour hours include 2,270 hours of idle time. This was caused by an unexpected machine breakdown.

All of the materials purchased were used during the month.

Requirements

(a) Calculate the budgeted profit/loss for April.   **(2 marks)**

(b) Calculate the actual profit/loss for April.   **(6 marks)**

(c) Prepare a statement that reconciles the budgeted and actual profits/losses for April 2004 in as much detail as is possible.   **(15 marks)**

(d) Calculate the actual profit/loss that would be reported by QBD plc if it used marginal costing.   **(2 marks)**

(e) Explain with relevant calculations how the reconciliation statement that you prepared would have been different if QBD plc used standard marginal costing instead of standard absorption costing.   **(5 marks)**

(Total = 30 marks)

? Question 7

The basic principles of standard costing and variance analysis may be adapted to the requirements of relatively new methods of accounting such as activity-based costing and throughput accounting.

Requirements

(a) Explain the core concept behind Activity-based costing insofar as it relates to variance analysis and discuss the manner in which variance analysis must be adapted when in ABC mode.   **(5 marks)**

(b) Explain the core concept behind Throughput Accounting insofar as it relates to variance analysis and discuss the manner in which variance analysis must be adapted when in TA mode.   **(5 marks)**

Solutions to
Revision Questions

3

☑ Solution 1

1.1

Budgeted fixed cost	£100,000
Budgeted production	8,000 units
Absorption rate	$\dfrac{£100,000}{8,000\ units} = £12.50/unit$
Volume variance	$1,400 \times £12.50 = £17,500$ (F)

Therefore the answer is (B).

1.2

Budgeted fixed costs = budgeted contribution to breakeven = £100,000		
Budgeted breakeven sales volume =		2,000 units
Budgeted contribution/unit = $\dfrac{£100,000}{2,000}$ =		£50
Budgeted selling price	=	£125/unit
So budgeted variable cost	=	£75/unit
So actual variable cost	= £75 − £12 =	£63/unit
So actual contribution/unit	= £125 − £63 =	£62
So actual contribution	= 7,100 × £62 =	£440,200
Less: Actual fixed costs		£105,000
Profit		£335,200

Therefore the answer is (A).

1.3

The expenditure variance is (11,135 hours × £4.50) − £46,200 = £3,907.50 fav

Therefore the answer is (D).

1.4

The efficiency variance is ((10,960 units × 1 hr) − 11,135 hrs) × £4.50 = £787.50

Therefore the answer is (D).

1.5

Standard cost		$	$
9,450 miles × 10		94,500	
6,050 passengers × 0.4		2,420	92,080
Fixed cost			5,000
Total			97,080
Actual cost			99,035
Total variance			1,955 (A)

Therefore the answer is (C).

☑ Solution 2

(a)

Standard cost	520 units @£21.50	11,180	
Labour rate variance	£0.75 × 1,200 hours	−900	fav
Labour efficiency variance	160 hours × £5	800	adv
Materials price variance	£.0945 × 740 kg	70	adv
Materials usage variance	40 kg × £2	−80	fav
Variable overheads variance	£260 − £300	40	
Fixed overheads volume variance	20 Units × £8	−160	fav
Fixed overheads expenditure variance	£3,800 − £4,000	−200	fav
Actual cost		10,750	

(b)

Budget profit	500 Units × £3.50	1,750	
Sales volume profit variance	20 Units × £3.50	70	fav
Standard profit on actual sales	520 Units × £3.50	1,820	
Selling price variance	520 Units × £1	−520	adv
Cost variances (see (a) above)	£11,180 − £10,750	430	fav
Actual profit	(520 Units × £24) − £10,750	1,730	

☑ Solution 3

- Work methodically through the exercise, calculating each variance item in turn.
- Note that most of the cost variances are calculated by reconciling standard cost with actual cost – not budget cost to actual cost.
- Note that the question invites you to identify which the most significant variances are – using whatever criteria you consider most appropriate.

(a) Budgeted unit cost is £3.00. Therefore the budgeted profit for October 20X8 is

$$(750 \times (7.50 - 3.00)) = £3,375.$$

(b) The actual profit for October 20X8 is

$$(860 \times £7) - £2,548 \text{ actual costs} = £3,472.$$

(c)

	£	
Budgeted profit	3,375	
Sales volume variance (W1)	495	(F)
Budgeted profit on actual sales	3,870	
Sales price variance (W2)	430	(A)
	3,440	

Ingredients	Price £		Usage £		
Mushrooms	30	(A)	12	(A)	(42)
Cream etc	n/a	–	n/a	–	12
Beef	98	(A)	240	(F)	142
Potatoes	5	(F)	2	(A)	3
Vegetables	7	(A)	11	(A)	(18)
Other	n/a	–	n/a	–	(2)
Fresh fruit	30	(A)	33	(A)	(63)
Actual profit					3,472

Workings

1. Sales volume variance = 110 extra menus sold × £4.50 unit contribution = £495(F).
2. Sales price variance = £(7.00 − 7.50) × 860 menus = £430(A).
3. Mushroom price = £(3.00 − 3.33) × 90 kg = £30(A).
4. Mushroom usage = ((860 × 0.1 kg) − 90 kg) × £3 = £12(A).
5. Beef price = £(15.00 − 16.40) × 70 kg = £98(A).
6. Beef usage = ((860 × 0.1 kg) − 70 kg) × £15 = £240(F).
7. Potatoes price = £(0.25 − 0.22) × 180 kg = £5(F).
8. Potatoes usage = ((860 × 0.2 kg) − 180 kg) × 0.25 = £2(A).
9. Vegetables price = £(0.90 − 0.925) × 270 kg = £7(A).
10. Vegetables usage = ((860 × 0.3 kg) − 270 kg) × £0.90 = £11(A).
11. Fresh fruit price = £(3.00 − 3.21) × 140 kg = £30(A).
12. Fresh fruit usage = ((860 × 0.15 kg) − 140 kg) × £3 = £33(A).

 These workings are in short summary form. As you progress through your studies you should become comfortable with this form.

(d) Report

To:	Restaurant manager
Date:	25 November 20X8
From:	Management accountant
Ref:	RM99/25

Food variance report – October 20X8

- Sales volume variance (£495 favourable). There was an increase of 110 set menus over budget caused by an overall increase in the demand for meals within this restaurant. In isolation from any other factors this increase adds £495 to profit.
- Sales price variance (£430 adverse). Management has reduced prices in order to combat competition and to attract more business. The impact of this is considered to be £430.

Note that the above figures follow a conventional variance analysis model. The impact of the price change is applied to all the unit sales in order to calculate the price variance while the impact of the volume change is valued at the original selling price.

Signed: Management accountant

Solution 4

- The question invites you to work backwards from the variance items to the source figures used to calculate them. The student whose study of variance analysis has consisted of merely memorising formulae will find this exercise difficult. The student who understands the logic of variance analysis will find it much easier.
- Note that requirement (b) does not follow on from requirement (a). An imperfect answer to requirement (a) need not prevent an examinee from obtaining full marks for requirement (b).

(a) The first step is to present the given budgeted information in a more usable form.

Budgeted information

	£	£
Sales		20,000
Material: 750 kg @ £6/kg	4,500	
Labour: 1,125 hours @ £4/hour	4,500	
Variable overhead	2,250	
Fixed overhead	4,500	
		15,750
Profit		4,250

Standard cost per units

	£
Materials − 0.5 kg × £6/kg	3.00
Labour − 0.75 hour £4/hour	3.00
Variable overhead − 0.75 hour × £2/hour	1.50
Fixed overhead − £3/unit	3.00
Total	10.50

(i) The budget profit is £4,250 (that is, £20,000 sales less £15,750 costs) giving a standard profit per unit of £2.8333 (that is, £4,250/1,500 units). If the sales volume variance is £850 adverse, then it follows that unit sales must have been 300 less than budget (that is, £850/£2.8333). Hence, the actual sales volume was 1,200 units.

(ii) The material usage variance is £150 adverse and this corresponds to 25 kg usage above standard. Standard usage was 775 kg (that is, 1,550 units produced × 0.5 kg per unit) and it follows that actual usage was 800 kg.

(iii) The material price variance is £1 per kg favourable (that is £1,000 material price variance/1,000 kg purchased). It follows that the actual purchase price must have been £5 per kg (that is, £6 standard price per kg less £1 per kg variance) giving a total material cost of £5,000.

(iv) The labour efficiency variance corresponds to 37.5 hours adverse (that is, £150 variance/£4 per hour standard rate). Standard labour usage was 1,162.5 hours (that is, 1,550 units output × 0.75 hours per unit). Hence, actual labour usage was 1,200 hours.

(v) The rate variance was £0.1666 per hour adverse (that is, £200 rate variance/1,200 hours) giving an actual rate of £4.1666 per hour. It follows that the actual labour cost was £5,000 (that is, 1,200 hours × £4.1666).

(vi) The standard variable overhead cost was £2,325 (that is, 1,550 units output × £1.50 per unit). The variable overhead variances total £675 adverse, hence the actual variable overhead must be £3,000.

(vii) The actual fixed overhead cost is £2,000 (that is, £4,500 budget less £2,500 favourable expenditure variance).

(b) • The adverse direct materials usage variance is a valuation of the cost impact of materials usage in excess of that which is standard for the output achieved. By convention, the excess is valued at the standard price for the purposes of the valuation.

• The adverse direct labour rate variance arises from payment of a labour rate in excess of standard. By convention, the impact on cost of that excess is taken to be based on actual labour usage.

• The adverse sales volume variance arises from fewer unit sales having been achieved than budgeted for. Its value is calculated by multiplying the unit sales deficiency by the standard profit margin per unit.

 Solution 5

• Note that there are two sets of variable overheads each using a different overhead absorption basis. It follows that there will be two separate sets of variable overhead variances.

• Note that requirement (c) invites discussion of the principles of overhead absorption – a topic introduced in Foundation level studies.

Overhead cost variances

(a)

	£	
Variable overheads		
Machine-hour related		
Standard overhead for 22,000 machine hours	176,000	(22,000 machine hours × £8)
Actual overhead	176,000	
Variable overhead expenditure variance	–	
Standard overhead for standard machine hours	174,400	(5,450 units × 4 machine hours × £8)
Standard overhead for 22,000 machine hours	176,000	(22,000 machine hours × £8)
Variable overhead efficiency variance	1,600	Adverse
Labour-hour related		
Standard overhead for 10,800 labour hours	43,200	(10,800 labour hours × £4)
Actual overhead	42,000	
Variable overhead expenditure variance	1,200	Favourable
Standard overhead for standard labour hours	43,600	(5,450 units × 2 labour hours × £4)
Standard overhead for 10,800 labour hours	43,200	(10,800 labour hours × £4)
Variable overhead efficiency variance	400	Favourable
Fixed overheads		
Budgeted fixed overhead	110,000	(5,500 units × £20 per cent)
Actual fixed overhead	109,000	
Fixed overhead expenditure variance	1,000	Favourable
Budgeted fixed overhead	110,000	(5,500 units × £20 per unit)
Standard fixed overhead	109,000	(5,450 units × £20 per unit)
Fixed overhead volume variance	1,000	Adverse

THE THEORY AND PRACTICE OF STANDARD COSTING

(b)

Variance	Meaning	Comment
Machine-related		
Expenditure	The variable overhead costs incurred are exactly in line with those which would have been budgeted for the machine hours worked.	Nil.
Efficiency	The output from the machines is lower than would have been budgeted based on the machine hours worked, therefore less variable overhead has been absorbed.	This is the cost impact of reduced machine efficiency.
Labour-related		
Expenditure	The actual variable overhead cost incurred is lower than the standard cost allowance for the hours worked by the employees.	Rates paid to staff have been lower than the standard ones budgeted for.
Efficiency	The output produced was higher than would have been expected from the number of labour hours worked and therefore more variable overhead has been absorbed.	This suggests that employees were working faster or harder than they would be 'at standard'.

(c) The use of multiple activity bases for variable overhead absorption can have the following benefits:

- more realistic product costs may be produced, resulting in improved pricing and decision-making in general;
- management will be more aware of the link between activity and cost behaviour, and will have more incentive to focus on the relationships between these two variables;
- cost reduction activities within this area are more likely to be successful;
- it may become apparent that costs are not driven solely by output volumes, and therefore the focus of managerial attention may be significantly broadened. This may encourage managers to adopt a 'holistic' view of the organisation.

 Solution 6

(a)

Budgeted profit per unit	$10.00
Budgeted production and sales	5,000 units
Budgeted profit	$50,000

(b)

	$	$
Sales		164,800
Total costs incurred	223,370	
Closing stock:		
1,700 × $30	51,000	
Cost of sales		172,370
Actual loss		7,570

(c)

Cost variances	Adverse	Favourable	
	$	$	$
Material price		2,480	
($38,720 − (10,300 × $4))			
Material usage	5,200		
(10,300 − (6,000 × 1.5)) × $4			
Labour rate	14,100		
($71,200 − (11,420 × $5))			
Labour efficiency		2,250	
((11,420 − 2,270) − (6,000 × 1.6)) × $5			
Labour idle time	11,350		
2,270 × $5			
Variable overhead expenditure	6,775		
($29,650 − ((11,420 − 2,270) × $2.5)			
Variable overhead efficiency		1,125	
((11,420 − 2,270) − (6,000 × 1.6)) × $2.5			
Fixed overhead expenditure	23,800		
($83,800 − (5,000 × $12))			
Fixed overhead volume		12,000	
(6,000 − 5,000 units) × £12 per unit			
Totals	61,225	17,855	43,370 (A)
Actual loss			7,570

(d)

The actual loss would be greater under marginal costing due to the non absorption of fixed overhead costs into the unsold stock items.

The loss would increase by 1,700 units × $12 = $20,400 so that under marginal costing the loss would be $27,970.

(e)

There would be no change to the budgeted profit as there was no budgeted change in the level of stocks.

The sales volume variance would be valued on a contribution basis so that it increases to $15,400 Adverse (700 units × $22), an increase of $8,400 adverse.

The fixed overhead volume variance would not exist, thus removing favourable cost variances totalling $12,000.

There would be no other changes and so, by totalling the above, it can be seen that they equate to $20,400 adverse, which equals the increase in the size of the loss as per part (d) above.

☑ Solution 7

(a) Traditional management accounting proceeds on an understanding that the range of production costs have a variety of fixed and variable characteristics. Further, where costs are variable they are deemed to vary directly in relation to units output. Costs which do not vary directly with units output are generally considered fixed. The manner in which individual costs are analysed into variance components follows this understanding. A variable cost variance is split into price and efficiency components while a fixed cost variance is split into volume and expenditure components.

Activity-based costing (ABC) proceeds on the assumption that most costs are actually variable, provided one takes a long enough view of the situation and understands that costs may vary in relation to the number of activities undertaken rather than units output. Hence some costs which traditional accounting would consider fixed are considered to be variable under ABC. This alternative understanding may feed through to relevant cost elements.

For example, the variance associated with an overhead cost that might be considered 'fixed' under the traditional convention would be analysed into volume and expenditure components. The same cost variance might be analysed into activity and expenditure (in this case amounting to price) components under the ABC convention.

(b) Throughput accounting (TA) proceeds on the assumption that, in the short term, all costs other than those associated with direct materials are fixed. This concept provides a performance evaluation that offers a guide to decision-making with particular reference to the utilisation of bottleneck resources. TA is not normally associated with product costing and hence with variance analysis. However, the TA concept can be adopted for variance analysis purposes.

For example, the variance associated with a direct cost (e.g. labour) that might be considered 'variable' under the traditional convention would be analysed into efficiency and price components. The same cost variance would be considered fixed under the TA convention and would be analysed into volume and expenditure components.

Standard Costing and
Performance Evaluation

Standard Costing and Performance Evaluation

4

LEARNING OUTCOMES

After completing study of this chapter you should be able to

▶ interpret variances, distinguishing between planning and operational variances;

▶ prepare reports using a range of internal and external benchmarks and interpret the results.

4.1 Introduction

In this chapter we will explore further aspects of the practice of standard costing. In particular, we will consider more detailed analysis of particular variances, the separation of variances into operational and planning components and the preparation of performance reports for management based on standard costing.

We will also begin a general exploration of the role of standard costing in performance evaluation and consider how that role may be changing in the modern economic environment. You should become aware that the relevance of a number of traditional management accounting practices is being questioned in the era of flexible manufacturing and a service-based economy.

4.2 Material mix and yield variances

The direct material usage variance measures the change in total direct material cost brought about by using a non-standard amount of material in production. Sometimes it is possible to subdivide the usage variance into a direct material mix variance and a direct material yield variance. This subdivision is most likely to be found in process industries, where a standard input mix is the norm, and recognisable individual components of input are combined during the production process to produce an output in which the individual items are no longer separately identifiable. Paint manufacture provides a typical example: if a blue paint is required, the basic paint base will be introduced to the mixing process, along with the blue dye; at the input stage, both raw process materials are separately identifiable, but at the end of the process, blue paint emerges, with the individual components no longer separately identifiable.

In many process industries, it may be necessary from time to time to vary the input *mix* – perhaps because of shortages of raw material, or in order to take advantage of attractive input prices. Whether the input mix is a standard or a non-standard one, there is a possibility that the *outcome* from the process will differ from that which was expected. In addition to *unexpected* differences in yield, it is perfectly *normal* in some processes for the physical volume of output from the process to be less than the total volume of input, that is, there may be *unavoidable* losses inherent in the operation of an efficiently working process. In the blended whisky industry, for example, such losses arise from evaporation, and the volume of output from the process is *expected* to be less than the volume of the input. The direct material *mix* variance measures the change in cost brought about by an alteration to the *constituents* of the input mix, while the direct material *yield* variance measures the change in cost brought about by any deviation in output from the *standard* process output.

The data below will be used to calculate mix and yield variances in the subsequent examples.

Example

A company has the following standards for a mix to produce 500 kg of product C:

Input	kg	Cost/kg	Total cost of mix	
A	200	£1.00	£200	
B	400	£1.60	£640	
	600		£840	600 kg of input should produce 500 kg of C at a standard cost of £1.68/kg

In a particular period, the actual results of the process were as follows:

Actual input	kg	Actual cost/kg	Total actual cost
A	300	£1.00	£300
B	300	£1.60	£480
	600		£780

Actual output: 400 kg of C

Note that, in the above data, there is no direct material *price* variance, as the actual cost per kilogram of inputs A and B was the standard cost in each case. The *whole* of the direct material variance is thus due to changes in the *usage* thereof. The total variance is the difference between the standard cost of the *output* of 400 kg of C (400 × £1.68 = £672) and the actual cost of £780. This gives an adverse direct material usage variance of £108. This material usage variance may be split into mix and yield components.

(a) Direct material mix variance

For an input of 600 kg:

Material	Actual input kg	Standard mix of input kg	Mix variance kg	Standard price per kg £	Mix variance £
A	300	200	100 (A)	1.00	100 (A)
B	300	400	100 (F)	1.60	160 (F)
	600	600			60 (F)

The material mix variance demonstrates the cost impact of using an ingredient mix different from that which is standard. That standard mix of 600 kg input is 200 kg of A and 400 kg of B. The actual mix of the 600 kg input is 300 kg of A and 300 kg of B. In this case, ingredient A has been substituted for ingredient B in the mix – and the net cost impact of this is £60 favourable.

Material mix variance: (Actual material input × standard cost per unit) – (actual total material input in standard proportions × standard cost per unit).

The CIMA *Terminology* offers an alternative methodology for working the material mix variance.

This other methodology works the components of the mix variance on the basis of the difference between budget usage for output achieved and the difference between the standard average and the standard cost of the materials input. In this case the standard average price of the material used is £1.40 per kg (that is £840/600 kg). This may be illustrated by reworking the mix variance calculated above using the alternative methodology:

Material	(a) kg	(b) kg	(c) kg	(d) £	(e) £	(f) £	(g) £
A	300	160	140	1.40	1.00	0.40	56 (F)
B	300	320	−20	1.40	1.60	−0.20	4 (F)
						Total	60 (F)

Key:
(a) actual usage
(b) budget input for output achieved A = 200 kg/500 kg × 400 kg, B = 400 kg/500 kg × 400 kg
(c) mix variance (kg), (a) − (b)
(d) standard average price per kg
(e) standard price per kg
(f) (e) − (d)
(g) mix variance (£), (c) × (f).

The logic here is more complex but it may be argued that it gives a more rigorous analysis of the situation. We are using more of the cheap ingredient and less of the expensive ingredient. So, it might be argued, both components of the mixture variance should be favourable.

Material mix variance (*alternative methodology*): ((Actual input quantity − budget material input quantity for the output produced) × (standard weighted average cost per unit input − standard cost per input unit)).

When answering an examination question simply requiring the calculation of a mix variance, the student is advised to always use the simple method illustrated at the start of this section. However, students should be aware that alternatives do exist and that the examiner may invite the student to demonstrate familiarity with these.

(b) Direct material yield variance

Standard cost per kg of output = £840/500 = £1.68

	kg	
600 kg input should have yielded	500	of C
But did yield	400	of C
Yield variance	100	(A)
× standard cost per kg of output (£1.68)		
Yield variance	£168	(A)

The material yield variance demonstrates the cost impact of generating above or below standard output from a given quantity of input. In this case, the input of 600 kg is associated with a standard output of 500 kg, but the actual output was only 400 kg.

The yield variance is 100 kg adverse (that is, 500 kg standard output − 400 kg actual output).

The cost impact of this is £168 adverse.

Material yield variance: (Standard output for actual input − actual output) × standard cost per unit of output.

The current edition of the *Terminology* permits use of both methods and earlier editions specified use of a third method. All possible methods give the same end result. Students are often confused when they see a mix variance in a text or model answer calculated using a method they are unfamiliar with.

The sum of the direct material mix variance and the direct material yield variance can be seen to be £108 adverse, which, in the absence of a direct material price variance, is equal to the total direct material variance.

The direct material mix and yield variances must be interpreted with care, as there is a very strong interrelationship between them. If we consider the concept of a *standard* mix, it is clear that such a mix will represent the combination of inputs that provides an acceptable quality of output at the least possible cost. If some *other* combination of inputs could produce a *lower* cost output without detriment to quality, then *this* alternative would have been selected as the standard. Any change in the input mix must therefore be expected to have an impact on the *yield* from the process, as well as on the price of the input mix. It is highly unlikely that any meaningful control can be exercised over the output from a process independent of the input to it, and thus the two variances should be considered together.

4.3 Labour mix and yield variances

The same logic applied in the calculation of materials mix and yield variances can equally well be applied to labour costs. When several different classes of labour are engaged then the labour efficiency variance can be split into mix and yield components.

This is best demonstrated through study of a simple example.

Example

The standard labour input associated with the production of one unit is as follows:

- 4 hours of skilled labour at £15 per hour;
- 6 hours of unskilled labour at £10 per hour.

The standard labour cost of one unit is £120. The standard total labour input associated with production of one unit is 10 hours at an average hourly rate of £12 (that is, £120/10 hours). It can also be seen that the standard labour mix is 40% skilled and 60% unskilled.

During Period 6,

- 25 units are produced;
- 95 hours of skilled labour are used;
- 175 hours of unskilled labour are used;
- £3,267.50 wages are paid.

We are required to calculate the labour cost variance and analyse this into labour rate and labour efficiency component variances. We are then required to analyse the labour efficiency variance into labour mix and labour yield components.

Step 1 – calculation of labour cost variance
This is the difference between the standard labour cost of producing 25 units and the actual labour cost incurred.

	£
Actual labour cost incurred (given)	3,267.50
Standard labour cost of 25 units (25 × £120)	3,000.00
Labour cost variance	267.50 (A)

Step 2 – calculation of labour rate and labour efficiency variances
The labour rate variance is the difference belween (actual hours worked × standard rate) and the actual wages paid. The labour efficiency variance is (standard hours required for output achieved − actual hours worked) multiplied by the standard hourly rate.

	£
Labour rate variance	
(95 skilled hrs × £15) + (175 unskilled hrs × £10) − £3,267.50	92.50 (A)
Labour efficiency variance	
((100 standard − 95 actual skilled hrs) × £15) +	
((150 standard − 175 actual unskilled hrs) × £10)	175.00 (A)
Sum total (labour cost variance)	267.50 (A)

Step 3 – calculation of labour mix and labour yield variances

Labour mix variance
For 270 hours worked:

Grade	Actual hours	Standard mix of hours	Mix variance hours	Standard rate per hr £	Mix variance £
Skilled	95	(40%) 108	13 (F)	15	195 (F)
Unskilled	175	(60%) 162	13 (A)	10	130 (A)
	270	270			65 (F)

Labour yield variance

270 hours of work should yield (270 hr/ 10 hrs/units)	27 units	
But did yield	25 units	
Yield variance	2 units (A)	
x std cost £120 per unit		
Yield variance	£240 (A)	

Check: mix variance £65(F) + yield variance £240(A) = total efficiency variance £175(A).

The variance analysis carried out in Step 3 indicates that a cost advantage has been achieved by substituting unskilled for skilled labour in the production process. However, that advantage has been more than offset by a cost disadvantage arising from the diminished efficiency of the whole workforce.

Again, in dealing with the labour mixture variance, the *Terminology* offers an alternative methodology:

π *Labour mix variance (alternative methodology)*: ((Actual hours worked − budget hours worked for the output produced) × (standard weighted average cost per hour worked − standard cost per hour worked))

Reworking the earlier example using this alternative methodology gives the following result:

Labour	*(a)* hours	*(b)* hours	*(c)* hours	*(d)* £	*(e)* £	*(f)* £	*(g)* £
Skilled	95	100	−5	12.00	15.00	−3.00	15(F)
Unskilled	175	150	25	12.00	10.00	2.00	50(F)
						Total	65(F)

Key:

(a) actual hours
(b) budget hours for output achieved skilled = 25 units × 4 hours, unskilled = 25 units × 6 hours
(c) mix variance (hours), (a) − (b)

(d) std avg rate per hour, £120/10 hour
(e) standard rate
(f) (e) − (d)
(g) mix variance (£), (c) × (f).

The logic in this case is more complicated, but the result is the same as that given in the simple method above. Again, you are always recommended to use the simple method if the requirement is merely to calculate the labour mix variance.

It should be appreciated that the example given is set in a manufacturing environment, but the technique may be most applicable in a service or professional environment. For example, an audit operation typically makes use of several well-defined grades of staff ranging from Partner to Junior. The calculation of a labour mix variance in regard to an audit may give some powerful insights into the effectiveness with which particular jobs were run. One of the key factors that can determine the performance of a professional practice is the manner in which the work of senior/qualified staff is integrated with that of their juniors.

4.4 Sales volume variances

We have previously encountered the sales volume variance. In its simplest form, this variance is

(budget − actual sales units) × standard profit per unit

However, it is capable of being expressed in several different ways and is capable of more detailed analysis. The principal alternative ways in which the sales volume variance can be expressed are as follows:

(a)

π *Sales volume profit variance*: ((Budgeted sales units × standard gross profit per unit) − (actual sales units × standard gross profit per unit))

This is commonly used to reconcile budget and standard gross profit as part of a control report when an absorption costing system is in use (as seen in Chapter 3).

(b)

π *Sales volume contribution variance:* ((budgeted sales units × standard contribution per unit) − (actual sales units × standard contribution per unit))

This is commonly used to reconcile budget and standard contribution as part of a control report when a marginal costing system is in use.

(c)

π *Sales volume revenue variance*: ((budgeted sales units × standard selling price per unit) − (actual sales units × standard selling price per unit))

This is commonly used as a stand-alone element in a sales control report.

Example

The above three alternatives may be illustrated by the following simple example:
ABC Ltd sells the Unit. Details of Unit sales in September were as follows:

Budget – 1,200 units
Actual – 1,100 units

Standard profit per unit – £100
Standard contribution per unit – £150
Standard selling price per unit – £200.

The three alternative sales volume variances listed above are

(1) Profit – £10,000
(2) Contribution – £15,000
(3) Revenue – £20,000.

The sales volume variance (whichever version of it you are using) can be analysed into mix and quantity components using the same logic encountered in regard to materials usage and labour efficiency variances.

Example

XY Ltd sells two products, X and Y, details for the current period as follows:

	Standard mix (units)	Standard profit (£ pu)	Average profit (£ pu)
X	2	5	
Y	3	6	
Total	5	((2×5)+(3×6))/5	5.60

Budget sales – 200 units X and 300 units Y
Actual sales – 180 units X and 310 units Y

It is apparent that the sales volume profit variance for the period is £40 adverse (that is (20 units X adverse × £5) plus (10 units Y favourable × £6)
We can split this into a sales quantity profit variance and a sales mix profit variance as follows:

Sales quantity profit variance   £56 (A)
(500 units Budget – 490 units Actual) × £5.60 per unit

Sales mix profit variance

	Standard mix (units)	Actual mix (units)	Variance (units)	Variance (£)
X	196	180	16 (A)	80 (A)
Y	294	310	16 (F)	96 (F)
Total	490	490		£16 (F)

The standard mix is the total unit sales (490) multiplied by 2/5 to give X and 3/5 to give Y. The mix variances in units are multiplied by the individual standard profits per unit to give the mix variance in £.

As with the other mix variances, there are alternative means of calculating the sales mix profit variance. That used above is the simplest and they all produce the same final result.

The example used relates to the sales volume profit variance, but exactly the same procedure can be used for its contribution and revenue variance alternatives.

4.5 Planning and operational variances

Some variances will arise through factors that are entirely, or almost entirely, within the control of management. These may be referred to as *operational* variances. Other variances can arise from changes in factors external to the business, and may be referred to as *planning* variances.

The *Official Terminology* defines operational and planning variances as follows:

> *Operational variance*: A classification of variances in which non-standard performance is defined as being that which differs from an *ex post* standard. Operational variances can relate to any element of the standard product specification.

> *Planning variance*: A classification of variances caused by *ex ante* budget allowances being changed to an *ex post* basis. Also known as a revision variance.

Management will wish to draw a distinction between these two variances in order to gain a realistic measure of operational efficiency. As planning variances are self-evidently *not* under the control of operational management, it cannot be held responsible for them, and there is thus no benefit to be gained in spending time investigating such variances at an operational level. Planning variances may arise from faulty standard-setting, but the responsibility for this lies with *senior,* rather than *operational,* management.

The concept may be demonstrated by the following simple case:

ABC Ltd produces Units and incurs labour costs. Details of actual and budget for period 9 are:

	Budget	Actual	Std per unit
Units	500	550	
Labour hours	1,000	1,200	2
Labour costs £	5,000	5,100	10

We are told that a change in technology subsequent to the preparation of the budget resulted in a 25% increase in standard labour efficiency, such that it is now possible to produce 5 Units instead of 4 Units using 8 hours of labour – giving a revised standard labour requirement of 1.6 hours (thus £8 labour cost) per Unit.

The total labour cost variance for period 9 is £400 favourable (i.e. £5,500 standard cost less £5,100 actual cost). This may be analysed as follows:

Planning variance:

Original (ex-ante) standard less the revised (ex-post) labour cost
(550 Units × £10) − (550 Units × £8) = £1,100 favourable

Operational variances:

Labour efficiency: (standard (ex-post) hours less actual hours) × standard hourly rate
((550 Units × 1.6 hours) − 1,200 hours) × £5 = £1,600 adverse
Labour rate: (standard rate − actual rate) × actual hours
(£5 − £4.25) × 1,200 = £900 favourable

Note that the three component variances add up to £400 favourable.

In this case, the separation of the labour cost variance into operational and planning components indicates a larger problem in the area of labour efficiency than might otherwise have been indicated. The operational variances are based on the revised (ex-post) standard and this gives a more meaningful performance benchmark than the original (ex-ante) standard.

It should be noted that *all* deviations of cost between actual and budgeted can be subdivided and attributed to either planning or operational causes. The example below illustrates this more general application of the techniques.

Big plc set up a factory to manufacture and sell 'Advance', a new consumer product. The first year's budgeted production and sales were 1,000 units. The budgeted sales price and standard costs for 'Advance' were as follows:

	£	£
Standard sales price (per unit)		200
Standard costs (per unit)		
Raw materials (10 kg at £10)	100	
Labour (6 hours at £8)	48	
		(148)
Standard contribution (per unit)		52

Actual results for the first year were as follows:

	£'000	£'000
Sales (1,000 units)		316
Production costs (1,000 units)		
Raw materials (10,800 kg)	194.4	
Labour (5800 hours)	69.6	
		(264)
Actual contribution (1,000 units)		52

The managing director made the following observations on the actual results:

In total, the performance agreed with budget; nevertheless, in every aspect other than volume, there were large differences.

Sales were made at what was felt to be the highest feasible price, but we now feel that we could have sold for £330 with no adverse effect on volume. Labour costs rose dramatically with increased demand for the specialist skills required to produce the product, and the general market rate was £12.50 per hour – although we always paid below the general market rate whenever possible.

The raw material cost that was expected at the time the budget was prepared was £10 per kilogram. However, the market price relating to efficient purchases of the material during the year was £17.00 per kilogram.

It is not proposed to request a variance analysis for the first year's results. In any event, the final contribution was equal to that originally budgeted, so operations must have been fully efficient.

Despite the managing director's reluctance to calculate it, the traditional variance analysis is as follows:

	£	£
Sales volume contribution variance		
(Actual sales volume = budgeted sales volume)		–
Selling price variance		
(Actual selling price − standard selling price) × actual sales volume		
(£316 − £200) × 1,000		116,000 (F)
Material price		
(Standard price − actual price) × actual quantity		
(£10 − £194,400/10,800) × 10,800	86,400 (A)	

Material usage
(Standard quantity − actual quantity) × standard price
(10,000 − 10,800) × £10   8,000 (A)

                                                  94,400 (A)

Labour rate
(Standard rate − actual rate) × actual hours
(£8 − £69,600/5,800) × 5,800   23,200 (A)

Labour efficiency
(Standard hours − actual hours) × standard rate
((1,000 × 6) − 5,800) × £8   1,600 (F)

                                                  21,600 (A)

Total variances   –

Reconciliation:

	£
Budgeted contribution (1,000 × £52)	52,000
Add: adverse cost variances	116,000
Less: favourable sales variances	(116,000)
Actual contribution	52,000

As the managing director states, and the above analysis shows, the overall variance for the company was zero: the adverse cost variances exactly offset the favourable sales margin price.

However, this analysis does not clearly indicate the efficiency with which the company operated during the period, as it is impossible to tell whether some of the variances arose from the use of inappropriate standards, or whether they were due to efficient or inefficient implementation of those standards. In order to determine this, a revised *ex post* plan should be constructed, setting out the standards that, with hindsight, *should* have been in operation during the period. These revised *ex post* standards are shown under (B) below.

	(A) Original plan	£	(B) Revised ex post plan	£	(C) Actual result	£
Sales	(1,000 × £200)	200,000	(1,000 × £330)	330,000	(1,000 × £316)	316,000
Materials	(10,000 × £10)	100,000	(10,000 × £17)	170,000	(10,800 × £18)	194,400
Labour	(6,000 × £8)	48,000	(6,000 × £12.50)	75,000	(5,800 × £12)	69,600

	£	£
Planning variances (A − B)		
Selling price	130,000 (F)	
Material price (100,000 − 170,000)	70,000 (A)	
Labour rate	27,000 (A)	
		33,000 (F)
Operational variances		
Selling price (B − C)	14,000 (A)	
Material price (10,800 × £1)	10,800 (A)	
Material usage (800 × £17)	13,600 (A)	
Labour rate (5,800 × £0.50)	2,900 (F)	
Labour efficiency (200 hrs × £12.50)	2,500 (F)	
		33,000 (A)
Total variances		–

A comparison of (B) and (C) produces *operational* variances, which show the difference between the results that were actually achieved and those that might legitimately have been achievable during the period in question. This gives a very different view of the period's operations. For example, on the cost side, the labour rate variance has changed from adverse to favourable, and the material price variance, while remaining adverse, is significantly reduced in comparison to that calculated under the traditional analysis; on the sales side, the sales margin price variance, which was particularly large and favourable in the traditional analysis, is transformed into an *adverse* variance in the revised approach, reflecting the fact that the company failed to sell at prices that were actually available in the market. A comparison of the original plan (A) with the revised plan (B) allows the planning variances to be identified. As noted at the beginning of this section, these variances are uncontrollable by *operating,* staff, and may or may not have been controllable by the *original* standard-setters at the start of the budget period. Where a revision of standards is required due to environmental changes that were not foreseeable at the time the budget was prepared, the planning variances are truly uncontrollable. However, standards that failed to anticipate *known* market trends when they were set will reflect faulty standard-setting: it could be argued that these variances *were* controllable (avoidable) at the planning stage.

Example

It would be useful to give a second example of planning and operational variances. For this example, we shall return to the data from the earlier section on material mix and yield variances.

You will recall that the standard mix was one that gave a cost of good output of £1.68 per kg, being the input cost of £840 divided by the standard output of 500 kg. In determining this optimal mix, the interaction between the input, the output and the cost of the input had to be taken into account and minimised. Where there is substitutability between inputs, a number of possible mixes may be feasible, for example an alternative mix might be the one shown below:

Input	kg	Cost/kg £	Total cost of mix £
A	325	1.00	325
B	275	1.60	440
	600		765

In this case, let us assume that the 600 kg of input has an expected output of 450 kg, so that the cost per kg is

£765/450 = £1.70

Despite resulting in a product of the right quality, this mix would *not* be chosen as the standard, because it has a higher cost per kg than the optimal mix at the expected input prices.

However, suppose that the actual results recorded in a particular period were as follows:

Actual input	kg	Actual cost/kg £	Total cost £
A	200	1.00	200
B	400	2.00	800
	600		1,000

Actual output: 500 kg of C

The cost per kg of output is now

£1,000/500 = £2

In this case, there would be *no* mix or yield variance, as the input to the process was in the standard mix and produced the standard output. The only variance reported would be an adverse *price* variance of £160 (400 × (£1.60 − £2.00)), reflecting the higher cost per kg of material B in the period under consideration. However, it is clear that the increase in the *price* of B renders the current standard mix *suboptimal.* If B has a price of £2, the *alternative* mix of 325 kg of A and 275 kg of B gives a *lower* output price per kg than the current standard mix, as shown below:

Input	kg	Cost/kg £	Total cost of mix £
A	325	1.00	325
B	275	2.00	550
	600		875

With output of 450 kg, the cost per kg of this mix is

£875/450 = £1.9444

This cost is lower than the cost of £2 per kg that is obtained when the original 'optimal' standard mix is retained in the face of changed prices. A more sophisticated variance analysis system would compare the actions of the operational management with the standards that *would* have been set had the conditions that *actually* prevailed been known at the time the standard was set. In this example, had the price of B been known to be £2 per kg, the alternative mix would have become the standard, and would have been the basis for comparison with the actual result.

The revised standard cost of the actual output is

500/£1.9444 = £972.22

The actual cost incurred was £1,000, giving a material cost variance of £27.78 adverse.

The material mixture variance may be calculated as follows:

Input	Standard mix kg	Actual mix kg	Variance kg	Standard cost £	Variance £
A	325	200	125 (F)	1	125 (F)
B	275	400	125 (A)	2	250 (A)
					125 (A)

The material yield variance is simply the difference between standard (450 kg) and actual (500 kg) yield for the 600 kg input multiplied by the standard cost per kg output.

This gives a result of £97.22 favourable (that is 50 kg × £1,9444).

	£
Material mix variance	125.00 (A)
Material yield variance	97.22 (F)
Material usage variance	27.78 (A)

Suppose that, in the same circumstances, the following results had been recorded.

Actual input	kg	Actual cost/kg £	Actual cost £
A	325	1.00	325
B	275	2.00	550
	600		875

Actual output: 450 kg of C

The actual results are identical to that *would* be expected if the comparison is made with the *revised* standard, and thus there can be no *operational* variance. However, a *planning* variance has occurred. The expected cost of 450 kg of C, based on the original standard mix and input prices, was 450 × £1.68 = £756. The *revised* standard cost of 450 kg of C was £875. The difference of £119 between the two figures results from the change in the price of B, which represents a *planning* variance beyond the control of the operating management.

The formal calculation of the variance is

450 × (£1.68 − £1.94) = £119 adverse (remember the £1.94 is rounded)

It is interesting to note that a failure to revise the standard in these circumstances might encourage management to continue to operate with the *original* standard mix, which would, in fact, be against the company's best interests.

On the face of it, the calculation of operational and planning variances is an improvement over the traditional analysis. However, you should not overlook the considerable problem of data collection for the revised analysis: where does this information come from, and how can we say with certainty what should have been known at a particular point in time?

4.6 Investigation and interpretation of variances

The calculation of variances is not sufficient of itself to ensure better management control. Variances only become useful when *action* is taken as a result of their calculation. The aim of variance analysis is to facilitate management by exception, allowing management to concentrate on those areas where action is necessary, without wasting time on matters which are performing in line with expectations.

4.6.1 Whether to investigate

Once the variances have been calculated, management has the task of deciding which variances should be investigated. It would probably not be worthwhile or cost-effective to investigate every single variance. Some criteria must be established to guide the decision as to whether or not to investigate a particular variance. Some general factors which may be taken into account include the following and we will return to consider some of them in more detail later in this section:

(a) *The size of the variance.* Costs tend to fluctuate around a norm and therefore 'normal' variances may be expected on most costs. The problem is to decide how large a variance must be before it is considered 'abnormal' and worthy of investigation.

A rule of thumb may be established that any variance which exceeds, say, 5 per cent of its standard cost may be worthy of investigation. Alternatively control limits may be set statistically and if a cost fluctuates outside these limits it should be investigated.

(b) *The likelihood of the variance being controllable or its cause already known.* Managers may know from experience that certain variances may not be controllable even if a lengthy investigation is undertaken to determine their causes. They may also be immediately aware of the cause of a variance. For example, it may be argued that a material price variance is less easily controlled than a material usage variance because it is heavily influenced by external factors. The counter-argument to the latter is that a materials price variance may be caused by external market factors (uncontrollable) or the quality of procurement management – and one doesn't know which is the cause until it is investigated.

(c) *The likely cost of an investigation.* This cost would have to be weighed against the cost which would be incurred if the variance were allowed to continue in future periods.

(d) *The interrelationship of variances.* Adverse variances in one area of the organisation may be interrelated with favourable variances elsewhere. For example, if cheaper material is purchased this may produce a favourable material price variance. However, if the cheaper material is of lower quality and difficult to process, this could result in adverse variances for material usage and labour efficiency.

(e) *The type of standard that was set.* You have already seen that an ideal standard will almost always result in some adverse variances, because of unavoidable waste and so on. Managers must decide on the 'normal' level of adverse variance which they would expect to see.

Another example is where a standard price is set at an average rate for the year. Assuming that inflation or a known upward trend exist, favourable price variances might be expected at the beginning of the year, to be offset by adverse price variances towards the end of the year as actual prices begin to rise.

4.6.2 Percentage variance charts

We have seen that the size of a variance may be used as a guide to managers to indicate whether the variance is worthy of investigation. However, it may be difficult for managers to appreciate the significance or the trend of variances when they are presented in absolute terms.

A percentage variance chart can provide a useful graphical presentation of variances that is easier for managers to understand and interpret than a series of figures presented in a tabular format. By presenting the variances over time any trend can be identified, and this can be used to decide whether any control action is required.

Example

Product L has a standard material cost of £7 per unit. Details of output and the recorded material cost variances for the last four periods are as follows:

Period	Output Units	Usage variance £	Price variance £
1	5,800	8,120 (A)	6,090 (F)
2	2,470	2,940 (A)	2,075 (F)
3	4,600	4,185 (A)	3,220 (F)
4	3,100	2,170 (A)	1,520 (F)

The fluctuating output and the corresponding fluctuations in variances make it difficult for managers to see whether there is any trend in the recorded variances.

In order to prepare a percentage variance chart it is necessary to express each variance as a percentage of the total standard cost of material for the output achieved.

Period	Standard material cost of output @ £7 per unit £	Usage variance £	%	Price variance £	%
1	40,600	8,120 (A)	20 (A)	6,090 (F)	15 (F)
2	17,290	2,940 (A)	17 (A)	2,075 (F)	12 (F)
3	32,200	4,185 (A)	13 (A)	3,220 (F)	10 (F)
4	21,700	2,170 (A)	10 (A)	1,520 (F)	7 (F)

The percentage variances can now be plotted on a percentage variance chart (Figure 4.1).

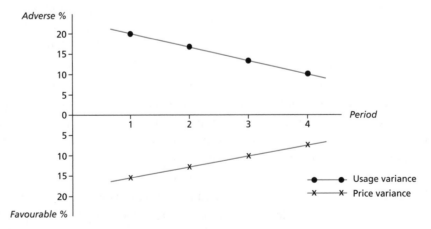

Figure 4.1 Percentage variance chart

The chart shows a clear trend in each variance. This trend was not clearly visible from the absolute figures. It appears that the variances may be interrelated; in Period 1 the material purchased was 15% cheaper than standard, which may have caused the 20% adverse usage variance, perhaps because the material was of inferior quality. However, the trend in variances shows that, as the price of material has increased (reducing percentage favourable price variance), the usage has tended to move closer to standard levels (reducing percentage material usage variance).

Since both variances are trending towards a zero percentage, it may not be necessary to undertake a detailed investigation at this stage. If you look back at the table of absolute variances, you will see that it would have been difficult to reach this conclusion from the information presented there.

4.6.3 The reasons for variances

Before we look in detail at variance investigation models, it will be useful to think about *why* actual performance might differ from standard performance. Four principal sources of variances can be identified, and we shall briefly examine each in turn:

(i) *Inefficient operations.* Currently attainable standards should be achievable by expending a reasonable amount of effort, and incorporate normal levels of machine efficiency, non-productive time, spoilage and waste. Variances from such standards may result from faulty machinery, departures from laid-down procedures or human error. The underlying cause of the inefficiency should be sought and eliminated.

(ii) *Inappropriate standards.* Setting standards can be time-consuming and expensive, particularly when there are large numbers of different products or services which consume large numbers of different inputs, and inaccurate standards may simply be the result of an unwillingness to invest sufficient resources to ensure their accuracy. It can be difficult not only to develop accurate standards in high-technology firms, but also to keep them up to date, as the rapid pace of change can overtake standards after only a short time in operation. If frequent changes occur in the *prices* of input factors, standards may quickly become out of date, and variances become less a measure of the purchasing department's efficiency or inefficiency than a reflection of general market conditions. When variances arise as a result of inappropriate standards, the standards need to be revised or updated – and kept under frequent review.

(iii) *Errors in recording actual results.* Humans being error prone, the amounts recorded for actual costs may be inaccurate. There can be few people who have never made an arithmetic slip, transposed numbers or misclassified a particular type of cost. It is improbable that any benefit would accrue to an investigation when the cause of the variance turns out to be a measurement error of this sort.

(iv) *Random or uncontrollable factors.* When setting a standard, it is usual to select a representative value; this well frequently be the mean, or other measure of central tendency. However, although this *single* value has been taken as a standard, the *reality* of the situation is that a *range* of outcomes is possible, even when the process is under control. This is an important point to bear in mind when considering the concept of a standard, because there is an implicit assumption that it represents a *single-point* acceptable measure. It should be understood to represent a band or *range* of possible acceptable measures. Although the band itself may be predictable, it is not possible to predict the *exact* value of an individual unit within it. As long as the process is under control (i.e. the value falls within the range of acceptable outcomes), an observation that *differs* from the standard would be regarded merely as a *random* or *uncontrollable* variance. By definition, a random deviation calls for no corrective action.

4.6.4 Investigation models

In an ideal world, variances would only be investigated when the benefits of an investigation exceed its cost. The difficulty arises in determining whether this is likely to be the case. Management can adopt one of two approaches to the problem: the application of a simple rule of thumb; or the use of a statistical model (with or without a built-in cost/benefit measurement).

Rules of thumb

By definition, these will be based on arbitrary criteria, but need not be quite as crude as the name suggests. For example, for key cost items, a small percentage deviation might prompt an investigation; for less significant cost items, either a higher percentage cut-off or a cutoff point expressed in absolute cost terms might be applied ('investigate all variances over £2,000 or 30 per cent of standard cost, whichever is the lower').

The obvious advantages of such a method are its inherent simplicity and ease of application. However, the choice of cut-off values is subjective: it relies on judgement and intuition rather than statistical probabilities, and thus fails to capture the statistical significance of variances, or to weigh the costs of an investigation against its potential benefits.

Statistical models

A formal statistical model enables management to determine the probability that a particular variance comes from a process that is in control, and an investigation will only be carried out when the probability of that falls below a particular predetermined level (typically expressed in terms of a number of standard deviations from the mean). The model assumes that two mutually exclusive states exist for a process – it is either 'in control' or 'out of control'. In the former case, variances will be due to random fluctuations around the standard, and merit no further action. In the latter case, variances indicate that investigation is called for, and that action will be able to bring the process back into line. A prerequisite of the model is that the 'in control' state is capable (or assumed to be capable) of being expressed in the form of a probability distribution.

Let us take as an example of the standard material content of a product. We shall assume that this figure, say 20 g of a particular chemical, represents the mean value of a large number of observations of the production process operating under conditions of normal efficiency, and that the observations display a normal distribution with a standard deviation of 2 g. On the particular day under review, 20,000 units were produced, with a total usage of 480 kg – an average of 24 g per product. This represents two standard deviations from the mean of 20 g. You should recall that, in a normal distribution, 95.45 per cent of all observations can be expected to fall within ± two standard deviations of the mean. Thus, in our example, if the process is under control, the probability of the average usage being two standard deviations from the mean is a mere 2.275 per cent (100 − 95.45%/2). In other words, it is highly *unlikely* that an observation of 24 g would come from a distribution with a mean of 20 g and a standard deviation of 2 g, the distribution representing a process under control. Such an observation is much more likely to derive from a totally *different* distribution, and, given the two mutually exclusive states mentioned above, this would imply to management that the process was out of control for the day under review, and investigation would be called for.

Statistical control charts

The formal means of distinguishing between random variations in an 'in control' process and variances indicating an 'out of control' situation is known as statistical quality control. A convenient means of recording and visually appraising variances is a *control chart*,

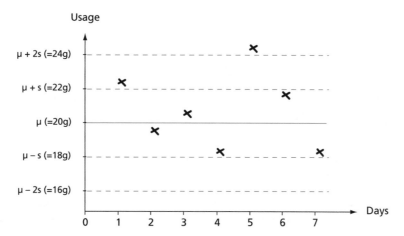

Figure 4.2 Control chart: normal distribution

on which successive cost observations are plotted in the form of a graph. The chart shows certain fixed points, representing the expected distribution of the particular item, and only actual observations which fall *outside* predetermined limits would be regarded as non-random and worth investigating. Visual analysis or statistical procedures can be employed to identify trends that indicate that a process is *heading* out of control, even though current observations are insufficient by themselves to prompt an investigation.

Figure 4.2 is a control chart of a normally distributed item, which takes as its 'in control' parameters – its *control limits* – two standard deviations from the mean (i.e. as there can only be a 4.55 per cent chance (100 − 95.45%) that an observation falling *outside* these parameters could result from a process in control, management considers that there is a high probability that such an observation would come from a process *out of control*). The data employed are those from our previous example, extended to include actual observations from prior and subsequent days to that previously examined. It can be seen that all observations, other than the one of 24 g, fall within the control limits, and would be considered random fluctuations of a process under control.

Not surprisingly, statistical quality control charts tend to be used to plot data measured in *physical quantity* terms, such as number of rejects or (as in our example) material usage. It should be noted, however, that they cannot distinguish between variances due to inappropriate standards or measurement errors, and those due to inefficient operations.

As indicated at the beginning of this section on investigation models, statistical decision models can be extended to incorporate the costs and benefits of an investigation. A discussion of such models lies outside the scope of this book, but interested readers are referred to Drury (see reading list) for an example. To the caveat mentioned above, however, should be added the severe difficulty of determining, or at least quantifying to an acceptable degree of accuracy, both the cost of an investigation and the benefits expected to accrue from it. This is, of course, a problem common to most mathematical decision-making models, and goes some way towards explaining the relatively infrequent use of many of them, including the techniques just mentioned.

4.6.5 Interrelationship of variances

We shall now consider the question of the interrelationship of variances in a little more detail. A simple example will illustrate the dangers of looking at variances in isolation.

Example

Let us assume that a purchasing manager takes a conscious decision to buy a quantity of slightly substandard direct material for a particularly low price. In order to meet the company's quality criteria, heavy spoilage and labour overruns are incurred when the material is put into production. The aim of the manager is to reduce the *total* costs of manufacturing for the company as a whole, by trading off a favourable price variance against expected adverse efficiency variances. If the manager's strategy works, the *overall* variance will be *favourable*, despite the substantial adverse labels attaching to the individual efficiency variances. Conversely, if the strategy *fails*, the overall variance will be *adverse*, despite the large favourable price variance. (An equally valid strategy might be to acquire more *expensive* material, which causes an *adverse* material price variance, in the expectation that product quality will be improved and give rise to reductions in warranty and servicing costs that exceed the increased material cost.) It is important to keep in mind that there are many interdependencies among a company's activities – the 'favourable' or 'adverse' label pinned on an individual variance should not lead management to make unwarranted value judgements and draw unjustified conclusions concerning a period's operations.

Managers should not regard a standard costing system as a straitjacket that constrains or stifles individual initiative, and prevents them from taking an overall view of the company and its objectives. For this reason, it would be wrong to give too much emphasis to any one performance measure. Such a narrow focus encourages managers to make decisions that maximise their own reported performance in terms of the measure, at the expense of profit maximisation for the company as a whole.

A further problem resulting from the interrelationship of variances results from the traditional focus of responsibilities within organisations. Responsibility for material price variances generally rests with the purchasing manager, and responsibility for material efficiency variances with the production manager. The problem revolves around the responsibility for the joint price/efficiency variance, which is invariably buried within the purchasing manager's variance, as the following example demonstrates.

Example

The product cost of X includes 2 Kg of direct material Y, at a standard cost of £2 per Kg. In a particular period, in order to produce a budgeted requirement of 1,000 units of X, 2,300 kg of Y are used, at an actual cost of £2.20 per Kg.

Conventional variance analysis on the above data would be as follows:

	£
Material price variance (£2.20 − £2.00) × 2,300	460 Adverse
Material usage variance (2,300 − 2,000) × £2.00	600 Adverse
Total material variance	1,060 Adverse

However, the buyer, while accepting responsibility for the price variance on the 2,000 kg in the *standard allowance* for actual production – £0.20 × 2,000 = £400 – might legitimately claim that the additional £60 (300 kg @ £0.20) included in the adverse variance ascribed to *his* activities is more properly attributable to the *production manager*. From the purchasing manager's point of view, if the production manager had operated efficiently, and produced in accordance with the standard quantities, only 2,000 kg would have been required for the actual production of 1,000 units. The extra 300 kg would not have been needed, and – certainly in a JIT system – not even purchased. However, in practice, this distinction between the *pure* price variance – £400 – and the *mutual* price/efficiency variance – £60 – is not often drawn (unless management bonuses depend upon individual variances – an undesirable situation for the reasons outlined above). The efficiency variance, other things being equal, is considered to be of greater significance than the price variance, in view of the more direct influence that the respective manager can exert over it. As a consequence, the management report may be prepared in a manner which seeks to minimise criticism on the part of the production manager of the measurement methods. A joint price/efficiency variance is less likely to cause disagreement – with its concomitant potential for organisational discord – if it is lost within the total *price* variance rather than the *efficiency* variance, particularly as price variances are often regarded more as reflections on forecasting ability than an ability to buy at a particular price.

Normal practice in assigning the joint price/efficiency variance may be rationalised by pointing out that, in reality, it is usual to calculate the material price variance at the point of *receipt* of material, rather than the point of use. Receipt and use will be separated by time in anything other than a JIT system. At the point of receipt, it is not known whether there will be a usage variance or not, and therefore it can be argued that the price variance is properly regarded as the sole responsibility of the buyer. However, this ignores the fact that purchases are ultimately a function of *usage,* and inefficiencies in the production department must inevitably be reflected in adverse price variances for the buyer, irrespective of the point at which the variance is calculated. It could also be argued in this situation that the buyer could generate favourable variances for himself by purchasing substandard material, which then causes inefficiencies in the production department and leads to greater quantities being bought, with concomitant increases in the buyer's favourable variance (this strategy should not be possible, however, in a situation in which a company pursues a policy of minimum standards in the quality of its purchases).

4.7   Standard costing in the modern business environment

4.7.1   Criticisms of standard costing

There has recently been some criticism of the appropriateness of standard costing in the modern business environment. The main criticisms include the following:

- Standard costing was developed when the business environment was more stable and operating conditions were less prone to change. In the present dynamic environment, such stable conditions cannot be assumed. If conditions are not stable, then it is difficult to set a standard cost which can be used to control costs over a period of time.
- Performance to standard used to be judged as satisfactory, but in today's climate constant improvement must be aimed for in order to remain competitive. The focus in a traditional standard costing environment is on minimising costs rather than on improving quality and customer care.
- Standard costing variances tend to be prepared on an aggregate basis. In today's manufacturing environment there is a need for variances specific to production lines and even individual batches.
- Product life cycles tend to be shorter with the result that standard costs become quickly out of date.
- The emphasis on labour variances is no longer appropriate with the increasing use of automated production methods.
- Standard costing variances are usually reported at the end of each month. In order to be flexible and responsive to changes in the external environment, managers need information more frequently.

4.7.2   Addressing the criticisms

An organisation's decision to use standard costing depends on its effectiveness in helping managers to make the correct planning and control decisions. Many of the above criticisms can be addressed by adaptations to traditional standard costing systems.

- Standard costs must be updated regularly if they are to remain useful for control purposes.
- The use of demanding performance standards can help to encourage continuous improvement.

- The standard costing system can be adapted to produce a broader analysis of variances that are less aggregated.
- It is possible to place less emphasis on labour cost variances and focus more on variances for quality costs, variable overhead costs, and so on.
- Real time information systems have been developed which allow for corrective action to be taken sooner in response to reported variances.
- Standard costing may still be useful even where the final product or service is not standardised. It may be possible to identify a number of standard components and activities for which standards may be set and used effectively for planning and control purposes.

4.7.3 Standards and variances: a cautionary note

An important theme running through this book is the search for continuous improvement, and its importance in the modern, globally competitive market. Thus, despite the heavy emphasis placed by the syllabus on variance accounting, and the calculation, investigation and interpretation of variances, it is appropriate that this discussion of standard costing concludes with the (slightly edited) words of Drury (2000):

> It is claimed that the concept of setting standards is not consistent with a . . . philosophy of continuous improvement. When standards are set, a climate is created whereby they represent a target to be achieved and maintained, rather than a philosophy of constant improvement. The . . . philosophy requires that actual performance measures be reported over time, rather than comparisons against a standard, so that the trend in performance can be monitored. Presenting performance measures over time communicates useful feedback information in the amount of rate of change in performance.

However, there is nothing in the process of variance analysis which makes it *inherently* incompatible with continuous improvement; rather, it may be argued that it is the way in which standards have *traditionally* been formulated and maintained which leads to the view quoted above. The standard against which actual performance is measured in variance analysis represents a type of *benchmark*. This benchmark is expressed in financial terms, and has traditionally been *internally* determined, by reference to a company's own costs and procedures.

4.8 Benchmarking

4.8.1 Benchmarking – the concept

There is now an increasing interest in the use of benchmarking as a means of establishing 'best practice', or standards, by the examination of the practices of *other* organisation relative to a company's own procedures. Benchmarking at its best establishes attainable standards by the examination of both *external* and internal information. If the standards which a firm employs are regularly reviewed in the light of information gained in external as well as internal benchmarking exercises, these standards will embrace continuous improvement by becoming increasingly demanding. The reporting of variances against these updated attainable standards will indicate progress towards them.

External benchmarking is the practice of comparing the critical performance indicators of different organisations. This is frequently carried out by groups of firms that agree to pool information. These firms may not operate in the same geographic areas or may not even be in the same sectors – it is unlikely that direct competitors will agree to voluntarily share information. One can benchmark against an unwilling partner, but the exercise then has to depend only on information that is in the public domain or that can be obtained by covert means.

Benchmarked performance indicators may include 'labour cost per unit of output' in a manufacturing concern or 'fee income per dental surgeon' in a dental practice. A benchmarking exercise will usually consider a range of appropriate performance indicators. If a firm finds that it is performing less well than others in respect of any one Indicator, then the relevant area of the operation will be a focus for attempted improvements.

Benchmarking can be used as a tool in the establishment of standard manufacturing costs. However, benchmarking is more widely used as a general performance evaluation tool. The use of internal benchmarking as an element in standard costing systems and the setting of standards has many advocates.

Extract from 'Looking in the mirror' (internal benchmarking)

John P. Puckett III and Philip S. Siegel, *Journal of Business Strategy,*
May–June 1997
Republished with permission, Emerald Group Publishing Limited.

Most senior executives view external benchmarking as an indispensable management tool. Finding out how their companies stack up against industry leaders provides a yardstick by which to measure performance and, equally important, role models to emulate. For some it has become an obsession to which they devote enormous resources.

But external benchmarking, despite its benefits, is overrated. Many companies are spending countless dollars and man-years seeking something that's right under their noses. By looking in the mirror and appreciating the divergence of performance within their own organisations, they can benchmark to make these internal differences apparent and to help uncover opportunities for capitalising on their unique strengths. The simple truth is a company's own best practices are usually superior to the best company's average practices.

Internal benchmarking will yield solutions that leverage existing knowledge and create more tangible value than external benchmarking. Six factors make this possible:

- It is easier to gather the data. External benchmarking relies on competitive data that is not readily available. When the data is available, it may be neither accurate nor timely. Moreover, it allows a comparison at only one point in time and does not provide a way to continually improve performance. With internal benchmarking, the data is always right at your fingertips.
- The comparisons are more relevant. They are more relevant because they relate to your business. You are not comparing yourself to a business that, in truth, is not the same as yours.
- It is easier to take action on the results. External benchmarking will identify differences between your company and competitors, but it will not tell you why you are different. Internal benchmarking lets you take that next step and, through a series of interviews and best practice sharing, really understand what behaviors are driving those differences.
- It allows you to set sound targets. Performance targets are no longer viewed as arbitrary and unrealistic. A process is in place. Individuals across the organisation are involved. The goals seem achievable because someone in the company is already achieving them. Buy-in increases; whining decreases.

- Internal champions exist. Internal benchmarking makes heroes out of the people who already have best practices in place. Pointing to Jane Doe in the phoenix branch, rather than company X or Y, personalises the effort. Everyone knows them and can identify with them. They may even be motivated by them. And, again, since someone in the company is currently doing it, there are no excuses.
- It allows continuous improvement. There is always going to be variance in performance across an organisation. Sharing best practices lets management keep raising the bar. One region achieves a record productivity level; a few months later, another region breaks that record. Now, all of the company's regions have an even higher target to shoot for.

Realising the maximum value

The factors most ripe for internal benchmarking are productivity ratios, efficiency response time, cost ratios and pricing performance. Many of the numerators for such ratios come from a company's finance department, while the denominators often come from information kept by the business units. For example, in many organisations, finance keeps overhead cost data and sales keeps account data, so if you want to benchmark overhead per account, you must combine data sources. You may have to do some digging. Usually, however, there are just one to four high-level metrics that make the most sense for a company to track, with a larger set of measures underlying them.

Internal benchmarking is most valuable when a company has multiple comparable units. These may be business units, branches, plants, sales offices, countries, even products. For example, how does widget plant A's reject rate compare with widget plant B's? Or what is the Asia/Pacific region's unit cost per account vis-à-vis that of Europe?

4.8.2 The selection, reporting and interpretation of benchmarks

An organisation can measure performance in many aspects of its operation using benchmarks. This may be a particularly important issue in not-for-profit organisations or service operations within commercial organisations. In these last cases it is often difficult to measure performance through use of conventional profit-based metrics.

A local authority may calculate and report the following metrics:

- cost per km of road maintained
- cost per child in school
- cost per library book maintained
- cost per tonne of sewage processed.

Such performance measures should be selected on the basis that they reflect some important aspect of the operation from the perspective of stakeholders.

These measures, taken on their own, may offer some insights to the stakeholder into how well or badly the organisation is performing. For example, the comparison of this year's cost per tonne of sewage processed with those for previous years might give some sense for what is happening. A steady increase in cost might suggest some decline in performance – although it might equally be indicative of other things such as an improvement in the standard of sewage disposal.

However, some clear reference point is needed in order to give such metrics clear meaning. That reference point should be a benchmark, derived from some internal or external source. An internal benchmark might be a standard cost calculated using work study methods or it might be an external benchmark provided by a benchmarking partner or through some consortium run by a third party.

However, caution should always be exercised in the interpretation of benchmarking reports. Fort example, let us say that Town A reports a sewage disposal cost of £250 per tonne whereas Town B reports a cost of £400 per tonne. Should stakeholders conclude from this that Town A is more efficient than Town B?. Not necessarily. Town A might be pumping raw sewage direct into the sea while Town B is processing the sewage before its disposal. Also Towns A and B may have subtly different accounting policies which mean that the two do not classify costs in the same way and hence the two figures compared in the benchmarking report are not strictly comparable.

Great caution should also be taken in the selection of appropriate benchmarks as a guide to action. For example, a given objective (e.g. 'containment of youth crime') can be achieved in a variety of different ways – through spending on police, education, social services and recreation. Town A may appear to run a very efficient police service (using a benchmarked measure such as 'arrests per police officer') but if the spending balance of police relative to social services is not right then Town A may not be containing youth crime in the most effective way. A small increase in spending on vocational education might allow a big cut in spending on police without an associated increase in youth crime.

Some government agencies have assisted in the provision of benchmarking systems. For example, in 1995 the Department of the Environment in association with CIMA published the 'Business Guide to Energy Costs in Buildings'. This guide collated energy consumption figures for business premises of all types and provided (1) a typical building benchmark and (2) a good practice benchmark for energy consumption in building of all types and sizes. Thus, the manager of an office building can look up appropriate energy consumption benchmarks for a building of the size, type and location that he/she is responsible for. Comparison of actual results with benchmarks will give a guide to performance and highlight those areas of energy consumption (e.g. power, heating, lighting) that offer the largest scope for improvement.

Benchmarking
Bob Scarlett – *CIMA Insider*, October 2003

Benchmarking is the process of improving performance by continuously identifying, understanding (studying and analysing), and adapting outstanding practices and process found inside and outside the organisation and implementing the results

(American Productivity and Quality Centre, 1997)

Benchmarking is an approach to performance management that starts with the premise that whatever the process (supply, production, sales or services), performance can best be measured and managed by comparing that process with an appropriate outside entity that is already achieving world-class performance. The outside entity used to provide the benchmark need not operate within the same sector as our process. Further the benchmark can be from either another organisation (an 'external' benchmark) or a different segment within the same organisation (an 'internal' benchmark).

A benchmark provides a standard of excellence against which to measure and compare. Benchmarks are performance measures – How many? (e.g. 'customers served per staff member per hour') How quickly? (e.g. 'delivery time to customer') How high? (e.g. 'proportion of sales giving rise to repeat business') How low? (e.g. 'proportion of output being defective'). To be meaningful, a benchmark should relate to a 'key performance indicator', that is something within the business process that has a major influence on results. Establishing benchmarks is a necessary part of benchmarking but of itself does not provide an understanding of best practices nor does knowledge of the benchmarks lead necessarily to improvement. Benchmarking is the learning of lessons about how best performance is achieved. Rather than merely measuring performance, benchmarking focuses on how to improve any given business process by exploiting 'best practices' by discovering the specific practices responsible for high performance, understanding how these practices work and adapting and applying them to the organisation. A benchmarking exercise may take the form of a process comparison which does not involve the use of metrics.

Some writers identify three distinct approaches to benchmarking:

(1) *Metric benchmarking.* The practice of comparing appropriate metrics to identify possible areas for improvement;
(2) *Process benchmarking.* The practice of comparing processes with a partner as part of an improvement process;
(3) *Diagnostic benchmarking.* The practice of reviewing the processes of a business to identify those which indicate a problem and offer a potential for improvement.

The Xerox corporation is often cited as the pioneer in benchmarking practice. When it wanted to improve performance in its warehousing and distribution operation it did not go down the then conventional road of process redesign. Rather, it identified the business which was acknowledged as being the very best at warehousing and distribution – the L.L. Bean catalogue merchant. L.L. Bean agreed to undertake a co-operative benchmarking project. Over a period the two exchanged data on various aspects of their inventory handling and processing of orders. As a result of this, Xerox identified those areas in its own operation which were performing at below Bean's standards and acted to implement improvements. One critical point to note is that Xerox did not adopt another office equipment business as its model – it adopted a business operating in a different sector altogether.

Benchmarking in all its varied forms is becoming increasingly widespread in industry, services and the public sector. In particular, it is perceived to offer a more sophisticated tool in performance management than more traditional approaches such as standard costing. The general thrust behind this idea is that standard costing belongs in the era when goods were produced in long continuous production runs and a high proportion of costs were 'product specific'. In the new economy, goods tend to be highly customised, contain a significant service element and are produced in short discontinuous production runs on a JIT basis. A large proportion of product costs are determined at the design stage or are 'customer specific', that is they relate to the manner in which the goods are provided to the customer. Efficiency is therefore very much a function of product engineering, the flexibility of the production operation and customer relationship management. It is argued that the traditional budgetary control report based on standard costing simply does not address these issues.

A comprehensive system of benchmarking can provide a much fuller impression of how well or badly an operation is performing. And, it is more likely to give an indication of those areas in the operation that are amenable to improvement. That said, benchmarking has its critics. For example:

Benchmarking relies on competitive data that isn't readily available. When the data is available, it may be neither accurate nor timely. Moreover, it allows a comparison at only one point in time and does not provide a way to continually improve performance.

John Pucket, Boston Consulting Group (quoted from 1997)

That is fair comment, but the discussion above indicates some of the ways in which such criticism might be answered. For one thing, benchmarking need not rely on competitive data. As with most business techniques, benchmarking has to be carried out well if it is to yield results.

4.9 Developments and current thinking in the application of standard costing

4.9.1 McDonaldisation – Another angle on things

Much contemporary discussion concerning the relevance of standard costing in the modern economic environment turns around the manner in which shortened product life cycles and increased customisation of products marginalise the whole concept of the standard cost. Furthermore, the associated 'static optimisation' approach to performance evaluation (through comparison of actual and standard) tends to avoid the whole thrust of modern thinking in areas such as total quality management, continuous improvement and business process re-engineering.

However, one should approach this discussion with a certain caution. In 1993 the American sociologist George Ritzer published his seminal work 'The McDonaldization of Society' (Pine Forge Press), a text which has been reprinted in revised editions on several subsequent occasions. The thrust of this text is that the delivery to market of large-volume, homogenous products (along the lines of McDonald's fast food) offers several advantages which may be grouped under the following headings:

- *Efficiency.* Such products are usually cheap to produce, quick to deliver and efficient in their use of resources. This follows the traditional 'scientific management' approach whereby standardisation of products and production methods leads to cost minimisation.
- *Calculability.* Such products place an emphasis on quantitative considerations such as weight, size, waiting time and price. For example, one measure of the real economic exchange rates of currencies is based on the price of a 'Big-Mac' in the different countries concerned.
- *Predictability.* Buyers can confidently purchase a product anywhere they are without having to give too much thought to the matter. A Big-Mac purchased in Chicago is the same as one purchased in Manchester.
- *Control.* The delivery of such products involves the use of a known set of materials and a simple, pre-determined set of tasks. It is therefore easy and meaningful to evaluate performance through comparison of actual inputs with standard inputs.

Ritzer claims that McDonaldisation is a social and organisational phenomenon. We need not explore this too deeply, but it is apparent that it is a phenomenon which is entirely consistent with 'Taylorism', scientific management and standard costing (see 'What is a Fair Day's Work?' in Chapter 3). The conceptual underpinning of McDonaldisation is pure 'scientific management'. It might be argued that the thrust of this is deeply traditional and runs counter to the 'new economy' concepts referred to in the first paragraph of this section.

4.9.2 Diagnostic reference groups

One specific area where standard costing currently appears to be flourishing is in healthcare management. For the purposes of remunerating healthcare providers and evaluating the performance of those providers, it is often deemed necessary to determine the standard cost of providing healthcare to persons suffering from specific medical conditions.

One response to this is the use of the diagnostic reference group (DRG) otherwise known as the healthcare resource group or case mix group. The medical conditions from which patients admitted to hospital are suffering can be classified into DRGs. Most practical applications of this approach involve the adoption of between 600 and 800 DRGs.

Patients within a given DRG all suffer from broadly the same medical condition and will receive broadly the same treatment.

Healthcare funders (insurance companies or the NHS) may undertake to pay a given amount per day to a hospital for the treatment of patients within a particular DRG. That per day rate will be determined with reference to the standard cost of treating a patient within the DRG – having regard to the resources required and the amount that the hospital has to pay for those resources. At the same time, the performance of a hospital may be evaluated by comparing its actual per day costs for given DRGs with the relevant standards. If a hospital incurs a cost of £5,000 per day for treating a patient requiring a liver transplant and the standard cost (or benchmark cost) is £4,000 per day, then this comparison offers a comment on the efficiency of the hospital concerned. Similarly, if a hospital takes 23 days to treat a particular DRG and the standard is 19 days, then this also is a comment on its efficiency.

However, the DRG approach is not without its critics. The clinical treatments available for any illness are varied. In the case of heart disease they range from a heart transplant at one extreme to merely counselling on lifestyle and diet at the other extreme. Each patient is different having regard to the detailed nature of the disease, its degree of progression and their own strength and state of general health. The clinician should evaluate each patient individually and decide on the programme of surgery, drugs and lifestyle counselling that is appropriate in each case. However, if a hospital is paid a fixed daily rate for treating a patient in a given DRG, then the clinician will be most reluctant to provide treatment above or below the standard package for that DRG. If treatment is provided above standard, then the hospital will not be paid any additional fee, and treatment below standard may result in unpleasant accusations of malpractice being levelled by both patients and funding providers.

The logic of the DRG approach is that each patient who presents with a given set of symptoms is offered a standard package of treatments – which may not always be entirely appropriate. A clinician may be tempted simply to offer the standard package to each patient in a DRG even though he or she may suspect that package to be inadequate in some cases and excessive in others. In effect, the approach may induce a degree of McDonaldisation with all patients served the medical equivalent of a Big-Mac. Unless great sensitivity is exercised in its application, the use of DRGs may result in clinical practice being distorted by what is essentially a financial control system.

4.10 Summary

In this chapter we have continued our exploration of the manner in which standard costing can be used as an element in performance evaluation. We have seen that many observers have suggested that standard costing may be in the process of becoming last year's model' in terms of its usefulness in the modern economic environment. The modern trend in performance evaluation is towards the use of internal and external benchmarking. Nevertheless, standard costing is a simple approach that is both well understood and widely used.

We will make further reference to various aspects of standard costing and benchmarking as we proceed through this text.

Self-test quiz

(1) Explain the manner in which a materials usage variance is split into mix and yield component variances (Section 4.2).

(2) In the context of a company audit exercise, what is the likely cause of an adverse labour mix variance (Section 4.3)?

(3) Explain the term 'planning variance' (Section 4.5).

(4) Explain the term 'operational variance' (Section 4.5).

(5) What is an 'ex-post standard' (Section 4.5)?

(6) List the factors that might influence the decision on whether or not to investigate a particular variance (Section 4.7).

(7) Explain the link between the standard cost concept and 'internal benchmarking' (Section 4.8).

(8) Explain the link between the standard cost concept and the 'Diagnostic Reference Groups' used in healthcare management (Section 4.9.2).

(9) How do 'Taylorism' and 'scientific management' contribute to the standard costing concept (Section 4.9.1)?

Revision Questions

❓ Question 1

The following data relates to both questions 1.1 and 1.2 below.

P Ltd operates a standard costing system. The following information has been extracted from the standard cost card for one of its products:

Budgeted production		1,250 units
Direct material cost	7 g @ £4.10 per kg	£28.70 per unit
Actual results for the period were as follows:		
Production		1,000 units
Direct material (purchased and used)	7,700 kg	£33,880

It has subsequently been noted that the market price of the material was £4.50 per kg during the period.

1.1 The value of the planning variance is

(A) £1,225 (A)
(B) £2,800 (A)
(C) £3,500 (A)
(D) £4,375 (A)
(E) £5,950 (A)   **(2 marks)**

1.2 The value of the material usage variance is

(A) £2,870 (A)
(B) £3,080 (A)
(C) £3,150 (A)
(D) £3,587.50 (A)
(E) £3,937.50 (A)   **(2 marks)**

The following data is to be used to answer questions 1.3 and 1.4 below.

SW plc manufactures a product known as the TRD100 by mixing two materials.
The standard material cost per unit of the TRD100 is as follows:

		£
Material X	12 litres @ £2.50	30
Material Y	18 litres @ £3.00	54

In October 2002, the actual mix used was 984 litres of X and 1,230 litres of Y. The actual output was 72 units of TRD 100.

1.3 The total material mix variance reported was nearest to

(A) £102 (F)
(B) £49 (F)
(C) £49 (A)
(D) £151 (A)   **(3 marks)**

1.4 The total material yield variance reported was nearest to

(A) £102 (F)
(B) £49 (F)
(C) £49 (A)
(D) £151 (A)   **(2 marks)**

The following data is to be used to answer questions 1.5, 1.6 and 1.7 below.
Q plc sells a single product. The standard cost and selling price details are as follows:

	£
Selling price per unit	200
Unit variable costs	124
Unit fixed costs	35

During October 2002, a total of 4,500 units of the product were sold, compared to a sales and production budget of 4,400 units. The actual cost and selling price details were as follows:

	£
Selling price unit	215
Unit variable costs	119
Unit fixed costs	40

1.5 The budgeted margin of safety is closest to

(A) 100 sales units
(B) £154,000 sales value
(C) £334,000 sales value
(D) £475,000 sales value   **(2 marks)**

1.6 The sales volume contribution variance for October was

(A) £4,100 (F)
(B) £5,600 (F)
(C) £7,600 (F)
(D) £9,600 (F)   **(2 marks)**

1.7 The selling price variance for October was

(A) £20,000 (F)
(B) £21,500 (F)

(C) £66,000 (F)

(D) £67,500 (F) **(2 marks)**

(Total = 20 marks)

1.8 The standard ingredients of 1 kg AB are 0.7 kg A (cost £5 per kg) and 0.3 kg B (cost £8 per kg). In the current period, 100 kg AB has been produced using 68 kg A and 32 kg B. The material mixture variance is

(A) nil.

(B) £10 (A)

(C) £6 (F)

(D) £12 (F)

(E) £6 (A)

1.9 Based on original standards, the standard requirement for the work achieved in the current period is 100 labour hours at a rate of £12 per hour. However, labour efficiency has increased by 20% (that is, 20% more output can be achieved from the same hours) and the standard has been revised to allow for this. The labour efficiency planning variance is

(A) £100 (F)

(B) £150 (F)

(C) £60 (F)

(D) nil.

(E) £200 (F)

The following data are to be used to answer questions 1.10 and 1.11 below.

The following extract from a standard cost card shows the materials to be used in producing 100 litres of an agricultural fertiliser.

Material H	30 litres	@ $4.00 per litre
Material J	50 litres	@ $3.50 per litre
Material K	40 litres	@ $6.50 per litre
	120	

During April 5,400 litres of the agricultural fertiliser were produced using the following materials:

Material H	1,860 litres
Material J	2,450 litres
Material K	2,740 litres
	7,050

1.10 The total material mix variance to be reported for April is nearest to

(A) $2,636 (A)

(B) $1,219 (A)

(C) $1,219 (F)

(D) $2,636 (F)

1.11 The total material yield variance to be reported for April is nearest to

(A) $2,636 (A)

(B) $1,219 (A)

(C) $1,219 (F)

(D) $2,636 (F)

Question 2

Super Clean products Ltd manufactures 'Whizzoh'. Whizzoh comprises three basic ingredients, the standard mix and price of which are as follows:

To produce 1 kg of Whizzoh:

HCB (hydrocarbon base)	0.9 kg at 5 p per kg
SHC (sodium hypochlorite)	0.1 kg at 21 p per kg
WM7 (a secret formula)	0.05 kg at 29 p per kg
	1.05 kg

SHC and WM7 are the active ingredients and are interchangeable. Super Clean Products Ltd's production facilities are highly automated and there is no direct labour. Fixed overheads are budgeted at £10,000 per month and production is budgeted to run at 20,000 kg of Whizzoh per month. Fixed overheads are absorbed through HCB usage. During the course of January, 21,500 kg of Whizzoh are produced with the following figures for material consumption:

HCB	19,100 kg at 5.1 p per kg
SHC	2,800 kg at 20 p per kg
WM7	980 kg at 33 p per kg
	22,880 kg

Fixed overheads during the period were £10,000.

Requirement

Reconcile standard and actual costs in January using a full variance analysis.   **(25 marks)**

 Question 3

PH plc operates a modern factory that converts chemicals into fertiliser. Because the demand for its product is seasonal, the company expects that there will be an average level of idle time equivalent to 20% of hours paid. This is incorporated into the company's standard costs, and the standard labour rate of £6.00 per hour paid is then adjusted accordingly. Any difference between the expected and the actual amount of idle time is reported as the 'idle time variance' and is valued at the adjusted wage rate.

Data for each of the 4 months from January to April 2002 is as follows:

	January	February	March	April
Actual hours paid	10,000	14,000	17,000	30,000
Actual productive hours	7,200	10,304	12,784	23,040
Standard hours produced	6,984	9,789	11,889	20,966
Idle time variance	£6,000 (A)	£6,720 (A)	£6,120 (A)	?
Efficiency variance	£1,620 (A)	£3,863 (A)	£6,713 (A)	?

Requirements

(a) Calculate the idle time variance and the efficiency variance for April.   **(4 marks)**

(b) (i) Using the data provided and your answer to (a) above as appropriate, prepare a percentage variance chart that shows the trend of these variances. (Use graph paper and show both variances on the same chart.)

   (ii) Comment on the usefulness of presenting the information in this format.

   (10 marks)

(c) Comment briefly on the possible inter-relationships between the idle time variance and the efficiency variance.   **(4 marks)**

(d) Explain briefly the factors that should be considered before deciding to investigate a variance.   **(7 marks)**

(Total = 25 marks)

Question 4

You are the management accountant of T plc. The following computer printout shows details relating to April 20X8.

	Actual		Budget	
Sales volume	4,900	units	5,000	Units
Selling price per unit	£11.00		£10.00	
Production volume	5,400	Units	5,000	Units
Direct materials				
Quantity	10,600	kg	10,000	kg
Price per kg	£0.60		£0.50	
Direct labour				
Hours per unit	0.55		0.50	
Rate per hour	£3.80		£4.00	
Fixed overhead				
Production	£10,300		£10,000	
Administration	£3,100		£3,000	

T plc uses a standard absorption costing system.
There was no opening or closing work in progress.

Requirements

(a) Prepare a statement that reconciles the budgeted profit with the actual profit for April 20 × 8, showing individual variances in as much detail as the above data permits.
   (20 marks)

(b) Explain briefly the possible causes of:

   (i) the material usage variance;
   (ii) the labour rate variance;
   (iii) the sales volume profit variance.   **(6 marks)**

(c) Explain the meaning and relevance of interdependence of variances when reporting to managers.   **(4 marks)**

(Total marks = 30)

Solutions to Revision Questions

 Solution 1

1.1

Planning variance		£
Ex-ante Standard	7 kg × £4.10 × 1,000	28,700
Ex-post Standard	7 kg × £4.50 × 1,000	31,500
Variance		2,800 (A)

Therefore the answer is (B).

Note: The £4.50 revised price per kg is stated to be a 'market' price and not a 'purchase' price. The £4.50 is therefore taken to be an ex-post standard on which a planning variance is to be calculated.

1.2

Material usage variance		kg
Ex-post standard	7 kg × 1,000	7,000
Actual		7,700
Variance		700 × £4.50/kg = £3,150 (A)

Therefore the answer is (C).

1.3

	Actual mix litres	Standard mix litres	Difference litres	Price £	Variamce £
X	984	885.6	98.4 (A)	2.50	246.0 (A)
Y	1,230	1,328.4	98.4 (F)	3.00	295.2 (F)
Totals	2,214	2,214.0	nil		49.2 (F)

Therefore the answer is (B).

1.4

$$\text{Expected output} = \frac{2,214}{30} \qquad = 73.8 \text{ units}$$

Actual output	= 72.0 units
Shortfall	= 1.8 units
1.8 units × £84/unit	= 151.2 (A)

Therefore the answer is (D).

1.5

Budgeted fixed costs = 4,400 units × £35/unit   = £154,000
Budgeted contribution/unit = £200 − £124   = £76

$$\text{Budgeted breakeven point (units)} = \frac{£154,000}{£76} \qquad = 2{,}026 \text{ units}$$

Budgeted sales units   = 4,400.00 units
Budgeted margin of safety (units) = 4,400 − 2,026   = 2,374
Budget margin of safety (sales value) = 2,374 × £200   = £474,800

Therefore the answer is (D).

1.6

100 units × (£200 − £124) = £7,600(F)

Therefore the answer is (C).

1.7

4,500 units × (£200 − £215) = £67,500(F)

Therefore the answer is (D).

1.8   Answer: (E)

£6 adverse – standard mix is 70 kg A plus 30 kg B, from which it follows that the mixture variance is 2 kg A @ £5 (favourable) plus 2 kg B @ £8 (adverse).

1.9   Answer: (E)

£200 favourable. Since output that required 100 hours under original standards now requires 83.333 hours (100 hours/1.2), it follows that the planning efficiency variance is 16.666 hours favourable with a cost of £200 (16.666 × £12).

1.10

	Actual mix litres	Standard mix litres	Difference litres	Standard price $/litre	Variance $
H	1,860	1,762.5	97.5	4.00	390.00 (A)
J	2,450	2,937.5	(487.5)	3.50	1,706.25 (F)
K	2,740	2,350.0	390.0	6.50	2,535.00 (A)
Total	7,050	7,050	nil		1,218.75 (A)

Therefore the answer is (B).

1.11

Standard cost per litre of output:

		$
H	30 litres @ $4.00	120.00
J	50 litres @ $3.50	175.00
K	40 litres @ $6.50	260.00
Total		555.00 per 100 litres

Actual input of 7,050 litres should yield 100/120 litres of output =	5,8750 litres	
Actual output	5,400 litres	
Shortfall	475 litres	

475 litres @ $555.00 per 100 litres = $2,636.25 (A)

Therefore the answer is (A).

 # Solution 2

- In answering this, it is critical to appreciate that you are being invited to reconcile standard and actual costs – not budget and actual costs. Failing to grasp this is one of the most common problems that student accountants have when undertaking variance analysis exercises.
- In specifying 'a full variance analysis' the question invites calculation of material mix/ yield variance and fixed overhead capacity usage/efficiency variances.
- Notes that since budget fixed overheads equals actual fixed overheads, there will be no fixed overhead expenditure variance.

Standard material cost of 1 kg of Whizzoh is

	Input	Unit cost	Total cost
	kg	*p/kg*	*£*
HCB	0.90	5	0.0450
SHC	0.10	21	0.0210
WM7	0.05	29	0.0145
	1.05		0.0805

Standard overhead cost of 1 kg Whizzoh is

0.9 kg of HCB @ £0.55555 = £0.50.

The £0.55555 absorption rate is budgeted overheads (£10,000) divided by budgeted HCB usage (18,000 kg).

Variance calculations	£	£
Standard cost of output		
Materials: (21,500 kg × £0.0805)	1,730.75	
Overheads: (21,500 kg × 0.9 hrs × £0.5555)	10,749.89	
Total		12,480.64
Actual cost of output		
Materials	1,857.50	
Overheads	10,000.00	
Total		11,857.50
Cost variance		623.14 (F)
	£	£
Material price variance		
A: 19,100 kg × (5 p − 5.1 p)	(19.10) (A)	
B: 2,800 kg × (21 p − 20 p)	28.00 (F)	
C: 980 kg × (29 p − 33 p)	(39.20) (A)	
Total		(30.30) (A)
Material mixture variance		
A: (19,611 kg standard − 19,100 kg actual) × 5 p	25.57 (F)	
B: (2,179 kg standard − 2,800 kg actual) × 21 p	(130.40) (A)	
C: (1,089 kg standard − 980 kg actual) × 29 p	31.76 (F)	
Total		(73.07) (A)

	£
Material yield variance	
$((22{,}880\,\text{kg}/1.05) - 21{,}500\,\text{kg}) \times £0.0805$	(23.38) (A)
Fixed overhead capacity	
$(19{,}100\,\text{kg actual} - 18{,}000\,\text{kg budget}) \times £0.55555$	611.11 (F)
Fixed overhead efficiency	
$(19{,}350\,\text{kg standard} - 19{,}100\,\text{kg actual}) \times £0.55555$	<u>138.89</u> (F)
Cost variance total	<u>623.00</u> (F)

Note: In calculating the mixture variance for A, the standard amount of A in the mix is 22,880 kg (actual input)/1.05 × 0.09.

 ## Solution 3

(a) Standard rate per hour worked $= \dfrac{£6.00}{0.8} = £7.50$

Idle time variance:

Expected idle time = 20% × 30,000 hours = 6,000 hours	
Actual idle time = 30,000 − 23,040	= <u>6,960</u> hours
	<u>960</u> hours
960 hours × £7.50 per hour	= £7,200 (A)

Efficiency variance:

Standard hours produced	= 20,966
Actual hours worked	= <u>23,040</u>
	<u>2,074</u> hours
2,074 hours × £7.50 per hour	= £15,555 (A)

(b) (i) Calculations for graph (expressing variances as % of standard)

Idle time	Standard cost of expected Idle time	Idle time variance	
	£	£	%
January	15,000	6,000 (A)	40 (A)
February	21,000	6,720 (A)	32 (A)
March	25,500	6,120 (A)	24 (A)
April	45,000	7,200 (A)	16 (A)

Efficiency	Standard cost of Standard hours Produced	Efficiency variance	
	£	£	%
January	52,380	1,620 (A)	3 (A)
February	73,418	3,863 (A)	5 (A)
March	89,168	6,713 (A)	8 (A)
April	157,245	15,555 (A)	10 (A)

See graph below.

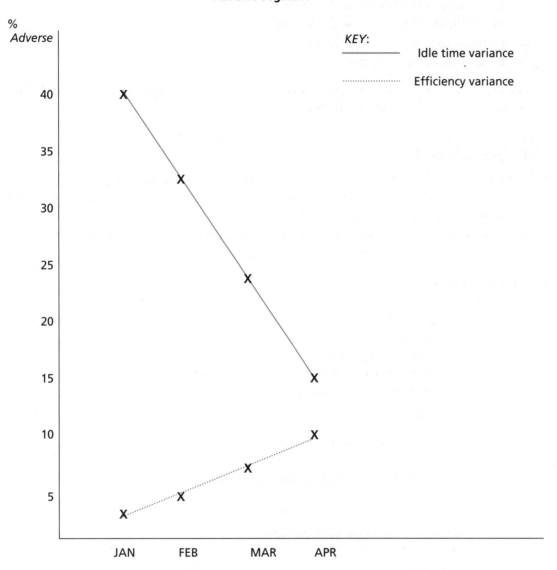

Variance Control Chart
Adverse Segment

(ii) Many managers find the graphical presentation of variances easier to understand than a series of figures presented in a tabular format. By presenting the variances over time the trend can be identified, and this is used to decide if any control action is required.

In this question, the variances have been expressed as percentages of the standard cost, rather than expressing them in monetary amounts. The use of percentages removes the changes in the monetary size of the variances caused by changing activity levels and this improves the trend information that is provided.

(c) The idle time variance and the efficiency variance are sub-variances of the overall efficiency variance.

As can be seen from the control chart, the idle time variance has reduced over the period, while the efficiency variance has increased. This could be because the employees are deliberately taking longer to complete their tasks to avoid being idle because of a lack of work.

(d) There are a number of factors to be considered before investigating a variance. These include
- the size of the variance;
- the likelihood of identifying the cause of the variance;
- the likelihood that the cause of the variance is controllable;
- the likely cost of correcting the cause;
- the cost of the investigation.

The overall factor that will determine whether or not to investigate a variance is whether or not there will be a positive benefit from the investigation.

 Solution 4

- Work methodically through the exercise, calculating each variance item in turn.
- Note that most of the cost variances are calculated by reconciling standard cost with actual cost – not budget cost to actual cost.
- Note that administration overheads are not absorbed into product costs and hence there is no associated volume variance.

(a) Standard product specification

	£	£
Sales price		10.00
Input costs:		
Materials 2 kg @ 50p	1.00	
Labour 0.5 hours @ £4	2.00	
Fixed production overhead	2.00	
		5.00
Profit		5.00

Note: The actual hours worked were 5,400 × 0.55 = 2,970.

T plc: budget/actual reconciliation statement – April 20X8

	£(F)	£(A)	£
Budgeted profit (5,000 × £5 − £3,000)			22,000
Sales volume profit variance (100 × £5)			500 (A)
Standard profit on actual sales			21,500
Variances:	£(F)	£(A)	
Direct material			
Price (£6,360 − £5,300)		1,060	
Usage (£5,300 − £5,400)	100		
Direct labour			
Rate (£11,286 − £11,880)	594		
Efficiency (£11,880 − £10,800)		1,080	
Fixed production overhead			
Expenditure (£10,300 − £10,000)		300	
Volume (£10,000 − £10,800)	800		
Sales price (4,900 × £1)	4,900		
Administrative cost expenditure	100		
Actual profit	6,394	2,540	3,854 (F)
			25,354

Calculation of actual profit

	£	£
Actual sales revenue		53,900
Actual costs		
Material	6,360	
Labour	11,286	
Production overhead	10,300	
	27,946	
Stock increase (500 units × £5)	2,500	
Cost of sales		25,446
		28,454
Fixed administration		3,100
Actual profit		25,354

The variance calculations shown above are in summary form. In an examination this is perfectly adequate, since the examiner does not need you to explain your calculations in expanded, narrative form. As we progress onwards through the text, we shall increasingly move to this abbreviated form of working. However, on this occasion a fuller explanation of the variance calculations is given below.

Explanation of cost variances

£

Direct materials
Price

Actual usage at standard cost	5,300	(10,600 kg × £0.50)
Actual usage at actual cost	6,360	(10,600 kg × £0.60)
Material price variance	1,060	Adverse

Usage

Standard usage for output at standard cost	5,400	(10,800 kg × £0.50)
Actual usage at standard cost	5,300	(10,600 kg × £0.50)
Material usage variance	100	Favourable

Direct labour
Rate

Actual hours at standard rate	11,880	(5,400 units × 0.55 hrs × £4)
Actual hours at actual rate	11,286	(5,400 units × 0.55 hrs × £3.80)
Labour rate variance	594	Favourable

Efficiency

Standard hours at standard rate	10,800	(5,400 units × 0.50 hrs × £4)
Actual hours at standard rate	11,880	(5,400 units × 0.55 hrs × £4)
Labour efficiency variance	1,080	Adverse

Fixed production overhead
Expenditure

Budgeted fixed overheads	10,000	
Actual fixed overheads	10,300	
Fixed overhead expenditure variance	300	Adverse

Volume

Budgeted fixed overheads	10,000	(5,400 units × £2)
Standard fixed overheads	10,800	
	800	Favourable

(b) (i) The material usage variance may be caused by:

- improved training of operating personnel;
- the sourcing of a better quality of material than was assumed in the standard cost.

(ii) The labour rate variance may be caused by:

- an unanticipated drop in bonus payments;
- the retirement of staff who have reached their maximum points on the salary scale and their replacement by low salary staff.

(iii) The sales volume profit variance may be caused by

- the increase in sales price discouraging customers;
- the adverse effect of a successful advertising campaign run by a competitor.

(c) The term 'interdependence of variances' describes a relationship in which an action taken by management or operating personnel causes more than one (related) variance to be reported. For example, the sourcing of better quality material, as mentioned in part (b), may result in lower usage (favourable material usage variance) but a higher price (adverse material price variance).

An understanding of interdependence is essential if responsibility for outcomes is to be correctly identified. It is therefore crucial to the success of a control system such as standard costing.

5

Developments in
Management Accounting

Developments in Management Accounting

5

LEARNING OUTCOMES

After completing study of this chapter you should be able to

▶ explain the impact of just-in-time manufacturing methods on cost accounting and the use of 'backflush accounting' when work-in-progress stock is minimal;

▶ explain the role of MRP and ERP systems in supporting standard costing systems, calculating variances and facilitating the posting of ledger entries;

▶ apply principles of environmental costing in identifying relevant internalised costs and externalised environmental impacts of the organisation's activities;

5.1 Introduction

In this chapter we will consider developments in the economic, business and manufacturing environments over the past 25 years and the impact that these developments have had on management accounting. One key issue in this area is the link between the Just-In-Time philosophy of management and its association with techniques such as total quality management, advanced manufacturing technologies, backflush costing and throughput accounting. We will also consider environmental accounting and identifying costs of complying with environmental requirements in areas such as CO_2 emissions, disposal of toxic waste and water usage.

5.2 The modern business environment

5.2.1 Traditional Production processes

In manufacturing industry (and one can identify parallels in the service sector), there have traditionally been three main methods of organising production, each one representing the least-cost method of satisfying customer needs:

(i) *Jobbing production.* Where customers require goods to be produced to their own particular specifications. In such an environment, each order is a one-off, manufactured to customer order. Typically, only low stocks are held and production is organised in a manner calculated to achieve flexibility. That is, machines and personnel are arranged in a manner that allows production to be shifted quickly from one job to another.

(ii) *Batch production.* Where production takes place in the form of discrete production runs. Typically, production is not to specific customer order and some stock holding of both finished goods and components may be essential. Given that production facilities have to switch quickly from output of one product to another, a degree of flexibility has to be incorporated in the operation. Such flexibility in plant arrangement and machine design may be at the expense of unit cost.

(iii) *Mass production.* Where a standard product is in continuous or near continuous production. This approach prioritises low unit cost at the expense of flexibility. If customer dispatches and supplier deliveries can be phased evenly (through use of JIT and SCM technique – discussed below), then it may be possible to operate with very low stock holdings.

The mass production model is typical of traditional industry. This approach is vulnerable to fluctuations in the market. A temporary down turn in customer demand may result in a build-up in stocks of finished goods and it may be difficult or expensive to suspend production when this happens. It may be very difficult to accommodate product features customised to the needs of individual customers. The weakness of the mass production model is that it lacks flexibility. It involves sacrificing a lot in exchange for low unit production cost.

5.2.2 The background to change

Cost is an important competitive weapon. Low-cost producers will have an advantage in the marketplace over those whose cost base is higher. However, cost is only one competitive weapon and it is one that has become of declining importance in recent years. Other dimensions of competition have become increasingly important: product reliability, product innovation, shortened time to market, and flexibility of response to customer demands – these last three being features of time-based competition.

It is obvious that a manufacturer would gain competitive advantage if he were able to produce the diversity of output seen in a jobbing system at a cost associated with mass production. In recent years, some manufacturers, most notably the Japanese, have been successful in moving towards this. Furthermore, the products of these manufacturers have an enviable reputation for reliability. These suppliers have clearly gained competitive advantage in the marketplace, forcing competitors to follow or exit the market. Consumers, given the opportunity to enjoy diversity and reliability at a mass-produced cost, have reacted not unexpectedly by requiring all manufacturers to offer these features. Further, a corollary of the requirement for greater diversity has been a shortening of product life cycles.

This fundamental shift in demand patterns dictates a need for companies to constantly review and redesign existing products, and to shorten the time to market of each new line in order to ensure satisfactory returns from it. Against this new background, companies will find it increasingly difficult to gain economic returns from an expensive, dedicated mass-production line operated in traditional way. Means must be found whereby manufacturing facilities cannot only accommodate the production of existing lines and their inevitable redesigned successors, but also facilitate the rapid introduction of new products at minimum cost. The challenge of the modern, globally competitive market is to offer an increased and increasing choice of high-quality products at a cost traditionally associated with mass production; to enjoy economies of scale, along with the economies of scope that result from the increased manufacturing flexibility. This challenge can be met by investment in new technology, and the adoption of alternative production management strategies. Those who successfully meet this challenge are the 'world-class manufacturers' that provide the benchmark against which other manufacturers are measured.

'World class' organisations make products using the latest manufacturing technologies and techniques. Those products are typically sold around the world and are generally viewed as being first rate in terms of quality, design, performance and reliability. Companies such as Toyota, BMW and Boeing have been described at various times as being world-class manufacturers. The world-class manufacturer will probably invest heavily in research, product design, CAD/CAM technology. It will also make extensive use of modern management concepts such as Total quality management (TQM), flexible manufacturing systems and customer relationship management. These concepts variously known as advanced manufacturing technologies (AMTs) or the new manufacturing are discussed in detail below.

5.3 The new manufacturing

5.3.1 Computer-aided design

At the initial design stage of a product, the considerable space occupied by the drawing tables of a typical design office has been replaced by computer terminals, and the time taken to work through an initial engineering drawing – and, more importantly, rework the drawing – has shortened dramatically as a result of the softwares currently available. Computer-aided design (CAD) allows huge numbers of alternative configurations to be analysed both for cost and utility. CAD allows quality and cost reduction to be built in at the design stage of a product. The advanced graphics facilities of the typical CAD program enable the draughtsman not only to move parts around the design, and instantly appreciate the effect of these changes on the finished product, but also to manipulate the drawing, and view the design from any desired angle (and even, in the case of the latest generation of software, 'walk through' it). The use of a database to match, where possible, the requirements of the new design with existing product parts will enable the company to minimise stockholdings by reducing the total number of product parts required.

5.3.2 Computer-aided manufacturing

The manufacturing process is carried out by a range of machinery that, together with its concomitant software, comes under the collective heading of computer-aided manufacturing (CAM). Significant elements of CAM are computer numerical control (CNC) and robotics. CNC machines are programmable machine tools that are capable of performing a number of machining tasks, such as cutting and grinding. A computer program stores all the existing manufacturing configurations and set-up instructions for a particular machine or bank of machines, facilitating a change in configuration in a matter of seconds via the keyboard; changes to existing configurations and new configurations are easily accommodated. CNC therefore offers great flexibility and dramatically reduced set-up times. Furthermore, unlike human operators, who tire and are error-prone, CNC machines are able to repeat the same operation continuously in an absolutely identical manner, to a completely consistent level of accuracy and machine tolerance. CNC also promotes flexibility through allowing machines to switch from output of one product to another very quickly.

Two brief examples will serve to illustrate the dramatic impact of CAM on manufacturing flexibility, and the time taken to develop a product and bring it to the market. Nissan, the car producer, found that the time taken to completely retool car body panel jigs in their intelligent body assembly system (IBAS) fell from 12 months to less than 3 months by reprogramming the process machinery by computer and using computerised jig robots. Similar advances have been made in the resetting of machines and in the exchange of dies. These changes have reduced the changeover time in moving from one process to another. Again it is a Japanese company, Toyota, that provides one of the best examples of the advances made in this area. As the speed of production changeover increases under CAM, the possibility of producing smaller and smaller batch sizes at an economic cost also increases, so that the production schedule can be driven more and more by customer requirements rather than the constraints of the traditional manufacturing process.

5.3.3 Computer-integrated manufacturing

The ultimate extension – and logical long-term direction – of AMT in the production environment is computer-integrated manufacturing (CIM), which brings together all the elements of automated manufacturing and quality control into one coherent system. The 'ideal' technological world of CIM – the fully automated production facility, controlled entirely by means of a computer network with no human interference – is not yet with us (and, indeed, with its overtones of 'ghost factories', would not necessarily be universally welcomed).

A somewhat watered-down version of CIM is already with us, however, in the form of a flexible manufacturing system (FMS) discussed below. The FMS cell is often referred to as an 'island of automation' in the context of a more traditionally organised facility.

5.3.4 Flexible manufacturing systems

The FMS is 'an integrated production system which is computer controlled to produce a family of parts in a flexible manner ... a bundle of machines that can be reprogrammed to switch from one production run to another'. It consists of a cluster of machine tools and a system of conveyor belts that shuttle the work piece from tool to tool in a similar fashion to the traditional transfer line used in mass (large-batch) production. Thus the benefits lie in being able to switch quickly from making one product to another.

The major strength of an FMS system is its ability to manufacture not just a family of parts, but a family of products. By using this system, General Electric has been able to produce a range of diesel engines that are of considerably different sizes on the same automated production line, without substantially retooling and time-consuming start-ups.

The FMS normally incorporates CAD and CAM features. It is an approach to manufacturing that is well attuned to modern market economics, where products have short life-cycles, are produced in short discontinuous runs (see discussion of JIT below) and are often highly customised to the needs of individual customers.

One notable aspect of an FMS (or any AMT environment) is that efficiency is a product of product design and plant flexibility rather than a direct result of low unit production costs. A traditional standard costing and variance analysis system may not be very effective in this environment. For one thing, once one moves away from a traditional mass production operation, a high proportion of production costs are either designed into a product or are facility costs not directly specific to any one product. Running a cost system that places a focus on things like the 'direct material usage variance' may tell one almost nothing about how well or badly a production operation is performing.

5.4 The value chain

The driving force behind the adoption of AMTs is a thorough appreciation of the relationship between *all* the factors within the value chain – the sequence of business factors by which *value* is added to the organisation's products and services. The value chain is illustrated in Figure 5.1.

- *Research and development.* The generation of, and experimentation with, ideas for new products, services or process.
- *Design.* The detailed planning and engineering of products, services or process.
- *Production.* The co-ordination and assembly of resources to produce a product or deliver a service.
- *Marketing.* The process by which potential customers learn about and value the attributes of the organisation's products or services, and are persuaded to buy them.
- *Distribution.* The mechanism by which the organisation's products or services are delivered to the customer.
- *Customer service.* The support activities provided to customers.

Functions within the value chain are not necessarily sequential; the organisation can gain important competitive advantages by activating individual parts of the chain concurrently. The major consideration is their smooth *co-ordination* within the framework of the organisation as a whole.

5.5 Political and social issues

The concept of 'social accounting' relates to the manner in which an organisation interacts with its social surroundings. Social accounting is the process of communicating the social and environmental effects of organisation's economic actions to particular interest groups within society and to society at large.

Social accounting emphasises the notion of corporate accountability. It may be defined as an approach to reporting a firm's activities which stresses the need for the identification of socially relevant behaviour, the determination of those to whom the company is accountable for its social performance and the development of appropriate measures and

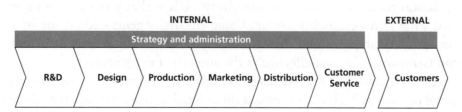

Figure 5.1 The value chain

reporting techniques. The main ideas underpinning social accounting as it impacts on an organisation are that its reporting system should:

- concern itself with more than only economic events;
- not be exclusively expressed in financial terms;
- be accountable to a broader group of stakeholders than owners;
- broaden its purpose beyond reporting financial success.

A business using social accounting will normally seek to identify and report the outcome of its activities to the community as a whole. Such a social outcome has cost and benefit dimensions. Social reporting (the output of social accounting) is intended to support the achievement of an organisation's social objectives. The objects of social accounting can be diverse, but the best known are gender, racial and environmental. Other issues are animal welfare, education, arts and sport.

The rise of social accounting has been influenced by a greater awareness of the impact of business activity on the whole community and on the environment. This awareness has been expressed through the work of pressure groups (such as Friends of the Earth) and through political and statutory means. South African law relating to 'Black Economic Empowerment' requires businesses to report on the racial mix of their employees and the amount invested in the advancement and promotion of black staff. Government departments apply positive discrimination in the awarding of contracts to businesses that have high levels of black ownership and management.

Environmental accounting, a subset of social accounting, focuses on the cost structure and environmental performance of a company. It involves the preparation, presentation, and communication of information related to an organisation's interaction with the natural environment. Environmental accounting is a legal requirement in some countries – such as Denmark, the Netherlands and Australia. The United Nations has been highly involved in the adoption of environmental accounting practices, most notably in the United Nations Division for Sustainable Development publication Environmental Management Accounting Procedures and Principles (2002).

One particular influence has been the EU Greenhouse Gas Emission Trading Scheme which was introduced in 2005. This was prompted by concerns over the impact of CO_2 emissions from industry on the global climate. The scheme gives each large industrial concern a GHG emission allowance which is capped. If its verified CO_2 emissions in any year exceed its allowance then a business has to buy additional allowances on the market. If its emissions are less than its allowance then it can sell its surplus on the market (where allowances usually trade at between €5 and €13 per tonne). This situation may create substantial liabilities or assets for a business which have to be accounted for. It also creates a complex decision-making situation in which businesses have to consider the cost–benefit trade off between alternative emission strategies. This scheme currently only applies to CO_2 although it is expected that it may be extended to other emissions and areas such as water usage.

One practical result of the above scheme in the UK is that a number of factories have established wind farms on their premises. Using electricity generated on-site by wind turbines reduces CO_2 emissions and thus avoids allowance purchase costs. It is unlikely that such wind farms would be cost-effective in the absence of the scheme.

The thrust behind these developments is an imperative to 'internalise' the external costs of an industrial operation. If a business impacts on the environment through the release of waste then the cost of that impact should be charged to the business in some way. The manner in which businesses must deal with this has a substantial management accounting dimension.

5.6 Production operations systems and management strategies

5.6.1 Material requirements planning

The traditional way to determine material requirements is to monitor stocks constantly; whenever they fall to a predetermined level, a preset order is placed to replenish them. This approach involves the replenishment of any one stock item independently of all others. In reality, the demand for a particular stock item is a function of the assemblies and sub-assemblies of which it forms a part. This traditional approach (involving re-order level and economic order quantity calculations) originates in the pre-computer era.

Material requirements planning (MRP or MRP1) is a technique that aims to ensure that material resources – raw materials, bought-in components and in-house subassemblies – are made available just before they are needed by the next stage of production or despatch. It also seeks to ensure that these resources are delivered only when required, so that stocks are kept to an absolute minimum. The technique enables managers to track orders through the entire manufacturing process, and helps the purchasing and production control departments to move the precise amount of material at the right time to the correct production/distribution stage. MRP1 is only practical with the availability of a full computer model of the production and associated materials procurement requirement for the coming period. MRP1 appeared in the 1960s with the arrival of computers in management.

The MRP is a computerised production planning system that begins with the setting of a master production schedule, and, working backwards, uses the information from this top-level schedule to determine the raw material, component and sub-assembly requirements at each of the earlier stages in the production process. Obviously, the ability of the system to deliver what is required in the correct place at the correct time will be dependant on the quality of the information that is put into the computer model.

The data in the system is analysed to produce a *material requirements* plan for purchasing and manufacturing. As the system is computerised, schedules can easily be reworked to accommodate changes to customer requirements. For example, if a customer requests that product X be delivered in the current month rather than product Y, which had previously been ordered, and that delivery of product Y be deferred until the following month, the MRP system can quickly reschedule all the activities that go to producing these requirements, in order to meet the new needs of the customer.

Prerequisites for the successful operation of an MRP system are as follows:

(i) *Strict schedule adherence.* The operation of informal expediting systems, or the informal alteration of production priorities, will quickly destroy the potential benefits of the system. Workers must be educated to understand the importance of schedule adherence, and controls should be in place to ensure this adherence. A further possible problem is that the system assumes unlimited capacity in all work centres, whereas in reality some work centres always behave as bottlenecks. This contradiction destroys the accuracy of MRP scheduling logic, and makes it ineffective for capacity planning and control.

(ii) *Accurate base data.* Data accuracy is vital to the system; if a plan is based on inaccurate data, it may be impossible to adhere to the schedule. For example, if the information in the inventory file is incorrect, perhaps stating that certain sub-assemblies are available when in fact they are not, the whole production schedule will be incapable of being completed in the manner envisaged. The difficulties encountered in keeping inventory records and 'bill of materials' (listing of materials and components required for products) up to date have been a major cause of failure in the implementation of MRP systems. Similarly, it is vital that the bill of materials file is accurate, and regularly updated to reflect any changes in product composition. An enormous effort is required in a typical company to bring the data inputs to a high enough level of accuracy to support an MRP system. However, without such accuracy, the MRP system will not bring about the expected benefits.

5.6.2 Manufacturing resources planning

When MRP is extended beyond the planning of raw materials, components and sub-assemblies to encompass other input resources, such as machine capacity and labour, so that the system provides a fully integrated planning approach to the management of all the company's manufacturing resources, it is known as manufacturing resources planning (MRP2). It is clear that the *caveats* mentioned above will only increase in importance when the system's database becomes larger and more complex.

Even if the data in an MRP system – either MRP1 or MRP2 – is accurate, and there is 100 per cent schedule adherence, this does not, of itself, mean that the company operating the system will be a world-class manufacturer. It has been argued that many western companies adopt an operations research focus in management, and this approach has been adopted in applying both MRP systems. An operations research approach takes input parameters as given. For example, production times, delivery times and design features are regarded as constants, and within this static framework the optimal production and purchasing plan is sought. This is the 'static optimisation' philosophy of performance management that is entirely consistent with the standard costing and budgeting models considered above.

This is not to argue that MRP systems are incompatible with world-class manufacturing or continuous improvement – indeed, Japanese companies such as Nissan use MRP2 – but simply to point out that applying MRP to an *existing* set of circumstances may improve the *efficiency* with which existing operations are carried out, but this efficiency may still lead to a level of cost that is *higher* than could be achieved if the parameters themselves were challenged. MRP2 appeared in the 1970s, very much as a straight line development from MRP1.

5.6.3 Optimised production technology

Like MRP systems, Optimised production technology (OPT) requires detailed information about inventory levels, product structures, routings and set-up and operation timing for each and every procedure of each product. However, unlike MRP, the technique actively seeks to identify and remove – or optimise the use of – bottleneck resources within a manufacturing process, in order to avoid unnecessary build-ups of stock. A bottleneck resource is the thing in the production process that limits overall output. We have already encountered this idea in the context of critical path analysis, limiting factor analysis and the principal budget factor.

Drury (2000) gives an excellent and concise description of the OPT approach, which is worth reproducing in full:

The OPT philosophy contends that the primary goal of manufacturing is to make money. Three important criteria are identified to evaluate progress towards achieving this goal. These are throughput, inventory and operating expenses. The goal is to maximise throughput while simultaneously maintaining or decreasing inventory and operating expenses.

The OPT approach determines what prevents throughput from being higher by distinguishing between bottlenecks and removing them or, if this is not possible, ensures that they are fully utilised at all times. Non-bottleneck resources should be scheduled and operated based on constraints within the system, and should not be used to produce more than the bottlenecks can absorb. The OPT philosophy therefore advocates that non-bottleneck resources should not be utilised to 100 per cent of their capacity, since this would merely result in an increase in inventory. Thus idle time in non-bottleneck areas is not considered detrimental to the efficiency of the organisation. If it were utilised, it would result in increased inventory without a corresponding increase in throughput for the plant.

With the OPT approach, it is vitally important to schedule all non-bottleneck resources within the manufacturing system based on the constraints of the system (i.e. the bottlenecks). For example, if only 70 per cent of the output of a non-bottleneck resource can be absorbed by the following bottleneck resources, then 30 per cent of the utilisation of the non-bottleneck is simply concerned with increasing inventory. It can therefore be argued that by operating at the 70 per cent level, the non-bottleneck resource is achieving 100 per cent efficiency.

The above description makes it clear that the objective of OPT is to maximise throughput of products, which necessitates the maximisation of output from bottlenecks. Everything else is subservient to this end, so, for example, buffer stocks might be held ahead of bottlenecks, and quality checked *before* product enters the bottleneck. Non-bottlenecks should be paced by the bottlenecks, and should not produce merely for stock.

It has been suggested that overheads should be changed to products on the basis of throughput time, defined as the time taken from initial input to the production line to removal from the line as a finished good. In using this as the allocation base, top management is flagging up to operating management that product costs can be reduced by cutting down throughput time.

5.6.4 ERP, CRM and SCM

MRP1, MRP2 and OPT are essentially business planning techniques, whereby the full resource requirements of a given plan of action can be identified and those requirements satisfied in the most cost-effective manner. The approach is entirely consistent with the budgeting model that we explored in earlier chapters. It is also compatible with standard costing since it incorporates a projection for what the resource requirements are for a budgeted level of production.

However, things have not stopped there and the 1990s saw further developments along this line. During the 1990s, enterprise resource planning (ERP) systems tended to displace the old MRP systems. ERP involves the use of elaborate computer systems to provide plans for every aspect of the business – not just confining attention to material supplies and manufacturing. ERP system design and installation became one of the major products sold by firms of business consultants. ERP systems are frequently associated and integrated with budgeting systems.

Another parallel development was customer relationship management (CRM) systems. These contained all the information about customers and customer requirements. They are often integrated with ERP systems and involve websites and e-commerce facilities. A CRM system may allow receipt of a customer order to automatically prompt the scheduling of necessary production facilities and the ordering of components.

The ultimate development of this kind was supply chain management (SCM), which became very much the 'hot topic' in business management circles in the late 1990s. SCM systems go beyond individual companies and seek to integrate the flow of information between different companies on a supply chain. Thus, if company A schedules production of a certain number of units, then information concerning this would feed through to A's component supplier B, via an SCM system. B's production control would automatically schedule production and delivery at the appropriate time of the components required by A.

To be effective, SCM system have to be associated with a high degree if mutual confidence among the participating businesses. This may involve placing personnel from one business in the premises of another to ensure that appropriate manufacturing standards and specifications are met. It may also involve sharing information about product design and cost structures.

The MRP, ERP and SCM represent a line of development associated with the use of computers and IT to undertake very detailed planning and resource scheduling exercises. However, many observers feel that this approach may be nearing the end of its life cycle. The elaborate, integrated ERP systems of the 1990s may be passing out of use. It is claimed that they involve unnecessary data collection, over-elaborate bills of materials and inefficient workflows. The current move is towards the alternative 'lean enterprise' and its associated information system requirements. The thrust of the lean enterprise concept is that production scheduling and resource acquisition should respond quickly and flexibly to customer demand rather than being the subject of an elaborate planning exercise. Once again, we encounter the idea that modern thinking in management places an emphasis flexibility and short response time rather than elaborate forward planning.

5.6.5 Just-in-time concept

There can be few students of business-related topics who have not heard of just-in-time (JIT) production methods. The CTMA *Official Terminology* defines JIT as follows.

> *JIT:* A system whose objective is to produce or procure products or components as they are required by a customer or for use, rather than for stock. A JIT system is a 'pull' system, which responds to demand, in contrast to a 'push' system, in which stocks act as buffers between the different elements of the systems, such as purchasing, production and sales.

JIT production is defined as follows.

> *JIT production:* A production system which is driven by demand for finished products whereby each component on a production line is produced only when needed for the next stage.

And JIT purchasing is defined as follows.

> *JIT purchasing:* A purchasing system in which material purchases are contracted so that the receipt and usage of material, to the maximum extent possible, coincide.

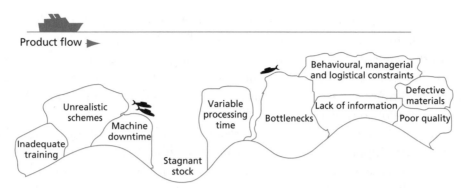

Figure 5.2 The just-in-time concept

The JIT is best described as a 'philosophy', or approach to management, as it encompasses a commitment to continuous improvement and the pursuit of excellence in the design and operation of the production management system. The logical thrust behind JIT is that production and resource acquisition should be 'pulled' by customer demand rather than being 'pushed' by a planning process. A JIT-based production operation responds quickly to customer demand and resources are required and utilised only when needed. In order to be able to operate in this manner, an organisation must achieve excellence in all areas of management.

An attempt to gains from the adoption of JIT usually exposes problems that were previously hidden. An analogy with a boat sailing along a river is often used to explain this result, as seen in Figure 5.2.

The production process in a multi-product plant represents the boat, and the levels of stocks that a company holds are the determinants of the water level of the river. A high level of raw material and component stocks, work in progress and finished goods would indicate that the river is extremely deep. As these stock are reduced, the water level reduces. The bed of the river may contain rocks, the height and quantity being determined by the number of problems that a company faces in its production. The 'rocks' may be caused by poor production scheduling, machine breakdown, absenteeism, inefficient plant layout, excessive rework, schedule interruption through order expediting and so on. However, these rocks do not cause a problem to the boat on the surface, provided that the water depth – the level of inventory – is sufficient to cover them. As the water level, the inventory goes down, the rocks – the problems within the company – will be exposed. The inevitable consequence of this is that the boat will crash into the rocks and will be damaged.

This damage can be avoided in one of the two ways. The first, the traditional western way, is to keep the water level deep – maintain high levels of stocks. An alternative way, and the way consistent with the JIT philosophy, is to remove the rocks, so that the boat can sail quite safely in a much lower level of water. Operating on a JIT basis with low inventories requires a first class operation in all the areas of:

- production scheduling,
- supplier relations,
- plant maintenance,
- information systems,
- quality controls,
- customer relations.

In a JIT environment, 'family groups' of products – products with similar production requirements – are manufactured in separate cells along production-line principles. That is, all the machines needed to carry out the manufacture of a particular product family are arranged in the form of a discrete 'mini' assembly line. The machines are grouped closely together in the sequential order required by processing, and products move from machine to machine in a constant flow, without 'queuing' by machines or returning to stores, thus minimising lead times and work in progress. The reader will recognise similar features and aims to those described earlier with an FMS.

The traditional manufacturing environment operates on a 'push-through' basis, in which one process supplies parts to the next process without regard to the latter's immediate ability to continue work on those parts. Work in progress in an unavoidable features of such a system. In contrast, the JIT system works on a 'pull' principle, whereby one workstation 'pulls' the part from the previous station; work will not begin in any workstation until the signal to part has been received from the next station in the process. The bin, or container, that is passed to the previous workstation to give the 'pull' signal, is known in Japanese as the 'kanban', hence the use of this word to describe JIT systems. As production only commences once the 'pull' signal has been received, this has the obvious consequence of keeping work in progress at a low level. One consequence of the 'pull' system, however, is that problems in any part of the system will immediately halt the production line, as earlier workstations will not receive the 'pull' signal and later stations will not have their own 'pull' signals answered. As noted above, this would have the powerful effect of concentrating all minds on finding a long-term solution to the problem.

The analogy of the boat and the river emphasised the role of buffer stocks in protecting the traditional manufacturing system against shortages caused by innate problems such as poor-quality production or machine breakdowns. JIT operates with minimal stock levels; its approach is to 'get it right first time', and the aim is 'zero defects'. In the absence of the attainment of this 'ideal' situation, JIT is still able to cut scrap and rework. If transfer batches are small, product is quickly manufactured and quality checked – any problems are quickly found and only a small amount of work in progress will need to be reworked.

The JIT manufacturer plays an active and constructive part in ensuring that cost savings are made by suppliers. Cost teams from the manufacturer regularly visit suppliers' plants, perform audits on the information supplied to them, and suggest ways in which the suppliers' operations might be carried out more efficiently and achieve greater synchronisation and harmony with the manufacturer's own specifications. This co-operation with a limited number of suppliers provides the manufacturer with a high degree of control of the upstream activities in the value chain, even though the supplier has legal ownership of these parts of the chain. There is an element of commonality with SCM (discussed above) in this.

5.7 Total quality management

Total quality management (TQM) may be defined as the continuous improvement in quality, productivity and effectiveness obtained by establishing responsibility for process as well as output. In this, every process has an identified process owner within the organisation and every person in an organisation operates within a process and contributes to its improvement. The idea is that quality is the key strategic variable in achieving strategic advantage. When a customer considers buying a product he is influenced in his choice of supplier by factors other than the technical specification of the product – such as speed of delivery, customisation, reliability, ease of placing an order and attractiveness of design. All these are quality-related factors. The TQM movement argues that ability to deliver these quality-related factors is a function of process, that is it is a function of how the organisation works.

The role that quality plays in ensuring an efficient and effective operation has already been encountered within the context of JIT. Operating on a demand-pull basis with minimal stocks requires a high level of quality at all levels in the manufacturing operation.

There are two recurring themes that run through much of the literature on TQM. These are 'terms' and 'empowerment'. Employee empowerment is considered to liberate talents and facilitate the deployment of skills. Teams are considered to improve the co-ordination of functions and skills within the organisation. The cooperative ethic lies at the heart of what TQM is all about.

The TQM is a philosophy and a movement rather than a body of techniques. There are many alternative definitions and models of TQM. However, the central idea is that quality is the key strategic variable in business and it is a variable that is amenable to organisational culture. The idea is that quality should be a feature that is rooted in the structure of the organisation. Quality should impact on the way that the organisation is run and on the way that staff are recruited, assessed, promoted and rewarded. The view that quality is something imposed on staff by inspectors is anathema to the TQM movement. W Edwards Deming, widely accepted as the founder of the TQM movement, argued that mass inspection of goods ties up resources and does not improve quality. Quality has to come from within the process rather than being imposed on it from without.

The main features of a TQM-oriented organisation include:

- Top priority is given to satisfying customers and the organisation is structured in a way that ensures interest convergence of owners, employees, suppliers and management in achieving this. Managers should act as facilitators rather than controllers.
- People are considered to be the key internal guarantors of success. Decision-making processes are participative. Management is both visible and accessible.
- Constant change is considered a way of life and the organisation is structured in a manner that readily embraces change. The organisation structure is flat, requiring employees to use initiative and communicate directly with customers and suppliers.
- The organisation pursues continuous improvement and not static optimisation. The concept of 'an optimum defects level' rooted in traditional cost accounting is entirely alien to TQM. Performance is measured against an external benchmark and not against an internal standard, in order to emphasise the possibility of improvement.
- The emphasis is on prevention of problems and faults rather than detection. Employees have a wide span of activity but a short span of control.

Achieving and improving quality is the central theme that runs through all of these features. This is particularly relevant in the era of flexible manufacturing when products are highly customised and product life cycles are short. Customer service and product innovation have become major elements in the quality of products that are being offered.

One feature of traditional management accounting is that it may not report the cost of quality failure and quality assurance. Poor-quality work results in costs, but those costs may be 'buried' at several points in the management accounting system and thus not be specifically reported. For example, the costs of quality failure may include:

- internally rejected and test-failed units (internal failure);
- compensation/replacement for units rejected and returned by customers (external failure);
- rectification costs;

DEVELOPMENTS IN MANAGEMENT ACCOUNTING

- compensation for units failed in service with customers;
- loss of customer goodwill and market reputation.

It is notable that some of these things are opportunity costs that have no immediate impact on accounting costs and are not reported through a conventional management accounting system.

The adoption of a TQM approach is likely to require the provision of comprehensive cost of quality reports that are supplied on a frequent basis to all levels in the organisation. This involves identifying the costs of quality control, quality failure and quality assurance – and collecting them together for management information and reporting purposes. It is only when the costs of quality are known that the measures needed to achieve and maintain high quality can be justified.

The role of design in determining product costs has already been encountered. Quality is engineered into products at the design stage. In the modern era, 90 per cent of product costs may be determined at the design stage – and a traditional costing system reporting costs and variances in discrete 1-month periods may be of limited relevance in evaluating performance. Reporting product costs on a life-cycle basis ('life cycle costing') therefore allows a much fuller understanding of the costs and benefits of quality.

TQM is a cultural thing and over the years it has attracted critics as well as followers. The debate between the two groups is explored in the article titled 'Quality streak' in the Readings section of this chapter.

TQM is a popular management topic but it has its critics.

Quality Streak

Bob Scarlett, *CIMA Insider*, 9 September 2001, (pp. 22–23)

The problems with TQM

There are two recurring themes that run through much of the literature on TQM. These are 'teams' and 'empowerment'. Employee empowerment is considered to liberate talents and facilitate the deployment of skills. Teams are considered to improve the co-ordination of functions and skills within the organisation. The cooperative ethic lies at the heart of what TQM is all about.

However, 20 years' experience of TQM has raised awkward questions.

Do employees and management really find 'empowerment' to be liberating? Empirical studies suggest that 'empowerment' often amounts to the delegation of additional duties to employees. Limits have to be placed on what employees can do, so empowerment is often associated with rules, bureaucracy and form-filing That apart, many employees find most satisfaction from outside work activities and are quite happy to confine themselves to doing what they are told while at work. The proponents of TQM are often very work-centred people themselves and tend to judge others by their own standards.

Do teams contribute to organisational effectiveness? Just calling a group of people who work in the same office 'a team' does not make it a team. A team requires a high level of co-operation and consensus. Many competitive and motivated people find working in a team environment to be uncongenial. It means that every time you want to do anything you have to communicate with and seek approval from fellow team members. In practice, this is likely to involve bureaucracy and form filling.

Is quality really a function of system? TQM tends to proceed from the assumption that variations in quality can be explained by features in the organisational system. The idea is that by changing the system you can improve quality. However, it can be argued that TQM merely moves empowerment from management to employees. It has been argued that the latter cannot be expected to succeed where the former have failed.

Experience with TQM

Management literature offers many examples of the success of TQM and the benefits that some organisations have obtained from it.

However, experience is not all good. Many organisations that have attempted TQM have found that it involves a great deal of additional bureaucracy. When the attempt is anything less than fully committed, then the results can be unfortunate. Some organisations have found themselves with two parallel structures. A new TQM structure is set up complete with committees and teams – but the old hierarchical structure remains in existence which actually amounts to 'the real organisation'.

One UK study (A.T. Kearney) reported found that only 20 per cent of organisations who had tried TQM reported positive results from it. A US study (Arthur D. Little) put the figure somewhat higher at 30 per cent. Celebrated failures include

- Florida Power and Light Company discontinued its TQ programme after extensive employee complains concerning excessive paperwork. This decision was taken in spite of the company having won Japan's 'Deming Prise' for quality management in 1989.
- British Telecom launched a TQ programme in the late 1980s but was reported (*The Economist,* 18 April 1992) to have abandoned most of it after 3 years. It was claimed that BT became bogged down in TQ-related bureaucracy and took some time to recover from it.

Conclusion

In appraising TQM one has to appreciate that it is not a well-defined technique that can offer a 'quick fix' solution to specific perceived problems. Rather, it is an organisational philosophy that embraces a wide variety of different techniques and ideas. For example, JIT and benchmarking are closely associated with TQM.

The general theme of TQM is the need to move away from a traditional hierarchic organisation structure in order to respond to the demands of an increasingly customer service–oriented business environment where quality is the key strategic variable. Those organisations which have made a success of TQM are ones which understand its limitations and are prepared to take the long view.

5.8 Synchronous manufacturing

The title 'synchronous manufacturing' was coined in 1984, when leading exponents of OPT felt that the focus of the latter, as evidenced by its nomenclature, had become too narrow. The change in name allowed the newly emerging procedures and concepts of JIT and TQM to be integrated with the basic principles of OPT. It is interesting to note, however, that the guiding force behind both OPT and synchronous manufacturing is the identification and management of 'bottleneck resources' – Eli Goldratt prefers to use the term 'theory of constraints'.

Synchronous manufacturing has been defined as follows.

> 🔑 *Synchronous manufacturing:* ... an all-encompassing manufacturing management philosophy that includes a consistent set of principles, procedures and techniques where every action is evaluated in terms of the common global goal of the organisation.

Note the use of the word 'philosophy' in the definition: this is the key to distinguishing it from its narrower, technique-based predecessor, OPT. The word 'optimised' in the latter implied that an 'optimum' position was possible, which runs counter to a belief in continuous improvement; and the words 'production' and 'technology' failed to capture the richness of the range of constraints and challenges faced by the firm in achieving its objectives – market constraints, and logistical, managerial and behavioural constraints need to be added to the physical constraints of production capacity.

A set of seven 'principles' are associated with synchronous manufacturing:

1. Do not focus on balancing capacities, focus on synchronising the flow.
2. The marginal value of time at a bottleneck resource is equal to the throughput rate of the products processed by the bottleneck.
3. The marginal value of time at a non-bottleneck resource is negligible.
4. The level of utilisation of a non-bottleneck resource is controlled by other constraints within the system.
5. Resources must be utilised, not simply activated.
6. A transfer batch may not, and many times should not, be equal to the process batch.
7. A process batch should be variable both along its route and over time.

Principle 5 requires a brief explanation: as we saw with OPT, it is possible to *activate* resource, particularly a non-bottleneck resource, beyond what is useful or productive for the system; however, that resource will only be *utilised* if the activation contributes positively to company performance. In other words, activating a resource without utilising it is both wasteful and costly.

An alleged weakness of the conventional JIT philosophy is its approach of improving the process everywhere in the system. According to synchronous manufacturing principles 2 and 3, the return on improvements at a *bottleneck* resource is enormous. But the return on improvement made at *non-bottlenecks* is marginal at best, and often of no consequence at all. In other words, whether *across-the-board* improvement activities have any impact on the organisational goal of making money is not known. The synchronous manufacturing philosophy, on the other hand, required managers to focus on those areas of operations that offer the greatest potential for *global* improvements. This process of *focused* improvement becomes a vital part of its own particular approach to continuous improvement throughout the entire organisation.

Another criticism of the basic JIT model is that it is unable to pre-plan the production schedule for any resource in the process except final assembly, and thus the schedule does not consider the resulting loads at the bottleneck work stations. Consequently, it may not effectively utilise the bottleneck resources and, since bottlenecks determine the throughput for the entire system, the resulting throughput may be less than optimum.

5.9 The emphasis on continuous improvement

What emerges from all the previous discussion is that a world-class business achieves its objectives by pursuing a policy of continuous improvement in those factors that have been shown to be important to customers in today's market place. These are:

   (i) Innovation in design
  (ii) Flexibility in process
 (iii) Short product lead times
 (iv) High quality at all levels in the operation
  (v) Low cost engineered into product and process.

It has been seen that the benefits from these features will not be realised through the slavish application of technologies and techniques. Similarly, a management accounting system which emphasises a compliance with standard costs over given short periods is not likely to be helpful. Long-term benefits will only be achieved by a commitment on the part of all employees to the philosophy of continuous improvement. The search for continuous improvement must become a personal as well as a corporate goal, or the full benefits of technologies and techniques – either individually or in combination – will not accrue to the firm, to the detriment of its competitive position.

Management accounting must assist a search for continuous improvement by supplying relevant information, that is information that helps management to choose the actions necessary to achieve the desired organisational goals, and information that measures the movement of the firm towards those goals. The onus is very much on the management accountant to develop new costing systems and performance measures that will support world-class manufacturing and world-class management.

5.10 Throughput accounting

In this chapter we are discussing the development of synchronous manufacturing, and the identification of bottleneck resources. In this context we will now go on to learn about throughput accounting, a new type of management accounting system that has been developed to provide management information that is more suited to the new manufacturing philosophy.

5.10.1 The theory of constraints

The concept behind the throughput accounting system was first formulated and developed by Goldratt and Cox (1986) in the United States of America in a book called *The Goal*. Godlratt (1990) developed the concept and eventually gave it the name the theory of constraints (TOC) by which name it is known today in the United States of America. The theory was picked up and turned into an accounting system in the United Kingdom, where it has become known as throughput accounting (TA). Goldratt and Cox developed the technique to help managers improve the overall profitability of the firm. The theory focuses attention on constraints or bottlenecks within the organisation which hinder

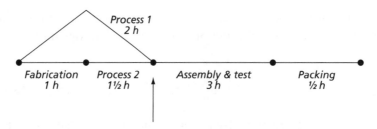

Figure 5.3 Network chart of a manufacturing process

speedy production. This main concept is to maximise the rate of manufacturing output, that is the throughput of the organisation. The idea being TOC is that raw materials should be turned into products that are immediately shipped to customers at the greatest possible speed, in a similar way to JIT system.

The important concept behind TOC is that the production rate of the entire factory is set at the pace of the bottleneck – the constraining resource. Hence, in order to achieve the best results TOC emphasises the importance of removing bottlenecks or, as they are called in the United States of America, binding constraints from the production process. If they cannot be removed they must be coped with in the best possible way so that they do not hinder production unduly. In order to do this, network diagrams need to be drawn to identify the bottlenecks or binding constraints. Figure 5.3 illustrates a simple network chart where the assembly and test process is the bottleneck.

In Figure 5.3 it can be seen that the assembly and test process is the bottleneck and that in order to maximise throughput, a buffer stock is needed prior to the assembly and test process so that its employees never have to wait for components from prior processes.

TOC identifies three types of cost.

1. Throughput contribution = sales revenue − completely variable costs this is usually = sales revenue – direct material cost.
   (Labour costs tend to be partially fixed and are excluded normally. Direct material cost includes purchased components and material handling costs.)
2. *Conversion costs.* These are all operating costs, excluding completely variable costs, which are incurred in order to produce the product, that is labour and overhead, including rent, utilities and relevant depreciation.
3. *Investments.* These include all stock, raw material, work in progress, finished goods, research and development costs, costs of equipment and buildings and so on.

The aim is to increase throughput contribution while decreasing conversion costs and investment costs. TOC is a short-term profit maximising technique that is very similar in approach to marginal costing. The only real difference is that the contribution may be more realistic in that all conversion costs are assumed to be fixed costs. Bottleneck decisions are in reality linear programming decisions as TOC attempts to do the following:

Maximise throughput contribution (sales revenue − direct materials) Subject to:

Production capacity (supply constraints)
Production demand (demand constraints)

The TOC is quite widely used in the United States of America by companies such as Ford Electronics, General Motors and Avery Dennison, some of which claim that it has revolutionised their business. It is also used by a number of UK companies, sometimes in the form of throughput accounting, discussed next.

5.10.2 Throughput accounting

In the United Kingdom Galloway and Waldron (1988/89) developed TA from the theory of constraints. It is very similar in concept to TOC but it is an accounting-based technique whereas TOC is not. Eli Goldratt has always stressed the differences between the two systems. This may have been because he is not over-fond of cost accountants or their methods and at one time one of his sayings was that 'cost accounting is the number 1 enemy of productivity'. TA is an extreme version of variable costing as, like TOC, it treats only direct material as variable and all labour and overhead costs as fixed. It operates through a series of ratios and differs from all other management accounting systems because it emphasises throughput first, stock minimisation second and cost control third.

Throughput accounting's primary concern is the rate at which a business can generate profits. In order to monitor this it focuses on the return on the throughput through the bottleneck resource.

Its key measure is:

$$\text{Return per time period} = \frac{\text{sales revenue} - \text{material costs}}{\text{time period}}$$

[Assuming materials are the only totally variable costs, Balderstone & Keef (1999)]

This ratio measures the value added by the organisation during a specific period of time, normally 1 hour. As time plays a crucial part in the ratio, managers' attention is automatically drawn to removing bottlenecks that might cause delay in the production process.

If one machine holds up production, because it is inefficient or has inadequate capacity, it is of little use to work the other machines at 100 per cent efficiency as the parts produced will be destined for stock until such time as the bottleneck machine can process them. Eventually when parts are spilling from the storeroom or piled all over the factory floor, the efficient machines will have to stop altogether for a time, in order to allow the bottleneck machine to catch up. Therefore, there is nothing to be gained by measuring and encouraging the efficiency of machines that do not govern the overall flow of work. The same applies to the efficiency of production staff working in the non-bottleneck processes. In fact bonuses that are paid to encourage fast working are at best simply wasted and at worst result in increased storage costs. Furthermore, if workers are encouraged to work too quickly, they are likely to produce more faulty goods and to waste materials. If the goods are destined for the storeroom, this increase in waste serves no purpose except to increase the average cost per unit.

A minor use of the return per time period ratio is to optimise production in the short term. Product return per time period ratio can be used in the same way as limiting factor ratios are used in order to plan how many units of each product should be made in order to maximise profit. The limiting factor is the first factor that prevents a manufacturing company expanding production towards infinity, and the ratio is contribution/limiting factor. The products are ranked according to this ratio; that is according to their use of the limiting factor, the one with the highest contribution per key or limiting factor being the best financially. In TA the key or limiting factor is the bottleneck. The return per time period ratio can be modified and used in a similar way to the P/V ratio. The amended ratio for ranking products is:

$$\text{Product return per minute} = \frac{\text{sales price} - \text{material costs}}{\text{minutes on key/bottleneck resource}}$$

This is illustrated in detail in the following example.

Exercise – contrasting TA with the limiting factor approach

A company produces two products, A and B, the production costs of which are shown below:

	A	B
	£	£
Direct material cost	10	10
Direct labour cost	5	9
Variable overhead	5	9
Fixed overhead	5	9
Total product cost	25	37

Fixed overhead is absorbed on the basis direct labour cost.

The products pass through two processes, Y and Z, with associated labour cost of £10 per direct labour hour in each. The direct labour associated with the two products for these processes is shown below:

	Time taken	
Process	Product A	Product B
Y	10 min	39 min
Z	20 min	15 min

Selling prices are set by the market. The current market price for A is £65 and that for B, £52. At these prices, the market will absorb as many units of A and B as the company can produce. The ability of the company to produce A and B is limited by the capacity to process the products through Y and Z. The company operates a two-shift system, giving 16 working hours per day. Process Z is a single-process line and 2 hours in each shift will be downtime. Process Y can process two units simultaneously, although this doubles the requirement for direct labour. Process Y can operate for the full 16 working hours each day.

Requirement

What production plan should the company follow in order to maximise profits?

Solution

In order to find the profit maximising solution in any problem, the constraints which prevent the profit from being infinite must be identified; the greater the number of constraints, the more difficult the problem is to solve. In the simplest case, where there is only one binding constraint, the profit maximising solution is found by maximising the contribution per unit of the scarce resource, that is binding constraint. Linear programming may be used to solve the problem where more than one constraint is binding for some, but not all, feasible solutions. Where the number of products is limited to two, and such constraints are relatively few in number, the problem can easily be expressed graphically to reveal the profit maximising solution, and/or the problem can be expressed in the form of a set of simultaneous equations. As the number of potentially binding constraints increases, the use of a computer becomes the only feasible way to solve the necessary number of simultaneous equations.

In this question, the only constraint is the company's ability to process the product. The total daily processing time for processes Y and Z are:

Maximum process time Y = 2 × 6 hours × 60 minutes = 1,920 minutes
Maximum process time Z = 12 hours × 60 minutes = 720 minutes

So the maximum number that could be produced of each of the two products is:

	Product A *Maximum units*	*Product B* *Maximum units*
Y	$\dfrac{1,920}{10} = 192$	$\dfrac{1,920}{39} = 49.23$
Z	$\dfrac{720}{20} = 36$	$\dfrac{720}{15} = 48$

In the case of both products, the maximum number of units which can be produced in Process Y exceeds the number that can be produced in Process Z, and thus the capacity of Process Y is not a binding constraint. The problem therefore becomes one of deciding how to allocate the scarce production capacity of Process Z in such a way as to maximise profit.

Traditional approach – maximising the contribution per minute in Process Z

Contribution of A = £65 (selling price) − £20 (variable cost) = £45
Contribution of B = £52 (selling price) − £28 (variable cost) = £24
Contribution of A per minute in process Z = £45 /20 = £2.25
Contribution of B per minute in process Z = £24/15 = £1.60

The profit maximising solution is therefore to produce the maximum possible number of units of A, 36, giving a contribution of £45 × 36 = £1,620.

Throughput approach – maximising throughput per minute in bottleneck resource Z

Throughput of A = £65 (selling price) − £10 (material cost) = £55
Throughput of B = £52 (selling price) − £10 (material cost) = £42

Throughput contribution of A per minute in process Z = £55/20 = £2.75
Throughput contribution of B per minute in process Z = £42/15 = £2.80

The profit maximising solution is therefore to produce the maximum number of units of B, 48, giving a throughput of £42 × 48 = £2,016.

It is clear that, given the different solutions, the two approaches cannot both lead to profit maximisation. Which technique is correct depends on the variability or otherwise of labour and variable overheads, which in turn depends on the time horizon of the decision. This type of profit maximisation technique is a short-term one and in today's world labour is likely to be fixed in the short term and so it can be argued that TA provides the more correct solution. Variable overheads would need to be analysed to assess their variability.

Marginal costing rose to popularity in the 1930s when labour costs were usually variable as the workforce was usually paid on a piece-rate basis. Since then textbooks, at least, have always assumed that labour is a variable cost in the short term. All that has happened with TA is that it tends to recognise the present reality, which is that most cost excluding materials are now fixed in the short term.

The marginal costing approach should of course be modified to accommodate this, as it requires only variable costs to be used to calculate contribution. If only material costs are variable, then only those costs should be used in the calculation of contribution. Thus there should be no difference between the two systems in this respect.

5.10.3 Throughput cost control and effectiveness measures

Although the measure of return per period is a valuable measure for speeding up the flow of work and eliminating bottlenecks it ignores the costs involved in running the factory. There is little to be gained if throughput and, therefore, revenue are increased marginally but in order to achieve this labour and overhead costs increase considerably. The throughput accounting ratio measures this:

$$\pi \quad \text{TA ratio} = \frac{\text{Value added per time period}}{\text{Conversion cost per time period}} \quad \text{i.e.} \quad \frac{\text{sales} - \text{Materials}}{\text{labour} + \text{overhead}}$$

This ratio will obviously be greater than one for a profitable company and the aim will be to increase it to an acceptably high level. If a product has a ratio of less than one, the organisation loses money every time it is produced.

Traditional efficiency measures such as standard costing variances and labour ratios can no longer be used with TA because traditional efficiency cannot be encouraged. (The labour force must not be encouraged to work to produce for stock.) A process efficiency ratio of throughput/cost can still be used.

Effectiveness is, however, the more important measure:

$$\pi \quad \text{Current effectiveness ratio} = \frac{\text{Standard minutes of throughout achieved}}{\text{Minutes available}}$$

This measures effectiveness and compares it to a current standard.

Traditional variances can also be misleading in a throughput environment. For example, if overtime was worked at the bottleneck to increase throughput an adverse labour rate variance would arise. Generally adverse variances are considered bad. However, in a throughput environment this would be good and would increase profits as long as the extra labour cost was less than the increase in value added.

TA's aim, like JIT, must always be to minimise production time taken and so all non-value-added elements in the production lead time need to be eliminated or minimised so that process time approaches the lead time.

Lead time = set-up time + waiting time + process time + inspection time + move time

5.10.4 Summary of throughput accounting

Table 5.1 highlights the difference between TA and traditional product costing.

Table 5.1 Difference between throughput accounting and traditional product cost systems

Throughput accounting	Traditional product costing
Value is added when an item is sold	Value is added when an item is produced
Schedule adherence and meeting delivery dates are the key to work effectively	Full utilisation of labour and machine time is the key to working efficiently
Variance analysis only investigates why the scheduled mix was not produced	Variance analysis investigates whether standards were achieved
Labour and traditionally defined variable overheads are not normally treated as variable costs	Labour and traditionally defined variable overheads are treated as variable costs
Stock is valued in the P&L and balance sheet at material cost only (i.e. variable cost)	Stock is valued in the P&L and balance sheet at total production cost

So far TA has only been considered in relation to manufacturing organisations but it has been used very successfully in service industries as well. For example, it has been used to speed up and reduce costs in checking customers' creditworthiness. In one company this process took a long time, often longer than a week, and held up further activities. Before TA was used, over-qualified people were used to make basic credit decisions and this caused the delays in deciding on creditworthiness. Afterwards ordinary members of staff were allowed to make decisions in the majority of cases and only difficult ones were referred to experts. This meant that decisions were made much faster, normally within 24 hours, and the cost of the function was reduced.

The TA has been criticised for being unduly short term because all costs apart from material costs tend to be treated as fixed. It could be argued that the use of traditional marginal costing is not always correct because those that use it tend to treat direct labour as a variable cost, which is not realistic. It could be argued, and has been by some that labour is more fixed than an item of machinery and its associated costs, as that can be removed and sold within a few weeks. Staff cannot be made redundant as quickly and the cost may be greater. Having said that, in the long term all costs are variable and all options possible but TA only considers the current situation and way of improving it.

Marginal costing and throughput accounting rely on the calculation of contribution (sales–variable cost) and as such there is no difference between them. Because direct labour was paid on a piece-rate, it was largely a truly variable cost when marginal costing was developed early in the twentieth century. Today, textbooks tend to use the same definition of variable costs for marginal costing purpose even though it is usually no longer relevant. Once this problem has been overcome the two systems are seen to be the same in principle, marginal costing dealing with short-term one-off decisions and throughput accounting providing a planning and control system.

Make or buy decisions should nearly always be made from a strategic viewpoint and not from a short-term marginal cost point of view. But assume for a moment that a short-term decision is needed and marginal costing is used, and that it suggests that the product under consideration should be made rather than bought in. If this product uses valuable capacity on the machine before the bottleneck machine, then the holding of buffer stock could be jeopardised under certain circumstances. This was a real scenario at Allied Signal Ltd. Because throughput accounting was used, management declined the opportunity to make the product under consideration (Darlington 1995). Again conflict occurred between the two systems, but the consequence of using spare capacity should have been considered in any system; throughput accounting simply drew attention to it.

It is also argued that by concentration on the relationship between sales and materials, TA neglects other costs. This is not a valid criticism as the TA ratio incorporates conversion costs per time period. However, the purpose of throughput accounting, and especially TOC, is not so much to control costs as to demonstrate ways of improving profit by increasing production flow. It is an attention-directing system. The criticisms can be countered but nevertheless throughput accounting is not a technique that will suit all organisations.

5.11　Backflush accounting

Traditional cost accounting systems track the sequence of raw materials and components moving through the production systems, and as a consequence are called 'sequential tracking systems'. As JIT is an entirely different system it requires its own cost accounting system. The absence of stocks makes choices about stock valuation systems unnecessary and the rapid conversion of direct material into cost of goods sold simplifies the cost accounting system. The approach is known as backflush accounting.

Backflush accounting delays the recording of costs until after the events have taken place, then standard costs are used to work backwards to 'flush' out the manufacturing costs. There are two events that trigger the records kept in most backflush accounting systems:

- The first is the purchase of raw materials, In a true JIT system where absolutely no raw material stock is held, even this trigger is not relevant and raw materials are 'flushed' when the second trigger is activated.
- The second trigger is either the transfer of goods to finished goods stock or, in a true JIT system, the sale of goods. Two examples of possible backflush accounting systems are given in Tables 5.2 and 5.3.

Table 5.2　System 1. A small stock of raw material is held but no finished goods stock

	Dr £	Cr £
1. Raw materials are purchased – £3,200		
Stock control	3,200	
Creditors control		3,200
2. Conversion costs are incurred – £3,000		
Conversion cost control	3,000	
Individual a/cs		3,000
3. Goods sold – £6,000 worth at standard cost		
Cost of goods sold	6,000	
Stock control		2,900
Conversion costs allocated		3,100
4. Under- or over-allocation of conversion costs		
Conversion costs allocated	3,100	
Cost of goods sold		100
Conversion costs control		3,000

Table 5.3 System 2. No raw material stock is held but same finished goods stock is held

	Dr £	Cr £
1. Raw materials are purchased – no entry		
2. Conversion costs are incurred – £3,000		
Conversion cost control	3,000	
Individual a/cs		3,000
3. Finished goods units produced £6,000		
Finished goods control	6,000	
Creditors control		2,900
Conversion costs allocated		3,100
4. Finished goods sold – £5,900		
Cost of goods sold	5,900	
Finished goods control		5,900
5. Under- or over-allocation of conversion costs		
Conversion costs allocated	3,100	
Cost of goods sold		100
Conversion costs control		3,000

The figures are the same as for System 1, but the transfer to finished goods is assumed to be £6,000 and the cost of goods sold is £5,900 leaving a finished goods stock of £100.

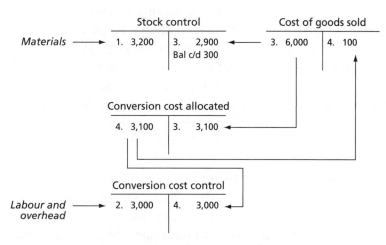

Figure 5.4 Ledger accounts for system 1

This is the system used by Toyota in its UK factory. The system seeks to induce employees to behave in a certain way. First employees must concentrate on achieving sales because cost of sales is the trigger – nothing gets recorded until the sale is made. Second there is no benefit in producing goods for stock. In traditional systems which have a finished goods, stock managers can increase profit by producing more goods than are sold in a period because an increase in finished goods stock reduces the cost of sales in traditional financial account (Figure 5.4).

The model just described may be altered to cope with work in progress in the system by using a raw and in progress account (RIP) in place of the stock control account. All other entries remain the same (Figure 5.5).

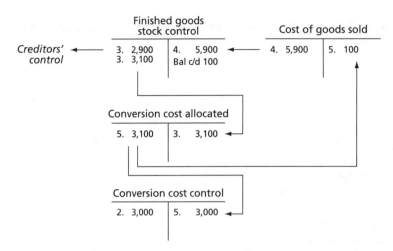

Figure 5.5 Ledger accounts for system 2

The backflush accounting model cannot be used by all organisations. It can only be used where a JIT-type system is in operation. Where it is used it does have advantages. The traditional system is time consuming and expensive to operate, as it requires a considerable amount of documentation, such as material requisitions and time sheets to support it in order to maintain the WIP records and job cards. If a company operates with low stock levels, the benefits of operating the traditional costing system are few. By introducing a black-flush system a considerable amount of clerical time is saved.

From the backflush accounting examples it can be seen that JIT eliminates direct labour as a cost category. Instead labour is treated as an indirect cost and is included in conversion cost with the overheads. This is because production is only required when demand requires it and so production labour will be paid regardless of activity. All indirect costs are treated as a fixed period expense. With JIT, failed or rework must be almost eliminated if the system is to work and so no accounts for this will exist in blakflush accounting whereas they are required in traditional systems.

The backflush accounting model does not conform to the accepted financial accounting proceducers for external reporting in the United Kingdom. This is because work in progress is treated as an asset in the financial accounts and in backflush accounting it is not shown to exist although in practice a small amount does. This can be countered by claiming, quite rightly, immateriality. If only one-tenth of one day's production is held in work in progress, then it is immaterial. It can also be claimed that it is immaterial if the work in progress does not change from one period to the next as opening and closing stock will cancel each other out.

Backflush accounting can be criticised because of the lack of information that it provides. Some argue, quite rightly, that in reality it is impossible to eliminate all stock as a truck arriving with raw material creates stock until it is moved to and used in production. If backflush accounting is used in a system where a substantial amount of stock is held, a physical stock-take will be needed, because the system does not record the quantity of stock. Instead it is derived on paper by the difference between the standard cost of material in the goods sold and the amount of materials purchased. This must be checked by a physical stock-take from time to time.

5.12 Environmental accounting

The political and social factors driving environmental accounting have been discussed earlier. A recent CACA research paper defined environmental accounting as:

> *The collection, analysis and assessment of environmental and financial performance data obtained from business management information systems, environmental management and financial accounting systems. The taking of corrective management action to reduce environmental impacts and costs plus, where appropriate, the external reporting of the environmental and financial benefits in verified corporate environmental reports or published annual reports and accounts*

Environmental accounting may involve a range of practices, including:

1. The identification, classification and reporting of costs incurred in complying with environmental legislation and regulation; this may include fines and penalties in failing to comply with relevant rules.
2. The reporting of costs incurred in voluntarily mitigating the impact of the business on the environment – which may relate to waste emissions, the protection of fauna and flora on-site and water conservation.
3. The identification and costing of assets and liabilities for inclusion in the balance sheet, arising from schemes such as the EU's CO_2 emission trading schemes.
4. The reporting of non-financial costs and benefits arising from environmental impacts.

External reporting issues arising from (3) have been the subject of consideration by regulatory bodies such as the International Accounting Standards Board. As early as 2003, the Board issued draft interpretation D1 (Emission Rights) on the matter of how emission allowances should be accounted for. The proposed treatment incorporated elements of earlier accounting standards on intangible assets, impairment of assets and contingent assets/liabilities.

Some bodies (one UK example being Business In The Community – BITC) publish green league tables of businesses. Rio Tinto is one company that has regularly featured high in the ranking on BITC tables. This appears to relate mainly to Rio Tinto's involvement in the development of carbon capture technology in coal fired power stations. EDF Energy has suffered from criticism for allegedly operating some of the world's dirtiest power stations and for dumping nuclear waste virtually on its own door step. A low ranking on green business tables attracts opprobrium that can hurt a business – through the resultant unpopularity of its products with customers and through the reluctance of governments to deal with it.

One practical result of the EU's GHG emission trading scheme is that a number of factories in the EU have established wind farms on their premises. Using electricity generated on-site by wind turbines reduces CO_2 emissions and thus avoids allowance purchase costs. It is unlikely that such wind farms would be cost effective in the absence of the scheme. The cost–benefit evaluation of alternative emission strategies for a business requires the support of a full management accounting exercise.

The identification of environmental costs through traditional management accounting practices has been the subject of some critical comment. It has been suggested that many environmental costs (such as those relating to energy, water and waste emission) tend to be lumped in with general production overheads and be attributed to product costs through a general overhead absorption base. An activity-based costing system may be developed to identify environmental costs more fully and then attribute them to products using meaningful cost drivers. Thus ABC should result in a particularly 'dirty' activity or product having the full costs of that dirt being attributed to them.

One recent research report outlined the full environmental costs of a business and associated benefits as follows:

Environmental costs and benefits

Capital costs	Expenses	Benefits	Cost liabilities
equipment	monitoring	green marketing	penalties & fines
facilities	testing	brand reputation	site decontamination
licenses	recording & reporting	risk avoidance	groundwater cleaning
	insurance	customer loyalty	landscape damage
	axes, fines & penalties	insurance savings	bans, boycotts & blacklists
	R&D	sale of recycled items	compensation to customers and
	recycling	public standing	employees
	waste disposal	allowance sales	

In addition, environmental issues may create liabilities that do not immediately give rise to expenses. For example, many businesses face liabilities arising from careless use of asbestos in products and buildings in years past. In many cases, an actuary is needed to estimate what the range of possible values for those liabilities might be.

Some of the issues grouped under the heading 'environmental accounting' influence the main management accounting and financial reporting systems. These include the use of ABC to sensitively trace environmental costs to products and the showing of GHG allowance assets / liabilities in the balance sheet.

Other issues may be more amenable to a dedicated annual environmental report. Such a report may list all the environmentally related costs, benefits, assets and liabilities that pertain to the current operations of the business. It may also give appropriate performance indicators (e.g. $ per kilo spent on waste recycling, $ per litre of water used spent on water conservation) that can be matched against previous year figures or industry-wide benchmarks.

Environmental accounting is partly an expression of the wider concept of Corporate Social Responsibility. It is also partly a means of accounting for certain classes of cost and benefit, the nature of which are becoming increasingly more prominent and better understood.

5.13 Summary

In this chapter, we have considered modern developments in the manufacturing, social, political, business and economic environment. We have explored the manner in which these developments have resulted in the adoption of new management philosophies such as TQM, JIT and TOC. Further, we have reviewed the new management accounting techniques such as ABC, throughput accounting and backflush accounting that have appeared in response to the modern environment.

This section concludes with an article on the manner in which modern management practices such as JIT, TQM and OPT interface with the more traditional management accounting practice of standard costing. The extract shown poses the possible incompatibilities between modern priorities and traditional practice.

Some writers have indicated that modern management philosophies may be incompatible with traditional financial control technique. In the article below, Lucas poses a number of issues for consideration in this regard.

Standard costing and its role in today's manufacturing environment

Mike Lucas, *Management Accounting,* April 1997. Reproduced by permission of the Institute of Management Accountants, Monteuale, NJ. www.imanet.org

In recent years, writers such as Kaplan and Johnson, Ferrara and Modern and Lee have argued that standard costing variance analysis should not be used for cost-control and performance-evaluation purposes in today's manufacturing world. Its use, they argue, is likely to induce behaviour which is inconsistent with the strategic manufacturing objectives that companies need to achieve in order to survive and prosper in today's intensely competitive international economic environment.

The case against standard costing

Drury, for example, has described how the scientific management principles of F.W. Taylor provided the impetus for the development of standard costing systems. The scientific management engineers divided the production system into a number of simple repetitive tasks in order to obtain the advantages of specialisation and to eliminate the time wasted by workers changing from one task to another.

Once individual tasks and methods have been clearly defined it is a relatively simple matter to set standards of performance using work study and time and motion study. These standards of performance then serve as the basis for financial control: monetary values are assigned to both standards and deviations from standard, that is variances. These variances are then attributed to particular operations/responsibility centers.

Companies operating in today's manufacturing environment, however, are likely to have strategies based on objectives such as improving quality, increasing flexibility to meet customer's individual requirements, reducing manufacturing lead times and delivery times, reducing inventories and unit costs. To help achieve these objectives, manufacturing strategies such as just-in-time (JIT), advanced manufacturing technology (AMT) and continuous improvement are often applied. Kaplan et al. argue that standard costing is counter-productive in such an environment. The major criticisms levelled at standard costing variance analysis are as follows:

1. *In a JIT environment, measuring standard costing variances for performance evaluation may encourage dysfunctional behaviour.*

The primary purpose of the JIT production system is to increase profits by decreasing costs. It does this by eliminating excessive inventory and/or work-force. Items will be produced only at the time they are needed and in the precise amounts in which they are needed – thus removing the necessity for inventories. Running the business without inventories requires the ability to produce small batch sizes economically. In order to do so, set-up times must be reduced. Performance measures should therefore be such as to motivate managers and workforce to work towards reducing set-up times in order to achieve the sub-goal of economic small batch size as a prerequisite for achieving the lower inventories. Performance measures that benefit from large batch sizes or from producing for inventory should therefore be avoided; standard costing variances are just such measures!

2. *In an AMT environment, the major costs are those related to the production facility rather than production volume-related costs such as materials and labour which standard costing is essentially designed to plan and control.*

Standard costing is concerned with comparing actual cost per unit with standard cost per unit. Fixed costs imputed to the product unit level are only notionally 'unit' costs. Any difference between the actual and the standard fixed cost per unit is not therefore meaningful for controlling operations, as it does not necessarily reflect under- or overspending – it may simply reflect differences in production volume.

What matters is the total fixed overhead expenditure rather than the fixed overhead cost per unit.

Therefore, in an AMT environment, standard costing variances have at best a minor role to play and at worst they may be counter-productive in so far as they force managers to focus on the wrong issues. An activity-based cost management (ABCM) system may be more appropriate, focusing on activities that drive the cost in service and support departments which form the bulk of controllable costs.

3. *In a JIT/AMT/continuous-improvement environment, the workforce is usually organised into empowered, multi-skilled teams controlling operations autonomously.*

The feedback they require is real time and in physical terms. Periodic financial variance reports are neither meaningful nor timely enough to facilitate appropriate control action.

4. *In a total quality management (TQM) environment, standard costing variance measurement places an emphasis on cost control to the likely detriment of quality.*

TQM requires a total managerial and worker ethos of improving and maintaining quality, and of resolving problems relating to this. The emphasis of standard costing is on cost control; variance analysis is likely to pull managerial and worker interest away from perhaps critical quality issues. Thus cost control may be achieved at the expense of quality and competitive advantage.

5. *A continuous improvement environment requires a continual effort to do things better, not achieve an arbitrary standard based on prescribed or assumed conditions.*

Ferrara has suggested that standard costing based on engineering standards – which in turn are predicted on the notion of a 'one best way' – is only appropriate in the static, bygone world of cost-plus pricing (the world in which the Scientific

Management School lived?). In such a world, a standard cost is established specifying what a product should cost and to this is added the required profit markup to arrive at the selling price. Cost management then consists of ensuring that standards are adhered to.

In today's intensely competitive environment (the argument goes), we no longer look to the total unit cost in order to determine selling price; instead, we use the selling price to help determine the cost the market will allow. This allowable or target cost per unit is a market-driven cost that has to be achieved if desired profits are to be achieved. In a highly competitive, dynamic world there is likely to be considerable downward pressure on this allowable cost. Cost management must therefore consist of both cost maintenance and continuous cost improvement.

In such a competitive improvement-seeking environment, of what value is standard costing based on predetermined engineering standards which create a mind-set of achieving the standard rather than of continuous cost reduction?

6. *In a largely automated production system, it argued, the processes are so stable that variances simply disappear.*

Gagne and Discenza, for example, contend that 'with the use of statistical quality control and automation, the production processes are very consistent and reliable. Variances often cease to exist.' If this is true, emphasis should be switched to the product design stage as most costs are effectively committed during this phase. A target cost that is achievable through the designer's efforts can be established and the designer then controls the design activities of a new product using the target cost as an economic guideline.

Self-test quiz

(1) Explain the terms MRP1 and MRP2 (Sections 8.5.1 and 8.5.2).
(2) How does the 'static optimisation' philosophy link MRP and standard costing concepts (Section 8.5.2)?
(3) How does IT contribute to the practices of ERP and SCM (Section 8.5.4)?
(4) What are the main features of JIT (Section 8.5.5)?
(5) How do the terms 'team' and 'empowerment' feature in TQM (Section 8.6)?
(6) List possible problems with the practice of TQM (Section 8.6).
(7) Explain the corporate social responsibility concept (Section 5.5).
(8) What information might a business include in its annual environmental report (Section 5.12).
(9) Explain the central feature of backflush accounting (Section 5.11).
(10) State why JIT, TQM and AMTs may not always be entirely compatible with the practice of standard costing (Section 5.13).

Revision Questions

? Question 1

1.1 What is a flexible manufacturing system and how does it relate to changes in the economy?

1.2 Explain materials requirements planning and contrast it with more traditional approaches to stock management.

1.3 Explain the Just-in-Time concept.

1.4 Explain the characteristics of a backflush accounting system.

1.5 Explain the features that make ABC more relevant to the modern manufacturing environment than traditional product costing technique.

1.6 Explain 'throughput accounting'.

1.7 Explain the 'total quality management' philosophy and its relevance to the modern economic environment.

1.8 Explain the meaning of the term 'the New Economy' and its relevance to the practice of management accounting.

? Question 2

'Japanese companies that have used just-in-time (JIT) for five or more years are reporting close to a 30 per cent increase in labour productivity, a 60 per cent reduction in inventories, a 90 per cent reduction in quality rejection rates, and a 15 per cent reduction in necessary plant space. However, implementing a JIT system does not occur overnight. It took Toyota over twenty years to develop its system and realise significant benefits from it.'

Source: Sumer C. Aggrawal, *Harvard Business Review*

Requirements

(a) Explain how the benefits claimed for JIT in the above quotation are achieved and why it takes so long to achieve those benefits. **(15 marks)**

(b) Explain how management information systems in general (and management accounting systems in particular) should be developed in order to facilitate and make best use of JIT. **(10 marks)**

(Total marks = 25)

> **!** The following two questions draw both on the issues explored in this chapter and on a wider range of management accounting and business management topics. In preparing answers to these questions you should consider your earlier studies of management accounting and general knowledge of business.

? Question 3

As part of a total quality management (TQM) programme in a large manufacturing company, quality costing has been introduced and is regarded as useful by senior managers. They are now planning to extend the TQM programme, and quality costing, from manufacturing to the whole of the company. You have been asked to devise a TQM programme, including appropriate quality measures and calculations of quality cost in the management accounting section of the finance department.

Requirements

(a) Briefly explain each of the four categories of quality cost (prevention cost, appraisal cost, internal failure cost and external failure cost). Give examples of each category appropriate to a manufacturing environment, and examples relevant to management accounting. **(8 marks)**

(b) Explain how this cost categorisation mentioned in (a) above can be used to help to develop performance measures within management accounting. Explain and justify a set of performance measures that can be used by the finance director in assessing the management accounting service. **(12 marks)**

(Total marks = 20)

? Question 4

(a) 'It may be argued that in a total quality environment, variance analysis from a standard costing system is redundant.'
Discuss the validity of this statement. **(8 marks)**

(b) Using labour cost as the focus, discuss the differences in the measurement of labour efficiency/effectiveness where (i) total quality management techniques and (ii) standard cost variance analysis are in use. **(7 marks)**

(Total marks = 15)

? Question 5

It has been suggested that much of the training of management accountants is concerned with *cost control* whereas the major emphasis should be on *cost reduction*.

Requirements

(a) Distinguish between cost control and cost reduction. **(10 marks)**

(b) Give three examples each of the techniques and principles used for
   (i) cost control and
   (ii) cost reduction. **(10 marks)**

(c) Discuss the proposition contained in the statement. **(5 marks)**

(Total marks = 25)

? Question 6

You are advising KL plc, a large scale manufacturing operation.

The lean enterprise [characterised by 'just in time' (JIT) total quality management (TQM) and supportive supplier relations] is widely considered a better approach to manufacturing. Some have suggested, however, that ABC hinders the spread of the lean enterprise by making apparent the cost of small batch sizes.

Comment by an academic accountant

Requirements

(a) Explain the roles that JIT, TQM and supportive supplier relations play in modern manufacturing management. How might the adoption of such practices improve KL's performance? **(10 marks)**

(b) Explain what the writer of the above statement means by 'the cost of small batch sizes'. Critically appraise the manner in which this cost is treated by KL's existing (single OAR-based) cost accounting system. Explain the benefits that KL might obtain through a full knowledge and understanding of this cost. **(10 marks)**

(c) Explain and discuss the extent to which academic research in the area of management accounting is likely to influence the practice of management accounting.

(5 marks)

(Total marks = 25)

? Question 7

X Ltd has recently automated its manufacturing plant and has also adopted a Total Quality Management (TQM) philosophy and a Just-in-Time (JIT) manufacturing system. The company currently uses a standard absorption costing system for the electronic diaries which it manufacturers.

The following information for the last quarter has been extracted from the company records:

	Budget	Actual
Fixed production overheads	$100,000	$102,300
Labour hours	10,000	11,000
Output (electronic diaries)	100,000	105,000

Fixed production overheads are absorbed on the basis of direct labour hours. The following fixed production overhead variances have been reported:

	$
Expenditure variance	2,300 (A)
Volume variance	5,000 (F)
Total	2,700 (F)

If the fixed production overheads had been further analysed and classified under an Activity-Based Costing (ABC) system, the above information would then have been presented as follows:

	Budget	Actual
Costs		
Material handling	$30,000	$30,800
Set up	$70,000	$71,500
Output (electronic diaries)	100,000	105,000
Activity		
Material handling (order executed)	5,000	5,500
Set up (production runs)	2,800	2,600

The following variances would have been reported:

		$
Overhead expenditure variance	Material handling	2,200 (F)
	Set ups	6,500 (A)
Overhead efficiency variance	Material handling	1,500 (A)
	Set ups	8,500 (F)
Total		2,700 (F)

Requirements

(a) Explain why and how X Ltd may have to adapt its standard costing system now that it has adopted TQM and JIT in its recently automated manufacturing plant.
(9 marks)

(b) Explain the meaning of the fixed production overhead variances calculated under the standard absorption costing system and discuss their usefulness to the management of X Ltd for decision-making. **(6 marks)**

(c) For the variances calculated under the ABC classification:
   (i) explain how they have been calculated;
   (ii) discuss their usefulness to the management of X Ltd for decision-making.
(10 marks)
(Total marks = 25)

? Question 8

You are employed as finance officer to Enterprise Bank plc. Your Chief Executive has recently attended a business seminar where he was told that 'throughput accounting is the most modern technique and can hugely increase profitability'. You are asked to prepare a briefing note on this technique.

Requirements

(a) Outline the theory of constraints and explain the main steps in its approach to the process of profit maximisation. **(11 marks)**

(b) List and explain three metrics associated with throughput accounting. **(3 marks)**

(c) Discuss the possible advantages and disadvantages associated with the use of throughput accounting. **(4 marks)**

(d) State and explain whether or not throughput accounting is appropriate for Enterprise Bank. **(2 marks)**
(Total marks = 20)

Solutions to Revision Questions

☑ Solution 1

1.1 An FMS is a manufacturing facility designed, organised and operated in a manner to facilitate swift changes in production. It is likely to be very different from a traditional production line which is organised for continuous production of a single product. FMS facilities typically consist of clusters of equipment which can be reprogrammed quickly as required. Such flexibility has a cost and makes demands on personnel. However, FMS facilities are adapted to the needs of a swiftly changing market and JIT production systems.

1.2 Traditional materials planning in the pre-computer era involved constantly monitoring stock levels and re-ordering whenever they fell below certain specified levels. This was an inherently passive approach. MRP involves preparing detailed procurement plans based on projected output and placing orders in order to ensure that materials are delivered as and when they are needed. The ability of a large, complex operation to operate with MRP (and its later variants – MRP2 and ERP) depends very much on the availability of reliable computer systems.

1.3 JIT is an approach to production that involves obtaining materials, components and use of facilities as and when they are needed. It also involves arranging to supply customers with goods only as and when they are required. It is therefore characterised by small but frequent deliveries, low stock levels and short, discontinuous batch production. Operating in this manner makes considerable demands on staff, facilities and the production planning operation.

1.4 Backflush accounting is an approach that avoids the cost-tracking approach that is characteristic of traditional accounting. The latter usually involves maintaining detailed records of costs incurred in order to determine the cost of products on a cumulative basis. Backflush costing and its variants work the other way. When production costs are incurred they are charged to a conversion cost account. When production is completed, the standard cost of the units concerned is credited to the conversion cost account. The balance outstanding on the latter at any time will therefore be the stock of raw materials and work in progress – sometimes described as the 'RIP' account. It is an approach considered well adapted to a JIT environment (where stocks are low and cost variances are few), but it is not new. It is similar in character to low-cost practice commonly used in the pre-computer era to prepare monthly management accounts.

1.5 ABC is an approach to cost determination which involves careful study of the activities that give rise to costs and the manner in which those activities vary with the level and structure of output. It seeks to attribute costs to products through the identification and use of appropriate 'cost drivers'. This contrasts with more traditional practice which involved the use of volume related, and often arbitrary, overhead absorption bases. ABC is more demanding than traditional practice but it is better attuned to the modern environment. A modern manufacturing operation typically involves a far more complex range of activities than was the case 30 years ago and a higher proportion of costs are likely to be indirect. A more sensitive approach to cost determination is therefore appropriate.

1.6 Throughput accounting is the term used to describe an approach to accounting which places an emphasis on production volumes, production times and contribution. In the practice of TA, the assumption is frequently made that the only truly variable cost in an operation is that of the materials used. The key TA performance indicator for any period is:

(Sales Revenue − Material Cost)/Production Time (hours).

By considering this indicator for 'the bottleneck facility' management may be guided in optimising the use of production facilities. Throughput accounting is therefore closely associated with the 'theory of constraints'.

1.7 TQM is a management philosophy which involves use of a range of advanced management techniques. Its central concept is that 'quality' is the key strategic variable in a business and that it is a variable that is amenable to organisational culture. The key concepts associated with the provision of quality in an organisation are 'empowerment' and 'teams'. TQM is very much the antithesis of the traditional 'command and control' concept associated with budgeting that we encountered earlier in this text. TQM involves the devolution of authority to multi-skilled, empowered teams in the organisation. It is claimed the TQM provides the organisational flexibility needed to cope with an environment where product life cycles are short, products are highly customised and products have a high service element. The empowerment and motivation of individual staff to deal directly with customers is therefore critical to success.

1.8 The 'New Economy' is a buzz word which became popular in management literature in the late 1990s. Essentially, it referred to a business environment in which it was expected that 'lean' and 'virtual' businesses would emerge as the dominant species. Traditional businesses with factories and offices would be replaced by loosely organised alliances which would obtain the use of facilities and resources only as and when needed. The goods being produced were expected to have an increasingly high service content (e.g. the software and associated system support in a PC costing more than the equipment). The key to success in this environment would be 'flexibility'. It was also claimed that new metrics (other than profit or return on investment) would be needed in order to evaluate the performance of such businesses. The spectacular collapse of many high profile New Economy businesses (Enron and World.com being examples) during the recession of the early 2000s has brought the term into some disfavour lately.

✓ Solution 2

In answering this question it is important to appreciate that JIT is not merely a stock management technique. Rather, it is a management philosophy.

(a) The benefits of JIT, as described by Aggrawal, are gained by a revolutionary change in work practices, company culture and external relationships. JIT is not just about running a production facility with less inventory, it is a way of working that reduces traditional practices which do not add value to the product. Such 'non-value adding' practices include warehousing and stock movement within the factory, testing for quality control, running machinery merely to accumulate large stocks of WIP at a bottleneck down the line and setting-up machinery to run a batch of different specification or product.

The new company culture gives workers the power to manage the production process by moving to where they are needed on the production line or by solving their own problems (quality circles). This requires co-operation between workers and a new approach to management. Furthermore, the workers self-test their work to provide quality assurance and must feel free to halt production if there is a problem. Workers need to be multi-skilled, that is there can be no demarcation across traditional skill boundaries, so that set-up times and maintenance downtime may be minimised. These new working practices coupled with new technology reduce inefficiencies in the production process and result in new working patterns.

New external relationships must be developed, especially with suppliers of materials and components. The supplies must be defect-free, on-time and delivered more frequently in smaller lots. There should be no inspection of goods received. Therefore, new standards need to be established with tighter tolerances, warranties and changed packing requirements. In return, the supplier will become the sole supplier, but will take on board the responsibility for R&D for the items supplied.

All of the above changes are quite radical and involve everyone concerned with the production process. The JIT philosophy will work only when workers are empowered, that is free to make decisions and own up to mistakes; this cultural change for both workers and management requires much training and much practice. Thus, the benefits of JIT do not appear overnight.

(b) The introduction of a JIT production process will result in smaller batch sizes, that is smaller production runs and more changeovers, lower inventory levels and more frequent deliveries, fewer direct labour and machine hours, but more indirect labour for quality assurance, software development, R&D and so on.

Thus, we see a need for faster gathering, grouping and analysis of performance for control purposes. Fortunately, computer-controlled processes capture much of the information required, such as what was done, when it was done, how long it took and what was produced. This enables traceable costs to be collected and monitored for each cost centre. This process must start at the component level, and for every stage in the production process the number of set-ups, orders, inspections, labour and machine time, and so on must be built into the product cost-control exercise.

Electronic data interchange will enable the system to match the pace of frequent deliveries on to the shop floor, and as a Kanban system will be used the day-to-day variation in inventory will be small. A complete production scheduling system will be required such as MRP2. This will allow for management accounting exercises such as capacity utilisation to be carried out.

The empowered workers will not require variance analysis, but motivational control will be more important and will use physical performance indicators, such as average set-up time or number of defects. Standard costing will still be required, but mainly as a foundation in preparing the financial accounting reports. To control the rising indirect costs, budget control will become more important. Cost planning will need to cater for blueprints for new products or production methods and for cost reduction as an ongoing process.

Thus, the development in management information systems is more of evolution and change in emphasis, as opposed to the revolution on the shop floor when JIT is introduced.

Solution 3

This question requires candidates to demonstrate their understanding of quality cost by providing examples, and to apply the approach to developing an appropriate set of performance measures for the management accounting function.

(a) *Prevention costs:*

These are investments made in machinery, technology and educational programmes with the intention of reducing the number of defective items. Examples are as follows:
- *Manufacturing:* Automated production processes such as robotics: the use of quality circles for process improvements.
- *Management accounting:* Replacing manual operations with computers; the use of regular staff training programmes.

Appraisal costs:

These are the costs of monitoring and inspection compared with predetermined standards of performance, before release to customers. Examples are as follows:
- *Manufacturing:* Product and process testing for quality by quality control staff; the costs of test equipment.
- *Management accounting:* The use of computer audits to check the reliability of computer software; the use of batch input controls to confirm the validity of data processing.

Internal failure costs:

These refer to failure costs discovered before delivery to customers. Examples are as follows:
- *Manufacturing:* The cost of scrapped production; the costs of rework and corrections.
- *Management accounting:* The costs of reprocessing input errors; the costs of producing replacement reports.

External failure costs:

These refer to failure costs discovered after delivery to customers. Examples are as follows:
- *Manufacturing:* The cost of meeting warranty claims from customers; the loss of repeat orders from customers.
- *Management accounting:* The costs associated with poor decision-making arising from inaccurate or untimely information to management; the costs associated with resolving external audit queries.

(b) How cost categorisation can help develop performance measures.

The breaking down of costs into the four categories identified in (a) provides a useful structure of data collection. Also, defining these cost categories helps to clarify an understanding of the issues involved in developing the objectives of management accounting within the organisation.

Rather than looking at the totality of quality costs within management accounting, a VFM approach can usefully be attempted in each quality cost area. For example, some of these quality cost areas are likely to be more critical than others, such as the provision of cost information for pricing purposes.

In this way, quality cost categorisation focuses attention on areas of both high expenditure and high importance, and may provide a basis for benchmarking the management accounting function against that of comparable organisations.

Appropriate quality and performance measures:
It needs to be recognised that management accounting has internal customers, that is other departments in the organisation and senior management. Their opinions on the service they receive are critical. Indeed many organisations are currently considering outsourcing their accounting functions.

Appropriate performance objectives should address issues such as:

- the usefulness of management accounting information – in other words, relevance to user needs;
- the timeliness of reports and cost exercises;
- the flexibility in response to user requests;
- the availability of accounting personnel to resolve queries;
- value for money.

Specific performance measures could then be, for example:

- the number of computer downtime hours in a period;
- the number of reports issued on time;
- ratings from internal customer satisfaction surveys;
- benchmarking management accounting costs and activities against those of comparable organisations.

Solution 4

(a) Standard costing involves the setting of standards at agreed levels of price and performance and the measurement of actual events against such standards in order to monitor performance. The variance analysis will measure changes in performance and price for sales, material, labour and overhead. A basic assumption is that the standards will apply over a time period during which they provide a suitable base against which to measure actual events.

A total quality environment adopts a different philosophy:
- It aims towards an environment of zero defects at minimum cost. This conflicts with the idea of standard costs, which, for example, accept that a planned level of yield loss has been built into material standards.
- It aims towards the elimination of waste, where waste is defined as anything other than the minimum essential amount of equipment, materials, space and worker time. Standard costs may be set at currently attainable levels of performance that built in an accepted allowance for 'waste'.
- It aims at continuous improvement. The focus is on performance measures that illustrate a continuous trend of improvement rather than 'steady-state' standard performance that is accepted for a specific period.
- It is an overall philosophy requiring awareness by all personnel of the quality requirements in providing the customer with products of agreed design specification. Standard costing tends to place control of each variance type with specific members of management and work-force. This view may cause conflicting decisions as to the best strategy for improvement.

(b) Standard costing will measure labour efficiency in terms of the ratio of output achieved: standard input. This measure focuses on quantity and does not address other issues of effectiveness. Effectiveness is a broader concept that incorporates the idea of trying to find the cheapest method of achieving a given result. Effectiveness in a total quality context implies high quality with a focus on value-added activities and essential support activities. Efficiency (in terms of output) may be achieved at a cost. In a total quality context, such costs may be measured as internal or external failure costs that will not be identified in the standard cost variance measure.

In a standard cost system, individual labour task situations are used as a basis for efficiency measurement. In a total quality environment it is more likely that labour will be viewed in multitask teams who are responsible for the completion of a part of the production cycle. The team effectiveness is viewed in terms of measures other than output, including incidence of rework, defect levels at a subsequent stage in production, and defects reported by the customer.

☑ Solution 5

In some types of popular management literature the terms 'cost control' and 'cost reduction' are used as if they are interchangeable. Actually, they mean very different things. The question invites students to explore relevant differences.

(a) Cost control is the process of containing costs to some predetermined norm. This is usually carried on by the formal comparison of actual results with those planned – the routine of budgets and standard costs and operating statements and the investigation of variances. Cost reduction is the wider-ranging attempt to reduce costs below the previously accepted norm or standard, preferably without reducing quality or effectiveness. This is a dynamic rather than routine process, quite possibly only carried out at infrequent intervals, for example at time of financial crisis.

(b) A wide range of examples can be given.

　(i) *Cost control:*

　　Budgetary control
　　Standard costing
　　Setting of spending limits by level of management
　　Procedures for formal authorisation of recruitment
　　Control of capital expenditure.

　(ii) *Cost reduction:*

　　Value analysis, value engineering
　　Systems analysis, O&M
　　Work study
　　Operations research (OR)
　　Standardisation of components and processes
　　Product range standardisation/simplification
　　Investment appraisal, terotechnology
　　Value-for-money analysis
　　Arbitrary cutting of overhead budgets
　　Zero-based budgeting.

　　Any three of the above are sufficient to answer the question.

(c) The cost-control techniques of standard costing and budgetary control would tend to support the proposal. However, a study of OR techniques (essentially cost-reduction techniques) and of recent developments, reported in *Management Accounting,* would lead to the conclusion that current practice is not purely control, but active cost reduction.

There has been considerable interest in a range of topics relating to new manufacturing techniques, and to Japanese methods – quality management, quality costs, JIT stock and production control, flexible manufacturing systems and computer-integrated manufacturing.

There has also been interest in a range of other innovations, in IT making management accounting faster and more effective especially with developments in data capture and transmission, in strategic management accounting and the links between management accounting and long-range planning, and in the extension of management accounting in areas where it has been relatively underdeveloped in service industries and the public sector, often with the development of new techniques such as data envelopment analysis.

☑ Solution 6

This is another question that invites students to draw on their general knowledge of modern development in management.

(a) The just-in-time (JIT) philosophy aims to enable scheduled production targets to be met while reducing to a minimum non-added-value activities of maintaining more than minimal stock levels of raw materials, subassemblies, work in progress and finished goods.

To achieve this aim, customer relations must be close to enable accurate demand forecasts and relevant product offerings. The factory layout and product design may need to be simplified and a multitask and teamwork culture needs to be established among the workforce. Supplier relationships are crucial and long-term contracts, including component research and development, will follow from a focus on reliable delivery of many on-specification and on-time batches of small quantities of materials.

These are all attributes of a world-class manufacturing standard in an advanced manufacturing technology environment. The old ways of mass production of a single product, in a dedicated production facility with large buffer stockholding, have been replaced with a flexible production facility producing small batches of different product variations, which have shorter life cycles.

Total quality management (TQM) aims to ensure that quality is the primary concern of every employee at every stage of producing a good or service. This implies empowerment of the workforce, that is each individual has responsibility and authority, for example, to stop the production line if necessary to maintain quality.

Both JIT and TQM radically alter the management function from directing to supporting, from organising to coaching, from deciding to facilitating, from problem-solving to providing resources. KL makes a wide variety to complex product and to be economic and to maintain customer satisfaction it will be forced to adopt such practices.

(b) It is not always economic to manufacture every product on a continuous basis. Therefore, a great deal of manufacturing is organised in the form of batches. Production lines periodically switch from one product to another. Operating in this manner will usually involve holding stocks of each product and producing fresh batches of each product as stocks are depleted by sales.

Manufacturing in large, infrequent batches incurs high inventory-holding costs. Manufacturing in small, frequent batches minimises holding costs but may give rise to certain additional costs. For example:

- set-up costs – that is, the opportunity cost of lost production capacity as machinery and the workforce reorganise for a different product;
- extra materials-handling costs as the materials and subassemblies and so on, used for the previous batch are replaced with those required for the next batch;
- quality costs – every time a new batch is commenced more emphasis (workers' and inspectors' time) must be put into assuring that quality is maintained;
- increased paperwork (or software data entry) and expediting corresponding to increased movements of smaller amounts of raw materials, subassemblies and finished products.

All the above factors give rise to costs and it is these costs that the writer is referring to.

These costs will be relatively higher in small-batch production than in large-batch production.

The purpose of any cost accounting system is to attribute production costs to individual products in a meaningful way. One weakness with KL's existing cost accounting system is that it may not adequately identify the full costs of small-batch production. Some of those costs (high labour and material usage in early production) are direct and will be correctly allocated to the products they relate to.

The factory overheads are distributed over all batches at a single overhead rate, for example labour hour rate, which takes no account of batch sizes. So, overheads are absorbed in a manner that discriminates in favour of small batches at the expenses of large batches.

Adopting a cost accounting system that allows a more meaningful treatment of small-batch costs (and ABC is not the only option) offers advantages including the following:

- by providing an accurate figure for batch-size costs, it allows the calculation of accurate optimum batch sizes for each production;
- by correctly treating and reporting small-batch costs, the need to control and manage those costs may become more apparent to managers;
- better short-term decision-making regarding whether to make a product or to buy it in, and better-informed pricing and portfolio decisions;
- better medium- to long-term decision-making, especially relating to reducing these overhead costs by use of IT, better systems and procedures, a better-trained and more flexible workforce, etc.

(c) Academic accountants are expected to carry out research and publish scholarly papers as well as teach undergraduates. Thus, such writers are likely to communicate new practices to the profession as a whole.

There are also numerous consultancy firms that generate business for themselves on the basis of new practices that produce superior results. They too are likely to communicate the general outline of their proprietary practices.

As to the development of new practices, this usually occurs as an empirical solution to a practical problem. This problem may be encountered by practising accountants, by academic accountants via their research, or by consultant accountants working for a client. The last two categories of accountant may have more resources and time to develop a radically new practice, but all three situations could lead to a new practice.

ABC is an example of a new practice based on old principles but applied in a new way to give new insights into production costing. The academic Kaplan is credited with publicising the idea via academic journals, a book, and in conjunction with a major group of consultants. All the ideas in ABC may have been developed and used individually by different practising accountants, but Kaplan took the time to develop them into a coherent theory for modern manufacturing and service sectors.

Some new practices have been developed by academics and all are communicated, tested, debated and explained to the accounting body as a whole by their activities. Thus academic research plays an important role in the development of new practices within the management accounting profession.

✅ Solution 7

(a) Increased competition and technology changes like computer-aided design (CAD), flexible-manufacturing systems (FMS) and computer-integrated manufacturing (CIM), along with the TQM philosophy and JIT manufacturing systems, will dramatically change the manufacturing environment for X Ltd.

To respond to these changes, many new costing systems, for example target costing, have been introduced and other more traditional costing systems have been adapted. One of the more traditional costing systems is standard costing which X Ltd is currently using. This is a control technique which compares standard costs and revenues with actual results to obtain variances which are used to stimulate control action to achieve improved performance.

The use of standard costing in today's manufacturing environment is criticised and as a result X Ltd may have to adapt it to cope with the changing nature of their business. Such criticisms and how they have been remedied are discussed below.

The changing nature of product cost structures has affected the application of standard costing in that overhead costs have become a more significant element of total cost and direct labour cost has decreased considerably. This is as a result of the large-scale investment made in production equipment. As standard costing is focused on controlling direct costs and therefore variable costs its usefulness is now being questioned where there is a large amount of fixed costs and indirect costs.

However, research shows that variable costs are still a significant proportion of total costs, such as direct material costs and variable overheads and under these circumstances standard costing is an important cost accounting method.

Standard costing in the new manufacturing environment now places less emphasis on direct labour cost variances. This environment has developed other variances which focus on critical inputs to the production process, for example machine hours, direct material costs, variable overhead costs and product quality.

Standard costing is inconsistent with many of the modern management philosophies today. Many of today's manufacturing organisations have adopted techniques like TQM, ABC and ABM which focus on cost control, the elimination of rejects and the maintenance of high quality products which are delivered to the customer at the right price and at the right time.

Standard costing in some ways contradicts these modern techniques, as it requires managers to be responsible for their own variances which, in some cases, motivates managers to achieve favourable variances at the detriment of quality, for example purchasing poor quality materials at a lower price. The same issues arise in relation to increasing actual volume above budgeted volume leading to favourable volume variances but increasing inventory levels. The emphasis is too much on cost minimisation rather than on the maintenance of product quality and customer care.

Standard costing has been adapted so that the cost driver analysis derived from an activity-based management system is now used to calculate variances beyond those traditionally calculated under standard costing. X Ltd's steps in introducing the ABC system will provide them with more useful variance information.

Traditionally, it was quite usual for variances to be reported on a monthly basis and this time delay in reporting is of little use to the control of day-to-day operations. Many manufacturing companies have implemented real-time information systems, which calculate the variances on a real-time basis and allow for corrective action to be taken sooner. CAD, for example, allows the control of production costs at the pre-production stage and can be used alongside target costing as a way of controlling costs before they are incurred and in a way which reflects market costs.

The variances calculated from a standard costing system are too aggregate, that is they are not normally specific to product lines or production batches and this makes it difficult for managers to determine their cause. Adapting the standard costing system to allow for a broader analysis has been undertaken by many manufacturing organisations.

Traditionally, one of the crucial factors of standard costing was a stable production process. Today's manufacturing environment has less stable production processes in that many different products are produced on the same production lines. It is, therefore, important that standard costing is customised to reflect this.

Shorter product life cycles mean that standard costing information can quickly become out of date and therefore needs to be regularly updated, otherwise its application will be very limited. The modern manufacturing environment has embraced the need to keep the standard cost data up-to-date.

The majority of manufacturing organisations still use standard costing and it is therefore unlikely that it will ever be completely abandoned. It has, however, become an integral part of the cost management systems in today's manufacturing environment and tends to be broadened to provide whatever variance information the organisation may need from time to time. So even if standard costing were to be abandoned for cost control and performance evaluation purposes, it will still have a specific use for inventory valuation, profit measurement and decision-making.

(b) *Fixed overhead expenditure variance – $2,300(A)*
This variance represents the difference between the fixed production overhead that should have been incurred in the period and that which was incurred. The adverse variance indicates that actual fixed production overhead incurred was more than budgeted for the period.

The total fixed overhead expenditure variance does not pinpoint the precise reason for the variance occurring as any difference will be the result of a combination of reasons. Therefore, it would be more appropriate to detail the actual fixed production overhead costs compared to that budgeted for each individual item. Without this level of detail, this variance would be difficult to use for decision-making purposes, for example the identification of specific fixed costs that would arise as a result of a decision being made.

Fixed overhead volume variance – $ 5,000(F)
This variance represents the over-or under-absorption of fixed production overhead costs, caused by the actual output differing from that budgeted for. A pre-determined OAR of £10 per labour hour gives a standard fixed overhead cost of £1 per unit. Hence, the standard fixed overhead cost for the 105,000 units produced incorporates a £5,000 absorption in excess of that budgeted for. This £5,000 over absorption corresponds to the favourable fixed overhead volume variance.

The purpose of the fixed overhead volume variance is to assist management's understanding of the causes of the variances. The use of this variance is limited in that it is only possible to calculate it under an absorption costing system. With an absorption costing system it is sometimes difficult to decide which costs are really fixed in nature. Also the usefulness of attaching a value for fixed overheads is questionable as fixed overheads often represent sunk costs and such costs are not appropriate for decision-making purposes. Perhaps it would be more appropriate to measure this variance in terms of lost contribution arising from lost sales. Also the use of labour hours as a driver of fixed costs may not be meaningful in the modern manufacturing environment in which X Ltd currently operates.

(c) (i) *Overhead expenditure variances*
These variances measure the difference between the actual production overhead costs and those in a budget flexed on the actual number of orders executed and the number of production runs.

Material handling has a $2,200 favourable variance indicating that the actual production overhead costs were less than the budget flexed on the actual number of orders executed.

This would be calculated as follows:

Material handling	$
Standard cost ($30,000/5,000 × 5,500)	33,000
Actual cost	30,800
Variance	2,200 (F)

The set up cost has a $6,500 adverse variance indicating that the actual production overhead costs were more than the budget flexed on the actual number of production runs.

This would be calculated as follows:

Set ups	$
Standard cost ($70,000/2,800 × 2,600)	65,000
Actual cost	71,500
Variance	6,500 (A)

These variances provide useful information as they compare each individual item of overhead expenditure against the budget.

Overhead efficiency variances

These variances measure the difference between the overhead cost budget flexed on the actual number of orders executed and the actual number of production runs and the overhead cost absorbed by the activity achieved.

Material handling – $ 1,500(A)

This variance indicates that the actual number of orders executed was more than expected for the output achieved resulting in this adverse variance.

This would be calculated as follows:

Material handling		
Standard orders executed		
(5,000/100,000 × 105,000)	5,250	
Actual orders executed	5,500	
Variance	250 × $6 = $1,500 (A)	

Set up – $8,500(F)

This variance indicates that the actual number of production runs was less than expected for the output achieved resulting in this favourable variance.

This would be calculated as follows:

Set ups		
Standard production runs		
(2,800/100,00 × 105,000)	2,940	
Actual production runs	2,600	
Variance	340 × $25 = $8,500 (F)	

(ii) When X Ltd implemented ABC the first stage in the process will have been to identify the major activities involved in the manufacturing of the electronic diaries. Examples of such activities are machine-related activities, direct labour-related activities and various support activities (ordering, receiving and so on). They will have identified the factors that influenced the cost of these activities, that is the cost drivers and a cost pool will then have been established for each activity and these costs will then have been traced to the electronic diaries based on the consumption estimates of these activities during the manufacturing process.

By implementing the ABC system it has become apparent that the traditional volume-based cost variances are replaced with activity-based cost driver variances which will provide more useful information as to the cause of such variances as these more accurately reflect the cause of resource consumption. So instead of aggregating all of the overhead costs as in the standard costing system, such overhead costs under an ABC system will be broken down based on the resources consuming those costs. The extent to which it leads to more accurate costing will depend on the analysis undertaken when determining the cost drivers.

The more detailed variances reported under the ABC system will allow the managers of X Ltd to gain better control of these areas and will assist in future planning and decision-making.

✓ Solution 8

(a) The principle underpinning throughput accounting is that profit is maximised by maximising throughput. Throughput is maximised by making the most effective use of the bottleneck resource within an operation. Typically, the production process in an organisation involves the sequential use of a series of discrete resources. One of these resources is generally the bottleneck that constrains production overall. The point of product performance evaluation in throughput accounting is therefore to identify the effectiveness with which individual products utilise the bottleneck resource and rank products accordingly. The relevant steps in the contruction of a throughput accounting report are:

(i) identify the key constraint which restricts output;
(ii) evaluate the return per time unit of the bottleneck resource generated by each product;
(iii) rank the products accordingly and adopt a plan that prioritises those products that perform at the highest levels;
(iv) concentrate investment on expanding capacity in the bottleneck resource.

In the short-term throughput accounting induces managers to prioritise products which give the largest possible return per unit of time they spend in the bottleneck resource. In the long-term throughput accounting induces managers to concentrate investment plans on developing capacity in the bottleneck resource.

The key performance metric in throughput accounting is 'throughput contribution' being sales less material costs. This incorporates no allowance for stock and inventory changes, so the accumulation of these items leads to a straight decline in reported performance. Managers are therefore induced to avoid stock and inventory build ups.

(b) Three key metrics associated with throughput accounting are:

1. throughput contribution – sales less material costs
2. return per time period – throughput contribution / time on key resource
3. TA ratio – throughput contribution / conversion cost (that is, labour plus overhead).

These three metrics place a focus on the performance of products in terms of their utilisation of key or bottleneck resources. Accordingly, they provide a guide to the prioritisation and ranking of products in the production planning process.

(c) The main advantage of throughput accounting is that it provides a continuing guide to resource utilisation. Specifically, it leads management to make the fullest possible use of the bottleneck or key resource which constrains production. In this sense it is an accounting expression of limiting factor and/or critical path analysis. The performance of individual products is presented in terms of how effectively they utilise the key resource in the business. This provides guide to which products should be prioritised and how usage of the key resource should be scheduled.

Throughput accounting is a utilitarian approach to performance evaluation and reporting based on the assumption that all costs, apart from materials, are fixed. That may be correct in the extreme short term but the approach takes an unsubtle view which is different to that which underpins other modern accounting technique such as ABC. ABC proceeds on the basis that most costs are variable provided a long enough view is taken and it is understood what costs vary with.

Furthermore, throughput accounting provides a wholly financial impression of performance which ignores strategic and long-term issues. Business decisions are unlikely to achieve an optimum outcome in the long term if they are guided solely by immediate financial considerations.

(d) Throughput accounting is most commonly associated with manufacturing and it is not an obvious candidate for use in a financial services environment. However, the system can be adapted to different circumstances. Banks offer a range of products such as personal loans, home loans, car loans and credit cards. These products may make use of a number of internal functions – such as processing loan applications, inputting system data, undertaking credit checks, processing cash disbursements and credit control.

Each of these functions will be undertaken by a specific resource set and one of these resource sets may be the bottleneck resource. For example, it may be that undertaking credit checks is a limiting factor that constrains the level of business that can be undertaken. Throughput accounting would concentrate attention on that and induce managers to adopt a business plan that makes fullest possible use of this resource.

Processing a large number of small personal loans may make a disproportionate use of credit check facilities relative to home loans. Throughput accounting would promote awareness of this and incline managers to concentrate on promoting home loans at the expense of personal loans.

Forecasting and Budgeting

Forecasting and Budgeting

6

6.1 Introduction

In this chapter we will consider the manner in which an understanding of cost and revenue structures can be applied in the construction of forecasts, plans and budgets. The preparation of budgets and their use in the control of operations are core management accounting functions. Budgets are widely used in the manufacturing, services, public and voluntary sectors.

The basic concepts and practices involved in budgeting are explored in this chapter.

6.2 The nature and purpose of budgeting

Budgets have two main roles:

1. They act as authorities to spend, that is, they give authority to budget managers to incur expenditure in their part of the organisation.
2. They act as comparators for current performance, by providing a yardstick against which current activities can be monitored, and they may be used as targets to motivate managers.

These two roles are combined in a system of budgetary planning and control.

6.2.1 Strategic planning, budgetary planning and operational planning

It will be useful at this stage to distinguish, in broad terms, between three different types of planning:

1. strategic planning
2. budgetary planning
3. operational planning.

These three forms of planning are interrelated. The main distinction between them relates to their time span which may be short, medium or long term.

Strategic planning

Strategic planning is concerned with preparing long-term action plans to attain the organisation's objectives.

Budgetary planning

Budgetary planning is concerned with preparing the short- to medium-term plans of the organisation. It will be carried out within the framework of the strategic plan. An organisation's annual budget could be seen as an interim term step towards achieving the long-term or strategic plan.

Operational planning

Operational planning refers to the short-term or day-to-day planning process. It is concerned with planning the utilisation of resources and will be carried out within the framework set by the budgetary plan. Each stage in the operational planning process can be seen as an interim step towards achieving the budget for the period.

Remember that the full benefit of any planning exercise is not realised unless the plan is also used for control purposes. Each of these types of planning should be accompanied by the appropriate control exercise covering the same time span.

6.2.2 Budgetary planning and control

Planning the activities of an organisation ensures that the organisation sets out in the right direction. Individuals within the organisation will have definite targets that they will aim to achieve. Without a formalised plan the organisation will lack direction, and managers will not be aware of their own targets and responsibilities. Neither will they appreciate how their activities relate to those of other managers within the organisation.

A formalised plan will help to ensure a co-ordinated approach and the planning process itself will force managers to continually think ahead, planning and reviewing their activities in advance.

However, the budgetary process should not stop with the plan. The organisation has started out in the right direction but to ensure that it continues on course it is management's responsibility to exercise control.

Control is best achieved by comparison of the actual results with the original plan. Appropriate action can then be taken to correct any deviations from the plan.

The two activities of planning and control must go hand in hand. Carrying out the budgetary planning exercise without using the plan for control purposes is performing only part of the task.

A budget could be defined as 'a quantified plan of action relating to a given period of time'.

For a budget to be useful it must be quantified. For example, it would not be particularly useful for the purposes of planning and control if a budget was set as follows: 'We plan to spend as little as possible in running the printing department this year'; or 'We plan to produce as many units as we can possibly sell this quarter'.

These are merely vague indicators of intended direction; they are not quantified plans. They will not provide much assistance in management's task of planning and controlling the organisation.

These 'budgets' could perhaps be modified as follows: 'Budgeted revenue expenditure for the printing department this year is £60,000'; and 'Budgeted production for the quarter is 4,700 units'.

The quantification of the budgets has provided:

(a) a definite target for planning purposes; and
(b) a yardstick for control purposes.

The thrust of this approach is that the budget provides an internal benchmark against which performance can be evaluated. If the department or business achieves its budget turnover and/or profit for the period that it is deemed to be performing well. Conversely, if it fails to achieve budget then it is deemed to be performing badly. This approach to performance evaluation has been subject to a variety of criticisms and we will explore these criticisms as we proceed through the text.

A budget can also have a variety of other uses relating to the legitimisation of decisions taken within an organisation. The process of preparing and obtaining approval for a spending budget may provide the channel through which authorisation is granted to commit resources.

In theory, a budget should be a motivating but 'neutral' tool. The practice of budgeting should not distort the processes it is meant to serve. However, at this point it should be noted that the process of establishing a budget and its subsequent use in control and performance evaluation can have a variety of behavioural effects within the organisation. These effects are not always obvious or intended. Sometimes, they can harm the organisation.

6.2.3 The budget period and the budget interval

The budget period is the time for which the budget is prepared. This is typically 1 year which reflects the fact that the financial reports for most organisations cover 1 year periods. But a budget can be for any length of time that suits management purposes.

Each budget period is normally split into control periods known as budget intervals. The budget interval is normally 3 months or 1 month. The 1 year budget is split into component parts for each budget interval and a budgetary control report is prepared at the end of each interval in which the budget and actual results are compared. The manner in which control reports may be prepared is explored later in this chapter.

6.3 The preparation of budgets

The process of preparing and using budgets will differ from organisation to organisation. However, there are a number of key requirements in the design of a budgetary planning and control process.

6.3.1 Co-ordination: the budget committee

The need for co-ordination in the planning process is paramount. The interrelationship between the functional budgets (e.g. sales, production, purchasing) means that one budget cannot be completed without reference to several others.

For example, the purchasing budget cannot be prepared without reference to the production budget, and it may be necessary to prepare the sales budget before the production budget can be prepared. The best way to achieve this co-ordination is to set up a budget committee. The budget committee should comprise representatives from all parts of the organisation: there should be a representative from sales, a representative from marketing, a representative from personnel and so on.

The budget committee should meet regularly to review the progress of the budgetary planning process and to resolve any problems that have arisen. These meetings will effectively bring together the whole organisation in one room, to ensure that a co-ordinated approach is adopted to budget preparation.

6.3.2 Participative budgeting

CIMA defines participative budgeting as:

 Participative budgeting: A budgeting system in which all budget holders are given the opportunity to participate in setting their own budgets.

This may also be referred to as 'bottom-up budgeting'. It contrasts with imposed or top-down budgets where the ultimate budget holder does not have the opportunity to participate in the budgeting process. The advantages of participative budgeting are as follows:

- *Improved quality of forecasts to use as the basis for the budget:* Managers who are doing a job on a day-to-day basis are likely to have a better idea of what is achievable, what is likely to happen in the forthcoming period, local trading conditions and so on.
- *Improved motivation:* Budget holders are more likely to want to work to achieve a budget that they have been involved in setting themselves, rather than one that has been imposed on them from above.

These factors contribute to the achievement of 'goal congruence' whereby managers are induced by the system to act in a manner which is consistent with the interests of the whole organisation.

The main disadvantage of participative budgeting is that it tends to result in a more extended and complex budgetary process. Furthermore, it may provide an opportunity for departmental managers to undertake 'budget padding'. This last practice involves managers negotiating budgets that are easy to achieve. Such budgets may include inflated cost estimates and/or relaxed revenue targets. However, the advantages are generally accepted to outweigh this disadvantage.

6.3.3 Information: the budget manual

Effective budgetary planning relies on the provision of adequate information to the individuals involved in the planning process.

Many of these information needs are contained in the budget manual.

A budget manual is a collection of documents that contains key information for those involved in the planning process. Typical contents could include the following:

(a) An introductory explanation of the budgetary planning and control process, including a statement of the budgetary objective and desired results.

Participants should be made aware of the advantages to them and to the organisation of an efficient planning and control process. This introduction should give participants an understanding of the workings of the planning process, and of the sort of information that they can expect to receive as part of the control process.

(b) A form of organisation chart to show who is responsible for the preparation of each functional budget and the way in which the budgets are interrelated.

(c) A timetable for the preparation of each budget. This will prevent the formation of a 'bottleneck' with the late preparation of one budget holding up the preparation of all others.

(d) Copies of all forms to be completed by those responsible for preparing budgets, with explanations concerning their completion.

(e) A list of the organisation's account codes, with full explanations of how to use them.

(f) Information concerning key assumptions to be made by managers in their budgets, for example the rate of inflation, key exchange rates and so on.

(g) The name and location of the person to be contacted concerning any problems encountered in preparing budgetary plans. This will usually be the co-ordinator of the budget committee (the budget officer) and will probably be a senior accountant.

6.3.4 Early identification of the principal budget factor

The principal budget factor is the factor that limits the activities of the organisation. The early identification of this factor is important in the budgetary planning process because it indicates which budget should be prepared first.

For example, if sales volume is the principal budget factor then the sales budget must be prepared first, based on the available sales forecasts. All other budgets should then be linked to this.

Alternatively, machine capacity may be limited for the forthcoming period and therefore machine capacity is the principal budget factor. In this case the production budget must be prepared first and all other budgets must be linked to this.

Failure to identify the principal budget factor at an early stage could lead to delays later on when managers realise that the targets they have been working with are not feasible.

The detailed mathematics of structuring a budget around the principal budget factor may be an exercise in limiting factor analysis of a kind encountered earlier in this text.

6.3.5 The interrelationship of budgets

The critical importance of the principal budget factor stems from the fact that all budgets are interrelated. For example, if sales is the principal budget factor this is the first budget to be prepared. This will then provide the basis for the preparation of several other budgets, including the selling expenses budget and the production budget.

However, the production budget cannot be prepared directly from the sales budget without a consideration of stockholding policy. For example, management may plan to increase finished goods stock in anticipation of a sales drive. Production quantities would then have to be higher than the budgeted sales level. Similarly, if a decision is taken to reduce the level of material stocks held, it would not be necessary to purchase all of the materials required for production.

6.3.6 Using spreadsheets in budget preparation

It is clear from just this simple example that changes in one budget can have a knock-on effect on several other budgets. For this reason spreadsheets are particularly useful in budget preparation. Budgetary planning is an iterative, or repetitive, process. Once the first set of budgets has been prepared they will be considered by senior managers. They may require amendments to be made or they may wish to see the effect of changes in key decision variables.

A well-designed spreadsheet model can take account of all of the budget interrelationships. This means that it will not be an onerous task to alter decision variables and produce revised budgets for management's consideration.

In modern times, the budgetary process has a major IT element.

Spreadsheets and databases as budgeting tools

Bob Scarlett, *CIMA student*, **July 1999**

Most organisations use the spreadsheet as the main tool in budgeting and business planning. However, the spreadsheet was developed and introduced as a personal productivity aid. Its use in budgeting for medium- to large-size organisations may be problematic. A new category of business software has recently emerged, designed for use in budget management. One US software supplier has claimed that sales of this category (including products such as Comshare Commander Budget and Hyperion Pillar) are among the fastest growing in business management software. These products are highly developed database systems.

The limitations of spreadsheets

The process of creating a budget in a large organisation is a complex operation. Each area in the organisation needs to prepare a plan and these plans need to be collated and consolidated. The system must then accommodate adjustments on a top-down and bottom-up basis. A budgeting operation based on spreadsheets has the following problems:

- *It is inflexible and error prone.* A large number of spreadsheets can be linked and consolidated but this process presents many difficulties. Calculations are complex and mistakes are easily made. Random 'what-if' analyses across centres may become very difficult to carry out.
- *It is a single-user tool in a multi-user environment.* A large number of spreadsheet users are involved using similar templates over periods of weeks. This involves massive duplication of effort and gives rise to risks relating to loss of data integrity and consistency of structure.

- *It lacks 'functionality'.* There are many users in the budget management process ranging from cost centre managers to the chief financial officer. All require ready access to the system in order to input data to it and draw information from it. The budget controller must be able to track revisions. Spreadsheet-based systems are notorious for complexity – and they can be anything but easy to use.

Spreadsheet-based budgeting systems may be perfectly adequate for the small and simple operation. However, the limitations of such systems may become increasingly apparent as larger and more complex operations are considered.

User requirements

Modern organisations operate in a dynamic environment where the budgeting process involves numerous iterations and changes carried out at very short notice. The type of changes the budget system must accommodate include basic figures, organisation structure and calculation logic. The budget users have to be able to revise the budget to allow for changed assumptions or changed structures in a matter of minutes.

To expand on this:

- Budget holders and cost centre managers need a simple interface with the system which allows them to input data to and draw information from the system without any major learning requirement. It should be possible to view data drawn from the system in simple tabular form.
- Budget managers and divisional mangers receive consolidations of the various departmental budgets. They need to be able to determine who has input their contribution to the consolidated budget and who has not. They need to be able to identify changes to the budget which have been entered at a subordinate level. Above all, they need to be able to carry out top-down changes to the budget to accommodate 'what-if' enquiries and changes in the organisational structure which move items of cost and revenue from one area of the budget to another.
- System administrators design, operate and update the system. They are usually qualified accountants who have a good knowledge of IT. They need a robust system which is easy to understand and where the various interfaces are not excessively technical. The system should allow its administrator to rearrange the system and bolt new modules onto the system without great IT sophistication.

What is needed is a system consisting of a group of linked modules which can be updated in two directions: changed data introduced at cost centre level should automatically feed up through to the various summaries; a new expense line, introduced just once, should feed its way down through to every cost centre. The impact of a departmental reorganisation on the budget should be accommodated by a simple re-coding of relevant data items.

The modern budget management system

The preparation of a large and complex budget is an exercise in data processing. The spreadsheet is, arguably, not well suited to this. The type of system that meets the above requirements is likely to be a database. Such systems have existed for many years but they have been associated mainly with the collation and reporting of large volumes of data. Specifically, they lacked a capability to allow random top-down, what-if analyses.

It is this last feature that distinguishes the modern budget management systems such as Comshare and Hyperion. Such systems contain a capability that allows the budget manager to undertake what-if analyses. For example, the budget manager can postulate the impact of a 12 per cent increase in fuel costs across all cost centers while all other data is held constant. This facility provides what many US budget managers call 'real-life budgeting'. A budget can be revised instantly without having to alter subordinate databases and rework the whole model.

A true multi-user capability allows shared access to a single database (or set of related databases) where users employ common definitions and data without any duplication of work. However, appropriate arrangements should be incorporated for the security and integrity of data. A developed budget management system should incorporate security features – including restricted access to certain account code items (e.g. management salaries).

Budgeting in a large operations is a complex process that requires the support of all the members of the organisation who are engaged in it. To gain the enthusiastic support of managers it is essential that the user interfaces, where data is input and information is extracted, are both familiar and 'user-friendly'.

6.3.7 The master budget

The master budget is a summary of all the functional budgets. It usually comprises the budgeted profit and loss account, budgeted balance sheet and budgeted cash flow statement. It is this master budget that is submitted to senior managers for approval because they should not be burdened with an excessive amount of detail. The master budget is designed to give the summarised information that they need to determine whether the budget is an acceptable plan for the forthcoming period.

6.4 Preparation of operational budgets

In this section, you will be working through an example of the preparation of operational budgets. Note that the preparation of an operational budget is an exercise in budgetary planning and it is not an exercise in operational planning (see earlier discussion). Try to apply your knowledge from your earlier studies of cost accounting to prepare the budgets before looking at our solution.

Exercise: preparing operational budgets

A company manufactures two products, Aye and Bee. Standard cost data for the products for next year are as follows:

	Product Aye per unit	Product Bee per unit
Direct materials		
X at £2 per kg	24 kg	30 kg
Y at £5 per kg	10 kg	8 kg
Z at £6 per kg	5 kg	10 kg
Direct wages		
Unskilled at £3 per hour	10 hours	5 hours
Skilled at £5 per hour	6 hours	5 hours

Budgeted stocks for next year are as follows:

	Product Aye units	Product Bee units
1 January	400	800
31 December	500	1,100

	Material X kg	Material Y kg	Material Z kg
1 January	30,000	25,000	12,000
31 December	35,000	27,000	12,500

Budgeted sales for next year: Product Aye 2,400 units. Product Bee 3,200 units. Prepare the following budgets for next year:

(a) production budget, in units;
(b) material purchases budget, in kg and by value;
(c) direct labour budget, in hours and by value.

 Solution

(a) Production budget

	Product Aye units	Product Bee units
Sales units required	2,400	3,200
Closing stock at end of year	500	1,100
	2,900	4,300
Less opening stock	400	800
Production units required	2,500	3,500

(b) Material purchases budget

	Material X kg	Material Y kg	Material Z kg	Total £
Requirements for production				
Product Aye	60,000	25,000	12,500	
Product Bee	105,000	28,000	35,000	
	165,000	53,000	47,500	
Closing stock at end of year	35,000	27,000	12,500	
	200,000	80,000	60,000	
Less opening stock	30,000	25,000	12,000	
Material purchases required	170,000	55,000	48,000	
	£	£	£	
Standard price per kg	2	5	6	
Material purchases value	340,000	275,000	288,000	903,000

(c) Direct labour budget

	Unskilled labour hours	Skilled labour hours	Total £
Requirements for production			
Product Aye	25,000	15,000	
Product Bee	17,500	17,500	
Total hours required	42,500	32,500	
	£	£	
Standard rate per hour	3	5	
Direct labour cost	127,500	162,500	290,000

6.4.1 Using inventory management and cost behaviour models

The construction of budgets involves the incorporation of a number of management models including those for inventories. Inventory holding policies may be determined by JIT (just-in-time) or EOQ (economic order quantity) models. You should be familiar with both of these models from your earlier studies and they are explored fully later in this text.

The thrust of the JIT model is that inventory levels are maintained as near as possible to zero through a high standard of production and procurement management. In this model, material requirements are delivered just as they are required thus avoiding the need for significant stocks. The thrust of the EOQ model is that optimum re-order levels and quantities can be mathematically identified to take account of holding and ordering costs.

The construction of budgets also involves an appreciation of the manner in which costs respond to changes in the level and structure of output. Cost behaviour models encountered earlier in this text are relevant here. It is normally assumed that most direct costs (materials and labour) are fully variable. Indirect costs (or overheads) plus some types of direct cost can be variable, semi-variable or fixed depending on their nature.

However, more refined models to predict overhead levels for particular output plans can be adopted. ABC links overhead costs to output through an appreciation of activities and cost drivers. The TOC model proceeds on the basis that all costs other than direct materials are fixed (at least in the very short term).

6.4.2 Budget interrelationships

The above example has demonstrated how the data from one operational budget becomes an input in the preparation of another budget. The last budget in the sequence, the direct labour budget, would now be used as an input to other budgets such as the cash budget. The material purchases budget will also provide input data for other budgets. For example, the material purchases budget would probably be used in preparing the creditors budget, taking account of the company's intended policy on the payment of suppliers. The creditors budget would indicate the payments to be made to creditors, which would then become an input for the cash budget and so on.

The cash budget is the subject of the next section of this chapter.

6.5 The cash budget

The cash budget is one of the most vital planning documents in an organisation. It will show the cash effect of all of the decisions taken in the planning process.

Management decisions will have been taken concerning such factors as stockholding policy, credit policy, selling price policy and so on. All of these plans will be designed to meet the objectives of the organisation. However, if there are insufficient cash resources to finance the plans, they may need to be modified or, perhaps, action might be taken to alleviate the cash restraint.

A cash budget can give forewarning of potential problems that could arise so that managers can be prepared for the situation or take action to avoid it.

There are four possible cash positions that could arise:

Cash position	Possible management action
Short-term deficit	Arrange a bank overdraft, reduce debtors and stocks, increase creditors.
Long-term deficit	Raise long-term finance, such as loan capital or share capital.
Short-term surplus	Invest short term, increase debtors and stocks to boost sales, pay creditors early to obtain cash discount.
Long-term surplus	Expand or diversify operations, replace or update fixed assets.

A detailed understanding of cash management is outside the scope of the IMPM syllabus. However, you should notice that the type of action taken by management will depend not only on whether a deficit or a surplus is expected, but also on how long the situation is expected to last.

For example, management would not wish to use surplus cash to purchase fixed assets, if the surplus was only short term and the cash would soon be required again for day-to-day operations.

Cash budgets therefore forewarn managers of the following:

(a) Whether there will be cash surpluses or cash deficits.

(b) How long the surpluses or deficits are expected to last.

6.5.1 Preparing cash budgets

You will have studied the basic principles of cash budget preparation at Foundation level. However, in case you have forgotten the basics we shall review them now and work through a basic example.

The examiner has stressed that your studies should emphasise the interpretive aspects of budget preparation. Therefore, we shall also look in outline at how to interpret the cash budget that you have prepared.

(a) The format for cash budgets

There is no definitive format that should be used for a cash budget. However, whichever format you decide to use, it should include the following:

(i) *A clear distinction between the cash receipts and cash payments for each control period.* Your budget should not consist of a jumble of cash flows. It should be logically arranged with a subtotal for receipts and a subtotal for payments.

(ii) *A figure for the net cash flow for each period.* It could be argued that this is not an essential feature of a cash budget. However, you will find it easier to prepare and use a cash budget in an examination if you include the net cash flow. Also, managers find in practice that a figure for the net cash flow helps to draw attention to the cash flow implications of their actions during the period.

(iii) *The closing cash balance for each control period.* The closing balance for each period will be the opening balance for the following period.

(b) Depreciation is not included in cash budgets

Remember that depreciation is not a cash flow. It may be included in your data for overheads and must therefore be excluded before the overheads are inserted into the cash budget.

(c) Allowance must be made for bad and doubtful debts

Bad debts will never be received in cash and doubtful debts may not be received. When you are forecasting the cash receipts from debtors you must remember to adjust for these items.

Exercise: cash budget

Watson Ltd is preparing its budgets for the next quarter. The following information has been drawn from the budgets prepared in the planning exercise so far.

Sales value	June (estimate)	£12,500
	July (budget)	£13,600
	August	£17,000
	September	£16,800
Direct wages	£1,300 per month	
Direct material purchases	June (estimate)	£3,450
	July (budget)	£3,780
	August	£2,890
	September	£3,150

- Watson sells 10% of its goods for cash. The remainder of customers receive 1 month's credit. No bad debts are anticipated.
- Payments to creditors are made in the month following purchase.
- Wages are paid as they are incurred.
- Watson takes 1 month's credit on all overheads.
- Production overheads are £3,200 per month.
- Selling, distribution and administration overheads amount to £1,890 per month.
- Included in the amounts for overhead given above are depreciation charges of £300 and £190, respectively.
- Watson expects to purchase a delivery vehicle in August for a cash payment of £9,870.
- The cash balance at the end of June is forecast to be £1,235.

Prepare a cash budget for each of the months from July to September.

 # Solution

Watson Ltd cash budget for July to September.

	July £	August £	September £
Sales receipts			
10% in cash	1,360	1,700	1,680
90% in 1 month	11,250	12,240	15,300
Total receipts	12,610	13,940	16,980
Payments			
Material purchases (1-month credit)	3,450	3,780	2,890
Direct wages	1,300	1,300	1,300
Production overheads	2,900	2,900	2,900
Selling, distribution and administration overhead	1,700	1,700	1,700
Delivery vehicle	–	9,870	–
Total payments	9,350	19,550	8,790
Net cash inflow/(outflow)	3,260	(5,610)	8,190
Opening cash balance	1,235	4,495	(1,115)
Closing cash balance at the end of the month	4,495	(1,115)	7,075

6.5.2 Interpretation of the cash budget

This cash budget forewarns the management of Watson Ltd that their plans will lead to a cash deficit of £1,115 at the end of August. They can also see that it will be a short-term deficit and can take appropriate action.

They may decide to delay the purchase of the delivery vehicle or perhaps negotiate a period of credit before the payment will be due. Alternatively, overdraft facilities may be arranged for the appropriate period.

If it is decided that overdraft facilities are to be arranged, it is important that due account is taken of the timing of the receipts and payments within each month.

For example, all of the payments in August may be made at the beginning of the month but receipts may not be expected until nearer the end of the month. The cash deficit could then be considerably greater than it appears from looking only at the month-end balance.

If the worst possible situation arose, the overdrawn balance during August could become as large as £4,495 − £19,550 = £15,055. If management had used the month-end balances as a guide to the overdraft requirement during the period then they would not have arranged a large enough overdraft facility with the bank. It is important, therefore, that they look in detail at the information revealed by the cash budget, and not simply at the closing cash balances.

6.5.3 Cash budget: second example

In the last example you saw how a cash budget can be used to forewarn managers of the cash effect of their planning decisions. A cash budget can also be used as a cash planning tool, as you will see when you work through the following example where it is used to decide on the payments to be made to suppliers.

Exercise

A redundant manager who received compensation of £80,000 decides to commence business on 4 January year 8, manufacturing a product for which he knows there is a ready market. He intends to employ some of his former workers who were also made redundant but they will not all commence on 4 January. Suitable premises have been found to rent. Material stocks costing £10,000 and second-hand machinery costing £60,000 have already been bought out of the £80,000. The machinery has an estimated life of 5 years from January year 8 and no residual value.

Other data is as follows:

1. Product will begin on 4 January and 25% of the following month's sales will be manufactured in January. Each month thereafter the production will consist of 75% of the current month's sales and 25% of the following month's sales.
2. Estimated sales are:

	Units	£
January	—	—
February	3,200	80,000
March	3,600	90,000
April	4,000	100,000
May	4,000	100,000

3. Variable production cost per unit:

	£
Direct materials	7
Direct wages	6
Variable overhead	2
	15

4. Raw material requirements for January's production will be met from the stock already purchased. During January, 50% of the materials required for February's production will be purchased. Thereafter it is intended to buy, each month, 50% of the materials required for the following month's production requirements. The other 50% will be purchased in the month of production.

5. Payment for raw material purchases will usually be made 30 days after purchase, but it will be possible to delay payment if necessary for another month. The manager does not intend to use this course of action too frequently because of the danger of adversely affecting the business's credit rating. Ten per cent of the business's purchases will be eligible for a 5% discount if payment is made immediately on delivery.

6. Direct workers have agreed to have their wages paid into their bank accounts on the 7th working day of each month in respect of the previous month's earnings.

7. Variable production overhead: 60% is to be paid in the month following the month it was incurred and 40% is to be paid 1 month later.

8. Fixed overheads are £4,000 per month. One-quarter of this is paid in the month incurred, one-half in the following month and the remainder represents depreciation on the second-hand machinery.

9. Amounts receivable: a 5% cash discount is allowed for payment in the current month and 20% of each month's sales qualify for this discount. Fifty per cent of each month's sales are received in the following month, 20% in the third month and 8% in the fourth month. The balance of 2% represents anticipated bad debts.

10. The manager's intended cash policy is to maintain a minimum month-end cash balance of £5,000. If cash balances are likely to be lower than this then supplier payment will be delayed as described above.

Prepare a cash budget for each of the first 3 months of year 8, taking account of the requirement to maintain a minimum month-end cash balance of £5,000. All calculations should be made to the nearest pound.

✓ Solution

Initial workings

	January	February	March	April
1. *Monthly production (units)*				
25% of following month's sales	800	900	1,000	1,000
75% of current month's sales	–	2,400	2,700	3,000
	800	3,300	3,700	4,000
2. *Material purchases*	£	£	£	£
Material cost of production	5,600	23,100	25,900	28,000
50% of following month's requirements	11,550	12,950	14,000	
50% of current month's requirements		11,550	12,950	
Purchases	11,550	24,500	26,950	

3. *Wages payments*

Previous month production volume (units)		800	3,300
× £6 = wages paid in month		£4,800	£19,800

4. *Variable overhead*

	January	February	March
	£	£	£
Variable overhead cost of production	1,600	6,600	7,400
60% paid in following month		960	3,960
40% paid 1 month later		–	640
		960	4,600

5. *Fixed overhead*

	£	£	£
One-quarter paid as incurred	1,000	1,000	1,000
One-half paid in following month	–	2,000	2,000
	1,000	3,000	3,000

6. *Sales receipts*

		£	£
Monthly sales		80,000	90,000
Received in current month × 95% × 20%		15,200	17,100
Received in following month × 50%			40,000
Total receivable		15,200	57,100

The next step is to begin to build up the cash budget so that it is possible to see how much cash is available to pay for the material purchases. The discount for early payment will be taken, as long as this does not cause the cash balance to fall below the minimum required balance of £5,000.

Cash budget for January to March, year 8

	January	February	March
	£	£	£
Sales receipts (W6)	–	15,200	57,100
Cash payments			
Wages (W3)	–	4,800	19,800
Variable overhead (W4)	–	960	4,600
Fixed overhead (W5)	1,000	3,000	3,000
Payments, excluding material purchases	1,000	8,760	27,400
Material payments (W7)	1,097	9,343	28,112
Total cash payments	2,097	18,103	55,512
Net cash flow	(2,097)	(2,903)	1,588
Opening cash balance	10,000	7,903	5,000
Closing cash balance	7,903	5,000	6,588

7. *Payments for material purchases*

	January	February	March
	£	£	£
Opening cash balance	10,000	7,903	5,000
Cash inflow (from budget)	–	15,200	57,100
Cash outflow, excluding materials (from budget)	1,000	8,760	27,400
	(1,000)	6,440	29,700
Cash available	9,000	14,343	34,700
Material payments			
January: 10% of January paid			
10% × 11,550 × 95% (Note 1)	(1,097)		

February: pay for January purchases			
(maximum amount possible) (Note 2)		(9,343)	
March			
Pay for January balance			(1,052)
February purchases (W2)			(24,500)
10% of March paid: 10% × 26,950 × 95%			(2,560)
Closing cash balance	7,903	5,000	6,588

Notes:

1. The remaining balance of January purchases (£11,550 × 90% = £10,395) is carried forward for later payment.
2. The remaining balance of January purchases (£10,395 − £9,343 = £1,052) must be paid in March.

6.6 Forecasting and planning

In preparing budgets it is usually necessary to develop the budget around a set of forecasts. The budget officer needs to know what sales of different products will be, what labour rates will be, what material costs will be and so on. It is not always possible to state with absolute certainty what these figures will be, so certain forecasting techniques may be deployed.

Time series analysis is one such technique. A time series is a series of values that vary over time. When plotted on a graph, a time series may reveal a trend or a relationship.

Such exercises can be carried out with varying levels of mathematical refinement. The simplest possible exercise in 'linear regression' is as follows:

Example

Month	Units produced	Costs
		£
1	100	1,200
2	150	1,550

We are required to forecast costs for month 3 when production of 120 units is planned.

On the assumption that the components of costs are either fixed or fully variable, then a model for cost behaviour can be developed using an equation in the form:

$$y = a + bx$$

where y is monthly costs, a is monthly fixed costs, b is variable cost per unit and x is output. As x rises by 50, y rises by 350, Hence b must be 7 and a is 500.

So we have deduced that the variable cost per unit (b) is £7, the fixed costs per month (a) are £500. So, if planned output (x) in month 3 is 120 units then we can forecast that costs in month 3 will be £1,340 (i.e. £500 fixed costs plus (£7 × 120 units) variable costs).

Example

A product called the Unit is on sale. The information below gives the actual monthly and cumulative sales of Units during the period month 1 to month 9.

Month	Total sales	Month sales
1	1,000	1,000
2	1,580	580
3	2,100	520
4	2,400	300
5	2,650	250
6	2,850	200
7	3,190	340
8	3,510	320
9	3,690	180

We are required to produce a forecast for sales of Units in month 10.

Inspection of these figures shows that there is a 'trend'. Monthly Unit sales are declining – but not at an even rate (such as sales each month being 150 Units lower than the previous month). The decline month 1 to month 2 is 420 Units, whereas the decline month 8 to month 9 is only 140 Units.

The figures may be represented graphically as in Figure 6.1.

The trend is apparent but the curve is not smooth. There are probably a number of random elements that are influencing sales – perhaps the amount of rain, what happens to be shown on television or developments in the political situation.

One approach to developing a forecast for month 10 Unit sales is to develop a mathematical model to relate time and Unit sales. Essentially, this involves producing an algebraic equation to link the two. One mathematical technique to do this is known as regression analysis.

The widespread use of PC systems has influenced how this technique is applied.

The relationship between time and cumulative sales is a curve. The simplest algebraic form of a curve is represented by the equation:

$$y = Ax^n$$

In this case we can adopt y as the cumulative sales, x as the months and A as Unit sales in month 1. The figure n is a constant and the analyst has to determine its value.

The figures can be set up on a computer spreadsheet as shown below. The months are entered in the left-hand column. The equation is entered in all the cells in the center column with x being set as the value of the matching month's figure. The value for n in all the cells is linked to a number entered in a reference cell below the main tabulation.

A series of iterations can then be carried out by changing the value of n. It can be determined very quickly that 0.6 gives 'a line of nearest fit'. The resulting tabulation appears as follows:

Spreadsheet

Month	Total sales
1	1,000
2	1,516
3	1,933
4	2,297
5	2,627
6	2,930
7	3,214
8	3,482
9	3,737

These figures are not a perfect match – but they closely fit the actual figures recorded above. They follow the general trend but do not allow for the random events that cause minor fluctuations around that trend.

These 'mathematically modelled' figures may be shown graphically as in Figure 6.2.

If the relationship between cumulative months (x) and cumulative Unit sales is

$$y = 1,000X^{0.6}$$

therefore, which x is 10, then y (cumulative month 1 to month 10 sales) is 3,981 and forecast month 10 sales is 244 Units. This forecast is unlikely to be perfect, but no forecast ever is.

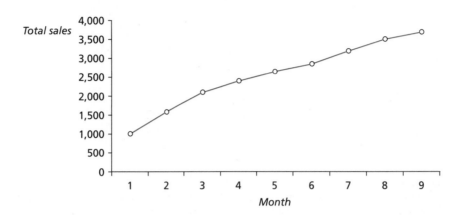

Figure 6.1 Cumulative sales of Units

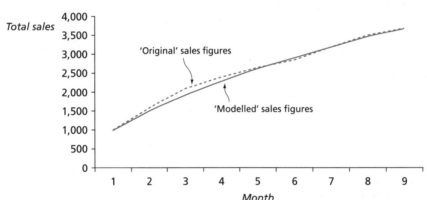

Figure 6.2 Mathematically modelled cumulative sales of Units

6.7 Time series

6.7.1 The concept

One practical application of regression analysis in business forecasting is time series analysis. This approach was implicitly used in the previous section, at an elementary level, to prepare forecasts of costs and sales. A time series is the name given to a set of observations taken at equal intervals of time, for example daily, weekly, monthly and so on. The observations can be plotted on a graph against time to given an overall picture of what is happening. Time intervals are usually plotted on the horizontal axis.

Time series can be constructed for total annual exports, monthly unemployment figures, daily average temperatures and so on.

Example

The following data relates to the sale of Units by ABC ltd. These are the quarterly totals taken over 4 years from 2002 to 2005.

Year	Q1	Q2	Q3	Q4
2002	25	20	22	36
2003	30	28	31	48
2004	41	40	47	61
2005	54	50	60	82

These sales figures may be presented graphically in the form of a time series as follows:

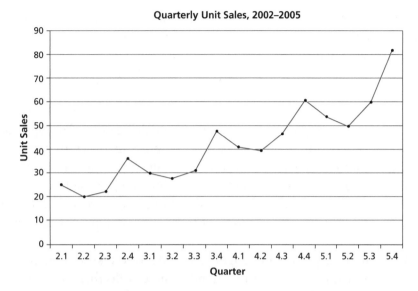

The graph gives a clear impression of how sales have moved over the 4-year period. It can be seen that sales have increased throughout the period but with seasonal variations. Sales seem to surge towards the end of the year then fall back during the middle of the year. Perhaps the Unit is a product with a seasonal sales pattern (e.g. Wellington boots being sold mainly in winter or electric razors being sold mainly around Christmas)?

The purpose of time series analysis is to examine the above graph in order to develop a model that will represent how Unit sales move over time. Typically, that model is represented in the form of an algebraic equation or a line drawn on a graph.

In the case shown, we may wish to use time series analysis to develop a model to predict what the Unit sales will be in 2006. One complication we have in doing this is that sales do not move over time in a neat, uniform manner. There are a number of factors that may influence how sales move over time.

6.7.2 Factors that cause variations

Various factors may cause a time series to move in the manner shown above. These factors include:

(a) *Long-term trend.* This is the key factor that causes the time series to move when the impact of short-term fluctuations has been ironed out. In the case illustrated above, the long-term trend is for Unit sales to rise. Long-term trends may relate to things such as change in the size or age structure of population, change in average income levels and technological progress.

(b) *Cyclical variations.* This is the way in which long-term cycles in trade cause demand to rise and fall. The UK economy has long been prone to 5-year trade cycles whereby the general level of demand in the economy tends to fluctuate around a long-term growth trend. Some observers have claimed that this cycle is associated with the frequency of general elections and the tendency of governments to stimulate the economy in the period before an election. The period considered in the illustrative example is too short to allow the impact of such cyclical variations to be visible.

(c) *Seasonal variations.* This is the way in which sales within a year follow a seasonal pattern. Such a pattern is clearly visible in the example, with sales peaking in winter and bottoming in summer.

(d) *Random (or stochastic) variations.* This is the tendency for sales figures to be influenced by utterly random and unpredictable factors. Examples of these are strikes, terrorist attacks, hurricanes and so on.

6.7.3 Time series modelling

As indicated above, the purpose of time series modelling is to develop a model based on past observations of some variable (e.g. unit sales) in order to forecast what unit sales will be in some future period. Typically, a time series model will incorporate the trend and the seasonal variations. Random variations are, by definition, impossible to forecast and are not incorporated in the model. Long-term cyclical variations normally lie outside the period for which the model is to be used and are not incorporated in the model.

The normal point of departure in designing a model is to take a number of observations of some variable over time and identify a trend. One can do this with varying degrees of mathematical refinement. The simplest approach is to plot the observations on a graph and draw a line of nearest fit through them. That line is the trend and it may be expressed as an equation in the form $y = a + bx$ (assuming it is a straight line). But, using a curve equation in the form $y = a + bx^n$ is possible and may be appropriate.

Another approach to identify a trend is to use moving averages. For example, go back to the figures used in the example in Section 6.7.1. If we take the observations for all quarters in 2002, add them up (giving 103) and then divide by 4, we arrive at 25.75. This figure may be taken as being on the trend line as at the end of quarter 2, 2002, since the averaging gives a 'de-seasonalised' figure. That exercise can be repeated for subsequent quarters (averaging the observations for the two previous and two subsequent quarters) and this gives a series of de-seasonalised trend figures as follows:

Quarter
2.2	25.75
2.3	27.00 (i.e. (20 + 22 + 36 + 30)/4)
2.4	29.00
3.1	31.25
3.2	and so on

One can identify a trend using a variety of different methods and alternative levels of mathematical refinement. Be aware that the whole modelling exercise is one in preparing a simplified representation of a complex reality. Using a very basic approach will usually give results of a quality very near to those obtained using a sophisticated approach.

Once a trend has been identified, variations from that trend can be averaged in order to determine the standard seasonal variations – and the time series model is then complete. The model can be used to forecast what sales will be in future time periods.

A time series model can be based on the assumption that the seasonal variations are either (a) fixed lump amounts (the additive model) or (b) constant proportions of the trend (the multiplicative model). One has to exercise judgement in determining which is most appropriate. Clearly, if the trend is rising and the seasonal variations appear to be increasing in absolute terms, then a multiplicative model will probably be most appropriate.

Example

C Ltd sells units, and quarterly unit sales in year 1 were as follows: 65 (q1), 80 (q2), 70 (q3) and 85 (q4).

Inspection of these figures indicates a trend in unit sales (see Solution) which may be represented by the equation:

$$y = 50 + 10x$$

where y = unit sales and x is the quarter number (with year 1 − quarter 1 being '1').

Solution

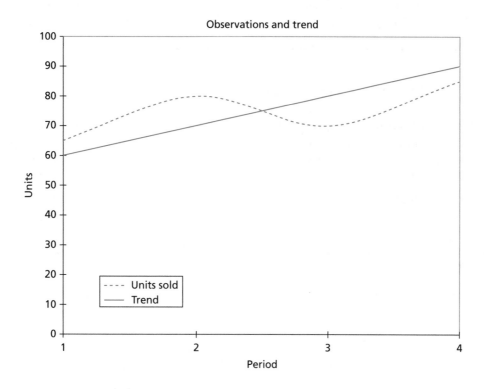

How might these figures be used to develop a time series model in order to forecast unit sales in each quarter of year 2, using (a) an additive modelling approach and (b) a multiplicative modelling approach?.

The point of departure is to take the actual unit sales and compare the trend figures with the actual figures for year 1 in order to determine the seasonal variation for each quarter. This variation can be expressed as (a) a lump sum for each quarter (the additive model) or (b) a percentage of trend (the multiplicative, or proportional, model).

C Ltd – unit sales time series analysis

	Period	Units sold	Trend	(a) Variation	(b) var %
Year 1 q1	1	65	60	5	8.333
Year 1 q2	2	80	70	10	14.286
Year 1 q3	3	70	80	−10	−12.500
Year 1 q4	4	85	90	−5	−5.556

Note that the multiplicative model season variations may be expressed in several different ways. For example, the quarter 3 factor may be expressed as an indexation 87.5% or 0.875.

One may then apply these variation figures to trend projections in order to produce a quarterly forecast for unit sales in Year 2. The two modelling approaches produce two alternative forecasts under headings (a) and (b).

Unit sales, budget for year 2

	Period	Trend	Add. (a)	Mult. (b)
			Year 2 forecast	
Year 2 q1	5	100	105	108
Year 2 q2	6	110	120	126
Year 2 q3	7	120	110	105
Year 2 q4	8	130	125	123

Note that this is the simplest possible example. In particular, we are basing our analysis on only one set of observations (those for year 1). In practice, one would prefer to calculate the seasonal variations on the basis of the average of two or three sets of observations. Thus, if one observed quarter 1 variations from trend (additive model) of 6 (year A), 5 (year B) and 7 (year C) then one would adopt the average of the three (6) as the quarter 1 seasonal variation. The averaging process has the effect of 'ironing out' the impact of random variations over the past period you are considering.

6.8 Sensitivity analysis

There is always a significant degree of uncertainty concerning many of the elements incorporated within a business plan or budget. The budget officer is often required to report on such uncertainty in some way. There are various approaches to this issue and one of the most widely used is 'sensitivity analysis'.

A sensitivity analysis exercise involves revising the budget on the basis of a series of varied assumptions.

Example

The budget for quarter 1 is as follows:

	£
Sales: 100 Units @ £40 per unit	4,000
Variable costs: 100 Units @ £20 per unit	(2,000)
Fixed costs	(1,500)
Profit	500

There is some uncertainty over the variable cost per unit and that cost could be anywhere between £10 and £30, with £20 as the 'expected' outcome. We are required to carry out a sensitivity analysis on this.

One approach to this would be to present the budget shown above as an 'expected' case but with two other cases as 'worst' and 'best' possible outcomes.

Worst-case budget (£30 Unit variable cost)

	£
Sales: 100 Units @ £40 per unit	4,000
Variable costs: 100 Units @ £30 per unit	(3000)
Fixed costs	(1,500)
Profit/(loss)	(500)

Best case budget (£10 Unit variable cost)

	£
Sales: 100 Units @ £40 per unit	4,000
Variable costs: 100 Units @ £10 per unit	(1,000)
Fixed costs	(1,500)
Profit	1,500

The position may be represented graphically as in Figure 6.3.

Figure 6.3 indicates that the operation remains profitable over 75% of possible outcomes. The budget user thus obtains an impression of the possible impact of the uncertainty.

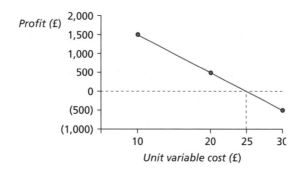

Figure 6.3 Sensitivity to unit variable cost

One can project the sensitivity cases through to the balance sheet as well as the profit and loss account. Let us say that the actual balance sheet at the start of quarter 1 is:

Balance sheet at the start of quarter 1

Fixed assets	5000
Debtors	1500
Cash/(Overdraft)	500
Net Assets	**7000**
Equity	5000
Profit & Loss	2000
Capital	**7000**

We determine that sales are all on 6 weeks' credit and all expenses are paid for immediately they are incurred. Then we can produce three alternative case budget end quarter 1 balance sheets as follows:

Budget balance sheets at the end of quarter 1

	Expected	*Worst*	*Best*
Fixed assets	5000	5000	5000
Debtors	2000	2000	2000
Cash/(Overdraft)	500	(500)	1500
Net Assets	**7500**	**6500**	**8500**
Equity	5000	5000	5000
Profit & Loss	2500	1500	3500
Capital	**7000**	**6500**	**8500**

Calculation of the individual balance sheet figures should be fairly obvious. But, let us consider the worst case cash balance as an example:

Cash inflow from Sales	£	2,000 (being 50% of Sales)
Cash outflow for expenses		−4,500
Cash inflow from opening debtors		1,500
Opening cash balance		500
End cash balance		−500

In practical budgeting, there may be uncertainty concerning a large number of factors within the budget, and sensitivity analysis may consist of a series of complex 'what if?' enquires – reworking the budget, on the basis of a range of different scenarios. In large organisations with complicated budgets, such exercises may be very demanding. In the pre-computer era, the relevant calculations were all carried out manually. This could be a time-consuming and error-prone exercise.

FORECASTING AND BUDGETING

Computer spreadsheets have made the task much easier. However, the spreadsheet has to be designed carefully in order to facilitate sensitivity analysis exercises. A well-designed spreadsheet allows a single correction (on a unit price or an hourly wage rate) to update the whole budget. Spreadsheet modelling is one of the most critical of the practical skills required by management accountants.

6.9 Zero-based budgeting

Certain approaches to the construction of budgets have been developed in recent years. In this and the following sections, we will consider three of these: zero-based budgeting (ZBB), programme-planning budgeting systems (PPBS) and activity-based budgeting (ABB). These three methods have one thing in common – they place an emphasis on the outputs of the process being budgeted for. They all tend to start from the results that the budget is intended to achieve and work backwards to the resources needed to achieve those results, the reverse of more traditional budgeting practices. In the modern context, the process of establishing a budget is an intelligent exercise in business planning wherein alternative means of achieving given objectives are identified and evaluated.

ZBB, PPBS and ABB are probably most applicable to costs which contain a substantial discretionary element, and as such they are most commonly encountered in service departments of commercial operations, the public sector and the not-for-profit sector.

 Discretionary cost: A cost whose amount within a time period is determined by a decision taken by the appropriate budget holder. Marketing, research and training are generally regarded as discretionary costs. Control of discretionary costs is through the budgeting process.

Like all budgeting techniques, ZBB is designed to be used in setting levels of *future* expenditures. As all cost-reduction techniques must, by definition, relate to the reduction of future costs (past costs being sunk), it follows that cost-reduction programmes and budgeting procedures are inextricably entwined. The CIMA *Official Terminology* defines zero-based/priority-based budgeting as:

Zero-based/priority-based budgeting: Method of budgeting that requires all costs to be specifically justified by the benefits to be expected.

This approach is particularly pertinent in public sector organisations, where funds are determined by tax revenues and government grants and allocations, that is, the income of the organisation is exogenously set. The aim of the fundholder is to achieve the best service levels possible within the given budget.

In traditional budgeting, *existing* expenditure levels form the baseline for discussions about future expenditure. Implicit in the traditional approach is an assumption and acceptance that current expenditure is adding value to the customer, and the focus of its attention is simply the justification of any proposed *increases* in that expenditure – it therefore adopts an incremental philosophy to budgeting. The rejection of this baseline as a starting point is what gives ZBB its name. An incremental approach is most likely to be applied to discretionary costs, as it is these costs that have no demonstrable relationship with volume or activity measures. The ZBB approach requires *all* activities to be justified and prioritised before the decision to devote resources to particular ones is taken.

All activities are subjected to the most basic scrutiny, and answers sought to such fundamental question as:

(a) Should the activity be undertaken at all?
(b) If the company undertakes the activity, how *much* should be done and how *well* should it be done (e.g. should an economy or a deluxe service level be provided)?
(c) How should the activity be performed – in-house or subcontract?
(d) How much would the various alternative levels of service and provision cost?

In order to answer these questions, all existing and potential organisational activities must be described and evaluated in a series of 'decision packages', giving the following four-step process to a ZBB exercise:

1. Determine the activities that are to be used as the object of decision packages – the provision of home support for the elderly or provision of catering facilities for the workforce, for example – and identify the manager responsible for each activity.
2. Request the managers identified in (1) above to prepare a number of alternative decision packages for those individual activities for which they are responsible. (At least three packages are normally requested: one that sets out what could be delivered with funding maintained at the *current* level; one for a *reduced* level of funding, e.g. 80% of the current level; and one for an enhanced level of funding, e.g. 120% of the current level.)
3. Rank the decision packages in order of their contribution towards the organisation's objectives.
4. Fund the decision packages according to the ranking established under (3) above until the available funds are exhausted.

6.9.1 Advantages of ZBB

The following advantages are claimed for ZBB:

 (i) It avoids the complacency inherent in the traditional incremental approach, where it is simply assumed that future activities will be very similar to current ones.
 (ii) ZBB encourages a questioning approach, by focusing attention not only on the cost of an activity, but also on the benefits it provides, as the relative benefits of different types and levels of expenditure. Forcing managers to articulate benefits encourages them to think clearly about their activities.
(iii) Preparation of the decision packages will normally require the involvement of many employees, and thus provides an opportunity for their view to be considered. This involvement may produce useful ideas, and promote job satisfaction among the wider staff.

6.9.2 Disadvantages of ZBB

The following disadvantages of ZBB need to be pointed out:

 (i) The work involved in the creation of decision packages, and their subsequent ranking by top management, is very considerable, and has given rise to the cynical description of the process as 'Xerox-based budgeting'.

(ii) The ranking process is inherently difficult, as value judgements are inevitable. This is a particular problem in public sector bodies, where choices between very disparate programmes must often be made: for example, it would be extremely difficult to formulate criteria that would allow an unambiguous ranking when decision packages related to public health must be measured against those relating to law and order. Nevertheless, such rankings are made, explicitly or implicitly, whatever funds allocation system is used; bringing the allocation problems into the open could be viewed as an advantage rather than a disadvantage of ZBB. However, without clear and explicit ranking criteria, the human brain finds ranking difficult. If 'a' is preferred to 'b', and 'b' is preferred to 'c', it should follow that 'a' is preferred to 'c'. Unfortunately, experiments have shown that humans are often unable to produce such logical progressions when faced with a large number of choices.

(iii) In applying ZBB, 'activities' may continue to be identified with traditional functional departments, rather than cross-functional activities, and thus distract the attention of management from the real cost-reduction issues. For example, in discussing value-added and non-value-added activities above, it was argued that the costs incurred in a warranty department are largely a function of the reliability of products, which itself is a function of actions and decisions taken elsewhere. If the warranty department is treated as an activity under ZBB, the focus of the decision packages is likely to be on providing the same level of customer service at reduced cost, or enhancing the level of customer service for the same cost. The main driver behind the department's cost – product reliability – may remain unaddressed in ZBB, as it is with the blanket cut approach.

6.9.3 ZBB in practice

ZBB has been adopted more widely in the public sector than the private, although examples of organisations regularly adopting a full ZBB approach are rare. Full-scale ZBB is so resource-intensive that critics claim that its advantages are outweighed by its implementation costs. However, it is not necessary to apply ZBB to the whole of an organisation; benefits can be gained from its application to specific areas. For example, in the public sector, a decision could be made regarding the overall size of the childcare budget, and ZBB could be applied to allocate resources within that particular field; similarly, in a business organisation, ZBB could be applied to individual divisions on a rotational basis. This selective application ensures that a thorough reappraisal of activities is undertaken regularly, but not so regularly that the process itself is a major drain on organisational resources.

Notwithstanding the criticisms, the main plank of the ZBB approach – the rejection of past budgets as a planning baseline – is being increasingly accepted. Two surveys of UK local authorities – the first undertaken in 1983 and the second in 1988 -showed the use of the approach increasing from 48% to 54% over the period.

6.10 Programme-planning budgeting systems

Programme-planning budgeting systems (PPBS) – a well-understood short title, in the absence of the acronym, is *programme budgeting* – is used quite widely in the public sector and not-for-profit organisation to avoid excessive costs and to ensure that expenditure is focused on programmes and activities that generate the most beneficial results.

As we have seen, traditional budgeting systems, whether in the public or the private sector, are heavily *input-oriented*, with the main emphasis on detailed financial controls. They also lean towards existing organisational units such as departments or divisions. In contrast, PPBS is expressed in terms of *programmes* (functional groups of activities with a common objective), rather than along traditional subdivisional lines, and is *output-* and *objective-oriented*, focusing on *end* items – the ultimate output of services of the organisation – rather than specific inputs. This form of budget structure has one obvious advantage, namely the ease with which it identifies the budget appropriations with the organisation's objectives, thus facilitating a more rational allocation of resources.

The steps involved in PPBS can be simply (if rather simplistically) stated:

1. specify the objectives of the various programmes;
2. measure the output in terms of the objectives;
3. determine the total costs of the programmes for several future periods;
4. analyse alternatives, and go for those with the greatest cost-benefit in terms of the objectives;
5. systematically implement the selected alternatives.

Some explanation of these steps is necessary. Effectiveness can be judged only against predetermined benchmarks set by the organisation. Yet the activities performed by public sector and not-for-profit organisations are often difficult to measure in a tangible way, and can take several years to be measurable, while requiring the annual funding of the related programmes; multiple measures will often be required to overcome these difficulties. Many programmes will also have multiple results, and a choice must usually be made regarding the relative weights attached to them. Further, there will often be questions regarding the legitimacy of causal relationships when measuring these results: particular outcomes could be brought about by the actions of more than one programme, given the nature of public sector and not-for-profit organisations and their objectives.

On a more positive note, one feature of PPBS that should be particularly beneficial is that managers making budget requests are expected to be able to state clearly what would happen if their requests were cut by, say, 10%. Thus the director of leisure services in a local authority should be in a position to say that such a cut would reduce the hours that a swimming pool could open, for example, or require that the grass in public parks be cut every 10 days instead of once a week. This feature of PPBS is, in its result, somewhat similar to ZBB, since different levels of service are associated with each level of requested funding. The interest in PPBS probably owes much to an increasing public demand for accountability by public and other not-for-profit organisations: taxpayers appear to have become dissatisfied with the performance of central and local government agencies; and donors to charitable causes have expressed concern about the proportion of contributed funds devoted to administrative expenses. PPBS specifies goals clearly, and allows people to see where their money is going and, eventually, to see whether or not it is spent *effectively*.

Exercise

The Alpha Sufferers Group is a national charity offering support to sufferers and funding medical research. You have been invited to attend a trustees' meeting at which the following report on this year's performance and next year's annual budget will be discussed. No further supporting information is provided for the trustees. The trustees have used an incremental approach to determine the budget.

FORECASTING AND BUDGETING

The treasurer has heard of 'PPBS' and wonders if it would be useful in the their not-for-profit organisation.

Criticise the current method of budgeting and explain the application (give specific examples) and possible advantages of PPBS to such an organisation.

	20X3		20X4	
	Budget £	Actual £	Budget £	Actual £
Income				
Subscriptions	20,000	18,000	20,000	
Donations received	160,000	200,000	220,000	
Fund-raising	500,000	440,000	484,000	
	680,000	658,000	724,000	
Expenditure				
Employees	60,000	60,000	60,000	
Premises	8,000	8,000	8,000	
Office expenses	28,000	33,000	30,000	
Administration	30,000	42,000	40,000	
Research	300,000	320,000	350,000	
Printing	25,000	30,000	25,000	
Room rental	15,000	12,000	15,000	
Donations made	200,000	230,000	260,000	
	666,000	735,000	788,000	
Excess of income over expenditure	14,000	77,000	(64,000)	

 ## Solution

The approach used to construct the budget is the 'traditional' approach to budgeting: looking at items line by line' and for a period of 1 year only. Presumably, the budget for the coming year was set by taking last year's actual figures and 'adding or subtracting' a bit to reflect expectations or intentions, and to use up the last year's 'unexpected' surplus of income over expenses.

The major criticisms of this approach in such a not-for-profit organisation are:

1. The emphasis is on annual figures, yet the activities of the charity (support and research) extend over a much longer time period.

2. There is no information in the budget about planned or actual achievements, such as the number of sufferer contacted and helped, the level of awareness of the condition, or increased knowledge of cause or treatment. All that is shown is whether the levels of expenditure were as authorised, and if income targets were achieved.

3. There has been no attempt to identify the costs of the different activities. For example, if one objective and activity is to put sufferers in touch with each other, then that would incur costs from several categories – employees, premises, office, administration, printing and so on. But it is impossible to tell from the figures presented how much was spent, or authorised, in achieving that individual objective.

4. There is no evidence that resources (cash, employee time, etc.) are being used in the most productive way. Indeed, there is no information at all as to how efficiently or effectively resources are being used.

A PPBS would overcome these problems with the traditional approach, because the emphasis would be on programmes and activities and how best to use resources to achieve the overall effectiveness of the charity in the medium and long term.

Application of PPBS

The trustees must undertake the following steps:

1. Review the charity's long-term objectives – for example, establish likely causes of the condition, put sufferers in touch with each other and so on.
2. Specify the activities and programmes necessary to achieve the overall objectives; for example, offer research grants to universities, fund a laboratory, maintain a database of sufferers, organise regional meetings and social events, distribute a regular newsletter or magazine and so on.
3. Evaluate the alternative activities and programmes in terms of both costs and likely benefits, that is, specify costs of putting sufferers in contact with each other via a newsletter and so on.
4. Select the most appropriate programmes.
5. Analyse the programmes selected, asking such questions as 'if we reduce the resources allocated to this programme by x per cent, what will happen to the level of achievement of objectives?'

Advantages of PPBS

By changing to a PPBS approach to budgeting, and thus taking a longer view than just 1 year, the trustees should be in a much better position to make informed decisions about the optimal use of their resources to achieve their clearly defined and understood objectives.

6.11 Activity-based budgeting

In recent years, a body of 'activity-based techniques' (ABTs) has been developed. These include activity-based costing, activity-based management and activity-based budgeting (ABB). The logical thrust behind all ABTs is that cost control and management should focus on the outputs of a process rather than on the inputs to that process.

ABT's are, arguably, most applicable to service-sector operations, the public sector, the not-for-profit sector and indirect costs in a manufacturing environment.

The traditional approach to budgeting presents costs under functional headings, that is, costs are presented in a manner that emphasises their nature. Thus, the traditionally arranged budget for a local authority public cleansing department over a given period might appear as follows:

Item of cost	£
Wages	140,000
Materials	28,000
Vehicle hire	35,000
Equipment hire	18,000
Total	221,000

The weakness of this approach is that it gives little indication of the link between the level of activity of the department and the cost incurred. The budget might be restated as an activity-based budget as follows:

Activity	£	Number of activities
Street sweeping	84,000	4,000
School cleaning	68,000	800
Park cleaning	39,000	130
Graffiti removal	30,000	150
	221,000	

This approach provides a clear framework for understanding the link between costs and the level of activity. Using the traditional approach, many of the costs listed under traditional functional headings might simply be considered 'fixed'. However, research often shows that, in the long run, few costs really are fixed. If one can identify appropriate 'cost drivers', then a very high proportion of costs reveal themselves to be variable.

For example, if the department is instructed to increase the frequency of street sweeping by 25% then this will increase the budgeted number of street sweepings (the 'cost driver') from 4,000 to 5,000. A single street-sweeping activity appears to cost £21 (i.e. £84,000 costs divided by 4,000 street sweepings); therefore, if the number of street sweepings rises from 4,000 to 5,000, then one might expect costs to increase by £21,000.

Another example is in the review of capacity utilisation. If it is known that the resources devoted to street sweeping have a capacity of 4,800 sweepings and only 4,000 sweepings are being budgeted for, then one might consider the possibility of reducing the capacity in some way.

Of course, ABBs and traditional budgets are not mutually exclusive. The two can be prepared in parallel or they can be integrated.

6.12 Efficiency and effectiveness in the not-for-profit sector

The not-for-profit (NFP) sector incorporates a wide range of operations including central government, local authorities, charitable trusts and executive agencies. The central thing about such operations is that they are not primarily motivated by a desire to make profit.

The ultimate objective of a commercial business is to generate a profit for its owners. Such a business may take a short or long-term view of the manner in which it wishes to do this. There are often alternative routes available which are capable of achieving this objective and management has to choose between them. However, there is a clear primary objective from which subsidiary objectives may be derived.

The objectives of NFP organisations may be partly legislated for, partly constitutional and partly political. For example, the Driver and Vehicle Licensing Agency (based at Swansea, UK) is charged with keeping records of vehicle registration and issuing driving licenses and road tax disks to motorists. This is a legal obligation. Mencap (a British Charity) has an obligation to act in order to provide assistance for the mentally handicapped written into its constitution.

Sunderland City Council has an obligation to run local schools – but has a wide measure of discretion over how it does this. It can spend money on salaries for teachers or it can switch some of that money into acquiring IT systems and making greater use of Computer Assisted Learning. It can provide teaching of classical Greek or it can reinforce its sports provision. The relevant choices the Council makes are determined by a political process. Parties contesting local elections will include their spending proposals in party manifestos and the voters will elect the Party with the most popular proposals.

However, practical problems with management in the NFP sector include the following:

- objectives may be vague or poorly understood;
- objectives may change regularly over time;
- radically different means may be available to achieve given objectives.

A further consideration is that the relationship between 'objectives' and 'means' is often poorly understood. For example, one public objective is 'to contain street crime within limits considered to be acceptable'. One means of achieving that objective is through the use of traditional police foot patrols. In fact, police foot patrols may be a poor method of containing many forms of street crime. The use of police response units using fast cars is much more cost effective. As soon as a crime is detected by video surveillance or a report from the public, the police can be on the scene quickly. A police officer in a fast car can cover much more ground than an officer on foot. That said, regular police foot patrols may make the public feel more relaxed as they go about their daily business.

However, many local politicians will advocate the need to 'have more bobbies on the beat' in their manifestos. This reflects some lack of clarity over objectives. Is the objective of policing to contain crime or to make the public feel more comfortable? The two are not the same at all. Are police foot patrols a means to achieve an objective, or are they an objective in themselves?

In recent years, much of the discussion concerning NFP sector management has concerned the promotion of the twin concepts of 'efficiency' and 'effectiveness'.

6.12.1 Efficiency

Efficiency concerns making the maximum possible use of a given set of resources; that is, it involves a straight comparison of output and input, for example the total cost per kilometre of road resurfaced.

Many UK local authorities in the 1970s were judged to be making an inefficient use of the resources available to them. They undertook most of their activities (such as road resurfacing or refuse disposal) using large numbers of directly employed council staff. It was often found that these in-house operations cost far more to achieve given outputs than comparable private sector operations.

Financial management initiatives in the 1980s required local authorities to put many of their works programmes 'out to tender'. Private contractors may submit bids in order to undertake specific works for the local authorities. The current private finance initiatives involve continuing private sector participation in the maintenance and operation of facilities such as schools and prisons. For example, in the past a contractor may have built a school for a local authority and simply handed it over to the authority. The more modern approach might involve the contractor building the school and then leasing it to the authority. The contractor thus remains responsible for aspects of its maintenance and management after completion. The contractor will now have an incentive to carefully consider the trade-off between construction costs and operating costs. Possible economies in the construction phase may be associated with higher operating costs later on and the contractor now has in interest in both.

Experience over the last 20 years suggests that this process has generally improved efficiency and achieved greater 'value for money' in local authorities – although the concept is not without its critics.

6.12.2 Effectiveness

Effectiveness concerns finding the cheapest combination of means to achieve a given objective.

This concept is a little more difficult to handle than efficiency. An NFP organisation will normally have a number of stated objectives. For example, a public authority may have 'containing youth crime within acceptable levels' as one of its objectives. It has several means by which it may achieve this objective, including:

- providing 'school attendance officers' to ensure that children are not truanting from school (Education Department);
- providing leisure facilities in the form of sports grounds and youth clubs (Recreation Department);
- providing assistance for disadvantaged or problem families (Social Services Department);
- providing police patrols to arrest or deter young criminals (Police Department);
- providing Young Offenders Institutions at which young criminals may be detained (Prisons Department).

All of these departmental activities contribute to achievement of the objective. The problem is to find the optimum combination of spending for all of the departments together. Practical solutions to this problem lie at the core of budgeting and planning techniques such as ZBB and PPBS.

An aggressive policy of arresting and detaining young criminals may achieve the required objective – but at high cost. Imprisoning a criminal is a very expensive 'last resort' and may turn a marginal criminal into a habitual one. Experience suggests that much crime can be deterred by less aggressive methods. A high proportion of crime is committed by young men in the 13–18 age group. Ensuring that children all attend school regularly and that adequate youth recreational facilities are available may address 'the causes of crime'.

An insensitive financial cut back in one area (e.g. making a school attendance officer redundant) can have a high cost impact in other areas when truanting schoolchildren commit petty crime. The key to effectiveness is in finding an optimum pattern of spending to achieve a given objective.

Finding that optimum pattern will usually involve determining a programme of activities which cuts right across traditional departmental boundaries. The emphasis in modern public sector planning tends to be on outputs rather than inputs. It should be appreciated that the departments within an organisation may be efficient – but the organisation as a whole may be ineffective if the overall pattern of departmental activity has not been carefully planned. Conversely, an organisation may have detailed inefficiencies in its operation, but be effective nevertheless.

Effectiveness is, by its very nature, rather more difficult to measure than efficiency. However, it should be appreciated that performance in an NFP organisation is a function of both efficiency and effectiveness. Performance management and measurement have to take account of this.

6.13 Budgetary control information

Budgetary control is achieved by comparing the actual results with the budget. The differences are calculated as variances and management action may be taken to investigate and correct the variances if necessary or appropriate.

- If costs are higher or revenues are lower than the budget, then the difference is an *adverse* variance.
- If costs are lower or revenues are higher than the budget, then the difference is a *favourable* variance.

6.13.1 Budget centres

The CIMA *Official Terminology* defines a budget centre as follows.

 Budget centre: A section of an entity for which control may be exercised through prepared budgets.

Each budget centre will have its own budget and a manager will be responsible for managing the centre and controlling the budget. This manager is often referred to as the budget-holder. Regular budgetary control reports will be sent to each budget-holder so that they may monitor their centre's activities and take control action if necessary. Costs attributed to individual budget centres may be classified as 'controllable' or 'uncontrollable'. Controllable costs relate to those factors over which the management of the budget centre have direct control, for example labour hours. Managers may be held fully responsible for controllable costs but less so for uncontrollable costs.

The structure of budget centres that an organisation adopts will normally correspond to its own organisational structure. Thus each division, department or section will have its own budget. For example, an equipment manufacturer may be organised in the form of three operating divisions, each working from its own factory site:

(1) heavy equipment manufacture division
(2) medium equipment manufacture division
(3) light equipment manufacture division.

Each division will have its own budget for both costs and sales revenues. Not only is each division a budget centre, but it is also a 'responsibility centre' for the purposes of management accounting. The costs and revenues associated with the operations of each division will be collated and reported periodically for the purposes of comparison with budget.

It should be appreciated that an organisation might be organised on regional rather than functional lines – and there might be North, South and East regional divisions. In such a case both the budget and the responsibility centres would match the organisational structure; the general point being that budgetary control would follow the responsibility accounting principal. Each divisional budget would relate to a clearly defined organisational unit with its own manager. That manager would be held responsible for achieving the budget.

The individual divisional budgets could be split into subsidiary departmental budget. For example, the costs contained in the budget for (1) heavy equipment manufacture division could be split into budgets for

(1.1) Assembly line A
(1.2) Assembly line B
(1.3) Paint Shop.

Again, each of these is a budget centre and a responsibility centre – with actual costs incurred being periodically reported for each and compared with a budget. The departmental managers would be responsible for keeping departmental costs within budget.

Key issues to consider in the design and operation of budget centres include:

- The budget centres should strictly match organisational units. Any departure from this breaches the responsibility accounting principal since no one manager is responsible for achieving a particular budget.
- The responsibility centres should strictly match the budget centres. Any departure from this means that the nature of the costs reported does not strictly match those being budgeted for. If some actual costs are being charged to one department but are in the budget of another, then the whole budgetary control exercise is debased.
- The extent to which 'uncontrollable' costs are attributed to individual departments should be minimised. But consider our earlier discussion (see Chapter 4) concerning activity-based costs. Few costs really are 'uncontrollable' – it is just a matter of determining which activities such costs relate to and who controls the level of those activities.

6.13.2 Budgetary control reports

If managers are to use the budgets to control effectively, they must receive regular control information. This control information provides "feedback" to managers on how the organisation has actually performed relative to budget.

The budgetary control reports should be

(a) *Timely.* The information should be made available as soon as possible after the end of the control period. Corrective action will be much more effective if it is taken soon after the event, and adverse trends could continue unchecked if budgetary reporting systems are slow.

(b) *Accurate.* Inaccurate control information could lead to inappropriate management action. There is often a conflict between the need for timeliness and the need for accuracy. The design of budgetary reporting systems should allow for sufficient accuracy for the purpose to be fulfilled.

(c) *Relevant to the recipient.* Busy managers should not be swamped with information that is not relevant to them. They should not need to search through a lot of irrelevant information to reach the part that relates to their area of responsibility. The natural reaction of an individual faced with this situation could be to ignore the information altogether.

  The budgetary reporting system should ideally be based on the exception principle, which means that management attention is focused on those areas where performance is significantly different from budget. Subsidiary information could be provided on those items that are in line with the budget.

  Many control reports also segregate controllable and non-controllable costs and revenues, that is the costs and revenues over which managers can exercise control are highlighted separately in the reports.

(d) *Communicated to the correct manager.* Control information should be directed to the manager who has the responsibility and authority to act upon it. If the information is communicated to the wrong manager its value will be immediately lost and any adverse trends may continue uncorrected. Individual budget-holders' responsibilities must be clearly defined and kept up to date in respect of any changes.

Budgetary control reports can be prepared with varying degrees of frequency, timeliness, accuracy and detail. For example, you can report at weekly, monthly or quarterly intervals. You can report figures accurate to the nearest £0.1 m or to the nearest penny.

Obviously, the greater the volume and sophistication of control reporting, the greater is its cost. In determining the style of reporting appropriate to an organisation one should have regard to the costs and benefits of reporting. The marginal benefits of additional reporting start to decline as the volume of reporting and the associated cost of reporting rise. An optimum position should be sought having regard to the needs of the organisation.

The design of a budgetary control report depends very much on the inclination of users. We have already seen examples of budgetary control reports in our earlier study of standard costing. In those cases, the reports took the form of reconciliations of budget and actual profit through the calculation of cost and sales variances.

But, alternative styles are possible. A simple example to illustrate a common format is as follows.

ABC Manufacturing Ltd

Operating Statement September 2004

£ millions	Quarter (01/06–30/09)			Year to Date (01/01–30/09)		
	Actual	Budget	Variance	Actual	Budget	Variance
Sales	24.1	22.9	15.2%	84.0	92.4	29.1%
Costs	18.6	18.8	21.1%	69.6	70.1	20.7%
Profit	5.5	4.1	134.1%	14.4	22.3	235.4%

In this case, the 'variances' are (actual–budget)/budget. These variances are not the same as the cost and sales variances we considered in Chapters 2 and 3. A plus percentage means that Actual exceeded Budget-it does not mean that it had an adverse impact on Profit.

A common feature in modern control reports is a forecast to year end position. Adding such a feature to the above report would involve inserting a third set of columns under the heading 'Forecast to Year End (01/01–31/12)'. This adds an element of feedforward to the report. Feedforward is the supply of information on what is forecast to happen in the future.

6.14 Fixed and flexible budgets

When managers are comparing the actual results with the budget for a period, it is important to ensure that they are making a valid comparison. The use of flexible budgets can help to ensure that actual results are monitored against realistic targets.

Example

A company manufactures a single product and the following data shows the actual results for the month of April compared with the budgeted figures.

Operating statement for April

	Actual	Budget	Variance
Units produced and sold	1,000	1,200	(200)
	£	£	£
Sales revenue	110,000	120,000	(10,000)
Direct material	16,490	19,200	2,710
Direct labour	12,380	13,200	820
Production overhead	24,120	24,000	(120)
Administration overhead	21,600	21,000	(600)
Selling and distribution o/head	16,200	16,400	200
Total cost	90,790	93,800	3,010
Profit	19,210	26,200	(6,990)

Note: Variances in brackets are adverse. Also, the figures described as variances (budget–actual) are not variances for standard costing and variance analysis purposes.

Looking at the costs incurred in April, a cost saving of £3,010 has been made compared with the budget. However, the number of units produced and sold was 200 less than budget, so some savings in expenditure might be expected. It is not possible to tell from this comparison how much of the saving is due to efficient cost control, and how much is the result of the reduction in activity.

Similarly, it is not possible to tell how much of the fall in sales revenue was due to the fall in activity. Some of the sales revenue variance may be the result of a difference in the sales prices but this budget comparison does not show the effect of this.

The type of budget in use here is a fixed budget. A fixed budget is one that remains unchanged regardless of the actual level of activity. In situations where activity levels are likely to change, and there is a significant proportion of variables costs, it is difficult to control expenditure satisfactorily with a fixed budget.

A flexible budget can help managers to make more valid comparisons. It is designed to show the expected revenue and the allowed expenditure for the actual number of units produced and sold. Comparing this flexible budget with the actual expenditure and revenue it is possible to distinguish genuine efficiencies.

6.14.1 Preparing a flexible budget

Before a flexible budget can be prepared managers must identify which costs are fixed and which are variable. The allowed expenditure on variable costs can then be increased or decreased as the level of activity changes. You will recall that fixed costs are those costs that will not increase or decrease over a given range of activity. The allowance for these items will therefore remain constant.

We can now continue with the example.

Management have identified that the following budgeted costs are fixed.

	£
Direct labour	8,400
Production overhead	18,000
Administration overhead	21,000
Selling and distribution overhead	14,000

It is now possible to identify the expected variable cost per unit produced and sold.

	Original budget (a)	Fixed cost (b)	Variable cost (c) = (a) − (b)	VC per unit (c)/l,200
Units produced and sold	1,200			
	£	£	£	£
Direct material	19,200	–	19,200	16
Direct labour	13,200	8,400	4,800	4
Production overhead	24,000	18,000	6,000	5
	21,000	21,000	–	–
Selling and distribution o/head	16,400	14,000	2,400	2
	93,800	61,400	32,400	27

Now that managers are aware of the fixed costs and the variable costs per unit, it is possible to 'flex' the original budget to produce a budget cost allowance for 1,000 units produced and sold.

The budget cost allowance for each item is calculated as follows:

Cost allowance = budgeted fixed cost + (number of units produced and sold × variable cost per unit)

For the costs that are wholly fixed or wholly variable the calculation of the budget cost allowance is fairly straightforward. The remaining costs are semi-variable, which you will recall means that they are partly fixed and partly variable. For example, the budget cost allowance for direct labour is calculated as follows:

Cost allowance for direct labour = £8,400 + (1,000 × £4) = £12,400

The budgeted sales price per unit is £120,000/1,200 = £100 per unit. If we assume that sales revenues follow a linear variable pattern (i.e. the sales price remains constant) the full flexible budget can now be produced.

Flexible budget comparison for April

| | Cost/revenue allowances | | | Actual | |
| | Fixed | Variable | Total | cost/revenue | Variance |
	£	£	£	£	£
Sales revenue			100,000	110,000	10,000
Direct material	–	16,000	16,000	16,490	(490)
Direct labour	8,400	4,000	12,400	12,380	20
Production overhead	18,000	5,000	23,000	24,120	(1,120)
Administration overhead	21,000	–	21,000	21,600	(600)
Selling and distn. o/h	14,000	2,000	16,000	16,200	(200)
	61,400	27,000	88,400	90,790	(2,390)
Profit	11,600	19,210	7,610		

Note: Variances in brackets are adverse.

This revised analysis shows that in fact the profit was £7,610 higher than would have been expected from a sales volume of 1,000 units.

The largest variance is a £10,000 favourable variance on sales revenue. This has arisen because a higher price was charged than budgeted. We know this because flexing the budget has eliminated the effect of changes in the volume sold, which is the only other factor that could have increased sales revenue.

Could the higher sales price have been the cause of the shortfall in sales volume? We do not know the answer to this, but without a flexible budget comparison it was not possible to tell that a different selling price had been charged. The cost variances in the flexible budget comparison are almost all adverse. These overspendings were not revealed when a fixed budget was used and managers may have been under the false impression that costs were being adequately controlled. In Chapter 2 we considered how each total cost variance can be analysed to reveal how much of the variance is due to higher resource prices and how much is due to higher resource usage.

6.14.2 Using flexible budgets for planning

You should appreciate that whereas flexible budgets can be useful for control purposes they are not particularly useful for planning. The original budget must contain a single target level of activity so that managers can plan such factors as the resource requirements and the product pricing policy. This would not be possible if they were faced were faced with a range of possible activity levels. The budget can be designed so that the fixed costs are distinguished from the variable costs. This will facilitate the preparation of a budget cost allowance for control purposes at the end of each period, when the actual activity is known.

6.14.3   Flexible budgets

Now that you have got the idea of how a flexible budget can be prepared, work through the following exercise to consolidate your understanding.

In this exercise, as in practice, you will need to investigate the cost behaviour patterns to determine which costs are fixed, which are variable and which are semi-variable.

The first step in investigating cost behaviour patterns is to look at the cost data. You should be able to easily spot any fixed costs because they remain constant when activity levels change.

The easiest way to identify the behaviour patterns of non-fixed costs is to divide each cost figure by the related activity level. If the cost is a linear variable cost, then the cost per unit will remain constant. For a semi-variable cost the unit rate will reduce as the activity level increases.

You will then need to recall how to use the high–low method to determine the fixed and variable elements of any semi-variable costs.

 Exercise

Lawrence Ltd operates a system of flexible budgets, and the flexed budgets for expenditure for the first two quarters of Year 3 were as follows:

Flexed budgets – Quarters 1 and 2

	Quarter 1 Units	Quarter 2 Units
Sales	9,000	14,000
Production	10,000	13,000
	£	£
Budget cost allowances		
Direct materials	130,000	169,000
Production labour	74,000	81,500
Production overhead	88,000	109,000
Administration overhead	26,000	26,000
Selling and distribution overhead	29,700	36,200
Total budget cost allowance	347,700	421,700

Despite a projected increase in activity, the cost structures in Quarters 1 and 2 are expected to continue during Quarter 3 as follows:

(a) The variable cost elements behave in a linear fashion in direct proportion to volume. However, for production output in excess of 14,000 units the unit variable cost for production labour increases by 50%. This is due to a requirement for overtime working and the extra amount is payable only on the production above 14,000 units.

(b) The fixed cost elements are not affected by changes in activity levels.

(c) The variable elements of production costs are directly related to production volume.

(d) The variable element of selling and distribution overhead is directly related to sales volume.

Prepare a statement of the budget cost allowances for Quarter 3. The activity levels during Quarter 3 were as follows:

	Units
Sales	14,500
Production	15,000

 ## Solution

If you divide each cost figure by the relevant activity figure, you will find that the only wholly variable cost is direct material, at £13 per unit.

You can also see that the only wholly fixed cost is administration overhead since this is a constant amount for both activity levels, £26,000.

For the remaining costs you will need to use the high–low method to determine the fixed and variable elements.

Production labour

	Production units	£
Quarter 2	13,000	81,500
Quarter 1	10,000	74,000
Change	3,000	7,500

$$\text{Variable cost} = \frac{£7,500}{3,000} = £2.50 \text{ per unit}$$

$$\text{Fixed cost} = £81,500 - (£2.50 \times 13,000) = £49,000$$

Production overhead

	Production units	£
Quarter 2	13,000	109,000
Quarter 1	10,000	88,000
Change	3,000	21,000

$$\text{Variable cost per unit} = \frac{£21,000}{3,000} = £7 \text{ per unit}$$

$$\text{Fixed cost} = £109,000 - (£7 \times 13,000) = £18,000$$

Selling and distribution overhead

	Sales units	£
Quarter 2	14,000	36,200
Quarter 1	9,000	29,700
Change	5,000	6,500

$$\text{Variable cost per unit sold} = \frac{£6,500}{5,000} = £1.30 \text{ per unit}$$

$$\text{Fixed cost} = £36,200 - (£1.30 \times 14,000) = £18,000$$

We can now prepare a statement of the budget cost allowances for quarter 3.

	£	Quarter 3 Budget cost allowance £
Direct material (15,000 units × £13)		195,000
Production labour:		
Fixed	49,000	
Variable up to 14,000 units (14,000 × £2.50)	35,000	
Variable above 14,000 units (1,000 × £3.75)	3,750	
		87,750
Production overhead:		
Fixed	18,000	
Variable (15,000 × £7)	105,000	
		123,000
Administration overhead: fixed		26,000
Selling and distribution overhead:		
Fixed	18,000	
Variable (14,500 × £1.30)	18,850	
		36,850
Total budget cost allowance		468,600

6.14.4 Extrapolating outside the relevant range

In the preceding example you were told that the cost structures would remain unaltered despite the increase in activity. In examinations, and in practice, if you need to do a similar extrapolation outside the range for which you have available data, you should always state the assumption that the observed behaviour patterns will still be applicable.

6.15 Budgets and motivation

The impact of budgets on the motivation of managers is the subject of an extensive body of research and writing. This body is not explored in any depth here. The key point to note is that an insensitive application of budgetary control may induce managers to do things that are not necessarily in the best interests of the organisation. For example, a manager attempting to keep his business unit within budget may cut back on quality control costs. This may achieve the required immediate result but only with adverse long-term consequences. Managers may attempt to negotiate budgets that they feel are easy to achieve which gives rise to the phenomenon of 'budget padding' that is the adoption of budgets that include inflated costs.

Much of the early academic work on budgets concerned the extent to which the 'tightness' or looseness' of a budget acted as an incentive or disincentive to management effort. This was the issue of 'budget stretch'. Seminal works in this general area included studies by A.C. Stedry (see his 1960 text 'Budget Control and Cost Behaviour') and G.H. Hofstede (see his 1968 text 'The Game of Budget Control').

The main thrust of the findings that emerged from these studies was:

- loose budgets (i.e. ones easily attainable) are poor motivators
- as budgets are tightened, up to a point they become more motivational
- beyond that point, a very tight budget ceases to be motivational.

The role of budget participation and the manner in which aspirations and objectives are stated was also explored in certain studies. It was suggested that the participation of managers in budget setting was a motivational factor – but see earlier discussion concerning budget padding and negotiation.

6.16 Summary

In this chapter, we have explored the budgeting concept. It has been seen that the process of establishing a budget is an exercise in business planning wherein alternative courses of action are identified and evaluated. Once it has been adopted, the budget may be used as a tool of control and a benchmark against which performance may be evaluated.

Modern approaches to budgeting place an emphasis on finding cost effective means of achieving given objectives. The point of departure is to identify the objectives of the organisation and then determine the cheapest combination of resources that can achieve those objectives. Hence, the emphasis is on the outputs of the operation rather than on the inputs.

Self-test quiz

(1) Define the term 'budget' (Section 6.2.2).
(2) Distinguish between 'budgetary planning' and 'budgetary control' (Section 6.2.2).
(3) Distinguish between 'strategic planning' and 'operational planning' (Section 6.2.1).
(4) What is the difference between 'bottom-up' and 'top-down' budgeting (Section 6.3.2)?
(5) What is the 'principal budget factor' (Section 6.3.4)?
(6) List problems that may be encountered in using a spreadsheet system to prepare and operate the budget of a large organisation (Section 6.3.6).
(7) State the main differences likely to be encountered between budget profit and budget cash flow (Section 6.5).
(8) Distinguish between an additive model and a multiplicative model in time series analysis (Section 6.7.3).
(9) What are the main factors that distinguish ZBB and PPBS from more traditional budgeting practices (Sections 6.9 and 6.10).
(10) Distinguish between efficiency and effectiveness in the not-for-profit sector (Section 6.12).

Revision Questions

6

? Question 1

1.1 AW plc is preparing its maintenance budget. The number of machine hours and maintenance costs for the past 6 months have been as follows:

Month	Machine hours	£
1	10,364	35,319
2	12,212	39,477
3	8,631	31,420
4	9,460	33,285
5	8,480	31,080
6	10,126	34,784

The budget cost allowance for an activity level of 9,340 machine hours, before any adjustment for price changes, is nearest to:

(A) £21,000
(B) £30,200
(C) £33,000
(D) £34,300

1.2 M plc uses time series analysis and regression techniques to estimate future sales demand. Using these techniques, it has derived the following trend equation:

$y = 10,000 + 4,200x$

where y is the total sales units and x is the time period.

It has also derived the following seasonal variation index values for each of the quarters using the multiplicative (proportional) seasonal variation model:

Quarter	Index value
1	120
2	80
3	95
4	105

The total sales units that will be forecast for time period 33, which is the first quarter of years 9, are:

(A) 138,720
(B) 148,720
(C) 176,320
(D) 178,320

1.3   Q limited used an incremental budgeting approach to setting its budgets for the year ending 30 June 2003.

The budget for the company's power costs was determined by analysing the past relationship between costs and activity levels and then adjusting for inflation of 6%.

The relationship between monthly cost and activity levels, before adjusting for the 6% inflation, was found to be:

$$y = £(14{,}000 + 0.0025x^2)$$

where y = total cost and x = machine hours.

In April 2003, the number of machine hours was 1,525 and the actual cost incurred was £16,423. The total power cost variance to be reported is nearest to:

(A) £3,391 (A)
(B) £3,391 (F)
(C) £3,740 (F)
(D) £4,580 (F)

1.4   H Limited uses a combination of regression analysis and time series analysis to predict its future sales volumes. An analysis of past data has shown that the underlying trend of the company's sales is well represented by the formula:

$$y = 100x + 2{,}400$$

where y is the total sales units for a period and x is the quarterly period number.

The seasonal variation index values based on the same past data is:

Quarter 1	105%
Quarter 2	96%
Quarter 3	90%
Quarter 4	109%

The increase in budgeted sales volumes between quarter 3 and quarter 4 next year, which are periods 17 and 18, will be:

(A) 100 units
(B) 119 units
(C) 432 units
(D) 888 units   **(Total = 20 marks)**

? Question 2

You are given the following information about a company's costs in the past two quarters.

	Q_1	Q_2
Production (units)	10,000	15,000
Sales (units)	9,000	15,000
Costs	£'000	£'000
Direct material		
A	50	75
B	40	60
Production labour	180	230
Factory overheads	80	95
Depreciation	14	14
Administration	30	30
Selling expenses	29	35

For accounting purpose, the company values inventory of units at a constant standard cost. In quarter 3:

- Sales and production will be 18,000 units.
- Material A will rise in price by 20% relative to earlier quarters.
- Production wages will rise by 12.5% relative to earlier quarters.
- The selling price per unit will remain constant at £40.
- Expenses are all paid in the month in which they are incurred.
- Sales are all on 2 month's credit terms. Seventy per cent sales are paid for on the due date while the remaining 30% are paid for 1 month after the due date.

Requirements
(a) Prepare a budget profit statement for quarter 3. **(12 marks)**
(b) Prepare a budget cash-flow statement for quarter 3. **(13 marks)**

(Total = 25 marks)

? Question 3

R plc is an engineering company that repairs machinery and manufactures replacement parts for machinery used in the building industry. There are a number of different departments in the company including a foundry, a grinding department, a milling department and a general machining department. R plc prepared its budget for the year ending 31 December 2003 using an incremental budgeting system.

The budget is set centrally and is then communicated to each of the managers who have responsibility for achieving their respective targets. The following report has been produced for the general machining department for October 2003:

	Budget	Actual	Variance
Number of machine hours	9,000	11,320	2,320 (F)
	$	$	$
Cleaning materials	1,350	1,740	390 (A)
Steel	45,000	56,000	11,000 (A)
Other direct materials	450	700	250 (A)
Direct labour	29,000	32,400	3,400 (A)
Production overheads	30,000	42,600	12,600 (A)
Total	105,800	133,440	27,640 (A)

The Manager of the general machining department has received a memo from the Financial Controller requiring him to explain the serious overspending within his department.

The Manager has sought your help and, after some discussion, you have ascertained the following:

- The cleaning materials, steel and other direct materials vary in proportion to the number of machine hours.
- The budgeted direct labour costs include fixed salary costs of $4,250; the balance is variable in proportion to the number of machine hours.

- The production overhead costs include a variable cost that is constant per machine hour at all activity levels, and a stepped fixed cost which changes when the activity level exceeds 10,000 machine hours. A further analysis of this cost is shown below:

Activity (machine hours)	3,000	7,000	14,000
Costs ($)	13,500	24,500	45,800

Requirements

(a) Prepare a revised budgetary control statement using the additional information that you have obtained from the Manager of the general machining department.   **(10 marks)**

(b) (i) Explain the differences between an incremental budgeting system and a zero-based budgeting system.   **(4 marks)**

(ii) Explain why R plc and similar organisations would find it difficult to introduce a system of zero-based budgeting.   **(4 marks)**

(c) Explain the benefits of involving the managers of R plc in the budget setting process, rather than setting the budget centrally as is R plc's current policy.   **(7 marks)**

(Total = 25 marks)

? Question 4

Y plc is currently preparing its budgets for the year ending 30 September 20x1.

The sales and production budgets have been completed and an extract from them is shown below.

	Production units	Sales units	Sales value
	£'000	£'000	£'000
January	900	1,000	50,000
February	850	800	40,000
March	1,000	900	45,000
April	1,200	1,100	55,000
May	1,250	1,300	65,000
June	1,175	1,200	60,000
July	1,100	1,150	57,500
August	*	1,050	52,500

* To be determined

Budgeted production costs are:

	£/unit
Direct materials	14
Direct labour	12
Variable overhead	6
Fixed overhead*	8
Production cost	40

*Fixed overheads are absorbed on a unit basis assuming a normal production level of 14 m units per year.

Direct materials are purchased in the month of usage and, where settlement discounts are available, Y plc's policy is to pay suppliers so as to receive these discounts. It is expected that 60% of Y plc's material costs will be received from suppliers who offer a 2% discount for payment in the month of purchase. Other material suppliers are to be paid in the month following purchase.

Direct labour costs are paid 75% in the month in which they are incurred, and 25% in the following month.

Variable overhead costs are paid in the month in which they are incurred.

Fixed overhead costs include £16 m depreciation. Fixed overhead expenditure accrues at a constant rate throughout the year and is paid 40% in the month in which it is incurred and 60% in the following month.

In addition to production costs, Y plc expects to incur administration overhead costs of £500,000 per month and selling overhead costs of 2% of sales value. These costs are to be paid in the month in which they are incurred.

Y plc's customers are expected to pay for items as follows:

- in the month of sale   20%
- in the month after sale   55%
- in the month 2 months after sale   15%
- in the month 3 months after sale   5%

Customers paying in the month of sale are given 1% discount. Five per cent of sales are expected to be bad debts.

In addition to the above, Y plc expects that

- new machinery is to be acquired on 1 February 20x1, costing £15 m, this is to be paid for in May 20x1;
- corporation tax of £ 10 m will be payable in June 20x1;
- a dividend of £ 7.5 m will be paid to shareholders in July 20x1;
- the bank balance at 1 April 20x1 will be £14.5 m.

Requirements

(a) Prepare Y plc's cash budget for the period April–July 20X1, showing clearly the receipts, payments and resulting balances for each month separately.   **(20 marks)**
(b) Use your answer to part (a) to explain clearly:
   (i) feed-forward control
   (ii) feedback control.   **(5 marks)**
(Total = 25 marks)

? Question 5

PMF plc is a long-established public transport operator that provides a commuter transit link between an airport and the centre of a large city.

The following data has been taken from the sales records of PMF plc for the last 2 years:

Quarter	Number of passengers carried	
	Year 1	Year 2
1	15,620	34,100
2	15,640	29,920
3	16,950	29,550
4	34,840	56,680

The trend equation for the number of passengers carried has been found to be:

$$x = 10,000 + 4,200q$$

where x = number of passengers carried per quarter and

q = time period (year 1 quarter 1: $q = 1$)
    (year 1 quarter 2: $q = 2$)
    (year 2 quarter 1: $q = 5$)

Based on data collected over the last 2 years, PMF plc has found that its quarterly costs have the following relationships with the number of passengers carried:

Cost item	Relationship
Premises costs	$y = 260,000$
Premises staff	$y = 65,000 + 0.5x$
Power	$y = 13,000 + 4x$
Transit staff	$y = 32,000 + 3x$
Other	$y = 9,100 + x$

where y = the cost per quarter (£), and x = number of passengers per quarter.

Requirements

(a) Using the trend equation for the number of passengers carried and the multiplicative (proportional) time series model, determine the expected number of passengers to be carried in the third quarter of year 3. **(7 marks)**

(b) Explain why you think that the equation for the Transit staff cost is in the form $y = 32,000 + 3x$ **(3 marks)**

(c) Using your answer to part (a) and the cost relationship equations, calculate for each cost item and in total, the costs expected to be incurred in the third quarter of year 3. **(3 marks)**

(d) Explain briefly why there may be differences between the actual data for the third quarter of year 3 and the values you have predicted. **(5 marks)**

(e) Prepare a report, addressed to the Board of Directors of PMF plc, that briefly explains the following in the context of measuring the *effectiveness* of the transport services:
- why the company should consider the use of non-financial performance measures;
- three non-financial performance measures that could be used. **(7 marks)**

(Total = 25 marks)

? Question 6

Nossex County Council (NCC) is responsible for the normal range of services associated with a major local authority. NCC is organised into departments each responsible for a particular activity, for example education, social services, parks and gardens and so on. Each department has an annual budget that is used in both the planning and control of activities.

After its budgets for 20x4/x5 had been approved by NCC's finance committee, it is found that due to government restrictions on the level of NCC's council tax, total expenditure will have to be reduced to a level 8% below that originally planned for.

Shortly after receiving news of this, NCC's Finance Committee Chairman (councillor Ron Scroggs) makes the following statement during the course of an interview on Radio Nossex:

We do not like what has happened but we shall have to make the best of things. It seems to me that the fairest thing to do is to cut back the present 20X4/X5 budget for each department by 8%. In this manner the misery will be spread evenly and everyone will suffer the same. The details of how this cut back will affect particular services can be left to the individual departmental heads to decide.

Requirements

In your capacity as chief executive of NCC write a report for NCC's Finance Committee on the situation explaining why you agree or disagree with the approach that Scroggs advocated in the radio interview. **(25 marks)**

Question 7

MNO Ltd manufactures a product known as the Unit. A large number of other companies also manufacture the Unit and the market price of the Unit is forecast to be £210 during 20x1. Market demand for the Unit is highest towards the end of the year. Customers prefer to place orders with manufacturers who are able to deliver Units immediately from their inventory.

A summarised version of MNO's balance sheet at 31 December 20x0 is shown below.

Summarised balance sheet of MNO Ltd as at 31 December 20X0

	£
Plant and equipment (net)	780,000
Inventory	80,000
Debtors	125,000
Cash at bank	30,000
Creditors	(20,000)
Net assets	995,000
Share capital	100,000
16% loan from shareholders	500,000
Retained earnings	395,000
Capital	995,000

During 20X1, MNO is committed to:

- repaying £125,000 of the 16% loan from shareholders in June and paying £40,000 interest on the loan in June and £30,000 interest in December;
- paying interest on its bank overdraft at a rate of 5% per quarter on the balance outstanding on the last day of each quarter;
- incurring fixed overhead costs (excluding depreciation) at a rate of £200,000 per quarter (all such costs are paid in the month in which they are incurred);
- incurring variable production costs at a rate of £100 per Unit (75% of these costs are paid for in the month they are incurred and 25% in the month after they are incurred).

MNO's accounting policies include:

- providing for depreciation at a rate of 5% per quarter on the net book value (i.e. cost less depreciation) of plant and equipment outstanding at the end of each quarter;

- valuing inventory (or 'stock') at a standard production cost of £160 per unit.

In early January 20X1, MNO's executives meet in order to discuss commercial strategy for the coming year. The sales director advocates an aggressive strategy (Strategy 1), involving new investment, high inventories and an expansion of sales. The finance director advocates a conservative strategy (Strategy 2) involving no new investment, minimising inventories and the adoption of a 'tight' credit policy on sales.

Relevant details concerning the two strategies are described in the following section.

Strategy 1

- In January, acquire new production equipment at a cost of £360,000.
- Offer 60% (by sales value) of customers, 2 months' credit and require the rest to pay immediately.
- Make sales at a rate of 900 units per month (quarters 1 and 2) and 1,300 units per month (quarters 3 and 4).
- Produce at the rate of 1,200 units per month (quarters 1 and 2) and 1,100 units per month (quarters 3 and 4).
- A review of outstanding debts at the end of 20X1 is forecast to result in a bad debt writeoff totalling £64,000 (all relating to quarter 4 sales).

Strategy 2

- Continue the existing credit policy of offering 50% (by sales value) of customers 1 month's credit and require the rest to pay immediately.
- Make sales at a rate of 800 units per month (quarters 1 and 2), 1,000 units per month (quarter 3) and 1,100 units per month (quarter 4).
- Produce at a rate of 850 units per month (quarters 1 and 2) and 1,000 units per month (quarters 3 and 4).
- A review of outstanding debts at the end of 20x1 is forecast to result in a bad debt writeoff totalling £10,000 (all relating to quarter 4 sales).

Requirements

(a) Prepare a cash-flow budget and a profit budget for MNO on the basis of Strategy 1. The budgets should be split into quarterly intervals showing cash-flow and profit forecasts for each individual quarter.   **(20 marks)**

(b) Prepare a cash-flow budget and a profit budget for MNO on the basis of Strategy 2. The budgets should be split into quarterly intervals showing cash flow and profit forecast for each individual quarter.   **(20 marks)**

(c) Compare and contrast the two sets of budgets you have prepared in answer to requirements (a) and (b). Advise MNO's management on the relative merits of the two alternative strategies. Advise which strategy should be adopted.   **(10 marks)**

(Total = 50 marks)

Note: In preparing your answer you may assume that cash is held on current account where it earns no interest and any cash deficit requirement is satisfied by drawing down on the overdraft facility.

? Question 8

'Traditional budgeting systems are incremental in nature and tend of focus on cost centers. Activity-based budgeting links business planning to the budgeting process with a view to finding the most cost-effective means of achieving objectives.'

Requirements

(a) Explain the weaknesses of an incremental budgeting system. **(5 marks)**

(b) Describe the main features of an activity-based budgeting system and comment on the advantages claimed for its use. **(10 marks)**

(Total = 15 marks)

Solutions to Revision Questions

 Solution 1

1.1

Use high and low points to determine the cost behaviour pattern based on past data:

	Machine hours	*£*
High	12,212	39,477
Low	8,480	31,080
Difference	3,732	8,397

$$\text{Variable cost per machine hour} = \frac{£8,397}{3,732} = £2.25$$

By substitution, the fixed cost is:
£39,477 − (12,212 × £2.25) = £12,000
For an activity level of 9,340 machine hours, the budget cost allowance would be:
£12,000 + (9,340 × £2.25) = £33,015
Therefore the answer is (C).

1.2

$x = 33$, so trend value is = 10,000 + (4,200 × 33) = 148,600
Seasonal variation index value = 120
Forecast sales units = 148,600 × 120% = 178,320
Therefore the answer is (D).

1.3

The budget cost allowance for 1,525 machine hours is:
= £14,000 + 0.0025 (1,525²)
= £14,000 + (0.0025 × 2,325,625)
= £14,000 + £5,814
= £19,814
Add 6% for inflation = £21,003
Thus the total variance is £16,423 − £21,003 = £4,580 (F)

Therefore the answer is (D).

1.4

Quarter 3 units = [(100 × 17) + 2,400] ×   90% = 3,690
Quarter 4 units = [(100 × 18) + 2,400] × 109% = 4,578
Difference   = 888

Therefore the answer is (D).

✓ Solution 2

- The question gives two sets of figures linked to alternative levels of output and sales. A simple linear regression approach can be used to determine the cost structure of the business and thus forecast costs for quarter 3.
- Note that some costs vary with production and some costs vary with sales.

Applying a linear regression approach to the figures supplied, the cost structure forecast for quarter 3 is as follows:

	Unit VC	*Quarter FC*
	£	£
Material A	6.00	
Material B	4.00	
Production labour	11.25	90,000
Factory overheads	3.00	50,000
Depreciation		14,000
Administration		30,000
Selling expenses	1.00	20,000
Total	25.25	204,000

(a) The budget profit statement for quarter 3 is:

	£	£
Sales revenue		720,000
Costs		
Materials	180,000	
Wages	292,500	
Factory overheads	104,000	
Depreciation	14,000	
Administration	30,000	
Selling expenses	38,000	
		658,500
Profit		61,500

(b) The budget cash-flow statement for quarter 3 is:

	£	£
Cash inflow:		
Q2 month 1		60,000
Q2 month 2		200,000
Q2 month 3		200,000
Q3 month 1		168,000
		628,000
Cash outflow		
Materials	180,000	
Wages	292,500	
Factory overheads	104,000	
Administration	30,000	
Selling expenses	38,000	
		644,500
Net cash flow		(16,500)

Seventy per cent of month 1 sales from Q₂ will be paid during Q₂. The other 30% of those sales will be paid in Q₃. Q₂ month 1 sales therefore give rise to a £60,000 cash inflow (i.e. 5,000 units × £40 × 30%) in Q₃. The same logic is applied to sales in later months.

Solution 3

(a) Analyse budget cost of direct labour:

	$
9,000 hours total cost	29,000
Fixed cost	(4,250)
Therefore variable cost of 9,000 hours	24,750

$$\text{Variable cost per houre} = \frac{\$24,750}{9,000} = \$2.75$$

Therefore,

Budget cost of 11,320 hours	$
Variable (11,320 × $2.75)	31,130
Fixed	4,250
	35,380

Use high/low technique to analyses production overheads (ignore 14,000-hour activity level to eliminate the effect of the step fixed cost):

	Hours	$
High	7,000	24,500
Low	3,000	13,500
Difference	4,000	11,000

$$\text{Variable cost} = \frac{\$11,000}{4,000} \text{ hours} = \$2.75 \text{ per hour}$$

Variable cost of 14,000 hours = 14,000 × $2.75 = $38,500
Total cost of 14,000 hours   = $45,800
Fixed cost (for activity levels above 10,000 hours) = $7,300

	Original budget	Flexed budget	Actual	Variance
Number of machine hours	9,000	11,320	11,320	
	$	$	$	$
Cleaning materials	1,350	1,698	1,740	42 (A)
Steel	45,000	56,600	56,000	600 (F)
Other direct materials	450	566	700	134 (A)
Direct labour	29,000	35,380	32,400	2,980 (F)
Production overheads	30,000	38,430	42,600	4,170 (A)
Totals	105,800	132,674	133,440	766 (A)

(b) (i) An incremental budgeting system is a system whereby budgets are prepared by adjusting the previous period's budget/actual values for expected changes in the level of activity and for expected price changes.

FORECASTING AND BUDGETING

A zero-based budgeting system is a system whereby all proposed activities have to be justified. Once the activity itself has been justified, then the method of carrying out the activity needs to be considered and the chosen method justified on a cost benefit basis.

(ii) R plc is an engineering company that operates in the repairs and maintenance sector of engineering.

This type of business has difficulty in predicting the exact nature of its customer's requirements as this depends on their needs in response to machinery failures.

For R plc and similar organisations to introduce zero-based budgeting, assumptions would have to be made as to the exact nature of the customer requirements. If these assumptions were to differ significantly from the actual customer requirements, the budget would be invalid.

(c) The main benefits of involving managers in the budget-setting process include:

Goal congruence – the manager will see their organisational target as a personal target because, by their setting it, they believe it to be achievable;

Motivation – the manager will be motivated to achieve the target, because not to do so would be a personal failure;

Accuracy/detail – the manager will have the detailed knowledge to prepare a budget that accurately identifies the resource requirements needed to achieve the target set.

Solution 4

(a) Cash budget

	April £'000	May £'000	June £'000	July £000
Receipts				
Sales	44,140	51,870	58,130	56,885
Payment				
Material	15,478	17,010	16,673	15,635
Labour	13,800	14,850	14,325	13,425
Variable overhead	7,200	7,500	7,050	6,600
Fixed overhead	8,000	8,000	8,000	8,000
Administrative overhead	500	500	500	500
Selling overhead	1,100	1,300	1,200	1,150
Machinery	–	15,000	–	–
Corporation tax	–	–	10,000	–
Dividend	–	–	–	7,500
	46,078	64,160	57,748	52,810
Balance b/f	14,500	12,562	272	654
Net cash movement	(1,938)	(12,290)	382	4,075
Balance c/f	12,562	272	654	4,729

Workings

	April £'000	May £'000	June £'000	July £'000
Direct material				
Purchases	16,800	17,500	16,450	15,400
Payment in month	9,878	10,290	9,673	9,055
1-month credit	5,600	6,720	7,000	6,580
	15,478	17,010	16,673	15,635
Direct labour				
Monthly cost	14,400	15,000	14,100	13,200
Payment in month	10,800	11,250	10,575	9,900
1 month in arrears	3,000	3,600	3,750	3,525
	13,800	14,850	14,325	13,425
Sales receipts				
20% in month (×99%)	10,890	12,870	11,880	11,385
55% in month after sale	24,750	30,250	35,750	33,000
15% 2 months after sale	6,000	6,750	8,250	9,750
5% 3 months after sale	2,500	2,000	2,250	2,750
	44,140	51,870	58,130	56,885

Each year	£'000
Fixed overhead	112,000
Less depreciation	16,000
Cash expense	96,000 = £8,000,000 per month

(b) (i) Feed-forward control occurs when, in compiling the budget, the cash flows predicted differ from those desired, resulting in the amendments to budgets or activities. Feed-forward is a proactive form of control, exercised before the event. For example, the capital expenditure on machinery might be deferred or financed differently to avoid the anticipated cash deficit in May.

(ii) Feedback control, on the other hand, is exercised after the activity has taken place, and involves comparing actual outcomes with those predicted in the budget. It is reactive control, and would result in an explanation being required should the cash expenditure on material in a given month differ by more than (say) 5% of budgeted value.

✅ Solution 5

(a) The trend values for quarter 3 of each year based upon the equation:

$$X = 4,200q + 10,000 \text{ d}$$

can be calculated as:

Year 1 (4,200 × 3) + 10,000 = 22,600 passengers
Year 2 (4,200 × 7) + 10,000 = 39,400 passengers

This can be compared with the past data provided to establish the seasonal variation:

	Trend	Past data	%
Year 1	22,600	16,950	75
Year 2	39,400	29,550	75

Thus it seems that the quarter 3 values are 75% of their equivalent trend values.

The trend value for the third quarter of year 3, adjusted for the seasonal variation, will thus be:

$$[(4,200 \times 11) + 10,000] \times 75\% = 42,150 \text{ passengers}$$

(b) The reason for the cost equation for the Transit staff being in the format shown is that it is a mixed cost, that is, it comprises a fixed element of £32,000 and a variable element of £3 for each passenger. This could be because the remuneration package provides for a fixed salary plus a bonus.

(c)

Cost item	Relationship	Cost
		£
Premises costs	$y = 260,000 + 0x$	260,000
Premises staff	$y = 65,000 + 0.5x$	86,075
Power	$y = 13,000 + 4x$	181,600
Transit staff	$y = 32,000 + 3x$	158,450
Other	$y = 9,100 + x$	51,250
		737,375

(d) There are a number of reasons why the actual data may differ from that predicted:

- The prediction of the number of passengers carried assumes that the underlying growth shown by the trend equation will continue into year 3.
- The prediction of the number of passengers carried assumes that the seasonal variation in the third quarter of year 3 will be the same as it was in the same quarter in previous years.
- The predicted costs are based on simple linear cost relationships that have probably been derived from past data using of linear regression analysis techniques on past data. In reality, costs rarely behave in a linear fashion, though this may be a reasonable approximation.
- Actual costs may be affected by a number of cost drivers other than, or in addition to, the number of passengers carried.
- The calculation does not consider the effects of price changes on the costs.

(e)

Report

To:	Board of Directors of PMF plc	*From:*	Management Accountant
Subject:	Non-financial performance measures	*Date:*	21 November 2001

Introduction

Further to our recent meeting, I have considered some of the non-financial performance measures that we may use in addition to our existing budgetary control procedures.

Findings

As a public transport operator, we operate in a service sector where the quality of the service we provide is paramount to our continued success. We should, therefore, focus on the needs of our customers and our employees to ensure that we continue to deliver the service required.

Among the measures that we can use to measure our effectiveness are

- the percentage of trains that arrive within 2 minutes of schedule;
- the percentage of trains that depart within 2 minutes of schedule;

- the percentage of trains cancelled in a period;
- the failure rate of our ticket machines;
- the failure rate of our ticketing gates;
- the failure rate of the escalators in our stations;
- the failure rate of our signaling system; and
- the number of injuries per thousand passengers carried.

> **Examiner's Note:**
> Candidates were required to identify any *three* suitable measures and briefly describe them.

Conclusion

These non-financial measures are as important as those that we currently use to control our costs and revenues. If we can improve our customers' perceptions of our performance, then we will continue to remain profitable and can improve still further in the future.

Signed: Management Accountant.

 Solution 6

- The critical thing to note here is that the approach advocated by Councillor Scroggs places an emphasis on 'inputs' to the process. It shows little awareness of outputs and objectives.
- The question invites you to discuss modern budgeting practices such as ZBB and PPBS.

From: Chief executive
To: Finance committee
Re: Budget savings

What the chairman is proposing is a course of action based on the incremental approach to budgeting. This approach seeks to determine budgets by taking past patterns of spending and using them as the basis for determining future patterns. For example, in establishing the budget for this year, one might take last year's budget and add or subtract an equal percentage to/from the spending of each department.

This approach is simple and avoids having to think too hard about what one is doing. It also avoids difficult political disputes by seeking to maintain an established *status quo* between spending departments.

However, the incremental approach to budgeting is essentially passive. It is generally considered to have various adverse features including the following:

- An 8% cut in the budget for parks and gardens may cause far less misery than a 5% cut in the budget for social services; blanket spending cuts can have very uneven effects in terms of the misery they cause.
- A given public objective (e.g. the welfare of old people) is best achieved by a carefully integrated pattern of spending within several departments (e.g. residential homes, meals on wheels, home helps and mobile libraries); unselective spending cuts in one area

(e.g. home helps) might cause substantial new requirements to be created in others (e.g. residential homes) if obligations are to be fulfilled.

- A selective rearrangement of spending may have far less impact on the standard of services than blanket cuts; for example, a reduction in police officer numbers might be partly offset by small increases in spending on 'traffic calming' measures and video surveillance in public areas.

The incremental approach to budgeting is not considered to be the most satisfactory available. A variety of proactive approaches to budget determination exists including PPBS and ZBB. It is suggested that these might be used to good effect on this occasion.

Solution 7

- This question addresses many of the issues explored in this and the preceding two chapters. It can be worked through without the use of a computer spreadsheet, but it provides a good spreadsheet modelling exercise. If you are adept in the use of a spreadsheet, then you may be able to construct the required four budgets very quickly indeed.
- Note that the profit budget tends to follow on from the cash flow budget because of the calculation of overdraft interest. This suggest the sequence in which the budgets should be arranged.
- The two sets of budgets should be constructed in a manner that allows them to be readily compared.
- When comparing the two strategies, be aware that profitability is not the sole relevant measure of performance.

(a) MNO Ltd: cash-flow budget for 20X1, Strategy 1

	Q1 £	Q2 £	Q3 £	Q4 £	20X1 £
Opening cash balance	30,000	(435,540)	(623,217)	(459,393)	30,000
Customer receipts	465,200	567,000	718,200	819,000	2,569,400
Capital expenditure	(360,000)				(360,000)
Variable costs	(350,000)	(360,000)	(332,500)	(330,000)	(1,372,500)
Fixed overheads	(200,000)	(200,000)	(200,000)	(200,000)	(800,000)
Loan interest		(40,000)		(30,000)	(70,000)
Loan repayment		(125,000)			(125,000)
Cash flow	(444,800)	(158,000)	185,700	259,000	(158,100)
'Initial' closing balance	(414,800)	(593,540)	(437,517)	(200,393)	
Overdraft interest	(20,740)	(29,677)	(21,876)	(10,020)	(82,312)
'Final' closing balance	(435,540)	(623,217)	(459,393)	(210,413)	(210,412)

MNO Ltd: profit budget for 20X1, Strategy 1

	Q1 £	Q1 £	Q3 £	Q4 £	20X1 £
Sales	567,000	567,000	819,000	819,000	2,772,000
Opening stock	(80,000)	(224,000)	(368,000)	(272,000)	(80,000)
Variable costs	(360,000)	(360,000)	(330,000)	(330,000)	(1,380,000)
Fixed overheads	(200,000)	(200,000)	(200,000)	(200,000)	(800,000)

Depreciation	(57,000)	(54,150)	(51,443)	(48,870)	(211,463)
Closing stock	224,000	368,000	272,000	176,000	176,000
Loan interest	(20,000)	(20,000)	(15,000)	(15,000)	(70,000)
Overdraft interest	(20,740)	(29,677)	(21,876)	(10,020)	(82,312)
Bad debt write-off				(64,000)	(64,000)
Net profit	53,260	47,173	104,681	55,110	260,225

(b) Cash-flow budget of MNO Ltd for 20X1, Strategy 2

	Q1 £	Q2 £	Q3 £	Q4 £	20X1 £
Opening cash balance	30,000	121,250	5,250	118,000	30,000
Customer receipts	545,000	504,000	609,000	682,500	2,340,500
Capital expenditure					–
Variable costs	(253,750)	(255,000)	(296,250)	(300,000)	(1,105,000)
Fixed overheads	(200,000)	(200,000)	(200,000)	(200,000)	(800,000)
Loan interest		(40,000)		(30,000)	(70,000)
Loan repayment		(125,000)			(125,000)
Cash flow	91,250	(116,000)	112,750	152,500	(240,500
'Initial' closing balance	121,250	5,250	118,000	270,500	
Overdraft interest	–	–	–	–	–
'Final' closing balance	121,250	5,250	118,000	270,500	270,500

Profit budget of MNO Ltd for 20X1, Strategy 2

	Q1 £	Q2 £	Q3 £	Q4 £	20X1 £
Sales	504,000	504,000	630,000	693,000	2,331,000
Opening stock	(80,000)	(104,000)	(128,000)	(128,000)	(80,000)
Variable costs	(255,000)	(255,000)	(300,000)	(300,000)	(1,110,000)
Fixed overheads	(200,000)	(200,000)	(200,000)	(200,000)	(800,000)
Depreciation	(39,000)	(37,050)	(35,198)	(33,438)	(144,685)
Closing stock	104,000	128,000	128,000	80,000	80,000
Loan interest	(20,000)	(20,000)	(15,000)	(15,000)	(70,000)
Overdraft interest	–	–	–	–	–
Bad debt write-off				(10,000)	(10,000)
Net profit	14,000	15,950	79,802	86,562	196,315

(c) The most conspicuous feature in comparing the two alternative strategies is that Strategy 1 yields about £60,000 more profit than Strategy 2. So, is Strategy 1 automatically preferable? The following observations are relevant in answering this question:

- Strategy 2 follows existing sales policies and the associated sales forecasts are, therefore, probably reliable; Strategy 1 follows new sales policies and the associated sales forecasts must incorporate estimates/assumptions about what will happen; the reliability of these estimates/assumptions may be uncertain and this makes Strategy 1 riskier than Strategy 2.
- Strategy 1 involves accumulating a £200,000 overdraft balance; this is a cause for some concern even though such a balance need not be a problem for a profitable company with an annual turnover approaching £3 m.

- Strategy 2 results in a cash surplus of £270,000 to be accumulated by the end of 20X1; this can be paid out to MNO's shareholders as dividends – thus reducing the capital employed in the business and without any adverse impact on its profitability.

Taking into account the above factors, it seems that Strategy 2 might be preferred under certain circumstances. Those circumstances might apply if the owners of MNO are anxious to follow a low-risk strategy and extract funds from the business.

✅ Solution 8

(a) Incremental budgeting uses year 1 budget as the starting point for the preparation of year 2 budget. It is assumed that the basic structure of the old budget is acceptable and that adjustments will be made to allow for changes in volume, efficiency and price levels. The focus, therefore, tends to be on the existing use of resources rather than on identifying objectives and alternative strategies for the future budget period. It is argued that incremental budgeting does not question sufficiently the costs and benefits of operating a particular resource allocation structure.

Incremental budgeting may, therefore, be argued to have weaknesses in that:

- the resource allocation is not clearly linked to a business plan and the consideration of alternative means of achieving objectives;
- there is a tendency to constrain new high-priority activities;
- there is insufficient focus on efficiency and effectiveness and the alternative methods by which they may be achieved;
- it often leads to arbitrary cuts being made in order to meet overall financial targets;
- it tends not to lead to management commitment to the budget process.

(b) The main features and potential advantages of activity-based budgeting are:

   (i) The major focus is on the planning of resource allocation that aims at efficiency, effectiveness and continuous improvement. Features may include:
      - the impact of change from the present activity levels are made more apparent;
      - key processes and constraints are identified and resource requirements related thereto are quantified;
      - efforts are made to identify critical success factors and the performance indicators that are most relevant for such factors.
   (ii) Activities are seen as the key to effective planning and control.
   (iii) It is argued that activities consume resources and that efforts should be focused on the control of the cause of costs not the point of incidence.
   (iv) Costs are traced to activities with the creation of 'cost pools' that relate to an activity.
   (v) It is easier to eliminate non-value-adding activities.
   (vi) Focus may be on total quality management with emphasis on process control through identification of cost drivers.

7

Dealing with Risk and
Uncertainty

Dealing with Risk and Uncertainty

7

7.1 Introduction

In this chapter we will recognise the uncertainty that exists when costs and revenues are estimated and how the risk associated with such uncertainty can be evaluated.

7.2 Probability

7.2.1 The probabilistic model and expected value

It would be rare for the outcome of a business decision to be known in advance, as a measure of risk or uncertainty is present in almost all situations. Risk and uncertainty have different specific meanings in decision theory. Risk exists where the decision-maker has knowledge, probably due to previous experience, that several alternative outcomes are possible. Previous experience enables the decision-maker to ascribe a probability to the likely occurrence of each alternative. On the other hand uncertainty exists where the future is unknown and so the decision-maker has no previous experience and no statistical evidence on which to base predictions. *Although clearly there is a difference between these two issues in practice, for the purposes of the syllabus the words are used interchangeably.*

Uncertainty can be incorporated into the forecasting by using a probabilistic model, which incorporates an allowance for uncertainty measured in terms of probabilities. A number of decision criteria have been developed to assist decision-makers in choosing between various options. By far the most commonly used criterion is that of selecting the option with the greatest expected value (EV), when dealing with profit or revenue, or with lowest EV, when dealing with costs. The EV is calculated by weighting the possible outcomes by their probabilities and then summing the result.

Example: calculating the expected value

An organisation is considering launching a new product. It will do so if the expected value of the total revenue is in excess of £1,000. It is decided to set the selling price at £10. After some investigation a number of probabilities for different levels of sales revenue are predicted; these are shown in Table 7.1.

Table 7.1 Situation I

Units sold	Revenue £	Probability	Pay-off £
80	800	0.15	120
100	1,000	0.50	500
120	1,200	0.35	420
		1.00	EV 1,040

The expected sales revenue at a selling price of £10 per unit is £1,040, that is [800 × 0.15] + [1,000 × 0.50] + [1,200 × 0.35]. In preparing forecasts and making decisions management may proceed on the assumption that it can expect sales revenue of £1,040 if it sets a selling price of £10 per unit. The actual outcome of adopting this selling price may be sales revenue that is higher or lower than £1,040. And £1,040 is not even the most likely outcome; the most likely outcome is £1,000, since this has the highest probability.

Probability data may be presented diagrammatically in the form of a histogram. The information given in the example immediately above might be presented as follows :

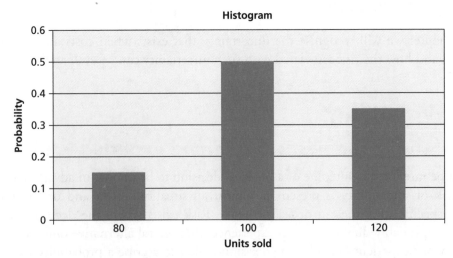

The single figure of the expected value of revenue can hide a wide range of possible actual results.

Furthermore, not all decision-makers will have the same attitude towards risk. There are three main types of decision-maker.

- *Risk neutral* decision-makers ignore the possible variations in outcome and are concerned only with the most likely outcome.
- *Risk seekers* are concerned only with the best possible outcome, no matter how unlikely it is to occur.
- *Risk averse* decision-makers prefer the alternative with the least variation associated with it.

Utility is another important aspect of risk and uncertainty that is described in detail later. The basis of the theory is that an individual's attitude to certain risk profiles will depend on the amount of money involved. For example, most people would accept a bet on the toss of a coin, if the outcome were that they would win £6 if it came down heads and if it came down tails they would pay £4. The average person would be happy to play secure in the knowledge that they would win if the game were repeated over a long enough period; if not it would still be a good bet. But if the stakes were raised so that the win was £6,000 on a single toss coming down heads and a loss of £4,000 if it came down tails, the average person might think twice and reject the bet as being too risky. Utility theory attaches weights to the sums of money involved; these are tailor-made to the individual's attitude towards winning and losing certain sums of money.

Therefore, considering a proposed option solely on the basis of its expected value ignores the range of possible outcomes.

Example: attitude to risk

For instance, after the investigation in the previous example the predicted revenues might have been different. They might have been as shown in Table 7.2.

Table 7.2 Situation II

Units sold	Revenue £	Probability	Pay-off £
40	400	0.15	60.0
100	1,000	0.50	500.0
137	1,370	0.35	479.5
		1.00	EV 1,039.5

Both situations give rise to the same expected sales revenue of £1,040 (to the nearest £), but the two situations are not the same. The second involves a wider dispersal of possible outcomes; hence it involves higher risk. If the decision-makers are risk averse they will judge the range of possible outcomes described in the second situation to be worse than the first. If the decision-makers are risk seekers they may prefer the second situation, because of the higher outcome in the best possible situation. However, in this case, the dire downside of £400 may put them off. Whatever the case it can be seen that the evaluation of the options solely on the basis of their expected value may not always be appropriate.

One possible approach to dealing with risk is to deploy sophisticated modelling technique in an attempt to improve the reliability of business forecasts. The use of trend analysis, encountered earlier in this text, is one possibility. Another possibility is the use of 'learning curve' and 'experience curve' theory to predict future production costs. The use of this theory is not explored here in any depth. But the key point is to develop a mathematical model to predict how future costs will behave having regard to labour becoming more adept at tasks (and hence unit resource requirements falling) the more times they are repeated.

7.2.2 Examples of expected value calculations

Two simple exercises of uncertainty follow. Try them yourself before looking at the answers.

 Exercise

A company buys in sub-assemblies in order to manufacture a product. It is reviewing its policy of putting each sub-assembly through a detailed inspection process on delivery, and is considering not inspecting at all. Experience has shown that the quality of the sub-assembly is of acceptable standard 90 per cent of the time. It costs £10 to inspect a sub-assembly and another £10 to put right any defect found at that stage. If the sub-assembly is not inspected and is then found to be faulty at the finished goods stage the cost of rework is £40.

Requirement

Advise the company whether or not they should change their policy.

 Solution

Four outcomes are possible:

  (i) Inspect and find no problems – cost £10.
 (ii) Inspect and find problems – cost £20.
(iii) Do not inspect and no problems exist – no cost.
(iv) Do not inspect and problems do exist – cost £40.

If sub-assemblies achieve the required standard 90 per cent of the time then there is a 10 per cent chance that they will be faulty.

    The expected value of the cost of each policy is as follows:

Inspect	$[0.9 \times £10] + [0.1 \times £20] = £11$
Do not inspect	$[0.9 \times £0] + [0.1 \times £40] = £4$

Taken over a long enough period of time, a policy of not carrying out an inspection would lead to a saving in cost of £7 per sub-assembly. On a purely quantitative analysis, therefore, this is the correct policy to adopt.

However, in the real world such a high level of failures is incompatible with a requirement for a 'quality product', and the concept of continuous improvement. It would be more useful to ask the supplier some basic questions regarding his quality management, in order to bring about a fundamental shift towards outcome (iii), rather than simply implementing a policy on the basis of such an uncritical analysis of the situation.

 Exercise

An individual is considering backing the production of a new musical in the West End. It would cost £100,000 to stage for the first month. If it is well received by the critics, it will be kept open at the end of the first month for a further 6 months, during which time further net income of £350,000 would be earned. If the critics dislike it, it will close at the end of the first month. There is a 50:50 chance of a favourable review.

Requirement

Should the individual invest in the musical?

Solution

The expected value of backing the musical is:

$$[0.5 \times £250,000] - [0.5 \times £100,000] = £75,000$$

As this provides a positive return it would be accepted on the basis of expected values as the alternative yields zero. However, the expected value can be misleading here as it is a one-off situation and the expected profit of £75,000 is not a feasible outcome. The only feasible outcomes of this project are a profit of £250,000 or a loss of £100,000.

While almost everybody would welcome a profit of £250,000, not many individuals could afford to sustain a loss of £100,000 and they would place a high utility on such a loss. Many investors would be risk averse in such a situation because they would not consider that a 50 per cent chance of making £250,000 was worth an equal 50 per cent risk of losing £100,000; the loss might bankrupt them. On the other hand, if the individual were a multi-millionaire the return of 250 per cent would be very appealing and the loss of a mere £100,000 would have a low utility attached to it.

The two exercises have only had single-point outcomes, that is conformity or otherwise with a pre-set quality standard and a successful show or a flop. It is obvious that the two outcomes of the first exercise represent the only possible alternatives and so quantification of the related pay-offs along the lines of the example appears reasonable. It is also obvious that the profit of £250,000 predicted for a successful show in the case of the second exercise is far too precise a figure. It would be more realistic to assume a range of possible successful pay-offs, which will vary, according to the number of seats sold and the price of the seats. If probabilities are attached to each estimate, the expected value of a successful outcome will take account of the range of possible outcomes, by weighting each of them by its associated probability. The range of possible outcomes might be as in Table 7.3.

Table 7.3 Range of outcomes

Outcome profit £	Probability	Expected value £
(100,000)	0.50	(50,000)
200,000	0.175	35,000
250,000	0.20	50,000
300,000	0.075	22,500
350,000	0.05	17,500
	1.00	75,000

The statement of a range of possible outcomes and their associated probabilities is known as a probability distribution. Presenting the distribution to management allows two further useful inferences to be drawn:

- *The most likely successful outcome.* That is the successful outcome with the highest probability (a profit of £250,000 in Table 7.3).
- *The probability of an outcome being above or below a particular figure.* The particular figure will either be the expected value or a figure of consequence, such as zero profit, where a lesser outcome might have dire consequences. By summing the probabilities for pay-offs of £200,000 and £250,000, it can be concluded that there is a 37.5 per cent probability that profits will be £250,000 or less if the musical is successful. By summing those for £300,000 and £350,000 it can be determined that the probability of a profit of £300,000 or more in the event of success is only 12.5 per cent.

So far only a very small number of alternatives have been considered in the examples. In practice a greater number of alternative courses of action may exist, uncertainty may be associated with more than one variable and the values of variables may be interdependent, giving rise to many different outcomes.

The following exercise looks at the expected value of a manufacturing decision, where there are three alternative sales volumes, two alternative contributions, and three alternative levels of fixed cost. The number of possible outcomes will be $3 \times 2 \times 3 = 18$.

Example

A company is assessing the desirability of producing a souvenir to celebrate a royal jubilee. The marketing life of the souvenir will be 6 months only. Uncertainty surrounds the likely sales volume and contribution, as well as the fixed costs of the venture. Estimated outcomes and probabilities are shown in Table 7.4.

Table 7.4 Estimated outcomes and probabilities

Sales units	Probability	Contn. per unit £	Probablity	Fixed cost £	Probablity
100,000	0.3	7	0.5	400,000	0.2
80,000	0.6	5	0.5	450,000	0.5
60,000	0.1			500,000	0.3
	1.0		1.0		1.0

Table 7.5 shows the expected value of the contribution to be £49,000. Totalling up the joint probabilities for each set of sales shows the project has a 56.5 per cent chance of making a net contribution, a 33 per cent chance of making a loss, and a 10.5 per cent chance of making neither a net contribution nor a loss.

Table 7.5 Expected value calculation

Sales units	Contn. per unit £	Total contn. a £	Fixed cost b £	Probability	Joint prob. c	Expected value of net contn. (a − b) × c £
100,000	7	700,000	400,000	0.3 × 0.5 × 0.2	0.030	9,000
	7	700,000	450,000	0.3 × 0.5 × 0.5	0.075	18,750
	7	700,000	500,000	0.3 × 0.5 × 0.3	0.045	9,000
	5	500,000	400,000	0.3 × 0.5 × 0.2	0.030	3,000
	5	500,000	450,000	0.3 × 0.5 × 0.5	0.075	3,750
	5	500,000	500,000	0.3 × 0.5 × 0.3	0.045	0
80,000	7	560,000	400,000	0.6 × 0.5 × 0.2	0.060	9,600
	7	560,000	450,000	0.6 × 0.5 × 0.5	0.150	16,500
	7	560,000	500,000	0.6 × 0.5 × 0.3	0.090	5,400
	5	400,000	400,000	0.6 × 0.5 × 0.2	0.060	0
	5	400,000	450,000	0.6 × 0.5 × 0.5	0.150	(7,500)
	5	400,000	500,000	0.6 × 0.5 × 0.3	0.090	(9,000)
60,000	7	420,000	400,000	0.1 × 0.5 × 0.2	0.010	200
	7	420,000	450,000	0.1 × 0.5 × 0.5	0.025	(750)
	7	420,000	500,000	0.1 × 0.5 × 0.3	0.015	(1,200)
	5	300,000	400,000	0.1 × 0.5 × 0.2	0.010	(1,000)
	5	300,000	450,000	0.1 × 0.5 × 0.5	0.025	(3,750)
	5	300,000	500,000	0.1 × 0.5 × 0.3	0.015	(3,000)
					1.000	49,000

This can be quite hard to visualise and it may be more useful to use a decision tree to express the situation, as shown in the next section.

7.3 Decision trees

7.3.1 Method and applications

A decision tree is another way of analysing risk and uncertainty. The decision tree model is only as good as the information it contains. The main difficulty is of course, as always, accurately predicting the probabilities that determine the uncertainty. However, a decision tree is a simple and visual way of presenting probabilistic information to management and as such can be quite a useful tool.

Table 7.6 Possible outcomes of plans A and B

	Plan A		Plan B	
	Profit £	Probability	Profit £	Probability
Adverse	20,000	0.5	(10,000)	0.3
Favourable	60,000	0.5	90,000	0.7
Expected profit	40,000		60,000	

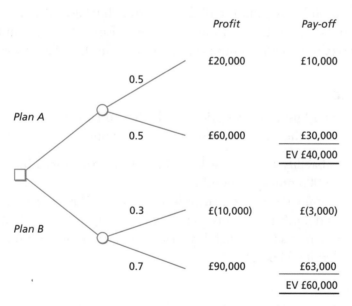

Figure 7.1 Decision tree: plans A and B

The options that management are seeking to evaluate may be very simple. For example, two alternative business plans, A and B, may be under consideration, both of uncertain outcome. Table 7.6 shows the likely possible outcomes of plans A and B.

When the expected profit is calculated it appears that plan B would be the best option. However plan B has a 0.3 chance of a loss of £10,000 whereas plan A will always generate a profit of some sort.

The information can be portrayed in a decision tree as shown in Figure 7.1. The squares and circles are symbols that have a special meaning. The square represents a point at which a decision is made; in this case there is only one decision to be made – the choice between plan A and plan B at the outset. A circle represents a point at which a chance event takes place. The lines, the branches of the tree, represent the logical sequence between the nodes to the different possible outcomes. The values under the heading 'Profit' in Figure 7.1 represent the possible outcomes. The 'Pay-off figures are calculated by multiplying the possible outcomes by their probabilities as in the earlier examples.

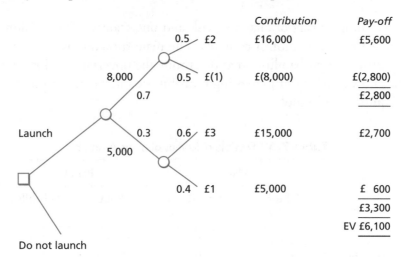

Figure 7.2   Decisions tree: product launch

This basic approach holds good for all decision trees but most decisions are more complicated and require decision trees with more complex features. For example, there may be two or more uncertainties within a business situation, as in the following exercise:

Exercise

The management of a business has to decide whether to launch a new product or not. If the product is launched there are two elements of uncertainty:

- There is a 0.7 probability that sales will be 8,000 units per month but a 0.3 probability that sales will be 5,000 units per month.
- If sales are 8,000 units per month, there is a 0.5 probability that the contribution per unit will be £2 and a 0.5 probability that it will be negative − £(1). If sales are 5,000 units per month there is a 0.6 probability that the contribution per unit will be £3 and a 0.4 probability that it will be £1.

Requirement
Draw a decision tree and advise management as to their best course of action.

☑ Solution

Figure 7.2 shows the decision tree for the product launch.

The sales units on each path are multiplied by the contribution per unit to give the total contribution. This is then multiplied by the probability of occurrence to give the pay-off. The pay-off on the first pathway is £16,000 × 0.7 × 0.5 = £5,600. All paths are summed to give an expected value of £6,100 if the product is launched and, obviously, if the product is not launched the return is zero. So in the absence of other considerations the decision-maker would decide to launch the new product.

Sometimes there are two or more decision points as in the following exercise.

Exercise

A company has prepared the design for a new product. It can either sell the design, for £100,000, or attempt to develop the design into a marketable product at a cost of £150,000. If the company decides to develop the product, the chances of success are 0.7. If the attempt fails the design can only be sold for £20,000. If the attempt succeeds the business has the choice of either selling the design and developed product for £180,000 or marketing the product. If the product is marketed then there is a 0.6 probability that the product will generate a cash inflow of £800,000 and a 0.4 probability that it will generate a cash outflow of £(100,000). Both figures exclude items previously mentioned.

Requirement

Draw a decision tree and advise management as to their best course of action.

Solution

The situation is shown in the form of a decision tree in Figure 7.3. For purposes of clarity the two decision points are labelled A and B.

Although in practice decision A precedes decision B, for the purposes of calculation decision B has to be decided first.

Decision B

The expected cash flow on the first path is £800,000 − £150,000 = £650,000. This is then multiplied by the probability of occurrence once the decision to market has been made, that is, by 0.6 to give £390,000. The second path shows that there is a 40% chance of making a loss of £250,000 [£100,000 − £150,000]. The expected value of marketing is therefore £290,000 compared with an expected value of only £30,000 from selling the designs and product [£180,000 − £150,000]. Therefore, it will pay to market the product if development goes ahead. The 'Sell' option can now be eliminated from our analysis.

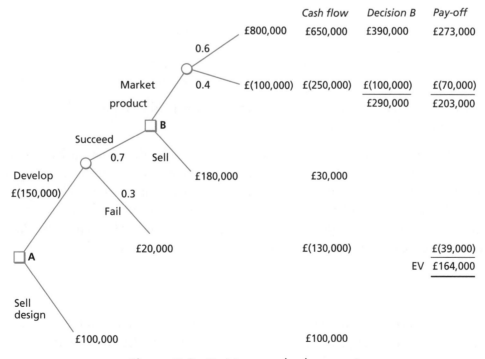

Figure 7.3 Decision tree: develop or not?

Decision A

The expected value of marketing and of failure are summed and compared with the £100,000 if the designs are sold. The £390,000 on the first path is multiplied by the probability of success, 0.7, etc. as shown under the 'Pay-off column. The expected value is £164,000. This is greater than £100,000 and so the product should be developed and marketed.

Factors to consider

A number of other factors arise from this exercise which should be taken into account when considering decision tree-type problems:

- *Time value of money.* The rejected option (the sale of the design) would bring an immediate income whereas the cash flow generated by product development is spread over time. If the span of time under consideration is in excess of a year or so, the time value of money should be incorporated in the calculations. The time value of money is discussed in detail later in this text, and we will return to this example at that stage.
- *Assumes risk neutrality.* As mentioned under probability, some decision-makers do not choose options which give the greatest expected value, because they are either risk seekers or risk averse. In the exercise, for instance, there is a 0.3 probability of losing £130,000 and the recommended course of action offers a 0.28 [0.7 × 0.4] probability of losing £250,000 if the product development is successful. The safe option of selling the design, with its guaranteed inflow of £100,000, could be the more attractive.
- *Sensitivity analysis.* The analysis depends very much on the values of the probabilities in the tree. The values are usually the subjective estimates of the decision-makers, and, no matter how experienced the people involved are, the values must be open to question. In the exercise, a small change in the estimated probabilities of success and failure in the product development phase from 0.7:0.3 to 0.6:0.4 would change the expected value from £164,000 to £122,000, which is much closer to the sell option.

	£
£650,000 × 0.6 × 0.6	= 234,000
£(250,000) × 0.6 × 0.4	= (60,000)
	174.000
Less: (130,000) × 0.4	(52,000)
	122,000

The decision is therefore very sensitive to changes in the predicted probabilities. Sensitivity analysis is discussed further later in this text.

- *Oversimplification.* In order to make the tree manageable, the situation has often to be greatly simplified. This makes it appear far more discrete than it really is. In reality the product in the exercise is unlikely to have just two possible values following successful development and marketing. In practice, it is much more likely that the outcomes would form a near continuous range of inflows and outflows. This cannot be shown on a decision tree, and so any decision tree usually represents a simplified situation.

7.3.2 The value of perfect information

One feature of uncertainty in business situations is that it is often possible to reduce it or even eliminate it. For example, market research can be used to determine with a reasonable degree of accuracy what the demand for a new product will be. However, market research costs money and the decision-maker has to decide whether it is worth paying for the research in order to reduce or eliminate the uncertainty of product demand.

The following exercise shows this.

 Exercise

The launch of a new product is being considered. There is a 0.6 chance that demand for the product will be strong and a 0.4 chance that demand will be weak. Two strategies for the launch are possible. Strategy 1 involves high promotion costs and will generate a net cash inflow of £120,000 if demand proves to be strong. However, if demand proves to be weak then a net cash outflow of £(30,000) will result. Strategy 2 involves low promotion costs. If demand proves to be strong then this will generate a net cash inflow of only £80,000 but if demand proves weak then a net cash inflow of £20,000 is still generated.

Requirement

(a) Draw a decision tree and advise which course of action generates the greatest expected profit.
(b) What is the maximum amount that should be paid for market research to determine with certainty whether demand will be strong or weak?

 Solution

(a) The required decision tree shown in Figure 7.4.

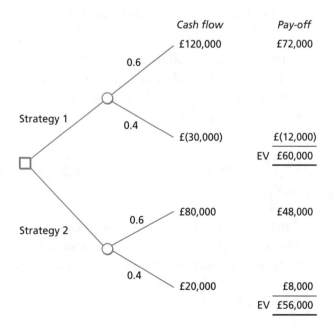

Figure 7.4 Decision tree: promotion cost strategies 1 and 2

The decision tree model suggests that Strategy 1 should be adopted since it generates the higher expected value. That is £60,000 as opposed to the £56,000 generated by Strategy 2. The problem with this is that if demand turns out to be weak Strategy 1 gives a negative cash flow of £30,000 compared with a positive cash flow of £20,000 from Strategy 2. In the case of weak demand Strategy 1 will turn out to have been the wrong choice.

(b) If the research predicted that demand would be strong then Strategy 1 would be adopted giving a cash inflow of £120,000. If the research predicted that demand would be weak then Strategy 2 would be adopted giving a cash flow of £20,000.

Hence the expected-cash flow outcome, with the research, will be £80,000, that is [£120,000 × 0.6] + [£20,000 × 0.4].

The expected cash inflow outcome without the research is £60,000.

Hence the value of the research and perfect information is £20,000, that is [£80,000 − £60,000].

The maximum amount that the decision-maker should pay for the research is £20,000.

Note that the probability that each type of demand will occur is unaltered. The research can only provide an accurate forecast of what might happen not change the outcome.

7.4 Uncertainty in investment appraisal

Later in this text you will be studying investment appraisal in detail. Investment appraisal involves the forecasting of cash flows associated with a project and clearly there will be some uncertainty attached to such forecasts.

The techniques for dealing with uncertainty that you have learned about in this chapter, using probabilities and sensitivity analysis, are useful for dealing with uncertainty in investment appraisal. However, these are not the only methods available to the management accountant.

You will see that it also possible to allow for uncertainty by other methods, including the following:

- Adjusting the required rate of return to allow for the perceived degree of risk; the cash flows from a more risky project might be discounted using a higher discount rate.
- Adjusting the payback time required; for a project that is perceived to be more risky, a shorter payback period might be required.

7.5 Standard deviations to measure risk and uncertainty

In order to measure the risk associated with a particular project, it is helpful to find out how wide ranging the possible outcomes are. The conventional measure is the standard deviation. The standard deviation compares all the actual outcomes with the expected value (or mean outcome). It then calculates how far on average the outcomes deviate from the mean. It is calculated using a formula.

If we have two probability distributions with different expected values their standard deviations are not directly comparable. We can overcome this problem by using the coefficient of variation (the standard deviation divided by the expected value) which measures the relative size of the risk.

Expected values, standard deviations or coefficient of variations are used to summarise the outcomes from alternative courses of action however it must be remembered that they do not provide all the relevant information to the decision maker. The probability distribution will provide the decision maker with all of the information they require. It would be appropriate to use expected values, standard deviations or coefficient of variations for decision making when there are a large number of alternatives to consider i.e. where it is not practical to consider the probability distributions for each alternative.

Example

A company is considering whether to make product X or product Y. They cannot make both products. The estimated sales demand for each product is uncertain and the following probability distribution of the NPVs for each product has been identified:

Product X		
NPV Outcome (£)	Estimated Probability	Weighted Amount (£)
£3,000	0.10	£300
£3,500	0.20	£700
£4,000	0.40	£1,600
£4,500	0.20	£900
£5,000	0.10	£500
	Expected Value	£4,000

Product Y		
NPV Outcome (£)	Estimated Probability	Weighted Amount (£)
£2,000	0.05	£ 100
£3,000	0.10	£ 300
£4,000	0.40	£1,600
£5,000	0.25	£1,250
£6,000	0.20	£1,200
	Expected Value	£4,450

Using an expected value approach the company's decision would be to produce product X. However, lets consider the standard deviation calculations for each product:

Product X			
NPV Deviation from Expected Value	Squared Deviation (£)	Probability	Weighted Amount (£)
£3,000 − £4,000 = −£1,000	1,000,000	0.10	100,000
£3,500 − £4,000 = −£500	250,000	0.20	50,000
£4,000 − £4,000 = £0	0	0.40	0
£4,500 − £4,000 = +£500	250,000	0.20	50,000
£5,000 − £4,000 = +£1,000	1,000,000	0.10	100,000

	Sum of weighted squared deviation		300,000
	Standard deviation		547.72
	Expected value		4,000

	Product Y		
NPV Deviation from Expected Value	Squared Deviation (£)	Probability	Weighted Amount (£)
£2,000 − £4,450 = −£2,450	£ 6,002,500	0.05	£300,125
£3,000 − £4,450 = −£1,450	£ 2,102,500	0.10	£210,250
£4,000 − £4,450 = −£450	£ 202,500	0.40	£81,000
£5,000 − £4,450 = +£550	£ 302,500	0.25	£75,625
£6,000 − £4,450 = +£1,550	£ 2,402,500	0.20	£480,500
	Sum of weighted squared deviation		£1,147,500
	Standard deviation		£1,071.21
	Expected value		£4,450

The expected net present value for each product gives us an average value based upon the probability associated with each possible profit outcome. If net present value is used for decision-making, then on that basis Product Y would be produced as it yields the highest return.

However, the net present value for each product does not indicate the range of profits that may result. By calculating the standard deviation, this allows us to identify a range of values that could occur for the profit for each product. Product Y has a higher standard deviation than Product X and is therefore more risky. There is not a significant difference in net present value for each of the products. However, Product X is less risky than Product Y and therefore the final selection will depend on the risk attitude of the company.

7.6 Maximin, Maximax and Regret Criteria

7.6.1 Attitude to risk

So far, we have concentrated on the manner in which risk and uncertainty can be modelled and expressed in a manner that may provide a guide to the decision-maker. However, information derived in that way does not itself usually give a full answer to decision-making problems. Typically, when the decision-maker is confronted with a choice between options then he/she has to accept a trade-off between risk and expected reward. Such a trade-off will normally involve behavioural issues.

It is normally assumed that a risk averse investor will, all other things being equal, prefer a low risk option to a high risk option. If option A and B offer the same expected outcome but A's range of possible outcomes has a lower standard deviation than B's – then A will be preferred. But practical decision-making problems are rarely as neat as this.

One behavioural model that is used to represent the behavioural dimension of attitudes to risk is commonly known as the maximin, maximax and minimax regret criteria model.

7.6.2 A practical example

A fruit trader plans to travel to market tomorrow. He has a small stall at the market and only a limited amount of cash available to buy stock to sell. Accordingly, he can select only one type of fruit to buy from the wholesaler today ready for tomorrow's market. There are four types of fruit from which the trader can make his selection; apples, pears, oranges and strawberries. From past experience, our trader expects that trading conditions tomorrow will fall into one of four headings; bad, poor, fair or good and each of these trading conditions has the same likelihood of occurring. Again using past experience, the trader has quantified the profit [+£] or loss [(£)] that he thinks he will earn tomorrow depending upon his choice of fruit and the trading conditions that emerge. These are as follows.

Fruit:	Apples	Pears	Oranges	Strawberries
Trading Condition				
Bad	(£1,000)	(£1,200)	(£300)	(£600)
Poor	(£200)	(£400)	(£100)	(£300)
Fair	+ £600	+ £700	+ £200	+ £100
Good	+ £1,000	+ £1,200	+ £400	+ £440

Let us now consider some of the alternative approaches that our trader might take to determine which type of fruit he will purchase and take to tomorrow's market, depending on the attitude to risk that is to prevail.

7.6.3 The maximin approach

This approach involves looking at the worst possible outcome only for each of the four types of fruit. That is to say we will focus on bad trading conditions only. We need to look for the best outcome amongst the four types of fruit in these conditions, although it might be more accurate to say that since all of these are loss-making we are looking for the least worst. In so doing, we completely ignore the outcomes that might emerge if trading conditions are other than bad. Clearly, the maximin choice will be oranges, since the anticipated loss of £300 is the least worst of the four types of fruit. This ultra-cautious approach indicates an aversion to risk that may be based upon some deep-rooted fear of failure.

7.6.4 The maximax approach

Here, we are looking to select the opportunity that offers the highest possible return. We will consider only good trading conditions, completely ignoring what might happen under fair, poor and bad. This would lead us to select pears with the highest possible profit of £1,200. In hoping that good trading conditions will emerge, we are taking an optimistic outlook on the situation and not worrying about the fact that, if trading conditions are bad, then pears will lead to the largest loss of £1,200.

7.6.5 The minimax regret approach

Sometimes known simply as 'Regret', this approach makes a decision today based upon how our trader might feel at the end of tomorrow's market. Having made his choice of the type of fruit he will sell, his success at the market will depend on the trading conditions that emerge and the trader has no control over this. His choice may turn out to be the best for the trading conditions that emerge and if so the trader will be happy. Alternatively, the trader may get to the end of tomorrow's market and have a feeling of regret, since he had not selected the type of fruit that would have been best under the trading conditions that emerged.

If for example, the trader selects oranges and trading conditions prove to be bad, then he will feel no regret as this type of fruit will have yielded the least worst loss of £300. But if, trading conditions turn out to be good, then the trader will regret having chosen oranges rather than pears which would have provided a much higher profit of £1,200 in this situation. Not only can we identify that this regret will exist, but we can also quantify it. Having earned a profit of £400 instead of £1,200, then the amount of regret will be £800.

For each trading condition, one of the types of fruit will yield no regret as it would represent the best choice as follows:

Trading Condition	Best choice
Bad	Oranges
Poor	Oranges
Fair	Pears
Good	Pears

From this, we can derive the following table that quantifies the regret that the trader would retrospectively feel for each combination of type of fruit and trading condition.

Fruit	Apples	Pears	Oranges	Strawberries
Trading Condition				
Bad	£700	£900	NIL	£300
Poor	£100	£300	NIL	£200
Fair	£100	NIL	£500	£600
Good	£200	NIL	£800	£760

In the above table, we have used bold figures to identify the maximum possible regret that the trader could feel for each of the four types of fruit. The key point here is that, although regret is a retrospective feeling, these figures are known in advance and the trader can use this information to select the type of fruit for tomorrow's market. The trader will select the type of fruit whose maximum potential regret is the lowest of the four. He will therefore choose apples with a maximum regret of £700.

There is evidence of aversion to risk here. The trader does not make profit/loss the prime focus of his decision-making but focuses on how badly he might feel tomorrow if things do not work out.

 Exercise

A company needs to decide which one of the three products to launch. Each of the products could lead to varying levels of profit and these have been constructed in the following payoff table:

	Profits £'000s		
Products	Worst	Most Likely	Best
X	10	12	22
Y	15	18	20
Z	8	11	15

Requirements

(a) Which product should be launched using the maximin decision rule?
(b) Which product should be launched using the maximax decision rule?
(c) Which product should be launched using the criterion of regret?

Solution

(a) Maximin decision rule

The maximin criterion suggests that a decision-maker should select the alternative that offers the least unattractive worst outcome, i.e. the manager will go for the product which gives the highest minimum profit. The highest minimum profit in this case is Product Y as this offers £15,000 as against £10,000 for Product X and £8,000 for Product Z.

(b) Maximax decision rule

The maximax criterion looks at the best possible results and therefore the decision-maker assumes that the best payoff will occur, i.e. maximise the maximum profit.

Applying the maximax decision rule, Product X would be chosen as this maximises the maximum profit possible.

(c) Applying the criterion of regret an investor will choose the alternative that will cause the least regret from making the wrong choice. You need to compare the options vertically and ask which is the best option under each set of conditions.

	Profits		
Products	**Worst** **£000**	**Most likely** **£000**	**Best** **£000**
X	10	12	22
Y	15	18	20
Z	8	11	15

The possible regret depending on demand conditions, will be:
If X is chosen

	Worst **£000**	**Most likely** **£000**	**Best** **£000**
X	5 less than Y	6 less than Y	Best choice – no regret

If Y is chosen

	Worst **£000**	**Most likely** **£000**	**Best** **£000**
Y	Best choice – no regret	Best choice – no regret	2 less than X

If Z is chosen

	Worst **£000**	**Most likely** **£000**	**Best** **£000**
Z	7 less than Y	7 less than Y	7 less than X

So the choice that has the lowest regret potential is Product Y – where the maximum potential regret is £2,000. (Compare Product Z which has the highest potential regret of £7,000)

7.7 Simulation

One other method used to analyse risk is the simulation or Monte Carlo technique. This method recognises that all the variables associated with a project are subject to change. Probabilities are assigned to all the likely outcomes for each variable in turn. Using random numbers and a computer program, multiple possible project scenarios are generated. The predicted probabilities are used such that the more likely the outcome associated with a particular variable, the more likely it will be selected in the simulation. The multiple scenarios can then be used to form a frequency distribution.

A simple set of results from such an exercise, where 100 simulations were run on a project, is presented below:

Profit	Frequency
<£0	2
£0–£2,500	12
£2,500–£5,000	26
£5,000–£7,500	35
£7,500–£10,000	17
£10,000–£12,500	7
>£12,500	1
	100

From this various conclusions can be drawn. For example, there is only a 2% chance of making a loss and there is a 25% chance of making more than £7,500.

One common application for this technique is in estimating counter queues in shops, banks, post offices and building societies. The length of waiting time predicted will determine the number of staff required. In this scenario there are two uncertainties: firstly, customers do not arrive at an even rate and secondly, some customers require more and some require less than the average service time. Thus two sets of frequency probabilities are used and two different sets of random numbers.

Stock holding systems are another area where simulation models can be used to good effect in order to minimise stock holdings without an undue risk of a stock-out.

7.8 Sensitivity analysis

This is the practice of assessing an uncertain situation by testing the impact on outcome of changes in key variables. A CVP chart (of the kind encountered earlier in this text) is a form of sensitivity analysis since it illustrates the impact on profit of changes in the sales level. In this case, the sales level is a key variable and the slope of the profit line, the break-even point and the margin of safety all provide impressions of sensitivity.

Sensitivity analysis can be carried out in many different ways and at varying levels of refinement.

Example: sensitivity analysis of a product

A business makes and sells the Unit. Relevant details are as follows:

Expected case:

Fixed costs £	1,000
Selling price per unit £	5
Variable cost per unit £	3
Units sold	600
Profit £	200

Consider the impact of a 20% adverse variance in each key variable in turn (with other variables held constant):

	Profit Revised	Profit £	%
Fixed costs £	1,200	0	−100%
Selling price per unit £	4	−400	−300%
Variable cost per unit £	3.6	−160	−180%
Units sold	480	−40	−120%

This analysis suggests that the profitability of the product is most sensitive to changes in the unit selling price. Management attention should therefore be concentrated most on this key variable. The overall 'riskiness' of the situation depends more on unit selling price than it does on fixed costs. That observation may be 'a statement of the obvious' in this particular case, but it serves to illustrate one key aspect of sensitivity analysis. The case also illustrates one possible weakness of sensitivity analysis in that it does not generally consider the probabilities of different outcomes. This last consideration is discussed in the article shown below.

Sensitivity analysis may be used as a guide in both 'go – no go' situations and in attempts to re-engineer a business situation in order to alter its risk-reward profile. For example, in the above case it might be judged acceptable to lower the unit selling price asked from £5 to £4.90 in exchange for a 600 unit customer advance order. This would reduce the expected profit from £200 to £140 but would significantly reduce uncertainty as both selling price and unit sales would become certain. The risk averse decision maker might find this change improves product viability.

Extract from 'The gentle touch'

Bob Scarlett, *CIMA Insider*, February 2003

(Note: the article refers to NPV (net present value) as the relevant performance measure. This is a foundation topic that you should be familiar with. But it is explored fully in the next chapter, so return to this item later in your studies if you have any doubts about it.)

You may be faced with a choice between alternative means of achieving given objectives. Where there are key variables, sensitivity analysis can help here as well. For example, say you need to provide a given standard of service for a five year period and there are two ways of achieving this:

(1) A high-capital approach involving the purchase of equipment that costs £14,000 and has a residual value of £1,400. This method uses 200 resource units annually.

(2) A low-capital approach involving the purchase of equipment that costs £2,800 and has a disposal cost of £1,200. This method uses 360 resource units annually.

The cost of capital is 10%. There is uncertainty regarding the likely average cost of a resource unit over the term but it will lie somewhere between £10 and £30.

A sensitivity analysis will offer useful insights in this case. You can project the NPV of costs at alternative resource unit prices as follows:

£ per unit	high cap	low cap
10	20,713	17,193
15	24,504	24,017
20	28,295	30,840
25	32,086	37,664
30	35,877	44,488

The sensitivity of the options to resource unit price can also be represented graphically.

The insights revealed by this analysis include:

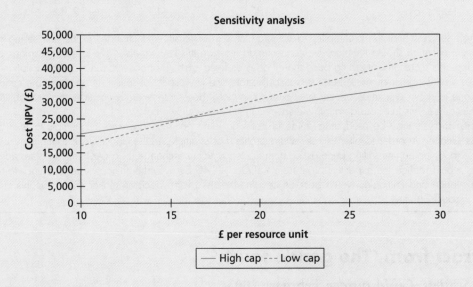

- The high-capital approach offers a cheaper solution in about 70% of the possible unit price outcomes, including the mean figure of £20 per unit
- The low-capital approach offers a cheaper solution only if the unit price is below £16. Even in the case of the lowest possible unit price (£10) the difference between the two alternatives is only around £3,500.

Purely on the basis of the information given, one would probably select the high-capital approach, but the process of using sensitivity analysis may distort decision-making. When considering issues related to risk and uncertainty, decision-makers commonly make certain working assumptions. One of these is that, in conditions of uncertainty, the probability distribution of possible outcomes is grouped symmetrically around a mean and most likely outcome. Indeed, many business projects are like that. The sensitivity analysis in this case uses a unit price of £20 as the median position, so you may be inclined to assume that this is the expected result and that outcomes close to this figure are more likely than ones remote from it. If you run similar projects often enough, then you might expect their average outcome to be very close to the median outcome.

Sensitivity analysis tends to focus on ranges of possible outcomes without considering the probabilities of different results within those ranges. It may be that outcomes at one extreme of the range are actually more likely than ones in the centre. In this case, the low-capital approach may be preferable if there is a high probability that resource unit prices will be at the lower end of the range.

Business decision-making is an art form. Sensitivity analysis is a general approach that can give the decision-maker powerful insights into the problem they are confronting, but it is not a technique that can provide the solution to that problem.

7.9 Summary

In this chapter we have learned how risk and uncertainty arise and how they affect decisions according to the risk attitude of the decision-maker.

Self-test questions

(1) What causes risk and uncertainty in a business context? (Section 7.2.1)

(2) What is an 'expected' outcome in conditions of uncertainty (Section 7.2.1)

(3) What is a decision tree? (Section 7.3.1)

(4) How is the value of information determined? (Section 7.3.2)

(5) How is a standard deviation calculated? (Section 7.5)

(6) What is a histogram? (Section 7.3)

(7) How might risk differentials be allowed for in investment appraisal? (Section 7.4)

Revision Questions

7

Question 1

1.1 If a particular marketing strategy is followed, there are four possible outcomes in terms of profit as follows:

Outcome	Profit £	Probability
A	100,000	0.1
B	70,000	0.4
C	50,000	0.3
D	−20,000	0.2

What is the expected outcome of this strategy?

The following scenario is common to 1.2 and 1.3.

A decision-maker is choosing between three alternative marketing strategies – A, B and C. The outcome of these strategies depends on whether the market condition will be weak, medium or strong. The outcomes of the respective strategies in the different possible market conditions, expressed in £ thousands of profit are as follows:

		Strategy	
Market	A	B	C
Weak	20	80	10
Medium	40	70	100
Strong	50	−10	40

1.2 What strategy should be adopted if the decision-maker acts on the maximin rule?

1.3 What strategy should be adopted if the decision-maker acts on the minimax regret rule?

1.4 A company has estimated the selling prices and variable costs of one of its products as follows:

Selling price per unit		Variable cost per unit	
$	Probability	$	Probability
40	0.30	20	0.55
50	0.45	30	0.25
60	0.25	40	0.20

Given that the company will be able to supply 1,000 units of its product each week irrespective of the selling price, and that selling price and variable cost per unit are independent of each other, calculate the probability that the weekly contribution will exceed $20,000. **(3 marks)**

1.5 A soft drinks company is preparing its sales budget for the coming season. It knows that its sales are dependent on the weather conditions that will prevail during the season. Weather conditions have two relevant characteristics – (a) windy (0.3 probability) or still (0.7 probability), and (b) wet (0.4 probability) or dry (0.6 probability). The outcomes (in terms of thousands of cans sold) in the possible weather scenarios are:

Scenario	Cans
Windy and wet	100
Windy and dry	140
Still and wet	110
Still and dry	200

What is the expected sales figure that should be included in the budget?

? Question 2

FRS Ltd is considering undertaking a project, the cash flow outcome of which depends on whether market demand proves to be weak (probability 0.25) or strong (probability 0.75).

Weak market demand will result in a negative cash flow of £180,000, while strong market demand will give rise to a positive cash flow of £500,000.

A market research consultant has offered to prepare a forecast on whether the market will be weak or strong for a fee of £80,000. Past experience with this firm indicates that it has a 0.8 chance of correctly forecasting strong market demand and a 0.6 chance of correctly forecasting weak market demand.

Requirements

(a) Advise FRS Ltd on whether or not the project is viable without the forecast.

(b) Advise FRS Ltd on whether or not the value of the forecast to FRS Ltd is greater or less than the fee requested by the consultant.

? Question 3

For the past 20 years a charity organisation has held an annual dinner and dance with the primary intention of raising funds.

This year there is concern that an economic recession may adversely affect both the number of persons attending the function and the advertising space that will be sold in the programme published for the occasion.

Based on past experience and current prices and quotations, it is expected that the following costs and revenues will apply for the function:

			£
Cost:	Dinner and dance:	Hire of premises	700
		Band and entertainers	2,800
		Raffle prizes	800
		Photographer	200
		Food at £12 per person (with a guarantee of 400 persons minimum)	
	Programme:	A fixed cost of £2,000 plus £5 per page.	
Revenues:	Dinner and dance	Price of tickets	£20 per person
		Average revenue from:	
		Raffle	£5 per person
		Photographs	£1 per person
	Programme:	Average revenue from:	
		Advertising	£70 per page

A sub-committee, formed to examine more closely the likely outcome of the function, discovered the following from previous records and accounts:

No. of tickets sold	No. of past occasions
250–349	4
350–449	6
450–549	8
550–649	2
	20

No. of tickets sold	No. of past occasions
24	4
32	8
40	6
48	2
	20

Several members of the sub-committee are in favour of using a market research consultant to carry out a quick enquiry into the likely number of pages of advertising space that would be sold for this year's dinner and dance.

Requirements
(a) Calculate the expected value of the profit to be earned from the dinner and dance this year.
(b) Recommend, with relevant supporting financial and cost data, whether or not the charity should spend £500 on the market research enquiry and indicate the possible benefits the enquiry could provide.

    NB: All workings for tickets should be in steps of 100 tickets and for advertising in steps of 8 pages.

? Question 4

The managing director of XYZ plc has devolved some decision-making to the operating divisions of the firm. He is anxious to extend this process but first wishes to be assured that decisions are being taken properly in accordance with group policy.

As a check on existing practice he has asked for an investigation to be made into a recent decision to increase the price of the sole product of Z division to £14.50 per unit due to rising costs.

The following information and estimates were available for the management of Z division.

(1) Last year 75,000 units were sold at £12 each with a total unit cost of £9 of which £6 were variable costs.
(2) For the year ahead the following cost and demand estimates have been made.

Unit variable costs

Pessimistic	Probability	0.15	£7.00 per unit
Most likely	Probability	0.65	£6.50 per unit
Optimistic	Probability	0.20	£6.20 per unit

Total fixed costs

Pessimistic	Probability	0.3	Increase by 50%
Most likely	Probability	0.5	Increase by 25%
Optimistic	Probability	0.2	Increase by 10%

Demand estimates at various prices (units)

			£13.50	£14.50
	Price per unit		£13.50	£14.50
Pessimistic	Probability	0.3	45,000	35,000
Most likely	Probability	0.5	60,000	55,000
Optimistic	Probability	0.2	70,000	68,000

(Unit variable costs, fixed costs and demand estimates are statistically independent.)

For this type of decision the group has decided that the option should be chosen which has the highest expected outcome with at least an 80 per cent chance of breaking even.

Requirements

(a) Assess whether the decision was made in accordance with group guidelines.
(b) Comment on the estimates for the decision and describe what other factors might have been considered.

? Question 5

CG is considering the launch of a new product. Launching the product will have three alternative possible outcomes in terms of profit, dependant on market conditions, as follows:

Market	*£ Profit*	*Probability*
Weak	−240,000	0.25
Medium	300,000	0.50
Strong	1,200,000	0.25

Abandoning the product, at any stage, will achieve a £60,000 income receipt from sale of the patent. An initial test-marketing exercise (costing £160,000) must precede the launch of the product. If the test marketing is 'positive' in terms of customer delight then the company may (or may not) go ahead with the launch. If the test marketing is 'negative' then the company will abandon the product. There is a 50/50 probability of the test marketing producing a positive result.

Requirement

Using probability analysis and such diagrammatic illustration as you see fit, advise CG on whether or not it should (a) abandon the project now, or (b) go ahead with the test marketing.

Solutions to Revision Questions

 Solution 1

1.1

	(a)	(b)	(a) × (b)
Outcome	*Profit £*	*Probability*	
A	100,000	0.1	10,000
B	70,000	0.4	28,000
C	50,000	0.3	15,000
D	−20,000	0.2	−4,000
expected			49,000

The expected outcome is £49,000 profit.

1.2 Strategy A gives the least-worst outcome (20) and it would be selected.

1.3 The 'opportunity cost' of each of the strategies in each of the market conditions as a result of having made a wrong decision is as follows:

	Strategy		
Market	*A*	*B*	*C*
Weak	60	0	70
Medium	60	30	0
Strong	0	60	10

There is a tie between A and B which both have a maximum opportunity cost of 60. If we then refer to the second largest maximum opportunity cost, then we would prefer B because its result is only 30 whereas that for A is 60.

1.4 Weekly contribution of $20,000 if sales demand = 1,000 units equals a contribution of $20 per unit.

The following combinations of selling price and variable cost per unit yield a contribution of more than $20 per unit:

Selling Price	Variable Cost	Probability
$50	$20	0.45 × 0.55 = 0.2475
$60	$30	0.25 × 0.25 = 0.0625
$60	$20	0.25 × 0.55 = 0.1375
		0.4475

Answer = 44.75%

1.5 Scenario outcomes and associated probabilities are as follows:

Scenario	(a) Cans	(b) Probability	(a) × (b)
Windy and wet	100	0.12	12
Windy and dry	140	0.18	25.2
Still and wet	110	0.28	30.8
Still and dry	200	0.42	84
Expected			152

The expected outcome is 152,000 cans and this figure might be incorporated in the budget. Note that the scenario probabilities are calculated by multiplying the individual probabilities of the two elements (e.g. the 'windy and wet' probability is 0.3 × 0.4 = 0.12).

✅ Solution 2

Tips
- A straightforward question on the value of information.
- Drawing a decision tree is a simple and visual way of presenting information and will help you in answering this question.

The position may be represented by the following decision tree diagram:

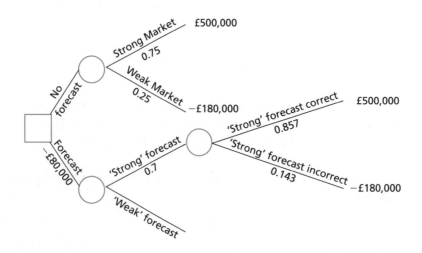

If a weak market is forecast then we may assume that it will be believed and the project will be abandoned at once – since there would be no point in proceeding with a project considered certain to result in a negative cash flow. The probability of the consultant forecasting strong market demand is 0.7, comprising two components, each with a separate outcome, as follows:

Probability of a correct forecast	$0.8 \times 0.75 = 0.6$
Probability of an incorrect forecast	$0.4 \times 0.25 = \underline{0.1}$
	$\underline{0.7}$

It follows that the probability of a strong market demand forecast being correct is 0.857 (i.e. 0.6/0.7) and the probability of a strong market demand forecast being incorrect is 0.143 (i.e. 0.1/0.7).

The expected cash flow generated by proceeding without a forecast is £330,000 (i.e. (£500,000 $\times$ 0.75) + (−£180,000 $\times$ 0.25)). Hence the project is viable without a forecast.

The expected cash flow generated by proceeding with a forecast is:

$$0.7[(£500,000 \times .857) + (−£180,000 \times 0.143)] − £80,000 = £201,932$$

The value of the forecast does not justify the fee. The forecast should not be commissioned.

 ## Solution 3

(a) The probability of ticket sales based on past experience is:

Number of t tickets sold	Probability	
250–349	0.2	(4 out of 20)
350–449	0.3	(6 out of 20)
450–549	0.4	(8 out of 20)
550–649	$\underline{0.1}$	(2 out of 20)
	$\underline{1.0}$	

Average revenue per person

	£
Price of ticket	20
Raffle	5
Photograph	1
	$\underline{26}$

Fixed costs for the event

	£
Hire of premises	700
Band and entertainers	2,800
Raffle prizes	800
Photographer	$\underline{200}$
	$\underline{4,500}$

Expected profit from the dinner and dance

Ticket sales (midpoint)	Income £	Food £	Fixed costs £	Profit £	Prob	Expected profit £
300	7,800	4,800	4,500	(1,500)	0.2	(300)
400	10,400	4,800	4,500	1,100	0.3	330
500	13,000	6,000	4,500	2,500	0.4	1,000
600	15,600	7,200	4,500	3,900	0.1	$\underline{390}$
					Expected profit	$\underline{1,420}$

The probability of the number of programme pages sold based on past experience is:

Programme pages sold	Probability	
24	0.2	(4 out of 20)
32	0.4	(8 out of 20)
40	0.3	(6 out of 20)
48	0.1	(2 out of 20)
	1.0	

Expected profit on programme advertising

Programme pages sold	Income £	Costs £	Profit/(loss) £	Prob. £	Expected profit £
24	1,680	2,120	(440)	0.2	(88)
32	2,240	2,160	80	0.4	32
40	2,800	2,200	600	0.3	180
48	3,360	2,240	1,120	0.1	112
				Expected profit	236

Total expected profit from the dinner and dance and programme advertising is
= £1,420 + £236 = £1,656

(b) If the policy is to hold a dinner and dance each year and to accept losses in some years and profits in others, there is no advantage in spending £500 on the market research enquiry. Market research is justifiable only if it affects action taken – a decision on whether or not to hold a dinner and dance and thus avoid any losses.

From the workings in (a) above, it can be seen that an overall loss will be incurred only when 300 tickets are sold. The expected loss that will be incurred if 300 tickets are sold is calculated as:

Loss from sale of 300 tickets £	Profit/(loss) on programmes £	Total loss £	Joint prob.	Expected value £
(1,500)	(440)	(1,940)	0.04	(77.6)
(1,500)	80	(1,420)	0.08	(113.6)
(1,500)	600	(900)	0.06	(54.0)
(1,500)	1,120	(380)	0.02	(7.6)
			Expected loss	(252.8)

The expected value of the market research is £252.80 and the cost of the research is £500. The expenditure on market research is not justified.

 Solution 4

Tips

- It is important to be clear on the group guidelines and to identify the various options available to the decision-makers before you begin your calculations.
- This is a question with three variables each of which can take three values. It is therefore important to plan your answer and work systematically.

(a) The group guidelines are to choose the option with the highest expected outcome and at least an 80 per cent chance of breaking even.

Expected contribution = Expected demand × expected contribution per unit.
Expected variable cost per unit = £7 × 0.15 + £6.50 × 0.65 + £6.20 × 0.20
$$= £6.515$$

Selling price = £13.50

Expected contribution per unit = £13.50 − £6.515
$$= £6.985$$

Expected demand	= 45,000 × 0.3 + 60,000 × 0.5 + 70,000 × 0.2
	= 57,500 units
Expected contribution	= 57,500 × £6.985
	= £401,637.50

Selling price = £14.50

Expected contribution per unit = £14.50 − £6.515
$$= £7.985$$

Expected demand	= 35,000 × 0.3 + 55,000 × 0.5 + 68,000 × 0.2
	= 51,600 units
Expected contribution	= 51,600 × £7.985
	= £412,026

Expected outcome is maximised at a selling price of £14.50.
Consider the probability of at least breaking even is 80% at a selling price of £14.50.

Selling price £14.50

Demand		35,000	55,000	68,000
Probability		0.3	0.5	0.2
Contribution per unit	Prob.			
£7.50	0.15	£262,500	£412,500	£510,000
Joint prob.		0.045	0.075	0.03
£8.00	0.65	£280,000	£440,000	£544,000
Joint prob.		0.195	0.325	0.13
£8.30	0.20	£290,500	£456,500	£564,400
Joint prob.		0.06	0.10	0.04

Last year's fixed cost = 75,000 × (£9 − £6) = £225,000
Expected fixed costs for this year are:

Increase	Fixed costs	Probability
50%	£337,500	0.3
25%	£281,250	0.5
10%	£247,500	0.2

Losses are incurred when contribution is less than fixed costs and the probability of these occurring is as follows:

Contribution	Fixed costs	Probability
£262,500	£337,500	0.045 × 0.3 = 0.0135
£262,500	£281,250	0.045 × 0.5 = 0.0225
£280,000	£337,500	0.195 × 0.3 = 0.0585
£280,000	£281,250	0.195 × 0.5 = 0.0975
£290,500	£337,500	0.060 × 0.3 = 0.0180
		0.2100

Probability of a loss = 0.21
Therefore probability of at least breaking even = 1 − 0.21
= 0.79

The guideline that the option chosen should have at least an 80 per cent chance of breaking even has not been met.

(b) Comments on the estimates for the decision:
- All estimates of costs are likely to be subjective, based on past costs and estimates concerning inflation.
- The probabilities will be subjective, since it is unlikely that sufficient past data is available to produce reliable data.
- The demand estimates are subjective, although it is possible that they were supported by market research.
- The three variables – variable costs, fixed costs and demand – may not be independent.

The main additional factors to take into account, apart from possible interdependence, are other selling prices, both outside this range and within it. Continuous probability distributions may be considered instead of discrete probabilities.

 Solution 5

The expected outcome of launching the product is:

Market	(a) Profit	(b) Probability	(a) × (b)
Weak	−240,000	0.25	−60,000
Medium	300,000	0.50	150,000
Strong	1,200,000	0.25	300,000
Expected			390,000

This is higher than the £60,000 gained from disposing of the product so it represents the outcome of a positive result from the test marketing. The expected results from the test marketing is therefore:

	(a)	(b)	(a) × (b)
Cost	−160,000	1	−160,000
Positive result	390,000	0.5	195,000
Negative result	60,000	0.5	30,000
Expected			65000

	(a)	(b)	(a) × (b)
Cost	−160000	1	−160000
Positive result	390000	0.5	195000
Negative result	60000	0.5	30000
Expected			65000

This expected outcome contrasts with the £60,000 to be gained from abandoning the product. So, CG should proceed to the test launch.

This reasoning may be represented diagrammatically as follows:

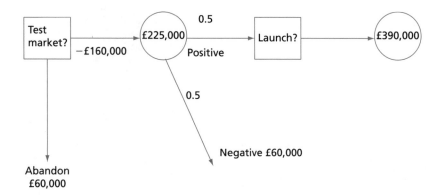

8

Project Appraisal

Project Appraisal

8

LEARNING OUTCOMES**LEARNING OUTCOMES**

After completing this chapter you should be able to:

► explain the processes involved in making long-term decisions;

► apply the principles of relevant cash flow analysis to long-run projects that continue for several years;

► calculate project cash flows, accounting for tax and inflation, and apply perpetuities to derive 'end of project' value where appropriate;

► apply activity-based costing techniques to derive approximate 'long-run' product or service costs appropriate for use in strategic decision-making;

► explain the financial consequences of dealing with long-run projects, in particular the importance of accounting for the 'time value of money';

► apply sensitivity analysis to cash flow parameters to identify those to which net present value is particularly sensitive;

► prepare decision-support information for management, integrating financial and non-financial considerations;

► evaluate project proposals using the techniques of investment appraisal;

► compare, contrast the alternative techniques of investment appraisal;

► prioritise projects that are mutually exclusive, involve unequal lives and/or are subject to capital rationing.

8.1 Introduction

In this chapter we will explore technique used in support of long-term decision-making. Long-term decision-making involves appraising proposed investments the costs and benefits of which are typically spread over a number of years. Such appraisal may involve determining whether a proposed investment is viable on a 'go or no-go' basis. Alternatively, it may involve ranking alternative investments to determine which is most attractive. The practice of investment appraisal will normally require the measurement of project performance using one or more of a number of possible metrics.

The future outcome of a proposed investment may be subject to variety of uncertainties. The viability and ranking of a project may therefore depend not only on its expected return but also on the degree of risk associated with that return. This raises issues relevant to the risk-reward trade off explored earlier in this text.

The practices described above are collectively described as 'capital budgeting'.

> 🔑 '*Capital budgeting*: Process concerned with decision-making in respect of the choice specific investment projects and the total amount of capital expenditure to commit.'

8.2 Approaches to capital budgeting and project appraisal

8.2.1 Basic concepts

This chapter deals with the various techniques of investment appraisal used in capital budgeting decisions.

Capital budgeting addresses two problems:

- How much should be spent on projects/assets?
- Which projects should be undertaken and which assets should be acquired?

This includes decisions on whether to:

- Invest in a new product line
- Acquire new premises or plant
- Enter a new market
- Undertake research and development
- Launch an advertising campaign
- Launch a new product
- In the case of the public sector – build a new school, new hospital or new road.

It is important to make sound capital budgeting decisions because:

- The decisions often involve large amounts of money.
- The commitment may be for a long period of time.
- It may not be easy to reverse a decision once implemented.
- Once a project is undertaken it may preclude other strategic choices being made.

The techniques discussed in this chapter are methods used to assess the *financial merits* of particular investments but there are other aspects to consider before making an investment decision. These include:

- The identification of all possible options/projects.
- The strategic direction of the organisation and whether the project under consideration will complement this.
- Whether the organisation has the skills to implement the project successfully.
- What will happen if the project is rejected – will the organisation be able to maintain its present status *vis-à-vis* its competitors, etc., without new investments? (Profitability will not be maintained over the years without new investment.)

The financial analysis of investment decisions must be seen as being only one part of the overall strategic analysis and this should be borne in mind throughout this chapter.

8.2.2 Relevant costs

A further consideration is that cost information must be incorporated in the appraisal of an investment. This may involve an understanding of the behaviour of the various costs incurred by a business. We have seen earlier in this text that the behaviour of some costs may be complex and not linked directly to output volume. Determining the cost impact of a particular course of action may therefore best be carried out using activity-based costing (ABC).

ABC seeks to offer an attribution of costs to products and services using an analysis of activities and cost drivers.

The relevant observation for current purposes concerning ABC is that traditional costing systems treat many categories of cost as being 'fixed' in the sense that they do not vary directly with output volume. However, ABC generally proceeds on the assumption that most costs are variable in the longer term if one understands the activities that they vary with. This understanding is particularly relevant when one is appraising a long-term investment.

Earlier in this text, we encountered the concept of whether or not a cost is 'relevant' to a given decision. We noted that many categories of cost such as sunk costs, committed costs and non-cash flow items such as depreciation are not normally relevant to a particular decision. We also noted that some categories of cost such as opportunity cost are relevant to a decision even though they are not directly attributable to the products or services being considered.

This concept of relevance is applicable to the kind of project appraisal that we are now considering. The merits of a proposed project are determined only by those costs and benefits (usually expressed in financial terms) that are relevant to it. Costs and benefits that do not depend on the outcome of a project are not relevant ones and are not normally incorporated in the project appraisal.

8.2.3 The different appraisal methods

The main evaluation methods are:

- Net present value (NPV)
- Payback (PB)
- Discounted payback (DPB)
- Internal rate of return (IRR)
- Accounting rate of return (ARR).

Each of these evaluation techniques will be discussed in turn. It is important to realise that the evaluation techniques are not mutually exclusive and most organisations today use more than one method. The most popular method used by organisations is payback; almost all organisations use it but the majority of firms now also use either net present value and/or internal rate of return. By using these methods in conjunction with payback they are able to bring into consideration several different aspects of the investment decision.

8.2.4 Processes involved

The emphasis in this chapter is on the means by which projects and options can be researched, evaluated and ranked. These means are essentially financial, using mathematical analysis of the forecast costs and benefits associated with proposed projects. This is capital budgeting. However, it should be appreciated that the merits of a project may also depend on factors which involve costs and benefits which cannot be expressed in immediate financial terms, such as:

- developing market share;
- promoting brand and company image;
- gaining expertise in a new technology.

It should be noted that the process by which an organisation identifies possible projects and options is essentially strategic. Strategic models incorporate issues relating to which sectors the organisation should operate in, what its objectives are and what measures might be taken to achieve those objectives. Organisational strategy will be explored fully in the later stages of your CIMA studies.

8.2.5 Net present value (NPV)

Shareholder value will be maximised by accepting those projects that offer a positive NPV and rejecting all others, under the normally assumed (but incorrect) investment conditions of perfect information, perfect capital markets and no risk. The other evaluation techniques do not necessarily produce results that maximise shareholder value, despite being widely used.

The NPV technique recognises that cash received in the future is less valuable than cash received today. This is because of the time value of money. If, for example, you inherited £10,000 today and did not wish to spend it immediately you might deposit the money in a bank or building society. By the end of the first year it would be worth more than £10,000. If the interest rate was 5 per cent, it would be worth £10,500.

The formula for this calculation is:

£1 invested today at 5% in 1 year's time is worth £1 + 0.05 = 1.05
£1 invested today at 5% in 2 year's time is worth $£(1 + 0.05)^2 = £1.103$
£1 invested today at 5% in 3 year's time is worth $£(1 + 0.05)^3 = £1.158$

This is compound interest and expresses what a £ invested today is worth at a particular moment in the future.

The management of an organisation do not wish to know this when making investment decisions. Instead they want to know what a £ received in the future is worth in terms of today's values. This is what NPV calculations do. The formula is:

£1 receivable in 1 year's time at 5% is worth $\dfrac{£1}{1.05} = £0.952$ today

£1 receivable in 2 year's time at 5% is worth $\dfrac{£1}{(1.05)^2} = £0.909$ today

£1 receivable in 3 year's time at 5% is worth $\dfrac{£1}{(1.05)^3} = £0.864$ today

The figures 0.952, 0.907 and 0.864 represent the present value of £1 received in 1, 2 and 3 years, respectively, at a cost of capital of 5 per cent. These figures are also known as discount factors.

If the present value of the future cash inflows exceeds that of the outflows, a positive NPV will result and the project should be accepted. If it does not, the NPV is negative and the project should be rejected.

The mathematical formula for calculating the discount factor is:

$$\text{Discount factor} = \frac{1}{(1+r)^n}$$

where r is the discount rate/opportunity cost of capital and n is the number of the time period.

The discount factors can also be obtained from tables, which are included at the end of this *Study System*. These tables will be supplied in the examinations.

Figure 8.1 gives information on four projects and Figure 8.2 uses the NPV technique to assess them. The layout is the generally accepted one and should always be used. It is important to remember that Year 0 is a day – the first day of the project. Year 1 is the last day of the first year and Year 2 is the last day of the second year, etc. It is generally assumed that all cash inflows received during a year are received on the last day of the year, even if in reality they are received earlier or throughout the year. It is possible in practice to use monthly or quarterly discount rates if this assumption could distort the result, but this is only done very rarely and will not be required in the examination. The discount rate is usually assumed to be the organisation's cost of finance also known as the cost of capital. Further discussion and calculation of this is beyond the scope of this syllabus.

		Project		
Cash flows	A	B	C	D
Year	£	£	£	£
0	(2,000)	(2,000)	(1,000)	(1,000)
1	1,000	20	640	0
2	1,000	20	640	0
3	50	1,600	20	0
4	50	1,600	20	1,800

Figure 8.1 Cash flows for projects A, B, C and D

Year	Discount factor 5%	A £		B £	C £	D £
0	1	(2,000)		(2,000)	(1,000)	(1,000)
1	0.952	952	(1,000 × 0.952)	19	609	0
2	0.907	907	(1,000 × 0.907)	18	580	0
3	0.864	43	(50 × 0.864)	1,382	17	0
4	0.823	41	(50 × 0.823)	1,317	16	1,481
	NPV? =	(57)		736	222	481

Figure 8.2 NPV calculations for projects A, B, C and D

Project A has a negative NPV and should be rejected because it provides a return that is less than the cost of capital, 5 per cent. But projects B, C and D show positive NPVs and they should all be accepted if the organisation has adequate funds.

Exercise: calculating the NPV without using present value tables

You might come across an examination question which requires you to calculate the NPV using a discount rate which does not feature on the present value table.

To deal with this you will need to calculate your own discount factors using the formula given earlier. To get some practise at doing this, try calculating the NPV for project B in the last example, using a cost of capital of 7.5 per cent.

 # Solution

Year		Discount factor	Cash flow £	Present value £
0		1.000	(2,000)	(2,000)
1	$1/(1 + 0.075)^1$	0.930	20	19
2	$1/(1 + 0.075)^2$	0.865	20	17
3	$1/(1 + 0.075)^3$	0.805	1,600	1,288
4	$1/(1 + 0.075)^4$	0.749	1,600	1,198
NPV =				522

Limitations of the NPV method

Although the NPV method provides managers with a simple decision rule: accept projects with a positive NPV, it does suffer from a number of disadvantages.

- The speed of repayment of the original investment is not highlighted.
- The cash flow figures are estimates and may turn out to be incorrect.
- Non-financial managers may have difficulty understanding the concept.
- Determination of the correct discount rate can be difficult.

Some of these limitations are not present in the payback method and as we have seen many organisations combine an assessment of the payback period with discounted cash flow in their appraisal.

8.2.6 Payback (PB)

Payback offers a different view of the investment decision and to some extent copes with an uncertain future by concentrating on early cash inflows. Payback is simply the time it takes for the cash inflows from a project to equal the cash outflows so that the project has paid back its initial investment. The payback period for the four projects is given in Figure 8.3 where the payback year is underlined.

Project	Initial outlay £	Year 1 £	Cumulative cash flows Year 2 £	Year 3 £	Year 4 £	Payback
A	2,000	1,000	2,000	2,050	2,100	2 years
B	2,000	20	40	1,640	3,240	4 years
C	1,000	640	1,280	1,300	1,320	2 years
D	1,000	0	0	0	1,800	4 years

Figure 8.3 Payback calculations for projects A, B, C and D

If you look carefully at the data you will see that, whereas project A pays back in exactly 2 years, project C would actually achieve payback some time during year 2, if we can ignore the end-of-year assumption concerning cash flows.

Occasionally, the payback period might be calculated assuming that cash flows occur evenly throughout the year. In this case the payback period for project C would be calculated as follows:

$$\text{Payback period for project C} = 1 \text{ year} + \frac{£(1,000-640)}{£640}$$
$$= 1.6 \text{ years}$$

Similarly, the payback period for project B would be 3.2 years, and project D would be 3.6 years.

$$\text{Payback period for project B} = 3 \text{ year} + \frac{£(2,000-1,640)}{£1,600}$$
$$= 3.2 \text{ years}$$
$$\text{Payback period for project D} = 3 \text{ year} + \frac{£1,000}{£1,800}$$
$$= 3.6 \text{ years}$$

However, the assumption of even cash flows during the year may be somewhat inaccurate; therefore the payback periods stated in Figure 8.3 are likely to be expressed with sufficient precision.

Management usually specifies a standard payback time for all investment decisions; this is normally quite short, say, 3 years. If the project pays back within this period it will be accepted, otherwise it will be rejected. If the project is not rejected on the payback criterion it is likely to be subjected to further analysis, probably using discounting techniques, before it is finally accepted.

In the previous example, assuming that the required payback is three years, projects A and C would be accepted, but using the NPV method projects B, C and D would be accepted. If the management judge projects by requiring them to meet both payback and NPV criteria, only project C would be accepted. This may seem to be prudent but it must be remembered that if no investments are made the organisation will decline relative to its competitors, as it will not be able to maintain its profitability in the long term. So care must be taken to make sure that the two hurdles, the discount rate and the payback period, are realistic ones and not overstated – the cost of capital must not be set unrealistically high or the payback period too short.

The advantages of using payback are as follows:

- It is the simplest evaluation method and is very easy to understand.
- It keeps organisations liquid by favouring projects with early cash inflows. NPV, of course, also does this by discounting, but not to such an extent. An organisation that is liquid tends to remain in business. The cash released by early inflows can also be re-invested in other profitable projects sooner.
- It helps to eliminate time risk. Using NPV an organisation might accept a long-term project with, perhaps, a 10-year payback. If predictions of market and costs beyond say, year 3 prove wrong, as they might well in an uncertain world, the project could in fact have a high negative NPV and even bring about corporate failure. Payback minimises this by selecting projects that recover their costs quickly.

However, academics criticise payback because:

- No weighting is given to the timing of the cash inflows, that is, an inflow received in year 2 is considered the same in terms of value as an inflow in year 1. In the example, the £1,000 received in year 2 in project A is accorded the same value as the £1,000 received in Year 1.
- Cash flows received after the cut-off point are ignored. This is the reason why projects B and D have been rejected.

The first criticism can easily be remedied by discounting the cash flows, thus creating discounted payback as described below. The second criticism, while true, is rather unnecessary as it is the counter to the key strengths of the payback technique which are the second and third advantages given above. The criticism can be overcome, however, by using a discounted payback index.

8.2.7 Discounted payback (DPB)

Discounted payback is simply the payback cash flows discounted by the cost of capital. Inspection of Figure 8.2 above reveals the DPBs for each of the four projects shown in Figure 8.4.

Project	Initial outlay £	Year 1 £	Year 2 £	Year 3 £	Year 4 £	Payback
		Cumulative discounted cash flows				
A	2,000	952	1,859	1,902	1,943	No payback
B	2,000	19	37	1,419	2,736	4 years
C	1,000	609	1,189	1,206	1,222	2 years
D	1,000	0	0	0	1,481	4 years

Figure 8.4 DPB calculations for projects A, B, C and D

Until very recently, most research did not differentiate between PB and DPB. But recent studies suggest that a significant proportion of manufacturing companies use DPB and many consider it the most 'important' investment appraisal method they use.

It has been argued by some that the DPB approach is just a truncated version of NPV, but this is not necessarily true. In practice the discount rates often differ. The discount rate used by companies in NPV calculations is often adjusted to take account of project risk and uncertainty and so the rate will be higher (this is dealt with later), whereas the discount rate used in DPB is the unadjusted cost of capital, as the decision-maker's function is to judge the payback period of the project against that required to deal with the uncertainty.

If DPB is used, the projects chosen will be those that maximise shareholder value modified by the payback so that the organisation remains liquid and flexible. By combining these two techniques management should be able to make the best possible decisions with the available information.

8.2.8 Profitability index (PI) or Discounted payback index (DPBI)

One of the questions that decision-makers often ask, apart from how quickly does the project pay for itself, is how many times does it recover the funds invested. This is particularly important if funds are scarce.

The PI provides one measure of this as follows:

$$PI = \frac{\text{Present value of net cash inflows}}{\text{Initial cash outlay}}$$

The PIs for the previous examples are calculated in Figure 8.5.

	A	B	C	D
Present value of net cash inflows (£)	1,943	2,736	1,222	1,481
Initial outlay (£)	2,000	2,000	1,000	1,000
DPBI	0.97	1.37	1.22	1.48

Figure 8.5 DPBI calculations for projects A, B, C and D

The higher the figure for PI, the greater the return. A figure for PI below 1.0 indicates, as in the case of project A, that the net cash inflows are lower than the initial cash outlay.

You might come across the index expressed in a slightly different way, in which case it might be referred to as the profitability index:

$$\text{Discounted payback index (DPBI)} = \frac{\text{Net present value of project}}{\text{Initial outlay}}$$

This index would be calculated as in Figure 8.6.

	A	B	C	D
Net present value (£)	(57)	736	222	481
Initial outlay (£)	2,000	2,000	1,000	1,000
Profitability index	–	0.37	0.22	0.48

Figure 8.6 PB calculations for projects A, B, C and D

This index provides similar information, but it shows the net present value per £1 invested in a project. The DPBI measure can be more meaningful than the simple + or − result presented by an NPV calculation, particularly, as stated earlier, if funds for investment are limited.

8.2.9 Internal rate of return (IRR)

The IRR is a variation of the NPV method. One of the main problems with using the NPV method is deciding on the correct discount rate. Judging the correct discount rate is not easy as it depends on interest rates, inflation, etc., and these factors can vary considerably from year to year, making it difficult to decide in year 0 what the correct discount rate to use in year 4 may be. IRR avoids this difficulty by not specifying a rate in advance.

IRR is the discount rate at which the sum of the discounted cash inflows equals the discounted cash outflow(s), so that the NPV is zero.

The IRR can be determined by trial and error. In the following example (Figure 8.7) for project C the trial discount rates used are 5 and 25 per cent.

Year	Cash flow £	Discount rate 5%	Discounted cash flow £	Discount rate 25%	Discounted cash flow £
0	(1,000)	1.000	(1,000)	1.000	(1,000)
1	640	0.952	609	0.800	512
2	640	0.907	580	0.640	410
3	20	0.864	17	0.512	10
4	20	0.823	16	0.410	8
			222		(60)

Figure 8.7   NPVs for project C for IRR calculations

The relationship between discount rate and NPV in this case may be represented graphically as follows:

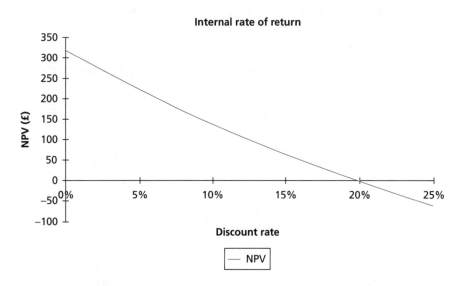

It can be seen that the IRR is near 20%. You can use a spreadsheet model to calculate an exact figure. It is actually 19.91%.

An approximation of the IRR can be calculated using interpolation or extrapolation from the figures that are available. In this case we have already calculated the NPV at reference point discount rates of 5% (222) and 25% (−60). If we assume that the function on the above chart is a straight line then it follows that each 1% rise in discount rate gives a 14.1 reduction in NPV (that is 282/20). It follows from this that a 15.74% rise in discount rate above 5% (that is 222/14.1) is required to reduce the NPV to zero. It follows from this that the estimated IRR is 20.74%. Since the IRR lies between the two reference points this exercise is described as interpolation.

A slight variation on this approach is extrapolation. Let us say we adopt 15% as one of our reference points instead of 25%. The NPV at 15% is 65. So, it follows that a 1% rise in discount rate gives a 15.70 reduction in NPV (that is 157/10). This indicates an estimated IRR of 19.14%. Since the IRR lies outside the two reference points this exercise is known as extrapolation.

Neither interpolation nor extrapolation give perfect results in this case – because they both assume that the NPV function is a straight line, whereas it is actually a slight curve. Consideration of the graph indicates that interpolation will normally overestimate the IRR while extrapolation will normally underestimate it. The degree of accuracy offered by both extrapolation and interpolation depends on how close the reference points are to the actual IRR.

The ERR of project C would then be compared to the organisation's cost of capital and accepted if the IRR was greater. This will always lead to the selection of an identical set of projects as the NPV method.

8.2.10 Mutually exclusive projects

Often, however, an organisation has to choose between projects rather than just selecting all those that meet the required hurdle rate. This will occur when the organisation's choice is limited for financial reasons or where there are different investment options within the same overall project.

Examples of the latter are: whether to build a hotel or a block of flats on a piece of land, or which of two types of manufacturing machinery to purchase for a new product. When making this type of decision, the decision-maker should be very wary of using ERR.

To illustrate this, suppose projects B and CC, whose cash flows are given in Figure 8.8, are mutually exclusive, that is, the decision-maker can only choose one of them. Figure 8.9 gives the ERR and two NPVs for the two projects. Use the cash flows from Figure 8.8 to check these for yourself.

Year	B	CC
	£	£
0	(2,000)	(2,000)
1	20	1,280
2	20	1,280
3	1,600	40
4	1,600	40

Figure 8.8 Cash flows for projects B and CC

	B	CC
IRR	15%	20%
NPV at 5%	£726	£448
NPV at 16%	£(59)	£102

Figure 8.9 IRRs and NPVs for projects B and CC

The NPV and ERR contradict one another if a discount rate of 5 per cent is used, but agree if a discount rate of 16 per cent is used. Only by using NPV will the organisation always make decisions that maximise shareholder value. The reason the two methods do not always agree is due to the timing of the cash inflows between the two projects. The cash inflows are relatively greater for project B, but because they come in the later years they are not so valuable if a high cost of capital is used. This can be seen when the 16 per cent discount rate is used. The graph in Figure 8.10 shows that the preference between the two projects changes between 11 per cent and 12 per cent. If the cost of capital is below 11 per cent B is better, if it is more than 12 per cent CC is preferred, until the NPV becomes negative at 20 per cent.

The general decision rule in DCF analysis is that where mutually exclusive projects are being considered, the one with the highest NPV is preferred. However, some caution should be exercised in the use of this rule. Our earlier exploration of attitude to risk indicated that a low-risk project with a lower expected NPV may be preferred to a high risk project with a higher NPV.

IRR is normally reported as part of a project appraisal. However, since it is a relative measure which lacks an element of scale it is not normally the deciding factor in selecting

PROJECT APPRAISAL

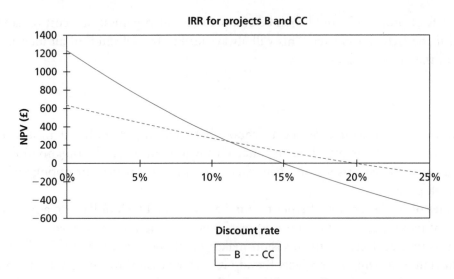

Figure 8.10 Net present values of Projects B and CC

between alternatives. A large project with a high NPV will normally be preferred to a small project with a lower NPV but a higher IRR. A tiny project can have a very high IRR. But IRR can still be informative since it offers insights into the return that alternative uses for capital offer and this can be a guide to future strategy and decision-making.

8.2.11 Multiple IRRs

A single figure for IRR will result only when the cash flows follow the normal pattern of an initial outflow followed by a series of inflows over the years. Where the cash flow signs change between positive and negative a number of times over the years, it is likely that a number of real solutions may exist. This is illustrated in the following example.

M is contemplating building a prototype machine, the cost of which will be paid for in two stages. Income can be expected from its demonstration. The machine will be expensive to break up and dispose of at the end of its life. The predicted cash flows are given in Figure 8.11, and Figure 8.12 shows the calculations at discount rates of 6 and 30 per cent, both of which give a NPV close to zero.

Year	Cash flow £
0	(3,910)
1	(10,000)
2	40,000
3	(26,510)

Figure 8.11 Predicted cash flows for project M

Year	Cashflow £	Discount rate 6%	NPV £	Discount rate 30%	NPV £
0	(3,910)	1.000	(3,910)	1.000	(3,910)
1	(10,000)	0.943	(9,434)	0.769	(7,692)
2	40,000	0.890	35,600	0.592	23,668
3	(26,510)	0.840	(22,258)	0.455	(12,067)
		NPV	(2)		(1)

Figure 8.12 NPVs for project M for use in IRR calculation

As both IRRs are equally valid, the decision whether or not to accept the project needs to be made using NPV. As seen in Figure 8.13, the discount rates between 6 and 30 per cent give positive NPVs and so if the organisation's cost of capital is in this range, the project should be accepted.

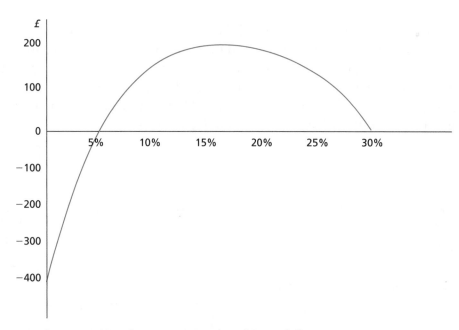

Figure 8.13 The net present value of the cash flows given in Figure 8.11

While projects with multiple sign changes are rare, care should also be taken if two projects are being compared, and if rather than discounting the cash flows of two projects separately one project is deducted from the other to give a single stream of cash flows prior to discounting. This method is likely to produce cash flows whose signs change from year to year and this can again give multiple IRRs.

Given the problems with the use of IRR, you may wonder why it is such a popular technique. Explanations for its popularity are:

● Users are familiar with using percentage rates, such as return on capital (ROC), mortgage rates, bank rates, etc. The yield of an investment is directly comparable to these and is easier to understand as a consequence.
● It avoids specifying a discount rate in advance. It can be a difficult matter predicting the cost of capital some years into the future.

8.2.12 Accounting rate of return (ARR)

This method is not recommended because it can produce incorrect results, but as it is still quite widely used in practice, it is discussed here. The ARR is the project's return on investment or ROI, but in this context it is known as the accounting rate of return. The ARR will tend to vary from year to year over the life of the project. This is because the cash inflows change, affecting profit, and the capital/investment gradually decreases as the assets are depreciated.

Annual ARRs/ROIs are not usually calculated; instead the average annual profit is normally expressed as a percentage of the average, or mid-point, investment:

$$\text{ARR} = \frac{\text{Average annual profit from the project}}{\text{Average investment}} \times 100$$

It is the only investment appraisal method that uses annual profit rather than annual net cash flow, and so depreciation must be deducted from annual net cash inflow to arrive at a figure that approximates to profit. If the initial investment has a residual or sales value at the end of the project's life this must be brought into the calculation of the average investment figure.

Using the previous data for projects A, B, C and D given in Figure 8.1, and making the following assumptions, the ARRs are as shown in Figure 8.14.

	A £	B £	C £	D £
Total cash inflow (A = 1000 + 1000 + 50 + 50)	2,100	3,240	1,320	1,800
Less depreciation	2,000	2,000	1,000	1,000
Accounting profit	100	1,240	320	800
Project life – years	4	4	4	4
Ave. accounting profit	25	310	80	200
Ave. investment (mid-point figure)	1,000	1,000	500	500
ARR	$\frac{25}{1,000} \times 100$	$\frac{310}{1,000} \times 100$	$\frac{80}{500} \times 100$	$\frac{200}{500} \times 100$
	2.5%	31%	16%	40%

Note: if the assets in project A had a disposal value at the end of Year 4 of, say, £500, the average investment would be:

$$\frac{£2,000 + £500}{2} = £1,250$$

Figure 8.14 ARR calculations for projects, A, B, C and D

Assumptions

- The initial outflow in year 0 represents the purchase of a fixed asset.
- Depreciation is the only difference between cash flow and profit.
- The asset will be depreciated to zero value over the life of the project.

Figure 8.13 shows that project D is the best project in terms of return but this must be compared with the organisation's required rate of return. If the required rate is the same as the rate used in the earlier NPV calculation, that is, 5 per cent, only A would be rejected and both methods would give the same results. But this is not always the case. If, on the other hand, the required rate of return was 16 per cent, the ARR would select projects B and D as being acceptable. The results of using a discount rate of 16 per cent in a NPV calculation are shown in Figure 8.15.

This shows that only project C would be accepted with a discount rate of 16 per cent. (From the previous ERR calculations it is known that project C has an IRR of about 20 per cent.)

This difference between ARR and NPV is of concern because managers are often judged by the return on capital of their division or business unit. They will only wish to invest in projects that increase the ROI of their division and at times this will clash with good decision-making which requires the use of NPV.

Year	Discount factor 16%	A £	B £	C £	D £
0	1.000	(2,000)	(2,000)	(1,000)	(1,000)
1	0.862	862	17	552	0
2	0.743	743	15	476	0
3	0.641	32	1,025	13	0
4	0.552	28	884	11	994
	NPV =	(335)	(59)	52	(6)

Figure 8.15 NPV calculations at 16% for projects A, B, C and D

On the other hand, ARR is still used by companies to assess projects – why is this if it can give misleading results? It may be due to:

- a familiarity with the use of profit as a measure;
- the desire to maintain a strong balance sheet – if this is so a project like D which is perfectly acceptable on a NPV basis would not be considered;
- the fact that it ties in with city analysis of the ROCE of the firm as a whole.

8.2.13 Example comparing ARR and NPV

Example

It is 2 January 20X1 and the management of G Ltd, a subsidiary of GER Group, has estimated the following results for the coming year ending 31 December 20X1:

	£000
Profit before depreciation	500
Fixed assets:	
Original cost	1,500
Accumulated depn at yr end	720
Net current assets (average for yr)	375

GER group assesses new projects using discounted cash flow and a cost of capital of 15 per cent. But it assesses the performance of its subsidiaries and their managers using ROI, based on the following:

(i) *Profit:* Depreciation of fixed assets is calculated on a straight-line basis on a presumed life of 5 years. Profit/loss on sale is included in the profit for the year.
(ii) *Capital employed:* Fixed assets are valued at original cost less depreciation as at the end of the year. Net current assets are valued at the average value for the year.

In addition to the normal transactions the management of G Ltd is considering submitting the following proposals to GER:

(i) At the start of the year it could sell for £35,000 a fixed asset which originally cost £300,000 and which has been depreciated by 4/5 of its expected life. If it is not sold the asset will generate a profit before depreciation of £45,000 which has been included in the current estimates for the coming year.
(ii) At the start of the year it could buy for £180,000 plant that would achieve reductions of £57,000 per annum in production costs. The plant would have a life of 5 years after which it would have no resale value.

Requirement

Evaluate the two proposals from the point of view of: (a) G Ltd's chief executive officer (CEO), and (b) GER group's chief accountant.

Solution

G Ltd's CEO will be interested in the ROI/ARR as the subsidiary's performance is judged on that basis, while GER's accountant will be concerned about the NPV for sound investment purposes.

Profit less depreciation £500,000 − (£1,500,000 × 1/5) = £200,000
Capital employed = £1,500,000 − £720,000 + £375,000 = £1,155,000

$$\text{Current expected ROI} = \frac{£200,000}{£1,155,000} \times 100\% = 17.3\%$$

(i) (a)

The current book value of the asset = £300,000 − (4 × £60,000) = £60,000
Loss on sale = £60,000 − £35,000 = £25,000
Depreciation for the coming year (part of the overall annual depreciation change of £300,000) = £60,000

To calculate the new ROI:

Revised profit = original profit + depreciation added back − loss on sale − profit forgone
Revised capital = original capital − book value of asset

$$\text{Revised ROI} = \frac{£(200,000 - 60,0000 - 25,000 - 45,000)}{£(1,155,500 - 60,000)} = 100\%$$
$$= 17.35\%$$

This ROI is marginally better than the current expected one and so the asset should be sold from the CEO of G Ltd's point of view.

(i) (b)

Using NPV

	Cash flow £	15% factor	Present value £
Year 0	35,000	1.000	35,000
Year 1	(45,000)	0.870	(39,100)
Net present value			(4,100)

This shows a negative NPV and so the asset should be retained.

(ii) (a)

$$\text{Revised ROI} = \frac{£(200,000 - 36,000 \text{ depreciation} + 57,000)}{£(1,55,000 + 1,44,000 \text{ year end net book value})} \times 100\%$$
$$= 17.01\%$$

As this is lower than the current expected ROI the new asset should not be purchased from the CEO of G Ltd's point of view.

(ii) (b)

	Cash flow £	15% factor	Present value £
Year 0	(180,000)	1.000	(180,000)
Years 1–5	57,000	3.352*	191,064
			11,064

*Note that, instead of multiplying 57,000 separately by each of the discount factors for years 1-5, we have used the cumulative total of the five discount factors. We will return to look of this in more detail in the next section.

As this is a positive NPV the asset should be purchased.

For the two projects in question the two methods give different answers. This will not always be the case but if a manager's performance is measured in terms of ROI the manager will assess all projects using ARR. If projects need a positive NPV in order to be accepted by head office the manager will only put forward proposals that give an increased ROI and a positive NPV. This will exclude some acceptable projects with positive NPVs but which have unacceptable ROI/ARRs.

8.2.14 Summary of the four investment appraisal methods

- The techniques which do not use discounting, that is straightforward payback and ARR, are still widely used in practice despite being theoretically inconsistent with the objective of maximising shareholder value.
- DPB is a widely used technique.
- IRR does not always select the best project where a choice has to be made between projects. This usually happens when the projects' IRR are many percentage points away from the organisation's cost of capital.
- Where cash flow signs change from year to year the IRR cannot be relied upon to give the correct answer.
- NPV is the only technique to always give a result that will maximise shareholder value.
- NPV is not used universally. For example, Japanese companies usually rely on payback techniques.

One final point should be made at this stage. DCF analysis (and related technique) is based on cash flow. When preparing the cash flow profile of a project, the impact of working capital should always be considered. For example, if £100 sales are made evenly over year 1 on 'cash terms' then it is conventional to class those sales as giving rise to a cash inflow at year 1 in the DCF analysis. However, if those sales are made on 6 months credit terms, then they will only give rise to a £50 cash inflow in year 1. £50 debtors will be outstanding at end year 1, giving rise to a £50 cash inflow in year 2.

We have already explored relevant technique for preparing cash budgets earlier in this text.

8.3 Other aspects of NPV analysis

8.3.1 Using the annuity rate

This is just a calculation short cut. It can be very time consuming to calculate the NPV of a project by hand if the project runs for a number of years. If the project has the same cash inflow every year, as many do, rather than discounting each year separately the annuity rate can be used. The annuity rate is the sum of the discount rates; see Figure 8.16.

These tables are given in the back of this *Study System*.

Year	Discount rate – 5%	Annuity 5%
1	0.952	0.952
2	0.907	1.859
3	0.864	2.723
4	0.823	3.546

Figure 8.16 Discount and annuity rates at 5%

For a project with an outflow of £30,000 in year 0 and inflows of £20,000 in years 1 and 2 the calculation of net present value is shown in Figure 8.17.

	Cash flow	Annuity	Net present value
	£	5%	£
Year 0	(30,000)	1	(30,000)
Years 1–2	20,000	1.859	37,180
			7,180

Figure 8.17 NPV at 5%

8.3.2 Unequal lives

Two mutually exclusive projects with different life spans cannot be compared adequately without making an adjustment for the difference in their lives. Projects X and Y are two such projects; their cash flows are given in Figure 8.18.

Year	X	Y
	£	£
0	(30,000)	(30,000)
1	20,000	37,500
2	20,000	

Figure 8.18 Cash flows for projects X and Y

In order to cope with this problem the projects' cash flows must be repeated for enough years until both projects finish in the same year. For example, if one project has a life of 4 years and the other a life of 3 years, year 12 would be the first time the projects both finish together. So the cash flows for the first would be repeated three times and for the second four times and the discounted cash flow would be carried out over 12 years. Projects X and Y fortunately have simpler cash flows and Y needs only to be repeated once as shown in Figure 8.19.

Year	X	Y
	£	£
0	(30,000)	(30,000)
1	20,000	37,500 + (30,000)
2	20,000	37,500

Figure 8.19 Comparative flows over two years for projects X and Y

These cash flows can now be discounted and the NPVs will be comparable. However, this method is rather time-consuming and a simpler method exists. It is to discount the projects once only and to divide the NPV by the annuity rate, that is the sum of the discount rates over the life of the project. This produces an average annual figure, known as an annualised equivalent, that allows the project returns to be compared fairly. This is done in Figure 8.20.

Figure 8.20 shows that project Y is the better investment when the difference in lives is removed.

It is not possible to stipulate that mutually exclusive investments should always be considered over the same period of time. Each case must be judged on its merits. The choice depends on the degree of freedom of action the organisation has when the shorter-lived project ends. If the organisation is forced to reinvest in similar assets at this point the projects should be compared over equal time periods. This situation will arise if the

Year	Discount rate 5%	NPV X £	NPV Y £
0	1	(30,000)	(30,000)
1	0.952	19,040	35,700
2	0.907	18,140	
	1.859	7,180	5,700
		÷	÷
		1.859	0.952
		=	=
Annualised equivalent =		£3,862	£5,987

Figure 8.20 Annual equivalents for X and Y

assets are manufacturing equipment and the organisation knows that the product will be made for many years ahead – longer than the life of the assets. Another example of this is when an organisation chooses between different types and sizes of vehicles for product distribution.

On the other hand, if the organisation is not going to invest in similar assets when the assets' productive lives end, the method described above should not be used. An example of this is if the two projects are marketing strategies for the launch of a novelty product. Under these circumstances it clearly makes no sense to repeat the cash flows as the product can only be launched once.

8.3.3 Asset replacement cycles

This is when a company has to make a decision to replace assets. The decision involves what to replace the asset with and when to replace.

If we are replacing assets we may be replacing them with a choice of more than one other asset, these assets may have different lifespans and therefore using NPV will not necessarily give us the right answer. To overcome this problem we have two methods available to us:

1. Lowest Common Multiple Method
2. Annualised Equivalent

Lowest common multiple method

This is where we find the smallest number, which we can divide into by each of a set of numbers. For example, if we have two projects, one with a life of 2 years and one with a life of 3 years the common multiple is 6 years. We then calculate the NPV of the two options over 6 years and compare the results.

Annualised equivalent

This is where the NPV is calculated and converted into an annual equivalent cost to allow comparisons of cost year on year.

Steps:

1. Calculate the NPV of the asset costs.
2. Based on the cost of capital and life of the assets find the cumulative discount factor from the cumulative discount tables.

3. Divide the NPV by the cumulative discount factor to find the annual equivalent cost for each asset.
4. Make your selection based on the least amount of annual cost.

Example

C Ltd. is considering replacing an asset with one of two possible machines.

Machine X	–	Initial Cost	£120,000
		Life	3 years
		Running Cost	£20,000 per annum
Machine Y	–	Initial Cost	£60,000
		Life	2 years
		Running Cost	£35,000 per annum
Cost of capital is 10%			

Requirements

(a) Calculate the NPV of each machine and on this basis make a decision.
(b) Considering the different lifespans of the machines, determine which machine should be purchased using:
   (i) Lowest Common Multiple Method
   (ii) Equivalent Annual Cost Method

Solution

(a)

NPV – Machine X

Years	Description	Cash flow	Discount factor		Present value
0	Outlay	£120,000	1.00		£120,000
1–3	Running Cost	£20,000	2.487		£49,740
				NPV	£169,740

NPV – Machine Y

Years	Description	Cash flow	Discount factor		Present value
0	Outlay	£60,000	1.00		£60,000
1–2	Running Cost	£35,000	1.736		£60,760
				NPV	£120,760

On the basis of the NPV calculation Machine Y should be selected as it has the lowest NPV cost.

(b)

(i) **Lowest common multiple method**
The lowest common multiple is 6 years and therefore each machine is evaluated on this timescale.

NPV – Machine X

Years	Description	Cash flow	Discount factor		Present value
0	Outlay	£120,000	1.00		£120,000
1–3	Running Cost	£20,000	2.487		£49,740
3	Replace	£120,000	0.751		£90,120
4–6	Running Cost	£20,000	1.868		£37,360
				NPV	£297,220

NPV – Machine Y

Years	Description	Cash flow	Discount factor		Present value
0	Outlay	£60,000	1.00		£60,000
1–2	Running Cost	£35,000	1.736		£60,760
2	Replace	£60,000	0.826		£49,560
3–4	Running Cost	£35,000	1.434		£50,190
4	Replace	£60,000	0.683		£40,980
5–6	Running Cost	£35,000	1.185		£41,475
				NPV	£302,965

Machine X should be purchased as it is the least cost option.

(ii) **Equivalent annual cost method**

	Machine X	Machine Y
NPV (from a)	£169,740	£120,760
Cumulative discount factor	2.487	1.736
Annual equivalent Cost	£68,251	£69,562

Machine X should be purchased as it is the least cost option.

Note that both methods will give the same answer but the second method is much quicker than the first for simple cash flows. However, it cannot be used where inflation must be taken into account – see below.

When to replace

The concept of annualised equivalents can be used in determining the optimum replacement cycle for an asset. This decision involves how long to continue operating the existing asset before it is replaced with an identical one. As the asset gets older, it may become less efficient, its operating costs may increase and the resale value will reduce.

In deciding on the replacement cycle, each project must be tested. This is achieved by:

1. Calculating the present value of the total costs incurred if the asset is kept for 1, 2 or 3 years.
2. Calculating the annual equivalent cost for each replacement cycle.
3. The lowest annual equivalent cost will then be the replacement cycle selected.

Example

JP Ltd operates a delivery vehicle, which cost £20,000 and has a useful life of 3 years. JP Ltd has a cost of capital of 5 per cent. The details of the vehicle's cash operating costs for each year and the resale value at the end of each year are as follows.

	Year 1 £	Year 2 £	Year 3 £
Cash operating costs	9,000	10,500	11,900
End of year resale value	14,000	11,500	8,400

Requirement

Determine how frequently the vehicle should be replaced.

Solution

The first step is to calculate the present value of the total costs incurred if the vehicle is kept for 1, 2 or 3 years.

		Keep for 1 year		Keep for 2 years		Keep for 3 years	
Year	5% discount factor	Cash flow £	Present value £	Cash flow £	Present value £	Cash flow £	Present value £
0	1.000	(20,000)	(20,000)	(20,000)	(20,000)	(20,000)	(20,000)
1	0.952	5,000*	4,760	(9,000)	(8,568)	(9,000)	(8,568)
2	0.907			1,000	907	(10,500)	(9,524)
3	0.864					(3,500)	(3,024)
Total present value			(15,240)		(27,661)		(41,116)

*−9,000 + 14,000

These present value figures are not comparable because they relate to different time periods. To render them comparable they must be converted to average annual figures, or annualised equivalents, by dividing by the cumulative discount factors as before:

	Keep for 1 year	Keep for 2 years	Keep for 3 years
Total present value of cost	£15,240	£27,661	£41,116
Cumulative 5% factor	0.952	1.859	2.723
Annualised equivalent	£16,008	£14,880	£15,100

The lowest annualised equivalent cost occurs if the vehicle is kept for 2 years. Therefore, the optimum replacement cycle is to replace the vehicle every 2 years.

Inflation and asset replacement cycles

If you are given inflation in an asset replacement cycle question it is not appropriate to use the annualised cost method. You must take account of the inflation and its impact on the individual cash flows and follow the lowest common multiple method.

8.3.4 Capital rationing

Sometimes the amount of capital that an organisation can invest in long-term projects is limited and so a choice must be made between a number of different projects. Management will obviously wish to select those projects that will give the greatest return per £ invested, provided the projects are compatible with the long-term strategic objectives of the organisation. The decision becomes more difficult if the time horizon is a long one and investments do not start at the same time. Figure 8.21 contains cash flow figures for five different projects.

Year	M £	N £	O £	P £	Q £
0	(100,000)	–	(60,000)	(120,000)	(80,000)
1	20,000	(160,000)	(40,000)	60,000	(100,000)
2	50,000	80,000	40,000	45,000	100,000
3	70,000	100,000	80,000	45,000	110,000

Figure 8.21   Cash flows for projects M, N, O, P and Q

If it is assumed that the organisation's cost of capital is 5 per cent and that the funds available in year 0 are £200,000, it is clear that even if the net present values are positive the organisation cannot invest in all four projects. N is irrelevant to the calculations if the capital rationing is in Year 0, but a choice must be made between the others.

The profitability index discussed earlier in this chapter can be used to rank the projects. The first step is to calculate the net present values of the projects and then express them as a percentage of the initial outflow so that comparable returns are obtained. This is done in Figure 8.22.

Year	Discount rate 5%	M £	O £	P £	Q £
0	1.000	(100,000)	(60,000)	(120,000)	(80,000)
1	0.952	19,040	(38,080)	57,120	(95,200)
2	0.907	45,350	36,280	40,815	90,700
3	0.864	60,480	69,120	38,880	95,040
Net present value		24,870	7,320	16,815	10,540
		÷	÷	÷	÷
		100,000	60,000	120,000	80,000
		24.87%	12.20%	14.02%	13.18%
Ranking		1st	4th	2nd	3rd

Figure 8.22   Profitability indexes for projects M, O, P and Q

Project N has been omitted because it is not relevant to the current decision – which is simply what funds to invest next year. All four projects have positive NPVs and so would be accepted if funds allowed. With £200,000 to invest project M would be chosen and five-sixths of project P assuming that the project allows partial investment. In many situations this would not be possible and so a decision would have to be made on the basis of NPVs. Investing in projects P and Q would give a gross NPV of £27,355. No other feasible combination could better this.

Capital rationing is not really a practical approach for the majority of organisations. It works well if the company is an investment company but for the majority of organisations providing a service or manufacturing products its solution will not be helpful. This simple view of capital rationing also takes no account of outflows in year 1 (which O and Q require) and whether there will be funds available in that year and in following years.

Capital rationing problems may present themselves in a variety of permutations of the issues involved.

Example

7 projects (A to G) are available but capital for investment is limited to £2 million pounds. Details of the projects (figures in £s) are:

Project	Investment	Inflow PV
A	250,000	325,000
B	1,000,000	1,082,500
C	500,000	757,500
D	1,000,000	1,235,000
E	1,250,000	1,335,000
F	250,000	300,000
G	500,000	590,000

Given that we cannot undertake all available projects, we are in a capital rationing situation. Analysis of the situation gives the following results:

Project	Investment	Inflow PV	PI	NPV	Ranking By PI%	By NPV
A	250,000	325,000	1.30	75,000	2	6
B	1,000,000	1,082,500	1.08	82,500	6	5
C	500,000	757,500	1.52	257,500	1	1
D	1,000,000	1,235,000	1.24	235,000	3	2
E	1,250,000	1,335,000	1.07	85,000	7	4
F	250,000	300,000	1.20	50,000	4	7
G	500,000	590,000	1.18	90,000	5	3

If we rank projects on the basis of NPV then this would have the following result:

Choice by NPV ranking

Rank	Project	Investment	NPV
1	C	500,000	257,500
2	D	1,000,000	235,000
3	G	500,000	90,000
Total		2,000,000	582,500

This is inappropriate since capital rationing is essentially a limiting factor problem, and the key measure is 'contribution per unit of the limiting factor'. In this case that is PV cash inflows per £1 invested – which is the PI index. Ranking projects on the basis of PI gives the following result:

Choice by PI index ranking

Rank	Project	Investment	NPV
1	C	500,000	257,500
2	A	250,000	75,000
3	D	1,000,000	235,000
4	F	250,000	50,000
Total		2,000,000	617,500

Clearly, this gives a better result. The example illustrates that PI index is the appropriate measure to be used in project ranking when capital rationing is the issue.

We have established a general rule for project ranking, but common sense has to be applied. There are always circumstances where general rules should not be followed.

Example

3 projects (A, B and C) are available with a total capital investment limit of £800,000. The details of the projects are:

Project	Investment	Inflow PV	NPV	PI	Rank
A	600,000	700,000	100,000	1.17	1
B	500,000	560,000	60,000	1.12	3
C	300,000	345,000	45,000	1.15	2

On the basis of the general rule, Project A only would be selected since it has the highest PI. But this precludes any other projects, generating an NPV of £100,000 and leaving £200,000 of the capital limit uncommitted. Consequently, NPV is maximised by adopting two projects (B and C) both of which have lower PIs than A. By adopting these two projects we raise total NPV to £105,000.

8.3.5 The discount rate

In all the examples considered so far a constant discount rate has been used, on the assumption that the cost of capital will remain the same over the life of the project. As the factors which influence the cost of capital, such as interest rates and inflation, can change considerably over a short period of time an organisation may wish to use different rates over the life of the project. NPV and DPB allow this but IRR and ARR present a uniform rate of return. Using NPV, for example, a different discount factor can be used for each year if so desired.

Perhaps one of the major problems in using a discounted cash flow method is deciding on the correct discount rate to use. It is difficult enough in year 1 but deciding on the rate for, say, year 4 may be very difficult because of changes in the economy, etc. If a very low rate is chosen almost all projects will be accepted, whereas if a very high discount rate is chosen very few projects will be accepted.

Looking back over the years it would appear that the majority of managers have probably used too high a discount rate and have, as a consequence, not invested in projects that would have helped their organisation to grow in relation to their competitors.

If there is any doubt over the correct discount rate to use, sensitivity analysis – described below – can help.

8.3.6 Sensitivity analysis

So far in this chapter it has been assumed that all the quantitative factors in the investment decision – the cash inflows and outflows, the discount rate and the life of the project – are known with certainty. In reality this is very rarely the case. Sensitivity analysis recognises this fact. The CIMA *Terminology* defines *sensitivity analysis* as:

> **!** A modelling and risk assessment procedure in which changes are made to significant variables in order to determine the effect of these changes on the planned outcome. Particular attention is thereafter paid to variables identified as being of special significance.

As the definition indicates, sensitivity analysis can be applied to a variety of planning activities and not just to investment decisions. For example it can be used in conjunction with breakeven analysis to ascertain by how much a particular factor can change before the project ceases to make a profit.

In sensitivity analysis a single input factor is changed at a time, while all other factors remain at their original estimates. There are two basic approaches:

- An analysis can be made of all the key input factors to ascertain by how much each factor must change before the NPV reaches zero, the indifference point.
- Alternatively specific changes can be calculated, such as the sales decreasing by 5 per cent, in order to determine the effect on NPV. The latter approach might generate results such as those in Figure 8.23, while the former approach is illustrated in the example that follows.

✋ **Exercise**

The initial outlay for equipment is £100,000. It is estimated that this will generate sales of 10,000 units per annum for four years. The contribution per unit is expected to be £6 and the fixed costs are expected to be £26,000 per annum. The cost of capital is 5 per cent.

Variable	Adverse variation	Revised NPV	% change in NPV
Project life	– overestimated by		
	1 year	£50	83%
	2 years	(£550)	192%
Cost of labour – underestimated by			
	5%	£300	50%
	10%	(£150)	125%
Sales volume	– overestimated by		
	2%	£150	25%
	5%	(£650)	208%

Figure 8.23 Effect of specific changes on a project

Requirements

(i) Calculate the NPV.

(ii) By how much can each factor change before the company becomes indifferent to the project?

 Solution

(i)

			£
Contribution = £6 × 10,000=			60,000
Less: fixed costs			26,000
Cash inflow per annum			34,000

		Cash flow £	Discount rate 5%	NPV £
Year 0	Outlay	(100,000)	1	(100,000)
Years 1–4	Annual cash inflow	34,000	3.546	120,564
				20,564

(ii) NPV can fall by £20,564 before the indifference point is reached.
This means that the annual cash flows can change by

X × 3.546 = £20,564
X = £5,800

Therefore, the fixed costs can rise by £5,800 to £31,800 – this is a change of 22 per cent.
The contribution can fall by £5,800 to £54,200 – this is a change of 9 per cent. This is the variation caused by price changes, volume changes and efficiency changes in costs.

Without more detailed knowledge of the project, it can probably be safely assumed that the project is not sensitive to a change in fixed costs as a change of 22 per cent seems very unlikely. This project is not particularly sensitive to changes in any of the factors calculated. On the other hand it is very difficult to predict future sales of some projects and an error of 10 per cent may be expected. The contribution is made up of many factors (the individual variable costs and the selling price) and without more detailed knowledge it is not possible to comment further.

Sensitivity analysis is very simple to carry out using a spreadsheet model and as a conse quence has become very popular in recent years. Once the model has been built a single cell can be altered by trial and error to determine the change needed to make the NPV zero.

As sensitivity analysis is carried out without the specification of the precise probability of a particular event occurring, it is easy to apply. Any outcome that appears critical as a result of the analysis can then be examined in more detail before a final decision is made. Its usefulness therefore lies in its role as an attention-directing technique as it directs atten tion to those factors that have the most significant impact on the outcome of the project. Armed with this knowledge management can take action to make sure that the events that are within their control stay within acceptable parameters.

In the example in Figure 8.22, wage rates may be critical. So management may seek to obtain a wage agreement that will limit rates of pay in the future so as to prevent the dan ger of even higher rates.

In the example in Figure 8.22, the life of the project and the sales volume are likely to be outside the control of management. If, after sensitivity analysis, the decision-makers are still unsure about a particular factor, such as sales volume, they may seek a full risk assessment based on a probability distribution for this particular factor and assess the resulting NPVs.

It is important that the output from a sensitivity analysis is not misinterpreted. Sensitivity analysis looks at the change in one factor in isolation but in the real world it is likely that several factors would move together and so the actual outcome of the project might depend on the combined performance of several or all of the variables. Figure 8.24 shows the proba bility of the occurrence of the 'most likely' figure for each of the factors given in Figure 8.23.

Variable	Probability of 'most likely' outcome
Project life	0.9
Cost of labour	0.7
Sales volume	0.5

Figure 8.24 Probability of most likely outcome

The figures in Figure 8.24 indicate a high degree of confidence in the estimate of the project life while there is less confidence in the other two factors. If it is assumed that the outcomes of each of the variables are independent, the probability of all three most likely outcomes occurring together is obtained by the multiplication of the probabilities, that is,

$$0.9 \times 0.7 \times 0.5 = 0.315$$

This shows that there is a 32 per cent probability that the most likely NPV will occur.

Exercise

Here is another exercise involving sensitivity analysis. Try it for yourself before looking at the solution.

A company is about to enter a new product market and has to determine which of two options it should select for its distribution strategy. The net present value for the project with each option has been calculated for two possible annual demand figures.

	Option X	Option Y
	NPV	NPV
Sales demand outcome	£000	£000
Lowest expected − 20,000 units	2.0	3.0
Highest expected – 55,000 units	15.5	10.0

The directors wish to compare the sensitivities of the two options to changes in forecast annual sales demand.

 Solution

The range of possible NPVs can be depicted on a graph. Although the NPV will not alter in a strictly linear fashion in response to changes in sales demand we can assume that the relationship will be approximately linear.

The graph helps the directors to assess the sensitivity of the options to variations in sales demand as follows.

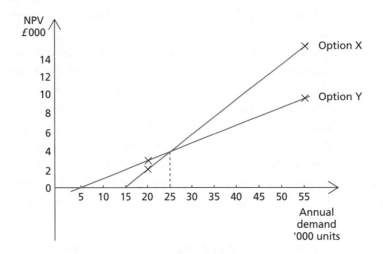

- Above a sales demand of 25,000 units per annum, option X results in the highest NPV. If there is an equal chance of any demand within the given range occurring, option X will be preferable for approximately 86 per cent of the possible outcomes.
- However, if a low sales volume is more likely then option Y would be preferable.
- Sales volume can reduce to as low as 5,000 units each year before option Y ceases to earn a positive NPV.

8.3.7 Risk

Risk in this context is business risk, that is the risk arising from the project rather than financing or financial risk. Rather obviously, the higher the risk the higher the required rate of return will be. There are many different ways of dealing with the perceived risk implicit in the project. They are:

- Sensitivity analysis, as previously discussed.
- The use of probability distributions and simulation modelling as discussed in Chapter 7.
- Adjustment of the required rate of return/cost of capital. This is a popular method in the UK. Individual projects are not normally assessed using individual rates specific to that project. Instead, say, three categories of risk are used (high, medium and low risk) and each has its own discount rate. Updating an existing manufacturing system will probably be considered low risk and be given a low discount factor, whereas bringing out an entirely new product concept may be considered high risk and be given a high discount factor.

- Adjustment of the payback time required; for a project perceived to be more risky, a shorter payback period would be required.
- Reduce cash inflows by, say, 20 per cent for a high-risk project.
- The use of decision tree analysis.

It is important that two methods are not used together otherwise there is a chance that double counting will take place and sound investments will not be made.

 ## Exercise

To give yourself some practice in taking account of the time value of money in decision tree analysis, it would be useful to return now to the example in Figure 7.3 of Chapter 7.

The time value of money can be incorporated quite simply, by multiplying the figures in the cash flow column by the relevant discount factor before multiplying by the probabilities.

Using the example data and assuming that it took one year to develop the designs and a further year before the contribution was received, and assuming the cost of capital is 10 per cent, the revised position is shown in Figure 8.25.

Outcome £	Cash flow £	Discount factor 10%	Net present value £	Pay-off £
800,000	650,000	0.826	536,900	225,498
(100,000)	(250,000)	0.826	(206,500)	(57,820)
			330,400	167,678
180,000	30,000	0.909	27,270	
20,000	(130,000)	0.909	118,170	(35,451)
				EV132,227
100,000	100,000	1.000	100,000	

Figure 8.25 Revised calculations for example in Figure 7.3 of Chapter 7

Taking account of the time value of money did not alter the final decision, but it did reduce the differential between the two expected value figures.

> The incorporation of risk and uncertainty into project appraisal is a popular exam topic, so make sure that you try the relevant practice questions.

8.3.8 Inflation

Inflation, which is the decline in purchasing power of the monetary unit, means that £1 received in 1 year's time is not as valuable in real terms as £1 received today. When inflation is low it is not a very important factor in the investment appraisal decision but when it rises above, say, 10 per cent it can become a major factor. During the 1960s and 1970s, several countries had inflation rates in excess of 100 per cent and this makes forward planning virtually impossible because of the unpredictability of future costs and revenues.

The cost of capital that a company uses is known as the monetary cost of capital and it includes an element that is due to inflation. That is, part of the rate includes a factor for the anticipated decline in the general purchasing power of the cash that the investment generates. If this element is stripped from the monetary rate the real rate of return is left.

The real rate of return is the return required to cover the investment risk and will of course vary from industry to industry.

There are two approaches for dealing with inflation in investment appraisal:

- *The real approach.* This uses the real rate of return rather than the monetary cost of capital. If this is done all cash flows must be predicted in terms of today's £. This method requires the discount rate to be adjusted but normally no adjustments are needed to future predicted cash flows because it is normal to predict them in terms of today's £. Thus it is a relatively simple method in terms of calculations.
- *The monetary approach.* This uses the monetary cost of capital. As a consequence future cash flows must be predicted in terms of their monetary value in years to come, which means adjusting the values by the predicted inflation rates. This is a lengthier calculation but is to be preferred as it allows for different inflation rates to be used for different types of cash flow. For example, materials may have a different inflation rate to direct labour.

The real rate of return can be found by using the following formula:

$$RR = \frac{(1 + MR)}{(1 + IR)} - 1$$

If the monetary rate (MR) = 13.4%

and the inflation rate (IR) = 5%, then

$$\text{the real rate (RR)} = \frac{(1 + 0.134)}{(1 + 0.05)} - 1$$
$$= 8\%$$

Conversely, the monetary rate is found using the formula:

$$MR = (1 + RR)(1 + IR) - 1$$
$$= (1 + 0.8)(1 + 0.05) - 1$$
$$= 13.4\%$$

 ## Exercise

A company is considering investing in a project which requires an initial investment of £150,000. The cash inflows during years 1–3 are expected to be £55,000 per annum. The company's monetary cost of capital is 10 per cent and inflation is expected to be 6 per cent during the life of the project.

Requirements

(i) Calculate the NPV of the project using the real rate of return as the discount rate.
(ii) Calculate the NPV of the project using the monetary cost of capital as the discount rate.

 ## Solution

(i)

$$\text{The real rate (RR)} = \frac{1.10}{1.06} - 1$$
$$= 3.8\%$$

We cannot look up discount factors for 3.8 per cent because they are not shown in the tables. Therefore, we will need to calculate the discount factors for ourselves.

Using the formula that we learned earlier in the chapter, the discount factor for each year is $1/(1 + r)^n$

Year		Discount factor 3.8%
1	$1 \times 1/(1 + 0.038)$	0.963
2	$0.963 \times 1/1.038$	0.928
3	$0.928 \times 1/1.038$	0.894

These discount factors can now be applied to the real cash flows.

Year	Cash flow £	Discount factor 3.8%	NPV £
0	(150,000)	1.000	(150,000)
1	55,000	0.963	52,965
2	55,000	0.928	51,040
3	55,000	0.894	49,170
			3,175

(ii) Inflation of cash flows:

Year	
1	$55,000 \times 1.06 = 58,300$
2	$58,300 \times 1.06 = 61,798$
3	$61,798 \times 1.06 = 65,506$

Year	Cash flow £	Discount factor 10%	NPV £
0	(150,000)	1.000	(150,000)
1	58,300	0.909	52,995
2	61,798	0.826	51,045
3	65,506	0.751	49,195
			3,235

The difference in final net present values is due to rounding up the real rate of return. Therefore, the same NPV results from both approaches; the real approach and the monetary approach.

We should also consider the possibility of general price deflation.

Extract from 'That sinking feeling' by Bob Scarlett, CIMA Insider, September 2002

Deflation affects various aspects of management accounting. In a situation of price deflation, the purchasing power of money rises over time: 5% annual deflation may be taken to indicate that £1 at year 0 and £0.95 at year 1 have the same purchasing power. This implies that 'real' interest rates are higher than the 'nominal' or 'money' rates quoted by banks. Take the following simple investment appraisal as an example. Consider a project that involves a £100 initial investment and which generates annual cash inflows of £40 (year 1), £40 (year 2) and £30 (year 3) at year 0 price levels. The current cost of money is 1% and the annual deflation rate is 5%. Using a 1% interest rate to discount the cash flows gives a positive NPV of +£7.93, which suggests that the project is viable. But the approach is wrong because it ignores deflation. To appraise the project properly, you have the option of using either a 'real' interest rate with cash flow figures projected at current (year 0) price levels (see figure), or a 'money' interest rate (1%) with cash flow figures projected at future price levels. Both methods give the same result:

'Real' interest rate and current price levels

Year	Cash flow	Discount	PV
0	−100	1.000	−100.00
1	40	0.941	37.62
2	40	0.885	35.39
3	30	0.832	24.96
		NPV	−2.02

The project is not viable, having an NPV of −£2.02. The critical issue to appreciate is that although the money interest rate is 1%, there is a 5% deflation rate. The principal on a loan therefore increases in real value by 5% each year. The real interest rate in this situation is $1.01/0.95 = 1.0632$, or 6.32%.

Deflation is not only a mathematical phenomenon. Deflation may affect business decision-making in several ways.

- Investing in projects that have long payback periods (or even no payback period) at projected future price levels may require some courage.
- Borrowing to finance the purchase of assets that are going to shrink in money value over time may also require some courage.
- It may be difficult to reduce some costs (e.g. wages) in line with deflation; this may make many projects less attractive than would otherwise be the case.
- Consumers may start to defer purchasing decisions if prices are falling; this may be irrational but it will make the general climate for investment less attractive.

8.3.9 Incorporating the effect of taxation

The effect of taxation can have a major impact on the viability of a capital investment project. The explanation of taxation given below is simplified because a detailed knowledge of tax is not required for this examination. Thus, it is assumed that tax is payable on profit without adjustment and that profit is the same as net cash inflow.

Corporation tax must be paid on annual profits thus creating cash outflows that reduce the annual net cash inflows. If the company's profit is £10,000 and the corporation tax rate is 30 per cent, the corporation tax liability is £3,000. On the other hand, a writing-down allowance is given if an asset is purchased; this reduces the cost of the purchase because the allowance can be set against annual profits thus reducing the tax liability.

Writing-down allowances (WDA) are expressed as a percentage, say 25 per cent. This percentage is applied to the cost of the asset, and any installation costs, etc., which are an integral part of the asset's use, on a reducing balance basis. Note that installation costs include preparing the site for the new asset and may include removing an old machine or knocking down old buildings and structures. So if the asset cost £950 and it cost £50 to install, the total cost would be £1,000. If the WDA is 25 per cent the allowance would be £250 in the first year. In year 2 it would be £1,000 − £250 = £750 × 25 per cent £187.5.

The allowances given are designed to match the fall in value of the asset over the period of ownership. So in the year in which the asset is sold there will be a balancing allowance or charge depending on whether the sale price is higher or lower than the initial cost less the total WDA given to date. In the previous example, if the asset were sold at the end of year 3 for £500 the balancing allowance would be £62.50. (The asset's value for taxation purposes in year 3 is £750 − £187.5 = 562.50; deduct the sales price of £500 to leave £62.50.) The writing-down allowances are set against the profit for the year and so they reduce a company's liability for corporation tax. For example, if the company made a profit of £10,000 during Year 1 and the rate of corporation tax is 30 per cent, its corporation tax payment will be £10,000 − £250 = £9,750 × 030 per cent = £2,925.

The effect of taxation will not necessarily occur in the same year as the relevant cash flow that causes it. Under the new taxation regime of corporation tax self-assessment the tax on the annual profit becomes due in four instalments. If it is assumed the organization has the standard 12-month accounting period the instalments are due in the 7th, 10th, 13th and 16th months from the start of the accounting period. This means that two instalments fall due within the same year as the causal profit/cash inflow, and the remaining two instalments fall due in the following year. Since we assume that cash flows occur at year ends this is simplified to become 50% of the tax paid in the year the profits are earned and 50% the following year.

Example

The management of a company are making a decision on whether or not to purchase a new piece of plant and machinery which costs £100,000. The new machine will generate a net cash flow of £30,000 each year for 4 years. At the end of the fourth year it will be sold for £20,000. The company's cost of capital is 5 per cent. Writing-down allowances are 25 per cent reducing balance and corporation tax is 30 per cent.

Calculation of writing-down allowances:

Year	Asset cost	30% Tax saved	Year 1	Year 2	Year 3	Year 4	Year 5
	£	£	£	£	£	£	£
	100,000						
Year 1 WDA (25%)	25,000	7,500	3,750	3,750			
	75,000						
Year 2 WDA (25%)	18,750	5,625		2,813	2,812		
	56,250			6,563			
Year 3 WDA (25%)	14,063	4,219			2,110	2,109	
	42,187				4,922		
Disposal proceeds	20,000						
Year 4 WDA	22,187	6,656				3,328	3,328
						5,437	

Calculation of corporation tax on profit:

Year 1 profit £30,000 − tax 30% = £9,000 − payable   Year 1 £4,500
                                                      Year 2 £4,500
Year 2 profit £30,000 − tax 30% = £9,000 − payable   Year 2 £4,500
                                                      Year 3 £4,500, etc.

The net present value of the project can now be calculated.

Year	Asset	WDA tax	Profit	Profit tax	Total	Disc. Factor	PV
	£	saved £	£	£	£	5%	£
0	(100,000)				(100,000)	1.000	(100,000)
1		3,750	30,000	(4,500)	29,250	0.952	27,846
2		6,563	30,000	(9,000)	27,563	0.907	25,000
3		4,922	30,000	(9,000)	25,922	0.864	22,397
4	20,000	5,437	30,000	(9,000)	46,437	0.823	38,218
5		3,328		(4,500)	(1,172)	0.784	(919)
NPV							12,542

Example

Using the data in the previous example, assume in addition that the company had to pay £5,000 to remove and dispose of an old machine before the new machine costing £100,000, which makes the same product, could be installed. The removal is treated as part of the cost of the new machine and the WDAs and the new calculation would be:

Calculation of writing-down allowances:

Year	Asset cost	Tax saved	Year 1	Year 2	Year 3	Year 4	Year 5
	£	£	£	£	£	£	£
	105,000						
Year 1 WDA (25%)	26,250	7,875	3,938	3,937			
	78,750						
Year 2 WDA (25%)	19,688	5,906		2,953	2,953		
	59,062			6,890			
Year 3 WDA (25%)	14,766	4,430			2,215	2,215	
	44,296				5,168		
Disposal proceeds	20,000						
Year 4 WDA	24,296	7,289				3,645	3,644
						5,860	

Calculation of corporation tax on profit:

Year 1 profit £30,000 − tax 30% = £9,000 − payable   Year 1 £4,500
                                                      Year 2 £4,500
Year 2 profit £30,000 − tax 30% = £9,000 − payable   Year 2 £4,500
                                                      Year 3 £4,500, etc.

Year	Asset £	WDA tax saved £	Profit £	Profit tax £	Total £	Disc. Factor 5%	PV £
0	(105,000)				(105,000)	1.000	(105,000)
1		3,938	30,000	(4,500)	29,438	0.952	28,025
2		6,890	30,000	(9,000)	27,890	0.907	25,296
3		5,168	30,000	(9,000)	26,168	0.864	22,609
4	20,000	5,860	30,000	(9,000)	46,860	0.823	38,566
5		3,644		(4,500)	(856)	0.784	(671)
NPV							8,825

> **!** If questions requiring taxation calculations are included in the examination the rate of corporation tax and the percentage writing-down allowance will be given in the question. This is because in reality they may change from year to year.

Now try this example. It incorporates tax and inflation and will demonstrate again the two possible ways of dealing with inflation in NPV calculations.

Either:

• discount real cash flows at the real rate of return;

or:

• discount money cash flows at the monetary (nominal) rate of return.

Example

The management of a company are making a decision on whether or not to purchase a new piece of office equipment, which costs £75,000. The equipment will generate a net cash flow of £35,000 per annum. At the end of the fourth year the equipment can be sold for £25,000. The equipment does not qualify for writing-down allowances. The corporation tax rate is 30 per cent.

Requirement

Assume that all cash flows are given in real terms, that 5 per cent is the real cost of capital and that annual inflation will be 4 per cent.

Calculate the NPV for this project using:

(a) the real cost of capital; and then
(b) the nominal (money) cost of capital.

Solution

(a) *Real cost of capital 5%*

Year	Asset £	Profit £	Corp. tax £	Total £	Discount factor 5%	Present value £
0	(75,000)			(75,000)	1.000	(75,000)
1		35,000	(5,250)	29,750	0.952	28,322
2		35,000	(10,500)	24,500	0.907	22,222
3		35,000	(10,500)	24,500	0.864	21,168
4	25,000	35,000	(10,500)	49,500	0.823	40,739
5			(5,250)	(5,250)	0.784	(4,116)
					NPV	33,335

(b) *Monetary (nominal) cost of capital*

$$(1 + m) = (1 + r)(1 + i)$$
$$(1 + m) = (1 + 0.05)(1 + 0.04)$$
$$m = 9.2\%$$

The required discount factors are:

Year		9.2% Discount factor
1	1 × 1/1.092	0.916
2	0.916 × 1/1.092	0.839
3	0.839 × 1/1.092	0.768
4	0.768 × 1/1.092	0.703
5	0.703 × 1/1.092	0.644

The monetary or nominal discount rates will be applied to the actual money cash flows. Disposal proceeds allowing for inflation

$$£25,000 \times (1.04)^4 \times £29,246$$

The corporation tax calculation

	Profit £	30% tax £	Payable Year 1 £	Payable Year 2 £	Payable Year 3 £	Payable Year 4 £	Payable Year 5 £
Year 1 £35,000 × (1.04)[1]	36,400	10,920	5,460	5,460			
Year 2 £35,000 × (1.04)[2]	37,856	11,357		5,678	5,679		
Year 3 £35,000 × (1.04)[3]	39,370	11,811			5,906	5,905	
Year 4 £35,000 × (1.04)[4]	40,945	12,284				6,142	6,142
			(5,460)	(11,138)	(11,585)	(12,047)	(6,142)

The project money cash flows can now be displayed.

Year	Asset £	Profit £	Corporation tax £	Total £	Discount factor 9.2%	Present value £
0	(75,000)			(75,000)	1.000	(75,000)
1		36,400	(5,460)	30,940	0.916	28,341
2		37,856	(11,138)	26,718	0.839	22,416
3		39,370	(11,585)	27,785	0.768	21,339
4	29,246	40,945	(12,047)	58,144	0.703	40,875
5			(6,142)	(6,142)	0.644	(3,955)
					NPV	34,016

You will note that both approaches give the same answer. The small difference between the two figures is simply due to rounding.

8.4 Post-completion appraisal

8.4.1 The investment cycle

As stated at the beginning of the chapter, the financial evaluation of projects is only part of the investment process. The full process is represented in Figure 8.26. This shows that the investment process is a cycle, rather than a discrete event.

The post-completion appraisal of projects provides a mechanism whereby experience gained from past projects can be fed into the organisation's decision-making processes to aid decisions on future projects. In other words, it aids organisational learning. A post-completion appraisal reviews all aspects of a completed project in order to assess whether it has lived up to initial expectations. This is a forward-looking rather than backward-looking technique. The task is often carried out by a small team, which typically consists of an accountant and an engineer who have had some involvement in the project. Surprisingly, it is rare to find that post-completion appraisal is the responsibility of the internal audit department. This is because it is not considered an audit of past events but a means of improving future decisions.

Studies suggest that it is practised by around 80 per cent of large companies.

8.4.2 Benefits of post-completion appraisal

The following benefits may be gained from a post-completion appraisal; the benefits are split into three types as classified by Mills and Kennedy (1993).

A – Benefits relating to the performance of the current project

- It enables speedy modification of under-performing/over-performing projects, by identifying the reasons for the under-/over-performance.
- It makes it more likely that 'bad' projects are:
  (i)   terminated; and
  (ii) terminated at an earlier stage.

B – Benefits which relate to the selection and performance of future projects

- It improves the quality of decision-making by providing a mechanism whereby past experience can be made available to future decision-makers.

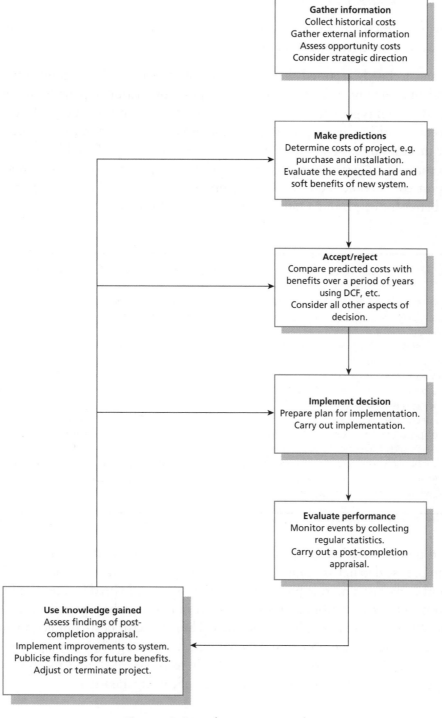

Figure 8.26 The Investment cycle

- It encourages greater realism in project appraisal as past inaccuracies in forecasts are made public. It tends to stop managers looking at their pet projects in a favourable light and ensures a more realistic approach to predicting future outcomes.
- It highlights reasons for successful projects. This may be important in achieving greater benefits from future projects.

C – Benefit to the investment appraisal system itself

- It provides a means of improving control mechanisms, by formally highlighting areas where weaknesses have caused problems.

Mills and Kennedy reported that at the time of their research the companies they surveyed had all gained type C benefits from their post-completion appraisals and that 40 per cent hoped to gain type B benefits. However, only 20 per cent sought type A benefits. This might seem surprising, but is probably because projects can be monitored more effectively by other means. For example, regular and routine monitoring of weekly sales or the time taken to complete stages in a research and development project would prove more effective than a post-completion audit. Thus post-completion appraisal is a management tool to assist in better future planning rather than a control technique.

F R Gulliver (1987) reported on BP's experience with post-completion appraisal. Four main benefits had arisen:

- Before post-completion appraisal existed BP's management approved unrealistically low budgets because planners inaccurately predicted the scope of the project when they submitted the budget. Now BP approves budgets in phases, and each phase becomes more accurate as planners work out the project's details. Because managers know that the projects are to be subjected to post-completion appraisal the plans they draw up are more accurate and realistic.
- The knowledge that rushing into a project, such as a company acquisition, in order to forestall action by competitors is often unwise. If there is any doubt about the soundness of the project the company has rarely regretted not going ahead with it.
- Before post-completion appraisal BP's management made some bad decisions on which contractors to use. As a result of post-completion appraisal a contractor evaluation unit was set up which monitors contractors' performance and aids future choice.
- BP found that engineers do not automatically make good managers. As a result of post-completion appraisal a department was set up to help engineers develop control techniques and procedures and to ensure that the right person manages the right project.

A good post-completion appraisal does not set out to identify the costs and benefits of a project in precise detail. (As pointed out above, this particular task will normally have been carried out as part of a routine project monitoring system.) Instead it seeks to identify general lessons to be learned from a project. It is not intended to be a policing exercise and, if it is to be effective, should not be seen as such. Thus the term post-completion appraisal is a more accurate term than post-completion audit. Even though it is not a policing exercise any attempts to hide or ignore realities are likely to be revealed, and its effect will be to encourage honesty in facing problems at all levels of the organisation.

8.4.3 Project abandonment

During a post-completion appraisal it may be realised that the project is not likely to be so profitable as first thought and the possibility of abandoning it or terminating it early should be considered. Past cash flows are, of course, irrelevant to the decision – only future cash flows need to be considered. Abandoning the project is only necessary when the net discounted expected future cash flow of the project becomes negative.

Example

Case I
A project, P, has expected cash flows as shown in Figure 8.27.

Year	Expected cash flow £	Discount rate 10%	Discounted cash flow £
0	(3,500)	1.000	(3,500)
1	2,000	0.909	1,818
2	2,000	0.826	1,653
3	2,000	0.751	1,503
		Expected net present value	1,474

Figure 8.27   Expected cash flows for project P

The initial investment of £3,500 in project P represents the purchase of a customised machine, the price of which is known with certainty. Because it is a customised machine its resale value is low; it can only be sold for £1,000 immediately after purchase. Once the machine is bought, therefore, the expected value of abandoning the project would be £1,000 (1.0 × £1,000). This must be compared with the expected value of continuing with the project, which is £4,974 (£1,818 + £1,653 + £1,503). In this case the expected benefits of continuing with the project far outweigh the returns from abandoning it immediately.

Case II
The decision to abandon a project will usually be made as a result of revised expectations of future revenues and costs. These revisions may be consistent with the data on which the original investment decision was based, or represent an alteration to earlier expectations. If the decision is consistent with the original data, the possibility, but not the certainty, that the project might have to be abandoned would have been known when the project was accepted. In these circumstances, project abandonment is one of a known range of possible outcomes arising from accepting the project. The cash flows in Table 8.28 were the expected ones, based on the probabilities given in Figure 8.28.

Year 0 £	Year 1 p	Year 1 £	Year 2 p	Year 2 £	Year 3 p	Year 3 £
(3,500)	0.33	3,000	0.33	3,000	0.33	3,000
	0.33	2,000	0.33	2,000	0.33	2,000
	0.33	1,000	0.33	1,000	0.33	1,000
Expected value		2,000		2,000		2,000

Figure 8.28   Probabilities for project P

In year 0, the expected net cash inflow in each year of project P's 3-year life is £2,000. The actual outcome of any of the 3 years is unknown at this point, and each of the three possible outcomes is equally likely. The factors that will cause any one of these results to occur may differ each year, or they may be the same each year. In some instances, a particular outcome in the first year may determine the outcome of years 2 and 3 with certainty. For example, the outcome of £3,000 in year 1 may mean that this same outcome will follow with certainty in years 2 and 3. Similarly outcomes of £2,000 and £1,000 in year 1 may be certain to be repeated in years 2 and 3. In year 0, the investor can only calculate the expected net cash flow in years 2 and 3, but with perfect correlation of flows between years these future flows are known with certainty at the end of year 1. If the year 1 inflow is either £3,000 or £2,000, perfect correlation between years will ensure that the actual NPV of the project will be positive. But if the first year's outcome is £1,000, the investment will have a negative NPV of £1,014, that is (£[3,500] + £1,000 × 2.486). Should the project be abandoned? The information is now certain and so the decision on whether to abandon should be made using a risk-free interest rate and not the company's normal cost of capital. If we assume that the risk-free rate is 5 per cent, the present value of continuing at the end of year 1 will be:

Year	Cash flow £	Discount rate 5%	Discounted cash flow £
0	(1,000)	1.000	(1,000)
1	1,000	0.952	952
2	1,000	0.907	907
A			859

Clearly, the project should not be abandoned.

Case III

Suppose a buy-back clause had been part of the sale agreement for the machine, which requires the supplier to repurchase the machine on demand for £2,000 at any time up to and including the first anniversary of the sale. The abandonment value of the project at the end of year 1 will be £2,000. When this is compared with the £1,859 present value of continuation, it is clear that the company should plan to terminate the project at the end of year 1, if the actual outcome of that year proves to be £1,000. When the buy-back option is included, the possible outcomes will change as shown in Figure 8.29.

Year 0		Year 1		Year 2		Year 3
£	p	£	p	£	p	£
(3,500)	0.33	3,000	0.33	3,000	0.33	3,000
	0.33	2,000	0.33	2,000	0.33	2,000
	0.33	1,000⎱	0.33	0	0.33	0
		2,000⎰				
Expected value		2,667		1,667		1,667

Figure 8.29 Possible outcomes with buy-back option

Including abandonment in the plan increases the expected NPV of the project by £80:

Year	Cash flow £	Discount rate 10%	Discounted cash flow £
0	(3,500)	1.000	(3,500)
1	2,667	0.909	2,424
2	1,667	0.826	1,378
3	1,667	0.751	1,252
			1,554

This type of problem can be analysed using a decision tree. Figure 8.30 sets out the data in this format.

The method outlined below can be utilised even where the correlation of cash flows between years is less than perfect. The correlation can range from perfectly positive (as in our example) to perfectly negative. Where the correlation is zero, that is total independence of cash flows between years, the method cannot be used. But in all other instances the knowledge gained in Year 1 will enable the forecast for later years to be refined to a greater or lesser extent. This in turn will allow the expected present value of continuing with the project to be compared with the present value of termination.

Case IV

During a project's life, events that were unforeseen at the time of the original decision may occur and have an impact on the expected cash flows of the project. Such events will require a revision of future predictions.

In the previous example the announcement of a new tax charged on revenues during the course of year 1 would necessitate a review of the project's profitability. If the effect of the new tax would be to reduce the project's revenues after year 1 by 50 per cent, the position would be as shown in Figure 8.31.

The introduction of the new tax means that a cash flow of £2,000 in year 1 will now be followed by only £1,000 in years 2 and 3. This will mean that the project should be abandoned in year 1. At the time the project was being considered, this situation was not, and could not have been, foreseen by the decision-maker.

Under these circumstances it would be surprising if there was any resistance to the idea of terminating the project, as external events, for which no one could be held responsible, had made it necessary. But when a revision in future expectations arising from errors in the original forecasts, or due to problems in project implementation,

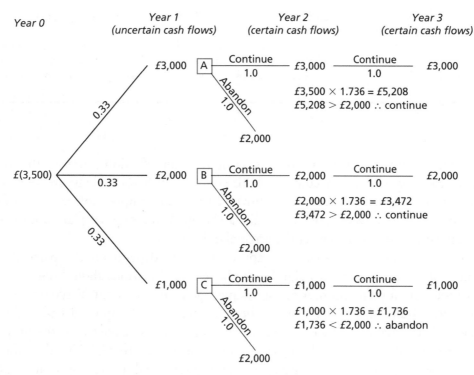

Figure 8.30 Decision tree for the cash flows in Figure 8.30

Year 0	Year 1		Year 2		Year 3	
£	p	£	p	£	p	£
(3,500)	0.33	3,000	0.33	1,500	0.33	1,500
	0.33	2,000	0.33	1,000	0.33	1,000
	0.33	1,000	0.33	500	0.33	500
Expected value		2,000		1,000		1,000

Figure 8.31 Effect of new tax charge on project revenues

indicate that abandonment is necessary, it can be much more difficult to acknowledge and accept. The post-completion audit team will play a significant role in identifying and highlighting the changed circumstances in such situations.

Example

Project X had the following expected cash-flow pattern at the time of its approval:

	Discounted cash flow
Year	£m
1	(8)
2	(16)
3	(24)
4	55
Net present value	7

The company experienced great difficulty in implementing the project in year 1, and the actual costs incurred during that year were £16m. The company must then ask itself whether the actual outcome in year 1 necessitates any revision in the expected outcomes of later years. If no revision is required, further costs of £40m (year 0 values) must be incurred to secure inflows of £55m (year 0 values). The expected net present value of continuing with project X beyond year 1 will thus be £15m (year 0 values). (Note that adjusting the figures to year 1 values would increase the expected NPV slightly, strengthening the case for continuation.)

The overall result of the investment would, of course, be negative by £1m, if years 2–4 costs and revenues are as forecast. The excess spend of £8m in year 1 is greater than the £7m net present value originally predicted. However, at the end of year 1 the £16m is a sunk cost and does not influence a decision on termination made at that time.

8.4.4 Role of post-appraisal in project abandonment

Those intimately involved with a project may be reluctant to admit, even to themselves, that early problems with a project are likely to continue. When problems are being experienced in project implementation, those involved may be tempted to try to resolve the situation in one of two ways. They can make a change in the original plans and/or incur further expenditure in order to meet the original objective.

Whether either of these responses is appropriate will depend on the particular circumstances of the project but any significant changes or deviations should not be undertaken without the formal approval of higher management. The control systems in place will normally require changes of scope to be documented and approved before they are undertaken. It is usually the responsibility of the engineers associated with the project to ensure that this is done. Expected project cost overruns should be highlighted by the routine monitoring of project expenditure by accounting staff, and formal approval should be obtained for the anticipated overspend. A prerequisite of approval by top management will often be the provision of the same level of detailed justification as was required when the initial funds were sanctioned. These controls ensure that significant changes to the character of a project cannot be made without top management's approval. However, they do not, of themselves, ensure that the option to terminate a project is considered, although it would be unlikely that management would fail to consider this possibility.

Some companies require an audit on all projects that need additional funds. The request for further funding would then be considered alongside the audit report. Routine monitoring of projects tends to focus almost exclusively on costs. An audit will review both costs and revenues, and, most importantly, focuses on the future. By checking the continuing validity of both forecast costs and revenues, the post-audit team is in a position to prepare a report to advise management on the wisdom of continuing with the project.

8.5 Summary

This chapter has dealt with the methods for determining whether to invest in a particular long-term project and has considered measures for assessing an investment centre's performance. Key points are as follows:

- The net present value (NPV) method of investment appraisal always produces the correct investment decision if the aim is to maximise shareholder value.
- The internal rate of return (IRR) of a project is the discount rate at which the NPV is zero.
- IRR can give multiple rates of return if cash flows are unusual.
- Payback is widely used in practice and has a number of advantages and disadvantages. It is the time taken for the cumulative cash inflows from a project to equal the initial outflow.

- Accounting rate of return is based on the accounting profit after depreciation. It is profit rather than cash based and its use has a number of limitations.
- Discounted payback may also be used to appraise projects. It combines the simplicity of payback with the theoretical validity of NPV.
- Calculation of a discounted payback index or profitability index can be useful if funds are scarce.
- Annuity rates can be used to simplify PV calculations when annual cash flows are equal.
- When projects with lives of unequal lengths are being considered they can be adjusted to a comparable basis through the use of annualised equivalents.
- Sensitivity analysis is a useful technique for assessing risk in a project.
- Inflation may be incorporated into discounted cash flow analysis in two ways: discount monetary cash flows at the monetary cost of capital, or discount real cash flows at the real cost of capital.
- Taxation affects the cash flows associated with a project, often also in the year following that in which the taxable profit is earned.
- Writing-down allowances are spread over the life of a capital asset, affecting cash flows throughout the life of a project.
- A post-completion appraisal has a number of benefits, many of which relate to future investment decisions and to the investment appraisal system itself.
- The project abandonment decision is based on relevant, future costs and revenues.

Self-test questions

(1) What role might ABC play in project appraisal? (Section 8.2.1)

(2) Explain the term 'present value' (Section 8.2.2)

(3) Explain the term 'payback' (Section 8.2.3)

(4) Explain the term 'profitability index' (Section 8.2.5)

(5) Compare and contrast ARR and NPV as project performance metrics. (Section 8.2.9)

(6) How might the optimum plant replacement cycle be determined? (Section 8.3.3)

(7) How does sensitivity analysis contribute to project appraisal? (Section 8.3.6)

(8) How might allowance for risk be incorporated in project appraisal? (Section 8.3.7)

(9) What role does the 'post completion audit' of projects play? (Section 8.4.2)

(10) Why might a part-complete project be abandoned? (Section 8.4.3)

Revision Questions

8

? Question 1

1.1 A company is evaluating a new product proposal. The proposed product selling rice is £180 per unit and the variable costs are £60 per unit. The incremental ash fixed costs for the product will be £160,000 per annum. The discounted ash flow calculation results in a positive NPV:

		Cash flow £	Discount rate £	Present value £
Year 0	Initial outlay	(1,000,000)	1.000	(1,000,000)
Years 1–5	Annual cash flow	320,000	3.791	1,213,120
Year 5	Working capital released	50,000	0.621	31,050
Net present value				244,170

What is the percentage change in selling price that would result in the project having a net present value of zero?

(A) 6.7%
(B) 7.5%
(C) 8.9%
(D) 9.6%
(E) 10.5%

1.2 A company has determined that the net present value of an investment project is 12,304 when using a 10% discount rate and $(3,216) when using a discount ate of 15%.
Calculate the Internal Rate of Return of the project to the nearest 1%.

(2 marks)

1.3 A company has a nominal (money) cost of capital of 18% per annum. If inflation is 6% each year, calculate the company's real cost of capital to the nearest 0.01%.

(2 marks)

1.4 A company is considering investing in a manufacturing project that would have a 3-year life span. The investment would involve an immediate cash outflow of £50,000 and have a zero residual value. In each of the 3 years, 4,000 units would be produced and sold. The contribution per unit, based on current prices, is £5. The company has an annual cost of capital of 8 per cent. It is expected that the inflation rate will be 3 per cent in each of the next 3 years.

The net present value of the project (to the nearest £500) is:
(A) £4,500
(B) £5,000
(C) £5,500
(D) £6,000
(E) £6,500

Data for Questions 1.5, 1.6 and 1.7

Details of the cash flows (figures in £ millions) associated with three projects (A, B and C are as follows):

Investment	Year 0	1	2	3	4	5
A	−400	100	120	140	120	100
B	−450	130	130	130	130	130
C	−350	50	110	130	150	100

The relevant company discount rate is 10%.

1.5 Calculate the payback period of investment A. **(2 marks)**

1.6 Calculate the discounted payback period of investment B. **(3 marks)**

1.7 Calculate the Internal Rate of Return (IRR) of investment C. **(3 marks)**

1.8 An investment company is considering the purchase of a commercial building at a cost of £0.85 m. The property would be rented immediately to tenants at an annual rent of £80,000 payable in arrears in perpetuity.

Calculate the net present value of the investment assuming that the investment company's cost of capital is 8% per annum.

Ignore taxation and inflation. **(2 marks)**

? Question 2

A manager is evaluating a three-year project which has the following relevant pre-tax operating cashflows:

Year	1	2	3
	$'000	$'000	$'000
Sales	4,200	4,900	5,300
Costs	2,850	3,100	4,150

The project requires an investment of $2 m at the start of year 1 and has no residual value.

The company pays corporation tax on its net relevant operating cashflows at the rate of 20%. Corporation tax is payable in the same year as the net relevant pre-tax operating cashflows arise. There is no tax depreciation available on the investment.

The manager has discounted the net relevant post-tax operating cashflows using the company's post-tax cost of capital of 7% and this results in a post-tax net present value of the project of $ 1.018 m.

Requirements

(a) Briefly explain sensitivity analysis and how the manager may use it in the evaluation of this project. **(4 marks)**
(b) Calculate the sensitivity of the project to independent changes in
    (i) the selling price;
    (ii) the cost of capital. **(6 marks)**

(Total for Question Two = 10 marks)

? Question 3

A business project is being considered, details as follows:

    Initial capital investment in equipment – $100,000
    Annual sales, year 1 to year 5 – 5,000 Units at $ 10 per Unit
    Variable costs (labour and material) – $3 per Unit
    Life of project – 5 years, with equipment having nil residual value

All sales and costs are on 'cash' terms. That is, there are no debtors or creditors. You may assume that all cash flows take place on the final day of the year in which they occur with the exception of the initial capital investment which takes place at the very start of the project. All surplus cash is paid out as dividends.

Requirements

(a) Calculate the profit earned each year of the project.
(b) Calculate the capital employed at the end of each year of the project.
(c) Calculate the ROCE generated each year of the project and its ARR.
(d) Calculate the payback period of the project.
(e) Calculate the NPV of the project using a 10% discount rate.
(f) Construct a chart (Chart 1) to identify the IRR of the project.

You are now told that all sales are to be on 6 months' credit terms. That is, at the end of each year, 6 months' sales will be outstanding in the form of debtors.

Requirements

(g) Calculate the profit earned each year of the project.
(h) Calculate the capital employed at the end of each year of the project.
(i) Calculate the ROCE generated each year of the project and its ARR.
(j) Calculate the payback period of the project.
(k) Calculate the NPV of the project using a 10% discount rate.
(l) Construct a chart (Chart 2) to identify the IRR of the project.

Requirement

(m) Having regard to all the foregoing, comment on a claim to the effect that 'methods of investment appraisal based on DCF analysis are invariably superior to the alternatives'.

Note: For the purposes of your analysis you may assume that sales and production costs are incurred evenly throughout the year.

[?] Question 4

A group consists of three operating divisions. Divisions A and B are long established and situated at the main site using old plant and equipment. The two divisions make much use of shared facilities. Division C is recently established at an independent site using its own new equipment. The three divisions are treated as profit centres with performance assessed on the basis of 'divisional return on capital employed', calculated as follows:

$$\frac{\text{Divisional net income before tax and interest, less share of HO costs}}{\text{Share of fixed assets at book value plus share of current assets}}$$

In the case of assets or head office costs not clearly attributable to any one division, the relevant figures are apportioned between divisions on a turnover basis. The divisions are currently generating a ROCE of about 10 per cent each.

In order to improve profitability a new system of investment appraisal has been introduced requiring that all new investments should be able to show an independent ROCE (judged on the above criteria) of at least 15 per cent.

Division B proposes a new project, detailed as follows:

Cost of new dedicated equipment	£75,000 (assumed to have a 5-year life)
Working capital	£75,000
Share of old equipment	£20,000 (assumed to have an indefinite life)
Life of project	5 years
Sales per year	140 units at £390 each
Variable costs	£150 per unit
Fixed costs per year	£17,000 including depreciation

Requirements

(a) Comment on the present methods of performance appraisal and investment analysis.
(b) Comment on the viability of B's proposal in the light of the foregoing.

[?] Question 5

A company is considering which of two mutually exclusive projects it should undertake. The finance director thinks that the project with the higher NPV should be chosen whereas the managing director thinks that the one with the higher IRR should be undertaken especially as both projects have the same initial outlay and length of life. The company anticipates a cost of capital of 10 per cent and the net cash flows of the projects are as follows:

Year	Project X	Project Y
	£000	£000
0	(200)	(200)
1	35	218
2	80	10
3	90	10
4	75	4
5	20	3

Requirements

(a) Calculate the NPV and IRR of each project.
(b) Recommend, with reasons, which project you would undertake (if either).
(c) Explain the inconsistency in ranking of the two projects in view of the remarks of the directors.
(d) Identify the cost of capital at which your recommendation in (b) would be reversed.

Note: You might find it interesting to answer this question using a computer spreadsheet.

? Question 6

You are considering the purchase of a new truck which will be required to travel 50,000 miles per year. Two suitable models are available, details of which are as follows:

- The Kam, having a life of 4 years and a price of £20,000; the running cost is initially 20p per mile but this figure will rise by 5p per mile for each year the truck is in service; a new engine will need to be fitted at a cost of £5,000 after the truck has been in service for 3 years;
- The Tru, having a life of 6 years and a price of £35,000; the running cost is initially 15p per mile but this will rise by 3p per mile for each year the truck is in service.

The cost of capital is 12 per cent.

Requirement

Explain which truck (the Kam or the Tru) should be purchased.

? Question 7

Camp plc has produced and marketed sleeping bags for several years. The sleeping bags are much heavier than some of the modern sleeping bags being introduced to the market. The company is concerned about the effect this will have on its sales. Camp pic are considering investing in new technology that would enable them to produce a much lighter and more compact sleeping bag. The new machine will cost £250,000 and is expected to have a life of four years with a scrap value of £10,000. In addition an investment of £35,000 in working capital will be required initially.

The following forecast annual trading account has been prepared for the project:

	£
Sales	200,000
Materials	(40,000)
Labour	(30,000)
Variable overheads	(10,000)
Depreciation	(20,000)
Annual profit	(100,000)

The company's cost of capital is 10 per cent. Corporation tax is charged at 30 per cent and is payable quarterly, in the 7th and 10th months of the year in which the profit is earned and the 1st and 4th month of the following year. A writing-down allowance of 25 per cent on reducing balance is available on capital expenditure.

PROJECT APPRAISAL

Requirement

Advise the management of Camp plc on whether they should invest in the new technology. Your recommendation should be supported with relevant calculations.

? Question 8

Apex Ltd has just completed the development of a new personal alarm device. Development costs totalled £50,000 and marketing costs to date total £5,000. A market survey suggests that the optimum price for the personal alarm is £49.90, at which price 2,000 units would be sold each month.

The personal alarm market changes rapidly and the market survey indicated that the probability of demand being maintained for:

> 2 years is 0.1
> 3 years is 0.5
> 4 years is 0.4

In order to start commercial production of the new device Apex Ltd must install a new automated assembly line at a cost of £1.2 million. The assembly line can produce the required quantity of the product but cannot be used for any other purpose and has nil disposal value. Because nobody has used this type of assembly line before, its life expectancy is uncertain. The best estimate available suggests that there is a 50 per cent chance that it will last for 4 years and an equal chance that it will last for only 3 years.

The unit variable cost of the personal alarm is £20.00 and attributable fixed costs totalling £100,000, excluding depreciation, will be incurred each year the personal alarm is produced.

The cost of capital is 14 per cent per annum.

Requirements

(a) Calculate the expected net present value of going ahead with the production of the new personal alarm device.
(b) Advise the management on the viability of the project. You should:
   (i)   refer to your calculations in (a) above
   (ii) include details of any assumptions made
   (iii) discuss any other factors you consider should be taken into account when making the final decision on whether to begin commercial production or not.

? Question 9

MN pic has a rolling programme of investment decisions. One of these investment decisions is to consider mutually exclusive investments A, B, and C. The following information has been produced by the investment manager.

	Investment decision A £	Investment decision B £	Investment decision C £
Initial investment	105,000	187,000	245,000
Cash inflow for A: years 1–3	48,000		
Cash inflow for B: years 1–6		48,000	

Cash inflow for C: years 1–9			48,000
Net present value (NPV) at 10% each year	14,376	22,040	31,432
Ranking	3rd	2nd	1st
Internal rate of return (IRR)	17.5%	14%	13%
Ranking	1st	2nd	3rd

Requirements

(a) Prepare a report for the management of MN pic which includes:
- a graph showing the sensitivity of the three investments to changes in the cost of capital;
- an explanation of the reasons for differences between NPV and IRR rankings – use investment A to illustrate the points you make;
- a brief summary which gives MN pic's management advice on which project should be selected.

(b) One of the directors has suggested using payback to assess the investments. Explain to him the advantages and disadvantages of using payback methods over IRR and NPV. Use the figures above to illustrate your answer.

Question 10

A company is considering the replacement of its delivery vehicle. It has chosen the vehicle that it will acquire but it now needs to decide whether the vehicle should be purchased or leased.

The cost of the vehicle is £15,000. If the company purchases the vehicle it will be entitled to claim tax depreciation at the rate of 25% per year on a reducing balance basis. The vehicle is expected to have a trade-in value of £5,000 at the end of three years.

If the company leases the vehicle, it will make an initial payment of £1,250 plus annual payments of £4,992 at the end of each of three years. The full value of each lease payment will be an allowable cost in the computation of the company's taxable profits of the year in which the payments are made.

The company pays corporation tax at the rate of 30% of its profits.

50% of the company's corporation tax is payable in the year in which profits are made and 50% in the following year. Assume that the company has sufficient profits to obtain tax relief on its acquisition of the vehicle in accordance with the information provided above.

The company's after tax cost of capital is 15% per year.

Note: Tax depreciation is not a cash cost but is allowed as a deduction in the calculation of taxable profits.

Requirement

Calculate whether the company should purchase or lease the vehicle and clearly state our recommendation to the company. **(10 marks)**

Question 11

A printing company is considering investing in new equipment which has a capital cost of £3 million. The machine qualifies for tax depreciation at the rate of 25% per year on a reducing balance basis and has an expected life of five years. The residual value of the machine is expected to be £300,000 at the end of five years.

An existing machine would be sold immediately for £400,000 if the new machine were to be bought. This existing machine has a tax written down value of £250,000.

The existing machine generates annual revenues of £4 million and earns a contribution of 40% of sales. The new machine would reduce unit variable costs to 80% of their former value and increase output capacity by 20%. There is sufficient sales demand at the existing prices to make full use of this additional capacity.

The printing company pays corporation tax on its profits at the rate of 30%, with half of the tax being payable in the year that the profit is earned and half in the following year.

The company's after tax cost of capital is 14% per year.

Requirements

(a) Evaluate the proposed purchase of the new printing machine from a financial perspective using appropriate calculations, and advise the company as to whether the investment is worthwhile. **(15 marks)**

(b) Explain sensitivity analysis and prepare calculations to show the sensitivity of the decision to independent changes in each of the following:

(i) annual contribution;

(ii) rate of corporation tax on profits. **(10 marks)**

(Total for Question Five = 25 marks)

Solutions to Revision Questions

 Solution 1

Tip

- You will need to use some accurate workings for Question 1.6. Although your workings will not receive any marks, if you keep them neat you will reduce the likelihood of errors.

1.1 Answer: (C)

To find the number of units:
Contribution per unit: £180 − £60 = £120

	£
Annual cash flow	320,000
Fixed costs	160,000
Total contribution	480,000 ÷ £120 = 4,000 units

The net present value of the project is £244,170. Therefore, the net present value of the revenue can fall by £244,170.

Current net present value of the revenue: £180 × 4,000 × 3.791 = £2,729,520

Therefore the fall in selling price: £244,170 ÷ £2,729,520 = 8.9 %

1.2 The internal rate of return of the project is 10% + [($12,304/$15,520) × 5%] = 14%

1.3 1.18/1.06 = 1.1132

Real cost of capital = 11.32%

1.4 Answer: (A)

Annual inflow = £5 × 4,000 × £20,000

$$\text{Real rate} = \frac{1 + 0.08}{1 + 0.03} - 1 = 0.0485$$

Discount factors: Year 1 $\dfrac{1}{1.0485}$ 0.954

           Year 2 $\dfrac{1}{1.0485^2}$ 0.910

           Year 3 $\dfrac{1}{1.0485^3}$ 0.868

           2.732 × £20,000 = £54,640

NPV = £4,500 (to the nearest £500)

Alternative method:

	Annual cash inflow inflated		8%	Present value
	£	£		£
Year 1	$20,000 \times 1.03$	20,600	0.926	19,076
Year 2	$20,000 \times 1.03^2$	21,218	0.857	18,184
Year 3	$20,000 \times 1.03^3$	21,855	0.794	17,353
				54,613

1.5

Year	£'000	£'000 to date
1	100	
2	120	220
3	140	360
4	120	480

Payback period = 3 years + 40/120ths of year 4 = **3.33 years**

1.6 Discounted cashflow are:

Year	£'000	£'000	£'000
1	130×0.909	118.17	
2	130×0.826	107.38	
3	130×0.751	97.63	
4	130×0.683	88.79	411.97
5	130×0.621		80.73

Discounted payback occurs in year 5 and can be estimated as:
4 years plus $(450 - 411.97)/80.73$ of year five = **4.47 years**

1.7 Discount using 20% cost of capital

Year	Cash flow	Discount factor	Present value
	£'000		£'000
0	(350)	1.000	(350)
1	50	0.833	42
2	110	0.694	76
3	130	0.579	75
4	150	0.482	72
5	100	0.402	40
NPV			(45)

	Discount Factor	NPV £'000
	10%	(48)
	20%	(45)
Change	10%	(93)

IRR = 10% + (48/93 $\times$ 10%) = 15% **(approx)**

1.8 £80,000 $\times$ 1/0.08 = £1 m therefore NPV = **£0.15 m**

✓ Solution 2

(a) Sensitivity analysis identifies the most critical elements of a decision by measuring the extent to which each individual element must change before it causes the decision-maker to change their decision.

The manager may use this technique to identify whether the acceptability of the project is more sensitive to changes in sales, costs, rate of taxation, or cost of capital. If more information were available the manager could consider the effects of changes to individual items of cost.

(b)

(i) The NPV of sales must reduce by $1,018 m before the manager's decision changes. The post tax present value of sales is:

Year		
1	$4.2 m × 80% × 0.935 =	$ 3.142 m
2	$4.9 m × 80% × 0.873 =	$ 3.422 m
3	$5.3 m × 80% × 0.816 =	$ 3.460 m
		$10.024 m

The % change required (i.e. sensitivity) = $1,018 m/$10.024 m = 10%

(b)

(ii) The sensitivity of the cost of capital is found by determining the discount % that causes the NPV to equal zero (i.e. the IRR).
Discount using 20%:

Year		
1	($4.2 m − $2.85 m) × 0.8 × 0.833 =	$0.900 m
2	($4.9 m − $3.10 m) × 0.8 × 0.694 =	$0.999 m
3	($5.3 m − $4.15 m) × 0.8 × 0.579 =	$0.533 m
		$2.432 m
	Less: Initial Investment	$2.000 m
	NPV	$0.432 m

	Discount Factor	NPV $
	7%	1.018 m
	20%	0.432 m
Change	13%	0.586 m

IRR = 7% + (1.018/0.586 × 13%) = 29.6%
The % change required is 22.6/7 = 323%

☑ Solution 3

No debtors

Year	Profit (a)	Capital (b)	ROCE (c)	Cash flow	Discount	PV
0				−100,000	1	−100,000
1	15,000	80,000	18.75%	35,000	0.909	31,818
2	15,000	60,000	25.00%	35,000	0.826	28,926
3	15,000	40,000	37.50%	35,000	0.751	26,296
4	15,000	20,000	75.00%	35,000	0.683	23,905
5	15,000	0	infinity	35,000	0.621	21,732
					NPV (e)	32,678
					p.back (d)	year 3
					ARR (c)	30%

PROJECT APPRAISAL

With debtors

Year	Profit (g)	Capital (h)	ROCE (i)	Cash flow	Discount	PV
0				−100,000	1	−100,000
1	15,000	105,000	14.29%	10,000	0.909	9091
2	15,000	85,000	17.65%	35,000	0.826	28,926
3	15,000	65,000	23.08%	35,000	0.751	26,296
4	15,000	45,000	33.33%	35,000	0.683	23,905
5	15,000	25,000	60.00%	35,000	0.621	21,732
6				25,000	0.564	14,112
					NPV (k)	24,062
					p.back (j)	year 4
					ARR (i)	20%

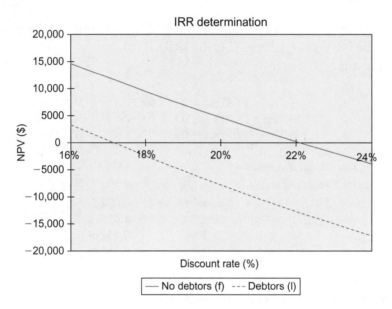

The IRR without debtors (f) is 17% while with debtors (l) it is 22%. (m) DCF-based methods of investment appraisal all incorporate subjective elements concerning the discount rate to be used and the projected cash flow profile being used. They can be as ambiguous as any of the alternatives. The payback method and its variants address subtle behavioural considerations that DCF does not. When people make an investment they attach a high priority to recovering that investment and may consider any return beyond that as a bonus. The payback period of an investment therefore incorporates a robust measure of the risk-reward trade off.

☑ Solution 4

(a) This general approach to project appraisal is open to criticism on a number of grounds, including the following:

- ROCE is a moving target which will rise as the life of the project proceeds due to the depreciation of fixed assets; it is difficult to see any logic behind basing project appraisal on performance in year 1 only;
- accounting profit is a subjective concept which is vulnerable to choice of accounting methods;
- there is no automatic reason why the use of existing facilities and equipment should be brought into consideration; these represent sunk costs which need not be considered (on the principle of marginality) unless there is some special reason to do so;

- the cost of new equipment and working capital receive exactly the same treatment; this is not appropriate since the working capital is fully recovered at the end of the project's life.

(b) An approach which avoids these problems is DCF analysis.

The annual income from the project is $[(140 \text{ units} \times £(390 - 150)) - £17,000] = £16,600$. Based on an annual income of £16,600 and capital employed of £170,000 the project yields an independent ROCE of 9.8 per cent. As such, it falls well below the Group's threshold of 15 per cent and is unlikely to be approved.

The project has a cash flow profile as follows:

Year	£
0	−150,000
1–4	31,600*
5	106,600**

* l33,600 contribution less £2,000 fixed cost cash flow (depreciation = £75,000/5 = £15,000)

** includes £75,000 recovery of working capital

DCF analysis of the above figures given an IRR of around 14 per cent. This could be viable – depending on the risk inherent in the project and the IRR of alternatives.

 Solution 5

Tip

- The key to this question is in understanding the reinvestment assumptions implicit in NPV and IRR calculations.

(a)

Factor 10%	Factor 20%	Project X £000	PV 10% £000	PV 20% £000	Project Y £000	PV 10% £000	PV 20% £000
1.000	1.000	(200)	(200.00)	(200.00)	(200)	(200.00)	(200.00)
0.909	0.833	35	31.82	29.16	218	198.16	181.59
0.826	0.694	80	66.08	55.52	10	8.26	6.94
0.751	0.579	90	67.59	52.11	10	7.51	5.79
0.683	0.482	75	51.23	36.15	4	2.73	1.93
0.621	0.402	20	12.42	8.04	3	1.86	1.21
		NPV	29.14	(19.02)	NPV	18.52	(2.54)

@ 10%   NPV Project X = £29,140
@ 10%   NPV Project Y = £18,520
@ 20%   NPV Project X = (£19,020)
@ 20%   NPV Project Y = (£2,540)

IRR Project X = 16%
IRR Project Y = 18%

(b) Undertake Project X:
- it has a positive NPV, indicating that it exceeds the company's cost of capital;
- assuming that the company's objective is to maximise the present value of future cash flows X offers the higher NPV.

X offers a higher NPV, whereas Y offers a high IRR. Where such conflicting indications appear it is generally appropriate to accept the NPV result, NPV being regarded as technically more sound than IRR.

(c) The two projects have radically different time profiles. X's cash inflows are grouped in the three middle years of the project, while nearly 90 per cent of Y's inflows come in the first year of the project. This leads to Y showing a higher IRR.

Risk, uncertainty and timing of cash flows may be considered by the directors in making the final investment decisions.

(d) Mutually exclusive project

The recommendation would be reversed at a cost of capital of approximately 14 per cent.

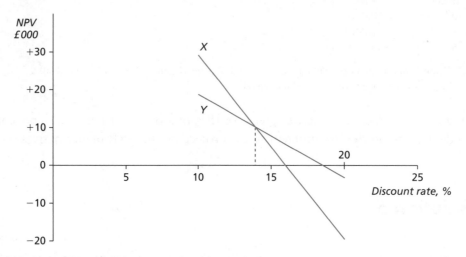

Note: You should appreciate that the true relationship between NPV and discount rate is a curvilinear one. A straight-line assumption is made to simplify calculations.

Solution 6

Tips

- Comparison of the two projects is complicated by their unequal lives.
- Use annualised costs to compare the two projects.

The annualised cost of the Kam is £21,160.

Workings

Year	Costs	12% DCF	PV
	£		£
0	20,000	1.000	20,000
1	10,000	0.893	8,930
2	12,500	0.797	9,963
3	20,000	0.712	14,240
4	17,500	0.636	11,130
		3.037	64,263

The annualised equivalent of £64,263 is £21,160 (£64,263/3.037). This is determined by calculating the NPV of acquiring and operating a Kam over four years and converting it to an equal annual equivalent cost by dividing the NPV by 3.037, the cumulative discount factor for four years at 12 per cent.

The annualised cost of the Tru is £19,270.

Workings

Year	Costs £	12%DCF	PV £
0	35,000	1.000	35,000
1	7,500	0.893	6,698
2	9,000	0.797	7,123
3	10,500	0.712	7,476
4	12,000	0.636	7,632
5	13,500	0.567	7,655
6	15,000	0.507	7,605
		4.112	79,239

The annualised equivalent of £79,239 is £19,270 (£79,239/4.112).

If follows that the Tru is the best option as it has a lower annualised cost.

☑ Solution 7

Tips

- This question incorporates taxation in capital investment appraisal.
- Begin by calculating the writing-down allowance (WDA) for the new investment and the tax relief.
- Calculate the net cash flow by working systematically in columns taking account of initial investment, working capital, scrap value, contribution, tax relief on WDA and tax on contribution, before calculating the present value.
- Remember that the working capital will be recovered at the end of the project.

Writing-down allowance

Year	Asset value £	30% Tax saved £	Year 1 £	Year 2 £	Year 3 £	Year 4 £	Year 5 £
	250,000						
Year 1 25% WDA	62,500	18,750	9,375	9,375			
	187,500						
Year 2 25% WDA	46,875	14,062		7,031	7,031		
	140,625						
Year 3 25% WDA	35,156	10,546			5,273	5,273	
	105,469						
Year 4 scrap value	10,000						
Year 4 bal. adj.	95,469	28,640				14,320	14,320
			9,375	16,406	12,304	19,593	14,320

NPV calculation for new investment

Year	Machine/ Wl capital on WDA £	Tax relief on WDA £	Contribution £	Tax on contribution £	Net cash flow £	DCF 10%	PV £
0	(250,000)						
	(35,000)				(285,000)	1	(285,000)
1		9,375	120,000*	(18,000)	111,375	0.909	01,240
2		16,406	120,000	(36,000)	100,406	0.826	82,935
3		12,304	120,000	(36,000)	96,304	0.751	72,324
4	10,000	19,593	120,000	(36,000)	148,593	0.683	101,489
	35,000						
5		14,320		(18,000)	(3,680)	0.621	(2,285)
				Net present value of new investment			70,703

*Contribution = Annual + Depreciation (1000,000 − 20,000)

As the net present value of the new investment is positive the advice to management should be to invest in the new technology.

 Solution 8

Tips
- A question that combines the time value of money, and decision trees which you encountered in Chapter 2.
- The marketing and development costs already incurred are sunk costs that are not relevant to the decision.

(a)

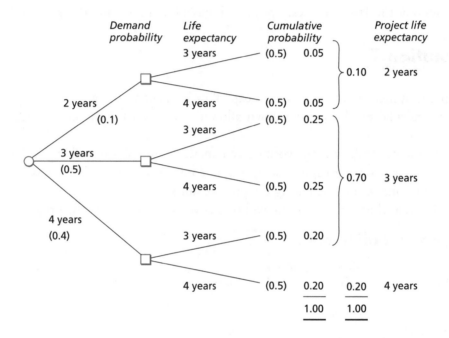

	£
Selling price per unit	49.90
Variable cost per unit	20.00
Contribution per unit	29.90
No. of units sold per annum	24,000
Total contribution	£717,600
Less fixed costs	£100,000
Relevant cash flow	£617,600

Year	Cash flow £	Probability	Disc. Factor	Present value £
0	(1,200,000)		1.000	(1,200,000)
1	617,600	1.0	877	541,635
2	617,600	1.0	769	474,934
3	617,600	0.9	675	375,192
4	617,600	0.2	592	73,124
	Expected net present value			264,885

(b) (i) The financial analysis in (a) above shows that the production and sale of the new personal alarm will result in a positive expected net present value of £264,885. As it is a large positive value the project will not be sensitive to slight errors in the estimation, for example of probabilities. The maximum NPV the project could earn is:

$$£617,600 \times 2.914 - £1,200,000 = £599,686$$

and there is a 0.2 probability of this occurring.

The minimum NPV the project could earn is, if the demand lasts for only 2 years

$$£617,600 \times 1.647 - £1,200,000 = £182,810$$

and there is 0.1 probability of this occurring.

(ii) The assumptions made include the following:
- Forecasts made are reasonably accurate.
- Taxation and inflation are ignored.
- The capital investment required is available.
- The cost of capital of 14 per cent is a reasonable estimate.

(iii) Other factors Apex Ltd should consider before making a decision are as follows:
- The availability of space, raw materials, etc.
- The reliability of the assembly line.
- Labour skills required-is additional training required?
- Threat of competitors and substitutes.
- Could the additional investment in this project be put to better use elsewhere?

✅ Solution 9

(a) **Report**

To:	The Management of MN plc
From:	Management Accountant
Re:	Investment opportunities A, B & C
Date:	21 November 20X1

Introduction

The three projects have different investment and return profiles as can be seen from the graph below. This graph can be used to select the best project for a particular cost of capital/discount rate. It shows that project C is better at 10 per cent discount rate, followed by B and then A, as shown by the NPV result. At 15 per cent, A is the only project yielding a positive NPV.

Differences between the NPV and IRR ranking

Normally, the NPV method provides the correct answer and maximises shareholder value, but in this instance other factors need to be considered. The three projects have two factors that differ. First, the length of the project, and second, the size of the initial sum of money invested. These two factors cause the difference in the results given in the question.

PROJECT APPRAISAL

The length of the project

Project A only lasts for 3 years, whereas the others last for 6 and 9 years. The NPV method assumes that at the end of year 3 no further investment is made in a project of a similar nature and funds earn the cost of capital/discount rate. This is the reason why Project A is ranked in third place. In reality, funds could probably be reinvested in a similar project earning 17.5 per cent or at least in another project of a different nature earning above 10 per cent, the cost of capital.

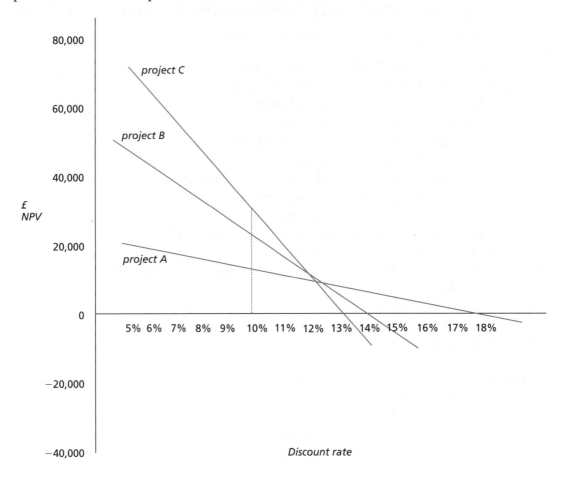

The calculation below shows the present value earned each year.

	Project A	Project B	Project C
Net present value at 10% a year	£14,376	£22,040	£31,432
Cumulative discount rate	2,487	4,355	5,759
	= £5,780	£5,061	£5,458
Ranking	1st	3rd	2nd

If funds could be reinvested in a project equal to A at the start of year 4 and again in year 7, the investment flow would generate an annual present value of £5,780 for 9 years and would be ranked first.

It could also be argued that where projects have similar returns, the one with the shorter life (Project A) should always be undertaken, because of the difficulty in predicting the future correctly. A fairly certain short term project may be better than a much longer term project generating a similar return. This is because the longer term project ties up funds that might not be as profitably used as originally predicted because of a change in circumstances, for example a rise in inflation.

The size of the investment

The other point to bear in mind is the size of the initial investment. If the NPV is expressed as a percentage of the initial investment, the following rankings are obtained:

	Project A	Project B	Project C
Net present value	£14,376	£22,040	£31,432
Initial investment	105,000	187,000	245,000
	= 13.69%	11.79%	12.83%
Ranking	1st	3rd	2nd

Project A gives a marginally better return, but if the money is not invested in Project C what will be done with it? The question implies that other investment opportunities exist which would allow for the additional investment of £140,000. If these do not exist, Project C may well be better. As can be seen in the following table, project C gives an additional positive net cash flow of £17,056 on the additional investment. This represents a return of 13 per cent each year on the excess investment. 48,000 × (5.132 − 2.361) = £133,008. Therefore, Project C is a better investment if the company has no alternative investment and can only reinvest at the time value of money during years 4–9.

	Project A £	Present value 10% Project C £	Additional cash flow £
Year 0	(105,000)	(245,000)	(140,000)
Year 1–3	119,376	119,376	–
Year 4–9	–	157,056	157,056
			17,056

Summary

- Project A is the best project if similar investment opportunities can be made in years 4 and 7. If this is not the case, Project C should be selected.
- Adopting Project A has the added advantage of keeping future options open and keeping the company liquid by returning the capital outlay quickly.

Signed: Management Accountant.

(b) Payback is a very simple method for assessing projects, which can be easily understood and calculated. Its main virtue is that it keeps the business liquid by returning funds quickly. This is obviously an advantage when the future is uncertain. However, by concentrating on the short term, projects with good returns after the payback date may be turned down and the longer-term strategic position of the company may be jeopardised. This is because investments in new technology, for example, may not be made at an early stage.

Payback is a traditional assessment method, but today discounted payback is more widely used.

If a payback method is to be used discounted payback is preferable. As can be seen from the calculations below, discounted payback alters the return time considerably and with a 10% cost of capital Project C's payback is in excess of 7 years when the returns are discounted.

	Project A	Project B	Project C
Payback	2.2 years	3.9 years	5.1 years
Discounted payback	2.6 years	5.2 years	7.5 years

Many companies use several investment appraisal methods – often NPV and payback. Perhaps MN pic should consider replacing IRR with discounted payback.

 Solution 10

Purchase

Tax Depreciation

			Tax relief @ 30%
			£
Cost		15,000	
Yr 1 WDA		(3,750)	
		11,250	1,125
Yr 2 WDA		(2,812)	
		8,437	844
Yr 3 Disp Bal All'ce		(5,000)	
		3,437	1,031

Cash flow

Year	0	1	2	3	4
	£	£	£	£	£
Investment	(15,000)			5,000	
Tax savings:					
Current Year		563	422	516	
Previous Year			563	422	515
	(15,000)	563	985	5,938	515
DF @ 15%	1.000	0.870	0.756	0.658	0.572
PV	(15,000)	490	745	3,907	295
	NPV = £(9,563)				

Lease

Cash flows

		Tax relief @ 30%
	£	£
Year 0	1,250	375
Years 1–3	4,992	1,498

NPV Calculation

		£	£
Yr 0	Lease	(1,250) × 1.000	(1,250)
	Tax saving	188 × 1.000	188
Yr 1	Tax saving	187 × 0.870	163
Yrs 1–3	Lease	(4,992) × 2.284	(11,402)
Yrs 1–3	Tax saving	749 × 2.284	1,711
Yrs 2–4	Tax saving	749 × 1.986	1,488)
			(9,102)

Leasing is the preferred option.

✓ Solution 11

(a) New sales = £4.0 m × 1.20 = £4.8 m

Variable costs are 60% of sales now but will reduce by 20% to 48% of sales (60% × 80%).

Thus contribution will be 52% of sales:
New contribution = £2.496 m/year
Old contribution = £1.600 m/year
Increase in contribution = £0.896 m/year

Cash flows

Year	0	1	2	3	4	5	6
	£m	£m	£m	£m	£m	£m	£m
Investment	(3.000)					0.300	
Old m/c	0.400						
Contribution		0.896	0.896	0.896	0.896	0.896	
	(2.600)	0.896	0.896	0.896	0.896	1.196	–
DF @ 14%	1.000	0.877	0.769	0.675	0.592	0.519	
PV	(2.600)	0.786	0.689	0.605	0.530	0.621	

Pre Tax NPV = 0.631
Tax NPV   = (0.368)
Post Tax NPV = 0.263   Worthwhile

Tax Depreciation

	Old	New	
Year 1	£	£	£
WDV b/f	250,000		
Disposal	400,000		
	(150,000)		
Bal chg	150,000		(150,000)
	NIL		
Addition		3,000,000	
WDA @ 25%		(750,000)	750,000
			600,000
		2,250,000	
Year 2			
WDA @ 25%		(562,500)	562,500
		1,687,500	
Year 3			
WDA @ 25%		(421,875)	421,875
		1,265,625	
Year 4			
WDA @ 25%		(316,406)	316,406
		949,219	
Year 5			
Disposal		(300,000)	
		649,219	
Ball All'ce		(649,219)	649,219
		NIL	

Tax

Year	Contribution	CA's	Taxable
	£m	£m	£m
1	0.896	0.600	0.296
2	0.896	0.563	0.333
3	0.896	0.422	0.474
4	0.896	0.316	0.580
5	0.896	0.649	0.247

Tax payable

Year	£m	Payable 1 £m	2 £m	3 £m	4 £m	5 £m	6 £m
1	0.296 × 30% = 0.088	0.044	0.044				
2	0.333 × 30% = 0.100		0.050	0.050			
3	0.474 × 30% = 0.142			0.071	0.071		
4	0.580 × 30% = 0.174				0.087	0.087	
5	0.247 × 30% = 0.074					0.037	0.037
		0.044	0.094	0.121	0.158	0.124	0.037
DF @ 14%		0.877	0.769	0.675	0.592	0.519	0.456
PV		0.039	0.072	0.082	0.094	0.064	0.017

NPV of tax = £0.368 million

(b) *Sensitivity analysis* is carried out before a decision is finally made. It is used to test how sensitive a potential decision is to a change or inaccuracy in the variables that have been used to reach the initial decision. Each variable is tested independently. The smaller the change required to change the initial decision then the more sensitive is that variable and the more justified is a manager in taking more care over the value of that variable. A key issue is the extent to which each variable is controllable by management. These factors enable management to decide whether or not to proceed with the initial decision.

In the context of this question sensitivity analysis

- measures the effect on NPV of changes in input variables.
- identifies the most critical input variable to the decision.

Contribution
The PV of contribution can reduce by £0.263 million before the proposal has a zero NPV.

Presently	£m
Pre tax contribution has a PV of	
2.496 × 3.433 =	8.569

Tax on contribution has a PV of
2.496 × 30% × 50% (yrs 1–5) = 0.3744
0.3744 × 3.433 = (1.285)

Plus

2.496 × 30% × 50% (yrs 2–6) = 0.3744
0.3744 × 3.012 = (1.128)
6.156

Thus a reduction of $\dfrac{0.263}{6.156}$ = 4.3% is needed before NPV = zero.

Tax rate
The PV of the tax payable = £0.368 million
This would have to increase by £0.263 million before the proposal has an NPV of zero.

That is to say, tax rates would have to increase by = $\dfrac{0.263}{0.368}$ = 71.5%

Thus the solution is more sensitive to changes in contribution than it is to changes in the rate of tax.

9

Managing Working
Capital: Cash Flow

Managing Working Capital: Cash Flow

LEARNING OUTCOMES

After completing this chapter you should be able to:

- explain the importance of cash flow and working capital management;
- analyse cash – flow forecasts over a twelve-month period;
- discuss measures to improve a cash forecast situation;
- identify sources of short-term funding;
- identify alternatives for investment of short-term cash surpluses;
- identify appropriate methods of finance for trading internationally.

9.1 Introduction

In this chapter, we explore the management of cash. Specifically, we will consider the manner in which cash budgets are used to support practices which facilitate the efficient operation of a business and minimise its financing costs. We will then consider the financial instruments, practices and products that may be used to support particular types of business transaction.

9.2 Cash management

The management of cash resources holds a central position in the area of short-term financing decisions. Results of investment decisions are estimated in cash terms and the value of an entity to a shareholder lies in its ability to add to their command over resources over time, which means to add to the shareholder's command over cash.

Cash management is part of the wider task of treasury management, which covers not only the management of the entity's cash in the normal course of business – making sure the entity always has enough cash on hand to meet its bills and expenses, and investing any surplus cash – but also other things too. Examples include foreign exchange dealings when the entity either imports or exports goods, arranging suitable mixes of short-, medium- and long-term borrowing, and dealing on the foreign currency markets and the

Eurocurrency market to maximise investment opportunities or to borrow funds on the most advantageous terms.

However, holding cash carries with it a cost – the opportunity cost of the profits that could be made if the cash were either used in the entity or invested elsewhere. Therefore, an entity has to balance the advantages of liquidity against profitability: cash should be held until the marginal value of the liquidity it gives is equal to the value of the interest lost.

Cash management is therefore concerned with optimising the amount of cash available to the entity and maximising the interest on any spare funds not required immediately by the entity.

9.2.1 The time value of money

A recurring theme of financial management is the time value of money – or the money value of time, depending on your point of view. It needs to be remembered, however, that there is not one generally applicable, constant price of money. Interest rates vary, according to the length of time of the investment, as portrayed in the familiar yield curve, and the yield curve itself varies over time. Interest rates are different according to whether you are lending to, or borrowing from, the banking system, and according to the flexibility of the arrangement, for example, how much notice is required to move funds into or out of an account.

Other things being equal, in what amounts to a reflection of their expected costs, the banks:

- pay higher interest on accounts subject to longer notices of withdrawal than they do on current accounts;
- charge higher interest on fluctuating overdrafts than they do on term loans.

A key task for the treasury function in any entity, therefore, is the management of the various accounts. Money is switched between them, so as to minimise aggregate costs (or maximise net income, as the case may be), recognising both transaction costs and interest rate differentials.

9.3 Cash flow forecasts

It is vital for entities to identify their cash requirements, in order to:

- minimise the cost of finance;
- maximise the returns from surplus funds;
- avoid embarrassment caused by unexpected inability to make required payments.

We have already explored the cash budget as part of our study of budgeting. It was seen that a cash budget is based on the cash flows of a business which are quite distinct from its profit or loss. The cash flow forecast is normally considered to be a component element in the cash budgeting exercise.

Cash flow forecasts are vital for the management of cash. They incorporate the expected or forecast inflows and outflows of cash through the organisation. They identify the cash surpluses or deficits that will occur from time to time. Cash flow forecasts are based on intervals which may be a single day, a week or a month. But, usually these intervals are short since cash flow management is very much a day-to-day operation. It should be noted that even a well capitalised organisation may encounter short-term cash flow difficulties caused by the pattern of its receipts and payments. The need to make a large payment or a delayed customer receipt may create a short-term cash shortage which can be difficult and expensive to cover if it was not foreseen in advance. If a business is suddenly forced to approach its bank for an emergency overdraft then this may harm the banking relationship in the long term.

Conversely, the accumulation of a large cash surplus may yield far less income if held on a current account than if it is invested in a timed deposit. In order to place money on timed deposit (e.g. for a month or a quarter) the business must be confident that it will not be needed during its term. Cash flow forecasting is an essential element in effective cash management. Cash management is generally considered to be a distinct exercise from long-term financing. Providing for the capitalisation and funding of a business over a time horizon of several years lies within the study of financial management and this is not considered here.

The basic techniques of cash flow forecasting have been considered earlier in this text in the context of cash budgets. The following exercise offers a full example of the preparation of a cash budget.

Exercise 9.1

The following information relates to Mansel, a publishing entity.

The selling price of a book is $15, and sales are made on credit through a book club and invoiced on the last day of the month.

Variable costs of production per book are materials ($5), labour ($4), and overhead ($2).

The sales manager has forecast the following volumes:

	Nov	Dec	Jan	Feb	Mar	Apr	May	Jun	Jul	Aug
No. of books:	1,000	1,000	1,000	1,250	1,500	2,000	1,900	2,200	2,200	2,300

Customers are expected to (with no bad debts anticipated) pay as follows:

One month after the sale	40%
Two months after the sale	60%

The entity produces the books 2 months before they are sold and the trade payables for materials are paid 2 months after production.

Variable overheads are paid in the month following production and are expected to increase by 25 per cent in April; 75 per cent of wages are paid in the month of production and 25 per cent in the following month. A wage increase of 12.5 per cent will take place on 1 March.

The entity is going through a restructuring and will sell one of its freehold properties in May for $25,000, but it is also planning to buy a new printing press in May for $10,000. Depreciation is currently $1,000 per month, and will rise to $1,500 after the purchase of the new machine.

The entity's income tax (of $10,000) is due for payment in March.

The entity presently has a cash balance at bank on 31 December 2003 of $ 1,500.

Requirement

Produce a cash budget (incoporating monthly intervals) for the subsequent 6 months from 1 January to 30 June.

Solution

Workings

1. Sales receipts

Month	Nov	Dec	Jan	Feb	Mar	Apr	May	Jun
Forecast sales (S)	1,000	1,000	1,000	1,250	1,500	2,000	1,900	2,200
	$	$	$	$	$	$	$	$
S × 15	15,000	15,000	15,000	18,750	22,500	30,000	28,500	33,000
Trade receivables pay:								
1 month 40%	–	6,000	6,000	6,000	7,500	9000	12,000	11,400
2 month 60%	–	–	9,000	9,000	9,000	11,250	13,500	18,000
Total sales receipts	–	6,000	15,000	15,000	16,500	20,250	25,500	29,400

2. Payment for materials – books produced two months before sale

Month	Nov	Dec	Jan	Feb	Mar	Apr	May	Jun
Qty produced (Q)	1,000	1,250	1,500	2,000	1,900	2,200	2,200	2,300
	$	$	$	$	$	$	$	$
Materials (Q × 5)	5,000	6,250	7,500	10,000	9,500	11,000	11,000	11,500
Paid (2 month after)	–	–	5,000	6,250	7,500	10,000	9,500	11,000

3. Variable overheads

Month	Nov	Dec	Jan	Feb	Mar	Apr	May	Jun
Qty produced (Q)	1,000	1,250	1,500	2,000	1,900	2,200	2,200	2,300
	$	$	$	$	$	$	$	$
Var. overhead (Q × 2)	2,000	2,500	3,000	4,000	3,800			
Var. overhead (Q × 2.50)						5,500	5,500	5,750
Paid (one month later)		2,000	2,500	3,000	4,000	3,800	5,500	5,500

4. Wages payments

Month		Dec	Jan	Feb	Mar	Apr	May	Jun
Qty produced (Q)		1,250	1,500	2000	1,900	2,200	2,200	2,300
		$	$	$	$	$	$	$
Wages Q × 4		5,000	6,000	8,000				
Wages Q × 4.50					8,550	9,900	9,900	10,350
75% this month		3,750	4,500	6,000	6,413	7,425	7,425	7,762
25% next month		–	1,250	1,500	2,000	2,137	2,475	2,475
cash paid in wages		3,750	5,750	7,500	8,413	9,562	9,900	10,237

Cash budget – 6 months ended June

	Jan	Feb	Mar	Apr	May	Jun
	$	$	$	$	$	$
Receipts:						
Credit sales	15,000	15,000	16,500	20,250	25,500	29,400
Premises disposal	–	–	–	–	25,000	–
	15,000	15,000	16,500	20,250	50,500	29,400
Payments:						
Materials	5,000	6,250	7,500	10,000	9,500	11,000
Var. overheads	2,500	3,000	4,000	3,800	5,500	5,500
Wages	5,750	7,500	8,413	9,562	9,900	10,237
Non-current assets	–	–	–	–	10,000	–
Income tax	–	–	10,000	–	–	–
Net cash flow	1,750	(1,750)	(3,413)	(3,112)	15,600	2,663
Balance b/f	1,500	3,250	11,500	(11,913)	(15,025)	575
Cumulative cash flow	3,250	1,500	(11,913)	(15,025)	575	3,238

9.3.1 Managing cash deficits

Short-term cash deficits are usually financed (by default) by utilising the entity's overdraft facility. In the example above, we are not aware of any *overdraft facility* and as such need to identify a suitable method of financing the deficit that exists in March and April.

Efficiency improvements arising from prompt banking (see below) are unlikely to release sufficient funds to cover a cash requirement of $15,025, so Mansel should consider the following steps:

- *Delay major items of capital expenditure.* The purchase of the new printing press could be delayed and although this would not affect the deficit in March or April, delaying the purchase until, say June or July would ease the cash drain in a very difficult month – particularly if the premises sale did not go through in May.
- *Improve collection period or delay trade payable collection period.* This was referred to above and there are associated problems (such as lost customers). However, if Mansel could increase the trade receivable collection period so that 80 per cent of money was collected 1 month after the sale and only 20 per cent 2 months after the sale, the cash flow would benefit significantly.

Similarly, if payments for materials could be delayed by another month (although this would seem unlikely) this would also have a beneficial effect.

- *Reduce inventory levels.* Mansel is effectively holding 2 months' inventory. Cash flow would improve if this figure was reduced.
- *Delay non-essential payments.* Delaying the income tax could be problematic: would the Revenue authorities consider payment by instalments?

If none of the above is possible, then the entity must consider approaching a bank to obtain an *overdraft facility*, consider some form of *factoring, invoice discounting*, or *sale and leaseback or raise additional long term funding through a bank loan or a share issue.*

9.3.2 Float

Float refers to the money tied up because of the time lag between a customer initiating payment (perhaps posting a cheque), and those funds being available for use by the recipient once the cheque has been cleared by the bank. This time lag will mean that the entity's cash at bank figure will be different in its own books of account from the figure on its bank statement.

There are three elements of time delay that cause float:

1. *Transmission delay.* This is the time delay caused by sending a cheque through the post.
2. *Lodgement delay.* When a cheque is received, there may be a delay in presenting the cheque to the bank for clearance.
3. *Clearance delay.* When a cheque is presented to a bank for clearance, it may take 3 days or more to clear.

Float could be reduced if customers paid by electronic funds transfer. Payment by electronic funds transfer has the advantage over cheque payment of being more secure, and it will reduce administrative time. However, these systems can be expensive to introduce.

9.4 Efficient-cash management

The amount of cash available to an entity at any given time is largely dependent on the efficiency with which cash flows are managed. Purely from the point of view of efficiency, for a given level of sales, debts should be collected and banked as quickly as possible while payments owed (to suppliers, etc.) should be delayed as long as possible. This approach is something of an oversimplification – it ignores the fact that a reduction in the credit granted to customers may reduce the overall sales level. Also, excessive delay in paying trade payables may reduce the entity's credit standing so that suppliers will only be prepared to deal with the entity on slightly less favourable terms. Cheques normally take three working days to progress through the banking system and be credited to or debited from the entity's account. The delay will, of course, be greater if the cheque is posted! These delays can be both advantageous to the entity (payments that have been made remaining in the entity's account a few days longer, either to earn interest or to keep overdraft interest down) or disadvantageous (cash not becoming available for the entity's use until a few days after debts have been paid by customers).

Part of the efficient management of cash is the practice of prompt banking of cash takings. By banking takings only once or twice a week, the entity misses the opportunity to earn interest on a positive cash balance or to reduce interest payments on an overdraft.

9.5 The link between cash, profit and the statement of financial position

 Examination questions in this area can require you to calculate profit forecasts from cash forecasts or cash flow forecasts from profit and statement of financial position forecasts.

Exercise 9.2

CBA is a manufacturing entity in the furniture trade. Its sales have risen sharply over the past six months as a result of an improvement in the economy and a strong housing market. The entity is now showing signs of 'overtrading' and the financial manager, Ms Smith, is concerned about its liquidity. The entity is 1 month from its year-end. Estimated figures for the full 12 months of the current year and forecasts for next year, on present cash management policies, are shown below.

	Next year $'000	Current year $'000
Income Statement		
Turnover	5,200	4,200
Less		
Cost of sales (Note 1)	3,224	2,520
Operating expenses	650	500
Operating profit	1,326	1,180

Interest paid	54	48
Profit before tax	1,272	1,132
Tax payable	305	283
Profit after tax	967	849
Dividends declared	387	339
Current assets and liabilities as at the end of the year		
Inventory/work in progress	625	350
Trade receivables	750	520
Cash	0	25
Trade payables	(464)	(320)
Other payables (tax and dividends)	(692)	(622)
Overdraft	(11)	0
Net current assets/(liabilities)	208	(47)
Note 1:		
Cost of sales includes depreciation of	225	175

Ms Smith is considering methods of improving the cash position. A number of actions are being discussed:

Trade receivables

Offer a 2 per cent discount to customers who pay within 10 days of despatch of invoices. It is estimated that 50 per cent of customers will take advantage of the new discount scheme. The other 50 per cent will continue to take the current average credit period.

Trade payables and inventory

Reduce the number of suppliers currently being used and negotiate better terms with those that remain by introducing a 'just-in-time' policy. The aim will be to reduce the end-of-year forecast cost of sales (excluding depreciation) by 5 per cent and inventory/work in progress levels by 10 per cent. However, the number of days' credit taken by the entity will have to fall to 30 days to help persuade suppliers to improve their prices.

Other information

- All trade is on credit. Official terms of sale at present require payment within 30 days. Interest is not charged on late payments.
- All purchases are made on credit.
- Operating expenses will be $650,000 under either the existing or proposed policies.
- Interest payments would be $45,000 if the new policies are implemented.
- Capital expenditure of $550,000 is planned for next year.

Requirements

(a) Provide a cash flow forecast for next year, assuming:
  (i) the entity does not change its policies;
  (ii) the entity's proposals for managing trade receivables, trade payables and inventory are implemented.
  In both cases, assume a full twelve-month period, i.e. the changes will be effective from day 1 of next year.
(b) As assistant to Ms Smith, write a short report to her evaluating the proposed actions. Include comments on the factors, financial and non-financial, that the entity should take into account before implementing the new policies.

MANAGING WORKING CAPITAL: CASH FLOW

 Solution

(a) *All figures in $'000s*

	No change in policy	Changes implemented
Profit from operations	1,326	1,424
Add depreciation	225	225
+/−change in trade receivables	−230	72
+72 +/−change in trade payables	144	−86
Cash flow from operations	1,465	1,635
Interest paid	−54	−45
Tax paid	−283	−283
Dividends paid	−339	−339
Investing activities		
Non-current assets	−550	−550
Inventory	−275	−212
Net cash flow	−36	206
Opening balance	25	25
Closing balance	−11	231

Changes implemented

1. Profit from operations:

Turnover	=	5,200
Less discounts	=	−52
CoS (3,224 − 225) × 95% + 225	=	−3,074
Operating expenses (unchanged)	=	−650
		1,424

2. Decrease in trade receivables:
   $520 − [($2,600/365 × 53*) + ($2,600/365 × 10*)] = 72$
   Decrease in trade payables:
   $[$320 − ($2,849**/365 × 30)] = 86$
3. Inventory:
   $[$350 − (625 × 90\%)] = 212$
   *Forecast receivables = $750/5,200 × 365 = 53 reduces to 10 for 50% of turnover.
   **Payables forecast are $3,224 − 225 = $2,999; these reduce by 5% to $2,849.

(b) **Report**

To: Ms Smith
From: Assistant
Subject: Proposed working capital policy changes

The answer should be set out in report format and include the following key points:

- Comment that cash flow is improved by almost a quarter of a million pounds if the proposed changes are made.
- Problems appear to have arisen because trade receivables and inventory control have not been adequate for increased levels of turnover.
- Liquidity: current ratio was 0.95:1 (all current assets to trade and other payables), will be around 1.2:1 under both options. Perversely, ratio looks to improve even if the entity takes no action and causes an overdraft. This is because of high receivables and inventory levels. Moral: high current assets do not mean high cash. Cash ratio perhaps a better measure.
- Receivables' days last year was 45, forecast to rise to 53 on current policies despite 'official' terms being 30. Entity could perhaps look to improve its credit control before offering discounts.

- Trade payables' days were 46, forecast to rise to 52. Are discounts being ignored? Are relationships with suppliers being threatened?*
- Dramatic increase in inventory levels forecast: 50 days last year, 71 days forecast this year. If change implemented, inventory will still be 67 days.*
- Operating profit percentage forecast to fall to 25.5 per cent from 281.1 per cent if no changes made. Percentage will fall to 27.4 per cent if changes implemented; a fall probably acceptable if cash flow improved and overdraft interest saved.
- Non-financial factors include relationships with customers and suppliers.
- Other financial factors, is increase in turnover sustainable?
- * Using cost of sales figures including depreciation.

9.6 Sources of short-term finance

In dealing with a forecast cash deficit, short-term finance may be obtained from a variety of sources including:

- trade credit from suppliers
- overdrafts
- short-term loans
- using trade receivables as security for a loan, through factoring or invoice discounting.

There are other sources that tend to be specifically associated with financing export sales such as:

- bills of exchange
- documentary credits.

9.6.1 Trade credit

Trade credit is an important source of finance for most businesses. Trade credit is the money owed to the suppliers of goods and services as a result of purchasing goods or services on one date, but paying for those goods on a later date. Trade credit is often viewed as being a free source of finance as interest is not usually charged by a supplier unless payment is overdue. Trade credit does have a cost, although those costs may be hidden.

As interest is not usually charged on trade credit, the temptation is to maximise the use of trade credit, but it is important that this is not abused. Exceeding the normal credit terms may lead to a number of potential problems:

- difficulty in obtaining credit terms from new suppliers;
- cash flow problems for key suppliers that could adversely affect the viability of both organisations;
- existing suppliers may be unwilling to extend further credit;
- supplier goodwill will be eroded;
- suppliers may refuse to supply in the future;
- credit rating may be reduced.

The problems of late payment have been a particular concern for smaller entities selling goods on credit to large entities in a number of countries. For example, the difficulties in obtaining payment from large entities prompted the UK government to introduce legislation in 1998 to help smaller entities. In the UK, smaller entities now have a statutory right to charge larger entities interest at a high interest rate (base rate + 8 per cent) on any overdue amounts. Entities that suffer from late payment usually have to resort to additional overdraft finance while waiting for their customers to pay.

9.6.2 Overdrafts

One of the most important external sources of short-term finance, particularly for small firms, is the overdraft. Features that make the overdraft popular are:

- *Flexibility.* The bank will agree to a maximum overdraft limit or facility. The borrower may not require the full facility immediately, but may draw funds up to the limit as and when required.
- *Minimal documentation.* Legal documentation is fairly minimal when arranging an overdraft. Key elements of the documentation will be to state the maximum overdraft limit, the interest payable and the security required.
- Interest is only paid on the amount borrowed, rather than on the full facility.

The drawback of overdraft finance is that it is, strictly speaking, repayable on demand, which means that the facility could be withdrawn at any time. Entities with few assets to offer as security will find it difficult to arrange further overdraft finance. The interest rate charged by the bank will vary depending on the perceived credit risk of the borrower.

9.6.3 Term loans

Term loans are offered by the high street banks and their popularity has increased for a number of reasons, not least their accessibility, which is of importance to smaller businesses. A term loan is for a fixed amount with a fixed repayment schedule. Usually the interest rate applied is slightly less than for a bank overdraft. The lender will require security to cover the amount borrowed and an arrangement fee is payable dependent on the amount borrowed.

Term loans also have the following qualities:

- *They are negotiated easily and quickly.* This is particularly important when a cashflow problem has not been identified until recently and a quick but significant fix is needed.
- *Banks may offer flexible repayments.* High street banks will often devise new lending methods to suit their customers; for example, no capital repayments for, say 2 years, thus avoiding unnecessary overborrowing to fund capital repayment.
- *Variable interest rates.* This may be important given the uncertainty that exists with interest rates.

9.6.4 Factoring

Entities selling goods on credit may have to wait 30, 60 or more days to receive payment from the customer. In the meantime, they have to finance their day-to-day activities, and purchase more supplies. Factoring organisations may help improve cash flow by speeding up the cash receipt relating to outstanding invoices. This is achieved by advancing, say 80 per cent of invoice value immediately, a balance being settled when the client's customer settles the debt.

Factoring is explored more fully later in this text.

9.7 Export finance

Selling goods overseas may involve offering longer credit periods than for similar domestic sales. The credit customer may not be as well known as a domestic customer. There is potentially a greater risk of delay or non-payment for goods. Entities may seek to raise finance in such circumstances to ease cash flow problems.

9.7.1 Export factoring

Export factoring is essentially the same as for domestic factoring described above, with the factor providing a cash advance, typically of about 80 per cent of invoice value. The credit insurance element of the factor's service will also protect against bad-debt risk.

Whereas factoring and the methods of finance mentioned above are relevant to an entity to finance domestic or export sales, there are methods of finance that are specifically associated with financing export sales.

9.7.2 Bill of exchange

A bill of exchange is defined in CIMA's *Management Accounting: Official Terminology* as follows:

> 🔑 A negotiable instrument, drawn by one party on another, for example, by a supplier of goods on a customer, who by accepting (signing) the bill, acknowledges the debt, which may be payable immediately (a sight draft) or at some future date (a time draft). The holder of the bill can thereafter use an accepted time draft to pay a debt to a third party, or can discount it to raise cash.

The bill of exchange is essentially a written acknowledgement of a debt. They are more commonly used for export transactions than for domestic transactions.

A bill of exchange is a device that may enable the supplier to receive the benefit of payment well before the customer actually pays. The way it works is like this:

1. The *supplier* draws up a simple document (the bill of exchange) requiring the customer to pay the amount due at some fixed future date. (The supplier is the *drawer* of the bill.)
2. The supplier signs the bill and sends it to the customer, who also signs it to signify that he/she agrees to pay, and returns the bill to the supplier. (The customer is the *acceptor* of the bill.)
3. The supplier now has a piece of paper that is worth money, because it constitutes an agreement on the customer's part to pay the debt on the due date. The supplier can now do one of three things:
    (a) hold the bill until the due date and collect the money;
    (b) arrange to transfer the benefit of the bill to the bank in exchange for immediate cash. The bank will make a charge for what is effectively a loan, so the amount received by the supplier will be less than the face value of the bill. This is called *discounting* the bill of exchange with the bank;
    (c) transfer the bill to his/her own supplier in a settlement of the debt. That supplier may in turn pass the bill to one of his/her own supplier, discount it or hold it to maturity.

4. When the due date of the bill arrives, the person holding it at that time presents it to the original acceptor for payment. If the acceptor pays, that is the end of the matter. If the acceptor does not pay on the due date, the bill is said to be dishonoured. Legal action by the parties concerned may then be initiated to recover the money from the original acceptor. A bank bill is a bill of exchange drawn on a bank and is typically used for arranging payment for imports.

Calculating the amount of discount on a bill

When a financial instrument such as a bill of exchange is sold or issued at a discount and redeemed at face value, we may need to calculate the amount of discount or the selling price.

The amount of discount is the rate of discount or discount yield (R) multiplied by the face value (F) multiplied by the time to redemption expressed as a number of days (T) over the days in the year (Y). The price is the face value less the discount amount. To calculate the price, use the formulae:

$$\text{Price} = F \times [1 - RT/Y]$$

Example

> A bill of exchange with a face value of $1,000 has 91 days to maturity. The discount yield required by the investor is 5%. Assume a 365 day year. What is the price the investor is willing to pay for the bill?
>
> $$\text{Price} = \$1,000 \times [1 - (0.05 \times 91)/365] = \$987.53$$

Advantages of bills of exchange

- provides a convenient method of collecting debts from foreign customers;
- foreign buyer receives full period of credit and the exporter can use the bill to raise immediate finance by discounting the bill;
- if the bill of exchange is dishonoured, it may be used by the drawer to support legal action against the drawee in the drawee's country.

9.7.3 Documentary credits

Documentary credits, or letters of credit as they are also called, provide an exporter with a secure method of obtaining payment for overseas sales. Documentary credits also provide the exporter with a method of raising short-term finance from a bank.

CIMA's *Management Accounting: Official Terminology* defines a letter of credit as follows:

> A document issued by a bank on behalf of a customer authorising a person to draw money to a specified amount from its branches or correspondents, usually in another country, when the conditions set out in the document have been met.

The process of payment using a documentary credit would be as follows. An exporter and a foreign buyer would complete a sales contract with payment agreed to be by documentary credit. The foreign buyer would then advise its bank (the issuing bank) to provide credit in favour of the exporter. The issuing bank would then ask the exporter's bank to advise and/or confirm credit to the exporter. The issuing bank would at this stage be providing a guarantee of payment for the goods. The exporter would then dispatch the goods and present the documents of title for the goods to its bank. Once the exporter's bank has checked the documents, it will be prepared to advance finance to the exporter and will forward the documents to the issuing bank. The issuing bank will check the documents and, if satisfied, will reimburse the exporter's bank. The issuing bank will release the documents to the foreign buyer after payment has been received, which will then enable the foreign buyer to take delivery of the goods.

Documentary credits are time-consuming and expensive to arrange and so will only tend to be used in situations where there is a high risk of non-payment.

9.7.4 Forfeiting

Forfaiting is an arrangement whereby exporters, normally of capital goods or raw materials, can obtain medium-term finance. The forfaiting bank buys at a discount to face value a series of promissory notes (or bills of exchange) usually extending over a period of between 6 months and 5 years. The promissory notes may be in any of the world's major currencies. For promissory notes to be eligible for forfaiting (and to provide the forfaiting bank's security), the notes must be guaranteed or avalised by a highly rated international bank (often in the importer's country). Forfaiting is non-recourse, with no claim on the exporter after the notes have been purchased by the bank; payment of the notes is guaranteed by the avalising bank.

Advantages of forfaiting include the following:

  (i) trade receivables are turned into immediate cash;
 (ii) as it is non-recourse, no liability appears on the statement of financial position;
(iii) future foreign-exchange and interest-rate risk is eliminated;
(iv) overdraft and other credit limits are not affected;
 (v) forfeited notes are negotiable.

Forfaiting was developed for East European trade, where governments sought finance for capital equipment purchases, but the time span of the projects was too long for bank or government export credits financing. Forfaiting enables exporters to offer clients medium-term fixed-rate finance with which to fund the order, while at the same time offering the exporter a means of obtaining immediate cash payment for the order, transferring default risk to the forfaiter.

9.8 Managing cash surpluses

When the cash budget of an organisation indicates a cash surplus, the financial manager needs to consider opportunities for short-term investment. A cash surplus may arise as a result of profitable trading, an uneven trade cycle or from a lack of suitable long-term investment opportunities, or perhaps as a result of a disposal programme. In principle, where there is no foreseeable use for the surpluses, the cash should be returned to shareholders or used to repay debt. Usually, cash will be retained to protect against unexpected losses or to fund unexpected investment opportunities.

Any cash surplus beyond the immediate needs should be put to work, even if only invested overnight. The following considerations should be made in assessing how to invest short-term cash surpluses:

- length of time for which the funds are available;
- amount of funds available;
- return offered on the investment in relation to the amount involved;
- risks associated with calling in the investment early (e.g. the need to give three months' notice to obtain the interest);
- ease of realisation.

The aim would be to maximise the post-tax return from the investment, but also to minimise the risk to the original capital invested.

9.9 Debt yields

The rate of return, or yield, on debentures, loan stocks and bonds is measured in two different ways.

9.9.1 Interest yield

Interest yield is also referred to as running yield or flat yield and is calculated by dividing the gross interest by the current market value of the stock as follows:

$$\text{Interest yield} = \frac{\text{gross interest}}{\text{market value}} \times 100\%$$

Example

A 6 per cent debenture with a current market value of $90 per $100 nominal would have an interest yield of:

$$\frac{6}{90} \times 100\% = 6.7\% \text{ grass or pre-tax}$$

Compound interest yield

If interest is paid half yearly, quarterly or even monthly, the interest rate will need to be compounded to give the annual yield.

Example

An investment pays 5% interest quarterly. What is the annual yield?

$$[[1 + 0.05]^4 - 1] \times 100 = 21.55\%$$

9.9.2 Yield to maturity (redemption yield)

The yield to maturity (or redemption) is the effective yield on a redeemable security, taking into account any gain or loss due to the fact that it was purchased at a price different from the redemption value.

Exercise 9.3

You are asked to put a price on a bond with a coupon rate of 8 per cent. It will repay its face value of $100 at the end of 15 years. Other similar bonds have a yield to maturity (YTM) of 12 per cent.

 Solution

The price of the bond is:

$8 × (annuity factor for $t = 15$, $r = 12$) + $100 × (discount factor $t = 15$, $r = 12$) = ($8 × 6,811) + ($100 × 0.1827) = $72.76

Note: The annuity factors and discount factors are obtained from tables at the end of this chapter. These tables will be provided in the examination.

What we are doing here is adding the NPV of 15 years of interest payments to the present value of the sum receivable on redemption.

We can turn this example round to calculate the YTM. If the price of the bond is known to be $78.40, what is the yield to redemption? This is basically an internal rate of return calculation and the answer is approximately 11 per cent.

The calculation is as follows. Assume two discount rates as for an IRR interpolation, between which the required percentage is likely to fall. Let us say, in this case, 10 per cent and 14 per cent. Then the equations are:

$t = 15$, $r = 10$, so $8 × 7.606 + $100 × 0.239 = $84.75

$t = 15$, $r = 14$, so $8 × 6.142 + $100 × 0.140 = $63.14

Then, by interpolation, bearing in mind that $r = 10$ is closer to $78.40 than is $r = 14$, so that the required rate must be nearer 10, then:

$$\text{Redemption yield} = 10\% + \left[\frac{84.75 - 78.40}{84.75 - 63.14}\right] \times 4$$
$$= 10\% + 1.17\% = 11.17\%$$

When selecting the two discount rates, it can sometimes be useful to estimate the likely rate by using simple annual returns. In the above example, it would be the return each year, without compounding, divided by the cost. The return is $100 − $78.40 = $21.60 over 15 years is $1.44 a year. Add the annual interest of $8 on to this and we get $9.44, divide by the cost of $78.40 and we get 12%. We would then select rates either side of this rough estimate, say 10% and 14%. This saves picking two rates to find that the yield is not between them.

9.9.3 Coupon rate

A connected issue that is often misunderstood is the relationship of face value to market value and coupon rate (on debt) to rate of return.

When a bond or debenture or any fixed-interest debt is issued, it carries a 'coupon' rate. This is the interest rate that is payable on the face, or nominal, value of the debt. Unlike shares, which are rarely issued at their nominal value, debt is frequently issued at par, usually $100 payable for $100 nominal of the bond. At the time of issue, the interest rate will be fixed according to interest rates available in the market at that time for bonds of similar maturity. The credit rating of the entity will also have an impact on the rate of interest demanded by the market.

Example

An entity issues bonds at par (the face or nominal value) with a coupon rate of 12 per cent. This means that for every $100 of debt the buyer will receive $12 per annum in gross interest. Assume that interest is payable annually (it is usually paid bi-annually but this would require more tricky calculations). Mr A bought $1,000 of this debt on 1 January 2002. He will receive $120 in interest every year as long as he owns the bond. This might be until it matures or it might be when he sells it in the market. If the opportunity cost to investors of bonds of similar risk and maturity is 12 per cent, then the coupon rate and the rate of return are the same.

However, assume that inflation increases at a much higher rate than expected by the market when the bond was issued. In January 2004, the opportunity cost to investors of similar bonds has risen to 15 per cent. Mr A continues to receive $120 on his $1,000 nominal value, but no new buyer would now pay $1,000 to get a return of 12 per cent – they now want 15 per cent. The price of the bond therefore falls to the level where the return on the debt is 15 per cent. This is $80 per $100 nominal of the bond.

Mr B buys $1,000 nominal of the bond in January 2004. He will receive $120 per year in interest, just like Mr A, but as Mr B paid only $800, his return is 15 per cent ($120/800 \times 100$). The coupon rate stays at 12 per cent, the nominal value at $1,000, but the rate of return is 15 per cent and the market value $800.

9.10 Short-term investments

Examples of short-term investment opportunities that might be considered by an organisation include the following.

9.10.1 Treasury bills

Treasury bills are issued by central banks, they are guaranteed by the government of the country of issue. No interest is paid as such, but they are issued at a discount and redeemed at par after a fixed period, for example, UK Treasury Bills are 91 days. They are negotiable, so the bills can be sold on the discount market at any time before their maturity date. There is an implied rate of interest in the price at which Treasury bills are traded.

9.10.2 Bank deposits

A wide range of interest-earning investment opportunities are available from the banks. A *term deposit* offers a fixed rate of interest for a fixed period, usually from 1 month to 6 years. For shorter periods, typically up to 3 months, the interest may be at a variable rate based on money-market rates.

9.10.3 Certificates of deposit

Certificates of deposit (CDs) are issued by the banks at a fixed interest rate for a fixed term (usually between 3 and 5 years). CDs are negotiable documents for which there is an active secondary market, meaning that the holder of a CD can realise the investment on the discount market at any time.

9.10.4 Money-market accounts

Most major financial institutions offer schemes for investment in the money market at variable rates of interest. There is a large money market in the UK for inter-bank borrowing and lending, with terms ranging from overnight to 12 months or more. Large entities will be able to lend surplus cash directly to a borrowing bank on the inter-bank market.

9.10.5 Local authority deposits

Local authorities have a requirement for short-term cash, with terms ranging from overnight to 12 months or more. Interest would be payable on these deposits.

9.10.6 Commercial paper

Large entities may issue unsecured short-term loan notes, referred to as commercial paper. These loan notes will generally mature within 9 months, typically between a week and 3 months. Commercial paper is negotiable, so the bills can be sold on the discount market at any time before their maturity date. There is an implied rate of interest in the price at which the commercial paper is traded.

9.10.7 Local authority bonds

These bonds are issued by local authorities and may be purchased with their remaining maturity. They are tradable, but have a lower level of marketability than most marketable securities, although this is dependent upon the size of the particular local authority.

9.10.8 Corporate bonds

These are bonds issued by entities to raise debt finance. They are long term, but are tradable and thus can be sold in money markets at any time. The level of liquidity depends on the cumulative volume issued by the entity. The level of risk depends on the individual entity and on the terms of the bond, but a credit score is available from credit rating agencies.

9.10.9 Government bonds

These are bonds issued by a government. They normally have lower default risk than corporate bonds (depending upon the government that issued them). They are tradable in money markets and tend to be more liquid than corporate bonds as they are issued in higher volumes.

9.10.10 Risk and return

When investing surplus cash in short-term investments, consideration must be given to the trade-off between return and risk. The liquidity of the investments must also be considered, how quickly could the investment be realised if it is required.

- *Default risk.* The risk that interest and/or principal will not be paid on schedule on fixed-interest investments. Most short-term investment in marketable securities is confined to investments with negligible risk of default.
- *Price risk.* Where interest rates change and this has not been anticipated, this will have an impact upon the tradable value of a security. Thus, if interest rates rise unexpectedly, then the value of a tradable fixed interest security will tend to fall until its yield is equal to the equivalent market yield for that type of security. If securities are held to redemption, the full nominal value is repaid, but the risk still exists in the opportunity cost of the higher interest lost on alternative investments.

Financial managers normally wish to avoid substantial price risk.

- *Foreign exchange risk.* If the funds are invested in an overseas currency, there is the risk that exchange rate movements may reduce the value of the principal in terms of the domestic currency. Given that the entity may purchase an overseas entity, then the investment may represent hedging against this in terms of currency matching. This may actually reduce risk. This, of course, depends upon identifying the particular country in which the entity is to be purchased.
- *Taxation and regulation risk.* Unexpected changes in tax rates or other regulation changes may impact upon the tradable value of a marketable security.
- *Return.* Managers will usually try to achieve the maximum yield possible, consistent with a satisfactory level of risk and marketability. It is unlikely that short-term cash surpluses will be invested in equities owing to the risks associated with achieving that return over a short period.
- *Liquidity.* Managers need to consider the ease with which they can access the invested funds if their forecasts prove inaccurate. For example, treasury bills and certificates of deposit can be traded in the market and realised at any time, whereas a fixed term deposit may not be available until the end of the deposit term.

9.11 Summary

In this chapter we have considered the treasury practices that are used by businesses and organisations. These practices are intended to facilitate the flow of cash through a business in a manner that minimises finance cost, maximises the return from cash holdings and limits exposure to risk. An effective treasury operation contributes significantly to the performance and value of a business.

Self-test questions
(1) What distinguishes the cash budget from the operational budget? (Section 9.3)
(2) What factors contribute to efficient cash management? (Section 9.4)
(3) Compare overdrafts and term loans as sources of finance. (Section 9.6)
(4) Explain the term 'bill of exchange'. (Section 9.7.2)
(5) Explain the term 'letter of credit'. (Section 9.7.3)
(6) Explain the term 'forfaiting'. (Section 9.7.4)
(7) Compare the 'coupon rate' and 'rate of return' on a bond. (Section 9.9.3)
(8) How might the default risk on a bank deposit be assessed? (Section 9.10.10)

Revision Questions

? Question 1

An entity commenced trading on 1 January and total sales for January were $150,000. Sales are made up of 60% on credit and 40% for cash. Sales grow at a monthly rate of 10%. Bad debts were 3% of credit sales. Half of the remaining trade receivables paid in the month following the sale and the remainder in the month after that.

The cash received during February was:

(A) $103,650
(B) $107,670
(C) $109,650
(D) $153,300   **(2 marks)**

? Question 2

The following items were extracted from an entity's budget for next month:

	$
Purchases on credit	360,000
Expected decrease in inventory over the month	12,000
Expected increase in trade payables over the month	15,000

What is the budgeted payment to trade payables for the month?

(A) $333,000
(B) $345,000
(C) $357,000
(D) $375,000   **(2 marks)**

? Question 3

Which ONE of the following transactions would NOT affect the amount of a bank overdraft?

(A) A payment by direct debit
(B) A bad debt write off
(C) An investment in treasury bills
(D) Bank charges   **(2 marks)**

? Question 4

An entity commenced business on 1 April 2002. Sales in April 2002 were $20,000, but this is expected to increase at 2% a month. Credit sales amount to 60% of total sales. The credit period allowed is 1 month. Bad debts are 3% of credit sales, but other trade receivables pay on time. Cash sales represent the other 40% of sales. The cash expected to be received in May 2002 is:

(A) $19,560
(B) $19,640
(C) $19,800
(D) $20,160

(2 marks)

? Question 5

In no more than 120 words, explain how and why good quality cash flow forecasting contributes to the efficient use of short-term cash surpluses. **(5 marks)**

? Question 6

ABC commences business on 1 January with a £300,000 cash balance. It produces and sells units. Its operating budget for the coming year (with quarterly intervals) is:

Quarters	1	2	3	4(L)	4(M)	4(H)
Unit sales	9,000	17,000	15,000	15,000	18,000	21,000
Units produced	10,000	20,000	15,000	15,000	18,000	21,000
Costs £s:						
Material X	50,000	100,000	75,000			
Material Y	40,000	80,000	60,000			
Labour	180,000	285,000	230,000			
Production overheads	80,000	110,000	95,000			
Plant depreciation	14,000	14,000	14,000			
Admin. overheads	30,000	30,000	30,000			
S&D overheads	29,000	37,000	35,000			
Total	423,000	656,000	539,000			

Three alternative budgets (Low, Medium and High sales cases) have been postulated for quarter 4. Relevant facts are:

- The Unit selling price throughout will be £40 with all sales on 2 months' credit terms. 70% of customers will pay on time with the remaining 30% paying 1 month late.
- Sales and production take place at an even rate throughout the individual quarters. Materials are delivered on a JIT basis and on 1 month credit terms which ABC will comply strictly with.
- Prices and labour rates are expected to stay the same throughout the year except for product X which will rise in price by 20% in quarter 4 relative to earlier quarters.
- For quarterly levels of production over 19,000 units, a 50% overtime premium must be paid on the variable component of labour costs relating to that production over the 19,000 unit ceiling.

Requirement

Prepare a 1 year cash flow forecast for ABC's management. You may arrange this forecast in the manner you consider most informative and make the most obvious assumptions concerning cost behaviour. **(20 marks)**

Question 7

A $100, 1 year bond is offered which pays $28 at the end of each quarter up to the time of final maturity. What is the equivalent annual rate of interest offered by this bond?

(5 marks)

Question 8

Which ONE of the following most appropriately describes *forfaiting*?

(A) It is a method of providing medium-term export finance
(B) It provides long-term finance to importers
(C) It provides equity finance for the redemption of shares
(D) It is the surrender of a share because of the failure to make a payment on a partly-paid share **(2 marks)**

Question 9

Which of the following is NOT a method used for raising finance to fund export sales?

(A) Bills of exchange
(B) Credit insurance
(C) Documentary credits
(D) Countertrade **(2 marks)**

Question 10

Which of the following would NOT be regarded as a source of short-term finance?

(A) Trade credit from suppliers
(B) Treasury bills
(C) Factoring of trade receivables
(D) Bank overdraft **(2 marks)**

Question 11

List six sources of short-term investments. **(3 marks)**

Question 12

In no more than 40 words, define the meaning of 'yield to maturity'. **(2 marks)**

? Question 13

After a bill of exchange has been accepted, there are a number of possible actions that the drawer could take. Which ONE of the following is NOT a possible course of action?

(A) Ask the customer for immediate payment
(B) Discount the bill with a bank
(C) Hold the bill until the due date and then present it for payment
(D) Use the bill to settle a trade payable **(2 marks)**

? Question 14

CX purchased $10,000 of unquoted bonds when they were issued by Z. CX now wishes to sell the bonds to B. The bonds have a coupon rate of 7% and will repay their face value at the end of five years. Similar bonds have a yield to maturity of 10%. Calculate the current market price for the bonds. **(3 marks)**

? Question 15

BH purchased a bond with a face value of $1,000 on 1 June 2003 for $850. The bond has a coupon rate of 7%. BH intends holding the bond to its maturity on 31 May 2008 when it will repay its face value.

? Requirements

(i) Explain the difference between the coupon rate of a security and its yield to maturity.
 (2 marks)
(ii) Calculate the bond's yield to maturity. **(3 marks)**
 (Total marks = 5)

? Question 16

Explain the main sources of short-term and medium-term funds. **(5 marks)**

? Question 17

Discuss a situation where it is better to obtain overdraft facilities rather than a term loan. **(5 marks)**

? Question 18

'Delaying payment to suppliers of goods and services is always a cheap form of borrowing funds.' Discuss this statement. **(5 marks)**

? Question 19

A bond has a current market price of $83. It will repay its face value of $100 in 7 years' time and has a coupon rate of 4%.

If the bond is purchased at $83 and held, what is its yield to maturity? **(4 marks)**

Solutions to Revision Questions

✅ Solution 1

The correct answer is (C), see Section 9.3.

Jan (0.6 × 150,000 × 0.97)/2 = $43,650
Feb (0.4 × 150,000 × 1.1) = $66,000
Total = $109,650

✅ Solution 2

The correct answer is (B), see Section 9.3.
$360,000 − $15,000 = $345,000

✅ Solution 3

The correct answer is (B), see Section 9.5.

✅ Solution 4

The correct answer is (C), see Section 9.3.

(20,000 × 1.02 × 40%) + (20,000 × 60% × 0.97) = $19,800

✅ Solution 5

An organisation's cash flow position will often incorporate wide oscillations around a long-term trend. The pattern of payments and receipts may therefore leave the business holding large cash surpluses for short periods, although these surpluses are likely to disappear when scheduled payments have to be made. If surplus cash is held on a current account then it may generate no interest income. If it is held on no-notice deposit then it may generate little interest. But, timed deposits (30 days, 60 days and 90 days being common) then a more attractive interest rate may be possible. The ability to accurately forecast how long a surplus will be available for allows interest on the surplus being maximised.

MANAGING WORKING CAPITAL: CASH FLOW

 Solution 6

The structure of ABC's costs (quarters 1 to 3) may be deduced as follows:

£	Fixed	Per unit
Material X		5
Material Y		4
Labour	80,000	10
Production overheads	50,000	3
Plant depreciation	14,000	
Admin. overheads	30,000	
S&D overheads	20,000	1

The variable labour cost per unit rises to £15 for production over 19,000 units. The S&D overheads (variable component) varies with unit sales rather than production.

The 1 year cash budget for ABC is as follows:

Cash flow forecast

Quarters	1	2	3	4 (L)	4(M)	4(H)
Sales	84,000	434,667	661,333	600,000	628,000	656,000
Costs:						
Material X	33,333	83,333	83,333	85,000	97,000	109,000
Material Y	26,667	66,667	66,667	60,000	68,000	76,000
Labour	180,000	285,000	230,000	230,000	260,000	300,000
Production overheads	80,000	110,000	95,000	95,000	104,000	113,000
Admin. overheads	30,000	30,000	30,000	30,000	30,000	30,000
S&D overheads	29,000	37,000	35,000	35000	38000	41000
Net cash flow	−295,000	−177,333	121,333	65,000	31,000	−13,000
Cumulative cash flow	5,000	−172,333	−51,000	14,000	−20,000	−64,000

 Solution 7

The cash flows associated with the bond are an initial (quarter 0) outflow of $100 followed by 4 quarterly (quarters 1 to 4) inflows of $28. The quarterly interest rate may be derived using the same interpolative methodology used to calculate IRR or by using a scientific calculator. It is 4.69%.

The annual rate equivalent to that quarterly rate is $1.0469^4 − 1 = 20.1\%$.

 Solution 8

The correct answer is (A).

 Solution 9

The correct answer is (B).

 Solution 10

The correct answer is (B).

Solution 11

Any six from the following list:

- treasury bills,
- bank deposits,
- certificates of deposit,
- bills of exchange,
- money-market accounts,
- local authority deposits,
- commercial paper,
- local authority bonds,
- corporate bonds,
- government bonds.

See Section 9.10.

 Solution 12

The yield to maturity is the effective yield on a redeemable security, taking into account any gain or loss due to the fact that it was purchased at a price different from the redemption value, see Section 9.9.2.

 Solution 13

The correct answer is (A), see Section 9.7.2.

 Solution 14

$700 × (annuity factor for $t = 5$; $r = 10$) + 10,000 × (discount factor $t = 5$; $r = 10$) = ($700 × 3.791) + (10,000 × 0.621) = 2,653.7 + 6,210 = $8,863.7 Annuity factor and discount factor are from tables, see Section 9.7.2

 Solution 15

 (i) The coupon rate is the interest rate payable on the face, or nominal, value of the debt. BH's bond has a coupon rate of 7% on $1,000, which equals $70 interest.

    The yield to maturity, or redemption yield, is the effective yield on a redeemable security. It takes into account the actual interest receivable and any gain or loss due to the fact that it was purchased at a price different from the redemption value. BH's yield to maturity takes into account that the $1,000 bond was purchased for $850.

 (ii) The yield to maturity can be calculated as the discounted annual rate of return at which the present value of future interest payments and redemption value of the bond at maturity equals the current market value of the bond.

    Let $t = 5$ and $r = 9$ and
    ($70 × 3.890) + ($1,000 × 0.650) = 272.3 + 650 = 922.3

Let $t = 5$ and $r = 12$ and
(70×3.605) + ($1,000 \times 0.567$) = 252.35 + 567 = 819.35

See Section 9.9.2.

 ## Solution 16

An overdraft from a bank is a common form of short-term loan and most businesses would have overdraft facilities arranged with their bank. However, term loans are also used widely to provide medium-term finance.

By being able to withdraw more than was deposited in a bank account, a business can use an overdraft to fund temporary shortages of cash resources. The problem is that the bank can withdraw the right to use the overdraft at any time and so there is an element of uncertainty. However, banks tend to treat their customers fairly and so will usually try to assist them in difficult times.

Trade credit is another form of short-term credit that is used by businesses. By delaying payments to suppliers, credit can be obtained without incurring cost unless cash discounts are forgone or suppliers increase prices recognising that payments are delayed unduly by some of their customers, see Section 9.6.

 ## Solution 17

An overdraft provides the management with flexibility. The exact amount of funding required and the timings, especially of repayment, can be adjusted to suit the funding needs of the organisation.

If the overdraft facilities are only used when it is essential, the cost of borrowing can be kept to a minimum. The interest on an overdraft is calculated on the daily balance and so interest will only be incurred when the facilities are used. It is likely, however, that the rate of interest charged will be high.

At any time, the bank can ask for the amount outstanding to be repaid. The bank manager will regularly require cash-flow projections in order to judge the borrower's creditworthiness, and it is not unusual for the owners or the managers responsible for the organisation to be asked to provide collateral security to reduce the default risk of the lender.

It is generally recognised that bank overdrafts are a convenient form of short-term borrowing that is used by most businesses because of the flexibility that it provides at a relatively low cost, see Section 9.6 and 9.6.3.

 ## Solution 18

By delaying payments to suppliers, it is possible for a business to obtain short-term finance. Thus, by taking a relatively long time before settling the amounts owed to trade payables, the funds can be used for other purposes. In the simplest position, inventory will be delivered and sold before a payment is made to the supplier of the inventory. It is possible that the firm's customer has already paid before the amount is paid to the supplier.

Provided that the selling price is not increased or cash discounts lost, trade credit is provided free and is particularly beneficial to small firms, although it is used by all businesses. It is extremely important that opportunities to receive cash discounts are not lost, as the annualised rate of interest forgone can be significant. However, as the annualised cost of offering cash discounts is high, it is relatively unusual to be offered this form of discount and so it is not often necessary to pay trade payables early. The period that is acceptable will be a matter that will be negotiated at the time of placing the order and it is not unusual to delay payments and so enjoy the 'free loan' for a longer period of time, see Section 9.6.1.

 Solution 19

Yield to maturity:

Using $t = 7$ and $r = 6$ and 8, from tables

$$(4 \times 5.582) + (100 \times 0.655) = 22.328 + 66.5 = 88.828$$
$$(4 \times 5.206) + (100 \times 0.583) = 20.824 + 58.3 = 79.124$$

$$6 + \frac{88.828 - 83.00}{88.828 - 79.124} \times 2 = 6 + \frac{5.828}{9.704} \times 2$$

$$= 6 + 1.20 = 7.20\%$$

See Section 9.9.2.

10

Managing Working Capital – Receivables, Payables and Inventory

Managing Working Capital – Receivables, Payables and Inventory

10

LEARNING OUTCOMES

After completing this chapter, you should be able to:

▶ interpret working capital ratios for business sectors;

▶ analyse trade debtor and creditor information;

▶ analyse the impacts of alternative debtor and creditor policies;

▶ analyse the impacts of alternative policies for stock management.

10.1 Introduction

In this chapter we consider the manner in which working capital management activities may be gauged and represented through the calculation of various business ratios. These ratios use figures drawn from financial and management accounting reports. Consideration is also given to the manner in which optimum policies may be identified in regard to the management of debt, trade credit and inventory.

10.2 Working capital management

In CIMA's *Management Accounting: Official Terminology,* working capital is defined as follows:

 The capital available for conducting the day-to-day operations of an organisation; normally the excess of current assets over current liabilities.

In accounting terms, this is a static statement of financial position concept, referring to the excess at a particular moment in time of permanent capital plus non-current liabilities over the non-current assets of the business. As such, it depends on accounting rules, such as what is capital and what is revenue, what constitutes retained earnings, the cut-off between long term and short term (twelve months from the end of the reporting period for published accounts) and when revenue should be recognised.

If working capital, thus defined, exceeds net current operating assets (inventory plus receivables less payables), the entity has a cash surplus (usually represented by bank deposits and investments); otherwise it has a deficit (usually represented by a bank loan and/or overdraft). On this basis the control of working capital can be subdivided into areas dealing with inventory, receivables, payables, and cash.

A business must be able to generate sufficient cash to be able to meet its immediate obligations and therefore continue trading. Unprofitable businesses can survive for quite some time if they have access to sufficient liquid resources, but even the most profitable business will quickly go under if it does not have adequate liquid resources. Working capital is therefore essential to the entity's long-term success and development and the greater the degree to which the current assets cover the current liabilities, the more solvent the entity.

The efficient management of working capital is important from the point of view of both liquidity and profitability. Poor management of working capital means that funds are unnecessarily tied up in idle assets, hence reducing liquidity and also reducing the ability to invest in productive assets such as plant and machinery, so affecting profitability.

An entity's working capital policy is a function of two decisions:

- First, the appropriate level of investment in, and mix of current assets to be decided upon, for a set level of activity. This is the investment decision.
- Second, the methods of financing this investment – the financing decision.

10.2.1 The investment decision

All businesses, to one degree or another, require working capital. The actual amount required will depend on many factors such as the age of the entity, the type of business activity, credit policy, and even the time of year. There is no standard fixed requirement. It is essential that an appropriate amount of working capital is budgeted for to meet anticipated future needs. Failure to budget correctly could result in the business being unable to meet its liabilities as they fall due. If a business finds itself in such a situation, it is said to be *technically insolvent*. In conditions of uncertainty, firms must hold some minimal level of cash and inventories based on expected sales plus additional safety inventory. With an *aggressive working capital policy*, a firm would hold minimal safety inventory. Such a policy would minimise costs, but it could lower sales because the firm may not be able to respond rapidly to increases in demand.

Conversely, a *conservative working capital policy* would call for large safety inventory levels. Generally, the expected return is lower under a conservative than under an aggressive policy, but the risks are greater under the aggressive policy. A *moderate policy* falls somewhere between the two extremes in terms of risk and returns.

10.2.2 The financing decision

Working capital financing decisions involve the determination of the mix of long-versus short-term debt.

There is a basic difference between cash and inventories on the one hand and receivables on the other. In the case of cash and inventories, higher levels mean safety inventory, hence a more conservative position. There is no such thing as a 'safety level of receivables' and a higher level of receivables in relation to sales would generally mean that the firm was extending credit on more liberal terms. If we characterise aggressive as being risky, then lowering inventories and cash would be aggressive but raising receivables would also be aggressive.

The financing of working capital depends upon how current and fixed asset funding is divided between long-term and short-term sources of funding. Three possible policies exist.

1. *Conservative.* A conservative policy is where all of the permanent assets both non-current assets and the permanent part of the current assets (i.e. the core level of investment in inventory and receivables, etc.) are financed by long-term funding, as well as part of the fluctuating current assets. Short-term financing is only used for part of the fluctuating current assets. The conservative policy is the least risky but also results in the lowest expected return.
2. *Aggressive.* An aggressive policy for financing working capital uses short-term financing to fund all the fluctuating current assets as well as some of the permanent part of the current assets. This policy carries the greatest risk of illiquidity, as well as the greatest return (because short-term debt costs are typically less than long-term costs).
3. *Moderate.* A moderate (or maturity matching) policy matches the short-term finance to the fluctuating current assets, and the long-term finance to the permanent part of current assets plus non-current assets. This policy falls between the two extremes.

10.3 Working capital ratios

Working capital management may be analysed using ratio analysis. We shall consider two groups of ratios: liquidity ratios and those concerned with the calculation of the working capital cycle.

10.3.1 Illustration

The financial statements of Alpha are shown below:

Alpha income statement for the year ended 31 December 20X9

	$	$
Sales revenue		500,000
Opening inventory	25,000	
Purchases	305,000	
Closing inventory	(30,000)	
Cost of goods sold		(300,000)
Gross profit		200,000
Other operating expenses	60,000	
Finance cost Profit	24,000	(84,000)
		116,000

Alpha statement of financial position as at 31 December 20X9

	$	$
Non-current assets		540,000
Current assets		
Inventory	30,000	
Receivables	62,500	
Bank	7,000	99,500
Capital and reserves		639,500
Share capital		125,625
Accumulated profit		256,000
		381,625
Non-current liabilities		
Loan notes		200,000
Current liabilities		
Payables		57,875
		639,500

All sales are on credit. Ignore taxation.

We will use this set of financial statements to illustrate the calculation of the working capital ratios.

10.3.2 Liquidity ratios

Liquidity refers to the amount of cash in hand or readily obtainable to meet payment obligations. Liquidity ratios indicate the ability to meet liabilities from available assets and are calculated from statement of financial position information. The most commonly used are the current ratio and the quick ratio.

10.3.3 The current ratio

The current ratio is the ratio of current assets divided by current liabilities:

$$\text{Current ratio} = \frac{\text{current assets}}{\text{current liabilities}}$$

Alpha's current ratio is:

$$\frac{99,500}{57,875} = 1.7\text{:}1$$

Note that this figure is usually expressed as a ratio rather than as a percentage.

The current ratio provides a broad measure of liquidity. A high current ratio would suggest that the business would have little difficulty meeting current liabilities from available assets. However, if a large proportion of current assets is represented by inventory, this may not be the case as inventories are less liquid than other current assets.

10.3.4 The quick ratio

The quick ratio, or *acid test,* indicates the ability to pay payables in the short term. The quick ratio recognises that inventory may take some time to convert into cash and so focuses on those current assets that are relatively liquid.

$$\text{Quick ratio} = \frac{\text{current assets} - \text{inventory}}{\text{current liabilities}}$$

Alpha's quick asset ratio is:

$$\frac{99,500 - 30,000}{57,875} = 1.2\text{:}1$$

By ignoring inventory, the ratio concentrates on those current assets which are immediately available to meet payables as and when they fall due.

There are no general norms for these ratios and 'ideal' levels vary depending on the type of business being examined. Manufacturers will normally require much higher liquidity ratios than retailers. If a norm is required, the best guide will usually be the industry average if one is available. The industry average should indicate whether the current and quick ratios required in the industry are generally quite high or relatively low. This will be determined by the trading conditions in the sector. For example, a retailer such as a supermarket will be able to purchase on credit and sell for cash. Therefore, there will be virtually no receivables other than credit card entities and very little inventory. The current and quick ratios will be quite low as a result. Whereas a manufacturing organisation will need to hold inventory in various stages of completion, from raw materials to finished products and the majority if not all of the sales will be on credit. As a result both liquidity ratios will be higher.

When analysing liquidity ratios, the absolute figure calculated for a particular year is less important than the trend from one year to the next. It is important to assess whether the organisation's liquidity is improving or declining over time.

10.4 Efficiency ratios

The efficiency ratios are related to the liquidity ratios. They give an insight into the standard of the entity's management of the components of working capital.

10.4.1 Inventory turnover

It is possible to calculate the average number of days taken by the business to sell an item of inventory, if there are several types of inventory each type must be calculated separately:

$$\frac{\text{Inventory}}{\text{Cost of sales}} \times 365$$

Note: Cost of sales should be the cost of inventories sold, it should not include other expenses, such as depreciation.

This is equivalent to taking the amount of inventory held by the business, dividing by the rate at which inventory is consumed in a year and multiplying by the number of days in a year. Alpha's inventory turnover is:

$$\frac{30,000}{300,000} \times 365 = 37 \text{ days}$$

This means that, on average, any given item of inventory will spend 37 days 'on the shelf before it is sold.

Obviously, it is desirable for this period to be as short as possible. The shorter the inventory turnover period, the more quickly inventory can be converted into cash. The inventory turnover ratio can, however, be too short. It is easy to reduce the figure produced by this ratio: the entity can simply allow its inventory to run down. This could, however, be counter productive if this led to stoppages in production because there were inadequate inventories of materials or components. Similarly, holding inadequate inventories of finished goods could cost the entity both trade and goodwill if it is unable to meet customer demand.

It is difficult to tell whether 37 days is 'good' or 'bad'. It would be helpful if Alpha could be compared to a similar entity or if previous years' figures were available.

Sometimes this ratio is calculated using constants of 52 or 12 to express the turnover in terms of weeks or months. It is also possible to invert the formula and leave out the constant to show how often inventory has 'turned over' during the year:

$$\frac{\text{Cost of sales}}{\text{Closing inventory}} = \frac{300,000}{30,000} = 10 \text{ times}$$

The inventory turnover ratios may be based on either end-year, mid-year or year average inventory figures. The analyst has to select which is most appropriate. For example, if the end-year position is unusual for some reason, then the mid-year position might be more meaningful. On the other hand, the end-year position is the most current figure and the impression it gives is therefore the most up to date possible. In any event, when inventory is comprised of a mixture of material stock, work-in-progress and finished goods – then the link between 'closing inventory' and cost of sales may be ambiguous.

The critical thing in any business ratio analysis is to be consistent. Year-on-year comparison requires that the figures for different years are prepared on the same basis. Even though the absolute ratio figures for any given year may be vulnerable to interpretation, the year-on-year comparison of figures will offer useful insights into how the business is developing.

10.4.2 Receivables turnover

This is a measure of the average length of time taken for credit customers to settle their balance:

$$\frac{\text{Trade receivables}}{\text{Sales}} \times 365$$

Alpha's ratio is:

$$\frac{62{,}500}{500{,}000} \times 365 = 46 \text{ days}$$

Again, it is desirable for this ratio to be as short as possible. It will be better for the entity's cash flow if customers pay as quickly as possible. It can, however, be difficult to press for speedier payment. Doing so could damage the entity's relationship with its customers.

In general, most businesses request payment within 30 days of the delivery of goods. Most customers tend to delay payment for some time beyond this. Alpha's ratio appears reasonable: customers are not taking an unrealistic time to pay and there is nothing to suggest that Alpha is putting undue pressure on its customers.

If the entity sells goods for cash and for credit, then it is important to divide the trade receivables figure by credit sales only. If sales cannot be broken down, then the ratio will be distorted. The classic case of this occurred when a student divided the receivables of a supermarket chain by the sales revenue figure (virtually all of which was cash) and came to the conclusion that the receivables turnover ratio was approximately 0.007 days (about 10 minutes!).

Note: When calculating the receivables turnover, you should only include trade receivables, not total receivables.

As was the case with inventory-based ratios, one can debate whether the end-year, mid-year or year-average receivables gives the most meaningful impression. The critical thing is to be consistent from one year to the next.

10.4.3 Payables turnover

This is the average time taken to pay suppliers:

$$\frac{\text{Trade payables}}{\text{Purchases}} \times 365$$

Alpha's payables turnover was:

$$\frac{57{,}875}{305{,}000} \times 365 = 69 \text{ days}$$

While the entity should collect cash from its customers as quickly as possible, it should try to delay making payments to its suppliers. Effectively, this is equivalent to taking out an interest-free loan, which can be used to help finance working capital. Again, the entity must use some restraint. If it becomes regarded as a slow payer, then it might find it difficult to obtain credit. Indeed, there are credit-rating agencies which compile lists of entities that have poor reputations.

Alpha's ratio of just over 2 months does not seem too unreasonable, although it does seem fairly slow.

Published financial statements do not usually state the purchases figure. It is possible to obtain a crude estimate of the payables turnover by using the cost of sales figure instead. This method will often have to be used in examination questions.

Note: Only trade payables should be included, taxation, interest and other payables should be excluded.

10.5 The working capital cycle

The efficiency ratios are related to those which measure liquidity. The working capital cycle gives an indication of the length of time cash spends tied up in current assets.

The working capital cycle is the length of time between the entity's outlay on raw materials, wages and other expenditures, and the inflow of cash from the sale of the goods.

In a manufacturing entity, this is the average time that raw materials remain in inventory less the period of credit taken from suppliers plus the time taken for producing the goods plus the time the goods remain in finished inventory plus the time taken by customers to pay for the goods. On some occasions, this cycle is referred to as the cash cycle or operating cycle.

This is an important concept for the management of cash or working capital because the longer the working capital cycle, the more financial resource the entity needs. Management needs to ensure that this cycle does not become too long. The working capital cycle can be calculated approximately as shown in the calculation below. Allowances should be made for any significant changes in the level of inventory taking place over the period. If, for example, the entity is deliberately building up its level of inventory, this will lengthen the working capital cycle.

A statement of how the working capital cycle (sometimes called the 'cash conversion period') might be worked is given below. Note that the individual days figures can all be worked on a variety of different bases. The main thing is to select that basis which is most meaningful in each case and then to apply it consistently from year to year.

Calculation of the working capital cycle

Raw materials — **Days**

Period of turnover of raw materials inventory $= \dfrac{\text{average value of raw material inventory}}{\text{Consumption of raw material per day}}$ X

Less

Period of credit granted by suppliers $= \dfrac{\text{average level of payables}}{\text{purchase of raw materials per day}}$ X

Add

Period of production $= \dfrac{\text{average value of work in progress}}{\text{average cost of goods sold per day}}$ X

Period of turnover of finished goods inventory $= \dfrac{\text{average value of inventory of finished goods}}{\text{average cost of goods sold per day}}$ X

Period of credit taken by customers $= \dfrac{\text{average values of receivables}}{\text{average value of sales per day}}$ X

Total working capital cycle — X

Some writers advocate computation of an annual working capital cycle and of a cycle for each quarter, since with a seasonal business the cycle would vary over different periods. The numerators in the equations can be found by taking the arithmetic mean of the opening and closing balances for inventories, payables and receivables. If a quarterly statement is being prepared, the opening and closing balances for the quarter would be used.

The calculation of the working capital cycle may alternatively be expressed as:

		Days
Raw materials inventory turnover period	$= \dfrac{\text{average raw materials inventory}}{\text{purchases}} \times 365$	X
Less		
Payables payment period	$= \dfrac{\text{trade payables}}{\text{purchases}} \times 365$	X
Add		
Work in progress turnover period	$= \dfrac{\text{average work in progress}}{\text{manufacturing cost}} \times 365$	X
Finished goods turnover period	$= \dfrac{\text{average finished goods inventory}}{\text{cost of sales}} \times 365$	X
Receivables collection period	$= \dfrac{\text{average finished goods inventory}}{\text{credit sales}} \times 365$	X
		X

In an examination situation, the information supplied in order to calculate the length of the working capital cycle is often simplified as shown below.

Example

The table below gives information extracted from the annual accounts of Davis for the past 2 years.
You are required to calculate the length of the working capital cycle for each of the 2 years.
Davis Extracts from annual accounts

	Year 1 $	Year 2 $
Inventories: Raw materials	108,000	145,800
Work in progress	75,600	97,200
Finished goods	86,400	129,600
Purchases	518,400	702,000
Cost of goods sold	756,000	972,000
Sales	864,000	1,080,000
Receivables	172,800	259,200
Trade payables	86,400	105,300

Solution

	Year 1 %	Year 1 Days	Year 2 %	Year 2 Days
Raw materials inventory holding (raw materials inventory ÷ purchases)	20.83	76	20.77	76
Less: Finance from suppliers (trade payables ÷ purchases)	16.67	(61)	15.00	(55)
		15		21
Production time (work in progress ÷ cost of sales)	10.00	37	10.00	37

Finished goods inventory holding				
(finished goods inventory ÷ cost of sales)	11.43	42	13.33	49
Credit given to customers	20.00	73	24.00	88
(receivables ÷ sales)		167		195

Note that, owing to the nature of the simplified information provided, end-of-year values rather than average values have been used for inventory, receivables and payables. The percentages calculated are multiplied by 365 to give figures expressed in numbers of days.

In a non-manufacturing entity, the working capital cycle can be calculated as follows:

Inventory turnover + receivables turnover − payables turnover

The logic behind this is that inventory cannot be converted into cash until it has been sold and then the customer pays for the goods. This must be offset against the fact that no cash is actually invested until the entity has paid the supplier for the goods. Thus, Alpha's working capital cycle is:

37 + 46 − 69 = 14 days

This means that, on average, the entity's money is tied up in any given item of inventory for 14 days before it is recovered (with profit).

10.6 Overtrading

Overtrading is the condition of a business which enters into commitments in excess of its available short-term resources. This can arise even if the entity is trading profitably.

Entities are particularly at risk of overtrading when they are growing rapidly and they do not raise further long-term finance. The additional inventories and trade receivables are funded by increases in payables. Additional non-current assets may be required for the expansion and will be paid for out of current funds, reducing the working capital.

If this continues for too long without raising further long-term funds, the entity may run into problems of cash shortages. The entity may not be able to meet its liabilities as they fall due, and although the entity is trading profitably it may be forced into liquidation.

10.6.1 Symptoms of overtrading

Symptoms that may indicate overtrading include:

- increasing revenue
- increasing inventory and receivables
- increasing current and non-current assets
- increase in assets funded by credit
- current liabilities exceed current assets and there is a decrease in both current and quick ratios.

The solution is to issue more equity shares or raise more long-term loan funds.

10.7 Shortening the working capital cycle

A number of steps could be taken to shorten the working capital cycle:

- *Reduce raw materials inventory holding.* This may be done by reviewing slow-moving lines, reorder levels and reorder quantities. Inventory control models may be considered if not already in use. More efficient links with suppliers could also help. Reducing inventory may involve loss of discounts for bulk purchases, loss of cost savings from price rises, or could lead to production delays due to inventory shortages.

- *Obtain more finance from suppliers by delaying payments, preferably through negotiation.* This could result in a deterioration in commercial relationships or even loss of reliable sources of supply. Discounts may be lost by this policy.
- *Reduce work in progress* by improving production techniques and efficiency (with the human and practical problems of achieving such change).
- *Reduce finished goods inventory* perhaps by reorganising the production schedule and distribution methods. This may affect the efficiency with which customer demand can be satisfied and result ultimately in a reduction of sales.
- *Reduce credit given to customers* by invoicing and following up outstanding amounts more quickly, or possibly offering discount incentives. The main disadvantages would be the potential loss of customers as a result of chasing too hard and a loss of revenue as a result of discounts.
- *Debt factoring*, generating immediate cash flow by the sale of receivables to a third party on immediate cash terms.

The working capital cycle is only the *time span* between production costs and cash returns; it says nothing in itself about the amount of working capital that will be needed over this period.

10.8 Managing receivables

An entity may have a ratio of trade receivables to total assets in the region of 20–25 per cent. This represents a considerable investment of funds and so the management of this asset can have a significant effect on the profit performance of an entity.

By international standards, the UK does not have a good record for the collection of debts. In the UK manufacturing sector, it takes on average about 60 days for an entity to collect the funds due from a receivable. In contrast, in the USA, the average collection period for manufacturing industry is in the region of 40 days.

In order to reduce the trade receivable days to a more respectable figure, entities may offer customers inducements in the form of *cash discounts*. These discounts may well speed up collection but reduce the amount from each sale when collected.

Credit management involves balancing the benefits to be gained from extending credit to customers against the costs of doing so and finding the optimum level of credit and discounts that will maximise the entity's profits. It also involves such things as assessing the credit risk of customers wanting credit, collecting debts which are overdue, assessing what effect changing credit terms will have on the occurrence of bad debts and setting individual credit limits for customers.

10.9 The credit cycle

The credit cycle refers to the events that take place between the receipt of a customer's order, through to the receipt of cash from the customer. The credit cycle can be broken down into two elements: the order cycle, being the period between the receipt of a customer's order and the raising of an invoice; and the collection cycle, which is the period from raising the invoice until cash is received from the customer.

The stages in the credit cycle are as follows:

- receipt of customer order
- credit screening and agreement of terms
- goods dispatched with delivery note
- invoice raised stating credit terms
- debt collection procedures
- receipt of cash.

The longer the credit cycle, the more cash there is locked into working capital. Reducing the length of the credit cycle will improve cash flow and thus improve the entity's liquidity position.

10.9.1 Credit control

As stated above, to have good credit management you should assess the credit risk of your customer base. This would involve giving consideration to your credit control procedures. Detailed below are key elements that need to be taken into account in setting a *credit control policy.*

- The terms of trade, notably the period of credit to be granted and any discounts to be allowed for early settlement. This will largely be determined by practice within the industry, but there is usually some scope for differentiation – from competitors and between customers (the riskier prospects being put on a shorter-period, higher-discount arrangement). It is important to record all the terms agreed.
- On a customer-by-customer basis, it is necessary to assess creditworthiness and to establish limits in terms of amount and time. New customers should be checked for creditworthiness before being given a credit account.

Sources of credit information include:

- bank reference from the customers bank;
- trade references from other entities the customer deals with;
- credit reference agency report;
- sales representative visit to customers premises;
- checking legal sources of information for example records of court judgements;
- carry out an analysis of the entity's latest financial statements;
- view the customers website, if one exists, for information;
- ask prospective customers to complete a credit application form and carry out credit scoring;
- check the entity's credit rating if it is large enough to have one.

Late payment is seen as a major problem in UK industry, with large entities accused of pressurising small ones. Various ideas have been put forward to counteract this:

- legislation to give suppliers a statutory right to interest on overdue debts;
- disclosure in published accounts of credit taken;
- a code of practice, including paying according to agreed terms;
- inclusion of payment to agreed terms as a requisite for receiving a quality certificate.

10.9.2 Payment terms

The payment terms will need to consider the period of credit to be granted and how the payment will be made. The terms agreed will need to specify the price, the date of delivery, the payment date or dates, and any discounts to be allowed for early settlement.

Examples of payment terms may be:

- *Payment within a specified period.* For example, customers must pay within 30 days.
- *Payment within a specified period with discount.* For example, a 2 per cent discount would be given to customers who pay within 10 days, and others would be required to pay within 30 days.
- *Weekly credit.* This would require all supplies in a week to be paid by a specified day in the following week.
- *Related to delivery of goods.* For example, cash on delivery (COD).

10.9.3 Cash discounts

Cash discounts are sometimes offered by entities as a means of improving cash flow by encouraging customers to settle their accounts early. The cost of offering a cash discount in order to generate better cash flow is sometimes overlooked. The savings made by the entity from a lower receivable balance and shorter average collecting period should be compared with the cost of the discount to see if the reduced period of credit could be financed by alternative means, for example, a bank overdraft.

 Exercise 10.1

Tandijono normally offers its customers 50-day payment terms, but to improve its cash flow is considering a 2 per cent discount for payment within 10 days.

You are required to advise the entity on the cost of this proposed action.

Assume a 365-day year and an invoice for $100.

 Solution

The entity would receive $98 on day 10 instead of $100 on day 50. Tandijono would then be able to invest the $98 for 40 days (50 − 10).

If the prevailing interest rate is r per cent per annum, the entity will benefit as follows:

$$\$98 \times r\% \times \frac{40}{365}$$

However, to achieve this the entity has to grant $2 in discount. To break even on this scheme, we must have:

$$\$98 \times r\% \times \frac{40}{365} \geq \$2$$

Rearranging:

$$r\% \geq \frac{\$2}{\$98} \times \frac{365}{40} = 18.6\%$$

The 18.6 per cent would then be compared with the entity cost of capital to establish if this is an efficient method of financing the shorter credit period.

Note: A more accurate method can be used that deals with the compound interest effect.

The compound interest formula states that the value S attained by a single sum X, after n periods at r per cent, is:

$$S = X(1 + r)^n$$

Using this formula to quantify the cost of offering the cash discount:

$$100 = 98(1 + r)^1$$

where

r = periodic rate (in this case the rate is for a 40-day period)

$$1 + r = 1.0204$$

$$r = 2.04\%$$

This periodic rate must then be converted into an annual rate using the formula:

$$(1 + \text{annualised rate}) = (1 + \text{periodic rate})^n$$

where

n = number of compounding periods in the year (in this example $\dfrac{365}{40} = 9.125$)

$$(1 + \text{annualised rate}) = (1.0204)^{9.125} = 1.202$$
$$\text{annualised rate} = 20.2\%$$

This compounding process can be short cut as shown below:

$$1 + r = \left(\frac{100}{98}\right)^{9.125}$$
$$1 + r = 1.202$$

 The cost of offering the cash discount is then 20.2 per cent.

 For the examination, the compound interest approach should be used.

Use the formula:

$$1 + r = [fv/dv]^n$$

where:

fv = face value

dv = discounted value

n = number of compounding periods in the year

10.9.4 Methods of payment

Payments from customers may be accepted in a number of forms, including:

- cash
- Bankers Automated Clearing Service (BACS)
- cheques
- banker's draft
- standing orders
- direct debit
- credit cards
- debit cards
- Clearing House Automated Payments System (CHAPS).

10.9.5 The stages in debt collection

There is no optimal debt collection policy that will be applicable to all entities. Debt collection policies will differ according to the nature of the business and the level of competition.

An effective solution will require the following:

- dedicated, well-trained credit control personnel;
- well-defined procedures for collection of overdue debts that take account of the potential costs of collecting an outstanding debt, and the need to maintain good relationships with customers;
- monitoring of overdue accounts;
- flexibility to allow for changing circumstances.

The longer a debt is outstanding, the higher the probability of default. There need to be well-defined procedures for following up – allowing in the first instance for the possibility of a genuine query – and keeping notes that can be referred to later. If the worst comes to the worst, there will be a need to understand the law relating to contracts, insolvency, winding up and liquidation. In practical terms, the danger of 'throwing good money after bad' needs to be considered.

One way of encouraging customers to pay within the agreed credit period is to charge interest on any overdue debts. While this would normally have to be agreed by the parties at the time of the sale, small businesses in the UK are provided with some protection against late payment by the Late Payment Act.

Since 1 November 1998, small businesses – those with less than 50 employees – can choose whether to charge large entities interest at 8 per cent above base rate on bills that are paid more than 30 days after they fall due.

10.10 Age analysis of trade receivables

As an aid to effective credit control, an age analysis of outstanding debts may be produced. This is simply a list of the customers who currently owe money, showing the total amount owed and the period of time for which the money has been owed. The actual form of the age analysis report can vary widely, but a typical example is shown below.

Robins

Age analysis of trade receivables as at 30 September 2005

Account number	Customer name	Balance	Up to 30 days	31–60 days	61–90 days	Over 90 days
B002	Brennan	294.35	220.15	65.40	8.80	0.00
G007	Goodridge	949.50	853.00	0.00	96.50	0.00
T005	Taylor	371.26	340.66	30.60	0.00	0.00
T010	Thorpe	1,438.93	0.00	0.00	567.98	870.95
T011	Tinnion	423.48	312.71	110.77	0.00	0.00
Totals		3,477.52	1.726.52	206.77	673.28	870.95
Percentage		100%		6%	19.4%	25%

To prepare the analysis, either use a computer programme or manually analyse each customer, account. For each customer, every invoice is allocated to the month it was issued. Then when payment is received, the invoice is cancelled from the analysis, leaving the total of unpaid invoices for each month. Difficulties analysing the balance can occur if the customer pays lump sum on account, rather than specific invoices. Care must be taken to allocate all adjustments other than cash, such as credit notes, discounts given, etc.

The age analysis of trade receivables can be used to help decide what action should be taken about debts that have been outstanding for longer than the specified credit period. It can be seen from the table above that 41 per cent of Robins's outstanding trade receivable balance is due by Thorpe. It may be that Thorpe is experiencing financial difficulties. There may already have been some correspondence between the two entities about the outstanding debts.

As well as providing information about individual customer balances, the age analysis of trade receivables provides additional information about the efficiency of cash collection. The table above shows that over 50 per cent of debts at 30 September 2005 have been outstanding for more than 30 days. If the normal credit period is 30 days, there may be a suggestion of weaknesses in credit control. It may also be useful to show the credit limit for each customer on the report, to identify those customers who are close to, or have exceeded, their credit limit.

The age analysis can also provide information to assist in setting and monitoring collection targets for the credit control section. A collection target could be expressed as a percentage of credit sales collected within a specified period or it could be expressed in terms of the average number of trade receivable days outstanding. When trying to achieve a collection target the age analysis can be very useful in identifying large balances that have been outstanding for long periods; these can be targeted for action to encourage payment.

10.11 Credit insurance

To protect against the risk of bad debts, an entity can take out credit insurance. There are a number of entities specialising in this form of insurance, offering a wide variety of services with costs to match.

Policies may be arranged that cover the whole of an entity's turnover. The credit insurer will normally place a limit on value of a single invoice that will be insured without special approval. The insured entity will need to assess each customer's creditworthiness, using approved information sources to ensure it is covered under the terms of the insurance.

Alternatively, an entity may wish to take out insurance on specific invoices. The premium payable will be determined by the perceived risk of non-payment.

10.12 Factoring

In CIMA's *Management Accounting: Official Terminology* factoring is defined as follows:

> The sale of debts to a third party (the factor) at a discount, in return for prompt cash. A factoring service may be *with recourse,* in which case the supplier takes the risk of the debt not being paid, or *without recourse* when the factor takes the risk.

Specialist finance entities (usually subsidiaries of banks) offering factoring arrangements will provide three main services:

1. provide finance by advancing, say 80 per cent of invoice value immediately, the remainder being settled when the client's customer settles the debt (but net of a charge for interest, typically 3 per cent per annum above base rate);
2. take responsibility for the operation of the client's sales ledger, including assessment of creditworthiness and dealing with customers for an additional service charge, typically 2 per cent of turnover;
3. they may, for an additional fee, offer non-recourse finance, that is, guarantee settlement even if they are not paid by the customer.

In order to do this economically, they have developed their expertise in credit control in terms of market intelligence (including credit scoring), information management (sophisticated databases, processing and decision support systems) and the skills required for dealing with customers especially those who are in no hurry to pay!

Alternatively, they may offer a *confidential invoice discounting* facility under which they provide the finance as above, but do not get involved with the operation of the sales ledger or hence become known to the customers. This has, to date, been more popular than the overt factoring arrangement. It is cheaper, of course, and avoids creating a barrier between the business and its customers. It is less attractive to the providers of finance, however, being in the nature of supplying a commodity rather than adding value through expertise.

Though, as mentioned, these financiers are usually subsidiaries of banks, they like to distinguish their approach from that of their parents. They argue that the mainstream banks, when deciding on the extent to which they are prepared to lend, have traditionally looked backwards – to an entity's past profits and tangible assets. This explains why they are reluctant to lend just when the entity needs it, that is, ahead of a growth phase. A sales-based package is a logical, flexible alternative. Having siphoned off the trade receivables in this way, the returns from a business are going to be more uncertain, making it difficult to raise more traditional forms of finance except at high interest rates. It is also worth noting that factoring is associated in many people's minds with financial difficulties ('the banks do not refer their best prospects to their factoring subsidiaries') or at best with small businesses, which may have an impact on the image of the business in the eyes of its suppliers.

Apart from the factors and invoice discounters, it is worth noting some other players in the receivables industry:

- the specialist information providers, covering credit assessments, increasingly available electronically. This means that the sales function can have access, thereby reducing the potential for friction, for example, taking an order only to find that 'finance' reject it on the grounds of credit risk;
- *Credit insurance,* clients typically pay around 1 per cent of sales, depending on the industry into which they are selling and on their perceived credit control skills. It should be seen as complementary to, rather than a substitute for, in-house vigilance;
- debt collectors, often members of the legal profession, who take over responsibility for dealing with unpaid bills – sometimes on commission, otherwise for a fee.

These various services are mutually supportive and there have been signs of convergence, that is, of providers who offer a menu from which businesses can pick.

 Examination questions could ask you to consider whether it is beneficial for an entity to use factoring or to raise the finance by an alternative method, for example, bank overdraft.

Exercise 10.2

(a) *You are required to* summarise the services that may be obtained from various forms of agreement for the factoring of trade debts and from invoice discounting.

(5 marks)

(b) B has been set up for the purpose of importing commodities that will be sold to a small number of reliable customers. Sales invoicing is forecast at $300,000 per month. The average credit period for this type of business is 2½ months.

The entity is considering factoring its accounts receivable under a full factoring agreement without recourse. Under the agreement, the factor will charge a fee of 2½ per cent on total invoicing. He will give an advance of 85 per cent of invoiced amounts at an interest rate of 13 per cent per annum.

The agreement should enable B to avoid spending $95,000 on administration costs.

You are required:

(i) to calculate the annual net cost of factoring;

(ii) to discuss the financial benefits of such an agreement, having regard to current interest rate on bank overdrafts of 12½ per cent.

(10 marks)
(Total marks = 15)

Solution

(a) Factoring and invoice discounting are methods of raising finance from trade receivables. In factoring the debts are sold, while invoice discounting is the assignment of debts as security for a loan.

The main services associated with entities offering this finance are:

- Provision of finance of between 80 per cent and 85 per cent of approved debts from the moment the goods or services are invoiced.

- Sales ledger service covering credit-checking, invoicing and collection. In effect, the sales ledger function or part thereof is subcontracted.
- Bad-debt insurance to cover the firm in the event of default on an invoice or invoices.
- Confidentiality to prevent the arrangement being apparent to customers and others.

(b)   (i)

Annual sales: $300,000 × 12	$3,600,000
Annual net cost of factoring	$
Fee: 2.5% of $3,600,000	90,000
Annual interest* (85% × 2.5/12 × 3.6 m × 13%)	82.875
Total annual cost	172,875
Less: administration costs	95.000
Net cost	77.875

* Assuming the agreement is based on existing invoices and does not phase in.

(ii) The borrowing of $637,500 (2.5/12 × 3.6 m × 85%) from the bank would cost $79,687.50. Therefore, factoring offers a saving of around $2,000 as well as providing certain advantages:

- *Flexibility.* As sales increase with the corresponding demand for finance, so finance from this source increases.
- *Security.* It allows the firm to pledge other assets as security for the finance.
- *Last resort.* It may be the most cost-effective lender to a firm that has no assets to offer as security.
- *Responsibility.* Relieves management of the responsibility for the sales ledger and can probably perform credit-checking better than the firm. Management must balance the disruption from cutting back its administrative costs with the financial and other advantages of factoring. Before reaching a decision, management should consider the possibility that the financial advantages may change and that re-establishing a sales ledger function may be costly.

10.13   Assessing the effectiveness of credit control

An outsider wishing to assess the effectiveness of a credit control function is generally limited to using static information and ratios, for example:

	Year 1	Year 2
$m		
(a) sales for the year	100.0	120.0
(b) trade receivables at the end of the year	16.0	20.0
Times per annum		
Asset velocity (a)/(b)	6.3	6.0
Days		
Average collection period 365(b)/(a)	58.4	60.8

This would be interpreted as an apparent deterioration in performance, but such an approach inevitably ignores a number of possible explanations:

- changes in the pattern of sales across the year, for example, more towards the end;
- changes in the mix of sales as between customers, for example, more to those granted longer credit;
- changes in terms, for example, less attractive discounts to some or all customers;
- different degrees of window dressing, for example, sales pulled forward from subsequent year.

Internally, of course, these problems do not arise, thanks to the availability of management information, including daily sales and receipts. As sales are entered into the ledger, for example, it is possible to identify when they should be paid, thus providing an appropriate yardstick against which to measure performance.

Entities that seek to apply the principles of value assurance to activities characterised as giving rise to 'indirect costs' could do worse than start with credit control. Value in this context is the cost of the next best alternative, for example, handing over the job to the professional factors.

This amounts to regarding the function as a business unit. It is credited with its actual receipts, having been debited with:

- the price at which the factor would buy the debts, for example, 98 per cent of their face value;
- the cost of finance, say 0.03 per cent per day on the aggregate balance;
- the costs of administration, etc.

If the net result is positive, the function is adding value to the entity.

10.14   Evaluating a change in credit policy

In an examination, you may be required to evaluate whether a proposed change in credit policy is financially justified. The example below illustrates the approach required to carry out this evaluation.

Exercise 10.3

The table below gives information extracted from the annual accounts of Supergeordie.

	$
Raw materials	180,000
Work in progress	93,360
Finished goods	142,875
Purchases	720,000
Cost of goods sold	1,098,360
Sales	1,188,000
Trade receivables	297,000
Trade payables	126,000

The sales director of Supergeordie estimates that if the period of credit allowed to customers was reduced from its current level to 60 days, this would result in a 25 per cent reduction in sales but would probably eliminate about $30,000 per annum bad debts. It would be necessary to spend an additional $20,000 per annum on credit control. The entity at present relies heavily on overdraft finance costing 9 per cent per annum.

You are required to make calculations showing the effect of these changes, and to advise whether they would be financially justified. Assume that purchases and inventory holdings would be reduced proportionally to the reduction in sales value.

 Solution

The first stage is to identify the reduction in the level of working capital investment as a result of the change in policy. Inventory and trade payables are assumed to fall by 25 per cent in line with sales, but the new level of trade receivables will need to be calculated using the trade receivable collection formula.

Reduction in working capital

	Existing level		New level	Change
	$		$	$
Raw materials	180,000	× 75% =	135,000	45,000
Work in progress	93,360	× 75% =	70,020	23,340
Finished goods	142,875	× 75% =	107,156	35,719
Trade receivables	297,000	*	146,466	150,534
Trade payables	(126.000)	× 75% =	(94.500)	(31.500)
Total	587.235		364.142	223.093

$$\text{Receivable collection period} = \frac{\text{trade receivables}}{\text{sales}} \times 365$$

$$60 = \frac{\text{trade receivables}}{1,188,000} \times 75\% \times 365$$

$${}^*\text{Trade receivables} = \frac{891,000 \times 60}{365}$$

$$= \$146,466$$

The second stage is to consider the annual costs and benefits of changing the credit policy. A key element here is to recognise the saving in finance costs as a result of the reduction in the level of working capital investment recognised above.

Annual costs and benefits

		$
Saving in finance costs	223,093 × 9% =	20,078
Reduction in gross profit (1,188,000 − 1,098,360)	= 89,640 × 25% =	(22,410)
Reduction in bad debts	=	30,000
Credit control costs	=	(20,000)
Net saving per annum before tax		7,668

The change in credit policy appears to be justified financially, but it should be remembered that there are a number of assumptions built in that could invalidate the calculations.

10.15   Trade payables

The term trade payables refers to the money owed to suppliers for goods and services. Taking credit from suppliers is a normal part of business, and is often viewed as being a free source of finance. The policy adopted regarding trade payables often then tends to be to maximise this resource, paying suppliers as late as possible. This policy may lead to a number of potential problems, discussed in the previous chapter, Section 20.2.1.

Trade payable management will broadly reflect trade receivable management, as one entity's receivable will be another entity's payable. Trade payable management will involve trying to maximise the credit period without jeopardising relationships with suppliers, while also seeking to optimise the level of inventory held.

10.16   The payment cycle

The payment cycle refers to the events that take place between agreeing the order, through to making payment.

The stages in the payment cycle are as follows:

- agreeing the order;
- credit control – evaluating whether to accept settlement discounts and deciding which invoices to pay first;
- method of payment;
- making payment to supplier.

Example: Trade payable payment policy at Marks and Spencer plc

The annual report for 2003 of Marks and Spencer plc states that its policy concerning the payment of its trade payables is:

'For all trade payables, it is the company's policy to:

- agree the terms of payment at the start of business with that supplier;
- ensure that suppliers are aware of the terms of payment;
- pay in accordance with its contractual and other legal obligations.'

The main trading company's (Marks and Spencer plc) policy concerning the payment of its trade creditors is as follows:

- General merchandise is automatically paid for 11 working days from the end of the week of delivery
- Foods are paid for 13 working days from the end of the week of delivery (based on the timely receipt of an accurate invoice) and
- Distribution suppliers are paid monthly for costs incurred in that month, based on estimates, and payments are adjusted quarterly to reflect any variations to estimate.

Trade creditor days for Marks and Spencer plc for the year ended 29 March 2003 were 14.3 days (10.3 working days), based on the ratio of company trade creditors at the end of the year to the amounts invoiced during the year by trade creditors.

10.16.1   Cash discounts

An entity may benefit from paying a supplier early in order to take advantage of settlement discounts. However, the benefit of the discount must be evaluated against the finance cost involved.

Exercise 10.4

Claud has been offered credit terms from a supplier whereby, Claud may claim a cash discount of 2 per cent if payment is made within 10 days of the invoice or pay on normal credit terms within 50 days.

You are required to advise the entity whether it should take advantage of the cash discount.

Assume a 365-day year and an invoice for $100.

 Solution

This is the mirror image of Exercise 21.1 (Tandijono). There we calculated that offering the discount was equivalent to an interest rate of 18.6 per cent per annum.

The implied interest cost of 18.6 per cent would then be compared with the overdraft rate. If Claud Ltd could borrow $98 for 40 days at a rate less than 18.6 per cent, it would be worthwhile taking advantage of the cash discount.

As before, by using the compound interest formula we arrive at a more accurate figure of 20.2 per cent per annum for the interest rate.

10.16.2 Methods of payment

Businesses may use a number of methods of payment for goods and services provided, including:

- cash
- Bankers Automated Clearing Services (BACS)
- cheques
- banker's draft
- standing orders
- direct debit
- credit cards
- debit cards
- Clearing House Automated Payments System (CHAPS).

10.17 Age analysis of trade payables

As an aid to effective management, an age analysis of trade payables may be produced. This is similar to the age analysis of trade receivables we saw earlier and is simply a list of the suppliers to whom we currently owe money, showing the total amount owed and the period of time for which the money has been owed. The actual form of the age analysis report can vary widely, but a typical example is shown below.

Anglo-Dutch

Age analysis of trade payables as at 30 September 2003

Account number	Customer name	Balance	Up to 30 days	31–60 days	61–90 days	Over 90 days
B004	Van Basten	294.35	220.15	65.40	8.80	0.00
D002	Van Dalen	949.50	853.00	0.00	96.50	0.00
D005	Dunister	371.26	340.66	30.60	0.00	0.00
H001	Van den Hoeven	1,438.93	0.00	0.00	567.98	870.95
K006	Koeman	423.48	312.71	110.77	0.00	0.00
Totals		3,477.52	1,726.52	206.77	673.28	870.95
Percentage		100%	49.6%	6%	19.4%	25%

The age analysis of trade payables will highlight any supplier accounts that are overdue. In the table above, $870.95 owed to Van den Hoeven has been outstanding for more than 3 months. The age profile shows that of the debts outstanding at 30 September 2003, nearly 45 per cent have been outstanding for more than 60 days, with the majority of those being outstanding payments due to Van den Hoeven.

10.18 Inventory management

Inventory, like receivables, involve the commitment of a large amount of a firm's resources. Their efficient management is of great concern to the financial manager. Inventory should not be viewed as an idle asset, rather they are an essential part of a firm's investment and operations. The optimum holding of inventory will maximise the benefits less costs involved.

Holding higher levels of finished goods inventory will enable the entity to be more flexible in supplying customers. More customers would receive immediate delivery rather than waiting for new items to be produced, and they might obtain a greater choice of types of product. There would be a smaller chance of sales being disrupted through interruptions in production. These benefits would have to be balanced against the storage costs incurred, the capital costs of financing the inventory and the cost of inventory becoming obsolete.

10.19 The nature of inventory

There are three main categories of inventory: raw materials, work-in-progress and finished goods.

10.19.1 Raw materials

These are used in the manufacturing or production process, for example, components, materials, fuel, etc. Inventory of raw materials are important because they allow *the production* process to be kept separate from the *supply* of raw materials.

10.19.2 Work-in-progress

These are partly finished goods, sub-assemblies, etc., that arise at, or between, various stages of the production process. They allow these various stages of production to be treated independently of each other.

10.19.3 Finished goods

These are completed goods, ready for sale, and held in inventory to meet anticipated customer demand.

The distinction between the categories is somewhat arbitrary (e.g. the finished goods of one entity may be the raw material of another – the 'finished' flour from a mill is a raw material to a bakery).

10.20 The costs of inventory

Three main types of cost are distinguishable.

10.20.1 Holding costs

These include storage costs, insurance, handling, auditing, deterioration, etc. Also, when money is tied up in inventory, it clearly cannot be used for other purposes, so that the opportunity cost of holding inventory (e.g. interest on other capital investments) must be considered.

10.20.2 Order costs

This is the cost of placing a (repeat) order to replenish inventory, for example, administrative costs, computer time, postage, unloading, quality control, etc. – whether the goods are obtained from outside or inside the entity.

10.20.3 The cost of running out of inventory

The costs associated with the consequences of running out of inventory include the obvious loss of contribution to profit arising from lost sales, as well as the loss of goodwill and the effect on future sales of unsatisfied customers going elsewhere. These costs are often difficult to quantify. There is also the cost of interrupted production.

10.20.4 Unit cost

Although not a category of cost in the same sense as the three types above, this is a term widely used to indicate the cost of acquiring one unit of product, taking all costs into account.

10.21 Inventory control policy

Though often undervalued as a management activity, inventory control policy, or a lack of it, can have a critical effect on working capital requirements, on the liquidity of the entity, on the smooth working of the production system and on customer service levels.

Therefore, an inventory control policy should reflect the following four criteria (despite the fact that they usually operate against each other):

1. keep total costs down (ideally to a minimum);
2. provide satisfactory service levels to customers;

3. ensure smooth-running production systems;
4. be able to withstand fluctuations in business conditions, for example, changes in customer demand, prices, availability of raw materials, etc.

Entity policy will dictate which of these will take precedence.

10.21.1 Dependent or independent demand

Products may be loosely considered to be subject to 'dependent' or 'independent' demand. For example, a mountain bike would be considered to have an 'independent' demand, whereas its components – wheels, tyres, frame, pedals, saddle, gears, etc. – have a dependent demand. This chapter will consider only 'independent demand'.

10.22 Inventory control systems

Three main systems are used to monitor and control inventory levels:

1. reorder level system
2. periodic review system
3. mixed systems, incorporating elements of both of the above.

10.22.1 Reorder level system

With this system, whenever the current inventory level falls below a pre-set 'reorder level' (ROL), a replenishment (replacement) order is made. Since there is normally a gap (lead time) between the placing of an order and receipt of supplies, say T, this has to be allowed for. This is illustrated in Figure 10.1, with the reorder quantity (for the replenishment order) shown as Q. (The actual size of this Q is often the economic order quantity, which is defined in the next section.) Buffer inventory is usually held as insurance against variations in demand and lead time.

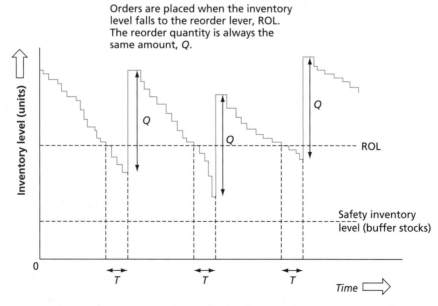

Figure 10.1 A simple reorder level system for inventory control

This system used to be known as the 'two-bin' system. Inventory is kept in two bins, one with an amount equal to the ROL quantity, and the rest in the other. Inventory is drawn from the latter until it runs out, whence a replenishment order is triggered.

A reorder level system is simple enough to implement if the variables (such as average usage, supplier lead time, etc.) are known with certainty. In practice, this is rarely the case.

10.22.2 Periodic review system

This is also referred to as a 'constant cycle' system. Inventory levels are reviewed after a fixed interval, for example, on the first of the month. Replenishment orders are issued where necessary, to top up inventory levels to pre-set target levels. This means that order sizes are variable (see Figure 10.2, where the *Q-values,* set by management, do not always ensure that the target is met, owing to variations in demand during the lead time, 7).

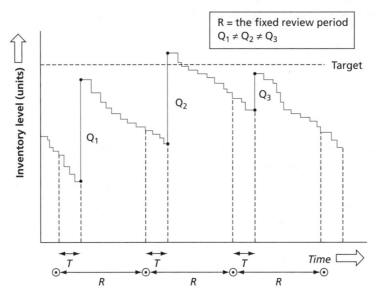

Figure 10.2 Periodic review system for inventory control

10.22.3 Mixed systems

In practice, mixtures of both systems are sometimes used, depending on the nature of the problem, the amount of computerisation and so on.

10.23 Economic order quantity (EOQ)

Consider the following simplified situation, in which an entity requires 24,000 boxes a year at a price of $8 per box. The order costs are $200 (delivery, admin, etc.) and the holding costs are 10 per cent per year, i.e. each order costs $200 to place and each box costs $0.80 per year to hold in inventory.

The table below shows a few simple calculations that illustrate how the economic order quantity operates. (These types of calculations are usually carried out using a spreadsheet.)

Order size (000)	Average orders/yr 24,000 ÷ Col 1	Annual order cost ($) Col 2 × 200	Mean inventory-holding Col 1 ÷ 2	Annual holding cost ($) Col 4 × $0.80	Total variable cost ($) Col 3 + Col 5	Total annual cost ($) Col 6 + cost of purchase
(1)	(2)	(3)	(4)	(5)	(6)	($192,000)
1	24	4,800	500	400	5,200	197,200
2	12	2,400	1,000	800	3,200	195,200
3	8	1,600	1,500	1,200	2,800	194,800
4	6	1,200	2,000	1,600	2,800	194,800
4.8	5	1,000	2,400	1,920	2,920	194,920
6	4	800	3,000	2,400	3,200	195,200

By inspection of the table (column 6), it appears that total variable cost is least when the order size is between 3,000 and 4,000 boxes, maybe about halfway between them since total variable cost is a curve. This is confirmed by Figure 10.3, which shows cost plotted against order size, using columns 1, 3, 5 and 7. The total annual cost (column 7) = total variable cost (column 6) + the purchase cost of 24,000 boxes at $8 ($192,000). The large differences between column 6 and column 7 should not be taken to imply that the basic purchase cost of inventory is always large in comparison to the variable costs of holding and ordering inventory and, of course, many entities have to hold a considerable range of inventory lines, so that a small saving in column 7, for many inventory lines, can mean big savings overall.

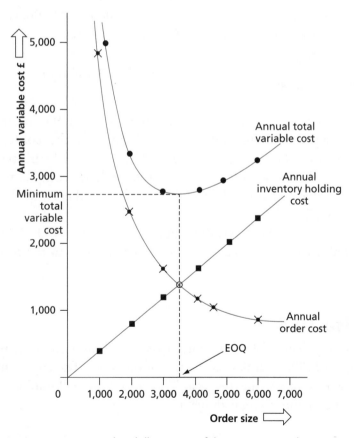

Figure 10.3 Graphical illustration of the economic order quantity

10.23.1 Comments on Figure 10.3

1. The annual total variable cost is minimised at the point where holding costs equal order costs, in this case when the order size is about 3,460 units.
2. The minimum annual total cost associated with a reorder quantity of 3,460 units is about $2,770 plus the purchase cost of $192,000, i.e. $194,770.
3. A reorder quantity of 3,460 units implies 6.93 orders per year, which is obviously impractical. In practice, this would clearly be rounded to 7 orders of 3,430 units. (24,000/7 = 3,430 to the nearest 10).
4. Such a reorder quantity is termed the *economic order quantity.*

The EOQ model assumes that there is a steady demand for a product, causing its level of inventory to be depleted at a constant rate. It is also assumed that inventory levels are replenished (replaced) by a reorder quantity (ROQ) at regular time intervals, with negligible lead time.

Two types of variable inventory costs have been considered above: order costs, which will be denoted C_0 per order, and holding costs, which will be denoted C_h per unit per year. Let the annual demand for the product be D units and the reorder quantity (ROQ) be shortened to Q for simplicity. Then the EOQ is

$$\text{EOQ} = \sqrt{\frac{2 \times C_o \times D}{C_h}}$$

Note: The EOQ formula is provided on the formula sheet in the examination. We shall use the data from the previous example to illustrate how it works.

The requirement is for 24,000 boxes a year; $\therefore D = 24,000$, $C_0 = 200$, $C_h = \$8 \times 10\% = \$0.80$. Substituting these numbers into the EOQ formula gives:

$$\text{EOQ} = \sqrt{\frac{2 \times \$200 \times 24,000}{\$0.80}} = \sqrt{\$12,000,000} = 3,464 \text{ units}$$

$\therefore$ The number of orders made per year = 24,000/3,464 = 6.93. In practical terms this means seven orders a year of about 24,000/7 = 3,430 units for the reorder quantity.

It could be seen from the costs graph (Figure 10.3) that total variable costs are minimised, theoretically, when total ordering cost = total holding cost, i.e. when the holding costs are $0.80 × 3,464/2, that is, $1,385.60. Therefore, in theory, total variable costs are 2 × $1,385.60 = $2,771.20.

In practice, C_0 = 7 × 200 = $1,400, and C_h = 0.5 × 3,430 × $0.80 = $1,372, giving a total variable cost of $2,772, which is extremely close to the theoretical value of $2771.20.

🖐 Exercise 10.5

A retailer has a steady demand for 600 units a year. Each unit costs the retailer $20. The costs of ordering are $100, regardless of the size of the order. The cost of holding a unit in inventory is 40 per cent of its value per year. What order size will minimise total inventory cost, and what is the minimum total annual inventory cost?

Solution

$D = 600 \; C_o = \$100 \; C_h = \$20 \times 40\% = \$8$

$$\text{EOQ} = \sqrt{\frac{2 \times C_o \times D}{C_h}}$$

$$\text{EOQ} = \sqrt{\frac{2 \times \$100 \times 600}{\$8}} = \sqrt{\$15,000} = 122.47 \text{ units}$$

In practice, this would be rounded to 120 units, which would be ordered $600/120 = 5$ times a year, i.e. every 10 weeks or so.

The annual order costs would be	$5 \times \$100$	=	$500
The annual holding costs would be	$0.5 \times 120 \times \$8$	=	$480
The purchase cost would be	$\$20 \times 600$	=	$12,000
∴ The total annual inventory cost would be			$12,980

10.24 Quantity discounts

It is quite common for some suppliers to offer discounts on items that are bought in large quantities. This not only reduces the unit purchase cost, but also the order cost because fewer orders will be made. In contrast, the higher average inventory levels result in increased holding costs. Although it may not be appropriate to use the EOQ formula (because the price per item is not fixed), the calculations shown below, manually, are quite easily done with a spreadsheet.

 Exercise 10.6

Suppose that our manufacturer (with $D = 24,000$, $C_0 = \$200$, $C_h = \$0.80$ and with the assumptions of the EOQ model), faced with buying from an external supplier, is offered a discount of 5 per cent on purchases of 5,000 boxes or more, all other factors being the same. What are the implications of this offer?

 Solution

A sketch graph will illustrate the situation (see Figure 10.4).

The total annual cost in column 7 of the table developed earlier is discontinuous at the point where the discount begins to operate. The EOQ formula can only be used up to the point where $Q = 5,000$.

The graph demonstrates this point clearly, where $Q = 5,000$. Some calculations at this value are now made to see if the discount is worth while and by how much.

At Q = 5,000 units, with the discount
Total order costs = $\$200 \times D/Q = \$200 \times 24,000/5,000 = \$960$
With the 5 per cent discount, the price per item falls from $8 to $7.60.
∴ Holding cost per item = $(\$7.60 \times 10\%) = \$0.76$
∴ Total holding cost = $(0.5 \times 5,000 \times \$0.76) = \$1,900$

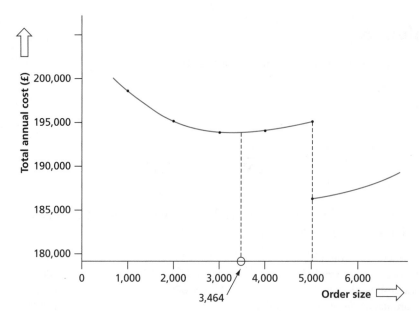

Figure 10.4 Total Annual Cost & over all size price discount of 5%

Total variable cost = ($960 + $1,900) = $2,860
The total annual cost = total variable cost + purchase cost
= ($2,860 + 24,000 × $7.60)
= ($2,860 + $182,400)
= $185,260

At Q = 3,464 units (EOQ), without the discount
The total variable cost was $2,772.
The purchase cost was $192,000.
The total annual cost was $194,772.
Therefore, the discount produces a saving of $(194,772 − 185,260), that is, $9,512.

10.25 Lead times

The models considered here assume that lead times (the time lags between the issuing of orders and their receipt) are negligible or at least constant. In practice, time lags occur and vary, so it is crucial to allow for them. We look here at constant lead times so that EOQ values remain the same, but the timings of placing orders have to change.

10.25.1 Lead times with constant demand

Suppose that our supplier requires 1 week to fulfil an order. The annual requirement of the manufacturer was for 24,000 units, so that 24,000/48 = 500 units are needed each week, assuming 48 working weeks to a year. Thus, whenever the inventory level falls to 500, a replenishment order to the EOQ value of 3,430 units should be made.

This leaves no margin for error and assumes constant usage, if 501 units were required in the week there would be a shortfall. If demand is not constant or lead times are variable, the ROL will need to be increased to ensure that inventory does not run out before the order is delivered.

In principle, a new order is placed whilst there is still sufficient inventory to cover the maximum demand over the maximum likely lead time. Setting ROL at this level will create a buffer inventory which is a quantity of inventory that will not usually be needed but could be needed if demand or lead times are above average.

10.26 Just-in-time purchasing

The JIT concept and JIT purchasing were considered earlier in this text. The general thrust behind the JIT concept is that good quality production management technique (covering areas such as production scheduling, quality inspection, customer and supplier relationships and equipment maintenance) may obviate the need for stock holding. The implications of this for procurement and purchasing are that:

- materials are delivered as and when required for use in production on a coupled-up basis; consequently buffer stocks, economic order quantities and re-order quantities are not relevant;
- material stocks are usually minimal;
- finished goods are produced only in response to customer requirements on a coupled-up basis; consequently optimum batch sizes are not relevant;
- inventories of finished goods are usually minimal and WIP should be small.

JIT is part of the wider new manufacturing concept whereby mass production of undifferentiated goods gives way to flexible production of customised goods. One implication of this is that procurement and purchasing have to become sophisticated operations closely integrated with the production and sales operations. Supplier and customer relationships need to involve a higher degree of engagement than was traditionally the case.

Traditional procurement practices based on re-order levels and EOQs imply a degree of decoupling between the procurement and use of materials. Modern JIT procurement requires that the purchasing operation is fully integrated with the sales and production operations. Business models supported by IT (considered earlier in this text) such as MRP, ERP and SCM are very much features of this.

10.27 Summary

In this chapter we have considered the manner in which the efficiency of working capital management impacts on business performance. We have also considered the techniques that have been developed in order to guide management towards optimum policies for the management of debt, trade credit and inventory. These practices are partly based on business culture and partly on mathematical models. It should be noted that there is a considerable overlap between inventory policy and other areas of policy in the management of a business.

Self-test questions

(1) What is 'working capital'? (Section 10.2)
(2) Compare the current and quick ratios (Section 10.3)
(3) Explain the working capital cycle. (Section 10.5)

(4) How does 'overtrading' manifest itself? (Section 10.6)

(5) State the advantages and disadvantages of credit insurance. (Section 10.11)

(6) State the advantages and disadvantages of debt factoring. (Section 10.12)

(7) List types of inventory holding cost. (Section 10.20.1)

(8) List the types of cost arising from a 'stock-out' situation. (Section 10.20.3)

(9) What are the main objectives in stock management? (Section 10.21)

(10) Compare the EOQ and JIT models. (Sections 10.23 and 10.26)

Revision Questions

? Question 1

An entity has a current ratio of 1.75. It has decided in future to pay its trade payables after 40 days, rather than after 30 days as it has in the past. What will be the effect of this change on the entity's current ratio and its cash operating cycle?

	Current ratio	Working capital cycle
(A)	Increase	Increase
(B)	Increase	Decrease
(C)	Decrease	Increase
(D)	Decrease	Decrease

(2 marks)

? Question 2

Which of the following is most likely to reduce a firm's working capital?

(A) Paying payables early
(B) Lengthening the period of credit given to receivables
(C) Repaying an overdraft out of cash
(D) Giving a discount to a customer for immediate cash settlement

(2 marks)

? Question 3

An entity has a current ratio of 1.5:1. It decides to use surplus cash balances to settle 30% of its total current liabilities. The current ratio will:

(A) decrease by more than 30%
(B) decrease by less than 30%
(C) increase by more than 30%
(D) increase by less than 30%

(2 marks)

? Question 4

An entity buys goods on credit and then, before payment is made, it is forced to sell all of these goods on credit for less than the purchase price. What is the consequence of these two transactions immediately after the sale has taken place?

(A) Inventory decreases and cash decreases
(B) Cash decreases and payables increase
(C) Inventory decreases and receivables increase
(D) Receivables increase and payables increase (2 marks)

? Question 5

A retailing entity has an annual turnover of $36 million. The entity earns a constant margin of 20% on sales. All sales and purchases are on credit and are evenly distributed over the year. The following amounts are maintained at a constant level throughout the year:

Inventory $6 million
Receivables $8 million
Payables $3 million

What is the entity's working capital cycle to the nearest day (i.e. the average time from the payment of a supplier to the receipt from a customer)?

(A) 81 days
(B) 111 days
(C) 119 days
(D) 195 days (4 marks)

? Question 6

Working capital is most likely to increase when:

(A) payments to trade payables are delayed
(B) the period of credit extended to customers is reduced
(C) fixed assets are sold
(d) inventory levels are increased (2 marks)

? Question 7

An entity's current assets exceed its current liabilities (which include an overdraft). The entity pays a trade payable, taking advantage of a cash discount. What will be the effect of this transaction upon the entity's working capital and on its current ratio?

	Working capital	Current ratio
(A)	Constant	Decrease
(B)	Constant	Increase
(C)	Decrease	Decrease
(D)	Increase	Increase

(2 marks)

? Question 8

Which ONE of the following transactions is most likely to affect the overall amount of working capital?

(A) Receipt of full amount of cash from a receivable
(B) Sale of a fixed asset on credit at its net book value
(C) Payment of a trade payable
(D) Purchase of inventory on credit **(2 marks)**

? Question 9

If the current ratio for an entity is equal to its acid test (that is, the quick ratio), then:

(A) the current ratio must be greater than one
(B) the entity does not carry any inventory
(C) trade receivables plus cash is greater than trade payables minus inventory
(D) working capital is positive **(2 marks)**

? Question 10

'Although many financial analysts use the current ratio to assess the liquidity position of firms, it is essential that care is taken in reaching any decision.'

The following information has been obtained from two small entities regarding the working capital that is being used at 30 September 2003.

	Entity A	Entity B
	$	$
Inventories	6,000	20,000
Trade receivables	5,800	10,000
Cash	2,200	–
Trade payables	7,000	7,000
Bank overdraft	–	3,000

Requirements

(a) Calculate the current ratio for each of the two firms. **(2 marks)**
(b) Discuss the implications of the ratios that you have calculated in terms of a request for credit from both of these entities. **(3 marks)**

(Total marks = 5)

? Question 11

DR has the following balances under current assets and current liabilities:

Current assets		$
Inventory	50,000	
Trade receivables	70,000	
Bank		10,000

Current liabilities	$	
Trade payables		88,000
Interest payable	7,000	

DR's quick ratio is:

(A) 0.80:1
(B) 0.84:1
(C) 0.91:1
(D) 1.37:1   (2 marks)

? Question 12

Which ONE of the following is most likely to increase an entity's working capital?

(A) Delaying payment to trade payables
(B) Reducing the credit period given to customers
(C) Purchasing inventory on credit
(D) Paying a supplier and taking an early settlement discount   (2 marks)

? Question 13

FGH requires a rate of return of 12.85% each year.

Two of FGH's suppliers, P and Q are offering the following terms for immediate cash settlement:

Entity	Discount period	Normal settlement
P	1%	1 month
Q	2%	2 months

Which of the discounts should be accepted to achieve the required rate of return?

(A) Both P and Q
(B) P only
(C) Q only
(D) Neither of them   (2 marks)

? Question 14

A retailing entity had cost of sales of $60,000 in April. In the same month, trade payables increased by $8,000 and inventory decreased by $2,000. What payment was made to suppliers in April?

(A) $50,000
(B) $54,000
(C) $66,000
(D) $70,000   (2 marks)

Question 15

Which ONE of the following services is NOT normally undertaken by a debt factor?

(A) Taking customer orders and invoicing
(B) Attempting to recover doubtful debts
(C) Making payments to entities before the cash is received from trade recievables
(D) Administering a entity's sales ledger **(2 marks)**

Question 16

If an entity regularly fails to pay its suppliers by the normal due dates, it may lead to a number of problems:

  (i) Having insufficient cash to settle trade payables
 (ii) Difficulty in obtaining credit from new suppliers
(iii) Reduction in credit rating
(iv) Settlement of trade receivables may be delayed.

    Which TWO of the above could arise as a result of exceeding suppliers' trade credit terms?

(A) (i) and (ii)
(B) (i) and (iii)
(C) (ii) and (iii)
(D) (iii) and (iv) **(2 marks)**

Question 17

BE has been offering 60-day payment terms to its customers, but now wants to improve its cash flow. BE is proposing to offer a 1 × 5% discount for payment within 20 days.
    Assume a 365-day year and an invoice value of $1,000.
    What is the effective annual interest rate that BE will incur for this action? **(4 marks)**

Question 18

DN currently has an overdraft on which it pays interest at 10% per year. DN has been offered credit terms from one of its suppliers, whereby it can either claim a cash discount of 2% if payment is made within 10 days of the date of the invoice or pay on normal credit terms, within 40 days of the date of the invoice.
    Assume a 365-day year and an invoice value of $100.

Requirement

Explain to DN, with reasons and supporting calculations, whether it should pay the supplier early and take advantage of the discount offered. **(5 marks)**

Question 19

An entity offers its goods to customers on 30 days' credit, subject to satisfactory trade references. It also offers a 2 per cent discount if payment is made within ten days of the date of invoice.

Requirement

Calculate the cost to the entity of offering the discount, assuming a 365-day year.

(4 marks)

? Question 20

Compare offering discounts to customers to encourage early settlement of bills with using debt factors. **(5 marks)**

? Question 21

AAD is a newly created subsidiary of a large listed entity. It commenced business on 1 October 2004, to provide specialist contract cleaning services to industrial customers. All sales are on credit.

More favourable credit terms are offered to larger customers (class A) than to smaller customers (class B). All sales are invoiced at the end of the month in which the sale occurs. Class A customers will be given credit terms requiring payment within 60 days of invoicing, while class B customers will be required to pay within 30 days of invoicing.

Since it is recognised, however, that not all customers comply with the credit terms they are allowed, receipts from trade receivables have prudently been estimated as follows:

Customer type	Within 30 days	31 to 60 days	61 to 90 days	91 to 120 days	Bad debts
Class A		50%	30%	15%	5%
Class B	60%	25%	10%		5%

The above table shows that trade receivables are expected either to pay within 60 days of the end of the credit period, or not at all. Bad debts will therefore be written off 60 days after the end of the credit period.

Budgeted credit sales for each class of customers in the first 4 months of trading are as follows:

Customer	October	November	December	January
	$'000	$'000	$'000	$'000
Class A	100	150	200	300
Class B	60	80	40	50

Assume all months are of 30 days.

Requirements

(a) Prepare a statement showing the budgeted cash to be received by AAD from trade receivables in each of the 3 months of November 2004, December 2004 and January 2005, based upon the prudently estimated receipts from trade receivables. **(7 marks)**

(b) Prepare a budgeted age analysis of trade receivables for AAD at 30 January 2005 for each of the two classes of customer. It should show the total budgeted trade receivables outstanding at that date analysed into each of the following periods:
   (i) within credit period
   (ii) up to 30 days overdue
   (iii) 30 to 60 days overdue. **(8 marks)**

(c) Explain the purposes of entities preparing an age analysis of trade receivables analysed by individual customers. **(5 marks)**

(Total marks = 20)

? Question 22

Which ONE of the following would not normally be considered a cost of holding inventory?

(A) Inventory obsolescence
(B) Insurance cost of inventory
(C) Lost interest on cash invested in inventory
(D) Loss of sales from running out of inventory   **(2 marks)**

? Question 23

An entity uses the economic order quantity model (EOQ model). Demand for the entity's product is 36,000 units each year and is evenly distributed each day. The cost of placing an order is $10 and the cost of holding a unit of inventory for a year is $2. How many orders should the entity make in a year?

(A) 60
(B) 120
(C) 300
(D) 600   **(2 marks)**

? Question 24

An entity uses the economic order quantity model (that is, the EOQ model) to manage inventory.

   Situation 1 – interest rates rise;
   Situation 2 – sales volumes increase.
   What would happen to the economic order quantity in each of these two situations?

	Situation 1	**Situation 2**
(A)	Increase	Increase
(B)	Increase	Decrease
(C)	Decrease	Increase
(D)	Decrease	Decrease

                                                                    (2 marks)

? Question 25

Calculate the economic order quantity (EOQ) for the following item of inventory:

- Quantity required per year 32,000 items
- Order costs are $15 per order
- Inventory holding costs are estimated at 3% of inventory value per year
- Each unit currently costs $40.   **(2 marks)**

? Question 26

BF manufactures a range of domestic appliances. Due to past delays in suppliers providing goods, BF has had to hold an inventory of raw materials, in order that the production could continue to operate smoothly. Due to recent improvements in supplier reliability, BF is re-examining its inventory holding policies and recalculating economic order quantities (EOQ).

- Item 'Z' costs BF $10.00 per unit
- Expected annual production usage is 65,000 units
- Procurement costs (cost of placing and processing one order) are $25.00
- The cost of holding one unit for one year has been calculated as $3.00.

The supplier of item 'Z' has informed BF that if the order was 2,000 units or more at one time, a 2% discount would be given on the price of the goods.

Requirements

  (i) Calculate the EOQ for item 'Z' before the quantity discount. **(2 marks)**
 (ii) Advise BF if it should increase the order size of item 'Z' so as to qualify for the 2% discount. **(3 marks)**

(Total marks = 5)

? Question 27

WCM is an entity that sells a wide range of specialist electrical and manual tools to professional builders through a trade catalogue.

The entity is considering the improvement of its working capital management in order to reduce its current overdraft. Most customers are required to pay cash when they place an order and thus there is little that can be done to reduce trade receivables. The focus of the board's attention is therefore on trade payables and inventory.

The working capital position at 30 April 2002 was as follows:

	$	$
Inventory	300,000	
Trade receivables	50,000	350,000
Trade Payables	150,000	
Overdraft	550,000	
		700,000
Net current liabilities		350,000

Trade payables

WCM has two major suppliers, INT and GRN.

INT supplies electrical tools and is one of the largest entities in the industry, with international operations. GRN is a small, local manufacturer of manual tools of good quality. WCM is one of its major customers.

Deliveries from both suppliers are currently made monthly, and are constant throughout the year. Delivery and invoicing both occur in the last week of each month. Details of the credit terms offered by suppliers are as follows:

Supplier	Normal credit period	Cash discount	Average monthly purchases
INT	40 days	2% for settlement in 10 days	$100,000
GRN	30 days	None	$50,000

WCM always takes advantages of the cash discount from INT and pays GRN after 30 days.

Inventory

The entity aims to have the equivalent of 2 months' cost of sales (equal to 2 months' purchases) in inventory immediately after a delivery has been received.

New working capital policy

At a meeting of the board of directors, it was decided that from 1 May 2002, all payments would be based upon taking the full credit period of 40 days from INT, and similarly taking 40 days before paying GRN.

A review of inventory is also to be commissioned to assess the level of safety (that is buffer) inventory held. In particular, it would examine the feasibility of a just-in-time inventory management system. Meanwhile, it was decided to make no purchases in May in order to reduce inventory levels.

While most of the board supported these changes, *the purchasing manager* disagreed, arguing that working capital would be even worse after the changes.

Requirements

(a) Calculate the annual rate of interest implied in the cash discount offered by INT. Assume a 365-day year. **(3 marks)**

(b) Calculate the anticipated current ratio of WCM at 31 May 2002, assuming that the changes in trade payable payment policy take place, and that there are no inventory purchases during May 2002.

Assume for this purpose that, in the absence of any change to trade payable policy, the overdraft would have remained at its 30 April 2002 level.

Clearly state any assumptions made. **(5 marks)**

(c) As a management accountant of WCM, write a memorandum to the directors that evaluates:

(i) the proposed changes to the trade payable payment policy;

(ii) the proposed policy to introduce a just-in-time system for inventory management.

(12 marks)
(Total marks = 20)

❓ Question 28

STK sells bathroom fittings throughout Europe. In order to obtain the best price, it has decided to purchase all its annual demand of 10,000 shower units from a single supplier. After investigation, it has identified two possible manufacturers – SSS and RRR. Each has offered to provide the required number of showers each year under an exclusive long-term contract.

Demand for shower units is at a constant rate all year. The cost to STK of holding one shower unit in inventory for 1 year is $4 plus 3% of the purchase price.

SSS is located only a few miles from the STK main showroom. It has offered to supply each shower unit at $400 with a transport charge of $200 per delivery. It has guaranteed such a regular and prompt delivery service that STK believes it will not be necessary to hold any safety inventory (i.e. buffer inventory) if it uses SSS as its supplier.

RRR is located in the Far East. It has offered to supply each shower unit at $398 but transport charges will be $500 per delivery. There is also a minimum order size of 1,000 shower units. Deliveries will be by ship and will therefore take some time to arrive. There is also significant uncertainty about the lead time which means that STK will need to hold a safety inventory of 600 shower units.

Requirements

(a) Using the EOQ model, calculate the optimal order size, assuming that SSS is chosen as the sole supplier of shower units for STK.   **(4 marks)**

(b) (i) Prepare calculations to determine whether SSS or RRR should be chosen as the sole supplier of shower nits for STK.   **(7 marks)**

    (ii) Describe any further factors that STK should consider before making a final choice of supplier.   **(4 marks)**

(c) Assume you are a consultant advising the Far East based entity RRR. Write a rief memorandum explaining how RRR could finance the necessary working capital for its proposed contract to supply STK.   **(5 marks)**

(Total marks = 20)

Solutions to Revision Questions

✓ Solution 1

The correct answer is (D), see Sections 10.3 and 10.5.

✓ Solution 2

The correct answer is (D), see Section 10.3.

✓ Solution 3

The correct answer is (D), see Section 10.3.
   Original ratio = 1.5/1 = 1.5
   Settlement = 0.3
   New current ratio = 1.2/0.7 = 1.71
   Increase = [(1.71/1.5) − 1] = 14%

✓ Solution 4

The correct answer is (D), see Section 10.3.

✓ Solution 5

The correct answer is (C), see Section 10.5.
   Receivable days = (8/36) × 365 = 81.11
   Inventory days = (6/36 × 0.8) × 365 = 76.04
   Payable days = (3/36 × 0.8) × 365 = (38.02)
   WCC = 81.11 + 76.04 − 38.02 = 119.13

✓ Solution 6

The correct answer is (C), see Section 10.3.

Solution 7

The correct answer is (D), see Section 10.3.3.

Payables fall more than the overdraft increases because of the discount. Current assets are unchanged. Thus working capital and the current ratio increase.

 Solution 8

The correct answer is (B), see Section 10.3.

 Solution 9

The correct answer is (B), see Section 10.3.3.

 Solution 10

(a) The current ratio is calculated as:
Current assets/Current liabilities

Entity A $ 14,000/7,000 = 2
Entity B $30,000/10,000 = 3

(b) From the ratios, it would appear that the liquidity position of Entity B is superior to that of Entity A. However, this does not reflect the real situation. Entity B owes more than Entity A and has an overdraft already. On the other hand, it also has significantly more inventory and trade receivables than Entity A.

To form an opinion on the liquidity position of these two entities, it is necessary to judge the likelihood of the inventory being sold and the amounts being collected from the trade receivables. It is necessary to focus on the time that will be needed to turn all these current assets into cash. The position of Entity B is not necessarily better as implied by the current ratio. In assessing the request for credit from both entities, the current ratio is not particularly helpful and should be used with caution, see Section 10.3.3.

 Solution 11

(70,000 + 10,000):(88,000 + 7,000)
80,000:95,000
0.84:1
Therefore the answer is (B), see Section 10.3.4.

 Solution 12

The correct answer is (D), see Section 10.2.

 Solution 13

The correct answer is (C), see Section 10.16.1
$P = (100/99)^{12} - 1 = 12.82\%$
$Q = (100/98)^{6} - 1 = 12.89\%$

Solution 14

The correct answer is (A), see Section 10.16

 Solution 15

The correct answer is (A), see Section 10.12

 Solution 16

The correct answer is (C).

 Solution 17

$s = x(1 + r)^n$
$1,000 = 985(1 + r)^{365/40}$
$1 + r = (1,000/985)^{9 \times 125}$
$1 + r = 1 \times 148$
$r = 14 \times 8\%$

 Solution 18

DN pays $98 on day 10 instead of day 40.
  Need to borrow $98 for 30 days

Effective annual interest rate is: $\dfrac{365}{30} = 12.1667$

$$1 + r = \left[\frac{100}{98}\right]^{12.1667}$$

$r = 0.2786$ or 27.86%

DN receives 27.86% interest if it takes the discount. If DN needs to borrow on overdraft to make the payment, it is to its advantage to borrow the money and take the discount as long as the interest rate is less than 27.86%.

If DN has surplus cash in its current account and it is earning less than 27.86% interest, it would be beneficial for DN to use the cash to pay early. If DN has any short-term investments yielding less than 27.86%, it may be worthwhile using these to fund early payment, see Section 10.16.1

 Solution 19

On the policy as described, the entity is offering 2 per cent for 20 days, i.e. 36.5 per cent per annum using simple interest. In accounting terms, the cost to the entity is 2 per cent of the sales in respect of which the discount is taken, but it will show correspondingly lower receivables. Assume sales of $1,000 per day, for simplicity: the discount would cost $7,300 per annum, but receivables would be $20,000 lower, 7,300/20,000 = 36.5 per cent. The cost of offering a cash discount should ideally be calculated using a compounded annual rate. In this example, the compounded annual rate is given by:

$$\frac{365}{20} - 1 = 1.446 - 1 = 44.6\%$$

This can be compared with the entity's cost of capital to arrive at an opportunity cost.

 Solution 20

The offering of a discount to customers is normally influenced by practice in the industry/trade in question and may therefore be unavoidable in principle although subject to customisation, firm by firm. The benefits (compared with factoring) are attributable to the maintenance of a direct relationship with the customer. In these days of developing long-term relationships, this can be very important. Also, sales ledger clerks and managers can pick up useful 'intelligence' from their contacts and head off potential problems, including bad debts, and all managers are prompted to think about the time value of money. There is a cost, however, that is not limited to the actual discount: keeping on top of the situation (e.g. reacting quickly to lapses) can be costly, though the latest computer systems have eliminated the need for clerks to go through ledgers.

Factoring, on the other hand, takes the administration of the sales ledger away from the entity and exploits the economies of scale and expertise of the specialists. Different payment terms can be negotiated, for example, some payment immediately on invoicing, thereby releasing further working capital, and/or the guaranteeing of payment. A particular advantage of this approach is that receipts are more predictable: customers may or may not pay in time to earn their discount, but the factor must pay to terms. There is a cost, of course, in respect of the administration and financing, and it must be acknowledged that the factor can be a barrier between the entity and its customers. A 'confidential invoice discounting' service can be an effective compromise.

Experience suggests that, thanks to avoiding double handling, a well-run sales accounting function adds value to a business; factoring is primarily attractive to entities who cannot raise funds from more traditional sources.

 Solution 21

(a)

Credit sales	Total sales	Cash received		
		November	December	January
Class A				
October	100		50	30
November	150		–	75
December	200		–	–
Total			50	105
Class B				
October	60	36	15	6
November	80		48	20
December	40	–	–	24
Total		36	63	50
Overall total (A + B)		36	113	155

(b)

Age Analysis of Receivables

	Total	Within credit period	Up to 30 days late	30 to 60 days late
Class A ,W1.	595	500	75	20
Class B ,W2.	78	50	16	12

Working 1–

Class A

	Total	Cash received (per (a))	Within credit period	Overdue up to 30 days	Overdue 31–60 days	Bad debts
Oct	100	80			20	
Nov	150	75		75		
Dec	200		200			
Jan	300		300			

Working 2 –

Class B

	Total	Cash received (per (a))	Within credit period	Overdue up to 30 days	Overdue 31–60 days	Bad debts
Oct	60	57				3
Nov	80	68			12	
Dec	40	24		16		
Jan	50		50			

(c) An age analysis of receivables is a useful control tool to identify those receivables that are at greatest risk of non-payment or late payment.

It provides an analysis of the total amounts outstanding according to their age. This may be based upon total receivables, a class of receivable or a particular receivable.

Individual receivable data can show accounts that are at risk and appropriate follow-up procedures can be entered into depending upon the period by which normal credit terms have been exceeded.

Progressively this might mean:

- a reminder letter
- telephone call
- personal visit
- withholding supplies
- debt collection agency
- legal action.

This progression is likely to be based upon the age of the receivable, but also the nature of the response to initial enquiries. More general age analysis data of classes of business or total or receivables will, when compared over time, enable credit managers to pick up trends in payments giving early warning signals. This might include problems with liquidity in the sector (e.g. through a downturn) or reduced internal efficiency in invoicing and follow-up procedures.

The information about the age of receivables may also help predict cash inflows from the business and decide appropriate action to speed up receipts arising from receivables (e.g. cash discounts, debt factoring, invoice discounting). The age analysis may also indicate when to make a provision for doubtful debts and how much this should be.

☑ Solution 22

The correct answer is (D), see Section 10.20.

☑ Solution 23

The correct answer is (A), see Section 10.24.

$$\text{EOQ} = \sqrt{(2 \times 36{,}000 \times \$10)/2} = 600$$
$$\text{Orders} = 36{,}000/600 = 60$$

☑ Solution 24

The correct answer is (C), see Section 10.24.

☑ Solution 25

Using the EOQ formula from the formulae sheet:

$$\sqrt{\frac{2 \times \$15 \times 32{,}000}{\$1.2}} = \sqrt{800{,}000} = 894.43$$

See Section 10.23.

☑ Solution 26

(i) Using the formula from the formula sheet:

$$\text{EOQ} = \sqrt{2C_o D/C_h}$$
$$= \sqrt{(2 \times 25 \times 65{,}000)/3} = \sqrt{1{,}083{,}333} = 1{,}040.83$$

EOQ for item 'Z' is 1,041 units per order.

(ii)

Total cost using EOQ		$
Unit cost 65,000 × $10	=	650,000
Holding cost $3 × 1,041/2	=	1,562
Ordering cost $25 × 65,000/1,041	=	1.561
Total cost		653.123

Assume order size = 2,000 units

		$
Unit cost 65,000 × $9.8	=	637,000
Holding cost $3 × 2,000/2	=	3,000
Ordering cost $25 × 65,000/2,000	=	813
Revised total cost		640.813

The total cost is $12,310 less, therefore it is worthwhile for BF to increase the order size and claim the discount, see Section 10.24

 ## Solution 27

(a)

$$(100/98)^{365/30} - 1 = 27.86\%$$

(b)

	$
Payables (April deliveries)	150,000
Overdraft (550,000 − 150,000)	400,000
Inventory (one month's purchases)	150,000
Receivables	50,000

$$\frac{\text{Current assets}}{\text{Current liabilities}} = 20,000{:}550,000 = 0.36 \text{ to } 1$$

(c)

Memorandum

To:	The Board of WCM	**From:**	Management Accountant
Subject:	Working capital Management	**Date:**	21 May 2002

Introduction

If the objective of the review is to reduce the entity's overdraft, then, while working capital can have a role, it must be viewed alongside other methods of reducing the overdraft including the raising of new long-term finance, divestment of assets and improvements in operating results.

The entity currently has negative working capital, but this is not of itself a problem and it is not unusual for cash business. If receivables are low because of mainly cash sales, but credit is taken from suppliers, then essentially cash is being received before the entity pays for the goods.

(i) Payable payment policy

INT

The entity currently pays after 10 days to take advantage of a cash discount. Delaying payment improves short-term liquidity, but loses the discount of 27.86% per year [see requirement (a)]. This is quite a high rate of return to lose, but must be weighed against the saving in overdraft interest.

In addition, while the overdraft will be lower in May than it was in April, this is a one-off benefit in the sense that continuing the policy will not lower the overdraft any further.

GRN

The current terms being offered by GRN are 30 days settlement. Taking 40 days is essentially a breach of this contract, although not uncommon in practice. The potential cost is that if this policy is decided upon unilaterally by WCM, then it may damage the relationship with the supplier.

Given that GRN is only a small entity, it may not wish to alienate WCM as a major customer. On the other hand, much may depend upon whether there are alternative suppliers at equivalent cost for WCM.

Moreover, GRN may seek to recover the cost of lost liquidity by other means: for example, higher prices, charging interest on overdue amounts, delaying deliveries until payment is made, reduced goodwill. More generally, the payment delay, if it becomes more widely known, may damage WCM's credit rating. This may make obtaining credit finance in future more difficult or more costly.

(ii) Just-in-time system (JIT)

Inventory

JIT may be defined as: 'A system whose objective is to produce or to procure products or components as they are required by a customer or for use, rather than for inventory' (from *CIMA Terminology* 2005 edition).

The basic decision for WCM is therefore whether it wishes to supply customers from inventory, or obtain supplies to match customer orders (i.e. obtaining inventory just in time). In the latter case, minimal (or even zero) inventory could be held.

The major disadvantage of supplying to order is that the delay in supplying customers may reduce sales and therefore profitability. Ultimately, this will feed through into reduced liquidity. If, however, demand is predictable, then very low levels of safety inventory could be maintained with orders being made on a JIT basis in anticipation of imminent sales, rather then responding to actual orders.

The advantages of holding lower inventory as a result of JIT include:

- Lower storage costs
- Less cash tied up in inventory
- Saved interest costs
- Lower costs from damage, wastage and obsolescence.

In order to obtain these advantages, certain procedures and relationships must be in place. However, the current policy of monthly deliveries is incompatible with JIT, which requires:

- frequent deliveries (preferably daily);
- small deliveries being economic;
- reliable and quick deliveries in terms of timing (i.e. a short and certain lead time);
- reliable deliveries in terms of product quality;
- good relationship with suppliers;
- supplier flexibility.

The credit policy of delaying may be seen as incompatible with maintaining the good supplier relationships necessary for JIT.

Comparing the current policy to JIT indicates the actions necessary for implementation. Historically, it appears that at the time of a new delivery, there are 1 month's sales in inventory. Immediately after the delivery, there are 2 months' sales in inventory.

The new policy of omitting May's purchases will mean that if the next order is in the last week in June, then inventory would have fallen to zero before the order and one month's sales immediately thereafter. This seems inappropriate as:

- monthly orders cause wide fluctuations in inventory levels;
- many different lines of inventory are held. Unless sales can be predicted a month in advance then rather than zero inventory, some lines of inventory are likely to run out while significant inventory could be held for other goods;
- while zero or near zero inventory is held for part of the month, none of the above conditions for JIT appears to be met.

Conclusion

Overall, the policy changes have worsened the current ratio from 0.5:1 to 0.36:1. Of itself, this does not matter if inventory and payables are being managed efficiently without affecting the service to customers.

This does not, however, appear to be the case at the moment and careful consideration of the conditions necessary for JIT need to be assessed and agreed with suppliers before the costs and benefits can be judged.

The issue of supplier payment management is inter-related to the issue of JIT inventory management and thus should be considered simultaneously.

Signed: Management Accountant

Solution 28

(a)

$$\text{Holding cost} = \$4 + (3\% \times \$400) = \$16$$

$$\text{EOQ} = \sqrt{(2C_o D/C_h)} = \sqrt{2 \times 10,000 \times \frac{\$200}{\$16}} = 500 \text{ units}$$

(b)

$$\text{Holding cost} = \$4 + (3\% \times \$398) = \$15.94$$

$$\text{EOQ} = \sqrt{\frac{(2 \times 10,000 \times \$500)}{15.94}} = 792$$

Examiner's note

It is necessary to check the EOQ to ascertain if the minimum delivery volume of 1,000 is a relevant (that is binding) constraint. In this case, it is, thus an order quantity of 1,000 applies.

	SSS	RRR
Order size	500	1,000
Annual demand	10,000	10,000
Number of orders	20	10

	$	$
Order cost	4,000	5,000
Holding cost	4,000	17,534
Purchase cost	4,000,000	3.980.000
	4.008.000	4,002,534

Thus ordering from overseas is $5,466 cheaper than the domestic purchase.

Ordering cost

SSS	$200 \times 20 =$	$4,000
RRR	$500 \times 10 =$	$5,000

Holding costs (EOQ/2 $\times$ C$_h$)

SSS

$$\frac{500}{2} \times \$16.00 = \$4,000$$

RRR

$$\frac{1,000}{2} \times \$15.94 = \qquad \$7,970$$

Plus safety inventorys:	$600 \times \$15,94 =$	$9,564
		$17,534

Purchase cost

SSS	$10,000 \times \$400 =$	$4,000,000
RRR	$10,000 \times \$398 =$	$3,980,000

Further factors that need to be considered are:

- The uncertainty of supply from RRR may lead to additional costs from running out of inventory, despite the safety inventories.
- Exchange rate movements may mean that the cost may increase if the contract with RRR has been written in the overseas currency. Hedging may lead to additional costs. Given that the two options are very close in terms of overall costs this may make a difference to the decision.
- If deliveries are incorrect or faulty, then re-supply may take a significant amount of time from RRR.
- The length of the lead time with RRR will require additional forward planning of inventory requirements.

(c)
Memorandum
To: RRR   **From:**   A Consultant
Subject: Financing STK contract   **Date:**   19 November 2002

Financing needs

In financing exports, there are a number of specific factors to be considered in addition to those present for domestic sales:

- The long lead time in delivering to STK by ship will mean additional working capital is tied up in inventory.
- International settlement may take longer as, for instance, it may be more difficult to put pressure on STK if it is slow in settling its debts.
- Foreign currency exchange may cause additional costs and/or risks depending on which of the two currencies forms the basis of the contract.
- Regulatory and compliance problems may cause additional delays in the transfer of goods or funds.
- There is an increased risk of bad debts where it is more difficult to obtain information due to geographic remoteness.

Methods of export finance

Examiner's note

Explanations by candidates do not require the level of detail supplied below in order to earn the required mark.

Export factoring

Debts may be sold to an export factor in much the same way as domestic factoring. This may include credit insurance to reduce bad debt risk.

Bills of exchange

A bill of exchange is an unconditional order by one person/entity to pay another a given sum at a specified future date. These are tradable, having a short date, normally within 180 days. They are, however, subject to default risk depending upon the creditworthiness of the drawee.

Bills of exchange are commonly used in export finance and will mean they can be sold at a discount to obtain more immediate cash.

Documentary credits (letters of credit)

This is a document issued by a bank on behalf of a customer authorising a person to draw money to a specified amount from its branches or correspondents, usually in another country, when the conditions set out in the document have been met.

It thus provides a secure means of obtaining payment from an overseas sale. These are, however, time consuming and expensive for trade and are thus only normally used where there is a high risk of a bad debt.

Forfaiting

This is normally most appropriate to capital goods where payment is over a number of years, but may also apply to a long-term contract such as that with STK as a means of obtaining medium-term export finance.

The buyer (STK) must undertake to make regular payments. It issues a series of promissory notesmaturing on a regular basis (for example, every 6 months). The buyer must also find a bank to guarantee (avalise) the notes.

RRR must find a bank to act as forfeiter. RRR will then receive the notes when STK receives the goods. It can then sell them to the forfeiting bank, at a discount, but without recourse, for immediate payment.

This reduces bad debt risk, reduces foreign exchange risk and provides immediate settlement – at a cost.

Advanced payment
As part of the contract, partial or full advanced payment might be arranged with STK (for example, when the goods are in transit).

Signed: A Consultant

Preparing for the
Examination

Revision Questions

The revision questions given below are mostly old CIMA examination questions, which have been lightly adapted in some cases. Although their content is relevant they should not all be viewed as practice examination questions.

Questions taken from examination papers under discontinued schemes do not all follow the style or arrangement of the current P1 Performance Operations paper. Such questions should therefore be considered as teaching or study exercises although you may be sure that their content and standard are appropriate for this purpose. Students should refer carefully to the P1 Pilot Paper and old P1 examination papers (when they become available) when preparing to sit the examination in order to ensure that they are familiar with the style and arrangement of questions that they are likely to encounter.

That said, the questions in this chapter have been split into three sections : A – multi-choice questions, B – short questions and C – long questions. These sections correspond to the arrangement of the P1 examination paper. Although a number of the questions may be considered as general study exercises which could relate to any section in the examination paper.

The relevance of the Revision Questions to the P1 learning outcomes is tabulated below. Note that the learning outcomes are listed in the order in which they appear in this text. That is the order which provides a logical study sequence. That is not entirely the same as the order in which the learning outcomes are listed in the published P1 syllabus.

Learning Outcomes	Questions
Chapter 1 – Basic Aspects of Management Accounting (A,B,C)	
Apply the principles of relevant cash flow analysis	4.4,4.10,10.1,
Chapter 2 – Cost Accounting Systems (A)	
Compare and contrast marginal (or variable), throughput and absorption costing methods in respect of profit reporting and stock valuation	1.1,1.2,2.5,4.7,4.8,4.9,5.1,5.2, 6.4,10.7,12.1,12.2,14.3,14.4,1 4.5,15.1,26,
Discuss a report which reconciles budget and actual profit using absorption and/or marginal costing principles	1.3,3.6,3.7,31,
Discuss activity-based costing as compared with traditional marginal and absorption costing methods including its relative advantages and disadvantages as a system of cost accounting	10.3,10.4,11.4,11.5,11.6,27, 28,31,

Chapter 3 – The Theory and Practice of Standard Costing (A)

Apply standard costing methods within costing systems including the reconciliation of budgeted and actual profit margins	1.4,1.5,3.1,3.2,3.3,4.5,4.6,6.1, 6.2,12.6,
Explain why and how standards are set in manufacturing and in service industries with particular reference to the maximisation of efficiency and minimisation of waste	2.4,6.3,17,19,20,
Interpret material, labour, variable overhead, fixed overhead and sales variances	10.2,15.2,17,23,

Chapter 4 – Standard Costing and Performance Evaluation (A)

Interpret variances … distinguishing between planning and operational variances	1.6,1.7,1.8,10.5,10.6,12.4,13.1, 13.2,14.1,14.2,
Prepare reports using a range of internal and external benchmarks and interpret the results	19,20,21,23,24,25,26,

Chapter 5 – Developments in Management Accounting (A)

Explain the impact of just-in-time manufacturing methods on cost accounting and the use of 'back-flush accounting' when work-in-progress stock is minimal	1.9,2.2,3.5,5.5,6.8,7.1,10.7, 10.8,19,29,
Explain the role of MRP and ERP systems in supporting standard costing systems, calculating variances and facilitating the posting of ledger entries	2.1,2.2,3.5,6.6,17,18,
Apply principles of environmental costing in identifying relevant internalised costs and externalised environmental impacts of the organisation's activities	1.10,11.2,18,

Chapter 6 – Forecasting and Budgeting (B)

Explain why organisations prepare forecasts and plans;	4.1,16,30,
Explain the purposes of budgets, including planning, communication, co-ordination, motivation, authorisation, control and evaluation, and how these may conflict	4.2,4.3,
Calculate projected product/service volumes employing appropriate forecasting techniques	2.3,2.7,11.1,13.5,15.3,
Calculate projected revenues and costs based on product/service volumes, pricing strategies and cost structures	2.6,12.5,14.3,14.4,14.5,
Prepare a budget for any account in the master budget based on projections/forecasts and managerial targets;	2.8,3.4,16,30,
Apply alternative approaches to budgeting;	5.3,5.6,6.5,12.5,16,28,

Chapter 7 – Dealing with Risk and Uncertainty (D)

Analyse the impact of uncertainty and risk on decision models that may be based on relevant cash flows, learning curves, discounting techniques etc.	5.4,7.3,7.4,
Apply sensitivity analysis to both short- and long-run decision models to identify variables that might have significant impacts on project outcomes	32,34,35,
Analyse risk and uncertainty by calculating expected values and standard deviations together with probability tables and histograms	33,
Prepare expected value tables;	5.4,34,37
Calculate the value of information;	7.4,34,
Apply decision trees;	33,

Chapter 8 – Project Appraisal (C)

Explain the processes involved in making long-term decisions;	33,35,36,37,
Apply the principles of relevant cash flow analysis to long-run projects that continue for several years	7.3,7.4,35,36,
Calculate project cash flows, accounting for tax and inflation, and apply perpetuities to derive 'end of project' value where appropriate	7.2,37,

Apply activity-based costing techniques to derive approximate 'long-run' product or service costs appropriate for use in strategic decision-making	10.3,10.4,
Explain the financial consequences of dealing with long-run projects, in particular the importance of accounting for the 'time value of money'	33,35,
Apply sensitivity analysis to cash flow parameters to identify those to which net present value is particularly sensitive	32,35,37,
Prepare decision support information for management, integrating financial and non-financial considerations	32,36
Evaluate project proposals using the techniques of investment appraisal	7.3,35,
Compare, contrast the alternative techniques of investment appraisal	36,
Prioritise projects that are mutually exclusive, involve unequal lives and/or are subject to capital rationing	7.2,

Chapter 9 – Managing Working Capital: Cash Flow (E)

Explain the importance of cash flow and working capital management	9.6,
Analyse cash-flow forecasts over a 12-month period	8.2,13.3,13.4,32,
Discuss measures to improve a cash forecast situation	9.3,9.4,
Identify sources of short-term funding	8.3,
Identify alternatives for investment of short term cash surpluses	6.7,
Identify appropriate methods of finance for trading internationally	9.7,

Chapter 10 – Managing Working Capital – Receivables, Payables and Inventory (E)

Interpret working capital ratios for business sectors	8.4,8.5,
Analyse trade debtor and creditor information	8.6,9.2,
Analyse the impacts of alternative debtor and creditor policies	8.1,8.6,9.1,9.5,12.3,22,
Analyse the impacts of alternative policies for stock management.	11.3,

Reference to syllabus items:

(A) Cost accounting systems
(B) Forecasting and budgeting techniques
(C) Project appraisal
(D) Dealing with uncertainty in analysis
(E) Managing short-term finance

Note: A significant number of the questions in this chapter draw on more than one of the specified learning outcomes. The indexing above relates questions to the main learning outcome or outcomes that those questions (and sub-questions, where appropriate) draw on. Some of the questions draw on several different topic areas in the course and are most accessible to students who have completed study of the whole course.

Section A – Multi-choice questions

 ## Question 1

The following data are given for sub-questions 1.1 and 1.2 below.
The following data relate to a manufacturing company. At the beginning of August, there was no inventory. During August 2,000 units of product X were produced, but only 1,750

units were sold. The financial data for product X for August were as follow:

	£
Materials	40,000
Labour	12,600
Variable production overheads	9,400
Fixed production overheads	22,500
Variable selling costs	6,000
Fixed selling costs	19,300
Total costs for X for August	109,800

1.1 The value of inventory of X at 31 August using a marginal Costing approach is

(A) £6,575
(B) £7,750
(C) £8,500
(D) £10,562   **(2 marks)**

1.2 The value of inventory of X at 31 August using a throughput accounting approach is

(A) £5,000
(B) £6,175
(C) £6,575
(D) £13,725   **(2 marks)**

1.3 A company has a budget to produce 5,000 units of product B in December. The budget for December shows that for Product B the opening inventory will be 400 units and the closing inventory will be 900 units. The monthly budgeted production cost data for product B for December is as follows:

Variable direct costs per unit	£6.00
Variable production overhead costs per unit	£3.50
Total fixed production overhead costs	£29,500

The company absorbs overheads on the basis of the budgeted number of units produced.

The budgeted profit for product B for December, using **absorption costing**, is

(A) £2,950 lower than it would be using **marginal costing**.
(B) £2,950 greater than it would be using **marginal costing**.
(C) £4,700 lower than it would be using **marginal costing**.
(D) £4,700 greater than it would be using **marginal costing**.   **(2 marks)**

1.4 Y has set the current budget for operating costs for its delivery vehicles, using the formula described below. Analysis has shown that the relationship between miles driven and total monthly vehicle operating costs is described in the following formula:

$$y = \pounds800 + \pounds0.0002x^2$$

where

y is the total monthly operating cost of the vehicles, and
x is the number of miles driven each month

The budget for vehicle operating costs needs to be adjusted for expected inflation in vehicle operating costs of 3%, which is not included in the relationship shown above.

The delivery mileage for September was 4,100 miles, and the total actual vehicle operating costs for September were £5,000.

The total vehicle operating cost variance for September was closest to

(A) £713 Adverse
(B) £737 Adverse
(C) £777 Adverse
(D) £838 Adverse   **(2 marks)**

1.5   The CIMA official definition of the 'variable production overhead efficiency variance' is set out below with two blank sections.

'Measures the difference between the variable overhead cost budget flexed on _____and the variable overhead cost absorbed by_____.'

Which combination of phrases correctly completes the definition?

	Blank 1	*Blank 2*
(A)	actual labour hours	budgeted output
(B)	standard labour hours	budgeted output
(C)	actual labour hours	output produced
(D)	standard labour hours	output produced

                                                                        (2 marks)

The following data are given for sub-questions 1.6 to 1.8 below.
The following data relate to Product Z and its raw material content for September.

Budget
Output   11,000 units of Z
Standard materials content   3 kg per unit at $4.00 per kg

Actual
Output   10,000 units of Z
Materials purchased and used   32,000 kg at $4.80 per kg

It has now been agreed that the standard price for the raw material purchased in September should have been $5 per kg.

1.6   The materials planning price variance for September was

(A) $6,000 Adverse
(B) $30,000 Adverse
(C) $32,000 Adverse
(D) $33,000 Adverse   **(2 marks)**

1.7   The materials operational usage variance for September was

(A) $8,000 Adverse
(B) $9,600 Adverse
(C) $9,600 Favourable
(D) $10,000 Adverse   **(2 marks)**

1.8 The materials operational price variance for September was

(A) $6,000 Adverse
(B) $6,400 Favourable
(C) $30,000 Adverse
(D) $32,000 Adverse **(2 marks)**

1.9 A company operates a just-in-time purchasing and production system and uses a back-flush accounting system with a single trigger point at the point of sale. A summary of the transactions that took place in June (valued at cost) is:

	£
Conversion costs incurred	890,000
Finished goods produced	1,795,000
Finished goods sold	1,700,000
Conversion costs allocated	840,000

The two items debited to the cost of goods sold account in June would be

	£		£
(A)	890,000	and	95,000
(B)	1,700,000	and	50,000
(C)	1,700,000	and	95,000
(D)	1,795,000	and	50,000 **(2 marks)**

1.10 In the context of environmental accounting, an external cost is:

(A) the cost of undertaking activities outside the boundaries of the normal premises of a business;
(B) the cost of remedial work arising from defective units of output;
(C) a cost incurred by the community as a result of activity undertaken by a business or organisation;
(D) a production cost which does not relate to a particular activity, product or service.

? Question 2

2.1 *Definition 1*: 'A system that converts a production schedule into a listing of materials and components required to meet the schedule so that items are available when needed.'

Definition 2: 'An accounting system that focuses on ways by which the maximum return per unit of bottleneck activity can be achieved.'

Which of the following pairs of terms correctly matches definitions 1 and 2 above?

	Definition 1	*Definition 2*
(A)	Manufacturing resources planning (MRP2)	Backflush accounting
(B)	Material requirements planning (MRP1)	Throughput accounting
(C)	Material requirements planning (MRP 1)	Theory of constraints
(D)	Supply chain management	Throughput accounting **(2 marks)**

2.2 Which of the following statements is/are true?

(i) Enterprise Resource Planning (ERP) systems use complex computer systems, usually comprehensive databases, to provide plans for every aspect of a business.

(ii) Flexible Manufacturing Systems (FMS) are simple systems with low levels of automation that offer great flexibility through a skilled workforce working in teams.

(iii) Just-in-time (JIT) purchasing requires the purchasing of large quantities of inventory items so that they are available immediately when they are needed in the production process.

(A) (i) only
(B) (i) and (ii) only
(C) (i) and (iii) only
(D) (ii) and (iii) only **(2 marks)**

2.3 If the budgeted fixed costs increase, the **gradient** of the line plotted on the budgeted Profit/Volume (P/V) chart will

(A) increase
(B) decrease
(C) not change
(D) become curvi-linear **(2 marks)**

2.4 A company operates a standard costing system and prepares monthly financial statements. All materials purchased during February were used during that month. After all transactions for February were posted, the general ledger contained the following balances:

	Debit	Credit
	£	£
Finished goods control	27,450	
Materials price variance	2,400	
Materials usage variance		8,400
Labour rate variance	5,600	
Labour efficiency variance		3,140
Variable production overhead variance	2,680	
Fixed production overhead variance		3,192

The standard cost of the goods produced during February was £128,500.

The actual cost of the goods produced during February was

(A) £96,998
(B) £124,448
(C) £132,552
(D) £160,002 **(2 marks)**

2.5 Overheads will always be over-absorbed when

(A) actual output is higher than budgeted output
(B) actual overheads incurred are higher than the amount absorbed
(C) actual overheads incurred are lower than the amount absorbed
(D) budgeted overheads are lower than the overheads absorbed **(2 marks)**

2.6 The following extract is taken from the production cost budget of L plc:

Output	2,000 units	3,500 units
Total cost	£12,000	£16,200

The budget cost allowance for an output of 4,000 units would be

(A) £17,600
(B) £18,514
(C) £20,400
(D) £24,000 **(2 marks)**

2.7 A company uses time series and regression techniques to forecast future sales. It has derived a seasonal variation index to use with the multiplicative (proportional) seasonal variation model. The index values for the first three quarters are as follows:

Quarter	Index value
Ql	80
Q2	80
Q3	110

The index value for the fourth quarter (Q4) is

(A) −270
(B) −269
(C) 110
(D) 130 **(2 marks)**

2.8 The budgeted profit statement for a company, with all figures expressed as percentages of revenue, is as follows:

	%
Revenue	100
Variable costs	30
Fixed costs	22
Profit	48

After the formulation of the above budget, it has now been realised that the sales volume will only be 60% of that originally forecast.

The revised profit, expressed as a percentage of the revised revenue, will be

(A) 20%
(B) 33.3%
(C) 60%
(D) 80% **(2 marks)**

❓ Question 3

The following data are given for sub-questions 3.1 to 3.3 below.
A company uses standard absorption costing. The following information was recorded by the company for October:

	Budget	Actual
Output and sales (units)	8,700	8,200
Selling price per unit	£26	£31
Variable cost per unit	£10	£10
Total fixed overheads	£34,800	£37,000

3.1 The sales price variance for October was

(A) £38,500 favourable
(B) £41,000 favourable
(C) £41,000 adverse
(D) £65,600 adverse   **(2 marks)**

3.2 The sales volume profit variance for October was

(A) £6,000 adverse
(B) £6,000 favourable
(C) £8,000 adverse
(D) £8,000 favourable   **(2 marks)**

3.3 The fixed overhead volume variance for October was

(A) £2,000 adverse
(B) £2,200 adverse
(C) £2,200 favourable
(D) £4,200 adverse   **(2 marks)**

3.4 A master budget comprises the

(A) budgeted income statement and budgeted cash flow only.
(B) budgeted income statement and budgeted balance sheet only.
(C) budgeted income statement and budgeted capital expenditure only.
(D) budgeted income statement, budgeted balance sheet and budgeted cash flow only.   **(2 marks)**

The following data are given for sub-questions 3.5 and 3.6 below.
The annual operating statement for a company is shown below:

	£'000
Sales revenue	800
Less variable costs	390
Contribution	410
Less fixed costs	90
Less depreciation	20
Net income	300
Assets	£6.75 m

The cost of capital is 13% per annum.

3.5 Which of the following definitions are correct?

(i) Just-in-time (JIT) systems are designed to produce or procure products or components as they are required for a customer or for use, rather than for inventory;

(ii) Flexible manufacturing systems (FMS) are integrated, computer-controlled production systems, capable of producing any of a range of parts and of switching quickly and economically between them;

(iii) Material requirements planning (MRP) systems are computer-based systems that integrate all aspects of a business so that the planning and scheduling of production ensures components are available when needed.

(A) (i) only
(B) (i) and (ii) only
(C) (i) and (iii) only
(D) (ii) and (iii)only **(2 marks)**

3.6 RJD Ltd operates a standard absorption costing system. The following fixed production overhead data is available for one month:

Budgeted output	200,000	Units
Budgeted fixed production overhead	£1,000,000	
Actual fixed production overhead	£1,300,000	
Total fixed production overhead variance	£100,000	Adverse

The actual level of production was

(A) 180,000 units
(B) 240,000 units
(C) 270,000 units
(D) 280,000 units **(2 marks)**

3.7 WTD Ltd produces a single product. The management currently uses marginal costing but is considering using absorption costing in the future.

The budgeted fixed production overheads for the period are £500,000. The budgeted output for the period is 2,000 units. There were 800 units of opening inventory at the beginning of the period and 500 units of closing inventory at the end of the period.

If absorption costing principles were applied, the profit for the period compared to the marginal costing profit would be

(A) £75,000 higher
(B) £75,000 lower
(C) £125,000 higher
(D) £125,000 lower **(2 marks)**

? Question 4

4.1 Which of the following best describes an investment centre?

(A) A centre for which managers are accountable only for costs.
(B) A centre for which managers are accountable only for financial outputs in the form of generating sales revenue.
(C) A centre for which managers are accountable for profit.
(D) A centre for which managers are accountable for profit and current non-current assets. **(2 marks)**

4.2 A flexible budget is

(A) a budget which, by recognising different cost behaviour patterns, is designed to change as volume of activity changes.
(B) a budget for a twelve month period which includes planned revenues, expenses, assets and liabilities.
(C) a budget which is prepared for a rolling period which is reviewed monthly, and updated accordingly.
(D) a budget for semi-variable overhead costs only. **(2 marks)**

4.3 The term 'budget slack' refers to the

(A) lead time between the preparation of the master budget and the commencement of the budget period.

(B) difference between the budgeted output and the actual output achieved.

(C) additional capacity available which is budgeted for even though it may not be used.

(D) deliberate overestimation of costs and/or underestimation of revenues in a budget. **(2 marks)**

4.4 PP Ltd is preparing the production and material purchases budgets for one of their products, the SUPERX, for the forthcoming year.

The following information is available:

SUPERX
Sales demand (units)	30,000
Material usage per unit	7 kgs
Estimated opening inventory	3,500 units
Required closing inventory	35% higher than opening inventory

How many units of the SUPERX will need to be produced?

(A) 28,775

(B) 30,000

(C) 31,225

(D) 38,225 **(2 marks)**

The following data are given for sub-questions 4.5 and 4.6 below.
X Ltd operates a standard costing system and absorbs fixed overheads on the basis of machine hours. Details of budgeted and actual figures are as follows:

	Budget	Actual
Fixed overheads	£2,500,000	£2,010,000
Output	500,000 units	440,000 units
Machine hours	1,000,000 hours	900,000 hours

4.5 The fixed overhead expenditure variance is

(A) £190,000 favourable

(B) £250,000 adverse

(C) £300,000 adverse

(D) £490,000 favourable **(2 marks)**

4.6 The fixed overhead volume variance is

(A) £190,000 favourable

(B) £250,000 adverse

(C) £300,000 adverse

(D) £490,000 favourable **(2 marks)**

4.7 A company operates a standard absorption costing system. The budgeted fixed production overheads for the company for the latest year were £330,000 and budgeted output was 220,000 units. At the end of the company's financial year the total of the fixed production overheads debited to the Fixed Production Overhead Control Account was £260,000 and the actual output achieved was 200,000 units.

The under/over absorption of overheads was

(A) £40,000 over absorbed
(B) £40,000 under absorbed
(C) £70,000 over absorbed
(D) £70,000 under absorbed   **(2 marks)**

4.8 A company operates a standard absorption costing system. The following fixed production overhead data are available for the latest period:

Budgeted Output	300,000 units
Budgeted Fixed Production Overhead	£ 1,500,000
Actual Fixed Production Overhead	£ 1,950,000
Fixed Production Overhead Total Variance	£150,000 adverse

The actual level of production for the period was nearest to

(A) 277,000 units
(B) 324,000 units
(C) 360,000 units
(D) 420,000 units   **(2 marks)**

4.9 Which of the following best describes a basic standard?

(A) A standard set at an ideal level, which makes no allowance for normal losses, waste and machine downtime.
(B) A standard which assumes an efficient level of operation, but which includes allowances for factors such as normal loss, waste and machine downtime.
(C) A standard which is kept unchanged over a period of time.
(D) A standard which is based on current price levels.   **(2 marks)**

4.10 XYZ Ltd is preparing the production budget for the next period. The total costs of production are a semi-variable cost. The following cost information has been collected in connection with production:

Volume (units)	Cost
4,500	£29,000
6,500	£33,000

The estimated total production costs for a production volume of 5,750 units is nearest to

(A) £29,200
(B) £30,000
(C) £31,500
(D) £32,500   **(2 marks)**

? Question 5

The following data are given for sub-questions 5.1 and 5.2 below.
Trafalgar Limited budgets to produce 10,000 units of product D12, each requiring 45 minutes of labour. Labour is charged at £20 per hour, and variable overheads at £15 per labour hour. During September 2003, 11,000 units were produced. 8,000 hours of labour were paid at a total cost of £168,000. Variable overheads in September amounted to £132,000.

5.1 What is the correct labour efficiency variance for September 2003?

(A) £5,000 Adverse
(B) £5,000 Favourable
(C) £5,250 Favourable
(D) £10,000 Adverse

5.2 What is the correct variable overhead expenditure variance for September 2003?

(A) £3,750 Favourable
(B) £4,125 Favourable
(C) £12,000 Adverse
(D) £12,000 Favourable

5.3 Which of the following definitions best describes 'Zero-Based Budgeting'?

(A) A method of budgeting where an attempt is made to make the expenditure under each cost heading as close to zero as possible.
(B) A method of budgeting whereby all activities are re-evaluated each time a budget is formulated.
(C) A method of budgeting that recognises the difference between the behaviour of fixed and variable costs with respect to changes in output, and the budget is designed to change appropriately with such fluctuations.
(D) A method of budgeting where the sum of revenues and expenditures in each budget centre must equal zero.

5.4 Nile Limited is preparing its sales budget for 2004. The sales manager estimates that sales will be 120,000 units if the Summer is rainy, and 80,000 units if the Summer is dry. The probability of a dry Summer is 0.4.

What is the expected value for sales volume for 2004?

(A) 96,000 units
(B) 100,000 units
(C) 104,000 units
(D) 120,000 units

5.5 MN plc uses a Just-in-Time (JIT) system and backflush accounting. It does not use a raw material stock control account. During April, 1,000 units were produced and sold. The standard cost per unit is £100: this includes materials of £45. During April, conversion costs of £60,000 were incurred.

What was the debit balance on the cost of goods sold account for April?

(A) £90,000
(B) £95,000
(C) £105,000
(D) £110,000

5.6 Which of the following statements are true?

(i) A flexible budget can be used to control operational efficiency.
(ii) Incremental budgeting can be defined as a system of budgetary planning and control that measures the additional costs that are incurred when there are unplanned extra units of activity.

(iii) Rolling budgets review and, if necessary, revise the budget for the next quarter to ensure that budgets remain relevant for the remainder of the accounting period.

(A) (i) and (ii) only
(B) (ii) and (iii) only
(C) (iii) only
(D) (i) only

? Question 6

The following data are given for sub-questions 6.1 and 6.2 below.
X40 is one of many items produced by the manufacturing division. Its standard cost is based on estimated production of 10,000 units per month. The standard cost schedule for one unit of X40 shows that 2 hours of direct labour are required at £15 per labour hour. The variable overhead rate is £6 per direct labour hour. During April, 11,000 units were produced; 24,000 direct labour hours were worked and charged; £336,000 was spent on direct labour; and £180,000 was spent on variable overheads.

6.1 The direct labour rate variance for April is

(A) £20,000 favourable
(B) £22,000 favourable
(C) £24,000 adverse
(D) £24,000 favourable   **(2 marks)**

6.2 The variable overhead efficiency variance for April is

(A) £12,000 adverse
(B) £12,000 favourable
(C) £15,000 adverse
(D) £15,000 favourable   **(2 marks)**

6.3 The fixed overhead volume variance is defined as

(A) The difference between the budgeted value of the fixed overheads and the standard fixed overheads absorbed by actual production
(B) The difference between the standard fixed overhead cost specified for the production achieved, and the actual fixed overhead cost incurred
(C) The difference between budgeted and actual fixed overhead expenditure
(D) The difference between the standard fixed overhead cost specified in the original budget and the same volume of fixed overheads, but at the actual prices incurred.   **(2 marks)**

6.4 Summary results for Y Limited for March are shown below.

	£'000	*Units*
Sales revenue	820	
Variable production costs	300	
Variable selling costs	105	
Fixed production costs	180	
Fixed selling costs	110	

Production in March	1,000
Opening inventory	0
Closing inventory	150

Using *marginal costing*, the profit for March was

(A) £170,000

(B) £185,750

(C) £197,000

(D) £229,250 **(2 marks)**

6.5 The CIMA definition of zero-based budgeting is set out below, with two blank sections.

'Zero-based budgeting: A method of budgeting which requires each cost element _____, as though the activities to which the budget relates _____.'

Which combination of two phrases correctly completes the definition?

	Blank 1	Blank 2
(A)	to be specifically justified	could be out-sourced to an external supplier
(B)	to be set at zero	could be out-sourced to an external supplier
(C)	to be specifically justified	were being undertaken for the first time
(D)	to be set at zero	were being undertaken for the first time **(2 marks)**

6.6 *Definition A*: 'A technique where the primary goal is to maximise throughput while simultaneously maintaining or decreasing inventory and operating costs.'

Definition B: 'A system whose objective is to produce or procure products or components as they are required by a customer or for use, rather than for inventory.'

Which of the following pairs of terms correctly matches the definitions A and B above?

	Definition A	Definition B
(A)	Manufacturing resource planning	Just-in-time
(B)	Enterprise resource planning	Material requirements planning
(C)	Optimised production technology	Enterprise resource planning
(D)	Optimised production technology	Just-in-time **(2 marks)**

6.7 Practical and productive possibilities for the investment of short term funds which may be required for business use in the near to medium term future include:

(i) Purchase of shares on the AIM (alternative investment market);

(ii) Leaving the money on bank current account

(iii) Holding the money as cash in the office safe

(iv) Purchase of fixed term bonds issued by banks and building societies

(v) Purchase of gold coins

(vi) Purchase of buy-to-let apartments

(vii) Making fixed term deposits with a bank

(viii) Making early repayment of long term borrowings

(A) (i) and (v)

(B) (iv) and (vii)

(C) (ii), (vi) and (viii)

(D) (iii) and (v)

6.8 Which of the following statements is/are true?

(i) Computer-integrated manufacturing (CIM) brings together advanced manufacturing technology and modern quality control into a single computerised coherent system.

(ii) Flexible manufacturing systems (FMS) are simple systems with low levels of automation that offer great flexibility through a skilled workforce working in teams.

(iii) Electronic data interchange (EDI) is primarily designed to allow the operating units in an organisation to communicate immediately and automatically with the sales and purchasing functions within the organisation.

(A) (i) only

(B) (i) and (ii) only

(C) (i) and (iii) only

(D) (ii) and (iii) only **(2 marks)**

? **Question 7**

7.1 In a TQM environment, external benchmarking is preferred to standard costing as a performance measurement technique because

(A) standard costs quickly become obsolete;

(B) TQM emphasises continuous improvement and reference to a predetermined internal standard gives no incentive to improve;

(C) TQM places an emphasis on employee empowerment, and the concept of a standard cost is alien to this;

(D) the use of standard costs is only possible in a traditional mass-production industry.

7.2 A supermarket is trying to determine the optimal replacement policy for its fleet of delivery vehicles. The total purchase price of the fleet is £220,000.

The running costs and scrap values of the fleet at the end of each year are

	Year 1	Year 2	Year 3	Year 4	Year 5
Running costs	£110,000	£132,000	£154,000	£165,000	£176,000
Scrap value	£121,000	£88,000	£66,000	£55,000	£25,000

The supermarket's cost of capital is 12 per cent per annum.

Ignore taxation and inflation.

The supermarket should replace its fleet of delivery vehicles at the end of

(A) Year 1

(B) Year 2

(C) Year 3

(D) Year 4

(E) Year 5.

The following data relates to both questions 7.3 and 7.4 below.

X Ltd can choose from five mutually exclusive projects. The projects will each last for 1 year only and their net cash inflows will be determined by the prevailing market conditions. The forecast annual cash inflows and their associated probabilities are shown below.

Market Conditions	Poor	Good	Excellent
Probability	0.20	0.50	0.30
	£000	£000	£000
Project L	500	470	550
Project M	400	550	570
Project N	450	400	475
Project O	360	400	420
Project P	600	500	425

7.3 Based on the expected value of the net cash inflows, which project should be undertaken?

(A) L

(B) M

(C) N

(D) O

(E) P   **(2 marks)**

7.4 The value of perfect information about the state of the market is

(A) Nil

(B) £5,000

(C) £26,000

(D) £40,000

(E) £128,000   **(3 marks)**

? **Question 8**

8.1 An entity is considering a proposal to offer a cash discount of 2 per cent to customers if they settle the amounts owing within 10 days. All sales offer 30 days' credit currently. What is the annualised compounded cost of giving this cash discount to a customer?

(A) 24.83%

(B) 36.5%

(C) 37.23%

(D) 44.6%

8.2 Cash-flow forecasts will be affected adversely by which one of the following?

(A) A reduction in the operating profit as a result of increased rates of depreciation being charged on the firm's plant and machinery

(B) A change in purchasing policy so that all cash discounts are now taken and this has reduced the payables in the statement of financial position

(C) Non-current assets have been sold at a substantial loss

(D) The working capital cycle has been reduced   **(2 marks)**

8.3 Which of the following statements about an overdraft facility is incorrect?

(A) The overdraft is repayable on demand

(B) Assets are normally required as security

(C) Interest is paid on the full facility

(D) Legal documentation is minimal compared with other types of loan. **(2 marks)**

8.4 The statement of financial position of KSS includes the following figures:

	$
Current assets	
Inventory	300,000
Trade receivables	200.000
	500,000
Current liabilities: Amounts due within one year	
Trade payables	200,000
Bank overdraft	50,000
	250,000

The quick ratio calculated from these figures is

(A) 0.8
(B) 1.0
(C) 1.2
(D) 2.0

8.5 Swinson, a retailing entity, has an annual revenue of $40 million. The entity earns a constant margin of 20% on sales. All sales and purchases are on credit and are evenly distributed throughout the year. The following amounts are maintained at a constant level throughout the year:

Inventory	$5 million
Trade receivables	$7 million
Trade payables	$2 million

What is the length of the entity's cash cycle to the nearest day?

(A) 64 days
(B) 92 days
(C) 98 days
(D) 114 days **(2 marks)**

8.6 Working capital is most likely to decrease when

(A) The period of credit extended to customers is increased
(B) Inventory levels are decreased
(C) Non-current assets are purchased
(D) Payables are paid before the balance is due **(2 marks)**

❓ Question 9

9.1 In October, an entity made credit purchases of $18,000 and credit sales of $24,000. All sales are made on the basis of cost plus 25%. By how much will working capital increase in October as a result of these transactions?

(A) $2,000
(B) $4,000
(C) $4,800
(D) $6,000 **(2 marks)**

9.2 The following items have been extracted from an entity's budget for next month:

	$
Sales on credit	240,000
Expected increase in inventory next month	20,000
Expected decrease in trade receivables next month	12,000

What is the budgeted receipt from trade receivables next month?

(A) $228,000
(B) $232,000
(C) $252,000
(D) $272,000 **(2 marks)**

9.3 An entity has a positive level of working capital but has an overdraft. What will be the impact of the following transactions on the current ratio?
Transaction 1:
Cash is received from trade receivables and is then used to reduce the overdraft.
Transaction 2:
A non-current asset is sold for cash thus is used to reduce the overdraft.

	Transaction 1	*Transaction 2*
(A)	Increase	Increase
(B)	Increase	Decrease
(C)	Decrease	Increase
(D)	Decrease	Decrease

(2 marks)

9.4 If payments to trade payables are delayed, what is the impact on the total level of working capital (ignore cash discounts)?

(A) Increase
(B) Decrease
(C) No effect
(D) Depends on whether working capital is positive or negative. **(2 marks)**

9.5 Invoice discounting normally involves

(A) Offering a cash discount for early settlement of invoices
(B) Selling an invoice to a discount house at a profit
(C) Selling individual invoice for cash to a factoring entity at a discount
(D) Writing off an invoice, partly or in total, as a bad debt. **(2 marks)**

9.6 Which of the following is not normally associated with overtrading?

(A) Falling sales
(B) Increase overdraft
(C) Falling current ratio
(D) Rising profit **(2 marks)**

9.7 Which of the following most appropriately describes *forfaiting*?

(A) It is a method of providing medium-term export finance
(B) It provides short-term finance for purchasing non-current assets which are denominated in a foreign currency

(C) It provides long-term finance to importers

(D) It is the forced surrender of a share due to the failure to make a payment on a partly paid share. **(2 marks)**

Section B – Short questions

? Question 10

Each of the sub-questions numbered 10.1 to l0.2 below require a brief written response.
This response should be in note form and should not exceed 50 words.
Write your answers to these sub-questions in your answer book.

10.1 The overhead costs of RP Limited have been found to be accurately represented by the formula

$$y \; 5 \; £10{,}000 \; 1 \; £0.25x$$

where y is the monthly cost and x represents the activity level measured as the number of orders.

Monthly activity levels of orders may be estimated using a combined regression analysis and time series model:

$$a = 100{,}000 + 30b$$

where a represents the de-seasonalised monthly activity level and b represents the month number.

In month 240, the seasonal index value is 108.

Requirement

Calculate the overhead cost for RP Limited for month 240 to the nearest £1,000.

(3 marks)

10.2 The following data have been extracted from the budget working papers of WR Limited:

Activity (machine hours)	Overhead cost £
10,000	13,468
12,000	14,162
16,000	15,549
18,000	16,242

In November 2003, the actual activity was 13,780 machine hours and the actual overhead cost incurred was £14,521.

Requirement

Calculate the total overhead expenditure variance for November 2003.

(4 marks)

The following data are given for sub-questions 10.3 and 10.4 below.
DRP Limited has recently introduced an Activity-based Costing system. It manufactures three products, details of which are set out below:

	Product D	Product R	Product P
Budgeted annual production (units)	100,000	100,000	50,000
Batch size (units)	100	50	25

Machine set-ups per batch	3	4	6
Purchase orders per batch	2	1	1
Processing time per unit (minutes)	2	3	3

Three cost pools have been identified. Their budgeted costs for the year ended 31 December 2004 are as follows:

Machine set-up costs	£150,000
Purchasing of materials	£70,000
Processing	£80,000

10.3 Calculate the annual budgeted number of:

(a) batches
(b) machine set ups
(c) purchase orders
(d) processing minutes **(2 marks)**

10.4 Calculate the budgeted overhead unit cost for Product R for inclusion in the budget for 2004. **(4 marks)**

The following data are given for sub-questions 10.5 and 10.6 below.
SW plc manufactures a product known as the TRD100 by mixing two materials. The standard material cost per unit of the TRD100 is as follows:

			£
Material X	12 litres	@ £2.50	30
Material Y	18 litres	@£3.00	54

In October 2003, the actual mix used was 984 litres of X and 1,230 litres of Y. The actual output was 72 units of TRD100.

10.5 Calculate the total material mix variance for October 2003. **(3 marks)**

10.6 Calculate the total material yield variance for October 2003. **(2 marks)**

The following data are given for sub-questions 10.7 and 10.8 below.
A company produces three products using three different machines. No other products are made on these particular machines. The following data is available for December 2003.

Product	A	B	C
Contribution per unit	£36	£28	£18
Machine hours required per unit			
Machine 1	5	2	1.5
Machine 2	5	5.5	1.5
Machine 3	2.5	1	0.5
Estimated sales demand (units)	50	50	60

Maximum machine capacity for December will be 400 hours per machine.

10.7 (a) Calculate the machine utilisation rates for each machine for December 2003. **(2 marks)**

(b) Identify which of the machines is the bottleneck machine. **(2 marks)**

10.8 (a) State the recommended procedure given by Goldratt in his 'Theory of Constraints' for dealing with a bottleneck activity. **(2 marks)**

(b) Calculate the optimum allocation of the bottleneck machine hours to the three products. **(3 marks)**

? Question 11

11.1 Z plc has found that it can estimate future sales using time-series analysis and regression techniques. The following trend equation has been derived:

$$y = 25,000 + 6,500x$$

where y is the total sales units per quarter and x is the time period reference number.

Z has also derived the following set of seasonal variation index values for each quarter using a multiplicative (proportional) model:

Quarter 1	70
Quarter 2	90
Quarter 3	150
Quarter 4	90

Using the above model, calculate the forecast for sales units for the third quarter of year 7, assuming that the first quarter of year 1 is time period reference number 1.

(3 marks)

11.2 Explain in less than 150 words what the logic is behind the EU Greenhouse Gas Emission Trading Scheme and what the likely impact of that scheme is on the energy usage and emission strategies of a business.

11.3 A company is preparing its cash budget for February using the following data. One line in the cash budget is for purchases of a raw material, J. The opening inventory of J in January is expected to be 1,075 units. The price of J is expected to be £8 per unit. The company pays for purchases at the end of the month following delivery. One unit of J is required in the production of each unit of product 2, and J is only used in this product. Monthly sales of product 2 are expected to be:

January	4,000 units
February	5,000 units
March	6,000 units

The opening inventory of product 2 in January is expected to be 1,200 units. The company implements the following inventory policies. At the end of each month, the following amounts are held:

Raw materials: 25% of the requirement for the following month's production
Finished goods: 30% of the following month's sales

Calculate the value for purchases of J to be included in the cash budget for February.

(4 marks)

The following data are given for sub-questions 11.4 to 11.6 below.

K makes many products, one of which is Product Z. K is considering adopting an activity-based costing approach for setting its budget, in place of the current practice of absorbing overheads using direct labour hours. The main budget categories and cost driver details for the whole company for October are set out below, excluding direct material costs:

Budget category	£	Cost driver details
Direct labour	128,000	8,000 direct labour hours
Set-up costs	22,000	88 set-ups each month
Quality testing costs*	34,000	40 tests each month
Other overhead costs	32,000	absorbed by direct labour hours

* A quality test is performed after every 75 units produced

The following data for Product Z is provided:

Direct materials	budgeted cost of £21.50 per unit
Direct labour	budgeted at 0.3 hours per unit
Batch size	30 units
Set-ups	2 set-ups per batch
Budgeted volume for October	150 units

11.4 Calculate the budgeted unit cost of product Z for October assuming that a direct labour-based absorption method was used for all overheads. **(2 marks)**

11.5 Calculate the budgeted unit cost of product Z for October using an activity-based costing approach. **(3 marks)**

11.6 Explain **in less than 50 words,** why the costs absorbed by a product using an activity-based costing approach could be higher than those absorbed if a traditional labour-based absorption system were used, and identify **two** implications of this for management. **(4 marks)**

? **Question 12**

12.1 JJ Ltd manufactures three products: W, X and Y The products use a series of different machines but there is a common machine that is a bottleneck.

The standard selling price and standard cost per unit for each product for the forthcoming period are as follows:

	W	X	Y
	£	£	£
Selling price	200	150	150
Cost			
Direct materials	41	20	30
Labour	30	20	36
Overheads	60	40	50
Profit	69	70	34
Bottleneck machine–minutes per unit	9	10	7

40% of the overhead cost is classified as variable

Using a throughput accounting approach, what would be the ranking of the products for best use of the bottleneck? **(3 marks)**

12.2 X Ltd has two production departments, Assembly and Finishing, and two service departments, Stores and Maintenance.

Stores provides the following service to the production departments: 60% to Assembly and 40% to Finishing.

Maintenance provides the following service to the production and service departments: 40% to Assembly, 45% to Finishing and 15% to Stores.

The budgeted information for the year is as follows:

Budgeted fixed production overheads	£
Assembly	100,000
Finishing	150,000
Stores	50,000
Maintenance	40,000
Budgeted output	100,000 units

At the end of the year after apportioning the service department overheads, the total fixed production overheads debited to the Assembly department's fixed production overhead control account were £180,000.

The actual output achieved was 120,000 units.

Calculate the under/over absorption of fixed production overheads for the Assembly department. **(4 marks)**

12.3 Dosh Ltd provides materials and services to a large number of local restaurants, bars and cafeterias. It is in established relationships with most of its customers although new customers do appear occasionally. The new customers are mostly facilities opening in the area for the first time or are temporary facilities relating to one-off events. As is customary in the catering trade, Dosh normally invoices its customers on 30 day credit terms.

In recent months, Dosh has periodically experienced problems arising from customers making late payment of invoices. The catering sector is passing through a cyclical downturn and a number of customers appear to be easing their cash flow position by deferring payment of supplier invoices.

The management of Dosh is considering introducing a system of discounts for early payments and penalties for late payment. The system would involve a provision for discounts and penalties being written into sale agreements. The following system has been proposed, based on a 360 day year:

(1) payments within the 30 day credit period allowed are allowed a discount based on the number of days early the payment is received and an 8% annual interest rate;

(2) payments beyond the 30 day credit period allowed are charged a penalty based on the number of days late the payment is received and a 12% annual interest rate.

Requirements

(a) Calculate the discount allowed on a $10,000 invoice paid 12 days early;

(2 marks)

(b) Calculate the penalty charged on a $10,000 invoice paid 17 days late;

(1 mark)

(c) Discuss the advantages and disadvantages that such a system might offer to Dosh Ltd. **(2 marks)**

12.4 PP Ltd operates a standard absorption costing system. The following information has been extracted from the standard cost card for one of its products:

Budgeted production	1,500 units
Direct material cost: 7 kg 3 £4.10	£28.70 per unit

Actual results for the period were as follows:

Production	1,600 units
Direct material (purchased and used): 12,000 kg	£52,200

It has subsequently been noted that due to a change in economic conditions the best price that the material could have been purchased for was £4.50 per kg during the period.

(i) Calculate the material price planning variance.

(ii) Calculate the operational material usage variance. **(4 marks)**

12.5 CJD Ltd manufactures plastic components for the car industry. The following budgeted information is available for three of their key plastic components:

	W	X	Y
	£ per unit	£ per unit	£ per unit
Selling price	200	183	175
Direct material	50	40	35
Direct labour	30	35	30
Units produced and sold	10,000	15,000	18,000

The total number of activities for each of the three products for the period is as follows:

Number of purchase requisitions	1,200	1,800	2,00
Number of set ups	240	260	300

Overhead costs have been analysed as follows:

Receiving/inspecting quality assurance	£1,400,000
Production scheduling/machine set up	£1,200,000

Calculate the budgeted profit per unit for each of the three products using activity-based budgeting. **(4 marks)**

12.6 SS Ltd operates a standard marginal costing system. An extract from the standard cost card for the labour costs of one of its products is as follows:

Labour cost	
5 hours × £12	£60

Actual results for the period were as follows:

Production	11,500 units
Labour rate variance	£45,000 adverse
Labour efficiency variance	£30,000 adverse

Calculate the actual rate paid per direct labour hour **(4 marks)**

❓ Question 13

The following data are given for sub-questions 13.1 and 13.2 below.

A company has a process in which three inputs are mixed together to produce Product S. The standard mix of inputs to produce 90 kg of Product S is shown below:

	$
50 kg of ingredient P at $75 per kg	3,750
30 kg of ingredient Q at $100 per kg	3,000
20 kg of ingredient R at $125 per kg	2,500
	9,250

During March 2,000 kg of ingredients were used to produce 1,910 kg of Product S. Details of the inputs are as follows:

	$
1,030 kg of ingredient P at $70 per kg	72,100
560 kg of ingredient Q at $106 per kg	59,360
410 kg of ingredient R at $135 per kg	55,350
	186,810

13.1 Calculate the materials mix variance for March.   **(3 marks)**

13.2 Calculate the materials yield variance for March.   **(2 marks)**

13.3 The following details have been taken from the debtor collection records of W plc:

Invoices paid in the month after sale	60%
Invoices paid in the second month after sale	20%
Invoices paid in the third month after sale	15%
Bad debts	5%

Customers paying in the month after the sale are allowed a 10% discount.

Invoices for sales are issued on the last day of the month in which the sales are made.

The budgeted credit sales for the final 5 months of this year are

Month	August	September	October	November	December
Credit sales	$80,000	$100,000	$120,000	$130,000	$160,000

Calculate the total amount budgeted to be received in December from credit sales.

(2 marks)

13.4 D plc operates a retail business. Purchases are sold at cost plus 25%. The management team are preparing the cash budget and have gathered the following data:

1. The budgeted sales are as follows:

Month	£'000
July	100
August	90
September	125
October	140

2. It is management policy to hold inventory at the end of each month which is sufficient to meet sales demand in the next half month. Sales are budgeted to occur evenly during each month.

3. Creditors are paid one month after the purchase has been made.

Calculate the entries for 'purchases' that will be shown in the cash budget for
   (i) August
   (ii) September
   (iii) October   **(3 marks)**

13.5 S plc produces and sells three products–X, Y and Z. It has contracts to supply products X and Y, which will utilise all of the specific materials that are available to make these two products during the next period. The revenue these contracts will generate and the contribution to sales (C/S) ratios of products X and Y are as follows:

	Product X	Product Y
Revenue	£10 m	£20 m
C/S ratio	15%	10%

Product Z has a C/S ratio of 25%.

The total fixed costs of S plc are £5.5 m during the next period and management have budgeted to earn a profit of £1 m.

Calculate the revenue that needs to be generated by Product Z for S plc to achieve the budgeted profit.   **(3 marks)**

? Question 14

14.1 D Limited manufactures and sells musical instruments, and uses a standard cost system. The budget for production and sale of one particular drum for April was 600 units at a selling price of £72 each. When the sales director reviewed the results for April in the light of the market conditions that had been experienced during the month, she believed that D Limited should have sold 600 units of this drum at a price of £82 each. The actual sales achieved were 600 units at £86 per unit.

Calculate the following variances for this particular drum for April:

(a) Selling price planning variance
(b) Selling price operating variance   **(4 marks)**

14.2 A company has a process in which the standard mix for producing 9 litres of output is as follows:

	$
4.0 litres of D at $9 per litre	36.00
3.5 litres of E at $5 per litre	17.50
2.5 litres of F at $2 per litre	5.00
	58.50

A standard loss of 10% of inputs is expected to occur. The actual inputs for the latest period were:

	$
4,300 litres of D at $9.00 per litre	38,700
3,600 litres of E at $5.50 per litre	19,800
2,100 litres of F at $2.20 per litre	4,620
	63,120

Actual output for this period was 9,100 litres.

You are required to calculate

(a) the total materials mix variance
(b) the total materials yield variance   **(4 marks)**

The following data are given for sub-questions 14.3 to 14.5 below.

SM makes two products, Zl and Z2. Its machines can only work on one product at a time. The two products are worked on in two departments by differing grades of labour.

The labour requirements for the two products are as follows:

	Minutes per unit of product	
	Z1	Z2
Department 1	12	16
Department 2	20	15

There is, currently, a shortage of labour and the maximum times available each day in Departments 1 and 2 are 480 minutes and 840 minutes, respectively.

The current selling prices and costs for the two products are shown below:

	Z1	Z2
	£per unit	*£per unit*
Selling price	50.00	65.00
Direct materials	10.00	15.00
Direct labour	10.40	6.20

Variable overheads	6.40	9.20
Fixed overheads	12.80	18.40
Profit per unit	10.40	16.20

As part of the budget-setting process, SM needs to know the optimum output levels. All output is sold.

14.3 Calculate the maximum number of each product that could be produced each day, and identify the limiting factor/bottleneck. **(3 marks)**

14.4 Using traditional contribution analysis, calculate the 'profit-maximising' output each day, and the contribution at this level of output. **(3 marks)**

14.5 Using a throughput approach, calculate the 'throughput-maximising' output each day, and the 'throughput contribution' at this level of output. **(3 marks)**

Question 15

15.1 S Ltd manufactures three products, A, B and C. The products use a series of different machines but there is a common machine, P, that is a bottleneck.

The selling price and standard cost for each product for the forthcoming year is as follows:

	A $	B $	C $
Selling price	200	150	150
Direct materials	41	20	30
Conversion costs	55	40	66
Machine P – minutes	12	10	7

Calculate the return per hour for each of the products. **(4 marks)**

15.2 PQR Ltd operates a standard absorption costing system. Details of budgeted and actual figures are as follows:

	Budget	Actual
Sales volume (units)	100,000	110,000
Selling price per unit	£10	£9.50
Variable cost per unit	£5	£5.25
Total cost per unit	£8	£8.30

(i) Calculate the sales price variance. **(2 marks)**
(ii) Calculate the sales volume profit-variance. **(2 marks)**

15.3 RF Ltd is about to launch a new product in June 2007. The company has commissioned some market research to assist in sales forecasting. The resulting research and analysis established the following equation:

$$Y = Ax^{0.6}$$

Where Y is the cumulative sales units, A is the sales units in month 1, x is the month number.
June 2007 is Month 1.
Sales in June 2007 will be 1,500 units.

Calculate the forecast sales volume for each of the months June, July and August 2007 and for that three-month period in total. **(4 marks)**

? Question 16

The following scenario is given for sub-questions (a) to (e).

X Plc manufactures specialist insulating products that are used in both residential and commercial buildings. One of the products, Product W, is made using two different raw materials and two types of labour. The company operates a standard absorption costing system and is now preparing its budgets for the next four quarters. The following information has been identified for Product W:

Sales

Selling price	£220 per unit
Sales demand	
Quarter 1	2,250 units
Quarter 2	2,050 units
Quarter 3	1,650 units
Quarter 4	2,050 units
Quarter 5	1,250 units
Quarter 6	2,050 units

Costs

Materials

A	5 kgs per unit @ £4 per kg
B	3 kgs per unit @ £7 per kg

Labour

Skilled	4 hours per unit @ £15 per kg
Semi-skilled	6 hours per unit @ £9 per kg
Annual overheads	£280,000
	40% of these overheads are fixed and the remain der varies with total labour hours. Fixed over heads are absorbed on a unit basis.

Inventory holding policy

Closing inventory of finished goods	30% of the following quarter's sales demand
Closing inventory of materials	45% of the following quarter's materials usage

The management team are concerned that X Plc has recently faced increasing competition in the market place for Product W. As a consequence there have been issues concerning the availability and costs of the specialised materials and employees needed to manufacture Product W, and there is concern that these might cause problems in the current budget setting process.

(a) Prepare the following budgets for each quarter for X Plc:
  (i) Production budget in units;
  (ii) Raw material purchases budget in kgs and value for Material B. **(5 marks)**

(b) X Plc has just been informed that Material A may be in short supply during the year for which it is preparing budgets. Discuss the impact this will have on budget preparation and other areas of X Plc. **(5 marks)**

(c) Assuming that the budgeted production of Product W was 7,700 units and that the following actual results were incurred for labour and overheads in the year:

Actual production	7,250 units
Actual overheads	
Variable	£185,000
Fixed	£105,000

Actual labour costs
Skilled–£16.25 per hour   £568,750
Semi–skilled–£8 per hour   £332,400

Prepare a flexible budget statement for X Plc showing the total variances that have occurred for the above four costs only. **(5 marks)**

(d) X Plc currently uses incremental budgeting. Explain how zero-based budgeting could overcome the problems that might be faced as a result of the continued use of the current system. **(5 marks)**

(e) Briefly explain how linear regression analysis can be used to forecast sales and briefly discuss whether it would be a suitable method for X Plc to use. **(5 marks)**

? Question 17

(a) A company uses variance analysis to monitor the performance of the team of workers which assembles Product M. Details of the budgeted and actual performance of the team for last period were as follows:

	Budget	Actual
Output of product M	600 units	680 units
Wage rate	£30 per hour	£32 per hour
Labour hours	900 hours	1,070 hours

It has now been established that the standard wage rate should have been £31 20 per hour.

  (i) Calculate the labour rate planning variance and calculate the operational labour efficiency variance.

  (ii) Explain the major benefit of analysing variances into planning and operational components. **(5 marks)**

(b) Briefly explain three limitations of standard costing in the modern business environment. **(5 marks)**

(c) Briefly explain three factors that should be considered before deciding to investigate a variance. **(5 marks)**

(d) G Group consists of several autonomous divisions. Two of the divisions supply components and services to other divisions within the group as well as to external clients. The management of G Group is considering the introduction of a bonus scheme for managers that will be based on the profit generated by each division.
Briefly explain the factors that should be considered by the management of G Group when designing the bonus scheme for divisional managers. **(5 marks)**

(e) Briefly explain the role of a Manufacturing Resource Planning System in supporting a standard costing system. **(5 marks)**

(f) Briefly explain the main differences between the traditional manufacturing environment and a just-in-time manufacturing environment. **(5 marks)**

? Question 18

The new manufacturing environment is characterised by more flexibility, a readiness to meet customers' requirements, smaller batches, continuous improvements and an emphasis on quality. In such circumstances, traditional management accounting performance measures are, at best, irrelevant and, at worst, misleading.

Requirements

(a) Discuss the above statement, citing specific examples to support or refute the views expressed.

(b) Explain in what ways management accountants can adapt the services they provide to the new environment.

? Question 19

Requirements

(a) J Limited has recently been taken over by a much larger company. For many years, the budgets in J have been set by adding an inflation adjustment to the previous year's budget. The new owners of J are insisting on a 'zero-base' approach when the next budget is set, as they believe many of the indirect costs in J are much higher than in other companies under their control.

   (i) Explain the main features of 'zero-based budgeting'.   **(2 marks)**

   (ii) Discuss the problems that might arise when implementing this approach in J Limited.   **(3 marks)**

(b) An analysis of past output has shown that batches have a mean weight of 90 kg and that the weights conform to the normal distribution with a standard deviation of 10 kg. The company has a policy to investigate variances that fall outside the range that includes 95% of outcomes. In September one sample batch weighed 110 kg.

   (i) Calculate whether the material usage variance for this batch should be investigated according to the company policy described above.   **(3 marks)**

   (ii) Discuss two other important factors that should be taken into account when deciding whether to investigate this variance.   **(2 marks)**

(c) UV Limited is a catering company that provides meals for large events. It has a range of standard meals at fixed prices. It also provides meals to meet the exact requirements of a customer and prices for this service are negotiated individually with each customer.

   Discuss how a 'McDonaldisation' approach to service delivery would impact on budget preparation and control within UV Limited.   **(5 marks)**

(d) A management consulting company had budgeted the staff requirements for a particular job as follows:

	£
40 hours of senior consultant at £100 per hour	4,000
60 hours of junior consultant at £60 per hour	3,600
Budgeted staff cost for job	7,600

The actual hours recorded were

	£
50 hours of senior consultant at £100 per hour	5,000
55 hours of junior consultant at £60 per hour	3,300
Actual staff cost for job	8,300

The junior consultant reported that for 10 hours of the 55 hours recorded, there was no work that she could do.

Calculate the following variances:

- Idle time variance
- Labour mix variance
- Labour efficiency variance **(5 marks)**

(e) ST plc is a medium-sized engineering company using advanced technology. It has just implemented an integrated enterprise resource planning system (ERPS) in place of an old MRP (manufacturing resource planning) system.

Discuss the changes that are likely to be seen after the implementation of the ERPS in

(i) the budget-setting process; and

(ii) the budgetary control process **(5 marks)**

(f) W Limited has conducted a review of its budget-setting procedures. The review coordinator frequently heard the following comment from staff interviewed:

'It's impossible to make this system work because senior managers want budgets to be a challenging target whereas the finance department require an accurate forecast.'

Discuss the issues raised in this comment, and advise the review coordinator on practical action that could be taken to alleviate the situation described. **(5 marks)**

? Question 20

Requirements

(a) A manufacturing company uses a standard costing system. Extracts from the budget for April are shown below:

Sales	1,400 units
Production	2,000 units
	$
Direct costs	15 per unit
Variable overhead	4 per unit

The budgeted fixed production overhead costs for April were $12,800.
The budgeted profit using marginal costing for April was $5,700.

(i) Calculate the budgeted profit for April using absorption costing. **(3 marks)**

(ii) Briefly explain two situations where marginal costing is more useful to management than absorption costing. **(2 marks)**

(b) The standard cost schedule for hospital care for a minor surgical procedure is shown below.

Staff: patient ratio is 0.75:1

	£
Nursing costs: 2 days × 0.75 × £320 per day	480
Space and food costs: 2 days × £175 per day	350
Drugs and specific materials	115
Hospital overheads: 2 days × £110 per day	220
Total standard cost	**1,165**

The actual data for the hospital care for one patient having the minor surgical procedure showed that the patient stayed in hospital for 3 days. The cost of the drugs and specific materials for this patient was £320. There were 0.9 nurses per patient on duty during the time that the patient was in hospital. The daily rates for nursing pay, space and food and hospital overheads were as expected.

Prepare a statement that reconciles the standard cost with the actual costs of hospital care for this patient. The statement should contain *five* variances that will give useful information to the manager who is reviewing the cost of hospital care for minor surgical procedures. **(5 marks)**

(c) C plc uses a just-in-time (JIT) purchasing and production process to manufacture Product P. Data for the output of Product P, and the material usage and material price variances for February, March and April are shown below:

Month	Output (units)	Material usage variance	Material price variance
February	11,000	£15,970 Adverse	£12,300 Favourable
March	5,100	£5,950 Adverse	£4,500 Favourable
April	9,100	£8,400 Adverse	£6,200 Favourable

The standard material cost per unit of Product P is £12.

Prepare a sketch (not on graph paper) of a percentage variance chart for material usage and for material price for Product P for the 3-month period. (*Note:* your workings must show the coordinates of the points that would be plotted if the chart was drawn accurately.)

(5 marks)

(d) Briefly discuss three reasons why standard costing may *not* be appropriate in a modern business environment. **(5 marks)**

(e) Compare and contrast marginal costing and throughput accounting. **(5 marks)**

(f) T plc is a large insurance company. The Claims Department deals with claims from policy holders who have suffered a loss that is covered by their insurance policy. Policy holders could claim, for example, for damage to property or for household items stolen in a burglary. The Claims Department staff investigate each claim and determine what, if any, payment should be made to the claimant.

The manager of the Claims Department has decided to benchmark the performance of the department and has chosen two areas to benchmark:

- the detection of false claims
- the speed of processing claims.

For each of the above two areas:
(i) state and justify a performance measure
(ii) explain how relevant benchmarking data could be gathered. **(5 marks)**

Question 21

A firm has recently commenced using a standard costing system but the manager is having some difficulty in identifying significant variances, that is, those that require further analysis and investigation.

Requirements

(a) Describe the factors which determine whether or not a variance is significant.

(5 marks)

(b) Suggest ways in which significant variances could be more easily identified.

(10 marks)

Question 22

AL's customers all pay their accounts at the end of 30 days. To try and improve its cash flow, AL is considering offering all customers a 1.5% discount for payment within 14 days.

Calculate the implied annual (interest) cost to AL of offering the discount, using compound interest methodology and assuming a 365-day year. **(3 marks)**

Section C – Long questions

? Question 23

Frolin Chemicals Ltd produces FDN. The standard ingredients of 1 kg of FDN are:

0.65 kg of ingredient F	@ £4.00 per kg
0.30 kg of ingredient D	@ £6.00 per kg
0.20 kg of ingredient N	@ £2.50 per kg
1.15 kg	

Production of 4,000 kg of FDN was budgeted for April 20X8. The production of FDN is entirely automated and production costs attributed to FDN production comprise only direct materials and overheads. The FDN production operation works on a JIT basis and no ingredients or FDN inventories are held.

Overheads were budgeted for April 20X8 for the FDN production operation as follows:

Activity	Total amount £
Receipt of deliveries from suppliers (standard delivery quantity is 460 kg)	4,000
Despatch of goods to customers (standard despatch quantity is 100 kg)	8,000
	12,000

In April 20X8, 4,200 kg of FDN were produced and cost details were as follows: Materials used:

	kg
F	2,840
D	1,210
N	860

at a total cost of £20,380.

Actual overhead costs: 12 supplier deliveries (cost £4,800) were made and 38 customer despatches (cost £7,800) were processed.

Frolin Chemicals Ltd's budget committee met recently to discuss the preparation of the financial control report for April, and the following discussion occurred:

- *Chief accountant*: 'The overheads do not vary directly with output and are therefore by definition 'fixed'. They should be analysed and reported accordingly.'
- *Management accountant*: 'The overheads do not vary with output, but they are certainly not fixed. They should be analysed and reported on an activity basis.'

Requirements

Having regard to this discussion:

(a) Prepare a variance analysis for FDN production costs in April 20X8: separate the material cost variance into price, mixture and yield components; separate the overhead

cost variance into expenditure, capacity and efficiency components using consumption of ingredient F as the overhead absorption base.
(b) Prepare a variance analysis for FDN production overhead costs in April 1998 on an activity basis.
(c) Explain how, in the design of an activity-based management system, you would identify and select the most appropriate activities and cost drivers.

? Question 24

X Ltd uses an automated manufacturing process to produce an industrial chemical, Product P.

X Ltd operates a standard marginal costing system. The standard cost data for Product P is as follows:

Standard cost per unit of Product P

Materials			
A	10 kgs	@ £15 per kilo	£150
B	8 kgs	@ £8 per kilo	£64
C	5 kgs	@ £4 per kilo	£20
	23 kgs		
Total standard marginal cost			£234
Budgeted fixed production overheads			£350,000

In order to arrive at the budgeted selling price for Product P the company adds 80% markup to the standard marginal cost. The company budgeted to produce and sell 5,000 units of Product P in the period. There were no budgeted inventories of Product P.
The actual results for the period were as follows:

Actual production and sales		5,450 units
Actual sales price		£445 per unit
Material usage and cost		
A	43,000 kgs	£688,000
B	37,000 kgs	£277,500
C	23,500 kgs	£99,875
	103,500 kgs	
Fixed production overheads		£385,000

Requirements

(a) Prepare an operating statement which reconciles the budgeted profit to the actual profit for the period. (The statement should include the material mix and material yield variances.) **(12 marks)**
(b) The Production Manager of X Ltd is new to the job and has very little experience of management information. Write a brief report to the Production Manager of X Ltd that
  (i) interprets the material price, mix and yield variances;
  (ii) discusses the merits, or otherwise, of calculating the materials mix and yield variances for X Ltd. **(8 marks)**

? Question 25

Marshall Limited operates a business that sells advanced photocopying machines and offers on-site servicing. There is a separate department that provides servicing. The standard cost for one service is shown below along with the operating statements for the Service

Department for the 6 months to 30 September 2003. Each service is very similar and involves the replacement of two sets of materials and parts.

Marshall Limited's budgets for 5,000 services per month.

Standard cost for one service

	£
Materials – 2 sets @ £20 per set	40
Labour – 3 hours @ £11 per hour	33
Variable overheads – 3 hours @ £5 per hour	15
Fixed overheads – 3 hours @ £8 per hour	24
Total standard cost	112

Operating Statements for 6 months ending 30 September 2003

Months	1	2	3	4	5	6	Total
Number of services per month	5,000	5,200	5,400	4,800	4,700	4,500	29,600
	£	£	£	£	£	£	£
Flexible budget costs	560,000	582,400	604,800	537,600	526,400	504,000	3,315,200
Less: Variances:							
Materials							
Price	5,150(F)	3,090(F)	1,100(F)	−2,040(A)	−5,700(A)	−2,700(A)	−1,100(A)
Usage	−6,000(A)	2,000(F)	−4,000(A)	−12,000(A)	−2,000(A)	0	−22,000(A)
Labour							
Rate	26,100(F)	25,725(F)	27,331(F)	18,600(F)	17,400(F)	15,515(F)	130,671(F)
Efficiency	5,500(F)	9,900(F)	12,100(F)	−12,100(A)	−4,400(A)	−11,000(A)	0
Variable overheads							
Spending	−3,500(A)	−3,500(A)	−2,500(A)	−4,500(A)	500(F)	2,500(F)	−11,000(A)
Efficiency	2,500(F)	4,500(F)	5,500(F)	−5,500(A)	−2,000(A)	−5,000(A)	0
Fixed overheads							
Expenditure	−3,000(A)	−5,000(A)	−5,000(A)	−15,000(A)	5,000(F)	5,000(F)	−18,000(A)
Volume	0	4,800(F)	9,600(F)	−4,800(A)	−7,200(A)	−12,000(A)	−9,600(A)
Actual costs	533,250	540,885	560,669	574,940	524,800	511,685	3,246,229

Requirements

(a) Prepare a summary financial statement showing the overall performance of the Service Department for the 6 months to 30 September 2003. **(4 marks)**

(b) Write a report to the Operations Director of Marshall Limited commenting on the performance of the Service Department for the 6 months to 30 September 2003.

Suggest possible causes for the features you have included in your report and state the further information that would be helpful in assessing the performance of the department. **(16 marks)**

? Question 26

You have been appointed as the management accountant of the DL Hospital Trust, a newly formed organisation with specific responsibility for providing hospital services to its local community. The hospital trust is divided into a number of specialist units: one of these, unit H, specialises in the provision of a particular surgical operation.

Although the trust does not have profit maximisation as its objective, it is concerned to control its costs and to provide a value-for-money service. To achieve this, it engages teams of specialist staff on a subcontract basis and pays them an hourly rate based upon the direct hours attributable to the surgical operation being carried out.

Surgical team fees (i.e. labour costs) are collected and attributed to each surgical operation, whereas overhead costs are collected and attributed to surgical operations using absorption rates. These absorption rates are based on the surgical team fees. For the year ended 31 December 20X3, these rates were:

Variable overhead	62.5% of surgical team fees
Fixed overhead	87.5% of surgical team fees

Each surgical operation is expected to take 10 hours to complete, and the total fees of the team for each operation are expected to be £2,000.

The budget for the year ended 31 December 20X3 indicated that a total of 20 such surgical operations were expected to be performed each month, and that the overhead costs were expected to accrue evenly throughout the year.

During November 20X2, there were 22 operations of this type completed. These took a total of 235 hours and the total surgical team fees amounted to £44,400.

Overhead costs incurred in unit H in November 20X3 amounted to:

Variable overhead	£28,650
Fixed overhead	£36,950

Requirements

(a) Prepare a statement that reconciles the original budget cost and the actual cost for this type of operation within unit H for the month of November 20X3, showing the analysis of variances in as much detail as possible from the information given.

(15 marks)

(b) The DL Hospital Trust has been preparing its budgets for 20X4, and the finance director has questioned the appropriateness of using surgical team fees as the basis of attributing overhead costs to operations.

You are required to write a brief report to her explaining the arguments for and against the use of this method. **(5 marks)**

? Question 27

F plc supplies pharmaceutical drugs to drug stores. Although the company makes a satisfactory return, the directors are concerned that some orders are profitable and others are not. The management has decided to investigate a new budgeting system using activity-based costing principles to ensure that all orders they accept are making a profit.

Each customer order is charged as follows. Customers are charged the list price of the drugs ordered plus a charge for selling and distribution costs (overheads). A profit margin is also added, but that does not form part of this analysis.

Currently, F plc uses a simple absorption rate to absorb these overheads. The rate is calculated based on the budgeted annual selling and distribution costs, and the budgeted annual total list price of the drugs ordered.

An analysis of customers has revealed that many customers place frequent small orders with each order requesting a variety of drugs. The management of F plc has examined more carefully the nature of its selling and distribution costs, and the following data have been prepared for the budget for next year:

Total list price of drugs supplied	£8 m
Number of customer orders	8,000

Selling and distribution costs	£'000	Cost driver
Invoice processing	280	See Note 2
Packing	220	Size of package – see Note 3
Delivery	180	Number of deliveries – see Note 4
Other overheads	200	Number of orders
Total overheads	880	

Notes:

1. Each order will be shipped in one package and will result in one delivery to the customer and one invoice (an order never results in more than one delivery).
2. Each invoice has a different line for each drug ordered. There are 28,000 invoice lines each year. It is estimated that 25% of invoice processing costs are related to the number of invoices and 75% are related to the number of invoice lines.
3. Packing costs are £32 for a large package and £25 for a small package.
4. The delivery vehicles are always filled to capacity for each journey The delivery vehicles can carry either 6 large packages or 12 small packages (or appropriate combinations of large and small packages). It is estimated that there will be 1,000 delivery journeys each year and the total delivery mileage that is specific to particular customers is estimated at 350,000 miles each year. £40,000 of delivery costs are related to loading the delivery vehicles and the remainder of these costs are related to specific delivery distance to customers.

The management has asked for two typical orders to be costed using next year's budget data, using the current method, and the proposed activity-based costing approach. Details of two typical orders are shown below:

	Order A	Order B
Lines on invoice	2	8
Package size	small	Large
Specific delivery distance	8 miles	40 miles
List price of drugs supplied	£1,200	£900

Requirements

(a) Calculate the charge for selling and distribution overheads for Order A and Order B using:
  (i) the current system; and
  (ii) the activity-based costing approach.   **(10 marks)**

(b) Write a report to the management of F plc in which you
  (i) assess the strengths and weaknesses of the proposed activity-based costing approach for F plc; and   **(5 marks)**
  (ii) recommend actions that the management of F plc might consider in the light of the data produced using the activity-based costing approach.   **(5 marks)**

(Total for requirement (b) = 10 marks)

? **Question 28**

The budget for the Production Planning and Development Department of ABC plc is currently prepared as part of a traditional budgetary planning and control system. The analysis of costs by expense type for the period ended 30 November 20X1 where this system is in use is as follows:

Expense type	Budget %	Actual %
Salaries	60	63
Supplies	6	5
Travel cost	12	12
Technology cost	10	7
Occupancy cost	12	13

The total budget and actual costs for the department for the period ended 30 November 20X1 are £1,000,000 and £1,060,000, respectively.

The company now feels that an activity-based budgeting approach should be used. A number of activities have been identified for the Production Planning and Development Department. An investigation has indicated that total budget and actual costs should be attributed to the activities on the following basis:

Activities	Budget %	Actual %
1. Routeing/scheduling – new products	20	16
2. Routeing/scheduling – existing products	40	34
3. Remedial rerouteing/scheduling	5	12
4. Special studies – specific orders	10	8
5. Training	10	15
6. Management and administration	15	15

Requirements

(a) Prepare *two* budget control statements for the Production Planning and Development Department for the period ended 30 November 20X1 that compare budget with actual cost and show variances using:
- a traditional expense-based analysis;
- an activity-based analysis.

(b) Identify and comment on *four* advantages claimed for the use of activity-based budgeting over traditional budgeting, using the Production Planning and Development example to illustrate your answer.

(c) Comment on the use of the information provided in the activity-based statement that you prepared in (a) in activity-based performance measurement and suggest additional information that would assist in such performance measurement.

? **Question 29**

PSA Ltd pays its operatives an hourly rate which at the start of 20X2 was forecast to be £10.50 throughout the year. Both hardwood and softwood are used on jobs, the 20X2 costs of which were forecast to be £55 per cubic metre (hardwood) and £9 per cubic metre (softwood). Overheads (absorbed on a labour hour overhead absorption rate [OAR]) for

20X2 were forecast to be £96,000 (fixed) and £ 72,000 (variable). It was forecast that 24,000 labour hours would be worked on all jobs at an even rate in 20X2. PSA Ltd uses a conventional cost accounting system and reports cost variances at the end of each month, with labour and material variances split into operational and planning components.

At the start of April 20X2 there was no work-in-progress and, during the month, work started on jobs 98, 107 and 109. Jobs 98 and 107 were fully complete by the end of the month. Job 109 was estimated to be 60% complete as regards labour and 80% complete as regards materials. The evaluator had calculated the following requirements for the jobs, based on the original standards specified above:

	Job 98	Job 107	Job 109
Standard labour hours	1,000	600	780
Hardwood (cubic metres)	200	180	120
Softwood (cubic metres)	320	400	300

During April, 2,200 labour hours were worked (wages paid were £24,500), 520 cubic metres of hardwood were used (cost £28,600) and 1,100 cubic metres of softwood were used (cost £9,200). Conditions in the labour market meant that operatives had to be engaged who were less able than those planned for. On average, operatives were able to work only at 4% below the original standard level of efficiency (i.e. expected output per hour is 4% less than standard). Hardwood available during 20X2 is 5% below forecast quality (that is, the output per cubic metre is 5% below standard). During March, the standard price of softwood for 20X2 was revised to £8 per cubic metre. April overheads were £7,800 (fixed) and £6,900 (variable).

Rapier Management Consultants have reported as follows:

Your cost system looks like something from an accounting textbook written 40 years ago. What you need is backflush costing. Rapier will be delighted to design you a backflush costing system for a modest fee.

Requirements
(a) Explain why conventional cost accounting systems use predetermined OARs.
(b) Construct PSA Ltd's April cost control report.
(c) Explain what backflush costing is and (as far as you can on the basis of available information) comment on the suitability of PSA Ltd's operation for backflush costing.

? Question 30

S Limited installs complex satellite navigation systems in cars, at a very large national depot. The standard cost of an installation is shown below. The budgeted volume is 1,000 units installed each month. The operations manager is responsible for three departments, namely purchasing, fitting and quality control. S Limited purchases navigation systems and other equipment from different suppliers, and most items are imported. The fitting of different systems takes differing amounts of time, but the differences are not more than 25% from the average, so a standard labour time is applied.

Standard cost of installation of one navigation system

	£	Quantity	Price (£)
Materials	400	1 unit	400
Labour	320	20 hours	16
Variable overheads	140	20 hours	7
Fixed overheads	300	20 hours	15
Total standard cost	1,160		

The Operations Department has gathered the following information over the last few months. There are significant difficulties in retaining skilled staff. Many have left for similar but better paid jobs and as a result there is a high labour turnover. Exchange rates have moved and commentators have argued this will make exports cheaper, but S Limited has no exports and has not benefited. Some of the fitters have complained that one large batch of systems did not have the correct adapters and would not fit certain cars, but this was not apparent until fitting was attempted. Rent, rates, insurance and computing facilities have risen in price noticeably.

The financial results for September to December are shown below.

Operating Statement for S Limited for September to December

	September £	October £	November £	December £	4 months £
Standard cost of actual output	1,276,000	1,276,000	1,102,000	1,044,000	4,698,000
Variances					
Materials					
Price	5,505 F	3,354 F	9,520 A	10,340 A	11,001 A
Usage	400 A	7,200 A	800 A	16,000 A	24,400 A
Labour					
Rate	4,200 A	5,500 A	23,100 A	24,000 A	56,800 A
Efficiency	16,000 F	0	32,000 A	32,000 A	48,000 A
Variable overheads					
Expenditure	7,000 A	2,000 A	2,000 F	0	7,000 A
Efficiency	7,000 F	0	14,000 A	14,000 A	21,000 A
Fixed overheads					
Expenditure	5,000 A	10,000 A	20,000 A	20,000 A	55,000 A
Volume	30,000 F	30,000 F	15,000 A	30,000 A	15,000 F
Actual costs	1,234,095	1,267,346	1,214,420	1,190,340	4,906,201

'A' = adverse variance 'F' = favourable variance

Requirements

(a) Prepare a report to the operations manager of S Limited commenting on the performance of the company for the 4 months to 31 December. State probable causes for the key issues you have included in your report and state the further information that would be helpful in assessing the performance of the company. **(15 marks)**

(b) Prepare a short report to the operations manager of S Limited suggesting ways that the budgeting system could be used to increase motivation and improve performance. **(5 marks)**

Question 31

RJ produces and sells two high performance motor cars: Car X and Car Y. The company operates a standard absorption costing system. The company's budgeted operating statement for the year ending 30 June 2008 and supporting information is given below:

Operating statement year ending 30 June 2008

	Car X $000	Car Y $000	Total $000
Sales	52,500	105,000	157,500
Production cost of sales	40,000	82,250	122,250
Gross profit	12,500	22,750	35,250
Administration costs			
Variable	6,300	12,600	18,900
Fixed	7,000	9,000	16,000
Profit/(loss)	(800)	1,150	350

The production cost of sales for each car was calculated using the following values:

	Car X Units	Car X $000	Car Y Units	Car Y $000
Opening inventory	200	8,000	250	11,750
Production	1,100	44,000	1,600	75,200
Closing inventory	300	12,000	100	4,700
Cost of sales	1,000	40,000	1,750	82,250

Production costs

The production costs are made up of direct materials, direct labour, and fixed production overhead. The fixed production overhead is general production overhead (it is not product specific). The total budgeted fixed production overhead is $35,000,000 and is absorbed using a machine hour rate. It takes 200 machine hours to produce one Car X and 300 machine hours to produce one Car Y.

Administration costs

The fixed administration costs include the costs of specific marketing campaigns: $2,000,000 for Car X and $4,000,000 for Car Y.

Requirements

(a) Produce the budgeted operating statement in a marginal costing format. **(7 marks)**
(b) Reconcile the total budgeted absorption costing profit with the total budgeted marginal costing profit as shown in the statement you produced in part *(a)*. **(5 marks)**

The company is considering changing to an activity based costing system. The company has analysed the budgeted fixed production overheads and found that the costs for various activities are as follows:

	$000
Machining costs	7,000
Set up costs	12,000
Quality inspections	7,020
Stores receiving	3,480
Stores issues	5,500
	35,000

The analysis also revealed the following information:

	Car X	Car Y
Budgeted production (number of cars)	1,100	1,600
Cars per production run	10	40
Inspections per production run	20	80
Number of component deliveries during the year	492	900
Number of issues from stores	4,000	7,000

Requirements

(c) Calculate the budgeted production cost of one Car X and one Car Y using the activity based costing information provided above. **(10 marks)**

(d) Prepare a report to the Production Director of RJ which explains the potential benefits of using activity based budgeting for performance evaluation. **(8 marks)**

? Question 32

RF Ltd is a new company which plans to manufacture a specialist electrical component. The company founders will invest £16,250 on the first day of operations, that is, Month 1.

They will also transfer fixed capital assets to the company.

The following information is available:

Sales

The forecast sales for the first four months are as follows:

Month	Number of components
1	1,500
2	1,750
3	2,000
4	2,100

The selling price has been set at £10 per component in the first four months.

Sales receipts

Time of payment	% of customers
Month of sale	20*
One month later	45
Two months later	25
Three months later	5

The balance represents anticipated bad debts.

* A 2% discount is given to customers for payment received in the month of sale.

Production

There will be no opening inventory of finished goods in Month 1 but after that it will be policy for the closing inventory to be equal to 20% of the following month's forecast sales.

Variable production cost

The variable production cost is expected to be £6–40 per component.

	£
Direct materials	1.90
Direct wages	3.30
Variable production overheads	1.20
Total variable cost	6.40

Notes:

Direct materials: 100% of the materials required for production will be purchased in the month of production. No inventory of materials will be held. Direct materials will be paid for in the month following purchase.

Direct wages: will be paid in the month in which production occurs.

Variable production overheads: 60% will be paid in the month in which production occurs and the remainder will be paid one month later.

Fixed overhead costs

Fixed overhead costs are estimated at £75,000 per annum and are expected to be incurred in equal amounts each month. 60% of the fixed overhead costs will be paid in the month in which they are incurred and 30% in the following month. The balance represents depreciation of fixed assets.

Calculations are to be made to the nearest £1.
Ignore VAT and Tax.

Requirements

(a) Prepare a cash budget for each of the first three months and in total. **(15 marks)**

(b) There is some uncertainty about the direct material cost. It is thought that the direct material cost per component could range between £1.50 and £2.20. Calculate the budgeted total net cash flow for the three month period if the cost of the direct material is:
  (i) £1.50 per component; or
  (ii) £2.20 per component. **(6 marks)**

(c) Using your answers to part *(a)* and *(b)* above, prepare a report to the management of RF Ltd that discusses the benefits or otherwise of performing 'what if' analysis when preparing cash budgets. **(9 marks)**

Question 33

A health clinic is reviewing its plans for the next three years. It is a not for profit organisation but it has a financial responsibility to manage its costs and to ensure that it provides a value for money service to its clients. The health clinic uses the net present value technique to appraise the financial viability of delivering the service, but it also considers other non-financial factors before making any final decisions.

The present facilities, which incur an annual total cost of £300,000, are only sufficient to meet a low level of service provision so the manager is considering investing in facilities to meet potential higher levels of demand. For the purpose of evaluating this decision the possible levels of demand for the health clinic's services have been simplified to high, medium or low.

The possible demand for the services in the first year and the level of demand that could follow that specific level in the next years, and their expected probabilities, are as follows:

Year 1	Probability	Years 2 and 3	Probability
Low	30%	Low 40%	
		Medium	60%
		High 0%	
Medium	50%	Low 30%	
		Medium	40%
		High 30%	
High	20%	Low 0%	
		Medium	30%
		High 70%	

The level of demand will be the same in years 2 and 3.

The manager is considering two alternative investments in facilities:

Facility A has the capacity to meet the low and medium levels of demand and requires an investment at the start of year 1 of £500,000. Thereafter it incurs annual fixed costs of £100,000 and annual variable costs depending on the level of operation. These annual variable costs are expected to be £150,000 at the low level of operation and £250,000 at the medium level of operation.

Facility B has the capacity to meet all levels of demand and requires an investment at the start of year 1 of £800,000. Thereafter it incurs annual fixed costs of £200,000 and annual variable costs depending on the level of operation. These annual variable costs are expected to be £100,000 at the low level of operation, £150,000 at the medium level of operation and £200,000 at the high level of operation.

Neither of these alternative investments has any residual value at the end of year 3.

If the facilities of the health clinic are insufficient to meet the level of service demand that occurs, the clinic must obtain additional facilities on a yearly contract basis at the following annual costs:

Level of service provision available internally	Level of service provision demanded	Annual cost of additional facilities
Low	Medium	£100,000
Low	High	£250,000
Medium	High	£150,000

These additional facilities are not under the direct control of the health clinic manager.

Note: All monetary values used throughout the question have been stated in terms of their present value. No further discounting is required.

Requirements

(a) Prepare a decision tree to illustrate the investment decision that needs to be made by the manager of the health clinic. (Numerical values are NOT required). **(6 marks)**

(b) Advise the manager of the health clinic which investment decision should be undertaken on financial grounds. **(15 marks)**

(c) Briefly discuss any non-financial factors that the manager should consider before making her final investment decision. **(4 marks)**

? Question 34

A ticket agent has an arrangement with a concert hall that holds pop concerts on 60 nights a year whereby he receives discounts as follows per concert:

For purchase of	*He receives a discount of*
200 tickets	20%
300 tickets	25%
400 tickets	30%
500 tickets or more	40%

Purchases must be in full hundreds. The average price per ticket is £3.

He must decide in advance each year the number of tickets he will purchase. If he has any tickets unsold by the afternoon of the concert he must return them to the box office. If the box office sells any of these he receives 60 per cent of their price.

His sales records over a few years show that for a concert with extremely popular artistes he can be confident of selling 500 tickets, for one with less known artistes 350 tickets, and for one with relatively unknown artistes 200 tickets.

His records show that 10 per cent of the tickets he returns are sold by the box office.

His administration costs incurred in selling tickets are the same per concert irrespective of the popularity of the artistes.

There are two possible scenarios in which his sales records can be viewed:

Scenario 1: that on average, he can expect concerts with lesser-known artistes;

Scenario 2: that the frequency of concerts will be:

	%
With popular artistes	45
With lesser-known artistes	30
With unknown artistes	25
	100

Requirements

(a) Calculate separately for each of scenarios 1 and 2:
   (i) the expected demand for tickets per concert;
   (ii) • the level of his purchases of tickets per concert that will give him the largest profit over a long period of time;
      • the profit per concert that this level of purchases of tickets will yield.

(12 marks)

(b) For scenario 2, only the maximum sum per annum that the ticket agent should pay to a pop concert specialist for 100 per cent correct predictions as to the likely success of each concert. **(8 marks)**

? Question 35

In 1994, Hulk Petroleum plc (HPC)constructed an oil production platform known as Claymore 4 (C4). After construction, C4 was positioned in the North Sea and wells were drilled from C4 into an oilfield below. The platform was designed to have a life of 25 years from 1 January 1995, with the original wells being productive for 10 years.

By 2004 the reservoirs in the oilfield tapped by the original wells will be almost exhausted. Untapped reservoirs in the oilfield below C4 are estimated to contain a maximum of 1,500,000 tonnes of extractable oil. Alternative strategies for the continuation of oil production from C4 have been identified as follows:

- low-intensity depletion strategy: involves drilling of new wells at a cost of £105 m. These would recover maximum extractable oil at an even rate over 15 years; the annual operating costs will be £3.2 million and the costs of decontaminating and dismantling C4 at year 15 will be £395 m.
- high-intensity depletion strategy: involves the drilling of new wells at a cost of £118 m. These would recover 1,300,000 tonnes of oil over eight years at an even rate; the annual operating costs will be £3.6 m and the costs of decontaminating and dismantling C4 at year 8 will be £280 m.

The average market price of oil throughout the period is forecast to be £325 per tonne. It is HPC's normal policy to require all new investment projects to generate an IRR in excess of 10 per cent (which is HPC's cost of money). In the case of mutually exclusive investments, the one with the highest IRR is adopted.

Requirements
(a) Write a memorandum in response to a letter from one of HPC's directors which includes the following statement:

Since cash flow and profit are the same thing in the long run, we should always adopt courses of action which maximise accounting profit. I do not understand the logic behind our investment appraisal policy.

(5 marks)
(b) Draw a graph in order to illustrate the sensitivity of the two strategies to the choice of discount rate (in the range 0–25 per cent) that may be used to appraise them.

(10 marks)
(c) In the light of your answer to (b), comment on the merits of HPC's existing investment appraisal policy. **(6 marks)**
(d) Advise HPC's management on which of the two strategies should be selected.

(4 marks)

? Question 36

Anmexsco is a mining company, which has discovered deposits of bauxite beneath Hyde Park in London. Anmexsco has negotiated a possible deal to undertake opencast bauxite mining in Hyde Park for a 5-year period. This would involve excavating most of the park to a depth of about 2,000 feet but restoring the park to its original condition at the end of the 5 years.

Details of the proposed deal are:

- an initial fee of £9,700,000 would be payable to the government;
- amounts of bauxite extracted are forecast to be:

Year	Tonnes
1	100,000
2	150,000
3	220,000
4	180,000
5	90,000

- the market price of bauxite is £90 per ton;
- annual operating costs will be £3,000,000 throughout;
- the costs of restoring Hyde Park are forecast to be:

Year	£
4	42,000,000
5	1,000,000

Anmexsco's investment appraisal rules require a project to show a minimum IRR of 17 per cent before it is allowed to proceed.

Financial analysts working for Anmexsco prepare a project evaluation, which shows the project yielding an IRR of 23.836 per cent and recommend that the project should proceed. On receiving this evaluation Anmexsco's chief executive makes the following statement:

I have checked these figures using only a pocket calculator and I would place the IRR of the project at around 11.5 per cent. This project is not viable and these analysts do not know what they are doing.

Requirements

(a) Explain and reconcile the two alternative evaluations of the project. (**18 marks**)
(b) Explain how you would use a standard computer spreadsheet to assist in this exercise.
(**7 marks**)

? Question 37

CH Ltd is a swimming club. Potential exists to expand the business by providing a gymnasium as part of the facilities at the club. The Directors believe that this will stimulate additional membership of the club.

The expansion project would require an initial expenditure of £550,000. The project is expected to have a disposal value at the end of 5 years which is equal to 10 per cent of the initial expenditure.

The following schedule reflects a recent market research survey regarding the estimated annual sales revenue from additional memberships over the project's 5-year life:

Level of demand	£000	Probability
High	800	0.25
Medium	560	0.50
Low	448	0.25

It is expected that the contribution to sales ratio will be 55 per cent. Additional expenditure on fixed overheads is expected to be £90,000 per annum.

CH Ltd incurs a 30 per cent tax rate on corporate profits. Corporation tax is to be paid in two equal instalments: one in the year that profits are earned and the other in the following year.

CH Ltd's after-tax nominal (money) discount rate is 15.5 per cent per annum. A uniform inflation rate of 5 per cent per annum will apply to all costs and revenues during the life of the project.

All of the values above have been expressed in terms of current prices.

You can assume that all cash flows occur at the end of each year and that the initial investment does not qualify for capital allowances.

Requirements

(a) Evaluate the proposed expansion from a financial perspective. **(13 marks)**
(b) Calculate and then discuss the sensitivity of the project to changes in the expected annual contribution. **(5 marks)**

You have now been advised that the capital cost of the expansion will qualify for writing down allowances at the rate of 25 per cent per annum on a reducing balance basis. Also, at the end of the project's life, a balancing charge or allowance will arise equal to the difference between the scrap proceeds and the tax written down value.

(c) Calculate the financial impact of these allowances. **(7 marks)**

Solutions to Revision Questions

Section A – Multi-choice solutions

☑ Solution 1

1.1 Marginal cost of inventory is an approximation of variable production cost of £62,000. l/8th production in inventory = £7,750

Therefore the correct answer is (B).

1.2 Throughput approach values inventory at direct materials cost = l/8th of £40,000 = £5,000

Therefore the correct answer is (A).

1.3 Absorption costing overhead rate is £29,500/5,000 units = £5.90 per unit

Absorption costing profit greater by £5.90 × 500 units = £2,950

Therefore the correct answer is (B).

1.4 $y = £800 + (0.0002 \times 4{,}100^2) = £4{,}162$

Total budgeted vehicle costs are £4,162 × 1.03 = £4,287

Variance is £4,287 − £5,000 = £713 Adverse

Therefore the correct answer is (A).

1.5 The correct answer is (C).

1.6 Planning price variance

30,000 × ($4.00 − $5.00) = $30,000 Adverse

Therefore the correct answer is (B).

1.7 Operational usage variance

(30,000 − 32,000) × $5.00 = $10,000 Adverse

Therefore the correct answer is (D).

1.8 Operational price variance

32,000 × ($5.00 − $4.80) = $6,400 Favourable

Therefore the correct answer is (B).

1.9 Items debited to cost of goods sold account will be:

Finished goods sold   £1,700,000

Difference between conversion costs incurred and conversion costs allocated, that is, £890,000 − £840,000 = £50,000

Therefore the correct answer is (B).

1.10 The correct answer is (C).

 Solution 2

2.1 The correct answer is (B).

2.2 The correct answer is (A).

2.3 Therefore the correct answer is (C).

2.4

	£	£
Std cost of goods produced		128,500
Plus adverse variances		
Materials price	2,400	
Labour rate	5,600	
Variable overheads	2,680	10,680
Less favourable variances		
Material usage	8,400	
Labour efficiency	3,140	
Fixed overheads	3,192	(14,732)
Actual cost of goods produced		**124,448**

Therefore the correct answer is (B).

2.5 The correct answer is (C).

2.6

			Difference
Output	2,000 units	3,500 units	1,500 units
Total cost	£12,000	£16,200	£4,200

Variable cost per unit = 4,200/1,500 = £2.80.

Fixed cost = 12,000 − (2,000 × 2.80) = £6,400 *(Note:* Alternatively, you could have used the figures for 3,500 units).

Therefore, the budget cost allowance for 4,000 units = £6,400 + (4,000 × 2.80) = £17,600.

Therefore the correct answer is (A).

2.7 The index values for a multiplicative model with four seasons add to 400.

Therefore the correct answer is (D).

2.8 Assuming the revenue was $100 will lead to the following revised figures:

	Original	*Revised*
Revenue	100	60
Variable costs	30	18
Fixed costs	22	22
Profit	48	20

Therefore the correct answer is (B) (20/60).

Solution 3

3.1

Standard selling price	£26
Actual selling price	£31
	£5 × 8,200 = £41,000 Favourable

The correct answer is (B).

3.2 Sales profit volume variance

	Units
Budgeted sales	8,700
Actual sales	8,200
	500 × (£26 − £10 − £4) = £6,000 Adverse

The correct answer is (A).

3.3 Fixed overhead volume variance

	Units
Budgeted output	8,700
Actual output	8,200
	500 × £4 = £2,000 Adverse

The correct answer is (A).

3.4 The correct answer is (D).

3.5 The correct answer is (B).

3.6 OAR 1,000/200 = £5 per unit

Total variance
Actual   £1,300,000
Absorbed   £1,200,000
                  £ 100,000 adverse
£1,200,000/£5 = 240,000

The correct answer is (B).

3.7

	Units
Opening inventory	800
Closing inventory	500
Decrease	300 × (£500,000/2,000) = £75,000 lower

The correct answer is (B).

☑ Solution 4

4.1 The correct answer is (D).

4.2 The correct answer is (A).

4.3 The correct answer is (D).

4.4

	Units
Sales	30,000
Req'd closing inventory	4,725
Less opening inventory	(3,500)
Production	31,225

The correct answer is (C).

4.5

Budget	£2,500,000
Actual	£2,010,000
Variance	£490,000 favourable

The correct answer is (D).

4.6

Budgeted volume	500,000 units
Actual volume	440,000 units
	60,000 units

OAR
2 hours × £2·50   ×£5 per unit
Volume variance   £300,000 adverse

The correct answer is (C).

4.7

	£
Absorbed (200,000 units × £1·50)	300,000
Incurred	260,000
Over absorbed	40,000

The correct answer is (A).

4.8   Actual fixed production

overhead cost	£1,950,000
Total variance	£150,000 adverse
Absorbed	£1,800,000
OAR per unit	£5
	360,000 units

The correct answer is (C).

4.9   The correct answer is (C).

4.10

High Low Method	Activity	Cost	
Highest	6,500	£33,000	
Lowest	4,500	£29,000	
Difference	2,000	£4,000	
Variable cost per unit		£2	
Substitute into highest activity	6,500	£33,000	Total cost
	6,500 × £2	£13,000	Variable cost
	Difference	£20,000	Fixed cost
Therefore	5,750 × £2	£11,500	Variable cost
		£20,000	Fixed cost
		£31,500	Total cost

The correct answer is (C).

☑ Solution 5

5.1 $[(11,000 \times 0.75) - 8,000] \times £20 = £5,000$ Favourable

Therefore the correct answer is (B).

5.2 $(8,000 \times £15) - £132,000 = £12,000$ Adverse

Therefore the correct answer is (C).

5.3   The correct answer is (B).

5.4 $(80,000 \times 0.4) + (120,000 \times 0.6) = 104,000$ units

Therefore the correct answer is (C).

5.5

	£
Cost of goods sold	100,000
Less material cost £45 × 1,000	45,000
Conversion cost allocated	55,000
Conversion cost incurred	60,000
Excess charged to cost of goods sold account	5,000
Total debit on cost of goods sold account £100,000 + £5,000 =	105,000

Therefore the correct answer is (C).

5.6   The correct answer is (D).

✅ Solution 6

6.1   Actual rate is £336,000/24,000 = £14 per hour

$$24,000 \times [£15 - £14] = £24,000 \text{ Favourable}$$

Therefore the correct answer is (D).

6.2 $[(11,000 \times 2) - 24,000] \times £6 = £12,000$ Adverse

Therefore the correct answer is (A).

6.3   The correct answer is (A).

6.4   Closing inventory would be valued at £300,000/1,000 = £300 per unit.

	£
Turnover	820,000
Production costs [£300,000 − (150 × £300)]	255,000
Other costs	395,000
Profit	170,000

Therefore the correct answer is (A).

6.5   The correct answer is (C).

6.6   The correct answer is (D).

6.7   The correct answer is (B).

6.8   The correct answer is (A).

✅ Solution 7

7.1 The Correct answer is (B).

7.2 Replacement at the end of the first year:

$$(\pounds220{,}000 \times 1.00) + ((\pounds110{,}000 - \pounds121{,}000) \times 0.893) = 210{,}177$$

$$\text{Annualised equivalent cost} = \frac{\pounds210{,}177}{0.893} = \pounds235{,}361$$

Replacement at the end of the second year:

$$(\pounds220{,}000 \times 1.00) + (\pounds110{,}000 \times 0.893) + ((\pounds132{,}000 - \pounds88{,}000) \times 0.797)$$
$$= \pounds353{,}298$$

$$\text{Annualised equivalent cost} = \frac{\pounds353{,}298}{1.69} = \pounds209{,}052$$

Replacement at the end of the third year:

$$(\pounds220{,}000 \times 1.00) + (\pounds110{,}000 \times 0.893) + (\pounds132{,}000 \times 0.797) + ((\pounds154{,}000 - \pounds66{,}000) \times 0.712) = \pounds486{,}090$$

$$\text{Annualised equivalent cost} = \frac{\pounds486{,}090}{2.402} = \pounds202{,}369$$

Replacement at the end of the fourth year:

$$(\pounds220{,}000 \times 1.00) + (\pounds110{,}000 \times 0.893) + (\pounds132{,}000 \times 0.797) + (\pounds154{,}000 \times 0.712) + ((\pounds165{,}000 \times 0.636) + ((\pounds176{,}000 - \pounds25{,}000) \times 0.567) = \pounds723{,}639$$

$$\text{Annualised equivalent cost} = \frac{\pounds723{,}639}{3.605} = \pounds200{,}732$$

Replacement at the end of the fifth year:

The fleet should be replaced at the end of four years.

Therefore the answer is (D).

7.3

		EV £000	Ranking
L	$(500 \times 0.2) + (470 \times 0.5) + (550 \times 0.3)$	500	2
M	$(400 \times 0.2) + (550 \times 0.5) + (570 \times 0.3)$	526	1
N	$(450 \times 0.2) + (400 \times 0.5) + (475 \times 0.3)$	432.5	4
O	$(360 \times 0.2) + (400 \times 0.5) + (420 \times 0.3)$	398	5
P	$(600 \times 0.2) + (500 \times 0.5) + (425 \times 0.3)$	497.5	3

Therefore the answer is (B).

7.4

Value of perfect information

Market prediction	Project £'000	Profit	Pr.	EV £'000
Poor	P	600	0.20	120
Good	M	550	0.50	275
Excellent	M	570	0.30	171
EV of profit with perfect information				566
Less the highest EV profit available without perfect information				526
Value of perfect information				40

Therefore the answer is (D)

✓ Solution 8

8.1 The correct answer is (D).

$$1 + r = (100/80)^{365/20}$$

$$1 + r = (1.0204)^{18.25}$$

$$1 + r = (1.446)$$

Cost of discount = 44.6%

8.2 The correct answer is (B).

Settling the amounts owed to trade payables earlier will reduce the cash balance sooner and so will affect the cash forecasts.

8.3 The correct answer is (C).

Interest is paid on the amount borrowed, rather than on the whole facility.

8.4 The correct answer is (A).

$$\text{Quick ratio} = \frac{\text{current assests} - \text{stock}}{\text{current liabilities}}$$
$$= \frac{200,00}{250,000} = 0.8 : 1$$

8.5 The correct answer is (C).

Cost of sales = 40 million × 80%	=	32 million	
Receivable days = 5/32 × 365	=	57	
Inventory days = 7/40 × 365	=	64	
Payable days = 2/32 × 365	=	(23)	
		98	

8.6 The correct answer is (C).

✅ Solution 9

9.1 The correct answer is (C).

Purchases increase inventory and increase trade payables, leaving working capital unchanged.

$$Profit\ on\ sales\ increase\ in\ WC = \$24,000 \times \frac{0.25}{1.25}$$
$$= \$4,800$$

9.2 The correct answer is (C).

$240,000 + $12,000 = $252,000

9.3 The correct answer is (A).

9.4 The correct answer is (C).

9.5 The correct answer is (C).

9.6 The correct answer is (A).

9.7 The correct answer is (A).

Section B – Short Questions

✅ Solution 10

10.1 Orders = [100,000 + (30 × 240)] × 1.08 = 115,776

Overhead cost = £10,000 + (£0.25 × 115,776) = £38,944

Answer is £39,000

10.2 Use high/low method to separate fixed and variable budgeted overhead cost:

	Hours	£
High	18,000	16,242
Low	10,000	13,468
Difference	8,000	2,774

Variable cost per machine hour

$$= \frac{£2,774}{8,000} = £0.34675$$

By substitution fixed cost

= £13,468 − (10,000 × £0.34675) = £10,000

Budget cost allowance		£
= £10,000 + (13,780 × £0.34675) =		14,778
Actual cost =		14.521
		257 (F)

10.3

Budgeted number of batches		
Product D (100,000/100)	=	1,000
Product R (100,000/50)	=	2,000
Product P (50,000/25)	=	2,000
		5,000
Budgeted machine set-ups		
Product D (1,000 × 3)	=	3,000
Product R (2,000 × 4)	=	8,000
Product P (2,000 × 6)	=	12,000
		23,000
Budgeted number of purchase orders		
Product D (1,000 × 2)	=	2,000
Product R (2,000 × 1)	=	2,000
Product P (2,000 × 1)	=	2,000
		6,000
Budgeted processing minutes		
Product D (100,000 × 2)	=	200,000
Product R (100,000 × 3)	=	300,000
Product P (50,000 × 3)	=	150,000
		650,000 minutes

10.4 *Budgeted cost/set-up*

$$= \frac{£150,000}{23,000} = £6.52 \quad \text{Budgeted unit cost of } \mathbf{R} = \frac{£6.25 \times 4}{50} = £0.52$$

Budgeted cost/purchase orders

$$= \frac{£70,000}{6,000} = £11.67 \quad \text{Budgeted unit cost of } \mathbf{R} = \frac{£11.67 \times 1}{50} = £0.23$$

Budgeted processing cost per minute

$$= \frac{£80,000}{650,000} = £0.12 \quad \text{Budgeted unit cost of } \mathbf{R} = £0.12 \times 3 = £0.36$$

Total budgeted unit cost of **R** *is*

		£	
Set-up costs	=	0.52	
Purchasing costs	=	0.23	
Processing costs	=	0.36	
Total cost	=	1.11	per unit

10.5

	Actual mix litres	*Standard mix litres*	*Difference litres*	*Price* £	*Variance* £
X	984	885.6	98.4 (A)	2.50	246.0 (A)
Y	1,230	1,328.4	98.4 (F)	3.00	295.2 (F)
Totals	2,214	2,214.0	nil		49.2 (F)

10.6

$$\text{Exected output} = \frac{2,214}{30} = 73.8 \text{ units}$$

Actual output	= 72.0 units
Shortfall	= 1.8 units
1.8units × £84/unit	= £151.2 (A)

An alternative would be only 73 complete units of output were expected, thus the shortfall would be 1 unit. The variance would be $1.0 \times £84$ per unit = £84 adverse.

10.7 (a) Machine utilisation rates

Product Required machine hours	A	B	C	Total
Machine 1	250	100	90	440
Machine 2	250	275	90	615
Machine 3	125	50	30	205

Utilisation rates:

Machine 1 (440/400)	=	10%
Machine 2 (615/400)	=	154%
Machine 3 (205/400)	=	51%

(b) Machine 2 is the bottleneck – it has the highest utilisation and this is greater than 100%.

10.8 (a) The Goldratt procedure is:

- identify the system's bottleneck,
- decide how to exploit or relieve the bottleneck,
- sub-ordinate everything else to relieving the bottleneck,
- elevate the system's bottlenecks,
- when one bottleneck is no longer a constraint, start procedure again (there will always be a new bottleneck).

(b) Optimal allocation would be on the basis of contribution from the bottleneck resource.

Ranking of contribution per product from machine 2 is:

Product	A	B	C
Contribution per unit	£36	£28	£18
Machine 2 hours	5	5.5	1.5
Contribution per machine hour	£7.20	£5.09	£12.00
Ranking	2	3	1

Thus allocation on this ranking

Product C	60 units	Using	90	hours
Product B	50 units	Using	250	hours
			340	hours

This use 340 hours, leaving an available balance of 60 hours.
This will make 60/5.5 = 10.9 units of Product B or 10 whole units.

Solution 11

11.1 $x = 27$ so trend value is $25,000 + (6,500 \times 27) = 200,500$ units

Quarter 3 adjustment is 150%, so forecast is 300,750 units

11.2 The GHG emission scheme gives each large industrial concern a GHG emission allowance which is capped. If its verified CO_2 emissions in any year exceed its allowance then a business has to buy additional allowances on the market. If its emissions are less than its allowance then it can sell its surplus on the market (where allowances appear to trade at between €5 and €13 per tonne).

　　This situation may create substantial liabilities or assets for a business which have to be accounted for. It also creates a complex decision making situation in which businesses have to consider the cost–benefit trade off between alternative emission strategies. The general idea is to 'internalise' the external costs from emissions and energy usage that a business causes thus influencing the policies of the business in a manner which benefits the common good.

11.3 Allocation of common process costs to R is £42,500 × (£9,800/£54,035) =£7,708

	January units	February units	March units
Sales	4,000	5,000	6,000
Closing inventory: 30% next month	1,500	1,800	
Less opening inventory	(1,200)	(1,500)	
Production in month	4,300	5,300	

Raw material requirement	January units
Monthly production	4,300
Closing inventory: 25% of next month's production	1,325
Less opening inventory	(1,075)
Material purchases	4,550

Payments for purchases for the cash budget in February are the actual purchases delivered in January, that is,

4,550 units at £8 per unit = £36,400

11.4

Total overhead cost	£88,000
Direct labour hours	8,000
Absorption rate	£11 per direct labour hour

Budgeted unit cost for product Z for October is:

	£
Direct materials	21.50
Direct labour 0.3 × £16	4.80
Overhead costs 0.3 × £11	3.30
Total unit cost	29,60

11.5 Cost driver rates are needed

Set-ups £22,000/88	=	£250 per set-up
Quality tests £34,000/40	=	£850 per test
Other overheads £32,000/8,000	=	£4 per direct labour hour
(note this is not a true cost driver)		

Activity-based cost of product Z

	£
Direct materials	21.50
Direct labour	4.80
Set-up costs 2 × £250/30	16.67
Quality tests £850/75	11.33
Other overhead costs 0.3 × £4	1.20
Total activity-based costs for October	55,50

An alternative approach to these calculations would be:

Set-up costs = [(150/30) × 2 × £250]/150 = £16.67

Quality costs = (2 × £850)/150 = £11.33

11.6 Costs under ABC could be higher where: there is production complexity not represented in direct labour hours; small batch sizes; or high levels of non-manufacturing activity. This may lead management to: increase batch sizes, simplify processes to reduce activities, or review pricing if this is not in line with ABC costs.

(Three implications are given, though only two are required).

		LD view (VC = 25 + 40)		**KL view (VC = 25 + 20)**	
Hours sold	*Price per hour*	*Contribution per hour*	*Contribution £*	*Contribution per hour*	*Contribution £*
	£	£		£	
0	100				
1,000	90	25	25,000	45	45,000
2,000	80	15	*30,000	35	70,000
3,000	70	5	15,000	25	*75,000
4,000	60	−5	−20,000	15	60,000
5,000	50	−15	−75,000	5	25,000

 Solution 12

12.1

	W	X	Y
	£	£	£
Selling price	200	150	150
Cost	41	20	30
Direct materials	159	130	120
Throughput contribution	159/9	130/10	120/7
TP/LF	£17.66	£13.00	£17.14
Ranking	1st	3rd	2nd

12.2

	Assembly (£)	Finishing (£)	Stores (£)	Maintenance (£)
Overheads	100,000	150,000	50,000	40,000
Reapportion				
Maintenance	16,000	18,000	6,000	−40,000
Stores	33,600	22,400	−56,000	
	149,600	190,400	Nil	Nil
OAR	149,600/100,000			
	£1.496 per unit			

Assembly

Absorbed 120,000 × £1.496	£179,520
Incurred	£180,000
Under absorbed	£480

12.3

(a) The daily interest rate corresponding to an 8% annual rate is (1.08 1/360) −1 = 0.0214%

The discount is therefore $10,000 x (1.000214 12) = $25.69

(b) The daily interest rate corresponding to a 12% annual rate is (1.12 1/360) −1 = 0.0315%.

The penalty is therefore $10,000 x (1.000315 17) = $53.66

(c) The advantages are :
- it provides a "gentle" incentive for customers to meet agreed credit terms; the application of a pre-agreed system need involve no confrontation or loss of goodwill;
- it matches charges to individual customers with costs and is hence an application of 'customer profitability analysis'; the activity of collecting overdue debts incurs costs and the system matches revenues to those costs;
- charging a "penal" interest rate on overdue debts may be a legitimate source of income.

The disadvantages are :

- the amounts of money involved are trivial and may not justify the administrative costs of running the scheme; it merely adds to the cost of doing business;
- it invites arguments with customers over the precise date on which a payment was "received";
- people should pay debts on the due date and should not require positive or negative incentives to do this.

12.4

Planning variance	£ per kg
Ex-ante standard	4.10
Ex-post standard	4.50
	0.40 × 11,200 = £4,480 Adverse
Usage variance	kg
Standard 7 × 1,600	11,200
Actual	12,000
	800 × £4.50 = £3,600 Adverse

12.5

	W	X	Y
	£ per unit	£ per unit	£ per unit
Selling price	200.00	183.00	175.00
Direct material	50.00	40.00	35.00
Direct labour	30.00	35.00	30.00
Overheads			
Receiving/inspecting etc	33.60	33.60	31.11
Production scheduling	36.00	26.00	25.00
Profit per unit	50.40	48.40	53.89

Cost driver rates
Receiving/inspecting quality assurance   £1,400,000/5,000 = £280 per requisition
Production scheduling/machine set up   £1,200,000/800 = £1,500 per set up

12.6

Efficiency variance
Standard hours   57,500
Actual hours   60,000
              2,500 × £12 − £30,000 Adverse

Rate variance
Standard rate   £12.00
Actual rate   £12.75
            £0.75 × 60,000 hours = £45,000 Adverse

 # Solution 13

13.1   Mix variance = $500 favourable

	Actual mix			*Standard mix*		
	kg	*$*	*$*	*kg*	*$*	*$*
P	1,030	75	77,250	1,000	75	75,000
Q	560	100	56,000	600	100	60,000
R	410	125	51,250	400	125	50,000
	2,000		184,500	2,000		185,000

13.2   Yield variance = $196,304 − $185,000 = $11,305 favourable   Output was 1,910 kg. The stanard input for this should be 1,910/90% = 2,122.22 kg

	Standard mix of input			*Standard mix for output*		
	kg	*$*	*$*	*kg*	*$*	*$*
P	1,000	75	75,000	1,061.11	75	79,583
Q	600	100	60,000	636.67	100	63,667
R	400	125	50,000	424.44	125	53,055
	2,000		**185,000**	2,122.22		**196,305**

Alternative method

Standard cost of 1 kg of output is $9,250/90 = $102.78

Expected output was 2,000 × 0.9 = 1,800 kg
Actual output was 1,910 kg

There is a favourable yield of 110 kg.
Therefore, the yield variance is 110 × $102.78 = $11,306 favourable

13.3

Month of sale	*Factor*	*Receive December $*
November	60% × 90%	70,200
October	20%	24,000
September	15%	15,000
Total		**109,200**

13.4 All figures are £'000

Month	Sales	Cost of sales	Opening inventory	Closing inventory	Purchase	Paid
July	100	80	40	36	76	
August	90	72	36	50	86	76
September	125	100	50	56	106	86
October	140	112	56			106

13.5 Budgeted profit = £1 m. Therefore total contribution = £6.5 m and contribution from Z must be £3 m.

	Product X	Product Y	Product Z	Total
Revenue	£10 m	£20 m	£12 m	
C/S ratio	15%	10%	25%	
Contribution (£m)	1.5	2.0	3.0	6.5
Fixed costs (£m)				5.5
Profit (£m)				1.0

✓ Solution 14

14.1

A – Original plan	600 × £72 = £43,200
B – Revised ex post plan	600 × £82 = £49,200
C – Actual results	600 × £86 = £51,600

Selling price planning variance is B − A = £6,000 Favourable
Selling price operating variance is C − B = £2,400 Favourable
(Total variance is C − A = £8,400 Favourable to check)

14.2 Mix variance

	Actual usage in standard proportions	$
D =	4,000 litres at $9 per litre	36,000
E =	3,500 litres at $5 per litre	17,500
F =	2,500 litres at $2 per litre	5,000
	10,000	58,500 (1)
	Actual usage in actual proportions	
D =	4,300 litres at $9 per litre	38,700
E =	3,600 litres at $5 per litre	18,000
F =	2,100 litres at $2 per litre	4,200
	10,000	60,900 (2)

Mix variance is (1) − (2) = $2,400 Adverse
Yield variance

Standard cost of 1 litre is $58.50/9	=	$6.50
Expected output is 10,000 × 90%	=	9,000 litres
Actual output	=	9,100 litres
Yield variance is (9,100 − 9,000) × $6.50 =		$650 Favourable

14.3

	Maximum no. of units of Z1	Maximum no. of units of Z2
Dept 1	480/12 = 40	480/16 = 30
Dept 2	840/20 = 42	840/15 = 56

Department 2 has more capacity than Department 1 for both products, therefore Department 1 is the limiting factor or bottleneck.

14.4

	Z1	Z2
Variable cost	£26.80	£30.40
Sales price	£50.00	£65.00
Contribution	£23.20	£34.60

Calculate contribution per limiting factor (Department 1 time)

Z1 = £23.20/12 = £1.933 per minute

Z2 = £34.60/16 = £2.1625 per minute

So, maximum contribution would be to make as many Z2 as possible, that is, 30 units × £34.60 = £1,038

14.5 Throughput or throughput contribution is sales less direct materials, so

Z1 is £50 − £10 = £40

Z2 is £65 − £15 = £50

Throughput per bottleneck minute is:

Z1 £40/12 = £3.333

Z2 £50/16 = £3.125

Thus, maximum throughput is by production of maximum number of Z1, that is, 40 units of Z1 giving throughput contribution of 40 × £40 = £1,600

 Solution 15

15.1

	A	B	C
	$	$	$
Selling price	200	150	150
Direct materials	41	20	30
Throughput	159	130	120
Machine P – minutes per unit	12	10	7
Return per factory hour			
	159/12	130/10	120/7
	13·25	13	17·14
×60 minutes	**795**	**780**	**1,028**

15.2

Sales price variance		
Budgeted selling price	£10·00	
Actual selling price	£9·50	
	£0·50	adverse
Actual sales volume (units)	110,000	
	£55,000	adverse

Sales volume profit variance

Budgeted sales volume (units)	100,000	
Actual sales volume (units)	110,000	
	10,000	favourable
Standard profit per unit	£2	
	£20,000	favourable

15.3 Forecast sales volume for June, July and August is:

Month	Cumulative sales (units)	Monthly sales (units)
June	1,500	1,500
July	2,274	774
August	2,900	626

☑ Solution 16

(a) Production budget in units

	Quarter 1	Quarter 2	Quarter 3	Quarter 4	Total
Required by sales	2,250	2,050	1,650	2,050	8,000
Plus required closing inventory	615	495	615	375	375
Less opening inventory	−675	−615	−495	−615	−675
Production Budget	2,190	1,930	1,770	1,810	7,700

Raw materials purchases budget

Material B	Quarter 1 kg	Quarter 2 kg	Quarter 3 kg	Quarter 4 kg	Total kg
Required by production	6,570	5,790	5,310	5,430	23,100
Plus required closing inventory	2,605.50	2,389.50	2,443.50	2,011.50	2,011.50
Less opening inventory	−2,956.50	−2,605.50	−2,389.50	−2,443.50	−2,956.50
Material Purchases Budget	6,219.00	5,574.00	5,364.00	4,998.00	22,155.00
Value	£43,533.00	£39,018.00	£37,548.00	£34,986.00	£155,085.00

(b) If material A is in short supply during the coming year, X pic will need to source a different supplier or find a substitute material. If they are unable to do this, then they will have to make best use of the materials in scarce supply and focus their efforts on producing the product which maximises contribution per limiting factor. Rather than starting with the sales budget they will now need to start with the production budget due to the scarcity of material A as there will be a limit to how many units of output they can produce. The production budget therefore becomes the key budget factor which will drive the preparation of all budgets. X plc could also review any wastage that may be occurring and aim to reduce this.

(c) Operating statement

	Fixed Budget	Flexed Budget	Actual	Flexible Budget Variance
Activity	7,700	7,250	7,250	
Overheads	£	£	£	£
Variable	168,000	158,182	185,000	26,818 adverse
Fixed	112,000	112,000	105,000	7,000 favourable
Labour				
Skilled	462,000	435,000	568,750	133,750 adverse
Semiskilled	415,800	391,500	332,400	59,100 favourable
	1,157,800	1,096,682	1,191,150	94,468 adverse

(d) Incremental budgeting builds in any inefficiency contained in the previous year's budget as it simply takes the previous year's budget or actual results and adjusts for anticipated changes. Incremental budgeting does not encourage building the budget from zero and justifying each item of cost. It also does not allow for the changing nature of the business environment as it is inward looking.

ZBB does require each cost element to be specifically justified, as though the activities to which the budget relates were being undertaken for the first time, thereby avoiding the problems encountered with incremental budgeting.

(e) The linear regression method determines mathematically the regression line of best fit. When forecasting sales a series of historical values for sales volume that vary over time would be plotted on a graph and a time series may then reveal a trend or relationship. This trend or relationship can then be adjusted for variations, for example cyclical, seasonal, long-term trend and random variations. Once the trend line has been adjusted for such variations a forecast of future sales can be made. However, it should be noted that linear regression analysis assumes that the past is an indication of what will happen in the future.

The linear regression method for sales forecasting may be useful to X pic in that it could provide a base from which other adjustments can be made according to the state of the market, availability and costs of material and labour.

☑ Solution 17

(a) (i) Difference in standard wage rate = £1.20 per hour

Planning variance	(standard hours for actual output) × difference in wage rate
	680 × (900/600) × £1.20
	1,020 × £1.20
	£1,224 Adverse
Operational efficiency variance	(standard hours for actual output − actual hours) × revised wage rate
	(1,020 − 1,070) × £31.20
	50 × £31.20
	£1,560 Adverse

(ii) The major benefit of analysing the variances into planning and operational components is that the revised standard should provide a realistic standard against which to measure performance. Any variances should then be a result of operational management efficiencies and inefficiencies and not faulty planning.

(b) The main limitations of standard costing in the modern business environment are as follows:

- The business environment in the past was more stable whereas the modern business environment is more dynamic and subject to change. As a result if a business environment is continuously changing standard costing is not a suitable method because standards cannot be established for a reasonable period of time.
- The focus of the modern business environment is on improving quality and customer care whereas the environment in the past was focused on minimising cost.
- The life cycle of products in the modern business environment is shorter and therefore standards become quickly out of date.
- The increase in automation in the modern business environment has resulted in less emphasis on labour cost variances.

(c) The benefit of investigating a variance should never exceed the cost of investigation. However this can be difficult to ascertain and therefore a manager should decide to investigate a variance based on the following:

Size
Criteria will be laid down which state that variances which are of a certain amount or percentage will be investigated. This is an extremely simple method to apply but the cut off values can be subjective.

Controllable/Uncontrollable
There is little point in investigating a variance if it is uncontrollable. The cost in this situation would outweigh the benefits of investigation since there would be no benefit obtained.

Interrelationships
An adverse variance in one part of the business may result in a favourable variance elsewhere. These interdependencies must be considered when deciding on investigation. For example a favourable labour rate variance may result in an adverse efficiency variance where less skilled workers are employed, costing less, as a result the workers take longer to do the job and an adverse efficiency variance arises.

Type of standard
If a company sets an ideal standard this will usually lead to adverse variances. The manager will need to decide at what size of adverse variance an investigation should take place on such variances.

(d) Firstly G Group must consider the transfer pricing system. The system must provide information that motivates divisional managers to make good economic decisions not just for themselves but for the company as a whole. It should also provide information that is useful for evaluating the managerial and economic performance of the divisions and should ensure that divisional autonomy is not undermined.

If there is unlimited demand for the output of the two divisions in the market then the transfer price should equal the market price less any savings as a result of internal transfer. This then allows the divisions to report a profit on the transfers and will not cause any issue for the calculation of the bonus.

However, if there is a limit on the amount that can be sold on the external market then the divisions would be transferring at marginal cost as there is no opportunity cost. In this case they will simply cover the marginal cost and have no contribution towards fixed costs or profit. This will mean that if the bonus is awarded on profit the divisional manager will not receive a bonus despite the fact that they have made internal supplies.

Therefore the company must ensure that in order for decisions to remain goal congruent the bonus scheme must allow for internal transfers that impact on the divisions' ability to earn bonuses.

Other areas to consider when implementing a bonus scheme include:
- It should be clearly understood by all personnel involved;
- There should be no delay between the awarding of the bonus and the subsequent payment of the bonus;
- It should motivate the personnel;
- It should not cause sub-optimal behaviour;
- Controllable and uncontrollable costs and revenues should be identified separately.

(e) A manufacturing resource planning system involves the planning of raw materials, components, subassemblies and other input resources, such as machine capacity and labour, so that the system provides a fully integrated planning approach to the management of all the company's manufacturing resources. The quality of the data which sets the parameters within a manufacturing resource planning system drives the company's operations and determines the optimal production and purchasing plan.

In order to ensure that a manufacturing resource planning system operates effectively it is essential to have:

- A master production schedule, which specifies both the timing and quantity demanded of each of the top-level finished good items.
- A bill of materials file for each sub-assembly, component and part, containing details of the number of items on hand, scheduled receipts and items allocated to released orders but not yet drawn from inventories.
- A master parts file containing planned lead times of all items to be purchased and sub-assemblies and components to be produced internally.
- A master labour and machine capacity file which specifies both the timing and quantity demanded to achieve planned production levels.

The data identified above that is used to ensure the manufacturing resource planning system operates effectively can then be used in a standard costing system to set parameters for materials, labour and overhead capacity. These will then be used to measure performance through variance analysis.

(f) Just-in-time is a system whose objective is to produce or procure products or components as they are required by a customer or for use, rather than for inventory. A just-in-time system is a 'pull system' which responds to demand, in contrast to a 'push system', in which inventories act as buffers between the different elements of the system, such as purchasing, production and sales.

The traditional business environment is a 'push system' in which one process supplies parts to the next process without regard to the ability to continue work on those parts.

This extends onto producing finished goods inventory ready for sale to customers. Work in progress, inventory of raw materials and finished goods inventory are an inherent part of such a traditional system.

On the other hand a just in time system is described as a philosophy, or approach to management, as it encompasses a commitment to continuous improvement and the pursuit of excellence in the design and operation of the production management system. A JIT system operates in such a way that production and resource acquisition should be pulled by customer demand rather than being pushed by a planning process. A JIT based production operation responds quickly to customer demand and resources are acquired and utilised only when needed. A JIT system operates with little or no inventories and in order to be able to operate in this manner, an organisation must achieve excellence in the following areas:

- Productvion scheduling
- Supplier relations
- Plant maintenance
- Information systems
- Quality controls
- Customer relations

Solution 18

(a) The traditional management accounting performance measures are best suited to a stable environment, which is programmable. These measures include budgetary control and standard costing which relies upon the ability to be able to predict the future with some accuracy. Standards are frequently set based upon past performance, the assumption being that the past is a good predictor of the future.

With the increase in competition in world markets and the ever-increasing rate of change of technology, the manufacturing environment has had to become more flexible in order to meet customer needs. Rather than being able to have long batch runs of the same product the emphasis is on small batches and constant product innovation and a requirement to improve and monitor quality.

Traditional management accounting techniques to monitor performance, such as standard costing, are unable to provide the information required because of the need to constantly revise standards. The move to more mechanised and computerised processes has also made the traditional labour variances obsolete because of the insignificant proportion of direct labour in total product cost. Taking the specific example of small batch manufacture, traditional standard costing spreads the set-up costs across the batch so that each item within the batch has a share. With small batch manufacture, this cost becomes a much larger proportion of total cost. The traditional costing system also lays little emphasis on the cost of quality and hence the system is not able to provide the information required by management to control this important aspect of modern manufacture. It is, therefore, true to say that traditional management accounting performance measures are, at best, irrelevant and, at worst, misleading in the new manufacturing environment.

(b) There are a number of ways management accounting can adapt to the new environment. Traditional standard costing systems can be modified to allow for the flexibility required. If the industrial engineering schemes are mechanised so that standard times can be calculated for each batch, these can be multiplied by the standard cost rate to give the standard cost against which actual costs can be measured. The standard cost rate would not have labour as a separate part, but would consider it as part of variable overhead.

An alternative is to move to a system of actual costing using statistical control charts to monitor costs. This is where a confidence interval is set about the mean and any deviations outside this are investigated.

In both standard and actual costing the move away from labour as the cost driver has meant that other bases of charging costs to products have had to be found. Although such methods have been used for many years, particularly in the metals industry, it has been recently formalised into activity-based costing.

Non-financial performance measures are also being developed to complement or replace the traditional measures. This is particularly true in the area of quality where control is essential for long-term survival.

☑ Solution 19

(a) (i) The main features of zero-based budgeting (ZBB) include:
- Each element of cost within the budget has to be explicitly justified each year; this is in contrast to adding an increment to the previous year's budget to allow for inflation;
- ZBB forces judgements to be made on priorities as to whether expenditure should be included in the budget and at what level;
- In practice, ZBB often forces an organisation to consider whether activities are best out-sourced or undertaken internally;
- One method of implementing ZBB requires the activities of an organisation to be described as a set of decision packages. For example, in the case of a local government organisation, providing day-care for the elderly could be a decision package. All the decision packages are then ranked in priority order and resources are allocated accordingly;
- ZBB seeks to act as a control to increase efficiency, and so, this approach is used particularly in the public sector where competitive markets do not provide a control on efficiency.

(ii) There are problems in implementing this approach. Successful implementation of ZBB is extremely difficult. There are very few examples of 'successful' implementations of ZBB, and many disaster stories; it is high risk.
- Implementation will only be effective if the staff of J are convinced of the value of undertaking ZBB. Thus, to effect the necessary 'culture change', additional problems may arise and additional expenditure is usually required.
- Some of the judgements needed in the ZBB process are very sensitive, particularly regarding reducing indirect costs of J. These decisions can prove difficult to make and can be divisive.
- It is usually expensive in terms of staff time; empirical evidence indicates this is frequently more so than expected. The business case for implementing ZBB prepared by the new owners of J must allow for this.
- ZBB usually needs consultants to aid the implementation. This adds the further problems of managing consultants and may add substantial cost. The benefits of implementing ZBB must be substantial to outweigh these costs and difficulties.
- Important aspects of work can be omitted from the activities included in the ZBB exercise, yet will still have to be undertaken.

(b) (i) 95% of outcomes will be within $\pm$ 1.96 standard deviations of the mean.
Thus 95% of outcomes will be the range 90 kg $\pm$ (1.96 3 10 kg), that is, in the range 70.4–109.6 kg.
The actual weight of this batch was 110 kg.
Thus, this batch falls outside the 95% limit and the variance should be investigated.

(ii) Other factors that should ideally be included in the decision include (only two needed):
- Trend of months – if there is a clear trend moving away from the mean, the company may wish to investigate before adverse variances go beyond the 95% limit;
- The cost of investigating the variance compared with the benefits of correcting it;

- The reliability of the standards set. Where standards are not reliable, there is a higher likelihood that an outcome outside the 95% limit is not worth investigating.

(c) 'McDonaldisation' is the phenomenon of producing large numbers of very similar products or services, such that they can be produced by repetitive processes, and with the minimum amount of variation. These processes would be well understood and would involve very low levels of uncertainty. The consequences for budgeting at UV are as follows:

- Standards can be set with a high degree of certainty and without great expense;
- Actual results are likely to be very close to budget if management perform well, thus budgetary control through comparison with variances is a reasonable strategy;
- For UV, the provision of set meals at events conforms to these characteristics. It should be possible to set accurate flexible budgets, and thus it would be possible to have published price schemes that will produce reliable profit margins;
- However, this only applies to part of the output of UV. The provision of specific meals to order for an event does not have the 'McDonaldisation' characteristics and thus budgeting for this output of the service provision will have to be different.

(d) Idle time variance is 10 hours at £60 per hour = £600 Adverse
The mi x and efficiency variances are calculated excluding the idle time hours.

Actual hours at standard rate	Senior consultant	50 × £100	£5,000
	Junior consultant	45 × £60	£2,700
			£7,700

Thus, the labour efficiency variance is

£7,600 − £7,700 = £100 Adverse

Labour mix variance:

	Actual hours	Standard mix		Mix variance hours	Rate per hour	£
Senior consultant	50	40%	38	12 Adverse	£100	1,200 Adverse
Junior consultant	45	60%	57	12 Favourable	£60	720
Favourable	95		95			480 Adverse

(e) (i) ERPS are integrated IT systems that include all aspects of the operations of a company and the financial accounting system. ERPS may affect the budget-setting process in the following ways:

- They are complex planning systems that will show the financial consequences of operational plans, and thus they can significantly improve efficiency in the budget-setting process;
- It is much easier with ERPS to conduct sensitivity analysis and budgets can be flexed with more precision;
- Some complex budget relationships are expensive to model and change, but this cost is reduced with effective ERPS;

- Some have argued that the budget-setting process almost disappears with an effective ERPS as the budget figures are a natural consequence of the planning process.

(ii) ERPS also has consequences for the budgetary control process, including:
- Actual data can be calculated and compared with budget data within very short time; periods, in fact, virtually in real-time with some systems This can lead to intensification of the budgetary control process;
- Far less resources are needed to operate a budgetary control system although vast resources may be needed to implement an ERPS;
- Accountants may play a much reduced role, as much of the data required for budgetary control is automatically prepared by the ERPS that operational managers are using.

(f) The comment highlights the well-known issue of forecast versus motivation and control. When preparing the whole company's budget it is important to have a realistic forecast of what is likely to happen, particularly for cash, purchases, labour and capital budgets. However, for a budget to be effective for motivation, targets must be set that are challenging. It is also argued that for control purposes, the budget must be a realistic benchmark against which actual performance can be compared, that is, it must be close to a forecast.

The difficulty is that both of these objectives are valid and beneficial. Thus, the issue becomes whether one budget can do both tasks or whether companies need to choose which task the budget will be used for.

Virtually, all companies prepare one version of the budget that is a forecast. Some have two sets of budgets – one as a forecast and another as a motivating and controlling budget for managers. However, having two budgets can cause other problems. Some companies separate forecasting and motivation. Thus, they set a single budget as a forecast, but have an incentive scheme that rewards performance that exceeds budget, or they have separate incentive targets for motivation purposes.

☑ Solution 20

(a) (i) OAR = $12,800/2,000 = $6.40 per unit

Inventory is budgeted to increase, and therefore absorption costing profit will be higher than marginal costing profit.

Absorption costing profit = 5,700 + (600 × $6.40) = $9,540

(ii) Marginal costing focuses on contribution. This changes proportionally with sales volume, and therefore can be easily manipulated to help management with many aspects of planning, control and decision-making For example, 'what if scenarios can be rapidly generated.

Note: Any two relevant situations would be accepted.

(b)

	£	£
Standard cost for 2-day procedure		1,165
Length of stay variances		
Nursing costs: 1 day × 0.75 × £320 per day	240	

Space and food costs: 1 day × £175 per day	175	
Hospital overheads	110	525
Standard cost for 3-day stay		1,690
Drug and specific cost variances		205
Nursing staffing variance: 3 days × (0.9 − 0.75) × £320		144
Actual cost		2,039

Note: All variances are adverse.

(c)

		February	*March*	*April*
1	Standard cost of output (£)	132,000	61,200	109,200
2	Usage variance (£)	15,970	5,950	8,400
3	Standard cost of actual purchases (£)	147,970	67,150	117,600
4	Price variance (£)	12,300	4,500	6,200
	Usage % variance (2/1)	12.1%	9.7%	7.7%
	Price % variance (4/3)	8.3%	6.7%	5.3%

(d)

1. Standard costing and variance analysis is a post-mortem. Management needs 'real-time' information.
2. Standard costing variances tend to be on an aggregate basis – much more detailed information may be needed.
3. Standard costs can be viewed as the benchmark. In the modern business environment, the emphasis is on constant improvement.
4. In the modern business environment, flexibility and the rapid response to changing demands may be more of a measure of good performance than adherence to standard.
5. Product life cycles are shorter and hence standards will need to be constantly reviewed. This extra work may invalidate the worth of the standard-setting process.

   Note: Any three relevant reasons would be accepted.

(e) The underlying methodology is the same except that throughput accounting (TA) takes a more extreme view of contribution and regards direct materials as the only 'variable' cost.

Marginal costing (MC) is used in many situations including aspects of decision-making, planning and control.

MC and TA both focus on contribution (but because of their differing classification of variable costs, their definition of contribution will be different). TA is based on the ideas of the 'Theory of Constraints' and seeks to maximise profits by maximising throughput by identifying and, where possible, removing bottlenecks. Maximising throughput on a bottleneck is similar to the MC idea of maximising contribution per unit of scarce resource.

(f) *Examiner's note*: There were many measures which candidates could have suggested. Candidates were expected to provide a justification of the measures suggested.

   • *Detection of false claims.* Calculate the percentage of false claims to total claims. Compare this to previous periods. Obtain data from other similar organisations, trade journals and/or industry groups. The measure would highlight the effectiveness of the staff handling the claims and internal procedures and training.

- *Speed of processing claims*, log claims and record the time from receipt to settlement. Compare to previous periods. Register and investigate complaints from policy-holders. Obtain data from other similar organisations, trade journals and/or industry groups. The measure would reflect internal efficiency and customer focus.

For both areas, every effort should be made to identify best practice and to use that to establish targets that are accepted.

☑ Solution 21

(a) Variances are significant if they materially affect the performance of a company. They may be positive, in which case the company performance is significantly better than planned; or negative, in which case the company's performance is significantly worse than expected. The level of significance will, therefore, depend upon the size of the company or department being considered.

There are a number of factors that determine whether a variance is significant or not. Its size relative to the budget is one measure of significance usually expressed as a percentage. This, however, is not sufficient on its own, as the size of the budget may be so small that a relatively large percentage may be insignificant in absolute terms. Also, a variance that always has the same sign, that is, positive or negative, is more significant than one that varies randomly. It is, therefore, necessary to monitor the cumulative variance, in addition to that for the current period.

(b) Significant variances can be identified in a number of ways. The simplest and most widely used method is that already described in (a) above where a percentage level is set, say 10%, outside of which all variances are investigated. A refinement of this is to only investigate those variances that are also above a predetermined level, say, £100. This is so that the cost of investigation does not outweigh the benefit, that is,

Cost of investigation\future cost saving $\times$ probability of successful investigation

As noted in (a), such criteria should be applied to both the period and cumulative variances. A refinement of the above is to set control limits using statistical techniques. Previous data is analysed, assuming normal distribution, and the standard deviation is calculated. A control chart is then drawn showing results against control intervals of one, two or even three standard deviations from the expected value, in effect confidence intervals for the actual results against budget.

☑ Solution 22

AL offers 1.5% interest for 16 days

$$(100/98.5)^{(365/16)} - 1 = (1.015)^{22.813} - 1$$

$$= 40.4\% \text{ or } 41.2\% \text{ depending on rounding}$$

Section C – Long Questions

 Solution 23

(a) Standard cost of materials

$$0.65 \times £4 + 0.3 \times £6 + 0.2 \times £2.50 = £490 \, kg \text{ of FDN}$$

Standard cost of overheads

£3 kg of FDN

Standard cost of actual output

	£
Materials: 4,200 × 4.90	20,580
Overheads: 4,200 × 3	12,600
	33,180

Actual cost of actual output

	£
Materials	20,380
Overheads	12,600
	32,980

Variance analysis

	£	
Cost variances		
Materials	200	(F)
Overheads	–	

Standard overhead cost of output

	£
Deliveries: (4,200/4,000) × 10 × 400 = 10.5 × 400	4,200
Despatches: (4,200/4,000) × 40 × 200 = 42 × 200	8,400
	12,600

	£	
Activity variances		
Deliveries: (12 − 10.5) × 400	600	(A)
Despatches: (38 − 42) × 200	800	(F)
Expenditure variances		
Deliveries: 4,800 − (12 × 400)	–	
Despatches: 7,800 − (200 × 38)	200	(A)
Total	–	

(c) The main characteristic of an ABC system is that it is structured around the outputs of the operation, rather than the inputs. In designing an ABC system, one is not concerned primarily with the nature of the costs, but rather with their purpose. The information given in the question suggests that overhead costs are associated with the activities of receiving consignments and sending out orders. The cost drivers in this case appear to be the number of deliveries received and orders despatched.

The best approach to identifying appropriate activities and cost drivers is to interview a representative sample of employees, carrying out the support services at all levels in the organisation, and invite them to identify the relevant factors. If a clear and consistent view emerges, then this may be adopted; if not, a detailed analysis of the activity patterns of these employees may be required.

 ## Solution 24

(a)

Operating Statement

	£	
Budgeted profit	586,000	
Sales volume contribution variance	84,240	Favourable
	670,240	

Variance	£	
Sales price	129,710	Favourable
Material price		
A	43,000	Adverse
B	18,500	Favourable
C	5,875	Adverse
Material mix		
A	30,000	Favourable
B	8,000	Adverse
C	4,000	Adverse
Material yield	222,300	Favourable
Fixed production overheads expenditure	£35,000	Adverse
Total variances	304,635	Favourable
Actual profit	**974,875**	

Workings
Mix variance

	A kg	B kg	C kg	Total kg
Actual materials in standard mix	45,000	36,000	22,500	103,500
Actual materials in actual mix	43,000	37,000	23,500	103,500
Difference	2,000	−1,000	−1,000	
Standard price	£15	£8	£4	
Variance	£30,000	£8,000	£4,000	£18,000
	favourable	adverse	adverse	favourable

Yield variance

Standard output from material input (103,500/23)	4,500 units
Actual output	5,450 units
Yield	950 units
	×£234
	£222,300 favourable

Material price variance

	A	B	C	
Standard price per kg	£15.00	£8.00	£4.00	
Actual price per kg	£16.00	£7.50	£4.25	
	−£1.00	£0.50	−£0.25	
	43,000	37,000	23,500	
×no of kg	£43,000	£18,500	£5,875	£30,375
	adverse	favourable	adverse	adverse

(b)   **Report**

To: Production Manager
From: Management Accountant
Date: 21 November 2006
Title: Material Price, Mix and Yield Variances

This report interprets the material price, mix and yield variances and also discusses the advantages and disadvantages of calculating the materials mix and yield variances.

(i) The material price variance is adverse because materials A and C cost more than standard and more than offsetting the favourable variance on B. Material, mix and yield variances are inter-related and, as individual variances, they should not be interpreted in isolation. By changing the mix this has led to a favourable mix and yield variance. This indicates that the decision to use less of material A and more of B and C has worked in the company's favour. The mix was also more efficient than the standard mix because the yield variance was also favourable. It should be remembered that substitution of one material for another can only occur up to a point, otherwise the identity of the product or the quality of the product can be seriously impacted upon.

(ii) The material mix and yield variances are sub-divisions of the material usage variance. X Ltd produces an industrial component where a standard input mix is the norm, and recognisable individual components of input are combined during the production process to produce an output in which the individual items are no longer separately identifiable. X Ltd may have decided to vary the input mix because of a shortage of material and or in order to take advantage of an attractive input price on material B. Whether X Ltd's input mix is a standard or non-standard one, there is a possibility that the outcome from the process will differ from that which was expected, that is the yield, in this instance the yield has been favourable. By calculating the mix and yield variances, X Ltd highlights the different aspects of the production process and provides additional insights to help managers to attain the optimum combination of materials input. You should note that mix and yield variances are appropriate only to those production processes where managers have the discretion to vary the mix of materials and deviate from engineered input-output relationships.

If X Ltd had not calculated the mix and yield variances they would have just calculated material usage variances which demonstrates how much of the direct material total variance was caused by using a different quantity of a material, compared with the standard allowance for the production achieved. The usage variance does not consider how a mix of different materials would have impacted on the yield and would not provide managers with an insight to attain the optimum combination.

Should you require any further information, please do not hesitate to contact me.

Solution 25

(a)

Summary Statement for 6 months to 30 September 2003

	Cumulative actual to date	Cumulative budget to date	Total variance	Price-spending variance	Efficiency volume
	£	£	£	£	£
Production	29,600	30,000	400		
Costs	£	£	£	£	£
Materials	1,207,100	1,184,000	(23,100)	(1,100)	(22,000)
Labour	846,129	976,800	130,671	130,671	0
Variable overheads	455,000	444,000	(11,000)	(11,000)	0
Fixed overheads	738,000	710,400	(27,600)	(18,000)	(9,600)
Total costs	3,246,229	3,315,200	68,971	100,571	(31,600)

( ) = Adverse variance

Note: Alternative statements that summarise the performance of the Service Department would be acceptable.

(b)

Report to the Operations Director of Marshall Limited

Re: Performance of the Service Department for the 6 months to 30 September 2003. A summary performance statement is attached to this report. The main features are set out below, along with issues that require further explanation or information.

- There has been a rise, then fall in volumes. Is this seasonal variation, such as less services required during the summer, or the result of other factors, such as action from competitors in months 4 to 6? If the trend in the last 3 months continues, this could be a serious problem that needs to be addressed promptly.

- A favourable material usage variance, as occurred in month 2 must mean that some parts were not replaced during the service. Is this acceptable? There seems to be a general inefficiency in material usage. Is this caused by a lack of care by service engineers or by poor quality sets? The price variance – see below – does not indicate cheap parts are being purchased.

- Material prices are on a general upward path. Is there a general drift in material places? Is there a material shortage? Are there other suppliers offering a better price?

- Labour price is massively out of line with budget yielding large favourable variances. Is this caused by a mistake in the budget or an unexpected change in the price, for example using different grades/mix of labour? This variance is more than 13% of budgeted cost and thus must be investigated quickly and thoroughly.

- Labour efficiency gets seriously worse after month 4. Has something unusual happened to labour during this month, perhaps a dispute? Is this significantly worse labour efficiency linked to the fall in output over the same months?

- Month 4 is significantly out of line with other months. What happened? Was production disrupted; was there a labour dispute or supplier problems or did another factor affect the result? It is important to find satisfactory explanations for the results in this month and attempt to ensure this performance is not repeated.

- Only total variable overhead variance has meaning and reveals a worsening position after the disaster in month 4, giving further evidence for some unusual circumstances.

- Fixed overhead spending seems to come under control from month 5, but what caused the problems in the early months? Has management acted to remedy matters?

- The fixed overhead volume variance is purely technical and represents differences between planned and actual production.

- Overall costs are 2% below budget, but this apparently satisfactory position masks considerable variation. Nevertheless, the general performance of the Service Department has been close to budget.

☑ Solution 26

(a) DL Hospital Trust: Unit H budget – actual reconciliation – November 20X3

	£	£	£
Original budgeted cost			
Direct labour (20 × £2,000)			40,000
Variable overhead			25,000
Budgeted variable cost			65,000
Fixed overhead			35,000
			100,000
Flexed to actual activity level (£65,000 × 2/20)			6,500
Flexed budget cost (see note below)			106,500
	(F)	(A)	
Surgical team fees rate variance	2,600		
Surgical team efficiency variance		3,000	
Variable overhead expenditure variance	725		
Variable overhead efficiency variance		1,875	
Fixed overhead expenditure variance		1,950	
	3,325	6,825	3,500 (A)
Actual cost			110,000

Note: A solution might alternatively show an activity adjustment to budgeted cost of £10,000 combined with a fixed overhead volume variance of £3,500(F).

Surgical team fees rate variance

Actual cost − actual hours at standard cost per hour

£44,400 − (235 × £200) = £2,600(F)

Efficiency variable

Actual hours at standard cost per hour − standard cost of operations performed

£47,000 − (£2,000 × 22) = £3,000(A)

Variable overhead − expenditure variance

Actual cost − budgeted cost

£28,650 − (£200 × 235 × 0.625) = £725(F)

Efficiency variance

Budgeted cost − standard cost of operations performed

£29,375 − (£2,000 × 0.625 × 22) = £1,875(A)

Fixed overhead expenditure variance

Actual fixed overhead − budgeted fixed overhead

£36,950 − (£2,000 × 0.875 × 20) = £1,950(A)

(b) *To:*   Finance director
     From: Management account
     Date:
     Subject: Absorbing overheads on a labour base

Overheads, in the context of the hospital, can be attributed to surgical operations on a labour cost basis on the grounds that it is an economic method to operate, it is a widely understood method of dealing with overheads cost, and as long as the mix of staff involved in surgical procedures does not vary too much, a labour cost-based system may be acceptable. There are, however, some potentially serious problems associated with this system.

It assumes that labour cost behaviour is reasonably closely related to overhead behaviour. In reality, there may be a number of 'drivers' of different elements of overhead cost.

As indicated above, if the mix of specialisms (with different levels of remuneration) change, there will be an impact upon the overhead charge to particular operations.

The use of labour cost as a basis for attributing overhead cost to operations therefore begs the question, why? If all that is required is a system that is both easy and cheap to operate, it may prove adequate; but if there is to be any managerial use made of the information assembled, then it is unlikely that this method will provide an acceptable quality of information, and therefore a study of the alternatives (focusing, in particular, on the identification of the causes of different elements of cost and on the possibility of using multiple absorption bases) should be considered.

Singed: Management accountant

Solution 27

(a) (i) Current system

£880,000/£8 m = 11 % of list price of drugs supplied
Thus, Order A will have a charge of £1,200 × 0.11 = £132
Order B will have a charge of £900 × 0.11 = £99

   (ii) Proposed system
         Cost driver rates

Invoice costs

Charge per invoice = £70,000/8,000=	£8.75 per invoice
Charge per invoice line = £210,000/28,000=	£7.50 per line

Delivery costs

Charge per delivery trip = £40,000/1,000=	£40 per trip
So, for large package = £40/6=	£6.67
For small package = £40/12=	£3.33
Charge per delivery mile = £140,000/350,000=	£0.40 per mile

Other overheads allocated by orders (this is not a genuine cost driver)

£200,000/8,000=	£25 per order

Overhead costs	Order A	£	Order B	£
Invoice costs	1 × £8.75=	8.75	1 × £8.75 =	8.75
	2 × £7.50=	15.00	8 × £7.50 =	60.00
Packing		25.00		32.00
Delivery	1 × £3.33=	3.33	1 × £6.67 =	6.67
	8 × £0.40=	3.20	40 × £0.40=	16.00
Other overhead costs		25.00		25.00
Total charge for overheads		80.28		148.42

(b)

Report to the management of F plc on the implications of implementing an activity-based costing approach

From:	Management Accountant
Date:	May 2005

This report covers two issues: (i) an assessment of the strengths and weaknesses of the proposed activity-based costing approach; and (ii) recommendations for action, the Management of F pic might take.

(i) All budgeting systems have strengths and weaknesses, and these are in part related to the specific circumstances of the company. For F the following are relevant.

Strengths include:

- Better understanding of the cost structure and what is driving costs.
- Ability to set prices that relate to the actual resources consumed, which should result in few or no loss-making orders being accepted.
- Highlights where costs are being incurred which should lead to action to reduce activities that have high costs.
- Prices could be defended if challenged by customers.
- Out-sourcing decisions can be analysed more easily.

Weaknesses might include:

- The costs may exceed benefits.
- The activity data is still very aggregated and may not be detailed enough to reveal important cost behaviour, for example the high cost of the longest distance category might be distorted by some very long deliveries.
- There are still arbitrary elements in the ABC system, particularly other overhead costs which means care must be taken with the data.

(ii) The following recommendations could be made to the directors of F plc.

The present policy is cost based. This approach is simple and relatively cheap to operate. However, such a policy is unlikely to be optimal, and will only be viable where the company is able to sell all its output. Thus, assuming that price is not closely linked to demand, a pricing policy that does no more than simply recover overheads and produce a profit may be deemed satisfactory. In this case, although the current charge for overheads is simple and cheap to calculate, it does not reflect the actual costs incurred by each order.

The new activity-based costing (ABC) system produces a measure of cost that better reflects the resources that have been used. This new ABC system produces very different costs to the previous system. However, the new costing system used, although a very simple version of ABC, is probably too complex for a pricing system.

As the first step in a review, it would be instructive to check whether some orders are actually losing money. The activity-based cost analysis indicates that orders with many different products and those delivered over a long distance are expensive, in comparison with orders for a larger volume of few products with shorter delivery distances.

F will need to develop a pricing structure that would enable some of the key cost drivers to be reflected in the prices charged, and to let customers know the charge in advance.

Another possible strategy would be to stop accepting long distance orders by imposing a distance limit. It might be possible to out-source long distance deliveries, possibly along with a high charge for the long distance band in the charging table, as mentioned above.

The costs based on the number of items on the invoice become very high when multiple products are ordered. This needs careful review. Would better systems using newer technology reduce these invoice costs – this is highly likely.

Solution 28

(a) Production Planning and Development: operating statement for period ended 30 November 20X1 (traditional expense-based analysis)

	Budget £'000	Actual £'000	Variance £'000
Salaries	600	667.8	67.8 (A)
Supplies	60	53.0	7.0 (F)
Travel cost	120	127.2	7.2 (A)
Technology cost	100	74.2	25.8 (F)
Occupancy cost	120	137.8	17.8 (A)
Total	1,000	1,060.0	60.0 (A)

Production planning and Development: operating statement for period ended 30 November 20X1 (activity-based analysis)

	Budget £'000	Actual £'000	Variance £'000
Routeing/scheduling – new products	200	169.6	30.4 (F)
Routeing/scheduling – existing products	400	360.4	39.6 (F)
Remedial rerouteing/scheduling	50	127.2	77.2 (A)
Special studies – specific orders	100	84.8	15.2 (F)
Training	100	159.0	59.0 (A)
Management and administration	150	159.0	9.0 (A)
Total	1,000	1,060.0	60.0 (A)

(b) Advantages claimed for the use of activity-based budgeting may include the following:
- Resource allocation is linked to a strategic plan for the future, prepared after considering alternative strategies.
- Traditional budgets tend to focus on resources and inputs rather than on objectives and alternatives. In the question, the traditional budget focuses on overall expenditure on resources such as salaries and the overall expenditure variance.
- New high-priority activities are encouraged rather than focusing on the existing planning model. Activity-based budgeting focuses on activities. This allows the identification of the cost of each activity, for example, special studies. It facilitates focus on control of the resources required to provide the activity. It will also help where financial constraints exist, in that activities may be ranked and their importance considered, rather than arbitrary cuts being made in areas such as production planning and development.
- There is more focus on efficiency and effectiveness and the alternative methods by which they may be achieved. Activity-based budgeting assists in the operation of a total quality philosophy. Focus within individual activities can be on areas such as waste reduction, inefficiency removal and innovation in methods.
- It avoids arbitrary cuts in specific budget areas in order to meet overall financial targets. Activities 1, 2 and 4 in the budget in (i) are primary activities that add value to products. Activity 3 (remedial rescheduling) is a non-value-added activity that should be eliminated. Activities 5 and 6 (training and management) are secondary activities that support the primary activities. Efforts should be made to ensure that their objectives are achieved in an efficient manner at minimum cost.
- It tends to lead to increased management commitment to the budget process. This should be achieved since the activity analysis enables management to focus on the objectives of each activity. Identification of primary, secondary and non-value-added activities should also help in motivating management in activity planning control.

(c) The statement in (i) shows the budget vs. actual cost comparison for each activity. This indicates that cost has fallen in all three primary activities – development of routeing, existing routeing and special studies. Remedial rerouteing is double the budget level, which must be investigated since it is a non-value-added activity. Training cost has increased by 50% from budget. This may be related to the high level of remedial rerouteing where staff under training have not been performing efficiently.

For each activity, it is also possible to prepare a cost analysis that compares budget vs. actual resources for salaries, and so on, in a similar way to the overall traditional budget statement given in the question. This will enable investigation of factors such as why salary costs for the activity exceed budget by £x or why supplies are below budget by £y.

The cost information does not specify the cost driver for each activity and the budget vs. actual comparison of these. For example, staff hours are likely to be the cost driver for an activity such as routeing/scheduling, whereas for training the cost driver may be number of staff trained. It is also necessary to determine the efficient cost-driver level, for example, staff hours per individual route development for a new product. How does this compare with the actual staff hours per individual route development? Again, a comparison of budget cost vs. actual cost per staff member trained will give an indication of efficiency of provision of the activity.

A further aspect of performance measurement is to determine the 'root cause' of each cost driver. For example, the staff hours required per route designed may be linked to the level of technology and software systems used. The root cause of employee training may be high labour turnover due to poor career prospects or a stressful work environment. It is important that such root causes are identified, since continuous improvement of the provision of an activity will only be achieved through improvement in the factors that influence its incidence.

✓ Solution 29

When you are calculating the standard allowances for the actual production in part (b) you will need to use the concept of equivalent units for job 109. Since the job is 60% complete as regards labour, the standard labour hours for variance calculations will be 60% of the original standard hours forecast for the job.

(a) Most organisations are required to set the price of their goods or services in advance of manufacturing and/or supplying them. The pricing policy for a product must be developed taking full account of the anticipated market conditions. As part of this decision-making process it is necessary to estimate all the costs involved to determine the profit generated by the forecast sales. This requires the use of a predetermined overhead absorption rate (OAR).

The timeframe used for calculating the OAR is usually the next budget year. Taking such a timescale will tend to even out seasonal or market fluctuations in demand. For example, a gas supply company making monthly calculations of OAR would have a much lower OAR in the winter months than in the summer. These short-term OARs send the wrong pricing signals, suggesting that one might reduce price when demand is high and increase price when demand is low. Alternatively, if the price is held constant, the profit per unit will fluctuate with the seasons. The use of predetermined OARs will almost certainly result in over-or under-absorption. This is shown in variance analysis as the fixed overhead volume variance.

(b)

PSA Ltd – Cost control report for April

	Standard cost £	Actual cost £	Variance £
Labour	21,714	24,500	2,786 (A)
Hardwood	26,180	28,600	2,420 (A)
Softwood	8,640	9,200	560 (A)
Fixed overhead	8,272	7,800	472 (F)
Variable overheads	6,204	6,900	696 (A)
	71,010	77,000	5,990 (A)

Labour variances

	£	£
Operational efficiency (W1)	483 (A)	
Operational rate (W2)	1,400 (A)	
Planning (W3)	903 (A)	
	2,786 (A)	2,786

Hardwood variances

	£	
Operational usage (W4)	1,045 (A)	
Price (W5)	0	
Planning (W6)	1,375 (A)	
	2,420 (A)	5,206

Softwood variances

	£	£
Operational usage (W7)	1,120 (A)	
Price (W8)	400 (A)	
Planning (W9)	960 (F)	
	560 (A)	5,766

Overhead variances

	£	
Variable overhead (W10)	696 (A)	
Fixed overhead volume (W11)	272 (F)	
Fixed overhead expenditure (W12)	200 (F)	
	224 (A)	5,990

Workings

Labour

Std hours = 1,000 + 600 + (780 × 60%) = 2,068, actual hours = 2,200
Actual cost per hour £11.136
Revised std hours 2,068/0.96 = 2,154

(W1)	(2,154 − 2,200) × 10.5	=	483 (A)
(W2)	2,200 × (11.136 − 10.5)	=	1,400 (A)
(W3)	(2,068 − 2,154) × 10.5	=	903 (A)

Hardwood

Std volume = 200 + 180 + (120 × 80%) = 476, actual volume = 520
Actual price 28,600/520 = £55 per cu.m.
Revised std volume 476/0.95 = 501

(W4)	(501 − 520) × 55	=	1,045 (A)
(W5)	(55 − 55) × 520	=	0
(W6)	(476 − 501) × 55	=	1,375 (A)

Softwood

Std use = 320 + 400 + (300 × 80%) = 960 cu. m., actual use = 1,100 cu. m.
Actual price 9,200/1,100 = £8.364 cu. m.

(W7)	(960 − 1,100) × 8	=	1,120 (A)
(W8)	(8.00 − 8.364) × 1,100	=	400 (A)
(W9)	960 × (9 − 8)	=	960 (F)

Overheads

'The OARs are £3 per hour for variable O/Hs (that is, £72,000/24,000 hours) and £4 per hour for fixed O/Hs (that is £96,000/24,000 hours). Consequently:

(W10) Variable O/H variance is (2,068 hours × £3) − £6,900 = £696 (A)
(W11) Fixed O/H volume variance is (2,068 × £4) − £8,000 = £272 (F)
(W12) Fixed O/H expenditure variance is £8,000 − £7,800 = £200 (F)

> Note: it is possible to undertake more detailed analysis on both the variable O/H variance and the fixed O/H volume variance – but the requirement does not specify this.'

(c) The traditional accounting system presently used by PSA Ltd follows all the costs as they are incurred for each product type, job or unit produced. These costs are classified and recorded forming an extensive database, which allows tight financial control to be exercised on the production process.

Specifically, PSA Ltd prepares a detailed monthly variance analysis as part of its control procedures. Its existing system is both flexible and powerful in that it incorporates adjustable standards to cater for external influences outside the control of PSA Ltd, for example the quality of labour or materials. The disadvantage of this system is that it is time-consuming and expensive to enter and manipulate the vast amount of data involved. In a modern AMT/JIT environment it may not be necessary to use such a complex system if

- all forms of stock inventory (raw materials, WIP and finished products) are kept at very low levels;
- production is highly automated and reliable, leading to low labour costs and efficient use of labour time;
- long-term relationships with suppliers ensure reliable delivery and fixed price and quality specifications.

Under these conditions, there will be little variation of input prices or efficiencies and therefore insignificant cost variations. Thus, there would be no need to use the traditional accounting technique, and backflush accounting may be used instead. The CEVIA *Official Terminology* defines backflush accounting as 'a method of costing, associated with a JIT production system, which applies cost to the output of a process. Costs do not mirror the flow of products through the production process, but are attached to output produced (finished goods stock and cost of sales), on the assumption that such back-flushed costs are a realistic measure of the actual costs incurred.' Thus, conversion costs are only attached to products when they are completed. This system only uses raw, in-process and finished goods accounts, which saves costs by reducing the amount of data required and the frequency of data entry, for example data on materials used only enters the system when a piece of work is completed. However, this system does not enable the valuation of WIP nor any variance analysis.

The variances for PSA Ltd are significant for efficiency of inputs (labour and materials) and there is also a noticeable change in WIP, and the price of inputs. If this is typical, then the proposal should be rejected, as backflush accounting is unsuitable. Rapier, like many consultants, may be too concerned with selling its services than with truly serving its customers.

Solution 30

(a) *Report to the operations manager of S Limited on performance for the period September to December*

From: Management Accountant
Date: December 2004

Four months is not a long period to recognise trends, but it is much better than a single month. The trends and significant features for this period include:

Output has fallen distinctly during the period. There are probably seasonal factors here. It is likely that more of these systems will be sold in Summer than in early Winter. It is also possible these differences are expected variations around the 1000 units per month budget? Were there some especially large contracts in September and October? This is not directly the responsibility of the operations manager but it will affect the operating results.

Material usage (efficiency) has varied over the 4 months, with October and December being poor. This is not related to volume, and so other explanations must be sought. One batch of systems has been more difficult to install and sometimes require additional or replacement parts. It would be important to ascertain whether other problems of material efficiency are linked to certain systems, certain fitters or specific stages of the installation process.

Material price – the buying in cost of the basic systems has risen over the 4 months. It appears that part of this increase has been the result of exchange movements. It would be important to quantify this effect. It would also be important to ascertain whether there are alternative sources. Have purchasing staff been active in seeking alternative sources? It might be possible to increase prices to reflect the rising cost, although this may be limited by its competitors or the firm's strategy, for example, to keep prices competitive to build market share.

The labour rate is higher than standard for all months and is deteriorating further. This clearly needs investigation. The most likely cause appears to be problems with keeping skilled staff and average labour rates may have risen to help retain staff. This may also have been caused by bad budgeting, or there may have been unexpected pay rises. As volumes have fallen during the months when hourly labour rates have risen, this rise is unlikely to have been caused by overtime payments.

More worrying than the rate variances are the labour efficiency variances that are also deteriorating. This may indicate that the cause of the higher wage rates is not the use of a higher proportion of skilled workers at higher wage rates. The problems with high staff turnover may have resulted in more staff learning the job and taking more time. Another possible cause is that fitters are taking longer on each vehicle as the monthly volumes are decreasing. This would indicate that labour is not actually a variable cost, although standard costing systems usually assume that it will be. Another explanation to be explored is whether the batch with the incorrect adapters has led to increased labour time being used. It might be that the average labour time is not as expected, purely as a consequence of the 25% variation that is known to occur.

For variable overheads only the total variable overhead variance has any real meaning. This also shows poor performance in November and December. This might indicate that variable overheads are not fully variable and as volumes fall, the variable overheads fall proportionately less.

A similar deteriorating pattern is seen with the fixed overhead spending variance. It is usually impossible to ascertain the causes of this without detailed investigation, as many different items of cost are included in this category. In this case it is clear that some of the main fixed costs have risen during the period, and these increases may not have been budgeted. It is important to enquire whether there has been effective control of costs by the department managers, although it also important to distinguish those costs where these managers have little control, such as rent, rates and insurance.

Overall there seems to be a worsening of operating performance in November and December, with no obvious cause apparent in the data. The total adverse variance is only 4.4% of the total standard cost and may not in itself require detailed investigation. However, this total includes some individual variances that are much larger in percentage terms, and these do need investigation. There are hints that lower volumes may be playing a part, and also hints that cost control needs to be tighter. As always, detailed questions will have to be asked to ensure that the causes of rising costs are understood. It may then be possible to manage these costs and reduce future costs.

The points above mention detailed additional information that would be helpful in assessing the performance for this period. There is other more general further information that would be helpful, including departmental information, market data, operating and quality data in physical units and details of the nature of the standards.

(b) *Report to the operations manager*

Subject: Ways to increase motivation and improve performance
From: Management Accountant
Date: December 2004

Motivation and performance improvement are complex subjects. Many aspects of the firm interact to produce the overall motivation for each individual employee. It is possible to use the budgeting system to increase motivation and improve performance. The following are possible means to achieve this in S Limited:

- Set budgets with the participation of managers. It may be possible do this in conjunction with an initiative to establish teams of fitters that have some autonomy over how they organise their work. There is evidence that this approach frequently produces improved results, but this is not guaranteed.
- Attempt to achieve acceptance of the standards in the budget. Participation is seen as one way to do this. Other approaches are through consultation and clear explanation to staff.
- Give clear and rapid feedback to the first-line managers and supervisors/team leaders. There is strong evidence that this improves motivation as people are keen to know how well they are doing and this reinforces any motivation to perform well.
- Link with appropriate incentives. It may be beneficial to introduce some incentive scheme linked to achieving the budget, but note that too strong a link will

lead to gaming behaviour. There is good evidence that incentives can improve performance, but also much evidence that where this emphasis is strong obtaining the reward becomes the objective and this may be achieved without making overall long run improvements in performance. For S Limited it would be very damaging for budgets to be met at the cost of damaging customer satisfaction.

- Encourage interchange between departments and teams, possibly by company-wide incentives not department-based incentives. This is particularly important where real improvements can best be achieved through improved cooperation.

- It may be important to note clearly the controllable and non-controllable elements within the budget. For example, the batch of systems that were difficult to fit was not the result of a decision by the fitters. There are strong arguments that managers should only be held responsible for performance where they have control, and that holding managers responsible for non-controllable results can be demotivating.

 ## Solution 31

(a) Total production cost:

Car X = $40,000 (standard unit cost from the table showing information for the cost of sales)

Car Y = $47,000

Fixed production overhead = $35,000,000

Budgeted machine hours = $(1,100 \times 200) + (1,600 \times 300) = 700,000$ machine hours

Fixed production overhead absorption rate = $\$35,000,000/700,000 = \$50$ per machine hour.

	Car X $ per car	Car Y $ per car
Total production cost	40,000	47,000
Fixed overhead absorbed	10,000	15,000
Variable production cost per car	30,000	32,000

Marginal costing operating statement – year ending 30 June 2008

	Car X $ 000	Car Y $ 000	Total $ 000
Sales	52,500	105,000	157,500
Variable production costs	30,000	56,000	86,000
Variable administration costs	6,300	12,600	18,900
Contribution	16,200	36,400	52,600
Specific fixed costs			
Marketing	2,000	4,000	6,000
Contribution to general fixed costs	14,200	32,400	46,600
General fixed costs			
Production			35,000
Administration			10,000
Profit			**1,600**

(b) The difference in the profit figures will be caused by the fixed production overheads that are absorbed into closing inventories. Changes in inventory levels will determine the amount of fixed production overheads that are 'moved' into the next accounting period and not charged in this period. If inventory levels increase, the absorption costing profit will be higher than the profit calculated using marginal costing.

	Car X	Car Y
Opening inventory (units)	200	250
Closing inventory (units)	300	100
Change in inventory (units)	+100	−150
Marginal profit will be	lower	higher
Fixed production overhead per car	$10,000	$15,000
Total difference in profits	$1,000,000	$2,250,000

Reconciliation

	$ 000
Absorption costing profit	350
Car X: inventory impact	(1,000)
Car Y: inventory impact	2,250
Marginal costing profit	1,600

(C)

Activity	Cost Driver	Calculation of drivers	Drivers
Machining costs	Machine hours	700,000	700,000
Set up costs	No. of production runs	(1,100/10) + (1,600/40)	150
Quality inspections	No. of inspections	(110 × 20) + (40 × 80)	5,400
Stores receiving	No. of deliveries	492 + 900	1,392
Stores issues	No. of issues	4,000 + 7,000	11,000

Activity	$000	Driver	Cost per driver
Machining costs	7,000	700,000	$10 per machine hour
Set up costs	12,000	150	$80,000 per set up
Quality inspections	7,020	5,400	$1,300 per inspection
Stores receiving	3,480	1,392	$2,500 per delivery
Stores issues	5,500	11,000	$500 per issue

	Car X		Car Y	
	Driver	$ 000	Driver	$ 000
Machining costs	220,000	2,200	480,000	4,800
Set up costs	110	8,800	40	3,200
Quality inspections	2,200	2,860	3,200	4,160
Stores receiving	492	1,230	900	2,250
Stores issues	4,000	2,000	7,000	3,500
Total overhead		17,090		17,910
Direct costs		33,000		51,200
Total production costs		50,090		69,110
Cars produced		1,100		1,600
Cost per car		**$ 45,536**		**$ 43,194**

(d)

Report

To: Production Director
From: Management Accountant
Date: 22 May 2007

Subject: Activity-based Budgeting – Performance Evaluation

As you are aware we are considering the implementation of an activity based costing system and moving away from the traditional absorption costing system which we currently operate.

There are many potential benefits associated with implementing activity based budgeting (ABB) for performance evaluation. Please find below an outline of some of the benefits that can be achieved from ABB.

Preparing budgets using a traditional absorption costing approach involves presenting costs under functional headings, that is, costs are presented in a manner that emphasises their nature. The weakness of this approach is that it gives little indication of the link between the level of activity of the department and the cost incurred. In contrast, activity based budgeting provides a clear framework for understanding the link between costs and the level of activity. This would allow us to evaluate performance based on the activity that drives the cost.

The modern business environment has a high proportion of costs that are indirect and the only meaningful way of attributing these costs to individual products is to find the root cause of such costs, that is, what activity is driving these costs. The traditional absorption costing approach does not provide this level of detail as costs under this system are attributed to individual products using a volume related measure. For our company this is machine hours which results in an arbitrary product cost. This makes it difficult to hold individual managers accountable for variances that arise. Whereas with an activity based costing approach responsibility can be broken down and assigned accordingly and individual managers can provide input into the budgeting process and subsequently be held responsible for the variances arising.

There is greater transparency with an ABB system due to the level of detail behind the costs. The traditional absorption costing approach combines all of the overheads together using a machine hour basis to calculate an overhead absorption rate and uses this rate to attribute overheads to products. ABB will drill down in much more detail examining the cost and the driver of such costs and calculates a cost driver rate which will be used to assign overheads to products. Therefore ABB has greater transparency than absorption costing and allows for much more detailed information on overhead consumption and so on. This then lends itself to better performance evaluation.

I would like to conclude that the traditional absorption costing approach to product costing does not enable us to provide a satisfactory explanation for the behaviour of costs. In contrast ABB will provide such details which will allow us to have better cost control, improved performance evaluation and greater manager accountability.

If you require any further information please do not hesitate to contact me.

 Solution 32

(a)

Cash Budget	Month 1	Month 2	Month 3	Total
	£	£	£	£
Sales receipts	2,940	10,180	15,545	28,665
Capital injection	16,250			16,250
Total receipts	**19,190**	**10,180**	**15,545**	**44,915**
Outflow				
Materials	0	3,515	3,420	6,935
Labour	6,105	5,940	6,666	18,711
Variable overhead	1,332	2,184	2,318	5,834
Fixed overhead	3,750	5,625	5,625	15,000
Total Outflow	**11,187**	**17,264**	**18,029**	**46,480**

Inflow-Outflow	8,003	(7,084)	(2,484)	(1,565)
Bal b/fwd	0	8,003	919	0
Bal c/fwd	8,003	919	(1,565)	(1,565)

Workings

Sales receipts	1	2	3
Sales units	1,500	1,750	2,000
	£	£	£
Selling price	10	10	10
Sales	15,000	17,500	20,000
Paid in month – 20%	3,000	3,500	4,000
Discount paid in month 2%	−60	−70	−80
45% in the following month		6,750	7,875
25% in 3rd month			3,750
Receipts	**2,940**	**10,180**	**15,545**

Production	1	2	3	4
	units	units	units	units
Required by sales	1,500	1,750	2,000	2,100
Opening inventory		(350)	(400)	
	1,500	1,499	1,600	
Closing inventory	350	400	420	
Production	1,850	1,800	2,020	
Material price	£1·90	£1·90	£1·90	
Material cost	£3,515	£3,420	£3,838	
Payment		**£3,515**	**£3,420**	

Labour			
Production units	1,850	1,800	2,020
Rate per unit	£3·30	£3·30	£3·30
Payment	£6,105	£5,940	£6,666

Variable Overhead			
Production units	1,850	1,800	2,020
Rate per unit	£1·20	£1·20	£1·20
Variable overhead cost	£2,220	£2,160	£2,424
Payment	£	£	£
60% in month	1,332	1,296	1,454
40% in following month		888	864
Payment	**1,332**	**2,184**	**2,318**

Fixed overhead	6,250	6,250	6,250
Payment			
60% in month	3,750	3,750	3,750
30% in following month		1,875	1,875
Payment	**3,750**	**5,625**	**5,625**

(b) (i)

	Month 1	Month 2	Month 3
£1.50			
£1.50 − £1.90	£0.40	£0.40	£0.40
Production units	1,850	1,800	2,020
Saving	£740	£720	£808
Saving		£740	£720
Total cash benefit	£1,460		
Current cash flow at £1.90	£(1,565)		
Revised cash flow at £1.50	**£(105)**		

(ii)

	Month 1	Month 2	Month 3
£2.20			
£2.20 − £1.90	£0.30	£0.30	£0.30
Production units	1,850	1,800	2,020
Additional cost	£555	£540	£606
Payment		£555	£540
Total additional payment	£1.095		
Current cash flow at £1.90	£(1,565)		
Revised cash flow at £2.20	**£(2,660)**		

(C)

To: Management
From: Management Accountant
Date: 22 May 2007
Subject: 'What if' analysis and cash budgets

This report addresses the benefits or otherwise of 'what if' analysis in relation to cash budgets. When there is a degree of uncertainty concerning elements incorporated within a budget 'what if' analysis allows us to revise the budgets on the basis of a series of varied assumptions.

In preparing the cash budgets we have identified that there is a degree of uncertainty concerning the direct material cost. We have used assumptions in part (b) to perform some calculations to estimate the effect of this uncertainty on the budgeted cash flow. The results were as follows:

Direct material cost per component	Increase/(decrease) in cash flow	Budgeted cash flow
£2·20	(£1,095)	(£2,660)
£1·50	£1,460	(£105)
£1·90		(£1,565)

If we perform some 'what if' analysis around these figures we can determine that a direct material cost of £2.20, that is, a 16% increase in material cost, results in a negative cash flow of − £2,660. This is a 70% increase in the closing cash negative balance. A direct material cost of £1.50, that is, a 21% decrease in direct material cost, results in a revised cashflow of − £105. This is a 93% reduction in the closing cash negative balance. The benefits of 'what if' analysis are that it allows us to:

- assess how responsive the cash flow is to changes in variables. Therefore we can assess how sensitive the variable is to changing conditions. From our calculations above obviously if the material cost increases it has a significant impact on the closing cash position;
- review critical variables to assess whether or not there is a strong possibility of the event occurring which leads to a negative cash flow;
- assess the variables that are most sensitive. These are the variables which cause the greatest variation with the lowest percentage change. It is important for the founders to pay particular attention to such variables and carefully monitor them.

It should however be noted that there are serious limitations when using 'what if' analysis. Two of the major ones are as follows.

- The changes in key variables are isolated whereas the management will be more interested in the effect on the cash flow of two or more key variables changing;
- There is no indication of the likelihood of a key variable changing and therefore the use of 'what if analysis is limited.

Should you require any further analysis or information please do not hesitate to contact me.

 Solution 33

(a)

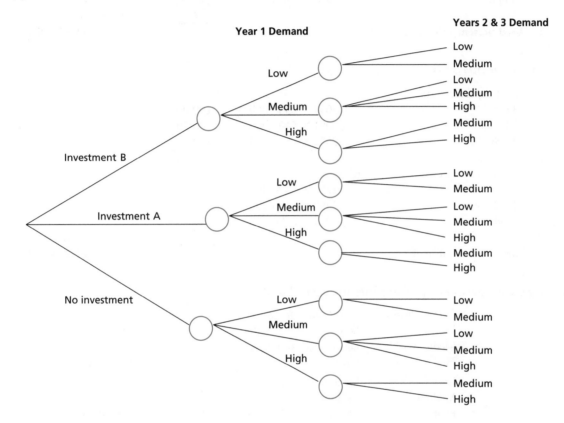

(b)

Investment in Facility B

Year 0 cost		£800,000	£800,000
Year 1 expected cost:			
Low	30% × £300,000 =	£90,000	
Medium	50% × £350,000 =	£175,000	
High	20% × £400,000 =	£80,000	
		£345,000	£345,000
Years 2 & 3 expected cost per year:			
Low	27% × £300,000 =	£81,000	
Medium	44% × £350,000 =	£154,000	
High	29% × £400,000 =	£116,000	
		£351,000	× 2 years = £702,000
Total present value of cost			**£1,847,000**

Investment in Facility A

Year 0 cost			£500,000	£500,000
Year 1 expected cost:				
Low	30% × £250,000 =	£75,000		
Medium	50% × £350,000 =	£175,000		
High	20% × £500,000 =	£100,000		
		£350,000		£350,000
Years 2 & 3 expected cost per year:				
Low	27% × £250,000 =	£67,500		
Medium	44% × £350,000 =	£154,000		
High	29% × £500,000 =	£145,000		
		£366,500	× 2 years = £733,000	
Total present value of cost				**£1,583,000**

No further investment

Year 1 expected cost:				
Low	30% × £300,000 =	£90,000		
Medium	50% × £400,000 =	£200,000		
High	20% × £550,000 =	£110,000		
		£400,000		£400,000
Years 2 & 3 expected cost per year:				
Low	27% × £300,000 =	£81,000		
Medium	44% × £400,000 =	£176,000		
High	29% × £550,000 =	£159,500		
		£416,000	× 2 years = £833,000	
Total present value of cost				**£1,233,000**

Note: Calculation of probabilities for years 2 and 3

Year 1 demand	Year 2 and 3 demand		Probability	
Low	Low	0.3 × 0.4	0.12	
Medium	Low	0.5 × 0.3	0.15	
High	Low	0.2 × 0.0	0.00	**Total 0.27**
Low	Medium	0.3 × 0.6	0.18	
Medium	Medium	0.5 × 0.4	0.20	
High	Medium	0.2× 0.3	0.06	**Total 0.44**
Low	High	0.3 × 0.0	0.00	
Medium	High	0.5 × 0.3	0.15	
High	High	0.2 × 0.7	0.14	**Total 0.29**

On purely financial grounds, using the expected cost basis, no further investment should be undertaken.

(c) By not undertaking further investment to increase the ability of the health clinic to service the increasing levels of demand the manager is becoming reliant on the use of other facilities that are not within her direct control. This could lead to a number of problems concerning the quality of the services provided, the reliability of the external service provision, and the vulnerability of the health clinic to increasing fees being charged by the external facility providers.

Furthermore the employees of the health clinic may become less motivated as they see that there is a tendency to utilise external facilities rather than invest within the business. This may illustrate a tendency towards short-term cost control to the detriment of the operation of the health clinic in the longer term.

Solution 34

Tips

- A straightforward question that involves probability theory and the calculation of expected values.
- Note that part (b) requires the maximum sum per annum. Don't forget to multiply the amount per concert by the number of concerts each year.

(a) (i) **Scenario 1**

Expected demand = 350 tickets per concert

Scenario 2

	Probability P	Demand X	EV
Popular artistes	0.45	500	225
Lesser known artistes	0.30	350	105
Unknown artistes	0.25	200	50
			380

Expected demand = 380 tickets per concert

(ii) Payoff table showing profit (W1, W2, WS3)

		Demand		
		200	350	500
	200	120	120	120
	300	(57)	225	225
Purchase level	400	(204)	219	360
	500	(246)	177	600

Expected values:

	EV
200 tickets 120 × 1	120
300 tickets (57) × 0.25 + 225 × 0.75	154.5
400 tickets (204) × 0.25 + 219 × 0.3 + 360 × 0.45	176.7
500 tickets (246) × 0.25 + 117 × 0.3 + 600 × 0.45	261.6

Scenario 1

If demand is 350 tickets on average, the ticket agent can purchase 200, 300, 400 or 500 tickets. The expected profits will be £120, £225, £219 or £177 respectively.

Optimum purchase level is 300 tickets per concert. This would give an expected profit of £225 per concert.

Scenario 2

The optimum purchase level is 500 tickets per concert, which will give an expected profit of £261.60 per concert.

(b) If demand is going to be 200 tickets for a concert then the optimum purchase level would be 200 tickets and the expected profit would be £120 per concert.

Similarly, if demand is going to be 350 tickets then the best profit would be £225 and if demand is going to be 500 then the best profit would be £600.

If the ticket agent has perfect information he will always make the best decision.

Expected profit	$= 120 \times 0.25 + 225 \times 0.3 + 600 \times 0.45$
	$= £367.50$ given perfect information.
Value of perfect information	$= £367.50 - £261.60$
	$= £105.90$
Annual value $= £105.90 \times 60$	$= £6,354$

Workings

(W1) Profit per ticket at different purchase levels

Purchase level	Discount	Profit per ticket sold
200	20%	$20\% \times £3 = 60p$
300	25%	$25\% \times £3 = 75p$
400	30%	$30\% \times £3 = 90p$
500	40%	$40\% \times £3 = £1.20$

(W2)

Purchase level	Demand	Sales
200	200	200
200	350	200
200	500	200
300	200	200
300	350	300
300	500	300
400	200	200
400	350	350
400	500	400
500	200	200
500	350	350
500	500	500

(W3) Each profit calculation consists of:

1. the profit of the units sold;
2. the cost of the units unsold and returned;
3. the value of the returns.

Value of returns $= £3.00 \times 60\% \times 10\% = 18$ p per return

Buy 200 demand 200:	Sales 200 tickets $\times$ 60 p $= £120$
Buy 200 demand 350:	Sales 200 tickets $\times$ 60 p $= £120$
Buy 300 demand 200:	Sales 200 tickets and returns 100 tickets

	£
Sales 200 tickets $\times$ ($£3.00 - £2.25$)	150
Returns 100 tickets $\times$ 18 p	18
	168
Cost of returns 100 tickets $\times$ £2.25 (30% disc)	(225)
	(57)

Solution 35

Tip

- When you are calculating the standard allowances for the actual production in part (b) you will need to use the concept of equivalent units for job 109. Since the job is 60 per cent complete as regards labour, the standard labour hours for variance calculations will be 60 per cent of the original standard hours forecast for the job.

(a) Most organisations are required to set the price of their goods or services in advance of manufacturing and/or supplying them. The pricing policy for a product must be developed taking full account of the anticipated market conditions. As part of this decision-making process it is necessary to estimate all the costs involved to determine the profit generated by the forecast sales. This requires the use of a predetermined overhead absorption rate (OAR).

The timeframe used for calculating the OAR is usually the next budget year. Taking such a timescale will tend to even out seasonal or market fluctuations in demand. For example, a gas supply company making monthly calculations of OAR would have a much lower OAR in the winter months than in the summer. These short-term OARs send the wrong pricing signals, suggesting that one might reduce price when demand is high and increase price when demand is low. Alternatively, if the price is held constant, the profit per unit will fluctuate with the seasons. The use of predetermined OARs will almost certainly result in over-or under-absorption. This is shown in variance analysis as the fixed overhead volume variance.

(b) *PSA Ltd – Cost control report for April*

	Standard cost	Actual cost	Variance	
	£	£	£	
Labour	21,714	24,500	2,786	ADV
Hardwood	26,180	28,600	2,420	ADV
Softwood	8,640	9,200	560	ADV
Fixed overheads	8,272	7,800	472	FAV
Variable overheads	6,204	6,900	696	ADV
	71,010	77,000	5,990	ADV

Labour variances

	£		£
Operational efficiency (W1)	483	ADV	
Operational rate (W2)	1,400	ADV	
Planning (W3)	903	ADV	
	2,786	ADV	2,786

Hardwood variances

	£		£
Operational usage (W4)	1,045	ADV	
Price (W5)	0		
Planning (W6)	1,375	ADV	
	2,420	ADV	5,206

	£		
Operational usage (W7)	1,120	ADV	
Price (W8)	400	ADV	
Planning (W9)	960	ADV	
	560	ADV	5,766

Overhead variances

800		FAV	
Expenditure (W11)	100	ADV	
Efficiency (W12)		ADV	
	224	ADV	5,990

Workings

Labour

Std hours = 1,000 + 600 + (780 × 60%) = 2,068, actual hours = 2,200
Actual cost per hour £11.136

Actual price $\dfrac{9,200}{1,100}$ = £8.364 per cu.m.

(W1)	(2,154 − 2,200) × 10.5	= 483 ADV
(W2)	2,200 × (11.136 − 10.5)	= 1,400 ADV
(W3)	(2,068 − 2,154) × 10.5	= 903 ADV

Hardwood

Std volume = 200 + 180 + (120 × 80%) = 476, actual volume = 520

Actual price $\dfrac{28,600}{520}$ = £55 per cu.m.

Revised std volume 476/0.95 = 501

(W4)	(501 − 520) × 55	= 1,045 ADV
(W5)	(55 − 55) × 520	= 0
(W6)	(476 − 501) × 55	= 1,375 ADV

Softwood

Std use = 320 + 400 + (300 × 80%) = 960 cu. m., actual use = 1,100 cu. m.

Actual price $\dfrac{9,200}{1,100}$ = £8.364 per cu.m.

(W7)	(960 − 1,100) × 8	= 1,120 ADV
(W8)	(8.00 − 8.364) × 1,100	= 400 ADV
(W9)	960 × (9 − 8)	= 960 FAV

Overheads

Monthly plan	2,000 labour hours × £4 = £8,000	
Revised plan	2,068 labour hours	
Actual	2,200 labour hours × £3 = £6,600	
(W10)	(2,200 − 2,000) × 4	= 800 FAV
(W11)	Fixed overhead expenditure variance	= 8,000 − 7,800 = 200 FAV
	Variable overhead expenditure variance	= 6,600 − 6,900 = 300 ADV
(W12)	Fixed overhead efficiency variance	= (2,068 − 2,200) × 4 = 528 ADV
	Variable overhead efficiency variance	= (2,068 − 2,200) × 3 = 396 ADV

(c) The traditional accounting system presently used by PSA Ltd follows all the costs as they are incurred for each product type, job or unit produced. These costs are classified and recorded forming an extensive database, which allows tight financial control to be exercised on the production process.

Specifically, PSA Ltd prepares a detailed monthly variance analysis as part of its control procedures. Its existing system is both flexible and powerful in that it incorporates adjustable standards to cater for external influences outside the control of PSA Ltd, for example, the quality of labour or materials. The disadvantage of this system is that it is time-consuming and expensive to enter and manipulate the vast amount of data involved. In a modern AMT/JIT environment it may not be necessary to use such a complex system if:

- all forms of stock inventory (raw materials, WIP and finished products) are kept at very low levels;
- production is highly automated and reliable, leading to low labour costs and efficient use of labour time;
- long-term relationships with suppliers ensure reliable delivery and fixed price and quality specifications.

Under these conditions, there will be little variation of input prices or efficiencies and therefore insignificant cost variations. Thus, there would be no need to use the traditional accounting technique, and backflush accounting may be used instead. The CIMA *Official Terminology* defines backflush accounting as 'a method of costing, associated with a JIT production system, which applies cost to the output of a process. Costs do not mirror the flow of products through the production process, but are attached to output produced (finished goods stock and cost of sales), on the assumption that such backflushed costs are a realistic measure of the actual costs incurred'. Thus, conversion costs are only attached to products when they are completed. This system only uses raw, in process and finished goods accounts, which saves costs by reducing the amount of data required and the frequency of data entry, for example, data on materials used only enters the system when a piece of work is completed. However, this system does not enable the valuation of WIP nor any variance analysis.

The variances for PSA Ltd are significant for efficiency of inputs (labour and materials) and there is also a noticeable change in WIP, and the price of inputs. If this is typical, then the proposal should be rejected, as backflush accounting is unsuitable. Rapier, like many consultants, may be too concerned with selling its services than with truly serving its customers.

Solution 36

Tips

- This is an investment appraisal question with multiple IRRs.
- Part (b) requires a graph with NPV on the 7-axis and discount rates on the X-axis.
- You will require a minimum of four data points in order to draw a fairly accurate curve.
- Make use of the cumulative DCF tables where appropriate – this will save you valuable time in an examination and avoids being lost in a mass of calculation.

(a) Memorandum

To:	Director, Managing Director
From:	Management Accountant
Date:	20 November
Re:	Maximising accounting profit

Thank you for your letter of 18 November. I appreciate that directors may be more familiar with the concept of profit as opposed to discounted cash flow analysis (DCF), but DCF analysis is the conventional and correct method to use.

The calculation of a profit figure is subjective in that different accounting conventions, such as straight-line or reducing balance depreciation, may be used to calculate the figure.

DCF analysis recognises the true cash flows in a project, the timing of these flows and the time value of money.

By using the internal rate of return, HPC can compare projects of different sizes in an equitable manner, using the DCF approach.

I suggest that we discuss these concepts further at our next meeting.

Signed: Management Accountant

(b) Workings

Low-intensity strategy

The annual revenue is $(1,500,000/15.0) \times £325 = £32.5\,m$. Thus, the annual net cash flow is $£32.5\,m - £3.2\,m = £29.3\,m$.

Time Years	Cash flow £m	DCF (0%)	PV £m	DCF (10%)	PV £m	DCF (15%)	PV £m	DCF (20%)	PV £m
0	(105)	1.000	(105.0)	1.000	(105.0)	1.000	(105.0)	1.000	(105.0)
1–15	29.3	15.000	439.5	7.606	222.9	5.847	171.3	4.675	137.0
15	(395)	1.000	(395.0)	0.239	(94.4)	0.123	(48.6)	0.065	25.7
NPV			(60.5)		23.5		17.7		6.3

High-intensity strategy

The annual revenue is $(1,300,000/8) \times £325 = £52.81\,m$.

Thus, the annual net cash flow is $£52.81\,m - £3.6\,m = £49.21\,m$.

Time		0%		10%		15%		20%	
Years	Cash flow	DCF	PV	DCF	PV	DCF	PV	DCF	PV
	£m		£m		£m		£m		£m
0	(118)	1.000	(118.0)	1.000	(118.0)	1.000	(118.0)	1.000	(118.0)
1–8	49.21	8.000	393.7	5.335	262.5	4.487	220.8	3.837	188.8
8	(280)	1.000	(280.0)	0.467	(130.8)	0.327	(91.6)	0.233	(65.2)
NPV			(4.3)		13.7		11.2		5.6

(c) Projects such as marine oil wells and nuclear power stations have negative cash flows at both the commencement and termination of the project. Under these conditions, there is more than one value of IRR that may be calculated for each strategy. Thus, a meaningful conclusion on IRRs is difficult to achieve.

In mutually exclusive options, such as this one, it is important to consider scale as well as a ratio of performance. Thus, the net present values should be compared and their effect on the organisation as a whole should be considered.

The project with the best IRR or NPV may be subject to greater risk than the alternative. Thus, HPC must decide upon its attitude to risks and rewards. In this scenario, the low-intensity strategy is better if the cost of money stays within the range 6–21 per cent per annum.

(d) The high-intensity option extracts the oil in a shorter period. If HPC does not intend to extract oil for the next 15 years this option may be beneficial. Also, if the cost of money is expected to be between 1 and 5 per cent per annum this option is preferable.

If the cost of money is expected to be between 6 and 21 per cent per annum the low-intensity option realises the larger NPV and is preferable. Normally, the project with the largest negative NPV would not be undertaken by a risk-averse company. The low-intensity option has this characteristic, but only if the cost of money is less than 1 per cent – which is very unlikely.

In this scenario, the lower capital investment option potentially offers the higher NPV, so a risk-taking company might choose the low-intensity operation. HPC must define its risk/reward attitude and the likely future cost of money in order to make a rational choice between the projects.

 Solution 37

Tip

- Because there are net cash outflows at both the beginning and the end of this project, two separate IRRs will arise.

(a) This is a case of multiple IRRs, as illustrated by the following diagram:

The project is viable because it yields a positive NPV at 17 per cent discount rate. However, it is also true that the cash flows show IRRs at both 11 and 24 per cent approximately and it is evident that in such a case only the NPV gives a reasonable basis for a decision.

Workings

Determination of project cashflows

Year	Initial fee £'000	Annual costs £'000		Sales value of bauxite £'000	Restoration costs £'000	Total cash flow £'000
0	(9,700)	–		–	–	(9,700)
1		(3,000)	100 × £90	9,000	–	6,000
2		(3,000)	150 × £90	13,500	–	10,500
3		(3,000)	220 × £90	19,800	–	16,800
4		(3,000)	180 × £90	16,200	(42,000)	(28,800)
5		(3,000)	90 × £90	8,100	(1,000)	4,100

Year	Cash flows £'000	0%	PVs at 11%	17%	24%
0	(9,700)	(9,700)	(9,700)	(9,700)	(9,700)
1	6,000	6,000	5,405	5,128	4,838
2	10,500	10,500	8,522	7,670	6,828
3	16,800	16,800	12,284	10,489	8,811
4	(28,800)	(28,800)	(18,971)	(15,369)	(12,182)
5	4,100	4,100	2,433	1,870	1,398
		(1,100)	(27)	88	(7)

(b) The cash flows and relevant discount factors for each year could be arranged in vertical columns. The sum of their products is the NPV. By linking the discount factors to an interest rate in a reference cell, considering alternative interest rates is fast and easy. Thus the calculation of precise IRRs is possible and a situation of multiple IRRs quickly established.

 ## Solution 38

(a)

Net Present Value
Cost of capital 10% (W1)

Year	Total cash flow £	DF £	PV
0	(550,000)	1.000	(550,000)
1	200,260	0.909	182,036
2	164,920	0.826	136,224
3	164,920	0.751	123,855
4	164,920	0.683	112,640
5	219,920	0.621	136,570
6	(35,340)	0.564	(19,932)
		NPV	121,393

The above NPV of £121,393, while an expedient calculation, does not allow for the benefit of the lag in the payment of taxation. When this is incorporated the NPV will be slightly larger which is even more in favour of the decision (see alternative below).

Alternative approach

If candidates use die nominal discount rate, and adjust all values for inflation, this reveals a slightly different NPV result because of the time lag of taxation.

Net Present Value
Cost of capital   15.5%

Year	Total cash flow	DF	PV
	£	£	
0	(550,000)	1.000	(550,000)
1	210,273	0.866	182,096
2	183,680	0.750	137,760
3	192,864	0.649	125,169
4	202,507	0.562	113,809
5	282,827	0.487	137,737
6	(45,104)	0.421	(18,989)
NPV			127,582

Workings

Project cash Flows	*Year 1*	*Year 2*	*Year 3*	*Year 4*	*Year 5*	*Year 6*
Contribution less fixed overhead		£247,380	£259,749	£272,736	£286,373	£300,692
Scrap value			£70,195			
Total tax payable on corporate profit	(£37,107)	(£76,069)	(£79,872)	(£83,866)	(£88,060)	(£45,104)
Net cash flow	£210,273	£183,680	£192,864	£202,507	£282,827	(£45,104)

Recommendation:

The project should be undertaken as it generates a positive net present value.

Workings

1. Real discount rate $\dfrac{(1 + 0.155)}{(1 + 0.05)} - 1 = 10\%$

2. Total cash flows

   Expected value of annual sales

Demand	x	P	Px
	£		£
High	800,000	0.25	200,000
Medium	560,000	0.50	280,000
Low	448,000	0.25	112,000
Expected value			592,000

Expected value of annual sales	£592,000
CS ratio	55%
Contribution	£325,600
Less: Fixed overheads	£90,000
Corporate profit	£235,600
Tax @ 30%	£70,680

Project cash flows	*Year 1*	*Year 2*	*Year 3*	*Year 4*	*Year 5*	*Year 6*
	£	£	£	£	£	£
Profit	235,600	235,600	235,600	235,600	235,600	
Scrap value					55,000	
Total tax payable on corporate profit	(35,340)	(70,680)	(70,680)	(70,680)	(70,680)	(35,340)
Net cash flow	200,260	164,920	164,920	164,920	219,920	(35,340)

(b)
Sensitivity of the project to changes in the expected annual contribution

The net (after tax) present value of the contribution
Cost of capital 10%

Year	Contribution £	Tax payment £	Cash flow £	DF	PV £
1	325,600	(48,840)	276,760	0.909	251,575
2	325,600	(97,680)	227,920	0.826	188,262
3	325,600	(97,680)	227,920	0.751	171,168
4	325,600	(97,680)	227,920	0.683	155,669
5	325,600	(97,680)	227,920	0.621	141,538
6		(48,840)	(48,840)	0.564	(27,546)
		NPV			880,666

The NPV of the project is £121,393. Therefore the PV of the contributions can fall by this amount. This means can fall by £121,393/£880,666, that is, a sensitivity of 13.78%.

(c)
Writing-Down Allowances schedule

	£	Tax saved @ 30% £	Year 1 £	Year 2 £	Year 3 £	Year 4 £	Year 5 £	Year 6 £
Initial expenditure	550,000							
WDA Year 1, 25%	137,500	41,250	20,625	20,625				
	412,500							
WDA Year 2, 25%	103,125	30,938		15,469	15,469			
	309,375							
WDA Year 3, 25%	77,344	23,203			11,602	11,601		
	232,031							
WDA Year 4, 25%	58,008	17,402				8,701	8,701	
	174,023							
Sale for scrap, year 5	70,195							
Balancing allowance	103,828	31,148					15,574	15,574
Total tax savings			20,625	36,094	27,071	20,302	24,275	15,574
Discount factor (nominal rate)			0.866	0.750	0.649	0.562	0.487	0.42
Present value			17,861	27,071	17,569	11,410	11,822	6,557
Total present value	92,290							

The net present value for the investment will increase by £92,290 due to savings in tax arising from writing down allowances.

Examiner's Note

The writing down allowances are not affected by inflation, except to the extent that the final asset value will increase.

Exam Q & As

At the time of publication there are no exam Q & As available for the 2010 syllabus. However, the latest specimen exam papers are available on the CIMA website. Actual exam Q & As will be available free of charge to CIMA students on the CIMA website from summer 2010 onwards.

Index

Index